THE PILLAR NEW TESTAMENT COMMENTARY

General Editor

D. A. CARSON

The Letter to the
PHILIPPIANS

G. WALTER HANSEN

WILLIAM B. EERDMANS PUBLISHING COMPANY
GRAND RAPIDS, MICHIGAN / CAMBRIDGE, U.K.

APOLLOS
NOTTINGHAM, ENGLAND

Published 2009
in the United States of America by
Wm. B. Eerdmans Publishing Co.
2140 Oak Industrial Drive N.E., Grand Rapids, Michigan 49505 /
P.O. Box 163, Cambridge CB3 9PU U.K.
www.eerdmans.com

and in the United Kingdom by
APOLLOS
Norton Street, Nottingham,
England NG7 3HR

Printed in the United States of America

28 27 26 25 24 12 11 10 9 8

Library of Congress Cataloging-in-Publication Data

Hansen, G. Walter, 1946-
The letter to the Philippians / G. Walter Hansen.
p. cm. — (The Pillar New Testament commentary)
Includes bibliographical references and indexes.
ISBN 978-0-8028-3737-0 (cloth: alk. paper)
1. Bible. N.T. Philippians — Commentaries. I. Title.

BS2705.53.H35 2009
227′.6077 — dc22

2009022366

British Library Cataloguing in Publication Data

A catalogue record for this book is available from the British Library.
Apollos ISBN 978-1-84474-403-9

Contents

COMMENTARY ON PHILIPPIANS

INDEXES

Editor's Preface

Commentaries have specific aims, and this series is no exception. Designed for serious pastors and teachers of the Bible, the Pillar commentaries seek above all to make clear the text of Scripture as we have it. The scholars writing these volumes interact with the most important informed contemporary debate, but avoid getting mired in undue technical detail. Their ideal is a blend of rigorous exegesis and exposition, with an eye alert both to biblical theology and the contemporary relevance of the Bible, without confusing the commentary and the sermon.

The rationale for this approach is that the vision of "objective scholarship" (a vain chimera) may actually be profane. God stands over against us; we do not stand in judgment of him. When God speaks to us through his Word, those who profess to know him must respond in an appropriate way, and that is certainly different from a stance in which the scholar projects an image of autonomous distance. Yet this is no surreptitious appeal for uncontrolled subjectivity. The writers of this series aim for an even-handed openness to the text that is the best kind of "objectivity" of all.

If the text is God's Word, it is appropriate that we respond with reverence, a certain fear, a holy joy, a questing obedience. These values should be reflected in the way Christians write. With these values in place, the Pillar commentaries will be warmly welcomed not only by pastors, teachers, and students, but by general readers as well.

* * *

Casual readers of the letter to the Philippians might think that it is one of the slighter contributions penned by Paul. Here one does not find, say, the massive theological reasoning of Romans, the emotional intensity of 2 Corinthians, or the contentious apologetic of Galatians. Some might almost find it bland. Yet those who have probed this letter more closely know that the first chapter finds Paul in one of his most reflective moods as, toward the end of his life, he contemplates the benefits of "departing" and "being with Christ" over against living on in this world to bring further gospel blessing to the churches for which he is responsible; that the second chapter includes one of the high points of New Testament Christology, the third is embroiled in contemporary debates about the New Perspective on Paul, and the fourth contains one of the most revealing pictures of the relationship between Paul and a supporting church. In all of this, the letter sings with the theme of joy and appeals to the Philippians to learn to "think the same thing." Small wonder that this letter is so embracing when all along it keeps trumpeting the gospel.

With themes and emotions so varied, the letter to the Philippians needs a commentator with a sure grasp and a warm heart. It helps that Dr Hansen writes with admirable clarity and simplicity, even when he is unpacking notoriously complex matters. Perhaps he brings so many qualifications to the table because he himself has not only served as a pastor and a seminary professor, but as a missionary in another cultural context. Certain it is that this commentary will become "must" reading for many pastors, students, and scholars as they try to think Paul's thoughts after him while reading this letter.

D. A. Carson

Author's Preface

In the process of writing this exposition of Philippians, I gained a deep appreciation for the importance of partnership not only from Paul's development of the theme of partnership in this letter but also from my partners in this work of producing a commentary. I could not have written this book in isolation; I depended on a community of friends who invested in my life and my work. As Paul's letter expresses his joy in his partnership with the Philippians, this preface celebrates my partnership with those who contributed significantly to this work.

Writers of previous commentaries, especially Barth, Beare, Bockmuehl, Bonnard, Fee, Fowl, Hawthorne, Martin, Müller, O'Brien, and Silva, became my constant dialogue partners in a long and exhilarating conversation about Philippians. I am deeply grateful for their insights, even at points where I respectfully disagree with them. My friends, John McEntyre and Ron Mahurin, read portions of this commentary and gave me the benefit of their thoughtful feedback. Gifted students in my courses on the Greek text of Philippians at Fuller Theological Seminary sharpened my interpretation by their tough questions and fresh perspectives. Conversations about my discoveries with numerous friends, especially the Monday lunch circle, enriched my own understanding. Ben Chang found many valuable journal articles. Annemarie Moody carefully compiled the bibliography and list of abbreviations. Nancy Bullock patiently proofread the entire manuscript. Don Carson, general editor of the Pillar New Testament Commentary, gave wise and gracious counsel for the clarification of key points. Milton Essenburg, Eerdmans editor, provided warm encouragement and meticulous attention to detail.

I express my deepest gratitude to my wife, Darlene, to whom I dedicate this book. Her joyful partnership in all aspects of our life made the process of writing this commentary an enjoyable adventure in our journey together.

I have used Today's New International Version (TNIV) as the basis for my exposition, except in my commentary on the Christ hymn (2:6-11) where I follow my own translation of the Greek text. For the most part, I have kept the body of the commentary free from technical language. The footnotes point to the academic research and contemporary debate related to my exposition of the text. My reason for using this style is to provide a commentary that is accessible to a wide audience of readers, especially Bible teachers and pastors. I hope that this commentary will be a way for me to enjoy a partnership with my readers as we seek to "live in a manner worthy of the gospel of Christ" (1:27).

G. WALTER HANSEN
July 2008

Abbreviations

I. ENGLISH TRANSLATIONS AND PARAPHRASES

ASV	American Standard Version
KJV	King James Version
NASB	New American Standard Bible
NEB	New English Bible
NIV	New International Version
NRSV	New Revised Standard Version
RSV	Revised Standard Version
TNIV	Today's New International Version

II. NEW TESTAMENT MANUSCRIPTS

$\mathfrak{P}^{46}$	Papyrus Chester Beatty II (ca. 200)
א	London: Sinaiticus (4th c.)
A	London: Alexandrinus (5th c.)
B	Rome: Vaticanus (4th c.)
C	Paris: Ephraemi Rescriptus (5th c.)
D	Paris: Claromontanus (6th c.)
F	Cambridge (9th c.)
Ψ	Athos (8th-10th c.)
$\mathfrak{M}$	The Majority Text, i.e., the text of the majority of Greek mss. (9th-15th c.)

III. APOCRYPHA

1 Macc	1 Maccabees
3 Macc	3 Maccabees
4 Macc	4 Maccabees
Sir	Sirach/Ecclesiasticus

IV. RABBINIC LITERATURE

m. Avot	*Mishnah Avot*

m. Sanh.	*Mishnah Sanhedrin*
Qidd.	*Qiddushin*
Yevam.	*Yevamot*

V. EARLY CHRISTIAN WRITINGS

Ignatius

Rom.	*To the Romans*

Polycarp

Phil.	*To the Philippians*

VI. CLASSICAL AND HELLENISTIC LITERATURE

Aeschylus

Pers.	*Persians*

Aristotle

Eth. nic.	*Nicomachean Ethics*
Pol.	*Politics*
Rhet.	*Rhetoric*
Virt. vit.	*Virtues and Vices*

Cicero

Amic.	*De amicitia*
Planc.	*Pro Plancio*

Epictetus

Diss.	*Dissertationes*

Homer

Il.	*Iliad*

Josephus

Ant.	*Jewish Antiquities*
C. Ap.	*Contra Apionem*
J.W.	*The Jewish War*
Life	*Life of Flavius Josephus*

Justinian

Dig.	*Digesta*

Plutarch

Amic. mult.	*De amicorum multitudine*
Mor.	*Moralia*
Alex. fort. virt.	*De Alexandri magni fortuna aut virtute*
Tranq. an.	*De tranquillitate animi*

Seneca

Vit. beat.	*De vita beata*

Sophocles

Ant.	*Antigone*

Philo

Cher.	*De cherubim*
Decal.	*De decalogo*
Migr.	*De migratione Abrahami*

VII. SECONDARY WORKS

AB	Anchor Bible
ABD	*Anchor Bible Dictionary*
ABRL	Anchor Bible Reference Library
ACCS	*Ancient Christian Commentary on Scripture*
ATR	*Anglican Theological Review*
BDAG	Bauer, W., F. W. Danker, W. F. Arndt, and F. W. Gingrich. *Greek-English Lexicon of the New Testament and Other Early Christian Literature.* 3rd ed. Chicago, 2000
BDF	Blass, F., A. Debrunner, and R. W. Funk. *A Greek Grammar of the New Testament and Other Early Christian Literature.* Chicago, 1961
BECNT	Baker Exegetical Commentary on the New Testament
Bib	*Biblica*
BNTC	Black's New Testament Commentaries
BSac	*Bibliotheca sacra*
BST	The Bible Speaks Today
BT	*Bible Translator*
BZAW	Beihefte zur Zeitschrift für die alttestamentliche Wissenschaft
CBQ	*Catholic Biblical Quarterly*
CIL	*Corpus Inscriptionum Latinarum*
DNTB	*Dictionary of New Testament Background*
DPL	*Dictionary of Paul and His Letters*
EDNT	*Exegetical Dictionary of the New Testament*
ETL	*Ephemerides theologicae lovanienses*
EvJ	*Evangelical Journal*
ExpT	*Expository Times*
FN	*Filología Neotestamentaria*
GTJ	*Grace Theological Journal*
HNT	Handbuch zum Neuen Testament
HTKNT	Herders Theologische Kommentar zum Neuen Testament
HTR	*Harvard Theological Review*
IBS	*Irish Biblical Studies*
ICC	International Critical Commentary
Int	*Interpretation*
JBL	*Journal of Biblical Literature*
JETS	*Journal of the Evangelical Theological Society*
JFSR	*Journal of Feminist Studies in Religion*
JGWR	*Journal of Gender in World Religions*
JSNT	*Journal for the Study of the New Testament*
JSNTSup	Journal for the Study of the New Testament: Supplement Series
JSOT	*Journal for the Study of the Old Testament*
JTC	*Journal for Theology and the Church*
JTS	*Journal of Theological Studies*
KEK	Kritisch-exegetischer Kommentar über das Neue Testament
LEC	Library of Early Christianity

LLt.	*Living Light*
LNTS	The Library of New Testament Studies
LS	*Louvain Studies*
LSJ	Liddell, H. G., R. Scott, and H. S. Jones. *A Greek-English Lexicon*
MM	Moulton, J. H., and G. Milligan. *The Vocabulary of the Greek Testament*
Neot	*Neotestamentica*
NIB	*The New Interpreter's Bible*
NIBCNT	New International Biblical Commentary on the New Testament
NICNT	New International Commentary on the New Testament
NICOT	New International Commentary on the Old Testament
NIDNTT	*New International Dictionary of New Testament Theology*
NIGTC	New International Greek Testament Commentary
NIVAC	The New International Version Application Commentary
Notes	*Notes on Translation*
NovT	*Novum Testamentum*
NovTSup	Novum Testamentum Supplements
NSBT	New Studies in Biblical Theology
NTD	Das Neue Testament Deutsch
NTG	New Testament Guides
NTS	*New Testament Studies*
PRSt	*Perspectives in Religious Studies*
QR	*Quarterly Review*
RevExp	*Review and Expositor*
SBLDS	Society of Biblical Literature Dissertation Series
SBLSBS	Society of Biblical Literature Sources for Biblical Study
SBT	Studies in Biblical Theology
SE	*Studia evangelica*
SHAW	Sitzungen der Heidelberger Akademie der Wissenschaften
SNTSMS	Society for New Testament Studies Monograph Series
SR	*Studies in Religion*
TDNT	*Theological Dictionary of the New Testament*
Them	*Themelios*
THKNT	Theologischer Handkommentar zum Neuen Testament
TJ	*Trinity Journal*
TJT	*Toronto Journal of Theology*
TLNT	*Theological Lexicon of the New Testament*
TNTC	Tyndale New Testament Commentary
TynBul	*Tyndale Bulletin*
TZ	*Theologische Zeitschrift*
WBC	Word Biblical Commentary
WTJ	*Westminster Theological Journal*
WUNT	Wissenschaftliche Untersuchungen zum Neuen Testament
ZNT	*Zeitschrift für die neutestamentliche Theologie*

ZNW	*Zeitschrift für die neutestamentliche Wissenschaft und die Kunde der älteren Kirche*
ZThK	*Zeitschrift für Theologie und Kirche*

VIII. TECHNICAL ABBREVIATIONS

A.D.	anno Domini
B.C.	before Christ
c.	century
ca.	circa, about
cf.	compare
ed.	editor, edition, edited by
e.g.	*exempli gratia*, for example
i.e.	*id est*, that is
LXX	Septuagint (Greek OT, 3rd c. B.C.)
ms., mss.	manuscript(s)
n.	footnote
NT	New Testament
OT	Old Testament
𝔭	Papyrus
repr.	reprint, reprinted
rev.	revised
trans.	translated by
v (v.)	verse(s)
vol(s).	volume(s)

Select Bibliography

I. COMMENTARIES ON PHILIPPIANS

Throughout this work I have referred to commentaries on Philippians simply by author surname and page number.

Barth, Karl. *Epistle to the Philippians.* Translated by James W. Leitch. Richmond: Westminster John Knox, 2002.

Beare, F. W. *A Commentary on the Epistle to the Philippians.* London: Adam & Charles Black, 1959.

Bockmuehl, Markus. *The Epistle to the Philippians.* BNTC 11. Peabody, Mass.: Hendrickson, 1998.

Bonnard, P. *L'épître de saint Paul aux Philippiens.* Neuchâtel: Delachaux & Niestlé, 1950.

Bruce, F. F. *Philippians.* NIBCNT 11. Peabody, Mass.: Hendrickson, 1995.

Calvin, John. *The Epistles of Paul the Apostle to the Galatians, Ephesians, Philippians, and Colossians.* Calvin's Commentaries 11. Edited by David W. Torrance and Thomas Forsyth Torrance. Translated by T. H. L. Parker. Grand Rapids: Eerdmans, 1965.

Caird, G. B. *Paul's Letters from Prison.* Oxford: Oxford University Press, 1976.

Collange, J. F. *L'épître de saint Paul aux Philippiens.* Neuchâtel: Delachaux & Niestlé, 1973.

Craddock, F. B. *Philippians.* Atlanta: John Knox, 1985.

Dibelius, M. *An die Thessalonicher I, II. An die Philipper.* HNT 11. Tübingen: Mohr-Siebeck, 1937.

Fee, Gordon D. *Paul's Letter to the Philippians.* NICNT. Grand Rapids: Eerdmans, 1995.

Fowl, Stephen E. *Philippians.* The Two Horizons New Testament Commentary. Grand Rapids: Eerdmans, 2005.

Friedrich, G. *Der Brief an die Philipper.* NTD 8. Göttingen: Vandenhoeck & Ruprecht, 1962.

Gnilka, J. *Der Philipperbrief.* HTKNT 10/3. Freiburg: Herder, 1968.
Hawthorne, Gerald F. *Philippians.* WBC 43. Nashville: Thomas Nelson, 1983.
Hooker, Morna D. "The Letter to the Philippians: Introduction, Commentary, and Reflections." Pages 467-550 in vol. 11 of *NIB.* Edited by Leander E. Keck. 12 vols. Nashville: Abingdon, 2000.
Lightfoot, J. B. *St. Paul's Epistle to the Philippians.* London: Macmillan, 1894. Repr., Grand Rapids: Zondervan, 1953.
Lohmeyer, Ernst. *Der Brief an die Philipper, an die Kolosser und an Philemon.* KEK 9. 13th ed. Göttingen: Vandenhoeck & Ruprecht, 1964.
Marshall, I. Howard. *The Epistle to the Philippians.* Epworth Commentaries. London: Epworth, 1992.
Martin, Ralph P. *The Epistle to the Philippians: An Introduction and Commentary.* TNTC. Grand Rapids: Eerdmans, 1959.
———, and Gerald F. Hawthorne, *Philippians.* WBC 43. Rev. ed. Nashville: Thomas Nelson, 2004.
Meyer, H. A. W. *Critical and Exegetical Handbook to the Epistles to the Philippians and Colossians, and to Philemon.* Repr. New York: Funk & Wagnalls, 1885.
Motyer, Alex. *The Message of Philippians: Jesus Our Joy.* BST. Downers Grove: InterVarsity Press, 1984.
Müller, Ulrich B. *Der Brief des Paulus an die Philipper.* THKNT 11/I. Leipzig: Evangelische Verlagsanstalt, 1993.
O'Brien, Peter T. *Epistle to the Philippians.* NIGTC. Grand Rapids: Eerdmans, 1991.
Schenk, Wolfgang. *Die Philipperbriefe des Paulus.* Stuttgart: W. Kolhammer, 1984.
Silva, Moisés. *Philippians.* BECNT. Grand Rapids: Baker Book House, 1992.
Thielman, Frank. *Philippians.* NIVAC. Grand Rapids: Zondervan, 1995.
Vincent, Marvin R. *A Critical and Exegetical Commentary on the Epistles to the Philippians and to Philemon.* ICC. Edinburgh: T&T Clark, 1897.
Witherington III, B. *Friendship and Finances in Philippi: The Letter of Paul to the Philippians.* New Testament in Context. Valley Forge, Pa.: Trinity Press International, 1994.

II. OTHER WORKS

Abrahamsen, Valerie. "Women at Philippi: The Pagan and Christian Evidence." *JFSR* 3 (1987): 17-30.
Achtemeier, Paul J., Joel B. Green, and Marianne Meye Thompson. *Introducing the New Testament: Its Literature and Theology.* Grand Rapids: Eerdmans, 2001.
Alexander, Loveday. "Hellenistic Letter-Forms and the Structure of Philippians." *JSNT* 37 (1989): 87-101.
Ascough, R. S. *Paul's Macedonian Associations: The Social Context of Philippians and I Thessalonians.* Tübingen: Mohr Siebeck, 2003.

———. "Recent Studies of Philippi." *TJT* 13 (1997): 72-77.

Bakirtizis, C., and H. Koester, eds. *Philippi at the Time of Paul and after His Death.* Harrisburg, Pa.: Trinity Press International, 1998.

Barclay, John M. G. *Jews in Mediterranean Diaspora from Alexander to Trajan: 323 BCE–117 CE.* Edinburgh: T&T Clark, 1996.

Barrett, C. K., ed. *The New Testament Background: Selected Documents.* Rev. ed. San Francisco: Harper & Row, 1987.

Bassler, J. M., ed. *Pauline Theology, Volume 1: Thessalonians, Philippians, Galatians, Philemon.* Minneapolis: Fortress, 1991.

Bateman, H. W. "Were the Opponents at Philippi Necessarily Jewish?" *BSac* 155 (1998): 39-61.

Bauckham, Richard J. "The Worship of Jesus in Philippians 2:9-11." Pages 128-39 in *Where Christology Began: Essays on Philippians 2.* Edited by Ralph P. Martin and Brian J. Dodd. Louisville: Westminster John Knox, 1998.

Bauer, W., F. W. Danker, W. F. Arndt, and F. W. Gingrich. *Greek-English Lexicon of the New Testament and Other Early Christian Literature.* 3rd ed. Chicago: University of Chicago Press, 2000.

Becker, J. C. "Erwägungen zu Phil. 3:20-21." *TZ* 27 (1971): 16-29.

Best, Ernest. "Bishops and Deacons in Philippians 1:1." *SE* 4 (1968): 190-231.

———. *One Body in Christ.* London: SPCK, 1955.

———. *Paul and His Converts.* Edinburgh: T&T Clark, 1988.

Bieringer, R., V. Koperski, and B. Lataire. *Resurrection in the New Testament: Festschrift J. Lambrecht.* Leuven: Leuven University Press, 2002.

Black, David A. "Paul and Christian Unity: A Formal Analysis of Philippians 2:1-4." *JSNT* 28/3 (1985): 299-308.

———. "The Discourse Structure of Philippians: A Study in Textlinguistics." *NovT* 37 (1995): 16-49.

Bloomquist, Gregory L. *The Function of Suffering in Philippians.* JSNTSup 78. Sheffield: JSOT Press, 1993.

Boers, H. "Judaism and the Church in Paul's Thought." *Neo* 32 (1998): 249-66.

Bonhoeffer, Dietrich. *Life Together.* Translated by John W. Doberstein. New York: Harper & Row, 1954.

Bormann, Lukas. *Philippi: Stadt und Christengemeinde zur Zeit des Paulus.* Leiden: Brill, 1995.

Böttger, Paul C. "Die Eschatologische Existenz der Christen: Erwägungen zu Philipper 3.20." *ZNW* (1969): 244-63.

Boyer, J. L. "First Conditions: What Do They Mean?" *GTJ* 2 (1981): 75-114.

Bradley, K. R. *Slavery and Society at Rome.* Cambridge: Cambridge University Press, 1994.

Brewer, R. R. "The Meaning of *Politeuesthe* in Philippians 1:27." *JBL* 73 (1954): 76-83.

Brown, Colin. "Ernst Lohmeyer's *Kyrios Jesus.*" Pages 6-42 in *Where Christology Began: Essays on Philippians 2.* Edited by Ralph P. Martin and Brian J. Dodd. Louisville: Westminster John Knox, 1998.

Blass, F., A. Debrunner, and R. W. Funk. *A Greek Grammar of the New Testament and Other Early Christian Literature.* Chicago: University of Chicago Press, 1961.

Brown, Raymond E. *An Introduction to the New Testament.* ABRL. New York: Doubleday, 1997.

Brown, W. P., ed. *Character and Scripture: Moral Formation, Community, and Biblical Interpretation.* Grand Rapids: Eerdmans, 2002.

Bruce, F. F. *The Canon of Scripture.* Downers Grove: InterVarsity Press, 1988.

———. *Paul: Apostle of the Heart Set Free.* Grand Rapids: Eerdmans, 1977.

Caird, G. B. *New Testament Theology.* Edited by L. D. Hurst. Oxford: Oxford University Press, 1994.

Campbell, G. "The Struggle for the Progress of the Gospel at the Heart of the Pauline Mission." *IBS* 21 (1999): 59-78.

Capper, B. J. "Paul's Dispute with Philippi: Understanding Paul's Argument in Phil 1–2 from His Thanks in 4.10-20." *TZ* 49 (1993): 193-214.

Carson, D. A. *Christ and Culture Revisited.* Grand Rapids: Eerdmans, 2008.

———. *Exegetical Fallacies.* Grand Rapids: Baker, 1984.

———, and Douglas J. Moo. *An Introduction to the New Testament.* 2nd ed. Grand Rapids: Zondervan, 2005.

Castelli, Elizabeth A. *Imitating Paul: A Discourse of Power.* Louisville: Westminster John Knox Press, 1991.

Chamblin, J. K. "Psychology." Pages 765-74 in *DPL.* Edited by Gerald F. Hawthorne, Ralph P. Martin, and Daniel G. Reid. Downers Grove: InterVarsity Press, 1993.

Cormack, Don. *Killing Fields: An Unfinished Portrait of the Cambodian Church — the Church That Would Not Die.* Crowborough: MARC, 1997.

Cotter, W. "Our *Politeuma* Is in Heaven: The Meaning of Philippians 3:17-21." Pages 92-104 in *Origins and Method: Toward a New Understanding of Judaism and Christianity.* Edited by B. H. McLean. JSJTSup 86. Sheffield: JSOT Press, 1993.

Croy, Clayton N. "'To Die Is Gain' (Philippians 1:19-26): Does Paul Contemplate Suicide?" *JBL* 122/3 (2003): 517-31.

Cullmann, Oscar. *Christ and Time: The Primitive Christian Conception of Time and History.* Translated by Floyd V. Filson. Rev. ed. Philadelphia: Westminster John Knox, 1964.

Davies, W. D. *Paul and Rabbinic Judaism: Some Rabbinic Elements in Paul's Theology.* London: S.P.C.K., 1948.

Deissmann, Adolf. *Light from the Ancient East.* Translated by Lionel R. M. Strachan. 4th ed. Grand Rapids: Baker, 1978.

deSilva, David A. "No Confidence in the Flesh: The Meaning and Function of Philippians 3:2-21." *TJ* 15 (1994): 27-54.

Doble, P. "'Vile Bodies' or Transformed Persons? Philippians 3:21 in Context." *JSNT* 86 (2002): 3-27.

Dodd, B. J. "The Story of Christ and the Imitation of Paul in Philippians 2–3." Pages 154-61 in *Where Christology Began: Essays on Philippians 2.* Edited by R. P. Martin and B. J. Dodd. Louisville: Westminster John Knox, 1998.

Donaldson, Terence L. *Paul and the Gentiles: Remapping the Apostle's Convictional World.* Minneapolis: Fortress, 1997.

Doty, William G. *Letters in Primitive Christianity.* Guides to Biblical Scholarship: New Testament Series. Philadelphia: Fortress, 1973.

Doughty, D. J. "Citizens of Heaven: Philippians 3.2-21." *NTS* 41 (1995): 102-22.

Duncan, G. S. *Paul's Ephesian Ministry: A Reconstruction with Special Reference to the Ephesian Origin for the Imprisonment Epistles.* New York: Charles Scribner's Sons, 1929.

Dunderberg, I., C. Tuckett, and K. Syreeni, eds. *Fair Play: Diversity and Conflicts in Early Christianity, Essays in Honour of Heiki Räisänen.* Leiden: Brill, 2002.

Dunn, James D. G. *Christology in the Making: An Inquiry into the Origins of the Doctrine of the Incarnation.* London: SCM, 1960.

———. *The Theology of Paul the Apostle.* Grand Rapids: Eerdmans, 1998.

Dupont, Jacques. "The Conversion of Paul, and Its Influence on His Understanding of Salvation by Faith." Pages 176-94 in *Apostolic History and the Gospel: Biblical and Historical Essays Presented to F. F. Bruce on His 60th Birthday.* Edited by W. W. Gasque and R. P. Martin. Grand Rapids: Eerdmans, 1970.

Ellis, E. E. "Paul and His Opponents." Pages 264-98 in *Christianity, Judaism and Other Greco-Roman Cults.* Edited by J. Neusner. Leiden: Brill, 1975.

Engberg-Pedersen, Troels. "Radical Altruism in Philippians 2:4." Pages 197-204 in *Early Christianity and Classical Culture: Comparative Studies in Honor of Abraham Malherbe.* Edited by John Fitzgerald, Thomas Olbricht, and L. Michael White. Leiden: Brill, 2003.

———. "Stoicism in Philippians." Pages 256-90 in *Paul in His Hellenistic Context.* Edited by Troels Engberg-Pedersen. Minneapolis: Fortress, 1995.

Ferguson, Everett. *Backgrounds of Early Christianity.* 2nd ed. Grand Rapids: Eerdmans, 1993.

Fitzgerald, John T. "Epistle to the Philippians." Pages 318-26 in vol. 5 of *ABD.* Edited by David Noel Freedman. 6 vols. New York: Doubleday, 1992.

———. "Philippians in the Light of Some Ancient Discussions of Friendship." Pages 141-60 in *Friendship, Flattery, and Frankness of Speech: Studies on Friendship in the New Testament World.* NovTSup 82. Edited by John T. Fitzgerald. Leiden: Brill, 1996.

———. "Virtue/Vice Lists." Pages 857-59 in vol. 6 of *ABD.* Edited by David Noel Freedman. 6 vols. New York: Doubleday, 1992.

Fitzgerald, J. T., ed. *Friendship, Flattery, and Frankness of Speech: Studies on Friendship in the New Testament World.* NovTSup 82. Leiden: Brill, 1996.

Fitzmyer, Joseph A. *The Acts of the Apostles.* AB 13. New York: Doubleday, 1998.

———. "The Aramaic Background of Philippians 2:6-11." *CBQ* 50 (1988): 470-83.

Fowl, Stephen E. "Imitation of Paul/of Christ." Pages 428-31 in *DPL*. Edited by Gerald F. Hawthorne, Ralph P. Martin, and Daniel G. Reid. Downers Grove: InterVarsity Press, 1993.

———. "Know Your Context: Giving and Receiving Money in Philippians." *Int* 56 (2002): 45-58.

———. "Philippians 1:28b, One More Time." Pages 205-23 in *New Testament Greek and Exegesis: Essays in Honor of Gerald F. Hawthorne*. Edited by Amy Donaldson and Timothy Sailors. Grand Rapids: Eerdmans, 2003.

———. *The Story of Christ in the Ethics of Paul: An Analysis of the Function of the Hymnic Material in the Pauline Corpus*. JSNTSup 36. Sheffield: JSOT Press, 1990.

Fox, Robin Lane. *The Classical World: An Epic History from Homer to Hadrian*. New York: Basic Books, 2006.

French, David. "Acts and the Roman Roads of Asia Minor." Pages 49-58 in *The Book of Acts in Its Graeco-Roman Setting*. Edited by David W. J. Gill and Conrad Gempf. Vol. 1 of *The Book of Acts in Its First-Century Setting*. Edited by Bruce W. Winter. Grand Rapids: Eerdmans, 1993.

Funk, Robert W. "The Apostolic *Parousia:* Form and Significance." Pages 249-68 in *Christian History and Interpretation: Studies Presented to John Knox*. Edited by W. R. Farmer, C. F. D. Moule, and R. R. Niebuhr. Cambridge: Cambridge University Press, 1976.

Furnish, V. P. "The Place and Purpose of Phil III." *NTS* 10 (1963-64): 80-88.

Garland, David E. "The Composition and Unity of Philippians: Some Neglected Literary Features." *NovT* 27 (1985): 141-73.

Garnsey, Peter. *Social Status and Legal Privilege in the Roman Empire*. Oxford: Clarendon, 1970.

Garter, Warren. *The Roman Empire and the New Testament*. Nashville: Abingdon Press, 2006.

Gathercole, Simon. *Where Is Boasting? Early Jewish Soteriology and Paul's Response in Romans 1–5*. Grand Rapids: Eerdmans, 2002.

Geoffrion, Timothy C. *The Rhetorical Purpose and the Political and Military Character of Philippians: A Call to Stand Firm*. Lewiston, N.Y.: Mellen Biblical Press, 1993.

Gill, David W. J. "Behind the Classical Façade: Local Religions in the Roman Empire." Pages 72-87 in *One God, One Lord: Christianity in a World of Religious Pluralism*. Edited by A. Clarke and B. Winter. Exeter: Paternoster, 1992.

———. "Macedonia." Pages 397-415 in *The Book of Acts in Its Graeco-Roman Setting*. Edited by David W. J. Gill and Conrad Gempf. Vol. 1 of *The Book of Acts in Its First-Century Setting*. Edited by Bruce W. Winter. Grand Rapids: Eerdmans, 1993.

Gillman, Florence M. "Early Christian Women at Philippi." *JGWR* 1 (1990): 59-79.

Green, J. B. "Resurrection of the Body: New Testament Voices concerning Personal Continuity and the Afterlife." Pages 85-100 in *What about the Soul? Neuroscience and Christian Anthropology.* Edited by J. B. Green. Nashville: Abingdon, 2004.

Greenlee, Harold J. "Saint Paul — Perfect but Not Perfected 3:12." *Notes* 4 (1990): 53-55.

Gundry Volf, Judith M. *Paul and Perseverance: Staying In and Falling Away.* WUNT 2/37. Louisville: Westminster John Knox, 1991.

Gundry, Robert H. "Style and Substance in 'The Myth of God Incarnate' according to Philippians 2:6-11." Pages 271-93 in *Crossing the Boundaries: Essays in Biblical Interpretation in Honour of Michael D. Goulder.* Edited by Stanley E. Porter, Paul Joyce, and David E. Orton. Leiden: Brill, 1994.

———. *SŌMA in Biblical Theology: With an Emphasis on Pauline Anthropology.* Grand Rapids: Zondervan, 1987.

Gunther, J. J. *St. Paul's Opponents and Their Background.* NovTSup 35. Leiden: Brill, 1973.

Hall, John F. "Caesar's Household." Page 798 in vol. 1 of *ABD.* Edited by David Noel Freedman. 6 vols. New York: Doubleday, 1992.

Hansen, G. Walter. *Abraham in Galatians: Epistolary and Rhetorical Contexts.* JSNTSup 29. Sheffield: JSOT Press, 1989.

———. "Paul's Conversion and His Ethic of Freedom in Galatians." Pages 213-37 in *The Road from Damascus: The Impact of Paul's Conversion on His Life, Thought, and Ministry.* Edited by Richard N. Longenecker. Grand Rapids: Eerdmans, 1997.

———. "Resurrection and the Christian Life in Paul's Letters." Pages 203-24 in *Life in the Face of Death: The Resurrection Message in the New Testament.* Edited by R. N. Longenecker. Grand Rapids: Eerdmans, 1998.

———. "Rhetorical Criticism." Pages 822-26 in *DPL.* Edited by Gerald F. Hawthorne, Ralph P. Martin, and Daniel G. Reid. Downers Grove: InterVarsity Press, 1993.

——— "Transformation of Relationships." Pages 181-204 in *New Testament Greek and Exegesis: Essays in Honor of Gerald F. Hawthorne.* Edited by A. M. Donaldson and T. B. Sailors. Grand Rapids: Eerdmans, 2003.

Harris, Murray J. "Appendix: Prepositions and Theology in the Greek New Testament." Pages 1192-93 in vol. 3 of *NIDNTT.* Edited by Colin Brown. 4 vols. Grand Rapids: Zondervan, 1975-85.

———. *Jesus as God: The New Testament Use of* Theos *in Reference to Jesus.* Grand Rapids: Baker, 1992.

———. *Raised Immortal: The Relation between Resurrection and Immortality in New Testament Teaching.* London: Marshall, Morgan & Scott, 1983.

———. "Resurrection and Immortality in the Pauline Corpus." Pages 147-70 in *Life in the Face of Death: The Resurrection Message of the New Testament.* Edited by Richard N. Longenecker. Grand Rapids: Eerdmans, 1998.

———. *Slave of Christ: A New Testament Metaphor for Total Devotion to Christ.*

NSBT 8. Series editor, D. A. Carson. Downers Grove: InterVarsity Press, 1999.

Harvey, J. D. "Orality and Its Implications for Biblical Studies: Recapturing an Ancient Paradigm." *JETS* 45 (2002): 99-109.

Hawthorne, Gerald F. "In the Form of God and Equal with God (Philippians 2:6)." Pages 96-110 in *Where Christology Began: Essays on Philippians 2.* Edited by Ralph P. Martin and Brian J. Dodd. Louisville: Westminster John Knox, 1998.

Hays, Richard B. *Echoes of Scripture in the Letters of Paul.* New Haven: Yale University Press, 1989.

———. *The Faith of Jesus Christ.* 2nd ed. Grand Rapids: Eerdmans, 2002.

———. *The Moral Vision of the New Testament: Community, Cross, New Creation: A Contemporary Introduction to New Testament Ethics.* San Francisco: HarperCollins, 1996.

Heen, Erik M. "Phil 2:6-11 and Resistance to the Local Timocratic Rule: *Isa theō* and the Cult of the Emperor in the East." Pages 125-53 in *Paul and the Roman Imperial Order.* Edited by Richard A. Horsley. Harrisburg, Pa.: Trinity Press International, 2004.

Hellerman, J. H. "The Humiliation of Christ in the Social World of Roman Philippi, Part 1." *BSac* 160 (2003): 321-36.

———. "The Humiliation of Christ in the Social World of Roman Philippi, Part 2." *BSac* 160 (2003): 421-33.

———. *Reconstructing Honor in Roman Philippi:* Carmen Christi *as* Cursus Pudorum. SNTSMS 132. Cambridge: Cambridge University Press, 2005.

Hendrix, Holland L. "Philippi." Pages 313-17 in vol. 5 of *ABD.* Edited by David Noel Freedman. 6 vols. New York: Doubleday, 1992.

Hengel, Martin. *Crucifixion.* Philadelphia: Fortress, 1977.

———. *Judaism and Hellenism: Studies in Their Encounter in Palestine during the Early Hellenistic Period.* 2 vols. Translated by John Bowden. Philadelphia: Fortress, 1976.

Holloway, Paul A. *Consolation in Philippians: Philosophical Sources and Rhetorical Strategy.* SNTSMS 112. Cambridge: Cambridge University Press, 2001.

Holmberg, Bengt. *Paul and Power: The Structure of Authority in the Primitive Church as Reflected in the Pauline Epistles.* Philadelphia: Fortress, 1978.

Holmes, Arthur F. *All Truth Is God's Truth.* Grand Rapids: Eerdmans, 1977.

Hooker, Morna D. "Interchange in Christ." *JTS* 22 (1971): 349-61.

———. "Philippians 2:6-11." Pages 151-64 in *Jesus und Paulus: Festschrift für W. G. Kümmel.* Edited by E. E. Ellis and Erich Grässer. Göttingen: Vandenhoeck & Ruprecht, 1975.

Hoover, R. W. "The HARPAGMOS Enigma: A Philological Solution." *HTR* 64 (1971): 95-119.

Horsley, Richard A., ed. *Paul and Empire: Religion and Power in Roman Imperial Society.* Harrisburg, Pa.: Trinity Press International, 1997.

Hurtado, Larry W. *Lord Jesus Christ: Devotion to Jesus in Earliest Christianity.* Grand Rapids: Eerdmans, 2003.

———. *One God, One Lord: Early Christian Devotion and Ancient Jewish Monotheism.* 2nd ed. Edinburgh: T&T Clark, 1998.

Jeremias, Joachim. "Zur Gedankenführung in den Paulinischen Briefen." Pages 146-54 in *Studia Paulina in Honorem J. de Zwaan.* Edited by J. N. Sevenster and W. C. van Unnik. Haarlem: Hohn, 1953.

Jewett, R. "The Form and Function of the Homiletic Benediction." *ATR* 51 (1969): 18-34.

Johnson, Luke Timothy. *The Writings of the New Testament: An Interpretation.* Rev. ed. Minneapolis: Fortress, 1999.

Jowers, Dennis W. "The Meaning of *morphē* in Philippians 2:6-7." *JETS* 49 (2006): 739-66.

Käsemann, Ernst. "A Critical Analysis of Philippians 2:5-11." *JTC* 5 (1968): 45-88.

———. "Kritsche Analyse von Phil. 2,5-11." *ZThK* 47 (1950): 313-60.

———. *Perspectives on Paul.* Philadelphia: Fortress, 1971.

Kennedy, George A. *New Testament Interpretation through Rhetorical Criticism.* Chapel Hill, N.C.: University of North Carolina Press, 1984.

Kilpatrick, G. D. "ΒΛΕΠΕΤΕ, Philippians 3:2." Pages 146-148 in *In Memoriam Paul Kahle.* Edited by M. Black and G. Fohrer. BZAW 103. Berlin: A. Töpelmann, 1928.

Kim, Seyoon. *Paul and the New Perspective: Second Thoughts on the Origin of Paul's Gospel.* Grand Rapids: Eerdmans, 2002.

Klijn, A. F. J. "Paul's Opponents in Philippians III." *NovT* 7 (1964): 278-84.

Knapp, D. T. "The Self-Humiliation of Jesus Christ and Christ-Like Living: A Study of Philipians 2:6-11." *EvJ* 15 (1997): 80-94.

Koester, Helmut. *Paul and His World: Interpreting the New Testament in Its Context.* Minneapolis: Fortress, 2007.

Koperski, V. "The Early History of the Dissection of Philippians." *JTS* 44 (1993): 559-603.

———. *The Knowledge of Christ Jesus My Lord: The High Christology of Philippians 3:7-11.* Kampen: Kok Pharos, 1996.

———. "The Meaning of *dikaiosynē* in Philippians 3:9." *LS* 20 (1995): 147-69.

———. "The Meaning of *Pistis Christou* in Philippians 3:9." *LS* 18 (1993): 198-216.

Koukouli-Chrysantaki. "Colonia Iulia Augusta Philippensis." Pages 8-14 in *Philippi at the Time of Paul and after His Death.* Edited by C. Bakritzis and H. Koester. Harrisburg, Pa.: Trinity Press International, 1998.

Kreitzer, L. J., and D. W. Rooke. "'Singing in a New Key': Philippians 2:9-11 and the 'Andante' of Beethoven's Kreutzer Sonata." *ExpT* 109 (1998): 231-233.

Krentz, E. "Meeting Paul Anew: Rereading an Old Friend in a New Age." *Dialog* 39 (2002) 267-83.

———. "Military Language and Metaphors in Philippians." Pages 105-27 in

Origins and Method: Towards a New Understanding of Judaism and Christianity: Essays in Honour of John C. Hurd. Edited by B. H. McLean. JSNTSup 86. Sheffield: JSOT Press, 1993.

Kruse, C. G. "Virtues and Vices." Pages 962-63 in *DPL.* Edited by Gerald F. Hawthorne, Ralph P. Martin, and Daniel G. Reid. Downers Grove: InterVarsity Press, 1993.

Ladd, George E. *A Theology of the New Testament.* Edited by Donald H. Hagner. Rev. ed. Grand Rapids: Eerdmans, 1974.

Lambrecht, J. *Pauline Studies.* Leuven: Leuven University Press, 1994.

Liddell, H. G., R. Scott, and H. S. Jones. *A Greek-English Lexicon: With a Revised Supplement.* 9th ed. Oxford: Oxford University Press, 1996.

Lincoln, Andrew T. *Paradise Now and Not Yet: Studies in the Role of the Heavenly Dimension in Paul's Thought with Special Reference to His Eschatology.* Grand Rapids: Baker, 1991.

Lloyd-Jones, Martin D. *The Life of Peace: An Exposition of Philippians 3 and 4.* Grand Rapids: Baker, 1992.

Loane, Marcus. *Masters of the English Reformation.* London: Hodder and Stoughton, 1954.

Lohmeyer, Ernst. *Kyrios Jesus: Eine Untersuchung zu Phil 2,5-11.* Sitzungsberichte der Heidelberger Akademie der Wissenschaften. Philosophisch-historische Klasse, Jahrgang 1927/28, 4. Abhandlung; Heidelberg: Carl Winter, Universitätsverlag, 2. Auflage 1961.

Longenecker, Richard N. *The Christology of Early Jewish Christianity.* SBT 17. London: SCM, 1970.

———. *Paul, Apostle of Liberty.* Grand Rapids: Baker, 1976.

———, ed. *Life in the Face of Death: The Resurrection Message in the New Testament.* Grand Rapids: Eerdmans, 1998.

———, ed. *Patterns of Discipleship in the New Testament.* Grand Rapids: Eerdmans, 1996.

———, ed. *The Road from Damascus: The Impact of Paul's Conversion on His Life, Thought, and Ministry.* Grand Rapids: Eerdmans, 1997.

Louw, Johannes P., and Eugene A. Nida, eds. *Greek-English Lexicon of the New Testament: Based on Semantic Domains.* Vol. 1. 2nd ed. New York: United Bible Societies, 1988-89.

Luter, A. B., and M. V. Lee. "Philippians as Chiasmus: Key to the Structure, Unity and Theme Questions." *NTS* 41 (1995): 89-101.

Malherbe, Abraham J. *Ancient Epistolary Theorists.* Atlanta: Scholars Press, 1988.

———. *Moral Exhortation: A Greco-Roman Sourcebook.* LEC 4. Philadelphia: Fortress, 1986.

———. "Paul's Self-Sufficiency (Philippians 4:11)." Pages 125-39 in *Friendship, Flattery, and Frankness of Speech: Studies on Friendship in the New Testament World.* NovTSup 82. Edited by John T. Fitzgerald. Leiden: Brill, 1996.

Marshall, I. Howard. "Incarnational Christology in the New Testament."

Pages 1-16 in *Christ the Lord: Studies in Christology Presented to Donald Guthrie.* Edited by H. H. Rowdon. Leicester: InterVarsity Press, 1982.

———. "The Theology of Philippians." Pages 117-74 in *New Testament Theology: The Theology of the Shorter Pauline Letters.* Edited by Karl P. Donfried and I. Howard Marshall. Cambridge: Cambridge University Press, 1993.

Marshall, J. W. "Paul's Ethical Appeal in Philippians." Pages 357-74 in *Rhetoric and the New Testament: Essays from 1992 Heidelberg Conference.* Edited by S. E. Porter and T. H. Olbricht. JSNTSup 90. Sheffield: JSOT Press, 1993.

Marshall, Peter. *Enmity in Corinth.* WUNT 23. Tübingen: J. C. B. Mohr, 1987.

Martin, Ralph P. *A Hymn of Christ: Philippians 2:5-11 in Recent Interpretation and in the Setting of Early Christian Worship.* Downers Grove: InterVarsity Press, 1997.

———, and B. J. Dodd, eds. *Where Christology Began: Essays on Philippians 2.* Louisville: Westminister John Knox, 1998.

Martyn, J. L. "De-apocalypticizing Paul: An Essay Focused on Paul and the Stoics by Troels Engberg-Pedersen." *JSNT* 86 (2002): 61-102.

Matera, F. J. "Imitating Paul in Order to Follow Christ." *Llt.* 38 (2001): 35-43.

Matlock, R. B. "Detheologizing the *pistis Christou* Debate: Cautionary Remarks from a Lexical Semantic Perspective." *NovT* 42 (2000): 1-23.

Mearns, Christopher. "The Identity of Paul's Opponents at Philippi." *NTS* 33 (1987): 194-204.

Meeks, W. A. *In Search of Early Christians: Selected Essays.* Edited by Allen R. Hilton and H. Gregory Snyder. New Haven: Yale University Press, 2002.

Metzger, Bruce M. *A Textual Commentary on the Greek New Testament.* Stuttgart: United Bible Societies, 1971.

Miller, E. C. "Πολιτεύεσθε in Philippians 1.27: Some Philological and Thematic Observations." *JSNT* 15 (1982): 86-96.

Moiser, J. "The Meaning of *koila* in Philippians 3:19." *ExpT* 108 (1997): 365-66.

Morgan, Robert. "Incarnation, Myth, and Theology: Ernst Kasemann's Interpretation of Philippians 2:5-11." Pages 43-73 in *Where Christology Began: Essays on Philippians 2.* Edited by Ralph Martin and Brian Dodd. Louisville: Westminster John Knox, 1988.

Moule, C. F. D. "Further Reflexions on Philippians 2:5-11." Pages 264-76 in *Apostolic History and the Gospel: Biblical and Historical Essays Presented to F. F. Bruce on His 60th Birthday.* Edited by W. W. Gasque and R. P. Martin. Grand Rapids: Eerdmans, 1970.

———. *An Idiom-Book of New Testament Greek.* 2nd ed. Cambridge: Cambridge University Press, 1963.

———. "The Manhood of Jesus in the NT." Pages 95-110 in *Christ, Faith, and History.* Edited by S. W. Sykes and J. P. Clayton. Cambridge: Cambridge University Press, 1972.

———. "St. Paul and Dualism: The Pauline Concept of Resurrection." *NTS* 13 (1966): 106-23.

Moulton, J. H., and G. Milligan. *Vocabulary of the Greek Testament.* Peabody, Mass.: Hendrickson, 1997.

Mullins, T. Y. "Disclosure as a Literary Form in the New Testament." *NovT* 7 (1964): 46-49.

———. "A Visit Talk in New Testament Letters." *CBQ* 35 (1973): 350-58.

Murphy-O'Connor, Jerome. *Paul, A Critical Life.* Oxford: Clarendon, 1996.

Murray, George W. "Paul's Corporate Witness in Philippians." *BSac* 155 (1998): 316-26.

Oakes, Peter. *Philippians: From People to Letter.* SNTSMS 110. Cambridge: Cambridge University Press, 2001.

O'Brien, Peter T. "Benediction, Blessing, Doxology, Thanksgiving." Pages 68-71 in *DPL.* Edited by Gerald F. Hawthorne, Ralph P. Martin, and Daniel G. Reid. Downers Grove: InterVarsity Press, 1993.

———. "Caesar's Household, Imperial Household." Pages 83-84 in *DPL.* Edited by Gerald F. Hawthorne, Ralph P. Martin, and Daniel G. Reid. Downers Grove: InterVarsity Press, 1993.

———. *Gospel and Mission in the Writings of Paul: An Exegetical and Theological Analysis.* Grand Rapids: Baker, 1995.

———. *Introductory Thanksgivings in the Letters of Paul.* NovTSup 49. Leiden: Brill, 1977.

———. "Letters, Letter Forms." Pages 550-553 in *Dictionary of Paul and His Letters.* Edited by Gerald F. Hawthorne, Ralph P. Martin, and Daniel G. Reid. Downers Grove, Ill.: InterVarsity Press, 1993.

O'Donovan, Oliver. *Resurrection and Moral Order.* Leicester: Inter-Varsity Press, 1986.

Otto, R. E. "If Possible I May Attain the Resurrection from the Dead (Philippians 3:11)." *CBQ* 57 (1995): 324-40.

Palmer, D. W. "To Die Is Gain." *NovT* 17 (1975): 203-18.

Pedersen-Engberg, T. *Paul in His Hellenistic Context.* Minneapolis: Fortress, 1995.

Peng, K. "Do We Need an Alternative Rendering for Philippians 1.3?" *BT* 54 (2003): 415-19.

Perkins, Pheme. "Finding Joy in the Lord." *QR* 22 (2002): 199-207.

———. "Philippians: Theology for the Heavenly *Politeuma.*" Pages 89-104 in *Pauline Theology: Thessalonians, Philippians, Galatians, Philemon.* Edited by Jouette M. Bassler. Vol. 1 of *Pauline Theology.* Edited by Jouette M. Bassler. Minneapolis: Fortress, 1991.

Perriman, A. "The Pattern of Christ's Sufferings: Colossians 1:24 and Philippians 3:10-11." *TynBul* 42 (1991): 62-79.

Peterlin, Davorin. *Paul's Letter to the Philippians in the Light of Disunity in the Church.* JSNTSup 79. Leiden: Brill, 1995.

Peterman, Gerald W. *Paul's Gift from Philippi: Conventions of Gift Exchange and*

Christian Giving. SNTSMS 92. Cambridge: Cambridge University Press, 1997.

———. "'Thankless Thanks': The Epistolary Social Convention in Philippians 4.10-20." *TynBul* 42.2 (1991): 261-70.

Peterson, Eugene. *A Long Obedience in the Same Direction: Discipleship in an Instant Society.* 2nd ed. Downers Grove: InterVarsity Press, 2000.

Plummer, Robert L. "The Mission of the Church in Paul's Letter to the Philippians in the Context of Ancient Judaism." *JETS* 49 (2006): 614-16.

Porter, S. E. *Idioms of the Greek New Testament.* Sheffield: JSOT Press, 1992.

———. "Word Order and Clause Structure in New Testament Greek: An Unexplored Area of Greek Linguistics Using Philippians as a Test Case." *FN* 6 (1993): 177-205.

———, and D. A. Carson., eds. *Discourse Analysis and Other Topics in Biblical Greek.* Sheffield: Sheffield Academic Press, 1995.

———, and T. H. Olbricht., eds. *The Rhetorical Analysis of Scripture: Essays from the 1995 London Conference.* Sheffield: Sheffield Academic Press, 1997.

———, and J. T. Reed. "Philippians as a Macro-Chiasm and Its Exegetical Significance." *NTS* 44 (1998): 213-31.

Poythress, V. S. "'Hold Fast' versus 'Hold Out' in Philippians 2:16." *WTJ* 64 (2002): 45-53.

Pretorius, E. "Role Models for a Model Church: Typifying Paul's Letter to the Philippians." *Neot* 32 (1998): 547-71.

Rapske, Brian. *The Book of Acts and Paul in Roman Custody.* Grand Rapids: Eerdmans, 1994.

Reed, Jeffrey T. *A Discourse Analysis of Philippians: Method and Rhetoric in the Debate over Literary Integrity.* LNTS. Sheffield: Sheffield Academic Press, 1997.

———. "Philippians 3:1 and the Epistolary Hesitation Formulas: The Literary Integrity of Philippians, Again." *JBL* 115 (1996): 63-90.

———. "The Infinitive with Two Substantival Accusatives, An Ambiguous Construction?" *NovT* 33 (1991): 1-27.

Reicke, B. "Caesarea, Rome, and the Captivity Epistles." Pages 275-86 in *Apostolic History and the Gospel: Biblical and Historical Essays Presented to F. F. Bruce on His 60th Birthday.* Edited by W. W. Gasque and R. P. Martin. Grand Rapids: Eerdmans, 1970.

Reumann, John H. P. "Justification and the *Imitatio* Motif in Philippians 3.2-21." Pages 17-28 in *Promoting Unity: Themes in Lutheran-Catholic Dialogue.* Edited by G. Anderson and J. R. Crumley Jr. Minneapolis: Augsburg, 1989.

———. "Philippians 3:20-21 — A Hymnic Fragment." *NTS* 30 (1984): 593-609.

———. "Philippians, Especially Chapter 4, as a 'Letter of Friendship': Observations on the Checkered History of Scholarship." Pages 83-106 in *Friendship, Flattery, and Frankness of Speech: Studies on Friendship in the New Testament World.* Edited by John T. Fitzgerald. Leiden: Brill, 1996.

Ridderbos, Herman. *Paul: An Outline of His Theology.* Grand Rapids: Eerdmans, 1975.

Saldarini, Anthony J. *Pharisees, Scribes and Sadducees in Palestinian Society.* The Biblical Resource Series. Grand Rapids: Eerdmans, 2001.

Sampley, Paul J. *Pauline Partnership in Christ: Christian Community and Commitment in Light of Roman Law.* Philadelphia: Fortress, 1980.

Sanders, E. P. *Paul and Palestinian Judaism: A Comparison of Patterns of Religion.* Philadelphia: Fortress, 1977.

———. *Paul, the Law, and the Jewish People.* Philadelphia: Fortress, 1985.

Sanders, J. T. "The Transition from Opening Epistolary Thanksgiving to Body in Letters of the Pauline Corpus." *JBL* 81 (1962): 348-62.

Schenk, Wolfgang. "Der Philipperbrief oder die Philipperbriefe des Paulus? Eine Antwort an V. Koperski." *ETL* 70 (1994): 122-31.

Schroeder, Frederic M. "Friendship in Aristotle and Some Peripatetic Philosophers." Pages 35-57 in *Greco-Roman Perspectives on Friendship.* Edited by John T. Fitzgerald. Atlanta: Scholars Press, 1977.

Schubert, Paul. *Form and Function of the Pauline Thanksgivings.* ZNT 20. Berlin: Töpelmann, 1939.

Schweitzer, Albert. *The Mysticism of Paul the Apostle.* Translated by William Montgomery. Baltimore: The John Hopkins University Press, 1998.

Seesemann, Heinrich. *Der Begriff KOINŌNIA im Neuen Testament.* Gießen: Töpelmann, 1933.

Seifrid, M. A. "In Christ." Pages 433-36 in *DPL.* Edited by Gerald F. Hawthorne, Ralph P. Martin, and Daniel G. Reid. Downers Grove: InterVarsity Press, 1993.

Sevenster, J. N. *Paul and Seneca.* NovTSup 4. Leiden: Brill, 1961.

Silva, Moisés. "Faith versus Works of Law in Galatians." Pages 217-248 in *Justification and Variegated Nomism, Volume 2: The Paradoxes of Paul.* Edited by D. A. Carson, Peter T. O'Brien, and Mark A. Seifrid. Grand Rapids: Baker Academic, 2004.

Spencer, A. B. *Paul's Literary Style: A Stylistic and Historical Comparison of II Corinthians 11:16–12:13, Romans 8:9-39, and Philippians 3:2–4:13.* New York: Oxford University Press of America, 1998.

Stanley, D. M. "'Become Imitators of Me': The Pauline Conception of Apostolic Tradition." *Bib* 40 (1959): 859-77.

———. "Imitation in Paul's Letters: Its Significance for His Relationship to Jesus and to His Own Christian Foundations." Pages 113-26 in *From Jesus to Paul: Studies in Honour of Francis Wright Beare.* Edited by Peter Richardson and John C. Hurd. Waterloo, Ont.: Wilfrid Laurier University Press, 1984.

Steenburg, David. "The Case against the Synonymity of MORPHĒ and EIKŌN." *JSNT* 37 (1988): 77-86.

Stendahl, Krister. *Paul among Jews and Gentiles.* Philadelphia: Fortress, 1976.

Stockton, David. "The Founding of the Empire." Pages 531-56 in *The Oxford*

History of the Classical World. Edited by John Boardman, Jasper Griffin, and Oswyn Murray. London: Oxford University Press, 1988.

Stowers, S. K. "Friends and Enemies in the Politics of Heaven: Reading Theology in Philippians." Pages 105-21 in *Pauline Theology: Thessalonians, Philippians, Galatians, Philemon.* Edited by Jouette M. Bassler. Vol. 1 of *Pauline Theology.* Edited by Jouette M. Bassler. Minneapolis: Fortress, 1991.

———. *Letter Writing in Greco-Roman Antiquity.* LEC 5. Philadelphia: Westminster, 1986.

Suggs, M. J. "*Koinonia* in the New Testament." *NovT* 4 (1960-61): 60-68.

Sumney, J. L. *"Servants of Satan," "False Brothers," and Other Opponents of Paul.* JSNTSup 188. Sheffield: Sheffield Academic Press, 1999.

Telbe, Mikael. *Paul between Synagogue and State: Christians, Jews, and Civic Authorities in I Thessalonians, Romans, and Philippians.* Stockholm: Almqvist & Wiksell, 2001.

———. "The Sociological Factors behind Philippians 3.1-11 and the Conflict at Philippi." *JSNT* 55 (1994): 97-121.

Thielman, Frank. "Ephesus and the Literary Setting of Philippians." Pages 205-23 in *New Testament Greek and Exegesis: Essays in Honor of Gerald Hawthorne.* Edited by Amy M. Donaldson and Timothy B. Sailors. Grand Rapids: Eerdmans, 2003.

———. *Paul and the Law.* Downers Grove: InterVarsity Press, 1994.

Thomas, Derek W. "The Place of Women in the Church at Philippi." *ExpT* 83 (1971-72): 117-20.

———. "Rejoice in the Lord? Cohesion in Philippians 3:1." *Notes* 10 (1996): 53-54.

Thompson, A. J. "Blameless before God? Philippians 3:6 in Context." *Them* (2002): 5-12.

Trebilco, Paul. "Asia." Pages 291-362 in *The Book of Acts in Its Graeco-Roman Setting.* Edited by David W. J. Gill and Conrad Gempf. Vol. 2 of *The Book of Acts in Its First-Century Setting.* Edited by Bruce W. Winter. Grand Rapids: Eerdmans, 1994.

Tyson, J. B. "Paul's Opponents at Philippi." *PRSt* 3 (1976): 82-95.

Udoh, F. E. "Paul's Views on the Law: Questions about Origin (Gal. 1:6–2:21; Phil. 3:2-11)." *NovT* 42 (2000): 214-37.

Waltke, Bruce K. "The Fear of the Lord: The Foundation for a Relationship with God." Pages 17-33 in *Alive to God: Studies in Spirituality Presented to James Houston.* Edited by J. I. Packer and Loren Wilkinson. Downers Grove: InterVarsity Press, 1992.

Wasink, C. S. *Chained in Christ: The Experience and Rhetoric of Paul's Imprisonments.* JSNTSup 130. Sheffield: Sheffield Academic, 1996.

Watson, D. F. "A Rhetorical Analysis of Philippians and Its Implications for the Unity Question." *NovT* 30 (1988): 59-60.

Wedderburn, A. J. M. "Paul's Collection: Chronology and History." *NTS* 48 (2002): 95-110.

Weidmann, F. W. "An (Un)accomplished Model: Paul and the Rhetorical Strategy of Philippians 3:3-17." Pages 245-47 in *Putting Body and Soul Together: Essays in Honor of Robin Scroggs.* Edited by V. Wiles, A. Brown, and G. F. Snyder. Valley Forge, Pa.: Trinity Press International, 1997.

Weima, J. A. D. *Neglected Endings: The Significance of the Pauline Letter Closings.* JSNTSup 101. Sheffield: Sheffield Academic, 1994.

Westerholm, Stephen. *Israel's Law and the Church's Faith: Paul and His Recent Interpreters.* Grand Rapids: Eerdmans, 1988.

———. *Perspectives Old and New on Paul: The "Lutheran" Paul and His Critics.* Grand Rapids: Eerdmans, 2004.

White, John L. *The Form and Function of the Body of the Greek Letter: A Study of the Letter-Body in the Non-Literary Papyri and in Paul the Apostle.* SBLDS 2. Missoula, Mont.: Scholars Press, 1972.

White, L. M. "Morality between Two Worlds: A Paradigm of Friendship in Philippians." Pages 201-15 in *Greeks, Romans, and Christians: Essays in Honor of Abraham J. Malherbe.* Edited by D. L. Balch, E. Ferguson, and W. A. Meeks. Minneapolis: Fortress, 1990.

Wiles, G. P. *Paul's Intercessory Prayers: The Significance of the Intercessory Prayer Passages in the Letters of St. Paul.* SNTSMS 24. Cambridge: Cambridge University Press, 1974.

Williams, Demetrius K. *Enemies of the Cross: The Terminology of the Cross and Conflict in Philippians.* JSNTSup 223. London: Sheffield Academic, 2002.

Winter, Bruce W. *Seek the Welfare of the City: Christians as Benefactors and Citizens.* First-Century Christians in the Graeco-Roman World. Grand Rapids: Eerdmans, 1994.

Wright, C. J. H. "Family." Pages 766-69 in vol. 2 of *ABD.* Edited by David Noel Freedman. 6 vols. New York: Doubleday, 1992.

Wright, N. T. *The Climax of the Covenant: Christ and the Law in Pauline Theology.* Minneapolis: Fortress, 1993.

———. *Paul in Fresh Perspective.* Minneapolis: Fortress, 2005.

———. "Paul's Gospel and Caesar's Empire." Pages 160-83 in *Paul and Politics: Ekklēsia, Israel, Imperium, Interpretation: Essays in Honor of Krister Stendahl.* Edited by Richard A. Horsley. Harrisburg, Pa.: Trinity Press International, 2000.

———. *What St. Paul Really Said.* Oxford: Lion Hudson, 1997.

Ziesler, J. A. *The Meaning of Righteousness in Paul: A Linguistic and Theological Inquiry.* SNTSMS 20. Cambridge: Cambridge University Press, 1972.

Introduction

Paul's letter to the Philippians exudes a joyful spirit and warm affection. As a "thank you" note to his friends for their generosity, Paul's letter wraps them in his warm embrace. Yet, as he affirms his friends, he also responds to their problems: rivalry and gossip in the church separate leaders; hostility and skepticism in the world challenge faith in Christ; and the spirituality of impressive religious teachers promoting a bogus formula for perfect success attracts recent converts. Since followers of Jesus in the twenty-first-century experience similar problems, Paul's first-century response to the Philippians sounds strangely applicable to the present time. Paul validates the authenticity of his message by speaking honestly about his own experience in prison and openly admitting his shortcomings in his journey of faith. His letter strengthens our faith in Christ in the face of suffering and death, encourages us to resolve our conflicts in our community, and teaches us how to embody the gospel so that the world can see and hear the grace of our Lord Jesus Christ. Above all, Paul's letter leads us to worship Jesus Christ as we contemplate his suffering on the cross, his exaltation as Lord, and his ultimate victory over all earthly powers.

To prepare the way for reading through this remarkable letter we will consider a few background issues: the historical setting of the church in Philippi, the nature of the letter, the occasion for the letter, and a brief preview of two major themes of the letter.

I. THE HISTORICAL SETTING OF THE CHURCH IN PHILIPPI

Philippi carried the name of Philip II, king of Macedon, since his fortification of the city in 356 B.C.[1] His patronage of Greek arts contributed to the

1. For historical overviews of Philippi see David Stockton, "The Founding of the Em-

ambition of his son, Alexander the Great, to make the world conform to Greek culture. Tutored by Aristotle, Alexander founded Greek cities across western Asia to be centers of Greek language and Greek entertainment. The conquests of Alexander made *koinē* Greek the means of communication in government and business throughout the Hellenized world.

After Mark Antony and Octavian defeated Brutus and Cassius, Julius Caesar's assassins, on the plains near Philippi in 42 B.C., Philippi became a Roman colony and home for discharged Roman army veterans. Antony, Octavian, and Lepidus ruled as a Triumvirate, a three-man dictatorship. But when Antony promoted Cleopatra's son, Caesarion, as the legitimate heir of Julius Caesar, he was caricatured by Octavian as a traitor to the ideals of Rome, a renegade in thrall to the Egyptian queen. The Triumvirate expired and civil war caused social and economic chaos. After Octavian defeated Mark Antony at the battle of Actium (31 B.C.), he was welcomed as a savior who restored peace and security to the Roman world. The *Pax Romana* created by Augustus enabled social and economic recovery in contrast to the times of distress during the civil war. Octavian gave his own propagandist report of his accomplishments in his *Res Gestae:*[2]

> In my sixth and seventh consulships, after I had extinguished the civil wars, having been put in supreme possession of the whole empire by the universal consent of all, I transferred the republic from my own control into the free control of the Senate and People of Rome. For this service I received the appellation of Augustus by a decree of the Senate.

In the colony of Philippi renamed by Augustus after the Julian family *(Colonia Iulia Augusta Philippensis),* Roman aristocracy flourished and Roman architecture became the standard.[3] More Roman soldiers were given allotments in Philippi. Since it was a Roman colony, the citizens of Philippi enjoyed all the privileges and rights of Roman citizens: they were exempt from taxes and governed under Roman law, the *ius Italicum.* Philippi was modeled after the mother city, Rome. Roman arches, bathhouses, forums, and temples dominated Philippi at the time of Paul. In a

---

pire," in *The Oxford History of the Classical World* (ed. John Boardman, Jasper Griffin, and Oswyn Murray; London: Oxford University Press, 1988), 531-56; Robin Lane Fox, *The Classical World: An Epic History from Homer to Hadrian* (New York: Basic Books, 2006); Holland L. Hendrix, "Philippi," *ABD* 5:313-17; David W. J. Gill, "Macedonia," in *The Book of Acts in Its Graeco-Roman Setting* (ed. David W. J. Gill and Conrad Gempf; vol. 2 of The Book in Its First-Century Setting, ed. Bruce W. Winter; Grand Rapids: Eerdmans, 1993), 411-13.

2. C. K. Barrett, ed., *The New Testament Background: Selected Documents* (rev. ed.; San Francisco: Harper, 1987), 3.

3. C. Koukouli-Chrysantaki, "Colonia Iulia Augusta Philippensis," in *Philippi at the Time of Paul and after His Death* (ed. C. Bakritzis and H. Koester; Harrisburg, Pa.: Trinity Press International, 1998), 8, 14; Lukas Bormann, *Philippi: Stadt und Christengemeinde zur Zeit des Paulus* (Leiden: Brill, 1995), 11.

Greek-speaking province, Latin became the official language of Philippi.[4] Although Greek, Phrygian, and Egyptian gods had their temples in Philippi, the imperial cult was the most prominent in the city. With impressive altars and temples dedicated to the emperor and members of his family, the city's religious life centered on the worship of the emperor.[5] Withdrawal from participation in the imperial cult was viewed as subversive activity.[6]

In the account of Paul's first visit to Philippi in A.D. 49, Acts captures the essence of this historical background by describing Philippi accurately as "a Roman colony" (Acts 16:12: *kolōnia*). Residents of Philippi expressed their pride in their Roman citizenship by accusing Paul and his associates of "advocating customs unlawful for us Romans to accept or practice" (Acts 16:21). Paul's complaint that he and Silas were treated unjustly as Roman citizens (Acts 16:37) also points to the high regard for Roman citizenship in this Roman colony. By reading Philippians in the light of the Roman character of Philippi and the importance of the imperial cult in this city, we gain an appreciation for the significance of Paul's report of his witness to the "whole palace guard" while in chains (1:12-13; 4:22), his references to our heavenly "citizenship" (1:27; 3:20), his description of external opposition to the faith (1:28-30), his use of the titles of the emperor ("Lord" and "Savior") for Christ (2:11; 3:20-21), his sorrow over those who have abandoned their faith because of the pressures of their surrounding culture (3:18-19), and his promise, not of a *Pax Romana,* but of the "peace of God" to guard the believers in Christ (4:7).[7]

When Paul arrived in Philippi after walking twelve miles with Silas, Timothy, and Luke[8] from Neapolis on the Roman road, Via Egnatia,[9] he sought to begin his witness to Christ as usual in a Jewish place of wor-

4. While Latin predominates in the inscriptions from the period, evidence of the continued use of Greek indicates that the Greek-speaking Paul would have been sufficiently understood to undertake his ministry in Philippi. See Hendrix, "Philippi," *ABD* 5:315. Evidently, Latin was an official veneer over a basically Greek culture

5. Erik M. Heen, "Phil 2:6-11 and Resistance to the Local Timocratic Rule: *Isa theō* and the Cult of the Emperor in the East," in *Paul and the Roman Imperial Order* (ed. Richard A. Horsley; Harrisburg, Pa.: Trinity Press International, 2004), 136: "It seems reasonable to assume that in Philippi at the mid-first century C.E., there was a flourishing imperial cult and that it had moved to the center of public discourse of the city."

6. Pheme Perkins, "Philippians: Theology for the Heavenly *Politeuma*," in *Pauline Theology: Thessalonians, Philippians, Galatians, Philemon* (ed. Jouette M. Bassler; vol. 1 of *Pauline Theology*, ed. Jouette M. Bassler; Minneapolis: Fortress, 1991), 93.

7. See the commentary on these texts below. See also Warren Carter, *The Roman Empire and the New Testament* (Nashville: Abingdon, 2006), 60-62; N. T. Wright, *Paul in Fresh Perspective* (Minneapolis: Fortress, 2005), 70-74.

8. Since this section is one of the so-called "we" sections of Acts, most interpreters suppose that Luke, the author of Acts, was with Paul at this time.

9. David French, "Acts and the Roman Roads of Asia Minor," in *The Book of Acts in Its Graeco-Roman Setting* (ed. David W. J. Gill and Conrad Gempf; vol. 1 of The Book of Acts in Its First-Century Setting; ed. Bruce W. Winter; Grand Rapids: Eerdmans, 1993), 49-58.

ship.[10] But apparently Philippi did not have a quorum of ten Jewish men necessary for the establishment of a synagogue.[11] In this city the place he found to keep the Sabbath was not a synagogue within the city but a "place of prayer" by the river outside the city gate where some women gathered on the Sabbath (Acts 16:13).[12] Lydia, Paul's first convert in Philippi, was in this group of women (Acts 16:14). She was an immigrant from Thyatira, a merchant in the trade of purple cloth, and a Gentile follower of the Jewish religion (a "God-fearer"). When "the Lord opened her heart to respond to Paul's message," she opened her home for the church (Acts 16:14-15).

The account of Paul's ministry in Acts also provides a sketch of the exorcism of a slave girl by Paul's command in the name of Jesus Christ for the spirit to depart (16:16-18). As a result of her deliverance from the spirit that gave her the ability to predict the future, her owners were enraged by their loss of income through the girl and dragged Paul and Silas before the magistrates. The charge against Paul and Silas demonstrates a strong aversion to Jewish proselytizing in Roman Philippi: "These men are Jews, and are throwing our city into an uproar by advocating customs unlawful for us Romans to accept or practice" (Acts 16:20-21). Evidently, Luke frames the charge in this way to raise the question of the legitimacy of Christianity in the Roman Empire.[13] Would the Christian religion be recognized as a *religio licita,* a licit religion by Roman authorities?

When the magistrates of Philippi were overwhelmed by the attack of the crowd against Paul and Silas, they stripped, beat, and imprisoned them (Acts 16:22-24). Paul's letter to the Philippians reminds the Christians in Philippi that the suffering of the church in Philippi is the same as the suffering that Paul experienced when he was in Philippi: "you are going through the same struggle you saw I had" (1:30).[14] This common experience of suffering for the sake of Christ forms the background for the theme of suffering in the letter. Paul writes the letter to explain how the suffering of Christ

10. Acts makes reference to Paul's practice of attending local synagogues in the accounts of his visits to Salamis (13:4), Pisidian Antioch (13:14), Iconium (14:1), Thessalonica (17:1), Berea (17:10), Athens (17:17), and Corinth (18:4, 7).

11. The requirement of ten men to form a synagogue is stated in the *Mishnah* (the compilation of oral law at the close of the second century A.D.): *m. Sanh.* 1:6: "Whence do we learn that a congregation is made up of ten?"; *m. Avot* 3:6: "If ten men sit together and occupy themselves with the Law, the Divine Presence rests among them."

12. There is some debate regarding this interpretation because the term "place of prayer" designates a synagogue in a few Jewish texts. See the discussion and references in Joseph Fitzmyer, *The Acts of the Apostles* (AB 31; New York: Doubleday, 1998), 585. In the light of the reports in Acts of Paul's practice of visiting local synagogues (see note 10 above), the lack of a reference to Jews or to a synagogue in the account of Paul's visit to Philippi indicates that Luke did not think that there was a synagogue in Philippi. Thus Luke's reference to a "place of prayer" (Acts 16:13, 16) outside of Philippi should not be taken as a reference to a synagogue of the Jews.

13. Fitzmyer, *Acts,* 588.

14. 1 Thessalonians also refers to this persecution in Philippi: "We had previously suffered and been treated outrageously in Philippi" (1 Thess 2:2).

and the suffering of the servants of Christ lead to ultimate vindication by God's triumphant grace.[15] By God's intervention, Paul and Silas were set free from their chains. After they led the jailer and his family to faith in the Lord Jesus (Acts 16:25-34), they went back to Lydia's house to meet with the believers (Acts 16:40).

According to this account in Acts, the first members of the church founded by Paul in Philippi included Lydia (a God-fearing, Gentile businesswoman), the members of her household, a Roman jailer, the members of his household, and perhaps a slave girl. Given the lack of evidence for a Jewish presence in Philippi, we can assume that all the members of the church were Gentile Christians. Paul's letter to the Philippians corroborates the evidence from the account in Acts that the church planted by Paul in Roman Philippi was a Gentile church. While the letter draws extensively from the vocabulary and social structures of Greco-Roman society, very little use is made of the Jewish Scriptures (except for allusions in 1:19; 2:10-11, 15) or customs. Where Paul does refer to a dangerous influence from a Jewish-Christian source (3:2-6), he seems to indicate that the threat came from outside the social setting of the church. Furthermore, three of the members of the church in Philippi mentioned by Paul have three Greek names and one has a Roman name: Epaphroditus, Euodia, Syntyche, and Clement (4:2-4). Another indication of the Gentile nature of the church is Paul's direct address to the Philippians with a Latin form of their name: *Philippēsioi* (4:15).

The account in Acts and Paul's letter to the Philippians inform us that some of the leaders in the church Paul planted in Philippi were women. Lydia invited Paul and his team to stay in her house (Acts 16:15). As head of her household, she evidently had the financial means to own or rent a home large enough for the initial gathering of believers. Paul's acceptance of her hospitality for himself and for the church confirmed her socially prominent position in the church. Paul's direct address to Euodia and Syntyche indicates that they were also significant leaders in the church (Phil 4:2). If their dispute was only a private matter between themselves, Paul's public appeal would have been unnecessarily embarrassing and inexplicable. Paul appealed to them by name because as influential leaders their personal dispute was causing a division within the church. The role of these women as leaders in the Philippian church would have been culturally acceptable in Philippi where women were well known for their religious devotion and prominent positions in society.[16] Rather than rejecting their position as leaders, Paul encouraged these women to be reconciled to

15. L. Gregory Bloomquist, *The Function of Suffering in Philippians* (JSNTSup 78; Sheffield: JSOT Press, 1993), 194-95.

16. Bockmuehl, 5, 8, 34; see W. Derek Thomas, "The Place of Women in the Church at Philippi," *ExpT* 83 (1971-72), 117-20; Valerie Abrahamsen, "Women at Philippi: The Pagan and Christian Evidence," *JFSR* 3 (1987), 17-30; Florence M. Gillman, "Early Christian Women at Philippi," *JGWR* 1 (1990), 59-79.

each other in their devotion to the Lord so that they would lead in a way that unified the church.

At the very beginning of the church in Philippi, the believers showed unusual commitment to support Paul in his mission to proclaim the gospel. Paul goes back to the beginning of his partnership with the Christians in Philippi to commend them for their generosity from the "first day" (1:5) and "the early days of your acquaintance with the gospel" (4:15). The Philippian church made regular contributions to Paul's mission even after he left Philippi (4:15-18). By sending Epaphroditus with gifts to serve Paul while he was in prison, the Philippian believers demonstrated that their concern for him never wavered even though at times they had no opportunity to show it (4:10). To a large extent, Paul's letter to the Philippians is his expression of gratitude for their constant friendship and faithful support.[17]

II. THE NATURE OF THE LETTER TO THE PHILIPPIANS

A. A Letter of Friendship

Paul's use of the language of friendship throughout his letter to the Philippians comes to its climax in an accumulation of friendship terms in 4:1: "my brothers and sisters, you whom I love and long for, my joy and crown, dear friends."[18] On the basis of this friendship language, many interpreters

17. Gerald W. Peterman offers valuable analysis of Paul's expression of gratitude in the light of first-century social conventions. See "'Thankless Thanks': The Epistolary Social Conventions in Philippians 4:10-20," *TynBul* 42.2 (1991), 261-70; also Gerald W. Peterman, *Paul's Gift from Philippi: Conventions of Gift Exchange and Christian Giving* (SNTSMS 92; Cambridge: Cambridge University Press, 1997). The absence of an explicit "thank you" in Philippians does not mean that Paul was ungrateful since verbal gratitude was not socially appropriate between intimate friends. Nor was Paul's lack of a material return to the Philippians a failure to fulfill his social obligation of reciprocity since he desired fruit that would be credited to their account (4:17) and promised them that God would discharge his debt by meeting their needs (4:19).

18. See John Reumann, "Philippians, Especially Chapter 4, as a 'Letter of Friendship': Observations on a Checkered History of Scholarship," in *Friendship, Flattery, and Frankness of Speech: Studies on Friendship in the New Testament World* (ed. John T. Fitzgerald; NovTSup 82; Leiden: E. J. Brill, 1996), 83-106; John T. Fitzgerald, "Philippians in the Light of Some Ancient Discussions of Friendship," in *Friendship, Flattery, and Frankness of Speech: Studies on Friendship in the New Testament World* (ed. John T. Fitzgerald; NovTSup 82; Leiden: E. J. Brill), 141-60; L. M. White, "Morality between Two Worlds: A Paradigm of Friendship in Philippians," in *Greeks, Romans, and Christians: Essays in Honor of Abraham J. Malherbe* (ed. D. L. Balch, E. Ferguson, and W. A. Meeks; Minneapolis: Fortress, 1990), 201-15; S. K. Stowers, "Friends and Enemies in the Politics of Heaven: Reading Theology in Philippians," in *Pauline Theology: Thessalonians, Philippians, Galatians, Philemon* (ed. J. M. Bassler; vol. 1 of *Pauline Theology*, ed. Jouette M. Bassler; Minneapolis: Fortress, 1991), 105-21.

of Philippians identify this letter as a letter of friendship.[19] In an ancient epistolary handbook, Demetrius describes the friendly letter as the first type of letter in his presentation of twenty-one types of letters. According to this classical book on letter writing, the essential elements of a letter of friendship are "1. two people separated, 2. one person attempting to converse with the other, 3. a relationship of friendship between the two, and 4. the writer attempting to maintain that relationship with the recipient."[20] A fascinating example of a letter of friendship illustrates these elements of a friendly letter. In this letter the author, Chairas, writes to his doctor-friend, Dionysius, requesting a medical prescription.[21]

> Chairas to his dearest Dionysius, many greetings and continual health. I was as much delighted at receiving a letter from you as if I had indeed been in my native place; for apart from that we have nothing. I may dispense with writing to you with a great show of thanks; for it is to those who are not friends that we must give thanks in words. I trust that I may maintain myself in some degree of serenity and be able, if not to give you an equivalent, at least to show some small return for your affection towards me. You sent me two prescription-copies, one of the Archagathian, the other of the caustic plaster. The Archagathian is rightly compounded, but the caustic does not include the relative weight of resin. Please tell me of a strong caustic which can safely be used to cauterize the soles (of the feet); for I am in urgent need. As to the dry (?) plaster, you wrote that there are two kinds. Send me the prescription for the resolvent kind; for the four-drug plaster is also dry. This letter is sealed with this (?). Farewell and remember what I have said. Year 5 of Nero the lord, month of Germanicaus 1. To Dionysius, physician.

In this first-century papyrus letter of friendship, Chairas provides an insight into a social custom of the time by explaining that friends need not express their thanks to each other in words. This insight helps us to understand why Paul does not explicitly verbalize his thanks to the Philippians for their gifts.[22] This letter from Chairas also expresses the social obligation of repayment: "to show some small return for your affection towards me." In his letter to the Philippians, Paul promised "repayment" from God: "my God will meet all your needs" (4:19).

19. See Stanley Stowers, *Letter Writing in Greco-Roman Antiquity* (LEC 5; Philadelphia: Westminster, 1986) 50-70; Loveday Alexander, "Hellenistic Letter-Forms and the Structure of Philippians," *JSNT* 37 (1989), 87-101; John T. Fitzgerald, "Philippians," *ABD* 5:320; Luke Timothy Johnson, *The Writings of the New Testament: An Interpretation* (rev. ed.; Minneapolis: Fortress, 1999), 372; Fee, 1-10.

20. Stowers, *Letter Writing in Greco-Roman Antiquity,* 54.

21. Stowers, *Letter Writing in Greco-Roman Antiquity,* 61-62. This is Stowers' translation of the papyrus letter, P. Merton 12, dated August 29, A.D. 58.

22. See a detailed analysis of this letter by Peterman, "'Thankless Thanks,'" 262-64.

Due to the complexity of Philippians, however, it is an oversimplification to restrict it to just one type of letter. Given Paul's multiple purposes, variety of styles, ethical exhortations, and theological reflections, his letter does not conform in a strict sense to a specific epistolary type identified by the ancient epistolary theorists.[23] But despite the mixed character of his letter, Philippians can still be appropriately identified in a broad sense as a friendship letter on the basis of the predominance of the friendship language in it.[24] We can see why this letter is labeled as a Hellenistic letter of friendship when we observe how Paul's use of friendship language reflects the language of friendship in his Hellenistic context. Ten expressions of friendship language in Philippians run parallel to common motifs in Hellenistic letters and essays on friendship.

1. Affection: Letters of friendship repeatedly express warm affection: "I long for you." "I love you."[25] Paul intensifies his expression of affection for the Philippians by pointing to the divine source and power of his affection: "I long for you with the affection of Christ Jesus" (1:8).
2. Partnership *(koinōnia):* Friendship is the basis of true partnership. "All friendship," says Aristotle, "involves *koinōnia.*"[26] Partnership *(koinōnia)* is a major theme in Philippians (1:5, 7; 2:1, 3:10; 4:15). In Paul's development of the meaning of partnership he moves from a *koinōnia* in the gospel (1:5) to the *koinōnia* of the Spirit (2:1) to the *koinōnia* in the sufferings of Christ (3:10).
3. Unity of soul and spirit: Paul's appeal to be of one soul (1:27), fellow soul (2:2), equal soul (2:20), and one spirit (1:27) represents the desire in Greco-Roman culture for friends to be of one soul. Aristotle repeats the proverbs of his day on this subject: "Friends have one soul between them; friends' goods are common property; friendship is equality."[27] In Paul's theology, unity of soul and spirit are formed and maintained in Christ.

23. Fitzgerald, "Philippians in the Light of Ancient Friendship," 142: "Viewed in terms of ancient epistolary theory, all of Paul's letters are 'mixed' in terms of their style and content. None conforms precisely to the epistolary types and styles identified by theorists such as Ps.-Demetrius and Ps.-Libanius." For texts and translations of ancient epistolary theorists such as Ps.-Demetrius and Ps.-Libanius, see Abraham J. Malherbe, *Ancient Epistolary Theorists* (SBLSBS 19; Atlanta: Scholars Press, 1988). Some interpreters of Philippians attempt to capture the mixed character of Philippians by calling it "primarily a friendly hortatory letter" (White, "Morality between Two Worlds," 206), "a hortatory letter of friendship" (Stowers, "Friends and Enemies," 107), and "a Christian hortatory letter of friendship" (Fee, 12).

24. Alexander, "Hellenistic Letter-Forms and the Structure of Philippians," 87-101, uses the term "family letters" in her analysis. Apparently, family letters may be viewed as a subcategory within the broader category of friendly letters.

25. See examples in Malherbe, *Ancient Epistolary Theorists,* 33; Stowers, "Friends and Enemies," 109.

26. Aristotle, *Eth. nic.* 8.12.1.

27. Aristotle, *Eth. nic.* 9.8.2.

4. Like-mindedness: Paul's letter sounds similar to the teaching of the Stoics on friendship when he urges the Philippian Christians to be "like-minded" and "of the same mind" (2:2; 4:2). According to Cicero, "There is no surer bond of friendship than the sympathetic union of thought and inclination."[28] The "whole essence of friendship" is the "most complete agreement in policy, in pursuits and in opinions."[29] Paul urges the Philippians to be like-minded by having "the same attitude of mind Christ Jesus had" (2:5).
5. Yokefellow: When Paul calls upon his "true companion" (4:3: true yokefellow; *gnēsie syzyge*) to help the women who are quarreling to be reconciled, he is drawing on a common appellation used for famous pairs of friends in Greco-Roman literature. The metaphor of the "yoke of friendship" was used by Plutarch to depict the relationship between pairs of friends such as Theseus and Perithous, Achilies and Patoclus, Orestes and Pylades, Phintias and Damon, and Epameinondas and Pelopidas. Euripides employed the metaphor "yokefellow" to depict the friendship between Orestes and Pylades.[30] Paul's yokefellow and co-workers are those who contended with him in the cause of the gospel (4:3).
6. Giving and receiving: Paul commends the Philippian community for the distinction of being the only church who shared with him in "the matter of giving and receiving" (4:15). Aristotle explains the ethics of "giving and getting" in the context of his treatise on friendship: "In regard to giving and getting money, the observance of the mean is liberality; the excess and deficiency are prodigality and meanness, but the prodigal man and mean man exceed and fall short in opposite ways of one another: the prodigal exceeds in giving but is deficient in getting, whereas the mean man exceeds in getting and is deficient in getting."[31]
7. Common struggles and joys: Friends share common struggles and common enemies. Paul reminds the Philippians of their common struggle: "you are going through the same struggle that you saw I had, and now hear that I still have" (1:30). And Paul warns against "enemies of the cross" (3:18). Plutarch expresses the view that friends share the same struggles and enemies: "Enmities follow close upon friendships, and interwoven with them, inasmuch as it is impossible for a friend not to share his friend's wrongs or disrepute or disfavor."[32] Friends also share common joys. Paul tells his friends in Philippi, "I rejoice, and I share my joy with all of you. In the same way, you also should rejoice and share your joy with me" (2:17-18; my

28. Cicero, *Planc.* 2.5.
29. Cicero, *Amic.* 4.15.
30. Fitzgerald, "Philippians in the Light of Ancient Friendship," 149.
31. Aristotle, *Eth. nic.* 2.7.4.
32. Plutarch, *Amic. mult.* 96 A-B; see Stowers, "Friends and Enemies," 113.

trans.). Dio Chrysostom expresses this view in his maxim: "Friends share one's joys while enemies gloat over one's misfortunes."[33]

8. Absence/presence: Friendship letters often refer to personal presence and absence.[34] At strategic points in his exhortations to the Philippians, Paul comments on his absence and promises that he will soon be present (1:27; 2:12, 24).
9. Virtue friendship: Aristotle asserts that "the perfect form of friendship is that between the good, those who resemble each other in virtue."[35] Cicero also insists that virtue is the basis of true friendship: "Let this be ordained as the first law of friendship: ask of friends only what is honorable; do for friends only what is honorable."[36] Aristotle describes two types of inferior friendship as the friendship of utility and the friendship of pleasure. In these types of friendship, friends do not love each other for what they are in themselves but for some useful benefit or pleasure to be gained through the friendship. "Friendships of this kind are easily broken off, in the event of the parties themselves changing, for if no longer pleasant or useful to each other, they cease to love each other."[37]

   Paul identifies his friendship with the Philippians as a virtue friendship by directing them to think about virtue (4:8).[38] He corrects any misconception that he had utilitarian motives for his friendship with the Philippians by insisting that he had not written because he was in need, for he had learned to be content (4:11). Friendship based on need is viewed negatively in ancient discussions of friendships. Genuine friendship can be given and experienced only by one who is self-sufficient and content.[39] "It is far from being true that friendship is cultivated because of need; rather it is cultivated by those who are abundantly blessed with wealth and power and especially virtue, which is man's best defense; by those least in need of another's help; and by those most generous and most given to acts of kindness."[40] Paul's self-sufficiency was empowered by God (4:13). And he led the Philippians to experience the same dependence on God to meet their needs (4:19).
10. Moral paradigm: Friendship is built on a moral paradigm of virtue. By calling his readers to think about the list of virtues in 4:8, Paul ele-

33. Dio Chrysostom, *Orations* 3.103; see Stowers, "Friends and Enemies," 113.

34. Stowers, "Friends and Enemies," 108-9.

35. Aristotle, *Eth. nic.* 8.3.6.

36. Cicero, *Amic.* 13.44.

37. Aristotle, *Eth. nic.* 8.3.3.

38. See Fitzgerald, "Philippians in the Light of Ancient Friendship," 157-60.

39. See Abraham J. Malherbe, "Paul's Self-Sufficiency (Philippians 4:11)," in *Friendship, Flattery, and Frankness of Speech: Studies on Friendship in the New Testament World* (ed. John T. Fitzgerald; NovTSup 82; Leiden: Brill, 1996), 124-39.

40. Cicero, *Amic.* 9.30.

vates his friendship with the Philippians to the level of a virtue friendship. But thinking about a list of virtues is not the ultimate goal of friendship. Paul connects the command to think with the command to practice (4:9). The virtues to be practiced are exemplified in the paradigm presented by Paul's message and life. The ultimate paradigm to guide true friendship is the paradigm of Christ's "all-surpassing act of selfless love."[41] The self-emptying, self-humbling of Christ is replicated in Paul's own person story (3:3-14). His life serves as an example to follow (3:17).

These ten parallels between friendship language in Philippians and Hellenistic letters of friendship and essays on friendship provide a framework for viewing Philippians as a letter of friendship. In his absence from his friends, his letter builds his friendship with them and promotes the qualities of true friendship in their church. Of course, Paul's letter is not merely a friendly letter that fits a Hellenistic pattern.[42] He transforms the meaning and experience of friendship by redefining each of the essential ideals of friendship given by Hellenistic essays on friendship in terms of communion with Christ and empowerment by Christ. As recipients and advocates of the gospel of Christ, Paul and his partner-friends in Philippi experience common sharing in the Spirit (2:1) and participation in the sufferings of Christ (3:10). Nevertheless, after recognizing Paul's transformation of Hellenistic patterns and concepts, we can still gain a basic understanding of the form and function of Paul's letter to the Philippians by viewing it as a letter of friendship.[43]

A simple outline of Philippians can be derived by observing the formal features of a letter of friendship in Philippians.[44]

41. White, "Morality between Two Worlds," 212-13.

42. William G. Doty, *Letters in Primitive Christianity* (Philadelphia: Fortress, 1973), 21: "I argue that Paul was the person who adopted Graeco-Roman letter models for Christian purposes, that in his letters a genre or subgenre was created, and that our task is that of identifying the stages and steps in generic construction." See also J. T. Reed, *A Discourse Analysis of Philippians: Method and Rhetoric in the Debate over Literary Integrity* (JSNTSup 136; Sheffield: Sheffield Academic, 1997), 176-77, for a discussion of the way that Philippians is an adaptation of the "epistolary genre to his own immediate situation" and a mix of epistolary traditions.

43. Bockmuehl, 35, appropriately notes several problems of using "friendship as the dominant social paradigm, at least in any formal and culturally documented sense." Paul never explicitly refers to friendship with the words *philos* or *philia;* his apostolic authority is implicit; he avoids the notion of mutual reciprocity central to the concept of friendship in Hellenistic moral essays. Despite Bockmuehl's cautionary note, however, the pervasive use of friendship language in this letter points to the basic structure of this letter. Fee, 14: "The letter reflects known first-century conventions; but the conventions themselves are mere scaffolding for Paul. He is altogether concerned for his friends in Philippi and their ongoing relationship to Christ."

44. See Alexander, "Hellenistic Letter-Forms and the Structure of Philippians," 87-101. These formal features are illustrated by parallels in papyrus "family letters" (a subcategory of friendly letters). My outline modifies and expands Alexander's outline.

1:1-2	address and greeting
1:3-11	prayer for the recipients
1:12-26	reassurance about the sender
1:27–2:18	request for reassurance about the recipients
2:19-30	travel plans and recommendation of intermediaries
3:1–4:1	additional information about the sender and instructions
4:2-9	practical instructions for recipients
4:10-20	acknowledgment of receipt of a gift from recipients
4:21-22	exchange of greetings with third parties
4:23	closing wish for health

Although this outline needs to be amplified by close attention to other unique features in Philippians, this list of conventional features of a letter of friendship in Philippians points to the function and basic structure of the letter.

B. A Deliberative Speech

Since Paul wrote his letter to be read aloud to the church in Philippi, it is helpful to study this letter in terms of its features as a public speech.[45] To understand Paul's "speech" to the Philippians, scholars use a method of study called rhetorical criticism.[46] According to Aristotle, "Rhetoric may be defined as the faculty of discovering the possible means of persuasion in reference to any subject whatever."[47] To explain the "means of persuasion" used by Paul in this letter rhetorical criticism seeks to describe the goal, *ethos*, and structure of the oratory of Paul in Philippians.

In terms of rhetorical criticism, a deliberative speech exhorts by recommending a course of action as better and dissuades by advising against behavior as worse.[48] Since a central goal of Paul's letter to the Philippians is to exhort believers to be "like-minded, having the same love, being one in spirit and of one mind" (2:2) and to warn against "selfish ambition or vain conceit" (2:3), his speech to the Philippians can be classified as an example

45. On the importance of "recapturing the ancient paradigm of orality" to understand Philippians, see J. D. Harvey, "Orality and Its Implications for Biblical Studies: Recapturing an Ancient Paradigm," *JETS* 45 (2002), 99-109.

46. See G. W. Hansen, "Rhetorical Criticism," *DPL* 822-26.

47. Aristotle, *The Art of Rhetoric* 1.2.1.

48. Aristotle, *The Art of Rhetoric* 1.3.5: "The end of the deliberative speaker is the expedient or harmful; for he who exhorts recommends a course of action as better and he who dissuades advises against it as worse; all other considerations, such as justice and injustice, honor and disgrace, are included as accessory in reference to this." The other two types of oration defined by classical rhetorical handbooks are forensic and epideictic. Forensic speech defends or accuses someone regarding past actions; epideictic speech affirms communal values by praise or blame.

of deliberative rhetoric.[49] Of course, Paul has other aims in this speech besides exhortation and dissuasion.[50] But by interpreting Philippians as a deliberative speech, we can see how the letter was constructed to fit the goal of recommending a course of action and warning against its opposite. Paul's first imperative — "as citizens of heaven live in a manner worthy of the gospel of Christ" (1:27) — sets the tone and direction of his deliberative speech. He calls for a course of action and Christ-like attitudes that will unify the church and warns against attitudes and enemies who will divide the church. His imperative to the two women in conflict — "be of the same mind" (4:2) — personalizes his call for unity heard all the way through the letter. The Christ hymn (2:5-11) serves to illustrate the choice set before the community. Just as Christ "humbled himself" (2:8), so believers must "in humility value others above [themselves]" (2:3).

An essential element in a persuasive speech is its *ethos*, determined by the moral character of the speaker.[51] Paul gives an account of his good moral character in his frequent references to himself: his imprisonment "served to advance the gospel" (1:12); for him "to live is Christ" (1:21); his life was "poured out like a drink offering" (2:17); he considered everything as "loss because of the surpassing worth of knowing Christ" (3:8); even though he was admittedly not perfect (3:12), he continued to "press on toward the goal" (3:14). All of these references attested to his role as an example and model to follow (3:17). He concludes his exhortation by appealing for his audience to put into practice all that they have learned, received, heard, and seen in him (4:9). The power of Paul's persuasive speech depends upon his good moral character.

The understanding of Philippians as deliberative speech and the appreciation of its *ethos* in Paul's ethical appeal are two useful contributions of rhetorical analyses of Philippians. Many studies have focused on the

49. Philippians is viewed as deliberative rhetoric by D. F. Watson, "A Rhetorical Analysis of Philippians and Its Implications for the Unity Question," *NovT* 30 (1988), 59-60; Bloomquist, *The Function of Suffering in Philippians*, 120; Witherington, 13.

50. Philippians cannot be restricted to one type *(genus)* of rhetoric. George Kennedy views the letter as epideictic rhetoric because he believes that the goal of the letter is to affirm communal values by praise and blame on the basis of what is honorable or disgraceful. See George A. Kennedy, *New Testament Interpretation through Rhetorical Criticism* (Chapel Hill: University of North Carolina Press, 1984), 77. Watson, "A Rhetorical Analysis of Philippians," 59-60, sees the use of epideictic rhetoric in 2:19-30. Bloomquist, *The Function of Suffering in Philippians*, 120, also admits that forensic and epideictic elements can be found in the letter, but thinks that the letter as a whole is an example of deliberative rhetoric.

51. Aristotle, *Art of Rhetoric* 1.2.4: "The orator persuades by moral character when his speech is delivered in such a manner as to render him worthy of confidence." According to Aristotle (*Art of Rhetoric* 1.2.3), persuasion depends upon three factors: the moral character of the speaker *(ethos)*, the emotions aroused in the hearers by the speech *(pathos)*, and the logical arguments in the speech *(logos)*. The discussion of Paul's references to his own moral character *(ethos)* is a contribution of the rhetorical analysis of J. W. Marshall, "Paul's Ethical Appeal in Philippians," in *Rhetoric and the New Testament: Essays from 1992 Heidelberg Conference* (ed. S. E. Porter and T. H. Olbricht; JSNTSup 90; Sheffield: JSOT Press, 1993), 357-74.

rhetorical structure of the letter, but with divergent and contradictory results. In the practice of the rhetorical criticism of Paul's letters, the Latin terms of classical rhetoric are used to designate the parts of the structure of the letter.[52] With the use of these terms, three rhetorical analyses of Philippians provide three different outlines of its rhetorical structure.[53]

	Watson	**Bloomquist**	**Witherington**
Exordium	1:3-26	1:3-11	1:3-11
Narratio	1:27-30	1:12-14	1:12-26
Propositio			1:27-30
Partitio	1:15-18a		
Probatio	2:1–3:21[54]	1:18b–4:7[55]	2:1–4:3
Peroratio	4:1-20[56]	4:8-20	4:4-20

These studies of the rhetorical structure of Paul's letter-speech to the Philippians provide valuable insights by drawing from the encyclopedic description of every conceivable feature of speech in the classical rhetorical handbooks.[57] Nevertheless, the description of the form of Paul's argumentation with the Latin terminology of these handbooks often tends to obfuscate rather than clarify the meaning of Paul's letter.[58] The significant disagreement between these studies observed in the chart above points to the difficulty of applying the canons of classical rhetoric to Philippians. When a rhetorical analysis of Paul's letter portrays Paul as someone devoted to following the dictates of rhetoricians of his time, the methodology becomes suspect.[59] A preoccupation with rhetorical form over substance is an obstacle to understanding the meaning of the theological themes and practical ex-

52. The Latin terms come from the Latin rhetorical handbooks: *Rhetoric to Herennius* (c. 84 B.C.); Cicero's *On Invention* and *Partitions of Oratory* (c. 87 B.C.); and the major work of Quintilian, *On the Education of the Orator* (A.D. 92). These handbooks provide comprehensive instruction on the theory and practice of rhetoric in Paul's time.

53. Watson, "A Rhetorical Analysis of Philippians," 57-88; Bloomquist, *The Function of Suffering in Philippians,* 119-38; Witherington, 11-20.

54. The *probatio* is divided into three subsections with an inserted *digressio* (2:19-30): 2:1-11; 2:12-18; 3:1-21.

55. The *probatio* is divided into five parts: *confirmatio* (1:18b-26); *exhortatio* (1:27–2:18); *exempla* (2:19-30); *reprehensio* (3:1-16); and *exhortatio* (3:17–4:7).

56. This section includes the *repetitio* (4:1-9) and *adfectus* (4:10-20).

57. The descriptive value of the system developed by the classical rhetoricians is highly regarded by many recent rhetorical critics. See, e.g., George Kennedy, *New Testament Interpretation through Rhetorical Criticism,* 10-11.

58. As Fee, 16 n. 43, says, Bloomquist "regularly lets his (very questionable) analysis of rhetorical form dictate meaning."

59. Bockmuehl, 39: "Despite claims to the contrary, highly precise models of rhetoric or social conventions are proving less than helpful as tools for the analysis of Philippians — not least because few of them tend to agree. What is more, the complexity of Paul's background and the *ad hoc* nature of his correspondence suggest that his letters are not conceived in terms of formal 'deliberative Graeco-Roman rhetoric' (thus Witherington 1994:11)."

hortation in Paul's letter. For this reason, I do not use the terminology of the classical rhetorical handbooks to define the structure of Philippians, even though I draw upon the insights of rhetorical criticism in the commentary.[60]

C. The Integrity of the Letter

An almost complete consensus accepts the letter's claim to Pauline authorship (1:1).[61] Paul's disclosure of his conversion and commitment to Christ, his description of his suffering and travels, his exposition of theology, his ethical appeals, and his opposition to false teachers all correspond to other letters universally accepted as Pauline (such as Romans, 1 and 2 Corinthians, and Galatians). Early church leaders quoted from Philippians as a letter from Paul.[62] Philippians is included in second-century lists of NT writings: the Muratorian canon and the canon of Marcion. For all these reasons, the authenticity of Philippians deserves the confident recognition it receives. The only serious question of authorship related to Philippians concerns the origin of the Christ hymn (2:6-11). That question is addressed in the commentary.

But while the authenticity of Philippians is commonly acclaimed, the integrity of Philippians is hotly contested. The traditional view that Philippians was composed as one letter in the form presented in the NT can no longer claim widespread support.[63] Many scholars propose that the present form of Philippians is a combination of two or three different letters written at different times.

A common argument against the unity of Philippians points to the abrupt change in tone at the beginning of chapter 3. The letter turns unexpectedly from warm encouragement (3:1: "my brothers and sisters, rejoice in the Lord!") to harsh warning (3:2: "Watch out for those dogs"). This rupture in the line of thought leads some to suggest that another letter was inserted at this point. Paul seems to be drawing to a close with the use of the clause "finally, my brothers and sisters, rejoice" (3:1). The reference to

60. On the basis of his detailed analysis of the strengths and weaknesses of rhetorical analyses of Philippians, Reed, *A Discourse Analysis of Philippians,* 170-77, concludes that interpretation of Philippians will be guided best by observing Paul's use of a mix of epistolary traditions rather than by imposing the canons of the rhetorical handbooks to the letter.

61. For a more extensive discussion of authorship with bibliography, see O'Brien, 9-10; Martin and Hawthorne, xxviii-xxx.

62. Including Polycarp of Smyrna, Irenaeus, Clement of Alexandria, and Tertullian.

63. David E. Garland, "The Composition and Unity of Philippians: Some Neglected Literary Features," *NovT* 27 (1985), 141: "A crescendo of voices now maintains that there is no reasonable doubt that all four chapters were *not* written as part of the same letter, *nor* in the order in which we have them." Garland (141-42 n. 3) lists twenty-four scholars who divide Philippians into three separate letters and six scholars who divide the letter into two separate letters. His list is only representative of a much wider scholarly perspective on this issue.

travel plans for himself and his associates in the previous section (2:19-30), usually found at the end of his letters, may also suggest that 3:1 marks the end of a letter. The contents of chapter 3 (3:1b–4:1) also seem to reflect a different situation than the background of chapters 1–2. The opponents (3:2: "dogs," "evildoers," "mutilators"; 3:18: "enemies of the cross") who threaten the church appear to be quite different from the ones mentioned in 1:15-17 and 1:28. And Paul no longer refers to his chains in chapter 3 as he did in chapter 1. Was he no longer in prison when he wrote chapter 3? Perhaps 3:1b–4:1 was written as a separate letter at a different time to combat the influence of Judaizers and libertines.

Another reason to infer the insertion of a separate letter comes from the observation that Paul's expression of gratitude for the Philippians' gift in 4:10-20 seems to come a long time after Paul's reception of the gift, if 4:10-20 was written at the end of the letter as we now have it. According to 2:25-30, sufficient time has passed since Epaphroditus delivered the gift for the Philippians to find out that he was sick and for Epaphroditus to hear about their concern for his health. Did Paul not communicate his gratitude to the church in Philippi for their gift during all this time when messages were being sent back and forth between Paul's location and Philippi to communicate information about the health of Epaphroditus? Perhaps 4:10-20 was written as a separate letter to the Philippians immediately after Paul received their gift from Ephaphroditus.

This line of reasoning leads to the supposition of two or three letters. According to the two-letter hypothesis, Paul's first letter (1:1–3:1a; 4:2-7, 10-23) expressed his gratitude for the gift, the impact of his imprisonment on the advance of the gospel, and his pastoral concern for unity in the church. The second letter (3:1b–4:1, 8-9) was written after his release from prison during a time when the church was seriously threatened by false teachers.[64]

According to the three-letter hypothesis, Paul's first letter (4:10-20) was a letter of thanks for the gift soon after Paul received it from Epaphroditus. The second letter (1:1–3:1; 4:2-9, 21-23) was sent with Epaphroditus on his return to Philippi to inform the Philippians of Paul's situation and to encourage them to be reconciled and united in their relationships in the church. The third letter (3:2–4:1) was composed sometime later as a severe warning against the dangerous influence of his opponents.[65] A visual presentation of these three letters is as follows:

1st letter:				4:10-20	
2nd letter:	1:1–3:1		4:2-9		4:21-23
3rd letter:		3:2–4:1			

64. Gnilka, 6-18.

65. Beare, 3-5; Collange, 21-30; Jerome Murphy-O'Connor, *Paul: A Critical Life* (Oxford: Clarendon, 1996), 215-30; Helmut Koester, *Paul and His World: Interpreting the New Testament in Its Context* (Minneapolis: Fortress, 2007), 72-75.

In his *To the Philippians*, Polycarp, the bishop of Smyrna (martyred in A.D. 155), refers to "letters" Paul wrote to them.[66] This reference to letters is taken by some as external evidence that Paul wrote two or more letters to the church in Philippi. Perhaps a leader in the church who collected Paul's letters combined them to make the final canonical form of the letter.[67]

Scholars convinced of the unity of Philippians as a single letter composed on one occasion without interpolations have forged counterarguments defending the integrity of this letter. Some of these arguments depend upon imaginative reconstructions of the circumstances in Paul's life and of Paul's psychological condition. Perhaps Paul was interrupted in his dictation by an alarming message about the harmful influence of false teachers in his churches. Distraught and deeply disturbed by this information, Paul decides that he will not end his letter as he had planned at 3:1. Instead he fires off a highly charged warning: "Watch out for those dogs" (3:2).[68] Such imaginative attempts to explain Paul's situation and state of mind are intriguing but unverifiable.

Better arguments for the unity of Philippians keep their focus on the text of Philippians. A thorough review of the textual tradition of Philippians reveals no evidence to support the multiple-letters hypotheses. From the earliest manuscripts (including the late-second-century papyrus text, 𝔓[46]) to patristic allusions and through all the later copies of the text, the complete diverse manuscript attestation to Philippians witnesses to one letter in the canonical form, without one hint that the letter contains a combination of separate letters written at different times or was ever circulated in a different form.[69] All the theories of multiple letters rest on conjectural speculation, not on textual evidence. The special appeal to Polycarp for external support of a hypothesis of two or more letters is speculative since his reference to the "letters" of Paul can be explained in other plausible ways. Perhaps, Polycarp used the plural form of "letters" as it was sometimes used in Greek to denote an epistle of great importance, such as a king's mandate, containing multiple directions and injunctions.[70] Or Polycarp could have been referring to other letters of Paul, such as, 1 and 2 Thessalonians, since he alludes to these letters as if they were addressed to the Philippians (Polycarp, *Phil.* 11:3-4). Polycarp may have inferred from Philippians 3:2 ("It is no trouble for me to write the same things to you again") that Paul had written previous letters to the

66. Polycarp, *Phil.* 3:2: "For neither am I, nor is any other like me, able to follow the wisdom of the blessed and glorious Paul, who, when he was among you in the presence of the men of the time, taught accurately and steadfastly the word of truth, and also when he was absent wrote letters to you, from the study of which you will be able to build yourselves up into the faith given to you."

67. Beare, 4.

68. Martin and Hawthorne, 171.

69. Silva, 14.

70. Lightfoot, 142.

Philippians.[71] These explanations of Polycarp's reference to "letters" obviate the necessity of taking it as proof that Philippians is a combination of two or more letters.

The case against the multiple-letter theories is strengthened by reviewing the wide diversity of these theories regarding the limits of the separate letters supposedly contained within Philippians. Is the hypothetical "third letter" 3:2–4:3, 8-9, or 3:2–4:1, or 3:1–4:9, or 3:1b–4:1, 8-9?[72] Such inability to agree about the beginning and ending of the hypothetical fragments within Philippians instills doubt about the credibility of these multiple-letter hypotheses. Related to this inability of the hypotheses to agree on the limits of the letters is their failure to explain the methodology of the editor who combined these "letters" in Philippians. Why did the editor place the "third letter" somewhere between 3:1 and 4:9 instead of after the first and second letters? Why did the editor place the "first letter" at 4:10-20 instead of before the second and third letters? Why did the editor not smooth out the objectionable abrupt breaks in the final edition? These unresolved questions intensify doubts about these hypotheses.

When Philippians is viewed as one letter without interpolations, the remarkable thematic continuity between different sections of the letter becomes clearly apparent. For example, the themes of progress in the faith (1:25; 2:12-14; 3:12-16), standing firm in the Lord (1:27; 4:1), humility (2:2, 5-8; 3:4-8), suffering (1:29-30; 2:8; 3:10), and the final victory of Christ (2:9-11; 3:20-21) bind the letter together into one harmonious whole.[73] Even the vocabulary employed to develop these themes ties the parts of the whole letter together. For example, the vocabulary of "citizenship," "standing firm," and "striving together" occur in the same order in 1:27 and in 3:20–4:3 to mark the beginning and the end of a unified section.[74] These observations

71. Garland, "The Composition and Unity of Philippians," 154. See below the interpretation of that phrase in this commentary as a reference to chapters 1–2. My interpretation of 3:1-2 is based on J. T. Reed, "Philippians and the Epistolary Hesitation Formulas: The Literary Integrity of Philippians, Again," *JBL* 115 (1966), 63-90.

See also Troels Engberg-Pedersen, "Stoicism in Philippians," in *Paul in His Hellenistic Context* (ed. Troels Engberg-Pedersen; Minneapolis: Fortress, 1995), 258 n. 5: "What Paul says he will repeat is the whole set of ideas that forms the content of 1:12–2:18, (a) using Paul's own example (1:12-26; cf. 3:4-16), as a model for (b) the desired reaction of joy and steadfastness on the part of the Philippians, (c) in the face of any supposed suffering they may have undergone. If this is right, then Paul is saying in 3:1b that he is now breaking up the smooth progression of letter topics in order to repeat the essential message of 1:12–2:18, culminating in the injunction to steadfastness (4:1, repeating 1:27). In other words, Paul himself says that he is going to do what analytics who assign the body of chapter 3 to a different letter than that of 1:12–2:18 say he cannot do!"

72. Garland, "The Composition and Unity of Philippians," 155 n. 50, presents a chart of eighteen different suggested limits for the "third letter."

73. Garland, "The Composition and Unity of Philippians," 157.

74. Garland, "The Composition and Unity of Philippians," 160. The terms for *citizenship* occur only here (1:27; 3:20) in Paul's letters.

provide a solid basis for accepting Philippians as one unified letter rather than as awkwardly disjointed fragments.[75]

The objection to the placement of 4:10-20 as a conclusion to a letter by the multiple-letter theorists seems to be inspired by modern etiquette for the polite way to say "thank you." Careful analysis of ancient Hellenistic letters reveals that expressions of gratitude could be reserved for the conclusion of letters between intimate friends or omitted altogether.[76] The verbal and thematic links between Paul's prayer of thanksgiving in 1:3-11 and his expression of gratitude in 4:10-20 demonstrate that Paul did not add his "thank you" as an afterthought but as a fitting conclusion to the theme of thanksgiving introduced at the beginning of his letter.

After weighing the evidence for and against the multiple-letter theories, we can reasonably conclude that we will be on firm ground if we take our journey through the text with the assumption that Paul composed this letter as one unified message on one occasion.[77]

III. THE OCCASION OF THE LETTER

A. Paul in Chains

Paul was motivated to write this letter by two aspects of his experience in prison: the advance of the gospel while he was in chains (1:12-25) and the gift from the church in Philippi through their messenger, Epaphroditus (2:25-30; 4:10-19).

The letter includes a report that Paul's imprisonment served to advance the gospel (1:12). His witness among the palace guard emboldened others to proclaim the gospel (1:13-14). Although some preached out of rivalry and others out of love, what mattered to Paul was that Christ was

75. See the commentary below for more detailed analysis of the "breaks" in continuity at such points as 3:1-2.

76. See Peterman, *Paul's Gift from Philippi,* 18; Peterman, "'Thankless Thanks,'" 261-70.

77. Some studies have argued for the unity of Philippians on the grounds of literary structures, but with mixed results: Watson, "A Rhetorical Analysis," 57-88; D. A. Black, "The Discourse Structure of Philippians: A Study in Textlinguistics," *NovT* 37 (1995), 16-49; A. B. Luter and M. V. Lee, "Philippians as Chiasmus: Key to the Structure, Unity and Theme Questions," *NTS* 41 (1995), 89-101. The attempt of Luter and Lee to describe a macrochiastic pattern in the letter is thoroughly refuted by S. E. Porter and J. T. Reed, "Philippians as a Macro-Chiasm and Its Exegetical Significance," *NTS* 44 (1998), 213-31. Rhetorical criticism is used to defend the unity of the letter by Watson, "A Rhetorical Analysis," and the multiple-letter hypotheses by W. Schenk, "Der Philipperbrief oder die Philipperbriefe des Paulus? Eine Antwort an V. Koperski," *ETL* 70 (1994), 122-31; Schenk is the only commentator who expresses his multiple-letter theory in the title of his commentary: *Die Philipperbriefe des Paulus* (The Letters of Paul).

preached (1:15-18). Facing the threat of execution and reflecting on his own death, Paul was torn between his desire to depart and be with Christ and his concern for the welfare of the church. He finally became convinced that he would remain to encourage the progress and joy in faith of the church (1:19-25).

While he was in prison, Ephaphroditus came from Philippi to take care of him and to convey a gift from the church. Unfortunately, Epaphroditus became ill and almost died (2:25-30). Epaphroditus was distressed when he learned that the church was worried about his health. Paul wrote this letter to express his gratitude for the support from the church (4:10-18) and to assure the church that their messenger was well and had honorably fulfilled his service. Paul urged the church to welcome Epaphroditus back home with joy (2:29). Paul probably sent this letter with him.

Paul's report of his imprisonment raises the question of the location of his prison. He boasted to the church in Corinth that he had "been in prison more frequently" than the other servants of Christ (2 Cor 11:23).[78] Unfortunately, he did not list the addresses of those imprisonments. As a result, the debate regarding his location when he wrote this letter continues. A decision regarding the place of Paul's prison inevitably determines the date of the letter.

Rome receives traditional and widespread current support as the location of Paul's imprisonment when he wrote Philippians.[79] The account in Acts confirms that Paul was held as a prisoner in his own rented house in Rome with a soldier to guard him (Acts 28:16). For two years, he received visitors and proclaimed the gospel unhindered (Acts 28:30-31). Paul's references in Philippians to the evangelization of the "palace guard" (Gk. *praitōrion,* 1:13) and to the Christian members of "Caesar's household" (4:22) seem to make Rome the most likely place for the composition of this letter. Although members of the "palace guard" and of "Caesar's household" (the imperial civil service) lived throughout the provinces of the Roman Empire, they were concentrated mainly in Rome. Citizens of Philippi, a Roman colony, would certainly have been impressed by the news that the gospel had advanced among the palace guard in Rome and that members of the imperial service in the capital city had become Christians.[80] If

78. *1 Clement* 5:5-6 confirms Paul's boast of multiple imprisonments: "Through jealousy and strife Paul showed the way to the prize of endurance; seven times he was in bonds, he was exiled, he was stoned."

79. In the early second century, the Marcionite "Prologue to Philippians" states that Paul wrote to the Philippians from prison in Rome. See F. F. Bruce, *The Canon of Scripture* (Downers Grove: InterVarsity Press, 1988), 142. Current support for Rome comes from Bruce, 14; Marshall, xix-xx; O'Brien 25; Silva, 8; Fee, 1; Bockmuehl, 32; Hooker, 473-75; Fitzgerald, "Epistle to the Philippians," *ABD* 5:323.

80. B. Reicke, "Caesarea, Rome, and the Captivity Epistles," in *Apostolic History and the Gospel* (ed. W. W. Gasque and R. P. Martin; Grand Rapids: Eerdmans, 1970), 285-86: "It was impossible for the readers to misunderstand the reference to Rome and Nero's clients in the greeting from 'those of Caesar's household' (Phil 4:22). Clients and servants of the

Philippians was written during Paul's imprisonment in Rome, its date of composition was about 61-62.

A problem with this view is that the distance between Rome and Philippi appears to be an obstacle to the number of journeys mentioned or implied by the letter. The letter reports four trips between Paul and Philippi and projects four more.

1. A messenger brought news to the Philippians of Paul's imprisonment.
2. The church sent Epaphroditus with a gift to Paul.
3. The church heard the news that Epaphroditus was sick.
4. Epaphroditus was distressed when he heard that the church knew about his illness.
5. Paul plans to send Epaphroditus back to Philippi.
6. Paul plans to send Timothy to Philippi as soon as he knows the outcome of his trial.
7. Paul plans to wait for Timothy to return with a report about the church in Philippi.
8. Paul plans to visit Philippi soon.

This number of journeys seems to imply an ease of communication and a relatively short distance between Paul's imprisonment and Philippi. From Rome to Philippi, a messenger had to travel at least 700 miles by the land route or at least 900 miles by the sea route.[81] To envision the first four journeys in this list taking over a year seems to conflict with the sense given by Philippians of messages being sent quickly back and forth.[82]

A second problem with accepting Rome as the origin of Philippians is Paul's communication of his plan to visit Philippi soon after he is released from prison (2:24). If Paul was writing from Rome, then returning to Philippi contradicted his stated plan not to return to the east where his work was done but to go on to Spain (see Rom 15:24, 28). Paul mentions his change of previous plans in 2 Corinthians 1:15-17, but he gives no indica-

---

emperor lived in several places, but primarily in Rome. . . . Paul is happy to be able to extend greetings from clients of the imperial house to the readers in Philippi. This fine point is lost if one does not accept Rome as the place where Paul had such success in important circles (Phil 1:12) and from where he writes to encourage the Philippian Christians to share his joy (2:18, etc.)."

81. Raymond Brown, *Introduction to the New Testament* (ABRL; New York: Doubleday, 1997), 495. D. A. Carson and Douglas J. Moo, *An Introduction to the New Testament* (2nd ed.; Grand Rapids: Zondervan, 2005), 504, estimate 1,200 miles.

82. Advocates of Rome suggest that the estimate of travel time could be reduced if (a) the church found out that Paul was going to be imprisoned in Rome before he got there, (b) Epaphroditus became ill on his journey and news was sent back, and (c) Epaphroditus's distress was based not on a message but on intuition that the church would be worried about him. Or he might have received a message while still on his journey a long way from Rome. See Silva, 7 n. 5.

tion in Philippians that his intention to visit Philippi after his imprisonment is a change of previous plans.

As an alternative to the traditional view, some scholars advocate Caesarea as the origin of Philippians.[83] If it was written in Caesarea, then its date would be 59-60. The record of Acts that Paul was imprisoned in the *praetorium* of Herod (Acts 23:35) fits with Paul's reference to the *praetorium* in Philippians 1:13. And as a major center of Roman power, Caesarea would have had a concentration of the emperor's administrative staff, "those who belong to Caesar's household" (4:22). Since Paul appealed to Caesar in Caesarea (Acts 25:11-12), he could have anticipated traveling to Rome by way of Philippi to make the visit he promised (Phil 2:24). Paul's harsh words against Judaizers in Philippians 3:2 may have been sparked by the Jewish attacks against him in Jerusalem and Caesarea (Acts 22–25).

This view faces the same problem of distance: in this case over a thousand miles by sea or land between Caesarea and Philippi. Even though Paul was in Caesarea for two years, the frequency of trips between Paul's imprisonment and Philippi assumed by Paul's letter to the Philippians seems implausible given that distance.[84] Furthermore, the connection between the account of the Jewish attacks against Paul in Acts 22–25 and Paul's polemic against Judaizers in Philippians 3 does not really work since Paul seems to be warning against a threat of Jewish Christians invading his churches.[85] And although Paul could have visited Philippi on his way from Caesarea to Rome, the account in Acts portrays Paul as having no hope of ever returning to that area again (see Acts 20:25, 38). In the light of these difficulties of positing Caesarea as the place of the composition of Philippians, even the strongest advocate of this position exclaims, "Not all questions can be answered or all problems solved, and to paraphrase Origen, 'Only God knows where Philippians was really written.'"[86]

Ephesus receives strong support as the origin of Philippians.[87] Since the distance between Ephesus and Philippi was only about a hundred miles, all of the trips mentioned in the letter would have been relatively short and easy compared to the trips between Rome and Philippi or

83. Hawthorne, xli-xliv.

84. Brown, *Introduction*, 494.

85. See the commentary below.

86. Hawthorne, xliii.

87. See G. S. Duncan, *Paul's Ephesian Ministry: A Reconstruction with Special Reference to the Ephesian Origin for the Imprisonment Epistles* (New York: Charles Scribner's Sons, 1929); Murphy-O'Connor, *Paul: A Critical Life*, 220; Brown, *Introduction*, 495-96; Thielman,19-20; Thielman, "Ephesus and the Literary Setting of Philippians," in *New Testament Greek and Exegesis: Essays in Honor of Gerald Hawthorne* (ed. Amy M. Donaldson and Timothy B. Sailors; Grand Rapids: Eerdmans, 2003), 205-23. Koester, *Paul and His World: Interpreting the New Testament in Its Context* (Minneapolis: Fortress, 2007), 72-75; Carson and Moo, *Introduction*, 503-6; Paul J. Achtemeier, Joel B. Green, and Marianne Meye Thompson, *Introducing the New Testament: Its Literature and Theology* (Grand Rapids: Eerdmans, 2001), 402-3; Gnilka, 20-25; Collange, 33-34; Müller, 16-23; Martin and Hawthorne, xxxix-l.

Caesarea and Philippi. In fact, some of the trips mentioned in Philippians may be mentioned in Acts and Paul's letters as well. Acts and 1 Corinthians (if Timothy was sent to Corinth by way of Macedonia) indicate that Paul sent Timothy to Macedonia while he stayed in Ephesus (Acts 19:22; cf. 1 Cor 16:10; Phil 2:23). And Acts and the letters to the Corinthians state that Paul went to Macedonia after his time in Ephesus (Acts 20:1; 1 Cor 16:5; 2 Cor 1:16; 2:13; 7:5; cf. Phil 2:24). Of course, the task of connecting Paul's letters with Acts is notoriously difficult, but these connections present a plausible way to solve the puzzle of relating Paul's travel plans in Philippians and the evidence for his journeys in Acts and his other letters.

Neither Acts nor Paul's letters record that Paul was imprisoned in Ephesus. But Acts describes a major riot in the city as a result of Paul's evangelistic work there (Acts 19:23–20:1). And Paul's letters speak of a serious threat to Paul's life while he was in Ephesus (1 Cor 16:8; 2 Cor 1:8-10: "we despaired of life itself. Indeed, we felt we had received the sentence of death"). Ephesus is certainly a good candidate for inclusion in Paul's reference to his numerous imprisonments (2 Cor 11:23). In Paul's time, Ephesus was the third largest city in the Roman Empire after Rome and Alexandria and the center of Roman military control, the Roman proconsul's headquarters, the Romans' communications network, and the Roman judicial courts for all of Asia.[88] First-century Latin inscriptions point to the presence of the palace guard and members of Caesar's household in Ephesus.[89] All of this evidence allows for Ephesus to be an excellent prospect for the place where imperial military and administrative forces heard the gospel while Paul was in chains (Phil 1:12-13).

Another line of reasoning in support of Ephesus as the place of Paul's imprisonment when he wrote Philippians traces the literary affinities between Philippians, Galatians, and 1 Corinthians.[90] In Philippians, Paul harshly warns against the influence of Jewish Christians who circumcise Gentile Christians and bring them under the Jewish law: "Watch out for those dogs, those evildoers, those mutilators of the flesh" (3:2). In Galatians, Paul issues a similar warning: "Mark my words! I, Paul, tell you that if you let yourselves be circumcised, Christ will be of no value to you at all"

88. Paul Trebilco, "Asia," in *The Book of Acts in Its Graeco-Roman Setting* (ed. David W. J. Gill and Conrad Gempf; vol. 2 of The Book of Acts in Its First-Century Setting, ed. Bruce W. Winter; Grand Rapids: Eerdmans, 1994), 307-9.

89. Adolf Deissmann, *Light from the Ancient East* (trans. Lionel R. M. Strachan; 4th ed.; Grand Rapids: Baker, 1978), 238; Brown, *Introduction*, 495 n. 35; Contested by F. F. Bruce, 12, on the grounds that the technical meaning of the three Latin inscriptions (*CIL* III.6085, 7135, 7136) refers to "a former member of the praetorian guard who later discharged police duties as a *stationarius* on a Roman road in the province of Asia." But Paul's use of the term *palace guard* (Phil 1:13: πραιτώριον) need not be limited to its technical, legal meaning. He may have used the common term in a wider sense as a reference to the Roman military personnel so prevalent in Philippi and Ephesus. See Thielman, "Ephesus and the Literary Setting of Philippians," 222.

90. See Thielman, "Ephesus and the Literary Setting of Philippians," 219-21.

(Gal 5:2). In both letters, Paul recounts his own conversion from Judaism to Christ (Phil 3:4-8; Gal 1:13-17) as a way to break the influence of the Judaizers. And both letters contrast righteousness that comes from law and righteousness that comes from God on the basis of faith (Phil 3:6-9; Gal 3:10-14).

In Philippians, Paul warns not only against Judaizers but also against libertines: enemies of the cross of Christ. Their destiny is destruction, their god is their stomach, and their glory is their shame (3:18-19).[91] This warning against libertinism and moral permissiveness is strikingly similar to the warnings against the same problem in the Corinthian church (see especially 1 Corinthians 3–6). Paul's final argument in both Philippians and 1 Corinthians against rampant immorality is the doctrine of the resurrection. Those who were seduced by the cultural philosophy — "Let us eat and drink, for tomorrow we die" (1 Cor 15:32) — were reminded that their earthly bodies would be transformed to be like the heavenly body of the resurrected Lord Jesus (1 Cor 15:35-58). In the same way, Paul warns the Philippians not to set their minds on earthly things (Phil 3:18-19), for "our citizenship is in heaven. And we eagerly await a Savior from there, the Lord Jesus Christ, who, by the power that enables him to bring everything under his control, will transform our lowly bodies so that they will be like his glorious body" (Phil 3:20-21). Both citizens in Roman Corinth and in Roman Philippi needed the strong encouragement of their heavenly citizenship to keep them from giving in to the immoral pressures of their surrounding culture.

If we place the writing of Philippians in the same place and time as the writing of Galatians and 1 Corinthians, these remarkable literary-theological parallels between these three letters make sense.[92] Paul's fight against Judaizers expressed in Galatians is summarized in Philippians. His warning to the Philippians about "the enemies of the cross," whose "god is their belly," recalls his extended polemic against the libertinism of the Corinthians who excused their immorality by chanting their slogans, "I have the right to do anything" and "food for the stomach and the stomach for food" (1 Cor 6:12-13). Philippians reflects the language and battles of the other two letters probably because it was written at the same time and place as they were: in Ephesus in the mid-50s.[93]

91. See the commentary below for evidence that Phil 3:18-19 addresses libertines enthralled by Roman culture, not Judaizers obsessed with Jewish law, as in Phil 3:2-9.

92. See Thielman, "Ephesus and the Literary Setting of Philippians," 223: "The battles that Paul fights in Philippians 3 are the battles of Galatians and 1 Corinthians, not those he undertook in Colossians, Philemon, and Ephesians during his Roman imprisonment."

93. The Ephesian provenance of 1 Corinthians is derived from 1 Corinthians 16:8. For defense of the Ephesian provenance of Galatians, see Murphy-O'Connor, *Paul: A Critical Life*, 180-82; Brown, *Introduction*, 474-77. For my advocacy of a mid-50s date for Galatians written to South rather than North Galatia, see G. W. Hansen, "Galatians, Letter to the," *DPL* 326-29.

Unfortunately, all of this discussion about the place of the composition of this letter is speculative and therefore inconclusive.[94] Fortunately, a decision one way or the other does not significantly affect our interpretation of the letter. What does matter for our understanding of Philippians is the indisputable evidence that Paul wrote this letter to express his joyful faith in Christ Jesus, his exalted Lord and eagerly expected Savior, while he was "in chains" (1:7, 13, 14, 17) and to communicate his appreciative love (1:7-8; 4:1, 10-18) for his generous friends in Philippi. His reports of his imprisonment and his receipt of the gift from Philippi give us a clear picture of the background of his letter in terms of his situation when he composed it. A full understanding of the occasion for the letter also needs to be derived from an investigation of problems in the church in Philippi alluded to by the letter.

B. The Church in Trouble

Paul's letter reveals that he was concerned about three problems in the church in Philippi: (1) disunity, (2) suffering, and (3) opponents.

1. *Disunity*

Paul's appeal to two women to "be of the same mind in the Lord" (4:2) does not come as a surprise but as a climactic conclusion to the letter. Selfish ambition and self-interest in the Philippian community come under Paul's censure (2:3-4); grumbling and arguing among the children of God also receive his stern rebuke (2:14). These glimpses of conflict in the life of the church give us some understanding of the reason for Paul's repeated appeals for the church to be united in spirit and of one mind (1:27; 2:1-5, 14; 3:17, 20; 4:2). We have to be careful not to use these frequent appeals to unity as a solid basis for extended speculation about the causes and nature of disunity in the church. Such speculation can be viewed as an example of the fallacy of "mirror-reading": projecting the opposite of Paul's words (a mirror-image) as a true picture of the situation. Fee makes this charge against Peterlin's elaborate reconstruction of "the church polarized around Euodia and Syntyche who were the focus of disunity" as a result of personal power struggles, disputes for and against Paul, debates for and against the collection for Paul, and theological controversies stirred up by some perfectionist members of the church.[95] Peterlin's theory goes beyond

94. Brown, *Introduction*, 496: "There is no way to decide this issue: the best arguments seem to be on the side of Ephesus, and the weakest on the side of Caesarea."

95. Davorin Peterlin, *Paul's Letter to the Philippians in the Light of Disunity in the Church* (NovTSup 79; Leiden: Brill, 1995), 221. See the criticism against Peterlin for mirror-reading by Fee, 7 n. 24; 66 n. 41.

the evidence in the text, especially in his description of an "anti-Pauline lobby" in the church. The warmth of Paul's compliments and the depth of his gratitude for the support of the church weigh heavily against Peterlin's hypothesis of hostility towards Paul. Nevertheless, Peterlin's insight into the personal power struggles reflected in the text provides a valuable answer to the question of the occasion and purposes of the letter. An overarching purpose of the letter is Paul's desire to resolve the dispute between leaders in the church by urging believers to "strive together with one accord for the faith of the gospel . . . by being like-minded, having the same love, being one in spirit and of one mind" (1:27; 2:2).

Winter suggests that the heart of Paul's concern was that "the private disagreement between two women was in danger of spilling over into the public place."[96] He provides abundant evidence from inscriptions and papyri to show that Paul's use of the verb "live as citizens" (1:27) reflects a widespread use of the same verb and concept in the literature of Paul's era to convey a similar concern that citizens live in "concord" and "harmony" with one another.[97] Paul's letter was motivated by the "politics of friendship" of his day as he urges the church to "give credibility in the public place to the implications of faith created by the gospel" by standing "firm in the one Spirit, striving together with one accord" (1:27).[98] Paul condemns disunity and calls for unity in the church so that it will give a clear witness to the gospel in the public square: "Do everything without grumbling or arguing, so that you may become blameless and pure, 'children of God without fault in a warped and crooked generation.' Then you will shine among them like stars in the sky" (2:14-15).

Clearly the problem of disunity in the church in Philippi was high on Paul's agenda as he wrote this letter. He addresses the problem not only in his direct appeal to the two women who are in conflict but also throughout the letter in his denunciations of envy, rivalry, selfish ambition, vain conceit, grumbling, and arguing and in his challenges to be one in spirit and of one mind. Above all, Paul's sense of urgency as he attends to the problem of disunity comes from his commitment to "defending and confirming the gospel" (1:7). The integrity of the gospel is negated by disunity in the church. While Paul works "to advance the gospel" even among "the palace guard" (1:12-13), he does not want disunity in the church to ruin the advance of the gospel in Philippi. Believers must be "of one mind" so that they will shine as stars in this dark world.

96. Bruce Winter, *Seek the Welfare of the City: Christians as Benefactors and Citizens* (Grand Rapids: Eerdmans, 1994), 101.

97. Winter, *Seek the Welfare of the City*, 82-104.

98. Winter, *Seek the Welfare of the City*, 103.

2. *Suffering*

Paul's letter to the Philippians addresses the painful, discouraging experience of suffering in the life of Christians.[99] Suffering is a major theme through his entire discourse: he describes his experience in chains facing execution (1:12-26); he explains that Christians are called to suffer for Christ (1:29); he quotes the hymn depicting Christ's death on a cross (2:8); he points to himself as one being poured out like a drink offering on the sacrifice and service coming from the faith of the Philippians (2:17); he relates how Epaphroditus suffered in the course of his service on behalf of the Philippians (2:27-30); he records his loss of all things to gain Christ (3:8); he expresses his desire to share in the sufferings of Christ (3:10); and he says that he knows what it is to be in need (4:12). Paul's emphasis on suffering has led interpreters from the early days of the church to our day to view Philippians as a letter of encouragement for martyrs. As Ignatius of Antioch (martyred 110) approached his execution, he was inspired by Paul's attitude: "Grant me nothing more than that I shall be poured out to God, while an altar is still ready" (cf. Phil 2:17).[100] Ignatius viewed his martyrdom as the way to perfect union with God: "Suffer me to be eaten by the beasts, through whom I can attain to God."[101]

In the modern era, Ernst Lohmeyer interpreted Philippians as a treatise on martyrdom giving the hope of corporeal transformation through the experience of martyrdom.[102] Lohmeyer's outline of the letter expresses his perspective:[103]

I. The Martyrdom of Paul (1:12-26)
II. The Martyrdom of the Community (1:27–2:16)
III. Help in Martyrdom (2:17-30)
IV. Dangers in Martyrdom (3:1-21)
V. Final Admonitions regarding Martyrdom (4:1-9)

While Lohmeyer's interpretation overemphasizes the theme of suffering at the expense of other themes, his approach does the service of highlighting the pervasive language of suffering in this letter. It is "a letter of consolation written to answer the Philippians' discouragement over Paul's imprisonment and their own suffering for the gospel."[104] In this letter Christians

99. Bloomquist, *The Function of Suffering in Philippians,* 193: "Suffering is central in Philippians as the occasion of the letter."

100. Ignatius, *To the Romans* 2:2. See Bloomquist's illuminating survey of the interpretation of the suffering passages in Philippians from the early church to the present time (*The Function of Suffering in Philippians,* 18-70).

101. Ignatius, *To the Romans* 4:2.

102. E. Lohmeyer, *Der Brief an die Philipper;* see Bloomquist, *The Function of Suffering in Philippians,* 50-52, for an analysis of Lohmeyer's position.

103. Lohmeyer, 5-6.

104. Paul A. Holloway, *Consolation in Philippians — Philosophical Sources and Rhetorical Strategy* (SNTSMS 112; Cambridge: Cambridge University Press, 2001), 161.

find solace and strength by understanding how their suffering is participation in the suffering and victory of Christ. Since vindication followed suffering for Christ (2:8-9), the suffering of Christians points to the final victory accomplished by Christ, who "will transform our lowly bodies so that they will be like his glorious body" (3:21).

3. *Opponents*

In his letter to the Philippians, Paul expresses his awareness of opponents of the church who threaten and seek to destroy the faith of Christians. He urges the believers to stand "firm in the one Spirit . . . without being frightened in any way by those who oppose you" (1:27-28). He recognizes that these "children of God" live in the midst of "a warped and crooked generation" (2:15). He strongly warns the church: "Watch out for those dogs, those evildoers, those mutilators of the flesh" (3:2). He writes with tears about "enemies of the cross": "Their destiny is destruction, their god is their stomach, and their glory is in their shame. Their mind is set on earthly things" (3:18-19). Paul also describes opposition to himself: "some preach Christ out of . . . selfish ambition, not sincerely, supposing that they can stir up trouble for me while I am in chains" (1:15-17).

The identification of the opponents alluded to in Philippians is the subject of a vast amount of secondary literature.[105] Current research proposes at least eighteen different identities for the opponents.[106] Some of the name tags pinned on the opponents are Jewish Christians, non-Christian Jews, Gentile Christians, non-Christian Gentiles, Jewish Gnostics, Hellenistic Jewish missionaries, Jewish Judaizers, Gentile Judaizers, and Roman authorities. A complete evaluation of the widely diverse identifications of the opponents requires the major monographs and dissertations dedicated to that task. My review of some of the options appears in the context of the commentary on verses referring to opponents. Our objective in this introduction is to outline the identifications made in this commentary with the caveat that other identifications receive worthy and reputable support. The

105. Fee, 7: "The secondary literature on this issue is second only to the huge output on 2:6-11." O'Brien, 26-27: "One of the most hotly debated issues in the contemporary study of Philippians is that of the nature and identity of the opponents to whom Paul alludes in his letter."

106. See the overview and extensive bibliography in P. W. Barnett, "Opponents of Paul," *DPL* 644-53. Also see especially H. W. Bateman IV, "Were the Opponents at Philippi Necessarily Jewish?" *BSac* 155 (1998), 39-61; E. E. Ellis, "Paul and His Opponents," in *Christianity, Judaism and Other Greco-Roman Cults* (ed. J. Neusner; Leiden: E. J. Brill, 1975), 264-98; J. J. Gunther, *St. Paul's Opponents and Their Background* (NovTSup 35; Leiden: E. J. Brill, 1973); J. Sumney, *Identifying Paul's Opponents* (JSNTSup 40; Sheffield: JSOT Press, 1990); J. B. Tyson, "Paul's Opponents at Philippi," *PRSt* 3 (1976) 82-95; D. K. Williams, *Enemies of the Cross of Christ: The Terminology of the Cross and Conflict in Philippians* (JSNTSup 223; Sheffield: Sheffield Academic, 2002).

following four categories of opponents defined here are described in more detail in the commentary.

1. Preachers of Christ who suppose they can stir up trouble for Paul (1:15-17)

Paul accuses these preachers of envy, rivalry, selfish ambition, and attempts to stir up trouble for him. But since he does not accuse them of false teaching, they do not deserve to be named as Jewish Judaizers, Gentile Judaizers, or Jewish Gnostics. Nor do they necessarily have the same name as those who are characterized by selfish ambition in Philippi (2:2). To take 1:15-17 as a double reference to anti-Paul parties in the place of his imprisonment and in Philippi requires an unsubstantiated leap.[107] All that can be accurately said about these preachers of Christ is that they illustrate the divisive, destructive results of envy and self-ambition.

2. Roman opponents to the gospel who are intimidating Christians in Philippi (1:28)

Since Paul tells the Philippians not to be frightened by these opponents in the same paragraph that refers to the common struggle that he and the Philippians are going through (1:29-30), he is referring to Roman authorities and Roman citizens: those who imprisoned him in Philippi ("the same struggle you saw I had") and in his present place of imprisonment ("and now hear that I still have") are also frightening the church and opposing the witness to the gospel of Christ. Paul did not underestimate the power of imperial agents to intimidate and persecute the fledgling group of believers in Christ. He calls Philippian believers to "stand firm in the one Spirit, striving together with one accord for the faith of the gospel" (1:27) so that they would not be overwhelmed by Roman Philippians who thought that subverting the imperial gospel that Caesar is Lord by proclaiming the gospel that Jesus Christ is Lord is evidence enough for execution (1:28).[108]

3. Jewish Christians who lead Gentile Christians to follow Jewish rituals (3:2)

Paul's harsh warning, "Watch out for those dogs, those evildoers, those mutilators," is followed by the claim for the church, "we are the [true]

107. Against Peterlin, *Paul's Letter to the Philippians*, 35-41.

108. See the commentary below for this interpretation. See also S. E. Fowl, "Philippians 1:28b, One More Time," in *New Testament Greek and Exegesis: Essays in Honor of Gerald F. Hawthorne* (ed. Amy M. Donaldson and Timothy B. Sailors; Grand Rapids: Eerdmans, 2003), 167-79: "This view reads this clause as asserting that the Philippians' steadfast faith in the face of opposition is a sign, but it is a sign that can be read two ways. The opponents will take it as a sign of the Philippians' imminent destruction. To the Philippians, however, it is a sign from God of their salvation" (178).

circumcision" (3:3). This contrast between the mutilators (those who impose circumcision) and the true circumcision points to the Jewish nature of these opponents. They would not have any access to the church if they did not claim to be Christians as well. These opponents are similar to or actually the same as the Jewish Christians who infiltrated Paul's churches in Galatia. As suggested above in the proposal that Ephesus was Paul's place of imprisonment when he wrote Philippians, Paul's invective against these opponents in Philippians 3:2 may have been ignited by his outburst in his letter to the Galatians against Jewish Christian agitators. Galatians and Philippians reflect the same severe censure of these troublemakers.

4. Gentile Christians who "live" (literally, are walking) "as enemies of the cross," as a result of the pressures of the pagan culture in Roman Philippi (3:18-19)

Paul writes with tears about many who "live as enemies of the cross." Living as a follower of Christ in a Roman colony was truly countercultural. The strong currents of pagan religions, hedonistic lifestyles, and especially the imperial cult could easily knock Christians off their feet and pull them away from walking in the way of the cross of Christ. The result of giving in to the pressures of their culture would cause Christians to live as enemies of the way of the cross: walking in the way of destruction, obeying their physical appetites as their god, making their boast in shameful activities, and setting their mind on earthly things (3:19). Instead of shining as stars "in a warped and crooked generation" (2:15), these (former? lapsed?) Christians were assimilating to their culture in Philippi in ways that denied the gospel. So Paul calls them to remember that they are citizens of heaven: "our citizenship is in heaven. And we eagerly await a Savior from there, the Lord Jesus Christ" (3:20).

Paul's references to the problem of disunity in the church, the experience of suffering, and the four categories of opponents (ambitious preachers, intimidating powers, Jewish Christian teachers, and enemies of the cross) form a matrix for interpreting the theology and ethical exhortations in his letter. When we put this matrix of the problems in Philippi together with the reports Paul gives of his own situation in prison and his receipt of the gift from Philippi, we have a full picture of the occasion for his letter.

IV. A PREVIEW OF TWO THEMES

All the different aspects and subjects of this letter point to two major themes: the gospel of Christ and the community in Christ.

A. The Gospel of Christ

Paul's driving passion in all of his work is "defending and confirming the gospel," "to advance the gospel," and "the defense of the gospel" (1:7, 12, and 16).[109] He writes this letter to thank the Philippians for their "partnership in the gospel" (1:5) since the early days of their "acquaintance with the gospel" (4:15). His first and overarching imperative to the Philippians is to "live as citizens in a manner worthy of the gospel of Christ, . . . striving together with one accord for the faith of the gospel" (1:27). The highest commendation Paul gives of his co-workers is that they "served with me in the work of the gospel" and "contended at my side in the cause of the gospel" (2:22, 4:3). The gospel of Christ takes first place in Paul's mission and his letter.[110]

The content of the gospel is the good news that Jesus Christ is Lord. Pulsating with praise for the humility and the exaltation of the Lord Jesus Christ, the Christ hymn (2:6-11) is the heart of the letter. This hymn expresses in lofty, lyrical language the narrative of Christ from his preincarnate glory to the universal praise of him as Lord to the glory of God the Father. The pathway of this divine person is marked by his humble obedience as a human slave all the way to death on a cross. Consequently, God exalted him by giving him the name "Lord" so that all creation will worship him as the ultimate sovereign above all earthly sovereigns. The church in Philippi is called by the hymn to express their worship of Jesus Christ as Lord in their humble service to one another (2:1-5).

This gospel of Christ has special relevance for recipients in a Roman colony. To "stand firm" for the gospel of Christ against the gospel of Caesar, they need to worship Jesus Christ as the Lord and Savior above all earthly powers. But the gospel of Christ reaches far beyond a contrast between Christ and the Roman emperor. No matter what earthly powers may oppose them, Christians everywhere are called to "live in a manner worthy of the gospel."

Living according to the gospel is a process of pressing on to apprehend the surpassing worth of Jesus Christ and being apprehended by him (3:12). Progress in the Christian life is not measured by "righteousness based on the law"; instead, it begins with the gift of "righteousness that comes from God through faith in Christ" (3:6-9). The "one thing" Paul desires to do in his life (3:13) is to know Christ, "to know the power of his resurrection and participation in his sufferings" (3:10). His pursuit of Christ serves as a model, an example, for the Philippians to follow (3:17). Paul's

109. I. Howard Marshall, "The Theology of Philippians," in Karl P. Donfried and I. Howard Marshall, *New Testament Theology: The Theology of the Shorter Pauline Letters* (ed. James D. G. Dunn; Cambridge: Cambridge University Press, 1993), 127: "The gospel controls the life of both Paul and his readers."

110. P. T. O'Brien, *Gospel and Mission in the Writings of Paul: An Exegetical and Theological Analysis* (Grand Rapids: Baker, 1995), 114-19.

life challenges his readers to exclaim with him: "For to me, to live is Christ" (1:21). With this goal in life they will face death courageously, knowing that they will be "with Christ" (1:23). Every day of their life will be oriented toward the "day of Christ Jesus" (1:6, 10; 2:16), when "the Lord Jesus Christ, the Savior," will come from heaven to "bring everything under his control and transform our lowly bodies so that they will be like his glorious body" (3:20-21).

B. The Community in Christ

Woven inseparably together with the theme of the gospel of Christ is the theme of the community in Christ. The phrase "in Christ" has a "dominating role in Philippians," occurring in various forms twenty-one times.[111] Although this phrase has a range of meanings and does not always refer to corporate union with Christ, the primary focus of the phrase in Philippians is the community in Christ. When Paul addresses his letter to "all God's holy people in Christ Jesus" (1:1), he is not simply addressing them as individual Christians. He is recognizing their corporate union with one another in their union with Christ. Paul introduces the Christ hymn by reminding them that they are a community in Christ. "Think this way among yourselves which also you think in Christ Jesus" (2:5; my trans.). My literal translation from the Greek text emphasizes the parallelism by using the same verb, "think," in both clauses and by understanding the phrases "in you" and "in Christ Jesus" as parallel references to the corporate union of Christians with Christ. Paul is calling Christians to "think the same in your community with each other as one is obligated to think in the community in Christ."[112]

The community in Christ is a "partnership in the gospel" (1:5). Paul develops this concept of partnership, fellowship, in his letter to emphasize the corporate nature of life in Christ. Standing behind the English word "partnership," the Greek word *(koinōnia)* connotes a variety of close relationships "involving mutual interests and sharing."[113] Marriage and family relationships, friendships, business partnerships, common possession of property, citizenship, and religious organizations were all considered to be examples of *koinōnia* in Paul's day. Paul's six references to partnership[114] in this letter draw from these various nuances of partnership and contribute to the development of his theology of community in Christ. A major purpose of this letter is to transform the experience of partnership in the light of life in Christ.[115]

111. Marshall, "The Theology of Philippians," 138.
112. Müller, 92. See the discussion of this verse in the commentary below.
113. BDAG, 552.
114. 1:5, 7, 2:1; 3:10; 4:14, 15.
115. L. T. Johnson, *The Writings of the New Testament: An Interpretation* (rev. ed.; Minne-

The kind of partnership enjoyed by Paul and the Philippians in their "partnership in the gospel" (1:5) is first of all their close association as friends who shared a common faith in the gospel. The partnership formed by mutual participation in the benefits of the gospel developed into a partnership to advance the proclamation of the gospel. The partnership of Paul and the Philippians in the work of proclaiming the gospel bears striking resemblance to business partnerships in Paul's day.[116] The Philippians' partnership in the appropriation and the proclamation of the gospel filled Paul with joyful thankfulness whenever he thought of them. A primary purpose of the letter was to express his gratitude to the church in Philippi for their partnership with him in the advance of the gospel.

Paul was aware that the problem of disunity in the church threatened this partnership. His partnership with the church in the mission of proclaiming the gospel would fail if members in the church were divided against each other. To strengthen the unity of the church, Paul draws on another meaning of partnership, that of common possession. Believers in Christ are heirs to the Holy Spirit; they have common possession of the Holy Spirit. They are bound together not only by their partnership to proclaim the gospel but also by their "common sharing in the Spirit" (2:1). Their "common sharing in the Spirit" is their way to experience participation in the sufferings of Christ (3:10). Paul's development of the concept of partnership places human partnership for the sake of the common venture of advancing the gospel (1:5) within communion with the Spirit (2:1), and communion with the Spirit within participation in the sufferings of Christ (3:10). The partnership in the gospel resulting from common sharing in the Spirit leads to common sharing in the sufferings of Christ.The term "participation in his sufferings" points to the solidarity of all believers who have chosen to participate in the sufferings of Christ. Paul is not presenting his participation as an individualistic enterprise reserved only for heroic martyrs. This participation in the sufferings of Christ does not happen in isolation from others. According to Paul, all believers are called to share together in the sufferings of Christ (1:29-30). By their experience in community of participation in his sufferings, believers grow in their knowledge of Christ. The longing to know participation in his sufferings is a longing for a community experience.

When Paul turns to the practical matter of writing a receipt for the financial contributions of the Philippians (4:10-19), he commends them for partnering with him in his trials (4:14) and for being the only church to partner with him in the arrangement of giving and receiving (4:15). By dis-

---

apolis: Fortress, 1999), 373, says that Paul "made fellowship the organizing principle of the letter."

116. J. Paul Sampley, *Pauline Partnership in Christ: Christian Community and Commitment in Light of Roman Law* (Philadelphia: Fortress, 1980); G. Walter Hansen, "Transformation of Relationships," in *New Testament Greek and Exegesis: Essays in Honor of Gerald F. Hawthorne* (ed. A. M. Donaldson and T. B. Sailors; Grand Rapids: Eerdmans, 2003), 182-89.

closing the deeper dimensions of the partnership as a common sharing in the Spirit and participation in his sufferings, he places his references to these financial aspects of the partnership within the unbreakable bonds of community life in union with Christ.

The community in Christ is the new people of God. Paul draws a strong contrast at the beginning of chapter 3 between the people of God identified by belonging to the Jewish people and the people of God identified by belonging to Christ. In harsh warnings (3:2), he depicts Judaizers (those who proselytize Gentile Christians to bring them within the circle of Judaism) as "dogs, evildoers, and mutilators."[117] By contrast, those who belong to Christ are "the circumcision, serving God by his Spirit, boasting in Christ Jesus, and putting no confidence in the flesh" (3:3). Paul's identification of the Gentile church in Philippi as "the circumcision" (a name for Israel, the Jewish people of God, because they were marked by the rite of circumcision) affirms their full inclusion in the true people of God because they are in Christ. Paul says that he considers all of his inherited privileges and moral accomplishments as a Jew (3:4-6) "a loss because of the surpassing worth of knowing Christ" (3:8). Christ is the center and circumference of the new people of God. All that matters is to "be found in him" (3:9). This radical redefinition of the community of believers in Christ as the true people of God gives the church a clear understanding of its identity before God and of its mission in the world.

Our understanding of the relationship of the community in Christ to the world is clarified by Paul's assertion to the Philippians, "our citizenship is in heaven" (3:20). The Philippians were Roman citizens under the authority of the emperor. But they had a more fundamental allegiance: they were citizens of a heavenly colony under the authority of the Lord Jesus Christ.[118] Because of his allegiance to the Lord in heaven, Paul faced death under the Roman emperor (1:19-24). He knew that the Philippians also faced fierce opposition from the Roman authorities for their commitment to the gospel of Christ (1:27-30). In the context of imminent execution and hostile persecution, Paul calls the church to a fearless proclamation of the gospel with the encouragement that even his imprisonment actually "served to advance the gospel, even among the whole palace guard" (1:12-13). Bold witness to the gospel that Jesus Christ is Lord brought some members of Caesar's household into the church (4:22). Believers in Christ fulfill their mission in the world when they "live as citizens of heaven in a manner worthy of the gospel of Christ" and "stand firm in the one Spirit, striving together with one accord for the faith of the gospel" (1:27; 4:1-2). By

117. See the commentary below for discussion of these terms.

118. D. A. Carson, *Christ and Culture Revisited* (Grand Rapids: Eerdmans, 2008), 166: "Inevitably, then, thoughtful Christians maintain some fundamental allegiances that set them apart from other citizens in the Empire who feel no loyalty whatsoever to a 'citizenship . . . in heaven.'"

their unity with one another in Christ they give solid evidence of the reality of their "citizenship in heaven."

Paul affirms the identity of believers as "the children of God" (2:15) by frequently referring to them as "brothers and sisters."[119] As a family letter, Philippians communicates news between members of the family. News about Paul's imprisonment, the suffering endured for Christ's sake, the illness of Epaphroditus, the plan to send Timothy, and his intention to visit are all the kinds of information shared between brothers and sisters. Paul's appeal for sisters who are in conflict to "be of the same mind" (4:2) comes from his concern for unity in the family. Only when brothers and sisters "do everything without grumbling or arguing" will they "become blameless and pure, 'children of God without fault in a warped and crooked generation'" (2:14-15). The mission of the family of God in the world depends upon their unity with one another.

The gospel of Christ and the community in Christ motivate Paul's exuberant outbursts of joy: he gives thanks with joy for their partnership in the gospel (1:5); he rejoices because Christ is preached and the community prays for him (1:18); he rejoices when he visualizes the children of God shining as stars and holding firmly the word of life (2:15-18); he asks the church to welcome Epaphroditus home with great joy (2:29); he calls the brothers and sisters to rejoice in the Lord (3:1; 4:4); and he rejoices greatly in the Lord because of the practical concern of the community for him while he was in prison (4:10). In a letter filled with reflections on the suffering of Paul and the Philippians, rejoicing in the Lord predominates over all the difficult circumstances of life. Like a mighty river surging through solid rock, joy flows from this letter through the suffering community of believers, giving them love for one another and the peace of God.

119. 1:12, 14; 2:25; 3:1, 13, 17; 4:1, 8, 21.

Philippians 1

I. GREETINGS AND GRACE (1:1-2)

[1]*Paul and Timothy, servants of Christ Jesus,*

To all God's holy people in Christ Jesus at Philippi, together with the overseers and deacons:

[2]*Grace and peace to you from God our Father and the Lord Jesus Christ.*

1 The threefold repetition of the name — *Christ Jesus, Christ Jesus, the Lord Jesus Christ* — presents the central theme that reappears throughout the letter and unites everything around the person of Christ. Paul defines his role and that of his co-workers as *servants of Christ Jesus.* He describes the relationship of the church to Christ as one of living *in Christ Jesus.* His blessing presents *God our Father and the Lord Jesus Christ* as the common source of grace and peace. The blessing anticipates the dramatic finale of the Christ hymn: *Jesus Christ is Lord, to the glory of God the Father* (2:11).

By beginning the letter with his own name, Paul follows the common form of Greek letters in his day.[1] Although Paul writes the entire letter in the first person singular, he also includes Timothy in the salutation.[2] Timothy is probably included because he served as Paul's secretary by writing down Paul's dictation of this letter.[3] Timothy may also be mentioned because Paul wanted to assure the Philippians that the points made in this letter were confirmed by Timothy, whom they knew from the time of Paul's

1. See W. G. Doty, *Letters in Primitive Christianity* (Philadelphia: Fortress, 1973); J. L. White, *Light from Ancient Letters* (Philadelphia: Fortress, 1986); P. T. O'Brien, "Letters, Letter Forms," *DPL* 550-53.

2. Timothy is included in the salutations of six of Paul's letters: 2 Cor 1:1; Phil 1:1; Col 1:1 Phlmn 1; 1 Thess 1:1; and 2 Thess 1:1.

3. Bruce, 25; Fee, 61; according to Martin and Hawthorne, 4-5, Paul included Timothy with himself in the address as *servants of Christ Jesus* to teach the Philippians that relationships in the church should be characterized by humble equality. See Collange, 38.

first visit to Philippi (Acts 16:1-12).[4] Timothy was one of Paul's closest associates. Paul speaks of him with great warmth and affection when he tells the Philippians that *as a son with his father he has served with me in the work of the gospel* (2:22).[5] Paul's description of Timothy's sacrificial service to others clearly echoes Paul's hymn to the self-giving love of Christ (2:6-8). From Paul's perspective, Timothy was a rare example of Christ-like humility and service.

After giving their names as the senders of this letter, Paul gives their titles. He and Timothy are *servants of Christ Jesus.* This is a significant departure from Paul's customary self-designation. Paul usually introduced himself as an apostle of Christ Jesus.[6] But in this letter he makes no reference to his apostolic position. In Romans 1:1 and Titus 1:1 the titles "slave" and "apostle" are combined and apply only to Paul. But in this letter Paul does something quite unusual: he uses the same title for both himself and Timothy. Their work together was that of "slaves," the literal meaning of the term *servants.*

In a Roman colony like Philippi, some slaves did menial work while others had great responsibilities in civil service. But in either case their lack of freedom and their subservience to their masters who owned them made their position as slaves ignominious compared to those who were free.[7] Paul's reference later in this letter to Christ's own obedience as a *slave,* obedience even to death on a cross (2:7-8), indicates that Paul's use of the title of slaves for himself and Timothy points to their total subjection to the will of their master: they were not autonomous; they were subject to the claims of the one who owned them.

Paul considered the position that he and Timothy had as *servants of Christ Jesus* to be a high privilege. It is a high calling to have the same position taken by Christ Jesus, who "emptied himself, taking the form of a slave" (2:7). And there is no one greater to serve than the one who was exalted by God and will be universally acclaimed to be the Lord of all (2:9-11). Paul's reasoning was simple: If Christ is our Lord, then we are his *servants.*[8]

4. O'Brien, 44.

5. Also 1 Cor 4:17: "I have sent to you Timothy, who is my beloved and faithful child in the Lord" (my trans.).

6. See Romans, 1 and 2 Corinthians, Galatians, Ephesians, Colossians, 1 and 2 Timothy, Titus. He omits the title "apostle" only in Philippians, 1 and 2 Thessalonians, and Philemon.

7. See Peter Garnsey, *Social Status and Legal Privilege in the Roman Empire* (Oxford: Clarendon, 1970); K. R. Bradley, *Slavery and Society at Rome* (Cambridge: Cambridge University Press, 1994).

8. Murray J. Harris, *Slave of Christ: A New Testament Metaphor for Total Devotion to Christ* (NSBT 8; ed. D. A. Carson; Downers Grove: InterVarsity Press, 1999), 138: "While for Christian leaders *doulos* was already a title of honour, it gained its positive connotations in the ears of all Christians because the divine Master they were serving was kind and generous and himself had blazed an exemplary trail of lowly service. What all the *douloi* of this *Kyrios* gained through being associated with him was not so much authority and power as

To be called servants of the Lord was a mark of distinction in the history of God's people. In the Greek translation of the Hebrew scriptures, the term "servant" is used as a title for Moses, Joshua, and David, who were each called servants of the Lord.[9] By announcing that he and Timothy were servants of Christ Jesus, Paul accepted a humble yet honored position taken by servants of the Lord among God's people.

The title of servants for himself and Timothy points to Paul's view of relationships in Christ: when believers in Christ freely and joyfully accept the position of servants of Christ Jesus, they will be united and effective in service.[10] Relationships are ruined by envy, rivalry, and selfish ambition (1:15-17; 2:3), but they will thrive when friends humbly serve each other before looking out for their own interests (2:3-4). At the beginning of his letter, Paul exemplifies the attitude he calls for all believers to have, the attitude of the one who accepted the form of a slave (2:5-8).

The double name, *Christ Jesus,* expresses Paul's belief that Jesus is the Messiah. In fact, the messianic role and work of Jesus was such a presupposition for Paul that he does not defend it but builds his theology upon it.[11] The great Christ hymn in this letter portrays both the humility of Christ in submitting to death on a cross and the sovereignty of Christ in receiving universal worship as the divine Lord (2:6-11). The attitude of those who are *servants of Christ Jesus* will be expressed in their Christ-like, humble service and their Christ-centered worship of Jesus as Lord.

The letter is written to *all God's holy people.* Such people are not in a special club of super-spiritual Christians. The phrase *God's holy people* is Paul's common designation for all believers in Jesus Christ. They are not simply common ordinary people. No, they are *holy,* and that means that they are separated from evil and consecrated to fulfill God's purposes.[12] The phrase *all God's holy people* is based upon God's call to Israel to be a "holy people." *In Christ Jesus* all God's people are holy. Their holiness is inherent in their calling and position *in Christ.*[13] It is not earned by social posi-

unparalleled honour and the assurance that their service, whatever its nature, was of supreme value, simply because it was done for *him.*"

9. Neh 10:29; Josh 24:29; Ps 89:20 (LXX 88:21).

10. Harris, *Slave of Christ,* 104: "The term *doulos* expresses both a vertical and a horizontal relationship of the Christian, who is both the willing vassal of the heavenly Master and the submissive servant of fellow-believers. The term epitomizes the Christian's dual obligation: unquestioning devotion to Christ and to his people. But the vertical relationship is prior and the horizontal secondary. Christians are devoted to one another as a direct result of being devoted to Christ. When they serve each other, they are demonstrating and expressing their slavery to the Lord Christ."

11. See N. T. Wright, *The Climax of the Covenant: Christ and the Law in Pauline Theology* (Minneapolis: Fortress, 1993), 41-49.

12. BDAG, 11.

13. Karl Barth (10): "'Holy people' are unholy people, who nevertheless as such have been singled out, claimed, and requisitioned by God for his control, for his use, for himself who is holy. Their holiness is and remains in Christ Jesus."

tion or moral performance, but by union with Jesus Christ. By addressing his letter to *all,* Paul shows that he is promoting the unity of all rather than recognizing any social or moral distinctions. The repetition of his references to *all* in the opening part of his letter[14] emphasizes Paul's concern to heal the divisions in the church by including opposing factions within his embrace.[15] Euodia and Syntyche (4:2) and others like them who were fighting against each other could not have missed the way Paul brings all of them together as one in his address to *all God's holy people in Christ Jesus.*

The residence of *all God's holy people* is indicated by the use of the preposition *in. All God's holy people* are *in Christ Jesus* and *at Philippi.*[16] The parallelism of these two prepositional phrases clarifies the meaning of this first instance of Paul's use of the important *in Christ* phrase in this letter. What does it mean to be *in Christ?* Is this simply Paul's way of referring to Christians? Does the preposition *in* point to a personal relationship with Christ by faith, to justification by faith in Christ, to mystical union with the risen Christ, to the participation of believers in the benefits of Christ's redemptive work, or to the church, the body of Christ (the church equals *all God's holy people in Christ Jesus*)? These interpretations and many more offer insights into the meaning of this key phrase *in Christ.*[17] Paul's use of the phrase is a shorthand summary of major themes in his theology. Throughout this letter Paul's use of this phrase expresses a range of nuances: a personal, subjective experience of the presence of Christ; a corporate, objective position in Christ's redemptive work; and an ethical activity by the indwelling power of Christ. The meaning of the phrase *in Christ* needs to receive a fresh evaluation in each particular context. At this point the phrase *in Christ* tells us where the Christian community lives, just as the phrase *in Philippi* tells us where the church resides.

Geographical, historical, and social factors contributed to the experience of residence in Philippi. The residents of Philippi lived in the northeastern corner of Macedonia on the famous Via Egnatia, a major Roman road. The city was founded in 42 B.C. as a colony for Roman veterans after the defeat of Brutus and Cassius by Mark Antony and Octavian (later

14. This is the first of five references to "all" (1:1, 3, 7 [twice], 8).

15. Paul also emphasizes his inclusion of "all" in his address to the Roman church (Rom 1:1) divided by animosity between Jews and Gentiles (Romans 14–15) and the Corinthian church (1 Cor 1:1; 2 Cor 1:1) renowned for its divisions and opposing factions (1 Cor 1:10-13).

16. The same preposition (ἐν) is used in the Greek text.

17. For interpretations of the phrase *in Christ,* see I. Howard Marshall, "The Theology of Philippians," in *New Testament Theology: The Theology of the Shorter Pauline Letters* (ed. Karl P. Donfried and I. Howard Marshall; Cambridge: Cambridge University Press, 1993), 138-48; E. Best, *One Body in Christ* (London: SPCK, 1955), 1-33; Richard N. Longenecker, *Paul, Apostle of Liberty* (Grand Rapids: Baker, 1976), 160-70; James D. G. Dunn, *The Theology of Paul the Apostle* (Grand Rapids: Eerdmans, 1998); 396-401; A. Oepke, "ἐν," *TDNT* 2:541-43; M. J. Harris, "Appendix: Prepositions and Theology in the Greek New Testament," *NIDNTT* 3:1192-93; M. A. Seifrid, "In Christ," *DPL* 433-36.

Caesar Augustus). Later the city was reestablished as a Roman colony, *Colonia Iulia Augusta Philippensium,* after Augustus defeated Mark Antony in the battle of Actium in 31 B.C. Augustus repopulated the colony with Roman soldiers and Italian farmers. As a result, the social relationships of the Philippians to their friends and business associates were defined by the social realities of life in a first-century Roman colony.[18]

Just as the Christians lived together as residents in Philippi, so they lived together as believers in Christ. Their life was centered in Christ; their new historical situation was created by the victory of the cross and resurrection of Christ; and as a result their social relationships to fellow believers were bound together by their common life in Christ.

As we consider Paul's frequent use of the *in Christ* phrase in this letter, we will see how Paul uses the experience of residence in Philippi to give believers a better understanding of their residence in Christ. The social realities of life *in Philippi* can be seen at many points behind Paul's language in this letter. He often uses the concepts and structures of the Greek and Roman culture of Philippi as analogies for life in Christ. For example, the common experience of partnership *(koinōnia)* in friendships and business in Philippi was a resource for Paul's theology of partnership in Christ (1:5, 7; 2:1; 3:10; 4:14, 15). Another prominent aspect of life at *Philippi* was the privilege of Roman citizenship. The concept of citizenship is the basis for Paul's exhortation to *live as citizens in a manner worthy of the gospel of Jesus Christ* (1:27) and his reminder that *our citizenship is in heaven* (3:20).

Paul's addition of the phrase *together with the overseers and deacons* is puzzling for two reasons. First, this is the only time in Paul's letters, except for the Pastorals,[19] where *overseers* and *deacons* are mentioned together as leaders of the church.[20] Second, there is no further reference to these people, at least not by these titles, in the rest of the letter. Two purposes may be adduced from the letter as a whole for Paul's direct address to these two groups of leaders in the church at the beginning of his letter. First, Paul's reference to his partnership with the Philippians at the beginning (1:5) and end (4:15-18) of his letter indicates that this letter serves as a "thank you" for their financial

18. David W. J. Gill, "Macedonia," in *The Book of Acts in Its Graeco-Roman Setting,* ed. D. W. J. Gill and C. Gempff (The Book of Acts in Its First-Century Setting; ed. B. W. Winter; Grand Rapids: Eerdmans, 1993), 1:411-13. See the Introduction to the commentary, 1-6.

19. "Overseer" (traditionally translated "bishop") in Tim 3:1, 2; Tit 1:7; "deacons" in 1 Tim 3:8, 12, 4:6. See also Acts 20:28 for the use of "overseers" in Paul's speech to the elders of the church in Ephesus.

20. Deacons mentioned by Paul are governmental authorities (Rom 13:4), Christ (Rom 15:8), Phoebe (Rom 16:1), Apollos and himself (1 Cor 3:5), himself and others as servants of the new covenant (2 Cor 3:6), himself and others as servants of God (2 Cor 6:4), servants of Satan masquerading as servants of righteousness (2 Cor 11:15), himself and others as servants of Christ (2 Cor 11:23), Christ (Gal 2:17), himself as a servant of the gospel (Eph 3:7), Tychicus, a faithful servant in the Lord (Eph 6:21), Epaphras, a servant of Christ (Col 1:7), himself as a servant of the gospel and the church (Col 1:23, 25), and Tychicus, a faithful servant and fellow slave in the Lord (Col 4:7).

support. Paul addressed the leaders of the church because they were the ones who administered this support and sent Epaphroditus bearing the gifts of the church to Paul (4:18).[21] Second, Paul addresses the bishops and deacons to emphasize their responsibility to make sure that the church will follow Paul's instructions.[22] By referring to these leaders, Paul commissions them to lead the church in *striving together with one accord for the faith of the gospel* (1:27). Especially in the light of Paul's appeal to Euodia and Syntyche to be united in one mind (4:2), Paul's address to the leaders seems to stress the role of leaders to resolve conflicts in the church so that the gospel of Christ will be embodied in the humility and unity of believers in Christ. Paul directs his opening greetings to leaders *(overseers and deacons)* in the church because they were the potential solution to the problem of disunity in the church.[23]

Two important inferences can be made from the way that Paul refers to these leaders. First, he refers to a plurality of leaders. The responsibilities of leadership were shared by a group of leaders in the church. On the basis of Paul's teaching in 1 Corinthians 12, we may expect that the members of this leadership group exercised a diversity of gifts and carried out diverse ministries in their service in the church. But by addressing his letter to the Philippians to the entire group of leaders — *the overseers and deacons* — Paul emphasizes the unity of this leadership group. Second, the leaders are not addressed as those who are *over* the church but rather as those who are *together with* the church. The terms themselves indicate that these leaders have the responsibility to exercise oversight and supervision in their service to the church. But these leaders are part of the church and serve *together with* the church. Perhaps the tendency of the leaders to seek superior positions for themselves caused Paul to alert them in the address of his letter that his call to serve with humility (2:3-4) was not only for the church members in general but especially for them in particular.[24] In fact, Paul's emphasis on humble service starts in the title he chose for himself and Timothy as *servants of Christ Jesus.*

21. Chrysostom, "Homily on Philippians 2.1.1-2," in *ACCS* 8:218: "Nowhere else does Paul write specifically to the clergy — not in Rome, in Corinth, in Ephesus, or anywhere. Rather, he typically writes jointly to all who are holy, faithful, and beloved. But in this case he addresses specifically the bishops and deacons. Why? Because it was they who had borne fruit and they who had sent Epaphroditus to him." See also Brian Capper, "Paul's Dispute with Philippi: Understanding Paul's Argument in Phil 1–2 from His Thanks in 4:10-20," *TZ* 49.3 (1993), 206-7.

22. Collange, 41-42.

23. Against Davorin Peterlin, *Paul's Letter to the Philippians in the Light of Disunity in the Church* (NovTSup 79; Leiden: Brill, 1995), 107, Paul's address includes this reference to the overseers and deacons "precisely because the conflict is most fierce among them." His speculative thesis depends upon giving the two women in 4:2 the title of overseers and/or deacons and imagining that they were leaders of an anti-Paul and a pro-Paul split in the church. His thesis goes beyond the evidence of the letter.

24. David E. Garland, "Philippians 1:1-26: The Defense and Confirmation of the Gospel," *RevExp* 77 (1980), 327.

2 *Grace* is Paul's adaptation of the "greetings" at the beginning of Greek letters of his day.[25] *Peace* echoes the common Jewish greeting *(Shalom)*. Paul's combination of the Greek and Jewish greetings reflects the intersection of Greek and Jewish cultures in Paul's expressions.[26] This greeting, *grace and peace to you,* is used in all of Paul's letters. Often referred to as a common formula or social convention in Paul's letters, this phrase of greeting is anything but an empty cliché for Paul. In fact, it expresses in condensed form the essence of his theology. His message is one of grace and peace: grace, the unmerited, undeserved saving work of God in Christ Jesus brings believers into peace, harmonious relationships with God and with each other.[27] The opening grace note is heard again in the last line of his letter: *The grace of the Lord Jesus Christ be with your spirit. Amen* (4:23). And the opening greeting of peace *(Shalom!)* is heard again in his promise of the *peace of God* and the *God of peace* (4:7, 9). All that Paul says in this letter is encompassed within this double emphasis on grace and peace. All of the outworking of salvation depends upon the gracious initiative of God, who *works in you to will and to act in order to fulfill his good purpose* (2:12-13). All who totally depend upon the grace of God will be protected by the peace of God and will enjoy the presence of the God of peace (4:6-9).

The source of grace and peace is God, known as *God our Father and the Lord Jesus Christ.* Before meeting the risen Christ, Paul's central affirmation of faith was the Jewish creed known as the *Shema:* "Hear, O Israel, the LORD our God, the LORD is one." After his encounter with Christ, Paul's faith included Jesus Christ within the *Shema:* "The Lord (Jesus Christ) (and) God (our Father), the Lord is one." This redefined monotheism is expressed in the great Christ hymn (2:6-11), which concludes with the universal confession that *Jesus Christ is Lord, to the glory of God the Father* (2:11).[28]

In his opening greetings, Paul begins to express the main points of his letter. His inclusion of Timothy in a partnership of servants of Christ Jesus, his inclusive address to *all* in Christ Jesus, and his rewording of the *Shema* to include the Lord Jesus Christ with God the Father as the common source of grace and peace introduce the themes of the gospel of Christ and the community in Christ. The "highly exalted" (2:9) Christ is the center of all the themes and the center of all life; he is the initiator and sustainer of the community. The only way to maintain unity in Christ Jesus is the way of Paul: keep your focus on Christ Jesus. Paul's threefold repetition of the

25. H. Conzelmann, "χάρις," *TDNT* 9:394: "χάρις echoes here the key-term χαίρειν in the greetings of Greek letters."

26. Doty, *Letters in Primitive Christianity,* 29.

27. Paul's understanding of *grace* is rooted in the Greek OT (LXX) use of this term to express God's covenant love *(ḥesed)* for his people (Conzelmann, "χάρις," *TDNT* 9:383).

28. See Wright, *The Climax of the Covenant,* 133: "What Paul has done . . . is to redefine both central Jewish doctrines, monotheism and election, and to do so by means of the crucified and risen Jesus. God and the people of God are both redefined through Jesus the Messiah." See also N. T. Wright, *Paul: A Fresh Perspective* (Minneapolis: Fortress, 2005), 86-90.

name of Christ Jesus in the opening address and greetings flows naturally from the one who exclaims: *For to me, to live is Christ* (2:21).

II. PRAYERS FOR PARTNERS (1:3-11)

[3]I thank my God every time I remember you. [4]In all my prayers for all of you, I always pray with joy [5]because of your partnership in the gospel from the first day until now, [6]being confident of this, that he who began a good work in you will carry it on to completion until the day of Christ Jesus.

[7]It is only right for me to feel this way about all of you, since I have you in my heart and, whether I am in chains or defending and confirming the gospel, all of you share in God's grace with me. [8]God can testify how I long for all of you with the affection of Christ Jesus.

[9]And this is my prayer, that your love may abound more and more in knowledge and depth of insight, [10]so that you may be able to discern what is best and may be pure and blameless for the day of Christ, [11]filled with the fruit of righteousness that comes through Jesus Christ — to the glory and praise of God.

After his greetings, Paul lets his readers listen in on his prayers of thanksgiving and intercession for them. Passionate prayers pour out of Paul's heart, expressing gratitude, joy, affection, longing, and love. These intimate prayers break through every attempt to define them simply in terms of letter forms and rhetorical structures. True enough, Paul developed a predictable letter form: at the beginnings of all his letters except Galatians,[29] Paul expresses his thanksgiving-prayers after his greetings.[30] This thanksgiving-prayer section functions rhetorically as an introduction to state the reason for the letter and prepare the audience for his instruction.[31] But surely the Philippians would not have heard these prayers as formulaic epistolary expressions and classical rhetorical strategies calculated to secure their goodwill. These prayers are authenticated as real

29. In his letter to the Galatian churches, Paul replaces his characteristic thanksgiving section with an expression of astonishment-rebuke. See G. Walter Hansen, *Abraham in Galatians — Epistolary and Rhetorical Contexts* (JSNTSup 29; Sheffield: JSOT Press, 1989), 33-43. In 2 Corinthians and Ephesians, the thanksgiving sections are somewhat modified by an inclusion of benedictions.

30. For major studies on the structure and significance of the Pauline thanksgiving sections, see Paul Schubert, *Form and Function of the Pauline Thanksgiving* (ZNT 20; Berlin: Töpelmann, 1939), and Peter T. O'Brien, *Introductory Thanksgiving in the Letters of Paul* (NovTSup 49; Leiden: Brill, 1977).

31. Duane F. Watson, "A Rhetorical Analysis of Philippians and Its Implications for the Unity Question," *NovT* 30 (1988), 61-65; L. Gregory Bloomquist, *The Function of Suffering in Philippians* (JSNTSup 78; Sheffield: JSOT Press, 1993), 121-23.

prayers, not merely formulas or rhetorical devices, by the way they are so intimately related to Paul's experience with the Philippians and his concerns for them expressed throughout the letter. Rather than general prayers of thanksgiving, they are specifically connected to the gifts and needs of the recipients. As they heard these prayers, they must have thought, "He really knows us; he is really praying for us."

3 The opening words of the prayer — *I thank my God* — convey more than a perfunctory habit. This thanksgiving is directly related to the close of the letter where Paul writes what reads like a formal receipt: *I have received full payment and have more than enough; I am amply supplied, now that I have received from Epaphroditus the gifts you sent* (4:18). From beginning to end, the letter needs to be read as a "thank you." But even more than an expression of gratitude for the Philippians' support, Paul's thanksgiving rises from his deep personal experience of God's grace. He directs his thanksgiving to *my* God. That personal pronoun communicates the transforming impact of God's gracious salvation in Christ Jesus on his own life. God's grace so transformed him that even in prison his gratitude to God guided his prayers, attitudes, and thoughts. Out of that personal experience of God, Paul assures the Philippians after his "receipt" for their gifts (4:18) that *my God will meet all your needs according to the riches of his glory in Christ Jesus* (4:19).

The connection between Paul's thanksgiving and the Philippians' financial gifts leads some to insist that the next phrase sets forth the Philippians' remembrance of Paul as the reason for Paul's thanksgiving: "I thank my God for all your remembrance of me."[32] According to this reading, the phrase points to their gifts as the evidence of their remembrance. When this phrase is read as Paul's explicit "thank you" for the Philippians' remembrance of him by their gifts, it fits neatly with the end of the letter where their gifts are acknowledged.[33] This translation makes good sense in the context of the letter as a whole and can also be justified by grammatical analysis.[34]

Although this translation receives strong support, the weight of evidence for the traditional reading — *every time I remember you* — decides the

32. O'Brien, 59-61; see also Martin (60), Gerald W. Peterman (*Paul's Gift from Philippi: Conventions of Gift Exchange and Christian Giving* [SNTSMS 92; Cambridge: Cambridge University Press, 1997], 93-98), and Witherington (36).

33. Peterman, *Paul's Gift from Philippi*, 95.

34. The translation, "for all your remembrance of me," reads the second person plural pronoun in the genitive case as a *subjective* genitive: the pronoun is related as *subject* to the verbal idea of the noun, "remembrance." This translation also reads the preposition ἐπί with the causal sense, "for" or "because of." The same preposition ἐπί in the next verse is used with the causal sense, *because of* (1:5). Although the preposition ἐπί does have a causal meaning in verse 5, Paul uses the preposition in 1 Thess 1:2 and Phlm 4 with a temporal sense to speak of the occasion when he was praying for his readers. And the occasion of his remembrance of the Philippians appears to be his focus here. Every remembrance of them leads him to give thanks to God.

case in its favor. The noun "remembrance" occurs six other times in the NT, all in Paul's letters. And in each other use of this noun, the pronoun in the genitive case associated with the noun is clearly the object of the remembering.[35] This pattern leads us to take the pronoun in the genitive case in our text as an objective genitive: the pronoun is the object of the remembrance. Paul remembers the Philippians in his thanksgiving-prayer to God. Any translation that reverses this so that the Philippians remember Paul runs counter to the consistent pattern of Paul's own use of this noun with a genitive. Such a translation also fails to explain the absence of any reference to the object of remembrance if the Philippians are the subject and not the object of remembrance. The suggestion that Paul is the unexpressed object assumes that Paul, as the subject of the verb in the previous phrase, *I thank my God,* is now switched to be the unexpressed object of remembrance. This is an unwarranted assumption. It is more reasonable to assume that Paul is the unexpressed subject of the verbal idea of remembrance since he is the subject of the verb in the previous phrase — *I thank my God.* The key point to remember from this technical discussion is that Paul remembers his friends in prayer.

4 This verse discloses four more elements in Paul's practice of prayer. First, Paul tells us about the frequency of thanksgiving in his prayers — *always.* Whenever he remembers the Philippians and in every prayer for them, he *always* thanks God for them. Thanksgiving to God for God's people was expressed in every prayer. A natural way of thinking about other people leads to praise for their favors and criticism for their faults. But Paul's thinking about the Philippians is not divided in this way between praise and criticism. All of his thinking about them causes Paul to thank God. There is only one way to see Paul's claim to complete thanksgiving in his remembrance of the Philippians as more than an exaggeration. Only in prayer to God can there be this consistent gratitude, for prayer with a Godward perspective focuses on God's gracious work in human lives no matter how fallen and needy.[36]

Second, Paul emphasizes that his prayers were on behalf of *all* the believers. Just as his letter was addressed to *all God's holy people* (1:1), so his prayers were for everyone in the church. Although some people in the church were fighting against each other (4:2), Paul does not exclude anyone from his prayers of thanksgiving. *All* are included in Paul's prayer. Prayer transcends the barriers that divide people. From the perspective of prayer, Paul sees the unity of God's people as an undivided whole in Christ. Just as Paul affirms at the end of the letter, the peace of God that surpasses all understanding is experienced in prayer (4:6-7). Peace, *shalom,* wholeness and

35. All seven occurrences of μνεία in the NT are in the Pauline letters: Rom 1:9; Eph 1:16; Phil 1:3; 1 Thess 1:2; 3:6; 2 Tim 1:3; Phlm 4. See BDAG, 654, for references to uses in nonbiblical Greek.

36. Barth, 14.

harmony, is expressed in Paul's own prayer that sees *all* of God's people united in God's presence.

Third, Paul's prayers focus on specific needs. The Greek word translated by TNIV as *prayers . . . pray* occurs twice in verse 4 and denotes an "urgent request to meet a need."[37] The same word also refers to the *prayers* of the Philippians for Paul's deliverance (1:19). And it is translated as *petitions* in Paul's exhortation to the Philippians to turn from anxiety by combining their *petitions* with thanksgiving (4:6). Paul follows his own counsel in his prayers for the Philippians: his urgent requests are combined with thanksgiving to God. Paul's prayers are not a way of escaping or denying reality. The emphasis on thanksgiving does not mean that prayers included only positive items and excluded any mention of problems. The real needs of the Philippians drove Paul to his knees to make urgent requests to God on their behalf.

Fourth, Paul's urgent requests were made *with joy*. This is the first of fourteen times that the joy note sounds in this letter.[38] The addition of each joy note develops the theme of joy. As we read through the letter, our understanding of the source and nature of joy expands. We first hear this theme of joy in Paul's prayers for his friends. Joy reverberates in the convergence of praying with urgency for the needs of his friends and giving thanks to God for them. Paul sees clearly all the pressures from without and the problems within the church. But his vision of the church is encompassed within the all-encompassing vision of God. As he addresses urgent requests for needs and thanksgiving to God, God fills the horizons of the past and the future: this sentence ends with the exuberant confidence that God began the good work in the past and will complete that work until the final consummation, the day of Christ Jesus (1:6). So the source of joy is the God who began the work of partnership *(koinōnia)* in the gospel (1:5) and who will complete that work. The nature of joy is confidence in God, who begins and finishes his good work. This joyful confidence does not deny any of the suffering of human existence. Paul's letter to the Philippians is brutally honest about suffering in Paul's life and in the lives of all believers. But in this opening prayer we see that urgent requests for needs are filled with joyful thanksgiving in the presence of God.

Paul's habit of praying for his friends discloses important dimensions of his spirituality. Every remembrance of his friends moves him to pray urgently for their needs. Every urgent request for them includes giving thanks to God for them. Giving thanks to God for his friends fills his heart with joy. Here we see a chain reaction in Paul's spirituality: memory of friends leads immediately to urgent requests for their needs; these petitions

37. BDAG, 213; "that which is asked with urgency based on presumed need" (Louw and Nida, 1.33.171.

38. The noun (χαρά): 1:4, 25; 2:2, 29; 4:1. The verb (χαίρω): 1:18 (twice); 2:17, 18, 28; 3:1; 4:4 (twice), 10.

prompt him to give thanks to God for his friends; thanksgiving to God lifts him to express joyful praise to God.

5 Paul tells the Philippians that their *partnership in the gospel from the first day until now* is the specific reason for his joyful thanksgiving.[39] Standing behind the English word *partnership,* the Greek word *(koinōnia)* connotes a variety of close relationships "involving mutual interests and sharing."[40] Marriage and family relationships, friendships, business partnerships, common ownership of property, citizenship, and religious organizations were all considered examples of *koinōnia* in Paul's day. Paul's six references to *koinōnia*[41] in this letter draw from these various nuances of *koinōnia* and contribute to the development of his theology of *koinōnia.* A major purpose of this letter is to transform the experience of *koinōnia* in the light of life in Christ.[42]

The kind of *koinōnia* enjoyed by Paul and the Philippians in their *partnership in the gospel* is first of all a close association as friends who share a common faith in the gospel. According to Aristotle, "All friendship involves *koinōnia.*"[43] This connection of friendship and *koinōnia* is emphasized in the immediate context by Paul's use of passionate friendship language: *I have you in my heart. . . . I long for all of you with the affection of Christ Jesus* (1:7-8). Throughout his letter, Paul continues to use friendship language to depict his affection for the Philippians. Their friendship started on *the first day* that Paul brought the gospel to them, and they responded positively. Their faith in the gospel brought them into mutual participation in the benefits of the gospel with Paul. They shared in the same experience of the grace of forgiveness and the peace of a covenant relationship with God, all made possible through the events of the cross and resurrection of Christ proclaimed in the gospel. The proclamation of the gospel had the transforming power to create a community *(koinōnia)* of believers in Christ.[44] This interpretation of *koinōnia* as a mutual sharing in the salvation proclaimed by the gospel is confirmed by Paul's reference to the *koinōnia* of the Spirit (2:1) and the *koinōnia* in the sufferings of Christ (3:10). Those who share in the benefits of the gospel participate in a friendship so deep that it may also be viewed as a family relationship. Hence, Paul refers to his friends nine times as *brothers and sisters.*[45]

The *koinōnia* initially formed by mutual participation in the benefits of the gospel developed quickly into a *koinōnia* to advance the proclama-

39. The English preposition *because* rightly translates the causal meaning of the Greek preposition ἐπί that introduces this phrase.

40. BDAG, 552.

41. 1:5, 7, 2:1; 3:10; 4:14, 15.

42. See the Introduction, 32-34.

43. Aristotle, *Eth. nic.* 8.12.1.

44. Mary Ann Getty, "Philippians: A Meditation on Community," *BT* 23 (1985), 374.

45. 1:12, 14; 2:25; 3:1, 13, 17; 4:1, 8, 21. That the term ἀδελφοί is gender inclusive and means *brothers and sisters* is demonstrated by Paul's direct address to two women in 4:2.

tion of the gospel. A false dichotomy is set up by some who interpret the phrase *partnership in the gospel* to mean participation in salvation,[46] and by others who take this phrase as a reference to cooperation in the work of evangelism.[47] For if there had not been personal appropriation of the gospel in the first place, there would not have been support for the propagation of the gospel. Their faithfulness in the work of proclaiming the gospel was evidence of the reality of their personal participation by faith in the benefits of the gospel.

The *koinōnia* of Paul and the Philippians in the work of proclaiming the gospel bears striking resemblance to business partnerships in Paul's day.[48] This dimension of *partnership in the gospel* as an active participation of the Philippians with Paul in the "business" of proclaiming the gospel message is highlighted by Paul's reference to the Philippians as "fellow-partners"[49] in the work of *defending and confirming the gospel* (1:7). Paul's mission was *to advance the gospel* (1:12), and this makes him rejoice whenever and by whomever *Christ is preached* (1:15-18). The Philippians actively participated in Paul's mission to spread the gospel by their prayers for him in his affliction (1:19), by their own suffering for their faith in Christ in the face of opposition (1:27-30), by their radiant witness (2:15-16), by the mission of Epaphroditus on their behalf to care for Paul's needs while in prison (2:25-30), and by their regular financial support of Paul (4:10-18). It is important to appreciate the breadth of the Philippians' involvement in this *partnership in the gospel* so that it is not reduced to either their belief in the message of salvation in Christ[50] or their financial support of Paul's mission to preach the gospel.[51] Paul's mention of the *first day* refers to their reception of the gospel. Since that day of personal appropriation of the gospel *until now,* they had continued to believe in the gospel and to support the propagation of the gospel. The Philippians' *koinōnia* in the appropriation and proclamation of the gospel filled Paul with joyful thankfulness whenever he thought of them.

6 After Paul declares his joy for his partnership with the Philippians (1:5), he expresses his confidence: *being confident of this, that he who began a good work in you will carry it on to completion until the day of Christ Jesus.*

46. H. Seesemann, *Der Begriff KOINŌNIA im Neuen Testament* (Gießen: Töpelmann, 1933), 73-74; F. Hauck, "κοινωνός," *TDNT* 3:805: Phil 1:5 "refers to the inward and undisturbed participation of the Philippians in the saving message of Christ."

47. Fee, 82-83; O'Brien, 60-61.

48. J. Paul Sampley, *Pauline Partnership in Christ: Christian Community and Commitment in Light of Roman Law* (Philadelphia: Fortress, 1980); G. Walter Hansen, "Transformation of Relationships," in *New Testament Greek and Exegesis: Essays in Honor of Gerald F. Hawthorne* (ed. A. M. Donaldson and T. B. Sailors; Grand Rapids, Eerdmans, 2003), 182-89.

49. "Fellow-partners" is my literal translation of the Greek term συγκοινωνούς (1:7). This Greek term is in the same (κοινωνός) word group as *koinōnia* (κοινωνία) and is translated by the verb *share* in the TNIV.

50. Hauck, "κοινωνός," *TDNT* 3:805.

51. Peterman, *Paul's Gift from Philippi,* 101.

Paul's confidence that this *partnership* with the Philippians would stand the tests of time was based upon his confidence in the creative power of God. Paul connects his confidence in the *good work* of God (1:6) directly to their *partnership in the gospel* (1:5). His joyful thanksgiving for their partnership in the gospel is based upon his conviction that this partnership is the good work of God.[52] Philippians 1:6 is widely interpreted as a basis for personal confidence: God began the good work of salvation in *me*, and he will complete that good work in *me*. Of course, the *good work* of God includes God's work of salvation in the individual. But as true as that individualistic application of the text is, it misses the connection of God's *good work* to *koinōnia*. The *good work* that God began was the formation of a corporate entity: the *partnership (koinōnia) in the gospel*. Those who belong to this *koinōnia* enjoy a friendship deeper than the blood relationship of brothers and sisters on the basis of their mutual participation in the saving work of Christ announced by the gospel.[53] Their *koinōnia* as friends is also a *koinōnia* as partners in the work of proclaiming the gospel. When Paul wrote his letter to the Philippians, this *koinōnia* was threatened by opposition from without (1:28) and conflict within (4:2). Intense suffering in a world hostile to the gospel and a bitter dispute between leaders in the church may have called into question the survival of their *partnership in the gospel*. Paul sought to strengthen his endangered *koinōnia* with the Philippians by raising it above mere human relationships. The survival of the *koinōnia in the gospel* did not depend merely on human initiative and human endurance. God is the founder of every true *koinōnia* in the gospel. And God will complete the purpose of every *koinōnia* in the gospel.[54]

The future of the *koinōnia* is secure as the *good work* of God *until* the completion of all God's work of salvation in the *day of Christ Jesus*. This *koinōnia* was not a short-term relationship. It will still be thriving at the *day of Christ Jesus*.

Paul's eager anticipation of the future *day of Christ Jesus* gave him confidence in the present time of suffering and conflict. Paul kept his eyes on that day when every knee will bow and every tongue confess that Jesus is Lord (2:9-11), and on that day when the Savior, the Lord Jesus Christ, will come from heaven to transform all the citizens of heaven living on earth to be like him (3:20-21). The bright light of that future day filled the darkest days in Paul's Roman prison. The darkness of anxiety and doubt about the

52. Verse 6 begins with a participle (πεποιθώς), "having been convinced." This is a causal use of the adverbial participle: *because* Paul is convinced of God's initiation and completion of the good work of the partnership, he gives joyful thanks to God for that partnership.

53. Müller, 43; Schenk, 96.

54. George W. Murray, "Paul's Corporate Witness in Philippians," *BSac* 155 (1998), 319: "Verse 6 continues the thought of verse 5. This cooperative evangelism, then, was not primarily the idea of Paul or the Philippians; it was a good work begun and continued by God."

future of his *koinōnia* with the Philippians vanished in the brilliance of that *day of Christ Jesus.* On that day of Christ Jesus, the new creation of God — the new community in Christ — will be perfect and complete. Paul prays that this new community *may be pure and blameless for the day of Christ* (1:10). The vision of the community in Christ on the future *day of Christ* inspires and guides the life of that community in the present. The hope of that future day of Christ gives strength to endure and persevere through all the trials, tensions, and disappointments of the present day.

7 Paul digresses from the report of his prayers to assert that it is entirely appropriate and even obligatory[55] for him to have such a joyful, confident attitude toward the Philippians: *It is right for me to feel this way about all of you. . . .* Paul's expression of intense affections for the Philippians in this passage confirms the TNIV use of the word *feel* for the Greek word *phronein.* But this Greek word points to more than Paul's emotional feelings; it also connotes thinking, being concerned, having an opinion or an attitude about something or someone.[56] This spectrum of nuances can be seen in the ten occurrences of this word in this letter. The word is used twice in Paul's appeal for unity and humility (2:2): being *like-minded* and *of one mind.*[57] Paul repeats this word in the introduction to his great Christ hymn: *have the same attitude of mind Christ Jesus had* (2:5). After telling of his own determination to press on toward the goal (3:14), Paul uses the same word in his appeal to all who are mature to *take such a view of things* and in his recognition that some may *think* differently (3:15). In his description of the enemies of the cross, Paul uses this word to indicate the focus of their *mind: Their mind is set on earthly things* (3:19). Paul uses the same word in his appeal to Euodia and Syntyche: *be of the same mind* (4:2). Finally, Paul uses this word twice in his commendation of the Philippians' *concern* for him: *. . . you renewed your concern for me. Indeed, you were concerned . . .* (4:10).

These uses of this significant word demonstrate that it refers to interior thoughts, attitudes, and feelings that motivate exterior directions and actions. In this letter Paul shows that one way of thinking and feeling leads to unity in the church, growth in Christ-likeness, and expressions of concern for those in need. Another way of thinking and feeling leads to divisions in the church, hostility toward Christ, and a preoccupation with selfish interests. In his first use of this word, Paul presents his own attitude toward all of the Philippians and asserts, *It is right for me to feel this way about all of you* (1:7). His positive attitude of joyful thanksgiving and warm

55. The phrase *It is right* (ἐστιν δίκαιον) "denotes that which is obligatory in view of certain requirements of justice" (BDAG, 247). The TNIV translation omits the conjunction καθώς at the beginning of this phrase in the Greek text. In this context this conjunction has a causal meaning and could be translated "because" (BDAG, 496). This causal use of καθώς indicates that Paul intends to spell out the reason why it is right for him to have the attitude he does toward the Philippians.

56. BDAG, 1065-66.

57. NRSV: "be of the same mind" and "of one mind."

affection for everyone is the *right* way to think and feel toward others in contrast to the negative attitude of envy, rivalry, and selfish ambition (1:15-17; 2:3-4). Although Paul does not make this contrast explicit in the context of his insistence that his way of feeling toward the Philippians is *right* (1:7), the strong contrast that he develops between a positive attitude and a negative attitude in other contexts (2:2-5; 3:15, 19) indicates that his positive attitude exemplifies the *right* attitude for the Philippians to have as well. The use of the same word in Paul's report of his own positive way of *thinking* (1:7) and in his appeal to all the believers to be *like-minded* (2:2) and to Euodia and Syntyche (4:2) to *be of the same mind* makes a connection between Paul's exemplary friendship love and his appeal to his friends to be united with each other. Paul presents himself as a model of the right way to think and feel about friends in Christ. At the end of the letter he calls for his readers to put into practice what they have seen in him (4:9). Practicing Paul's positive attitude toward friends promotes unity in the church and a credible witness for Christ in the world.

Paul's repetition of *all* hammers home the importance of unity. He greets *all* (1:1); he prays with thanksgiving for *all* (1:4); he feels the same way about *all* (1:7). Like a steady drumbeat, the steady repetition of *all* keeps reminding the reader that his love is not selective. He embraces *all.*

In the rest of this sentence in verse 7, Paul explains that his positive attitude toward all believers was motivated by (a) his heart and (b) their partnership in God's grace.

(a) Paul tells them of the condition of his heart in the phrase *since I have you in my heart.* The heart is the "center and source of the whole inner life, with its thinking, feeling and volition."[58] In a similar expression, Paul told the church in Corinth, "you have such a place in our hearts that we would live or die with you" (2 Cor 7:3). When Paul tells his friends that he has them in his heart, he is expressing more than a sentimental feeling; he is stating the commitment of his heart to give his life for his friends. In fact, he tells them later that he has poured out his life for them (2:17). His heart commitment to every one of the believers was demonstrated by his sacrificial love for them. The combination of this expression of heartfelt commitment for all of his friends in Philippi with the previous assertion of the positive way he thinks about all of them augments his model of friendship love. The commitment of the heart is the source of a positive way of thinking about friends.

The NRSV translates this phrase, "because you hold me in your heart." The Greek grammar allows for this translation. In Greek the subject and object of an infinitive are both in the accusative case. Both pronouns, "me" and "you," are in the accusative case. It is unclear which pronoun is the subject and which pronoun is the object. That explains why there are the different translations: *I have you* (TNIV); "you hold me" (NRSV). In fa-

58. BDAG, 508.

vor of the NRSV translation is the focus of Paul on his faithful partners: he opens his prayer with thanksgiving for their partnership (1:5); in the next phrase he commends them for their partnership in his suffering (1:7); and he ends his letter with gratitude for the way they *shared* with him (4:14, 15). Their partnership was evidence that they held Paul in their heart. Their heartfelt commitment to Paul motivated Paul's positive attitude toward them. The TNIV translation, however, is supported by the flow of the whole prayer report, which expresses Paul's friendship love for the readers. A high point in this expression of Paul's love for his friends comes in verse 8, where Paul actually takes a solemn oath that God is the witness of his longing and affection for them. This passage is all about Paul's heart for the believers.[59] So the TNIV translation correctly views Paul as the subject: *I have you in my heart.* Though geographically distant, Paul held them in his heart. Paul was not a friend who followed the common practice: "out of sight, out of mind." This kind of friendship is uniquely possible for Christians in *koinōnia* with each other and with the Lord.

(b) Paul's affection for the Philippians also flows from his experience of their *koinōnia* with him, especially in his time of imprisonment: *whether I am in chains or defending and confirming the gospel, all of you share in God's grace with me.* For the first time, Paul points to his *chains.* The way he repeatedly refers to his *chains* in the next few verses (1:13, 14, 17) indicates that he could not shake his conscious thoughts free from his chains. Paul's chains bound him to his Roman guards, chafed his skin, and severely restricted his mobility.[60] As a man who was accustomed to the freedom of extensive travel and the honor accorded to an esteemed rabbi, Paul now experienced the pull of chains against every motion of his body and the dishonor of his position as a prisoner.

As a Roman prisoner, Paul would be brought to trial in court before a Roman judge. The prospect of his trial is reflected in his use of two legal terms: *defending and confirming.* Paul viewed his trial as an opportunity to make a "speech of defense"[61] that would lead to the "validation"[62] of the *gospel.* Paul's reference to the defense and confirmation of the gospel could be interpreted as a way of describing his entire vocation: his whole life was dedicated to the defense of the gospel. But his use of the same terms in his recognition that he was in chains for *the defense of the gospel* (1:16) shows that these terms have a technical legal sense in this context.[63] Paul was led

59. Specific studies of the use of the Greek infinitive indicate that when an infinitive is followed by two accusatives, the first is normally the subject and second is the object. See Jeffrey T. Reed, "The Infinitive with Two Substantival Accusatives: An Ambiguous Construction?" *NovT* 33 (1991), 1-27.

60. Brian Rapske, *The Book of Acts and Paul in Roman Custody* (Grand Rapids: Eerdmans, 1994), 25-28.

61. BDAG, 117.

62. BDAG, 173.

63. H. Schlier, "βεβαίωσις," *TDNT* 1:603; Collange, 47-48.

by chains to make his legal defense in court. The chains that restricted Paul's power were the means by which the power of the gospel was released. The suffering of Paul leads to the vindication of the gospel. This experience of vindication through suffering becomes a major theme in this letter.[64]

Paul's suffering was the occasion for the Philippians to demonstrate their partnership with Paul. While he was *in chains, defending and confirming the gospel,* they shared with him. So Paul commends them in the final phrase of this sentence: *all of you share in God's grace with me.* This phrase gives the reason for Paul's joyful gratitude and heartfelt affection for them: that they all shared with him.[65] The simple word *share* translates a complex Greek word: the combination of the preposition *with* and the noun *koinōnos* (partner) in this word denotes "a sharer with someone in something."[66] Paul is clearly picking up the theme of partnership that he began with in his thanksgiving for *koinōnia* in verse 5.[67] Now he affirms that the Philippians were co-partners with him in *God's grace.*

Partnerships are usually based upon the ability of partners to share their wealth and skills to accomplish common objectives. For example, the Roman law codes describe a partnership between an architect and a landowner.

> Victor and Asianus had agreed that monuments should be erected with the exertions and skill of Asianus on land purchased with Victor's money. They would then be sold. Victor would recover his money with the addition of an agreed sum, and Asianus would get the rest in recognition of the hard work he had put into the *partnership* [*koinōnia*].[68]

From a human perspective, it would appear that Paul and his friends had entered into such a partnership based upon Paul's skills to evangelize and the Philippians' financial ability to support him in his work. But Paul did not view this partnership merely as a common human relationship. God's grace is the origin, basis, and purpose of this partnership. Yes, Paul and his co-partners were sharing their wealth and skills, but this sharing was viewed as a sharing *in God's grace.* God's unmerited, undeserved favor was the source of all that they were, all that they did, and all that they had.

The TNIV addition of the modifier *God's* to the word *grace* clarifies what Paul affirms in his salutation: God is the source of grace (1:2). But the absence of this modifier in the Greek text keeps the focus on the nature rather than the source of grace. What is the nature of grace in this context?

64. Bloomquist, *The Function of Suffering in Philippians.* 196.

65. The final word in this Greek sentence is the participle ὄντας. In this context the participle has a *causal* function: *Because* you are. . . .

66. BDAG, 952.

67. Müller, 45.

68. Justinian, *Digest* 17.2.52.7 (Ulpian).

That the Christians shared with Paul in the grace of salvation is certainly true, but that general sense of grace as salvation does not seem to be the specific focus in this context, since Paul is speaking of their sharing with him in a special way in his suffering. It is also true that Paul refers in other contexts to his apostolic ministry as "the grace given to me" (1 Cor 3:10; Gal 2:9), and it would be accurate to say that the Philippian Christians shared in his apostolic ministry by their own witness and their support of Paul.[69] But again that sense of grace as Paul's apostolic ministry seems too broad to fit the specific content that the Philippians shared with Paul while he was in chains.

Two meanings of *grace* that fit in this specific context are the grace of giving and the grace of suffering. Paul refers to financial support as the "grace of giving" (2 Cor 8:7). At the end of this letter to the Philippians, Paul's use of the same language of sharing and partnering to denote giving financial support (4:14-18) indicates that Paul has their financial gifts in mind in 1:7 when he speaks of sharing with him in grace when he was in chains.[70] While he was in chains, their generous sharing met his basic needs. Their sharing was an expression of God's grace. Another aspect of God's grace is also in view here: they shared with him in the *grace* of suffering for Christ.[71] Paul tells them that *it has been granted* [a verb form of the noun *grace*] *to you on behalf of Christ not only to believe on him, but also to suffer for him, since you are going through the same struggle you saw I had, and now hear that I still have* (1:29-30). Paul's friends in Philippi were co-partners in God's grace with Paul inasmuch as they participated with Paul in suffering for Christ by sending Epaphroditus with gifts to care for Paul in prison and by enduring the *same struggle* in their Roman colony that Paul was enduring in his Roman prison. In both places, the proclamation that Christ is Savior and Lord brought them into conflict with the Roman declaration that Caesar is Savior and Lord.[72]

When the Philippians partnered with Paul in the grace of giving to meet his needs in prison, they demonstrated that they were partners with him in the grace of suffering for the defense of the gospel. No wonder, then, that Paul can assert that he has them in his heart, because they were such faithful partners with him in grace while he was in chains, defending and confirming the gospel. Again Paul stresses that *all* of them were partners with him in grace. Sharing in God's grace brought them *all* together in the first place, and sharing in God's grace kept them *all* together.

8 Paul's reflection on the partnership of his friends with him moves him to make an exceptionally strong declaration of his love for them: *God can testify how I long for all of you with the affection of Christ Jesus.* Paul is not

69. Bonnard, 17, defines *grace* in terms of the grace of apostleship.

70. Peterman, *Paul's Gift from Philippi,* 105.

71. Lohmeyer, 26-27, defines *grace* in terms of suffering martyrdom.

72. See Richard A. Horsley, ed., *Paul and Empire: Religion and Power in Roman Imperial Society* (Harrisburg, Pa.: Trinity Press International, 1997), 140-41.

embarrassed to express his strong desire for his friends.[73] Insisting that *God can testify* stresses the intensity of his longing: his longing for his friends is so far beyond human description that only God can plumb its depths and attest to its strength.[74] Only God can measure his love because it exceeds human love: he longs for all his friends *with the affection of Christ Jesus.* The literal meaning of the Greek word translated *affection* by the TNIV refers to the physiological parts called the inward parts, entrails, or bowels. These inner body parts served as referents for the emotions of love, compassion, and affection.[75] Paul is saying that his longing for his friends is empowered by the strong emotions of the love of Christ Jesus for them. Paul's life in Christ Jesus brings all his relationships within the sphere of Christ's love. Paul's relationships were never only on the human level — human person with human person. No, they always involved the coinherence of Christ living within Paul, Paul living within Christ, Christ living within the church, and the church living within Christ. The passion of Paul's expression of longing is really astonishing. He discloses his own strong desire to be with his friends: *I long for all of you.* He intensifies his disclosure by calling on God to be his witness: *God can testify.* He asserts that his longing is beyond human limitations by insisting that it is really the love of Christ motivating and empowering him: *with the affection of Christ Jesus.*[76] And for the fifth time in this opening section of the letter we hear the emphasis on *all: all, all, all, all, all* are loved by Paul or, rather, by Christ in Paul and Paul in Christ. Human love cannot be so consistently inclusive; some are always excluded. Divine love embraces all and brings all inside. Divine love makes outsiders insiders.

9 So far Paul's report of his prayers for his friends focuses on thanksgiving. Now the focus shifts to intercession: *And this is my prayer: that your love may abound more and more in knowledge and depth of insight.* Paul told his friends that whenever he made his urgent requests he gave thanks for them (1:3-4). Now he lets them know that the content of his requests is related to the reasons for his thanksgiving.[77] He gave thanks to God for them because they shared with him when he was in chains and because he longed for them with the affection of Christ Jesus. In other words, their love for him and his love for them were the reasons for his thanksgiving. Now

73. The verb to "long" (ἐπιποθῶ) means "to have a strong desire for something with implication of need" (BDAG, 377).

74. Paul calls on God to be his witness in order to emphasize the purity of his motives (1 Thess 2:5, 10) and the integrity of his reports (Rom 1:9; 2 Cor 1:23).

75. BDAG, 938.

76. H. Köster, "σπλάγχνον," *TDNT* 7:556: "Paul's emotions, which might be regarded as personal inclinations, are an expression of his being ἐν Χριστῷ, and they have their origin here. Only in the light of this basic relation of the believer to Christ, which is usually called Christ mysticism, can one understand the addition of Χριστοῦ Ἰησοῦ to ἐν σπλάγχνοις. This love and affection which grip and profoundly move the whole man are possible only in Christ."

77. Müller, 46.

he prays that their love will grow. Although he gave thanks for the authenticity of their love, he prayed that the quality and generosity of their love would *abound more and more.*[78] Paul viewed love not as a static possession, but as a dynamic process. True love is not something you possess; true love constantly grows and increases.

In his autobiographical sketch later in the letter, Paul pictures his own life as a race toward the finish line; he is pursing the goal, but not yet attaining it (3:12-14). Because he envisioned life in Christ as a process of dynamic growth, he expressed his desire for believers in Christ to excel, increase, and *abound* in love (1:9; 1 Thess 3:12), joy (1:26), generosity (2 Cor 8:7), hope (Rom 15:13), and the work of the Lord (1 Cor 15:58). Paul is not content with the status quo in his life or in the lives of his friends. He prays that love will *abound,* and not only *abound,* but *abound more and more.* The addition of *more and more* emphasizes the ongoing dynamic process of growth and the ever-growing potential for better and purer expressions of love.

The kind of love that Paul prays will abound is *agapē*-love. Although *agapē* has a wide range of meaning, even in Paul's letters, the meaning of the term in this letter is clearly denoted by the immediate context.[79] Paul refers to *agapē* four times. He prays for *love* to abound (1:9); he commends those who preach Christ *out of love* (1:16); and he reminds the Philippians of the *encouragement from being united with Christ* and *the comfort from his love,* so that they will have *the same love* for one another (2:1-2). The meaning of *agapē* in this last reference is developed by a contrast between *selfish ambition or vain conceit* and humble service of others (2:3-4). The narrative of Christ, *who made himself nothing by taking the very nature of a servant* (2:8), provides the ultimate paradigm of self-giving love.

Paul's prayer for love to abound does not specify the object of love. But three clues in the context indicate an emphasis on love for one another. First, Paul's thanksgiving for *koinōnia* (1:5, 7) points to his interest in strengthening the love relationships with his friends. Second, his repeated reference to *all* in his greetings and thanksgiving demonstrates his concern for the inclusion and unity of all. This concern is developed throughout the letter. Third, Paul's extraordinary expression of his love for the Philippians (1:8) is linked by the simple conjunction *and* to his prayer for their love to abound. Paul's own love for them is a model for their love for one another. Paul urges them at the end of the letter to put into practice what they learned, received, heard, and saw in him (4:9). Paul seeks to stimulate them

78. The Greek word (περισσεύω) translated *abound* denotes "to be in abundance, to be extremely rich, overflow, grow, progress, excel" (BDAG, 805).

79. See D. A. Carson, *Exegetical Fallacies* (Grand Rapids: Baker, 1984), 30, for a warning against defining *agapē-love* without regard to the immediate context. As Carson reminds us, "There is nothing intrinsic to the verb ἀγαπάω or the noun ἀγάπη to prove its real meaning or hidden meaning refers to some special kind of love." The example of Demas (2 Tim 4:10), who deserted Paul "because he loved this world" (ἀγαπήσας τὸν νῦν αἰῶνα), illustrates the range of meaning of the *agapē-love* term.

to love each other by the strong assertion of his love. The need for this stimulus to love one another can be seen in the letter. Twice Paul refers to the divisive impact of *selfish ambition,* the very opposite of self-giving love (1:17; 2:3). Repeatedly Paul calls for the believers to be one in spirit (1:27; 2:2), to be like-minded, and to agree with each other (2:2; 4:2). Paul's concern that his friends grow in love for one another is heard in his prayer for them.

Love for one another, however, must not be cut off from the source of this love. Paul has just said that the source of his longing for his friends is the *affection of Christ* (1:8). Paul's insertion of the story of Christ's self-emptying, self-giving service in the context of calling believers to serve each other in humility (2:2-8) shows how knowing and loving Christ empower loving one another. When Paul prayed that the love of his friends would abound, he surely was praying for growth in their love for Christ as well as their love for one another. His own estimation of the *surpassing worth of knowing Christ* (3:7) would never have allowed him to refer only to the reciprocal love of believers for one another without rooting that love in loving and knowing Christ. While the prayer for love to abound focuses on the fruit of love for one another, the root of love for Christ is always Paul's highest priority for himself and his friends.

When Paul tells Christians that he is praying *that your love may abound more and more in knowledge and depth of insight,* he is pointing to the way for love to increase. Writing to the Corinthians, Paul speaks of love and knowledge as opposites: "knowledge puffs up; love builds up" (1 Cor 8:1). He also speaks of the futility of knowledge without love: "If I have all knowledge, but do not have love, I am nothing" (1 Cor 13:2). But in this letter to the Philippians, Paul prays that love will be multiplied *in knowledge and depth of insight.* The preposition *in* may refer to the context of love: Paul prays for love to abound in the sphere of knowledge.[80] When the domain of knowledge is devoid of love, knowledge has no value. But when love abounds in the domain of knowledge, knowledge then serves the goals of love and love multiplies. Alternatively, the preposition *in* expresses an instrumental sense: when knowledge is used as an instrument of love, love abounds more and more because of knowledge. Love is primarily a motive, a desire to give of one's self to serve the needs of others. But love needs to know how to serve others. Love needs to be instructed by knowledge in order to fulfill its desire to serve. Only a doctor who knows how to make a diagnosis and perform the operation can serve the patient in need of life-saving surgery. As G. K. Chesterton understood, "Love is not blind. Love is bound. And the more it is bound, the less it is blind."[81] Love needs to see clearly and speak truthfully. Love knows how to see and speak.

The knowledge Paul prays for is not ordinary knowledge. The word

80. So O'Brien, 75.

81. G. K. Chesterton, *Orthodoxy* (Image Books ed.; Garden City, N.Y.: Doubleday, 1959), 71.

for *knowledge* used here is a compound word that could be translated "full knowledge." It speaks of a "transcendent and moral" knowledge.[82] A study of the meaning of this word in Paul's letters shows that this knowledge is "recognition of the will of God that is effective in the conduct of one who knows God. Intellectual understanding and existential recognition belong together."[83] Paul's prayer for knowledge echoes the passionate concern expressed by the prophet Hosea: "There is no faithfulness, no love, no knowledge of God in the land. . . . My people are destroyed from lack of knowledge" (Hos 4:1, 6).[84] The knowledge of God is preeminently essential for the people of God. Although Paul does not specify the object of knowledge in his prayer, his letter emphatically states that the highest aim of his life is *to know Christ — yes, to know the power of his resurrection and participation in his sufferings* (3:10). The purpose of Paul's narrative of the humiliation and exaltation of Christ (2:6-10) is to lead his friends into the knowledge of Christ so that they will have the same love for one another (2:2). Knowledge of Christ multiplies love.

Paul's prayer combines knowledge with *depth of insight.* Although this is the only time that this word *insight* is used in the NT, it appears often in the Greek translation of the OT (the LXX), especially in Proverbs.[85] "Denoting moral understanding,"[86] *insight* guides the actions and words of those who are wise. *Insight* is "necessary for human relationships, where it must distinguish between good and evil and judge accordingly."[87] Paul adds the word *all* (translated by TNIV as *depth*) to *insight* to stress the need for wisdom to do the right thing and to speak the right word in every circumstance. Without *insight,* love does not know how to express itself with actions and words that are appropriate to each situation of life. Often love asks the question: I desire to love these people with such great needs, but what should I say and do to meet their needs? Only by insight does love have the direction to act wisely in ways that give healing, joy, and life to those who are loved.

The combination of *knowledge and depth of insight* unites the personal knowledge of Christ and a practical understanding of people. Knowing Christ and understanding people are both necessary for love to abound more and more.

10 Paul's prayer continues with two purpose statements: *so that you may be able to discern what is best and may be pure and blameless for the day of*

82. BDAG, 369.

83. W. Hackenberg, "ἐπίγνωσις," *EDNT* 2:25. ἐπίγνωσις appears fifteen times in Paul's letters: Rom 1:28; 3:20; 10:2; Eph 1:17; 4:13; Phil 1:9; Col 1:9, 10; 2:2; 3:10; 1 Tim 2:4; 2 Tim 2:25; 3:7; Tit 1:1; Phlm 6.

84. The same Greek word, ἐπίγνωσις, is used in the LXX translation of Hos 4:1, 6.

85. Prov 1:4, 7, 22; 2:3, 10; 3:20; 5:2; 10:14; 11:9; 12:1, 23; 14:6, 7, 18; 15:7, 14; 18:15; 19:25; 22:12; 23:12; 24:4.

86. BDAG, 29.

87. E. Schütz, "Knowledge," *NIDNTT* 2:391.

Christ. The reason why they should abound in love in knowledge and depth of insight is to *discern what is best.* Love seeks *what is best* for the other person, but *what is best* is not always obvious. Sometimes equally attractive good options compete for first place. It is necessary to examine the options in order to approve the one that is superior to all the others. The basic meaning of *discern* occurs in a description of testing gold by fire to prove that it is genuine as an illustration of the testing of faith to prove its genuineness (1 Pet 1:7). The same word is used in a parable of Jesus by a man who turns down an invitation to a banquet because he has to go and *examine* his oxen (Luke 14:19). *To discern* denotes this process of testing concluded by the decision to approve what is genuine and *what is best.*[88] The phrase *what is best* translates a word that simply means "things that differ." But in this context the word connotes those things that differ because they are superior.[89] Paul's concern here is not the choice between what is good and what is bad, but between what is good and *what is best.* His letter closes with the exhortation to concentrate on what is *excellent or praiseworthy* (4:8). Paul exemplified this choice of the best in his single-minded pursuit of his God-given goal (3:13). His prayer for all his friends is that their love will grow as it is informed by knowledge and insight so that they will be able to choose the best way to express love to one another.

Paul's letter to the Romans offers a fascinating use of the phrase *to discern what is best.* Paul refers to the discernment of what is best in his description of Jews who rely on the law and "approve of what is superior because you are instructed by the law" (Rom 2:18). In this case the approval of what is superior is guided by the law. The growth of the Jewish oral law was inspired by the desire to prescribe what was best for every situation in life. The basic principles of the written law were expanded by these oral traditions so that the Jews would know ahead of time what would be the best thing to do no matter what happened. In the autobiographical section of his letter to the Philippians, Paul says that when he was a Pharisee in regard to the law he was faultless according to righteousness prescribed by the law (3:5-6). But when he met Christ he considered all his achievements as a Pharisee as a loss compared to the surpassing value of knowing Christ. In his prayer for Christians, Paul prays that the expansion of their love, not the expansion of the law, will instruct them how to choose the best way to love in each situation. This may sound like the relativism of situation ethics: love, not law, guides the choices made in the situations of life. But whereas situation ethics generally will not allow love to be informed by any absolutes, Paul prays for love to be guided by knowing Christ, the ultimate standard for true love.

Not only does the knowledge of Christ guide love's choices, but the day of Christ will judge love's choices. For this reason Paul's prays that his

88. BDAG, 255.
89. BDAG, 239.

friends *may be pure and blameless for the day of Christ.* When this second reference to the day of Christ is viewed in parallel with the first reference to the day of Christ, then we clearly see that Paul's focus is on perfecting the community. In his thanksgiving, Paul expressed his confidence that God would carry his good work on *to completion until the day of Christ Jesus* (1:6). In that context, the good work that God is perfecting is the *koinōnia* — the partnership of the Philippians with Paul in the gospel. Now Paul prays that love will abound so that believers will be *pure and blameless for the day of Christ.* The purpose of love is to perfect a community so that it will be *pure and blameless.* Paul is not promoting individualistic perfectionism. An individual who takes Paul's words as inspiration for developing and polishing personal moral perfection, like a body builder working out every day to look like Mr. Universe or Miss America, misses the point of Paul's prayer. Paul is praying for the church to be *pure and blameless.* The moral meaning of *pure* denotes "being sincere, without hidden motives or pretense."[90] A few paragraphs after this prayer, Paul describes the way some preach Christ with motives of rivalry, envy, and selfish ambition, but others out of goodwill and love (1:15-17). Later he urges the community to be one in love rather than divided by the motive of selfish ambition (2:2-3). His prayer for purity expresses the same concern that the community will be united by pure love for one another rather than divided by rivalry, envy, and selfish ambition.

The word *blameless* simply means without offense and can express either "without fault because of not giving offense" or "not causing offense."[91] The only other occurrence of this word in Paul's letters is found in his command to the Corinthians: "Do not cause anyone to stumble" (1 Cor 10:31). Paul's concern that the Philippians not cause each other to stumble can be seen throughout his letter, especially in his appeals to be united (1:27; 2:2; 4:2) and to do everything without complaining or arguing (2:14). His prayer expresses this concern when he asks God to multiply their love so that they will not cause each other to stumble. The words *pure and blameless* are connected in this sentence to the word *love* and express the purpose of growth in love for one another. When love abounds in the community, the community is characterized by a pure desire to serve each other rather than envying and hurting each other. Paul's prayer asks God to do what Paul had already expressed confidence that God would do: perfect the community in Christ until the day of Christ. To be *pure and blameless* is not the result of a self-improvement program, but the good work of God. God's good work of multiplying love in the community is a work in progress and will continue to be under construction *for the day of Christ.*

The preposition *for* indicates a specific time up to which the good work of God continues.[92] This prepositional phrase, *for the day of Christ,* dispels

90. BDAG, 282.
91. BDAG, 125-26.
92. BDAG, 289.

any notion that Paul expected the perfection of the community to be completed before that day. In his autobiographical statements, Paul strongly asserts that he has not *already obtained all* or *already arrived* (3:12). Since Paul's letters were written in response to specific practical issues, his autobiographical statements aim to refute any version of perfectionism that expects perfect purity in the present. At the same time, however, Paul is praying for progress toward the goal of a community that is perfected in love for the day of Christ. Envisioning future perfection, he prays for growth in the present.

Paul's repeated references to the day of Christ (1:6, 10; 2:16) demonstrate his future orientation. The day of Christ's return cast its light over all of Paul's life and illuminated his prayers as well as his actions. His prayer expresses his desire for the church to grow in love each day until that day when Christ will *bring everything under his control* and *transform our lowly bodies so that they will be like his glorious body* (3:21). That vision of Christ's triumph gave Paul hope to pray for growth in love even in the severe trials of the present. The ultimate future transformation by Christ's power assured him of the present work of Christ in the community.

11 Paul's vision of people who are *pure and blameless* on the day of Christ is now expressed in a vivid picture of his friends as they would be on that day: *filled with the fruit of righteousness that comes through Jesus Christ — to the glory and praise of God.* Paul's vision may be inspired by a poetic picture of a beautiful orchard: "They are like a tree planted by streams of water, which yields its fruit in season" (Ps 1:3).[93] Or he may be using a prophetic picture of a vineyard that was planted, watered, and protected by God (Isa 5:1-4).[94] Although Paul's picture portrays flawless fruit, it also points to a process of growth. When Paul depicts people who are *filled,* he is pointing to the future completion of a process.[95] A fruitful orchard or vineyard does not happen in one day; it is the result of a long process of planting, watering, pruning, and fertilizing. Later in the letter, *fruit* is the result of the work of Paul (1:22) and the giving of the Philippians (4:17). But in this prayer, the *fruit of righteousness* is the result of God's power, as the passive voice and the next phrases indicate.[96] The fruit of Christ-like character and behavior is the fruit of the Spirit (Gal 5:22).[97]

Paul's description of fruit as the fruit *of righteousness that comes*

93. See also Jer 17:8; Ezek 19:10; Matt 7:17-20; Rev 22:2.

94. See also Ps 80:8; Jer 12:10; John 15:1-5.

95. See Stanley E. Porter, *Idioms of the Greek New Testament* (Sheffield: JSOT Press, 1992), 40-42, for Porter's list of the uses of the perfect tense form; he points to the rare future use of the perfect tense with 1 John 2:5 as an example ("the love of God is going to be complete"). Although this usage is rare, Paul's use of the perfect tense form in Phil 1:11 also looks to the future when God's people are going to be filled.

96. Although Beare (55) takes the verb *filled* in the middle voice, Porter, *Idioms of the Greek New Testament,* 66, lists this verb in Phil 1:11 as an example of the passive voice with an accusative case object: "being filled with respect to the fruit of righteousness." This use of the passive voice is sometimes called the "divine passive" (Bockmuehl, 69).

97. Bonnard, 20; Müller, 48.

through Jesus Christ keeps this focus on the divine source of fruitfulness. The prepositional phrase *through Jesus Christ* modifies the word *fruit,* not the word *righteousness.*[98] This fruit is organic fruit, organically produced from the river of life, Jesus Christ. Fruit that comes from roots that are nourished by this river is the best kind of fruit: *the fruit of righteousness.*

Paul's description of the fruit as *fruit of righteousness* may be interpreted in two ways: (a) righteousness is the source of the fruit, or (b) righteousness is the nature of the fruit.[99] The wide range of meaning encompassed by the word *righteousness* has received extensive attention.[100] In this context, however, the two meanings of righteousness most appropriate can be simply stated as legal (a right legal standing) or ethical (right moral behavior). A common line of interpretation sees *righteousness* as the source of *fruit* and understands it in the legal sense as a right legal standing with God. By God's judicial decision, justification, believers in Christ are given the position of *righteousness,* a right legal standing with God. This position of *righteousness,* a right relationship with God, produces the *fruit* of moral character and ethical qualities.[101]

The context, however, supports an interpretation of *righteousness* as a definition of the nature of the fruit. In this interpretation, righteousness has an ethical sense and refers to righteous behavior.[102] *Righteousness* is the content of this fruit. These are people whose lives are *filled with the fruit* of attitudes and actions that reflect the attitudes and actions of Christ (2:5-8). That kind of fruit is defined as *righteousness.*

98. The article τόν before the prepositional phrase *through Jesus Christ* agrees in gender with the neuter gender of the word *fruit,* but not the feminine gender of the word *righteousness.*

99. The genitive case in the Greek text can be either a genitive of source or a genitive of definition.

100. For a discussion of the range of meaning of *righteousness* in Paul's letters, see G. Schrenk, "δικαιοσύνη," *TDNT* 2:202-9; H. Seebass, "Righteousness," *NIDNTT* 3:362-65; J. A. Ziesler, *The Meaning of Righteousness in Paul: A Linguistic and Theological Inquiry* (SNTSMS 20; Cambridge: Cambridge University Press, 1972); Stephen Westerholm, *Perspectives Old and New on Paul: The "Lutheran" Paul and His Critics* (Grand Rapids: Eerdmans, 2004), 261-96; Mark A. Seifrid, "Paul's Use of Righteousness Language against Its Hellenistic Background," in *Justification and Variegated Nomism: Volume 2: The Paradoxes of Paul* (ed. D. A. Carson, Peter O'Brien, and Mark A. Seifrid; Grand Rapids: Baker, 2004).

101. Bruce, 38; Beare, 55-56; Gordon P. Wiles, *Paul's Intercessory Prayers: The Significance of the Intercessory Prayer Passages in the Letters of St Paul* (Cambridge: Cambridge University Press, 1974), 212 n. 3: "The phrase here means the fruit resulting from and demonstrating the righteousness (obj. genitive) rather than the fruit which is righteousness." O'Brien, 80.

102. Silva, 61; Fee, 104: "Paul's emphasis, therefore, is on 'the fruit consisting of righteousness.' . . . Paul's present emphasis is on Christian behavior, not on how one becomes related to God so as to produce such behavior." Martin and Hawthorne, 33-34: "The 'fruit of righteousness,' therefore, must be understood in an ethical sense as referring collectively to those 'truly good qualities' (GNB) in the Philippians that result in all kinds of noble acts and worthwhile deeds done toward each other and their neighbors." Motyer, 59: "the practical righteousness of holy living."

This phrase — *filled with the fruit of righteousness* — is at the end of a long sentence that begins with Paul's prayer that *your love may abound more and more.* Paul looks forward to the *day of Christ,* when his prayer will be completely answered. Paul prays that on that day, when Christ examines the fruit produced in his vineyard, the church, he will find fruit of *pure* motives to love and *blameless* service of love. That kind of fruit is the *fruit of righteousness.* In this context, *righteousness* describes the character and actions of a community totally permeated and controlled by love. Since love is a relational word, this use of *righteousness* points to relational righteousness, right relations with one another.

Later in this letter Paul shifts his focus in his use of the word *righteousness* by contrasting two kinds of righteousness: Paul's *own* righteousness *in law* and *from law* contrasted with righteousness *from God* and *in Christ* (3:6-9). When Paul introduces *the righteousness that comes from God on the basis of faith* (3:9), he is not talking about righteousness that people practice, but righteousness that God gives. These two different ways in which Paul uses the term *righteousness,* as moral behavior that comes through Christ Jesus (1:11) and as God's gift of a right relationship in Christ (3:9), provide a full and balanced picture of Paul's view of life in Christ. By God's gift of a right relationship in Christ, *righteousness from God* (3:9), the believer is empowered by Christ Jesus to produce the *fruit* that consists *of righteousness,* the self-giving love of Christ (2:5-8).[103]

Paul concludes his prayer with a doxology: *to the glory and praise of God.* Paul's prayer is an expression of hope in the continuation and final completion of God's work in the church. From now until *the day of Christ,* God will be forming a community of believers who grow in love so that on the day of Christ they will be pure and blameless and filled with the fruit of righteousness. The doxology gives glory and praise to God for every day leading to the ultimate day. The vision of the ultimate day fills every day with purpose to abound in love with pure motives and blameless service and to be filled with the fruit of righteousness to the glory and praise of God. All the glory and praise for God's new creation belongs only to God.[104] Paul's great hymn to Christ in this letter ends in the same way. The

103. Westerholm, *Perspectives Old and New on Paul,* 277 n. 39: "It has long been debated whether the claim that sinners are 'dikaiosified' [justified] means merely that they are treated as though they were *dikaios* [righteous] (though in themselves they are not) or whether their character is so transformed that they may now rightly be called *dikaios;* in this latter view, if the *dikaios* are people who do what God requires, then God makes sinners into that kind of people, even though in the past they were very different. Both positions capture important aspects of Paul's thought. Paul does think (as the latter position holds) that believers have been transformed; they belong to the 'new creation' (2 Cor 5:17); they are intended to practice 'dikaiosness' [righteousness] (Rom 6:13, 18-19; Phil 1:11). He also speaks (as the former positions insists) of believers as those who receive a δικαιοσύνη [righteousness] that is not inherently their own (Rom 5:17), of their being the beneficiaries of a divine exchange between Christ's δικαιοσύνη and their own sin (2 Cor 5:21; cf. 1 Cor 1:30)."

104. The early manuscript 𝔓[46] reads, "to the glory of God and praise of me." While

universal confession that Jesus Christ is Lord leads to *the glory of God the Father* (2:11).

Praise to God for the perfection of the church on the day of Christ gave Paul the ability to rejoice during his dark days in a Roman prison, even on days when he received reports of opposition to the church and division between leaders in the church. Confidence in the ultimate transformation of the church by God is the reason why Paul frequently interrupts this letter with outbursts of exuberant joy. Chains and divisions could not take away his joy. Since the cross was followed by the exaltation of Christ, Paul was convinced that all who shared in the suffering of Christ would also share in the victory of Christ. On the basis of that conviction, Paul begins this prayer with thanksgiving and ends it with praise. Paul has much to tell the church; his letter is full of exhortation. But before he speaks directly to the church, he speaks to God about the church. Most of what Paul says to God in prayer is heard again in his exhortation to the church. Since Paul prefaces his exhortation with prayer, the church is assured of the good result of all their suffering and striving. Paul does not motivate the church by guilt; no, he does so by the guarantee of the final victory in Christ. The vision of the perfect purity and unity of the church on the day of Christ empowers the church to be *like-minded, having the same love, being one in spirit and of one mind* (2:2) in the present.

III. REPORTS OF GOSPEL MINISTRY (1:12-26)

A. The Progress of the Gospel (1:12-14)

> [12]*Now I want you to know, brothers and sisters, that what has happened to me has actually served to advance the gospel.* [13]*As a result, it has become clear throughout the whole palace guard and to everyone else that I am in chains for Christ.* [14]*And because of my chains, most of the brothers and sisters have become confident in the Lord and dare all the more to proclaim the gospel without fear.*

12 Paul turns from his prayer to inform his readers of his own situation. He begins with an unconventional use of a conventional form. The introductory phrase — *I want you to know, brothers and sisters* — is often called a "disclosure formula" by analysts of Greek letter forms[105] and is found

Paul does say that church is his "joy and crown," other early and diverse MSS (ℵ A B Ψ 𝔐) give solid evidence for Paul's usual practice of giving all the glory and praise to God.

105. T. Y. Mullins, "Disclosure as a Literary Form in the New Testament," *NovT* 7 (1964), 46-49; J. T. Sanders, "The Transition from Opening Epistolary Thanksgiving to Body in Letters of the Pauline Corpus," *JBL* 81 (1962), 349; John L. White, *The Form and Function of the Body of the Greek Letter: A Study of the Letter-Body in the Non-literary Papyri and in Paul the*

with variations in Greek papyrus letters of Paul's day and in Paul's letters as an introduction to a new section of a letter.[106] The four parts of this conventional phrase are (1) some form of an expression of desire — I want or I desire, (2) a verb of knowing — to know, to be informed, or not to be ignorant, (3) the addressees — you, *brothers and sisters*,[107] and (4) the information disclosed. This conventional introduction opens the way for Paul's unconventional report on his circumstances. A conventional report would provide a detailed description of the letter writer's situation. But even though Paul says he wants his readers to know *what has happened*[108] to him and refers repeatedly to his *chains*,[109] he does not give a detailed account of the events and conditions of his imprisonment. In our day, a journalist would want to have a narrative of his arrest, imprisonment, and courtroom appearances, plus some drawings of his prison and his guards, a diary of his daily activities, menus of his meals, medical records of his physical condition, and, above all, a disclosure of his feelings.[110] But such personal matters were not Paul's priorities. From Paul's perspective the most important thing that had happened was the advance of the gospel. His most urgent concern is to demonstrate that his imprisonment *actually served to advance the gospel*. TNIV translates a Greek word as *actually* to emphasize the positive meaning, "to a greater or higher degree, more."[111] This word can also be a "marker of an alternative to" an expressed or unexpressed negative, in which case it would be translated "*rather* in the sense *instead* (of something)."[112] Twice in this sentence Paul holds up his *chains* for all to see. Chains are certainly an obstacle to progress, according to conventional wisdom. The close connection of the negative word *chains* and the positive word *advance* in this sentence indicates that Paul is using the word *actually* as a marker of a surprising alternative to a negative expectation. What had happened to Paul was the negative experience of imprisonment. But in-

Apostle (SBLDS 2; Missoula: Scholars Press, 1972), 11-15. See Stanley K. Stowers, *Letter Writing in Greco-Roman Antiquity* (LEC 5; Philadelphia: Westminster, 1986), 58-70, for examples of the way that letters of friendship substitute for actual companionship by disclosing personal information. Although Stowers does not refer to the disclosure formula, his illustrations of friendly letters amply demonstrate the importance of personal disclosure in letters of friendship.

106. Mullins provides nineteen examples from Greek letters and nine examples from Paul's letters: Rom 1:13; 11:25; 1 Cor 10:1; 11:3; 12:1; 2 Cor 1:8; Gal 1:11; 1 Thess 2:1; 4:13.

107. The Greek word ἀδελφοί is clearly a reference to both male and female siblings, as we can see from the end of the letter where Paul addresses the ἀδελφοί (4:1) and then immediately speaks directly to two women (4:2).

108. τὰ κατ' ἐμέ is a reference to his "circumstances" (BDAG, 513). See the use of the same phrase in Eph 6:21 and Col 4:7.

109. 1:7, 13, 14, 17.

110. For descriptions of prisons in the ancient Roman world, see Craig S. Wansink, *Chained in Christ: The Experience and Rhetoric of Paul's Imprisonments* (JSNTSup 130; Sheffield: Sheffield Academic, 1996); Rapske, *The Book of Acts and Paul in Roman Custody*.

111. BDAG, 613.

112. BDAG, 614.

stead of turning out to be a negative hindrance, Paul's chains served to *advance* the gospel. Perhaps Paul is employing a subtle play on words. The Greek word for *advance (prokopē)* sounds similar to the Greek word for hindrance *(proskopē)*. We would expect to hear Paul say that what had happened to him, his imprisonment, was a *proskopē*, a hindrance. But Paul surprises us by saying that imprisonment was a *prokopē*, an advance.

It is easy to understand the reasons why Paul focuses on the advance of the gospel. First, his partnership with the Philippians for the purpose of propagating the gospel (1:5) depended upon solid progress in his work. If the Philippians concluded that Paul's imprisonment hindered or terminated his work in proclaiming the gospel, as it would have been reasonable to conclude, then they would think that the purpose of their partnership had ended. They would surmise that their support of Paul's work was no longer needed since Paul, now in chains, could no longer work. Paul had to inform them that his chains turned out to be a great advantage for his work.

Second, Paul focuses on the progress of the gospel rather than on his personal experience in prison because it was the gospel that mattered most to him. He exclaims in this letter, *For to me, to live is Christ* (1:21). Since Christ was the center of Paul's life, all other details of his imprisonment were peripheral and secondary. The progress of the gospel was, in fact, the most personal concern in Paul's life.

Third, Paul tells his friends that his chains brought about an advance of the gospel to encourage them in their suffering. The Philippians were *going through the same struggle* (1:30) as Paul. They were not in chains, but they were facing stiff opposition for their faith in Christ. Paul encourages them not to be *frightened in any way by those who oppose you* (1:28). Paul presents the positive result of his imprisonment to give them courage, demonstrating that all who suffer for Christ and for the gospel will be vindicated, as Paul was, by the progress of the gospel. Though the messenger may be bound in chains, the message cannot be bound. Caesar's chains released the power of the gospel of Christ.

Paul provides evidence for his positive report by describing the impact of his imprisonment on the members of the emperor's bodyguard and entourage (1:13) and on the members of the Christian family (1:14).

13 Paul's reference to the *palace guard* points to the most elite group of Roman soldiers, who served as a special bodyguard for Caesar.[113] This

113. Πραιτώριον, the Greek word for *palace guard,* is derived from the Latin word *praetorium,* originally a reference to "the praetor's tent in the camp and its surroundings" (BDAG, 859). This word designates "the governor's official residence" in Matt 27:27; Mark 15:16; John 18:28, 33; 19:9. Whether these references point to the palace of Herod in the western part of Jerusalem or to the palace of Pilate in the temple area is unclear (Bargil Pixner, "Praetorium," *ABD* 5:447). Paul was imprisoned in the palace of Herod (ἐν τῷ πραιτωρίῳ τοῦ Ἡρῴδου) in Caesarea (Acts 23:35). The key question regarding the meaning of πραιτώριον in Phil 1:13 is whether it refers to a place or to people: to Caesar's or the governor's palace (in

group of 9,000 elite soldiers sometimes exerted control over Caesar himself. In fact, they deposed and promoted Caesars. After they assassinated Caligula, they put Claudius on the throne. Later they guided the directions of Nero's reign.[114] But Caesar's bodyguard could not intimidate Paul. He served a higher power than Caesar or Caesar's bodyguard; he was an agent of the one whom God had exalted to receive universal worship as Lord (2:9-11).

It has become clear, Paul reports, *throughout the whole palace guard and to everyone else that I am in chains for Christ.* Both the guards and others employed by Caesar[115] came to realize that Paul was in chains as a result of his identification with Christ. The word order in the Greek phrase ("my chains manifest in Christ became") is correctly rearranged in the TNIV so that *in Christ* modifies *my chains.* The palace guard would normally see chains on a prisoner as evidence of Caesar's power. These chains were Caesar's chains, demonstrating that Caesar was Lord, binding the prisoner for Caesar to fulfill Caesar's will. But in Paul's case the palace guard and everyone else associated with Caesar saw Paul's chains as evidence of Christ's power in Paul's life. He was in chains because he was in Christ. Paul's chains were the result of his proclamation that Christ is Lord.

Imagine a guard coming on duty to watch Paul. He has no idea who Paul is. So he asks Paul the most common question directed at prisoners, "Why are you in chains?" Paul's answer is Christ-centered: "I am in chains because I belong to Christ. I serve Christ. Jesus Christ in humility and in obedience to God's will died for our sins on a Roman cross under Roman power. Jesus Christ is now the risen and exalted Lord above all powers. Christ called me to proclaim the good news about him among the nations. Christ is the Savior of all who trust him. One day everyone will recognize and worship Christ as the Lord of all." Undoubtedly, something like this would have been Paul's answer. All the elements of this answer are prominent in his letters. A Roman guard would immediately recognize the subversive force of Paul's proclamation of Christ. Paul's acclamation of Christ as Lord and Savior (2:11; 3:20) challenged Caesar's claim to these titles. The guard would conclude that Paul is in chains because he is in Christ.

Paul's focus on Christ made him an expert at reframing his experience so that the negative became a positive. His chains could easily be

---

Rome, Ephesus, or Caesarea) or to the bodyguard of Caesar (in Rome, Ephesus, or Caesarea). The interpretation of this word as a reference to the imperial bodyguard is based on its close connection (in the same prepositional phrase) with the reference *to everyone else* (Phil 1:13). Since this phrase refers to people, it is probable that πραιτώριον is also a reference to people, the *palace guard.* See the Introduction, 19-23, for the significance of Paul's reference to the palace guard in the discussion of the provenance of this letter.

114. Everett Ferguson, *Backgrounds of Early Christianity* (2nd ed.; Grand Rapids: Eerdmans, 1993), 31-32.

115. The close connection in one prepositional phrase of the palace guard and everyone else indicates that everyone else should be considered in the same circle as those "who belong to Caesar's household" (4:22).

viewed as a tragic end to a brilliant career, a restriction of a gifted apostle, and an outrageous injustice against a Roman citizen. Instead of being led by his chains to a negative outlook, Paul used them to lead his guards to the knowledge of Christ. He valued his chains as evidence of his union with Christ. He saw his chains as a fulfillment of his ambition to know the participation in the sufferings of Christ (3:10).

14 The second line of evidence for Paul's positive report about the advance of the gospel is the salutary effect of his imprisonment on fellow believers. *Because of my chains, most of the brothers and sisters have become confident in the Lord and dare all the more to proclaim the gospel without fear.* The chains that bound Paul liberated others to speak the word of God fearlessly. Though Paul attributes this transformation to the chains themselves, the real source of inspiration was Paul's fearless witness to Christ while in chains, as the previous clause indicates. The chained inspired the unchained. When believers heard that Paul used his chains as an opportunity to express his faith in Christ, even to the palace guard, they were emboldened to proclaim Christ fearlessly even when they might have been intimidated to keep their mouths shut.

Paul's reference to *most* means more than many; it means that a majority of brothers and sisters were influenced by his bold witness in prison.[116] His life in prison motivated most of the church to take an open and public stand for Christ, even if that meant opposition and rejection. The life of one man in chains transformed the life of the church. Paul recognizes that it was not ultimately his own fearless witness but the Lord who really encouraged the church to speak boldly. Although the NIV takes the prepositional phrase *in the Lord* as a modifier of *brothers and sisters,* TNIV correctly connects this phrase to the verb *have become confident.* Since Paul addresses fellow believers in Christ as *brothers and sisters,* connecting the phrase *in the Lord* to this name for Christians would be unnecessarily redundant.[117] Paul sometimes uses the phrase *in the Lord* to modify attitudes and actions that he desires and commends, as he does seven other times in this letter (2:19, 24, 29; 3:1; 4:1, 2, 4). Believers are to rejoice *in the Lord,* agree *in the Lord,* and stand *in the Lord.* In these instances, the phrase *in the Lord* points to the Lord as the one who motivates and empowers the actions and attitudes of believers. Paul acknowledges the way God was using his difficult circumstance of imprisonment for the benefit of the church when he says that most believers *have become confident in the Lord.*

The TNIV translation, *have become confident,* expresses the meaning of the Greek word: "to be so convinced that one puts confidence in something."[118] Most believers were so convinced by the impact of Paul's witness to the palace guard while he was in chains that they, like Paul, put their

116. BDAG, 848.

117. Vincent, 17; Fee, 116; cf. Beare, 59.

118. BDAG, 792.

confidence in the Lord to empower their witness as well. "If the Lord can give courage to Paul to witness like that while he is in chains," they must have reasoned, "then he can give courage to us to witness in our difficult circumstances."

Having been convinced by the Lord to put their confidence in the Lord, they *dare all the more to proclaim the gospel.* The word *dare* indicates a willingness "to show boldness or resolution in the face of danger, opposition, or a problem."[119] Paul is not saying that the believers did not have any boldness at all; he asserts that they had *more* boldness as a result of his imprisonment. The comparative word *more* points to a remarkable increase in the bold proclamation of these believers. When the danger of speaking for Christ increased beyond their worst nightmares, their boldness increased beyond measure. Before they were witnessing, but timidly and hesitantly; now they dared to take big risks in their witness and speak out *without fear* in dangerous situations. Paul's example and the Lord's presence took away their fears and gave them amazing courage. Courage is contagious. The timid catch boldness from the brave.

The content of the bold proclamation is *the gospel* (TNIV), literally, "the word" (NRSV) or "the word of God" (NIV). The shorter reading, "the word," not modified by "of God," is found in an early manuscript and in the Majority Text.[120] Sometimes Paul refers to proclamation and teaching simply as "the word" (1 Thess 1:6; Gal 6:6; Col 4:3; 2 Tim 4:3), but more often he indicates the source and content of the word by speaking of "the word of God," "the word of the Lord," or "the word of Christ" (1 Thess 1:8; 2:13; 2 Thess 3:1; 1 Cor 14:36; 2 Cor 2:17; 4:2; Col 1:25; 3:16). The longer reading, "the word of God," is found in early and diverse manuscripts and probably reflects the addition of the modifier "of God" by early copyists to make this text conform to Paul's usual practice.[121] Although some doubt remains as to whether the original text of this letter read "the word" or "the word of God," we are not in doubt regarding the content of "the word," since the next paragraph repeatedly asserts that *Christ is preached* (1:15-18). This proclamation of Christ is *the gospel,* the most powerful "word" in the Roman Empire.

Many words can be spoken in human discourse without the slightest risk or need for courage. But speaking this particular word — a Christ-

119. BDAG, 1010.

120. The reading τὸν λόγον λαλεῖν ("to speak the word") is supported by 𝔓[46] D[c] 1739 1881 𝔐 Marcion Chrysostom.

121. The reading τὸν λόγον τοῦ θεοῦ λαλεῖν ("to speak the word of God") is supported by diverse MSS evidence (א A B P Ψ 33 81 629 1241 vg syr [p h] Clement). Two MSS (F G) have τὸν λόγον κυρίου λαλεῖν. The usual rule is that the shortest reading is the more reliable, since it is customary for scribes to add rather than delete. There is no good reason why scribes would delete the modifier τοῦ θεοῦ or κυρίου found so often in Paul's letters if it were already in the text. See Bruce M. Metzger, *A Textual Commentary on the Greek New Testament* (Stuttgart: United Bible Societies, 1971), 611-12: the shortest reading "best explains the origin of the other readings, which have the appearance of scribal expansions."

centered word — always requires courage. The message of Christ's humble obedience unto death on a cross (2:8) strikes a blow at every proud heart. The message of Christ's exaltation to be the universal Lord over all creation (2:9-11) requires every knee to bow before him. Anyone who dares to speak this word outside the church, outside the comfortable circle of Christian admirers, will be inspired by Paul's courageous witness when he was chained to the emperor's bodyguard. Ever since Paul, the courage of faithful witnesses for Christ has ignited courage in the hearts of other witnesses.

As the fires were lit in 1555 in Oxford to burn the English reformers, Hugh Latimer and Nicholas Ridley, for their faithful witness to Christ, Latimer shouted, "Be of good comfort, Master Ridley, and play the man. We shall this day light such a candle by God's grace in England as I trust shall never be put out!"[122] The example of these two martyrs has encouraged generations of Christians to proclaim the gospel without fear.

B. Motives for Preaching Christ (1:15-18a)

> [15]*It is true that some preach Christ out of envy and rivalry, but others out of goodwill.* [16]*The latter do so out of love, knowing that I am put here for the defense of the gospel.* [17]*The former preach Christ out of selfish ambition, not sincerely, supposing that they can stir up trouble for me while I am in chains.* [18a]*But what does it matter? The important thing is that in every way, whether from false motives or true, Christ is preached. And because of this I rejoice.*

15 After announcing the good news about the brothers and sisters who dare to speak the word courageously, Paul tells the bad news that they are divided by their different attitudes toward him. Although Paul draws a sharp line of contrast between these two groups, he is clear that they have the same identity and the same message. He introduces both groups with pronouns *(some . . . others)* that have as their antecedent the brothers and sisters referred to in verse 14.[123] So both groups have the same identity: they are all included within the Christian family of brothers and sisters. They are not wolves in sheep's clothing; they are not pseudo-Christians. They are really brothers and sisters in Christ. Paul also repeatedly asserts that both groups *preach Christ* (vv. 15, 17, and 18). So both groups have the same message. They all faithfully preach the gospel message of salvation through the cross and resurrection of Christ. They are not people who subtract from the gospel message, as some in Corinth did by their denial of the

122. Marcus Loane, *Masters of the English Reformation* (London: Hodder and Stoughton, 1954), 169.

123. The Greek pronouns (τινὲς . . . τινές) point back to Paul's reference in verse 14 to most of the brothers and sisters (τοὺς πλείονας τῶν ἀδελφῶν).

bodily resurrection. They are not people who supplement the gospel message, as some in the Galatian churches did by their requirement of circumcision and other Jewish rituals. The factor that divides these two groups of people is not their Christian identity or their Christian message but their different attitudes toward Paul.

Some preach Christ out of envy and rivalry. Envy and rivalry are often paired in Paul's letters in lists of reprehensible characteristics of evil people. *Envy and rivalry* are works of the flesh (Gal 5:20-21) and evidence of a depraved mind (Rom 1:28-29). Teachers of false doctrines are interested in controversies "that result in envy, rivalry" and other destructive attitudes and words (1 Tim 6:3-4). *Envy* is characteristic of people who are "enslaved by all kinds of passions" before their salvation and rebirth by the Holy Spirit (Tit 3:3). *Rivalry* should be avoided because it is a mark of warped and sinful people (Tit 3:9-11). Contemporaries of Paul, such as Plutarch and Dio Chrysostom, condemned envy and rivalry because these attitudes are destructive to harmony in the public arena.[124] Envy and rivalry cause personal enmity. The envious begrudge the successes of their opponents and celebrate their misfortunes. The envious person works to harm and ruin the object of envy. Readers of Paul today will observe that envy and rivalry are too often characteristic of preachers of Christ in our competitive churches.

In contrast to the envious with their ill will, Paul says, others out of *goodwill* preach Christ. Some commentators argue that *goodwill* refers to divine favor.[125] In some contexts goodwill refers to the divine will, as in 2:13. But in the immediate context the contrast with the ill will of the envious toward Paul and the reference to the love of Paul in the next phrase (v. 16a) confirm that Paul is describing human goodwill. When some were so hostile toward him, the goodwill of these preachers toward Paul must have been a welcome encouragement. The purpose of their preaching was to express their goodwill toward Paul.[126] They stepped into the gap left by Paul's imprisonment and carried on his work of gospel preaching because they desired to help Paul by continuing his mission.

16 Paul now expands his definition of the goodwill of these preachers. Their witness to Christ was given *out of love* (1:16a). The chiastic form used by Paul in his description of these two different groups can be diagrammed as follows:[127]

124. See Bruce Winter, *Seek the Welfare of the City: Christians as Benefactors and Citizens* (Grand Rapids: Eerdmans, 1994), 94-97.

125. O'Brien, 99-100; Bockmuehl, 78-79.

126. The grammatical construction here (the preposition διά with the accusative case of goodwill) expresses purpose. But this construction does not necessarily indicate that goodwill refers to the divine will, as Bockmuehl (79) insists. See Collange, 55.

127. The Byzantine MSS tradition (𝔐) transposes verses 16 and 17 so that the sequence in Paul's description is ABAB rather than ABBA. Early and diverse witnesses (𝔓[46] ℵ A B D*) support the chiastic form given in the text.

A *envy and rivalry*
B *goodwill*
B *love*
A *selfish ambition*

Those who proclaimed Christ *out of love* were seeking to serve Paul. Whatever effort, time, and personal sacrifice preaching Christ required, they were willing to pay the cost because they loved Paul. Their love for Paul was guided by knowledge: *knowing that I am put here for the defense of the gospel* (1:16b). In his prayer for the Philippians, Paul asks that their love may abound more and more in knowledge (1:9). Now we see an illustration of the way that knowledge increases and guides love. These preachers knew that Paul's imprisonment was actually a divine appointment[128] for the purpose of defending the gospel in his trial. They knew that Paul's goal was not a defense of himself to protect his life, but a defense of the gospel of Christ. Motivated by their knowledge of Paul's faithful defense of the gospel, they sought to express their love for Paul by their faithful proclamation of Christ.

17 In contrast to the preachers of goodwill, the envious preachers exhibited their ill will by their attempts to hurt Paul. Paul says that *they preach Christ out of selfish ambition, not sincerely, supposing that they can stir up trouble for me while I am in chains.* The Greek word for *selfish ambition* is translated by TNIV as "self-seeking" in Romans 2:8 and as "factions" in 2 Corinthians 12:20. In Aristotle's *Politics,* this word "denotes a self-seeking pursuit of political office by unfair means."[129] Paul condemns this attitude in his list of vices (2 Cor 12:20; Gal 5:20). He points to the danger of this attitude in Philippi by warning the Christians to *do nothing out of selfish ambition* (2:3). Those who preached Christ with the motive of selfish ambition were not preaching *sincerely,* "not from pure motives."[130] In fact, they were motivated to preach Christ because they were *supposing* that their preaching would cause Paul trouble while he was in chains. By his use of the word *supposing,*[131] Paul reveals a crucial difference between the preachers motivated by love and the preachers motivated by selfish ambition. Paul's supporters were motivated by *knowing* that his imprisonment was the result of God's appointment of him for the defense of the gospel. Their knowledge was true. Paul's rivals were motivated by *supposing* that Paul's imprisonment gave them a way to cause him trouble. Their supposition was false.

What kind of *trouble* they hoped to cause Paul is unclear. In Paul's let-

128. The words *put here* translate a Greek word (κεῖμαι) that literally means "to lie or recline," but metaphorically means "to be appointed or destined for something" (BDAG, 537).

129. BDAG, 392, with references to Aristotle, *Politics* 5, 3p. 1302b, 4; 1303a, 14.

130. BDAG, 14.

131. Οἴομαι *(suppose)* means to "consider something to be true but with a component of tentativeness" (BDAG, 701).

ters the word *trouble* refers to all kinds of outward circumstances that cause distress: persecution (1 Thess 1:6; 3:3), beatings, imprisonment, riots, hard work, sleepless nights, and hunger (2 Cor 6:4-5).[132] *Trouble* may also be an "inward experience of distress."[133] In 2 Corinthians 2:4 Paul uses the same word when he speaks of his own inner turmoil as "great distress [*trouble*] and anguish of heart." Were the envious preachers trying to cause Paul to experience emotional anguish by displaying their freedom to preach in contrast to his lack of freedom?[134] Or did Paul's rivals suppose that their preaching might actually cause Paul to receive harsher treatment in his imprisonment and trial?[135] Paul does not explain what kind of trouble these preachers had in mind, but he does expose their motives. They preached Christ *from false motives* (1:18). Their preaching, though true in content, was actually a façade, a pretense,[136] for their envious, self-seeking desire to hurt Paul. Their motive for preaching contradicted the content of their message. In contrast, those who preached Christ out of love for Paul had *true* motives. Their desire to serve Paul by preaching Christ was consistent with their message of Christ who came to serve.

Paul does not precisely identify these envious preachers. All we know for sure is that they were inside the church, because Paul includes them among the brothers and sisters. And they are not false teachers — such as Judaizers — because Paul does not object to the content of their message: they proclaim Christ.[137] But why did they envy Paul? We can imagine that they envied Paul because his effective preaching won a bigger following than they had. And how did they hope to stir up trouble for Paul? We can speculate that they expected their preaching to attract a bigger following than Paul had before he was restricted by chains and thus to cause Paul inner anguish because he was left so far behind. Perhaps they thought that Paul's imprisonment removed their competition and gave them a chance to take center stage and outshine Paul, who had been taken offstage. They supposed that the contrast between their spectacular ability to preach outside of prison and Paul's inability to preach in prison would cause Paul great pain.

We would like to have more description of these envious preachers to confirm or correct our imagination. But we already have more than enough description to challenge our own motivation in preaching. Paul's exposure of false motives for preaching Christ confronts all preachers of Christ with

132. See also the lists of hardships in 1 Cor 4:9-13; 2 Cor 6:4-10; 11:23-28.

133. BDAG, 457, includes our text, Phil 1:17, in this category.

134. O'Brien, 102.

135. Winter, *Seek the Welfare of the City*, 95.

136. προφάσει, translated *false motives* by TNIV, denotes "a falsely alleged motive, pretext, ostensible reason, excuse" (BDAG, 889).

137. Against Lightfoot (90), who identifies these teachers as Judaizers. Vincent (19) observes that "nowhere in his epistles does Paul speak of Judaizers as preachers of Christ unless it be of 'another Jesus' (2 Cor 11:4)."

the need to examine their motives. The motives of *envy and rivalry* contradict the message of the self-giving love of Christ. *Selfish ambition* is not consistent with the proclamation of the cross of Christ. A desire to *stir up trouble* for fellow Christians undermines the unity of all who proclaim Christ.

18a Paul's response to the envious preachers who desired to hurt him demonstrates his refusal to compete with other preachers. After exposing his opponents' supposition that their preaching would stir up trouble for him while he was in chains, he dismisses their attack with a question: *But what does it matter?* (1:18a). In other words, Paul writes, So what?[138] For Paul, *the important thing is that in every way, whether from false motives or true, Christ is preached* (1:18). If the message of Christ is compromised, diluted, or supplemented in any way, then Paul forcefully confronts those who tamper with the message itself. When he warns the Philippians about the influence of Judaizers, Paul blasts away with harsh words: *Watch out for those dogs, those evildoers, those mutilators of the flesh* (3:2). But as long as Christ is preached, Paul is unconcerned about his own position or fame in comparison to that of other preachers. So those who intended to cause Paul harm by exalting themselves above him as preachers of Christ actually caused him to rejoice because Christ was preached. *Because of this I rejoice,* he exclaims. The advancement of the message, not the advancement of Paul, is the source of Paul's joy.

The question of Paul's reason for including this description of these two different groups of preachers in his letter to the Philippians raises significant issues for the interpretation of the entire letter. If this story was told to reflect the situation in Philippi, then we may be led to conclude that the divisions in the church in Philippi were caused by similar opposing attitudes toward Paul. Peterlin draws this conclusion: "The excursus in 15-17 has a double reference. Paul recognized the overlapping between the circumstances of the two situations, and so in the letter to the Philippians he highlighted those aspects of the other situation which were closest to the Philippian reality and most appropriate for the purpose of the letter. . . . Envy and selfish ambition are at the heart of both situations."[139] Paul connects the two situations by using the same phrase — *selfish ambition* — when he describes those who preach Christ out of *selfish ambition* (1:17) and when he appeals to the Philippians to *do nothing out of selfish ambition* (2:3). If some Christians in both situations are characterized by selfish ambition and envy, then we have a valuable clue for understanding the cause of the problem of disunity in the Philippian church. Division was caused by different attitudes toward Paul. Some envied and were driven by their selfish ambition to take the glory away from Paul for themselves. Others loved and sought to serve Paul. By telling of his response to the envious preachers, Paul lets the church in Philippi know that the negative attitudes of

138. Literally, his question is, "For what?" (Τί γάρ;).

139. Peterlin, *Paul's Letter to the Philippians,* 40.

some toward him in that church are of little or no importance. He minimizes the significance of disputes caused by his personality, his position, and his prestige. As long as the gospel advances, his promotion or demotion does not matter to him. Paul's expression of tolerance toward some preachers who envy him is probably intended to assure those who are against him in Philippi that he does not reject them.[140]

This description of the conflict in the church in Philippi in the light of 1:15-18 as one between a pro-Paul faction and an anti-Paul faction is highly speculative and unwarranted by the evidence. What we know from the evidence of the letter about the conflict in the church in Philippi is derived from Paul's appeal to the church to be *of one mind,* to *do nothing out of selfish ambition or vain conceit* (2:3), and to *do everything without grumbling or arguing* (2:14) and from his appeal to two women to *be of the same mind* (4:2). From this evidence or from anything else in the letter, we do not have an adequate basis for speculating that some in the church were against Paul. In fact, Paul's expressions of his joy and delight in the church (1:7-8; 2:17; 4:1) and of his genuine appreciation for the church (4:14-18) contradict any theory that there was an anti-Paul faction in the church. His description of the opposing factions in 1:15-18 simply teaches how the church should focus on the proclamation of Christ with pure motives and love. To draw any other implications from this passage goes beyond the evidence and detracts from Paul's example of rejoicing in the proclamation of Christ above all else. As long as the focus is kept on Christ, there will be unity in the church. As soon as the focus shifts to interpersonal competition and conflict, unity will be destroyed. No wonder Paul urges Christians who are in conflict to *have the same attitude of mind Christ Jesus had* (2:5). All that really matters is to *know Christ* (3:10).

C. Courage to Honor Christ by Life or by Death (1:18b-26)

> [18b]*Yes, and I will continue to rejoice,* [19]*for I know that through your*
> *prayers and God's provision of the Spirit of Jesus Christ what has happened*
> *to me will turn out for my deliverance.* [20]*I eagerly expect and hope that I will*
> *in no way be ashamed, but will have sufficient courage so that now as always*
> *Christ will be exalted in my body, whether by life or by death.*
>
> [21]*For to me, to live is Christ and to die is gain.* [22]*If I am to go on living in*
> *the body, this will mean fruitful labor for me. Yet what shall I choose? I do*
> *not know!* [23]*I am torn between the two: I desire to depart and be with Christ,*
> *which is better by far;* [24]*but it is more necessary for you that I remain in the*
> *body.* [25]*Convinced of this, I know that I will remain, and I will continue with*
> *all of you for your progress and joy in the faith,* [26]*so that through my being*
> *with you again your boasting in Christ Jesus will abound on account of me.*

140. Peterlin, *Paul's Letter to the Philippians,* 41.

18b When Paul turns from his report of his present circumstances to a report of his future expectations, he expresses joyful confidence: *Yes, and I will continue to rejoice* (1:18b). He indicates both a transition to a new perspective and a continuation of his joyful attitude by combining an adversative conjunction ("but") with a coordinating conjunction ("and"): not only this, but also. These two conjunctions are translated *yes, and* by TNIV.[141] By changing from the present tense ("I rejoice") to the future tense *(I will rejoice),* Paul communicates his decision to rejoice in the future whether the outcome of his trial will be life or death. Paul's uncertainty about the future expressed at the end of this sentence in verses 18b-20 does not weaken the intensity of his decision asserted at the beginning of the sentence.[142] Whether he lives or dies, whether he is executed or released, Paul is determined to rejoice. The prospect of his trial drove him to prayer, but it did not drive him to despair. His joy did not depend on the prospect of keeping his life, but on honoring Christ, *whether by life or by death.*

19 Paul's decision to rejoice whether he lived or died was not completely irrational. His joy was based on knowledge, the knowledge of his *deliverance: for I know that . . . what has happened to me will turn out for my deliverance.* Paul's words, *will turn out for my deliverance,* are the same ones used by Job. While he was suffering, Job asserted, "Though he slay me, yet will I hope in him; I will surely defend my ways to his face" (Job 13:15). Then Job expressed his hope: "this will turn out for my deliverance" (Job 13:16). Paul recalled the scriptural account of Job's suffering while he was in chains. By appropriating the story of Job to his own experience of suffering, Paul was able to echo the hope of Job: *I know that . . . what has happened to me will turn out for my deliverance.*[143]

But what kind of *deliverance* does Paul mean in this context? Two common interpretations are deliverance from imprisonment and execution or deliverance in the sense of eternal salvation. Those in favor of the former interpretation[144] point out that the primary meaning of *deliverance* is "preservation, with focus on physical aspect: from impending death."[145] Acts 7:25 narrates the story of Moses, who "thought that his own people would realize that God was using him to rescue them [literally, "giving them deliverance"], but they did not." According to Acts 27:34, Paul assured those who were lost at sea in a terrible storm that they would experience deliver-

141. For the meaning of ἀλλὰ καί ("but and"), see BDAG, 45; BDF, §448 (6); MHT 3, 330: "Introducing a strong addition, ἀλλά or ἀλλὰ καί may be *yes, indeed.*"

142. 1:18-20 is one sentence in the Greek text.

143. Richard B. Hays, *Echoes of Scripture in the Letters of Paul* (New Haven: Yale University Press, 1989), 22: "By echoing Job's words, Paul the prisoner tacitly assumes the role of righteous sufferer, as paradigmatically figured by Job. Awaiting his trial, he speaks with Job's voice to affirm confidence in the favorable outcome of his afflictions; thereby, he implicitly transfers to himself some of the significations that traditionally cluster about the figure of Job."

144. See Martin and Hawthorne, 49-50.

145. BDAG, 985-86.

ance. Both of these uses of the Greek word for *deliverance* refer to a physical rescue.

Paul's confident expectation, *I know that I will remain, and I will continue with all of you* (1:25), appears to support the interpretation of *deliverance* as rescue from imprisonment and execution. If Paul's statement beginning with the verb *I know* in verse 25 is an elaboration of the statement beginning with the same verb *I know* in verse 19, then it seems that verse 19 expresses Paul's expectation of deliverance from Roman execution.

This interpretation of the word *deliverance* as acquittal and release from prison faces opposition for two reasons. First, Paul usually uses the word *deliverance* with a "focus on transcendent aspects."[146] Paul confirms the ultimate salvation of believers in the next section of this letter (1:28).[147] The interpretation of deliverance in 1:19 as eschatological deliverance from the judgment of God and ultimate vindication before God fits well with Paul's emphasis in this letter on God's vindication through suffering. Just as Christ was vindicated and exalted by God after death on a cross (2:9-11), so Paul eagerly anticipates ultimate deliverance and transformation when the *Savior* comes from heaven (3:20-21). Since the experience of the followers of Christ conforms to the narrative of Christ's vindication through suffering, Paul could be confident that he would ultimately be delivered and vindicated by God, whatever the outcome of his present suffering and trial might be.[148]

Second, a focus on immediate, physical *deliverance* reduces the full significance of the words, *whether by life or by death* (1:20). Hawthorne sees this phrase as simply a "stock expression that means 'totally,' or 'all-encompassing' . . . somewhat like the modern expression 'for dear life,' or 'on your life.'" "Thus," Hawthorne asserts, "this phrase carries in it no suspense regarding the outcome of his trial."[149] But he gives no good reason why the phrase *by life or by death* should not be taken at its face value as a reference to the possible outcome of his trial. Paul anticipates a deliverance that does not depend on Roman justice. Although he clearly indicates his expectation that he will be released (1:24-26), he confidently insists that his deliverance does not depend on release from prison; it will occur, *whether by life or by death.*

Both Paul's consistent use of the word *deliverance* to mean transcendent salvation and his insistence that deliverance is not dependent on release from prison and execution appear to support the interpretation of deliverance as eschatological, transcendent salvation — "vindication in the

146. BDAG, 986; W. Foerster, "σῴζω," *TDNT* 7:993

147. See also the use of this word (σωτηρία) in 1 Thess 5:8-9; Rom 5:9; 8:18-30.

148. See O'Brien (110) and Fee (131) for a defense of the interpretation of σωτηρία as ultimate salvation in heaven.

149. Hawthorne, 43-44; Martin and Hawthorne, 54: "The expression simply means that Paul's entire existence, as that of a responsible human being (σῶμα), is aimed at one goal, that of bringing praise to Christ."

heavenly court."[150] However, Paul's focus in verse 20 is neither temporal, physical release from prison and execution nor eschatological salvation and ultimate vindication before God in heaven. As verse 20 will show, Paul expects a deliverance that will happen *now as always*, a deliverance that will happen when *Christ will be exalted in my body.*

The deliverance Paul has in mind is accomplished through the combined power of the *prayers*[151] of his friends and *God's provision of the Spirit of Jesus Christ.* The way Paul combines *prayers* and *God's provision* of *the Spirit* shows how closely human prayers and God's provision are related.[152] Our prayers have no power in themselves to help apart from the work of the Spirit. In fact, genuine prayer is possible only with the help of the Spirit (Rom 8:26). While the help of the Spirit is not limited to the extent of our prayers, we cannot presume upon the Spirit's presence and power when there is not a concerted effort to pray for God's provision of the Spirit. Paul has already assured the Philippians of his prayers for them (1:4, 9-11). Now he tells them how much he counts on their prayers for him.[153] Paul openly admits that he depends on the prayers of his partners. By their prayers, they are investing in their partnership with Paul and are bringing about Paul's deliverance. Because of their prayers, Paul is filled with joy rather than anxiety. As Paul teaches, prayer is the sure cure for anxiety (4:6).

The answer to the prayers of his partners is the *provision of the Spirit.* The word *provision* bears the connotation of generous provision, as can be seen from its use in the cognate verb form in a first-century papyrus document where a man makes a complaint against his wife: "I for my part *provided* for my wife in a manner that exceeded my resources."[154] This man's use of this word "provided" was probably derived from the language of marriage contracts, which contain the same word to stipulate the responsibility to "supply" the needs of a spouse.[155] Paul uses the verb form of the word *provision* when he says that God "supplies" his Spirit (Gal 3:5). That parallel with our text indicates that the *provision of the Spirit* referred to here is not something that the Spirit gives, but the provision is the Spirit.[156] In re-

150. Gnilka, 65-66; Collange, 57; O'Brien, 110.

151. The singular form of *prayer* (δεήσεως) should be taken as a distributive singular with the plural pronoun *your: your prayers.*

152. Since one preposition and one article introduce both nouns *(prayer . . . provision),* both nouns are to be considered as parts of a unified whole.

153. In 1:4 and 1:19, Paul uses the same word to denote an "urgent request to meet a need, exclusively addressed to God" (BDAG, 211).

154. MM, 251, citing P. Oxy. 2.282 (dated A.D. 30-35).

155. Ibid.

156. The debate here centers on the ambiguous grammatical construction: in the phrase the *provision of the Spirit,* the word *Spirit* is in the genitive case. When the genitive case is used with a verbal noun such as *provision,* the genitive may be a subjective genitive: the word in the genitive case serves as a subject of the verbal aspect of the noun (the Spirit provides). Or the genitive case may be an objective genitive: the word in the genitive case

sponse to the prayers of Paul's partners, God gave the Spirit to be with Paul and to empower Paul.[157] A significant parallel in the words of Jesus confirms this connection between prayer and the gift of the Spirit: "If you then, though you are evil, know how to give good gifts to your children, how much more will your Father in heaven give the Holy Spirit to those who ask him!" (Luke 11:13).

The Spirit is the *Spirit of Jesus Christ.* The presence of the Spirit is the presence of Christ himself.[158] The declaration of Paul in the next sentence *(For to me, to live is Christ!)* shows that Paul is thinking of the presence of Christ when he refers to the *Spirit of Christ Jesus.* Paul knows that he is not alone in prison; he will not stand on trial alone; and if he is sentenced to die, he will not suffer and die alone. He counts on the prayers of his friends and the presence of the Spirit of Jesus Christ to fill the darkness of his prison with light and to turn his trial into deliverance.

20 Paul's knowledge of his deliverance is confirmed by what he has come to *eagerly expect and hope.* By speaking of the future in terms of expectation and hope, Paul does not mean to communicate any uncertainty or anxiety. Just as the pairing of expectation and hope in Romans 8:19-25 indicates a confident expectation of what will surely come to pass, so also in this context Paul combines these two words to emphasize his certainty that the future is essentially guaranteed.

What Paul so eagerly expects is expressed in negative and positive terms. First, in negative terms, Paul expects that he *will in no way be ashamed.* As shameful as imprisonment and execution were in the Roman world, that was not Paul's concern. He has already explained how his chains became a way to advance the gospel. And at the end of this sentence, he dismisses death itself as an obstacle to his mission. The shame Paul hoped to avoid had nothing to do with his personal reputation or the verdict at his trial. His sense of shame was directly connected to God's gracious appointment to defend the gospel (1:7, 16). He would be ashamed if he did or said anything that was not consistent with the proclamation of Jesus Christ.

Paul's focus on the proclamation of Christ comes into sharper focus in the positive side of his expectation, that he *will have sufficient courage so that now as always Christ will be exalted in my body.* The word *courage* refers to outspokenness, frankness, and boldness of speech, especially in the presence of a person of high rank.[159] Paul is eager to take his stand in the Roman

---

serves as the object of the verbal aspect of the noun (the Spirit is the provision). In support of the former, see O'Brien, 111-12. In support of the latter, see Fee, 133; Bockmuehl, 84.

157. TNIV adds *God's* to the text to modify *provision,* on the basis that the *provision of the Spirit* is *God's provision.*

158. Here again the ambiguous genitive case leaves room for various interpretations. The genitive case of Jesus Christ may mean that Jesus sent the Spirit or that Jesus is the Spirit. O'Brien, 112, supports the former; Fee, 134, supports the latter.

159. BDAG, 781.

court and defend the gospel. He believes that he has a divine appointment to do so. He knows that the prayers of his partners and the presence of the Spirit of Jesus Christ will empower him to speak with such boldness before the Roman tribunal that Christ will be exalted. That is the *deliverance* that Paul expects. God's salvation will be experienced in the *now* and in the *body.* What Paul is talking about in this context is neither a salvation from execution nor a salvation in heaven, but a salvation of the Spirit of Christ in the present, an empowering to be a bold witness for Christ his Lord. Paul is aware that his trial may be his last and greatest witness for Christ in his *body.* In fact, his witness may cause his execution. Nevertheless, Paul's goal in life is the exaltation of Christ, *whether by life or by death.* Paul's hope of salvation is that *now as always Christ will be exalted in my body.*

21 After asserting his eager expectation that Christ will be glorified in his body, whether by life or by death (v. 20), Paul now affirms what living and dying mean to him. The personal pronoun at the beginning of the sentence *(For me)* emphasizes the intensely personal nature of his affirmations. His bedrock convictions are set forth in the form of forceful, epigrammatic exclamations. English translations do not capture the rhetorical power of his words. But the reader can hear the drumbeat repetition of the same sounds in a transliteration.

to zēn — Christos	to live — Christ
to apothanein — kerdos	to die — gain

Paul's own heartbeats are heard in the rhythm of these words.

To live — Christ! The absence of a verb may be filled in many ways: to live is Christ; to live means Christ; to live depends on Christ; to live honors Christ. The foundation, center, purpose, direction, power, and meaning of Paul's life is Christ. Certainly, life so transformed and empowered by Christ is life on a higher level and of a different quality than common, ordinary human life. Yet, Paul repeatedly defines the kind of life he has in view as life *in my body* (v. 20) and life "in the flesh" (vv. 22, 24). Paul is not referring merely to his inner spiritual life, his private religious life, or his future eternal life. Life *in the body* and "in the flesh" is the outward expression of everyday earthly life in words and works. In the previous section, Paul is focused on the proclamation of Christ (vv. 15-20); in the next sentence he speaks of *fruitful labor.* His fruitful labor of proclaiming Christ is the outward expression of the life of Christ in his body and in his flesh.

Barth says that the meaning of life in verse 21 is not the same as life in the body (v. 20) or life in the flesh (vv. 22 and 24). In Barth's interpretation, "The life of Paul of which verses 20 and 22 speak has according to verse 21 been checkmated, so to speak, (although it is still there on the board) by *another* life. This other life is Christ himself."[160] Barth's analogy of a chess

160. Barth, 37.

game pictures the life of Paul and the life of Christ as opposing sides: Paul is checkmated by Christ. Although Paul does confess later that he was arrested by Christ (3:12), his claim here is that every aspect of his present, bodily, earthly existence is completely permeated by Christ. Instead of using the picture of chess to interpret Paul, it would be more helpful to use his own image of bearing fruit in his work (v. 22). The life of Paul is not opposed to the life of Christ, as in a game of chess. But as a tree depends totally on water, earth, and sun to bear fruit, so Paul depended totally on the life of Christ to bear fruit.

Taken as a definition of his life, the declaration — *to live is Christ* — implies perfection. If it is always and totally true that every breath, every movement, every thought of life is Christ, then not one aspect or moment of life would be lived apart from Christ. That would be perfection: life perfectly empowered by and conformed to Christ. But later Paul emphatically denies perfection: "Not that I have already obtained all this, or have already been made perfect" (3:12, NIV). The declaration — *to live is Christ* — expresses the meaning and goal of Paul's life. But that meaning and goal have yet to be fully realized. He desires to know Christ and be conformed to Christ (3:10). He presses on to take hold of that for which Christ Jesus took hold of him (3:12). *To live* is not a static position but a dynamic process of becoming and growing. For Paul the purpose of living is pressing forward to know and serve Christ each day.

When the goal of living is Christ, then living inevitably follows the way of Christ, the way of self-giving, self-humbling, and self-sacrifice (2:5-8). This way of living is not an escape from suffering. Paul writes that living is Christ while he is in chains for preaching the gospel. For Paul the reality that living is Christ meant that he considered *everything a loss because of the surpassing worth of knowing Christ,* and, in fact, Paul had lost all things and considered them rubbish, in order that he might *gain Christ* (3:8).

Gaining Christ more than covers any loss incurred for the sake of Christ, even the loss of life itself. If *to live is Christ,* then *to die is gain.* The word *gain* means something advantageous, a profit.[161] Since Paul uses the same word for *gain* here in 1:21 *(to die is gain)* as he does in 3:8 *(that I may gain Christ),* he appears to be saying that the gain of dying is Christ. He says as much in verse 23: *I desire to depart and be with Christ.* According to one common interpretation of this expression in verse 23, Paul's aspiration of knowing Christ more fully in the process of living would be completely fulfilled when he enjoyed the immediate presence of Christ after death.

Another way of interpreting the word *gain* builds on the use of this word in classical literature to express the relief that death brings from the pain of living. In Sophocles' play, Antigone says, "Whoever lives in as many ills as I — how does this one not get *gain* by dying."[162] Paul's life was

161. BDAG, 541.

162. Sophocles, *Antigone* 463-64; D. W. Palmer, "'To Die Is Gain,'" *NovT* 17 (1975),

so marked by suffering that he might be expected to view death as a way to escape the agony of life. That was a common view of death in his Hellenistic culture. Hawthorne says that Paul's words *(to die is gain)* "are the words of a very human Paul giving vent to a very human and universal sentiment: death is a gain to those whose life has become weighed down with well-nigh unbearable burdens."[163] But to view death as an escape from a painful life does not seem to be the perspective of Paul. He constantly asserts in this letter that his painful life is a joyful life since it is centered in Christ. Dying is gain, not because it is an escape from life, but because it leads to union with Christ, the goal of life.

Since Christ is the goal of life, dying is gain if it is a way of bearing witness to Christ. Paul expected that Christ would be exalted in his body, *whether by life or death* (1:20). If Christ was exalted in his body by his death, then his death was definitely a gain. As Martin notes, "The gain, then, is not only the apostle's own receiving of his heavenly reward in the presence of the Master (verse 23), but the promotion of the gospel in the witness which his fearless martyrdom for Christ will produce."[164] As Paul felt the weight of his chains and faced his imminent execution, he was overwhelmed not by the pain but by the gain of suffering and death. Paul viewed his suffering and death as a gain for the advance of the gospel because he expected that this death would be his final and most effective witness for Christ.[165]

This view of the martyr's death as the ultimate witness to the faith of the martyr is eloquently expressed in Jewish literature of Paul's day. 4 Maccabees picks up the martyrdom stories in 2 Maccabees and develops them rhetorically and philosophically to demonstrate that the death of righteous Jews under Antiochus Epiphanes (second century B.C.) was their ultimate witness to their faith in God and their devotion to the law. As Eleazar's flesh was burning away to bone, he prayed, "You know, O God, that though I could have saved myself I am dying in these fiery torments for the sake of the Law."[166] Early Christian martyrs also viewed their death as a gain because it gave them the opportunity to follow in the way of Christ and confess their faith in Christ. Early in the second century, Ignatius, bishop of Antioch in Syria, wrote seven letters on his way to his death as a martyr in Rome. He clearly states one of his reasons for writing: "I am writing to all the churches and am insisting to everyone that I die for God of my own free will — unless you hinder me. . . . Let me be food for the wild beasts. . . . then I will truly be a disciple of Jesus Christ. . . . It is better

---

203-18, presents a list of quotations from classical literature that view death as gain since it is a release from the pains and burdens of life.

163. Hawthorne, 45.

164. Martin, 76.

165. Bockmuehl, 89.

166. 4 Macc 6:27.

for me to die for Jesus Christ than to rule over the ends of the earth. . . . Allow me to be an imitator of the suffering of my God."[167]

The death of martyrs for Christ throughout the history of the church has been viewed as a great gain for the proclamation of the gospel. For example, Don Cormack's account of the church in Cambodia cites a letter from one of the church leaders on the eve of the horrific reign of terror by the Khmer Rouge.[168]

> Phnom Penh
> April 4, 1975
>
> My dear friends,
>
> "For me to live is Christ and to die is gain." Please pray that this will be worked out in my life.
>
> Your brother in Christ,
> Tiang Chhirc

Cormack comments:

> It was his final prayer request. Would we watch and pray with him in this moment of agony? He had underscored the word "die" three times. The Lord answered his prayer. In life he was one who lived single-mindedly for Christ. And in dying a martyr's death, making the ultimate sacrifice, he bore compelling witness to his Lord; and so it was not a waste, but a gain for the Cambodian church, and for the beloved Chhirc, those tears all wiped away now, joy in the immediate presence of his Lord.

This account of the gain of a martyr's death in the twentieth century echoes what Paul meant by the gain of death: gain for the glory of Christ through proclaiming Christ in dying a martyr's death. Though Paul's letter is not a manual on martyrdom or promoting martyrdom,[169] his words here have provided needed encouragement and inspiration for many facing a martyr's death.

22 Paul's reflection on living and dying leads him to consider a perplexing question: *If I am to go on living in the body, this will mean fruitful labor for me. Yet what shall I choose? I do not know!* What makes the choice between life and death so difficult is the benefit of each: living means *fruitful labor;* dying means to *be with Christ* (1:23). When Paul contemplates the real possibility that he may not be executed, but be released and continue to live, he is not in doubt about the positive consequence of "remaining in the flesh" (my

167. Ignatius, *Romans* 4–6.

168. Don Cormack, *Killing Fields, Living Fields: An Unfinished Portrait of the Cambodian Church — The Church That Would Not Die* (Crowborough: MARC, 1997), 155.

169. Against E. Lohmeyer, 57-59.

literal translation from the Greek). His reference to "remaining in the flesh" (TNIV, *living in the body*) in this context does not focus on the sinful connotations of "flesh" that often give a totally negative meaning to the word "flesh" in other contexts in his letters. For example, Paul told the Roman Christians that living according to the flesh leads to death (Rom 8:13). The works of the flesh listed in Galatians 5:19-21 are the most heinous sins. In Philippians 1:22, however, the words "living in the flesh" (my lit. trans.; TNIV, *living in the body*) simply means a continuation of his physical life.[170] In this context "living in the flesh" produces fruitful work, not sinful works. Paul is sure about the consequence of a continuation of his physical life. If he is allowed to continue living in the flesh, *this will mean fruitful labor for me.*[171] Paul has already asserted that *to live is Christ* (1:21). Now he describes the nature of that life: it is physical life (in the flesh), and it is a life of *fruitful labor.* What an amazing expression of enthusiasm for life! Paul did not say that this life is so wretched and so worthless that it would be better to die in order to escape its endless toil and drudgery. He did not list all the physical ailments and the emotional turmoil that he would surely have to endure if he continued to live. Just the opposite: Paul was totally confident that *this life,* this physical life, *means fruitful labor.* When Paul thought about the possibility of continuing to live, he focused on fruit, harvest, and profit. He knew that the great harvest of fruit that he would reap was produced by work. In the immediate context, the work Paul has in mind is that of proclaiming the gospel in the world (1:18) and of strengthening the faith of the church (1:25). But Paul emphasizes in this letter that God is at work in and through all our work: the God *who began a good work in you will carry it on to completion* (1:6), and God is the one *who works in you to will and to act to fulfill his good purpose* (2:13). Paul did not view his work as a grim duty or burdensome obligation, but as the fruitful out-flowing of God's faithful in-working.

This prospect of reaping the fruit of changed lives by participating in the gracious work of God makes continuing to live so attractive that Paul is genuinely perplexed: *Yet what shall I choose? I do not know!* When the *gain (kerdos)* of dying is compared to the *fruit (karpos)* of living, it is difficult to tell what the best alternative is. The question does not indicate that Paul actually has the power to choose life or death or that he is trying to make up his mind whether to petition God for life or death. Paul is asking himself a rhetorical question as he faces the possible alternatives before him. To his own question, *what shall I choose?*[172] he answers, *I do not know.*

170. BDAG, 914-16.

171. Hawthorne suggests that "if" really conveys the causal sense of "since" (47). But Paul appears to be using the "if" clause here in a process of logical reasoning about the alternatives of living and dying (see BDF §372.2.b), not as a statement of his assumption that he will live. So he first states the real possibility *(if I am to go on living in the body),* then the logical consequence of that possibility *(this will mean fruitful labor for me).*

172. "I prefer" is better than I *choose* as a translation of αἱρήσομαι in this context. See BDAG, 28.

In all the other seventeen uses of the verb *I know* in Paul's letters, this word means to "make known, reveal."[173] Although most translations make an exception to normal usage by translating the verb as *know*,[174] it is more likely that the meaning here is the same as in all the other NT uses: "I cannot make known." Paul is simply leading his readers step by step through his own process of thinking about the alternatives of life and death. At this point in the process, he admits that he is genuinely bewildered by the question of his own preference. Therefore, he "cannot make known" to himself or to his readers whether he will prefer life or death.

23 Paul now restates and describes in more depth the nature of his dilemma as he faces the real possibilities of his own death and the continuation of his life. *I am torn between the two,* he exclaims. The verb *I am torn* depicts the pressure of crowds "pressing against" Jesus (Luke 8:45), the siege of Jerusalem when her enemies "hem" her "in" on every side (Luke 19:43), and the controlling power of a high fever (Luke 4:38) or fear (Luke 8:37). Paul uses this word to convey the compelling and controlling force of Christ's love in his life (2 Cor 5:14).[175] In this text, the verb vividly portrays the strong inward pressures Paul feels from two conflicting desires: his desire to be with Christ by dying, and his desire to serve the needs of Christians by living.

First, he explains why he desires to die: *I desire to depart and be with Christ, which is better by far.* His *desire* for death is expressed with a term connoting a "great desire for something, longing and craving."[176] Paul used this word to speak of the intense cravings of the sinful human nature, the lust of the flesh (Gal 5:16).[177] The same word is used in a positive sense to express his strong desire to see believers face to face (1 Thess 2:17). And in this text Paul employs the word *desire* to express the intense longing he has *to depart and be with Christ.*

With his use of the metaphor *to depart,* Paul speaks of his own death with a common Greek euphemism for death.[178] The same word was used as a nautical term in Greek literature to describe a ship setting loose from its mooring or hoisting its anchor.[179] This euphemistic way of referring to his death does not necessarily carry with it the Greek metaphysical concept of the soul departing from the body. The context does not warrant importing

173. The verb occurs twenty-six times in the NT, eighteen times in Paul's letters. The meaning in all cases outside of this text is to "cause information to become known, make known, reveal" (BDAG, 203).

174. Also, BDAG (203) gives *know* as the meaning only in this one NT text, with support from extrabiblical Greek texts.

175. BDAG, 971.

176. BDAG, 372.

177. In the Pauline letters ἐπιθυμία is used to denote inordinate craving and lust in 1 Thess 4:5; Gal 5:16, 24; Rom 1:24; 6:12; 7:7, 8; Eph 2:3; 4:22; Col 3:5; 1 Tim 6:9; 2 Tim 2:22; 3:6; 4:3; Tit 2:12; 3:3.

178. BDAG, 67.

179. LSJ, 112.

Platonic philosophy into Paul's simple, metaphorical expression. Paul links his death *(to depart)* to his union with Christ — *to be with Christ.* The way both infinitives *(to depart . . . to be)* share one article in the Greek unites the two together. When Paul thinks of his death, he thinks of his union with Christ.

One way of understanding Paul's anticipation of being *with Christ* is to take this expression as a reference to his after-death experience. Death is the gateway to eternal union with Christ. What the after-death experience of being with Christ actually entails is the subject of two millennia of theological reflection. Is this after-death experience a conscious, personal fellowship with Christ in a bodiless, intermediate state between death and the future resurrection of the body? Is this after-death experience an unconscious soul-sleep with Christ until the awakening and bodily resurrection at the return of Christ? Does this after-death experience lead instantaneously to the resurrection of the body in the transcendent, eternal realm even though the resurrection of the dead is still future in temporal terms on earth? These and many related questions have been extensively debated in the long history of the interpretation of the simple phrase, *to depart and be with Christ.*

Paul's confidence in another context that "to be away from the body" means "to be at home with the Lord" (2 Cor 5:8) can certainly be heard in the expression of his desire in Philippians 1:23, *to depart and be with Christ.* The context of this phrase in Philippians, however, has a somewhat different focus. Paul is speaking primarily here about being *with Christ* in death, not only after death. He introduced his reflections on life and death by expressing his hope that *Christ will be exalted in my body, whether by life or by death* (1:20). He desires that his visible bodily death will be a witness to his invisible union with Christ. Paul is reflecting on the meaning of his death. He finds meaning in his death by focusing on the death of Christ. In his great hymn on Christ (2:6-11), Paul emphasizes the death of Christ by a twofold repetition: Christ *became obedient to death — even death on a cross!* (2:8). Paul views his own death as a special union with Christ: *the participation in his sufferings, becoming like him in his death* (3:10). In the conclusion of the passage where Paul links his death to being with Christ (1:23), he assures his readers that it has also been granted to them *on behalf of Christ not only to believe on him, but also to suffer for him* (1:29). In fact, they are *going through the same struggle* as Paul (1:30). Paul's way of dealing with the suffering in his life and in the life of all believers is not only by focusing on the great escape from suffering that comes after death, but also by focusing on communion *with Christ* and witness *for him* in suffering and in death. Barth captures this meaning of Paul's reflection on death: "The *analysai* [to depart], the departure and leave taking in order to die, means 'gain' because it means a perfect *syn Christō einai,* a 'being with Christ' now also in the death of the body, in dying with him — because Christ's 'being magnified' in the bodily life of his people is crowned by his taking them up also into this *einai syn autō* [*to be with him*], into the fellowship of his death (cf. 3:10)."[180]

Although the complete phrase *to be with Christ* occurs only in this text (1:23), a similar use of the preposition *with,* with Christ, Jesus, or the Lord, or of the pronoun "him" occurs eleven other times in Paul's letters.

"God will bring *with* Jesus those who have fallen asleep in him" (1 Thess 4:14)
"we will be *with* the Lord forever" (1 Thess 4:17)
"whether we are awake or asleep, we may live together *with* him" (1 Thess 5:10)
"the one who raised the Lord Jesus from the dead will also raise us *with* Jesus" (2 Cor 4:14)
"by God's power we will live *with* him in our dealing with you" (2 Cor 13:4)
"we died *with* Christ" (Rom 6:8)
"He who did not spare his own Son, but gave him up for us all — how will he not also, along *with* him, graciously give us all things?" (Rom 8:32)
"God made you alive *with* Christ" (Col 2:13)
"Since you died *with* Christ" (Col 2:20)
"For you died, and your life is now hidden *with* Christ in God" (Col 3:3)
"When Christ, who is your life, appears, then you also will appear *with* him in glory" (Col 3:4)

Paul also communicates the same concept of union with Christ by adding the preposition *with* to words to form new compound words.

Buried *with* (Rom 6:4; Col 2:12)
United *with* (Rom 6:5)
Crucified *with* (Rom 6:6; Gal 2:20)
Live *with* (Rom 6:7)
Heirs *with* (Rom 8:17)
Suffer *with* (Rom 8:17)
Glorify *with* (Rom 8:17)
Have the same form *with* (Rom 8:29; Phil 3:21)
Be conformed *with* (Phil 3:10)

A study of the twelve prepositional phrases and the nine compound words shows that the preposition *with* points to participation *with* Christ in the redemptive events of his suffering, crucifixion, burial, resurrection, and glorification. Participation *with* Christ in his redemptive events is ef-

180. Barth, 38.

fected through faith and baptism (Rom 6:4-8). Through baptism the believer in Christ becomes a participant in the story of Christ. The believer already participates in the past redemptive events with Christ (suffered with, crucified with, died with, raised with, live with) and eagerly anticipates participation in the future redemptive events with Christ (raised with, glorified with, heirs with, live with forever). If 1 Thessalonians 4:17 ("we will be with the Lord forever") is truly the closest parallel to Philippians 1:23, then both these texts point to future, eternal communion with Christ.[181] This interpretation then seeks to explain how Paul reconciled his reference to communion with Christ after death (Phil 1:23) with his reference to communion with Christ after the *parousia*, the return of Christ (1 Thess 4:17).[182] But the two different contexts of Philippians 1:23 and 1 Thessalonians 4:17 indicate that these texts are not exactly parallel. In the immediate context of Philippians 1:23, Paul is focusing on his suffering and execution, not on the *parousia* of Christ as in 1 Thessalonians 4:17. He sees his suffering and death as participation with Christ in Christ's suffering and death. His focus in 1:23 is explicitly expressed in 3:10: *participation in his sufferings, becoming like him in his death.* This last phrase *(becoming like him in his death)* contains one of Paul's compound words built on the preposition *with.* This compound word indicates that Paul wanted to be made into the same form *with* Christ as Christ was in his death. The form of Christ in his death is defined by Paul in the Christ hymn: "taking the form of a servant . . . he humbled himself and became obedient unto death, even death on a cross!" (2:7-8). Paul defines the meaning of his own death by looking at the cross of Christ. When he looked at the cross of Christ, Paul thought, "That is my destiny! As Christ embraced the cross in humble obedience to God, so I desire to embrace my death as a witness to my union *with* Christ."

Paul anticipates that his union *with* Christ in death will *be better by far.* The superiority of death over life is often interpreted in the light of the view that Paul is looking forward to eternal communion with Christ after death. The future face-to-face communion with Christ after death far surpasses even the present joy of life in Christ in the flesh. Other texts in Paul's letters leave no doubt that Paul eagerly anticipated being with Christ after death. In 2 Corinthians 5:8, he confidently asserts his expectation of communion with Christ after death: "Yes, we do have confidence, and we would rather be away from the body and at home with the Lord." The context for this expression of confidence in his eternal "home with the Lord" is an extended contrast between the temporal and eternal (2 Cor 2:13–5:10). Paul knows that "if the earthly tent we live in is destroyed, we have a building from God, a house not made with hands, eternal in the heavens" (2 Cor 5:1). In his development of this contrast between the temporary

181. So O'Brien, 132.
182. O'Brien, 135-36.

earthly life and the eternal heavenly life, Paul emphatically asserts his belief in the certainty of his eternal home with Christ.

Paul's focus in Philippians 1:12-30, however, is somewhat different from that in 2 Corinthians 5. As he writes to the Philippians, he is in chains and faces the real possibility of execution. As he reflects on the significance of his suffering and death, he realizes that suffering is a grace given to him and all believers (1:29), and he accepts his own death as *gain, better by far* than continuing to live in the flesh "because it is the final, consummate act in which Christ can be glorified in his bodily life."[183] Paul makes a positive evaluation of death as a gain because it is the way to know Christ, to share in the sufferings of Christ, and to become like Christ in his death (3:10), and the way for Christ to be glorified in his body (1:20).

Such a positive view of suffering and death would have been helpful for Paul's first-century readers who were also facing persecution and possible execution for their faith in Christ. They would have been reassured that their suffering and death were not meaningless tragedy, but an eloquent witness to the reality of their union with Christ. But what application does Paul's positive view of his death have for his twenty-first-century readers? Many twenty-first-century readers have experiences similar to Paul's: they face intense persecution and even martyrdom. They will be encouraged by Paul's words to believe that the Lord will be with them in the valley of the shadow of death. Others face no threat of persecution; they have every expectation of living a long, healthy, relatively pain-free life. But even though they are not in prison facing execution for their faith, they can be inspired by the courageous faith of Paul and many like him throughout the history of the church. When we see how others followed Christ through suffering and even martyrdom, we are challenged to be faithful to Christ in our own lives.

24 Although Paul desired to depart and be with Christ since that is *better by far,* he reassures his readers that *it is more necessary for you that I remain in the body.* Paul was willing to delay crossing the finish line in his own race in order to serve the needs of the believers in Philippi. He set aside his personal ambition so that he could do what was necessary for them. Serving the community outweighs individual desires. Remaining *in the body* (literally, "flesh") for the *progress and joy* (see v. 25) of others is more necessary than sacrificing the body in death as the ultimate witness to Christ. Paul's willingness to postpone his own goal to promote the welfare of others exhibits the self-emptying, self-humbling character of Christ (2:6-8).[184]

25 Paul's insight that remaining in the flesh was best for the believers led him to his conviction that he would stay alive and continue his service to them: *Convinced of this, I know that I will remain, and I will continue*

183. Barth, 41.

184. N. Clayton Croy, "'To Die Is Gain' (Philippians 1:19-26): Does Paul Contemplate Suicide?" *JBL* 122.3 (2003), 531: "Since Paul's rhetorical contemplation and eventual rejection of personal advantage occur in ch. 1, they effectively prepare for the Christ hymn in ch. 2."

with all of you for your progress and joy in the faith. At first it seems strangely contradictory to hear Paul emphatically express his strong conviction that he will continue living just after he has said that he did not know whether to choose life or death (v. 22). But as we follow the process of his thought, we can see how he reached this conviction. When he reflected on exalting Christ in his body by life or by death (vv. 20-23), he questioned whether he would choose life or death. He carefully weighed the benefits of each as a way to glorify Christ. Life meant fruitful work; death meant union with Christ in his sufferings and death. When he reached the point in his thinking where he clearly saw the real need for him to continue his work on behalf of the church (v. 24), the question of life or death was answered. He became *convinced* that he would continue to live so that he could continue to serve. The purpose of his continued service was *for your progress and joy in the faith.* Here we see Paul's concise definition of the need he saw in the life of these believers. They *all* needed to experience *progress and joy in the faith.* The words *progress* and *joy* are united as twin objects of the same preposition *(for),* and they are both modified by the phrase *in the faith.* Real progress in the faith will result in genuine joy in the faith. Progress without joy is spurious; joy without progress is counterfeit.

By the word *faith,* Paul could mean the subjective process of believing in Christ (see v. 29: *believe on him*) or the objective content of belief (see v. 27: *the faith of the gospel*). Since both meanings are found in the immediate context, Paul could have both in mind when he speaks of progress in the faith. His goal is to assist *all* believers to make solid progress in learning to trust Christ and in standing firm together to contend for the faith of the gospel. *Joy in the faith* will be the evidence of their *progress* in the faith. Just as Paul's life was characterized by joy (v. 18), so he expected that their lives would be characterized by joy.

26 Paul states his ultimate objective for his return visit to the church in Philippi: *that through my being with you again your boasting in Christ Jesus will overflow on account of me.* The word *boasting (kauchēma),* translated as "joy" by NIV, really means taking pride in, exulting in, glorying in, and boasting in something or someone.[185] The same word refers to the pride Paul expects to have in the effective witness of the church as a result of his mission to them: *as you hold firmly to the word of life. . . . then I will be able to boast on the day of Christ that I did not run or labor in vain* (2:16). The verb form of this word occurs in Paul's vision of the church as those *who boast in Christ Jesus* (3:3). When Paul uses this word to express the purpose of his return visit, he places two prepositional phrases side by side: "in Christ Jesus in me" (1:26, my literal translation). TNIV translates these two phrases as *in Christ Jesus . . . on account of me.* The preposition *in* has various meanings, depending on the context.[186] In this context the repetition of the preposition

185. BDAG, 537.
186. BDAG, 326-30, lists twelve meanings for ἐν.

in may express both the object of boasting and the means by which boasting takes place. According to some interpreters, the first use of the preposition *in* points to the object of boasting (boasting *in* Christ Jesus) and the second refers to the means of boasting (boasting *on account of* Paul).[187] According to O'Brien, however, the first use of this preposition refers to the sphere of boasting (in union with Christ Jesus), and the second refers to the object of their pride (Paul and his mission). "The apostle asserts that the Philippians would have ample cause to exult, and that reason would be found in Paul himself — but it would all be in the sphere of Christ."[188] The NEB version captures this understanding of the prepositions: "so that when I am present with you again, your pride in me may be unbounded in Christ Jesus."

Both lines of interpretation agree that Christ is the ultimate reason for boasting and Paul's mission is the specific occasion for boasting. Paul's total identification of his life with Christ *(For to me, to live is Christ!)* means that boasting in Paul really leads to boasting in Christ, the source of Paul's life, and boasting in Christ leads to boasting in Paul, the faithful manifestation of Christ's life. Fee explains that "in cases such as this one, where the boast is 'in someone,' the boast is still 'in Christ.' What he has done in and for Paul serves as the ground for their 'glorying in Christ' and the sphere in which boasting overflows."[189]

Paul was convinced that it was necessary for him to be with the church in Philippi again so that they would boast in Christ Jesus and take pride in his mission. Paul's expectation of a return visit to Philippi presents a challenge to constructing a chronology of Paul's life. The view that Paul was writing from prison in Rome has to suppose that Paul changed his travel plans to make this return visit. Paul had not planned to return to the regions east of Rome. Before going to Rome, he wrote, "now there is no more place for me to work in these regions" (Rom 15:23). He thought that he had finished his ministry east of Rome and was committed to extend his ministry to Rome and even to Spain. But the possibility that Paul may have changed his plans can be supported by the evidence in 2 Corinthians 1:12-24 that Paul did in fact change other travel plans on other occasions. If Paul wrote from Caesarea, then it makes sense to suppose that he planned to visit Philippi after his release on his way to Rome. If Paul wrote this letter from Ephesus, then Paul's return visit to Philippi is documented by 2 Corinthians 1:12-24 and Acts 20:1-5. No matter what position one takes regarding the origin of Paul's letter to the Philippians, reasonable explanations can be given for Paul's plans to make a return visit to Philippi. The question of origin has to be decided on other bases than Paul's travel plans

187. Hawthorne, 52; Silva, 86; Bockmuehl, 95.

188. O'Brien, 141; Peterlin, *Paul's Letter to the Philippians,* 45-47; see also Lightfoot: "The first denotes the sphere in which their pride lives; the second the object on which it rests" (94).

189. Fee, 155.

and itineraries. Once that question is settled, then his travel plans can add to an understanding of his chronology.[190]

This verse on boasting in Christ and in Paul is an apt conclusion to Paul's report of his mission (1:12-26). His report emphasizes that his time in chains has served to advance the gospel: the whole palace guard is hearing about Christ; others are boldly proclaiming Christ; and Christ will be exalted by Paul, whether by life or by death. Therefore, there is no need to be ashamed of Paul's imprisonment. Instead everyone should take pride in all that is being accomplished by Paul, even while he is in chains. And everyone should give Christ all the glory for all that he has done in and through Paul.

IV. IMPERATIVES FOR CITIZENS WORTHY OF THE GOSPEL (1:27–2:18)

A. Stand Firm Together in Suffering (1:27-30)

> [27]*Whatever happens, as citizens of heaven live in a manner worthy of the gospel of Christ. Then, whether I come and see you or only hear about you in my absence, I will know that you stand firm in the one Spirit, striving together with one accord for the faith of the gospel* [28]*without being frightened in any way by those who oppose you. This is a sign to them that they will be destroyed, but that you will be saved — and that by God.* [29]*For it has been granted to you on behalf of Christ not only to believe on him, but also to suffer for him,* [30]*since you are going through the same struggle you saw I had, and now hear that I still have.*

27 After reporting that his own circumstances *served to advance the gospel* (1:12-26), Paul encourages his readers: *as citizens of heaven live in a manner worthy of the gospel of Christ.* Paul's autobiographical account serves to set the standard for his ethical imperatives. His testimony that his mission served *to advance the gospel* even while he was in chains is the basis of authority for his challenge to *live in a manner worthy of the gospel of Christ* in the face of opposition. The all-important link between the previous section and this one, between Paul's life and theirs, is the *gospel of Christ.* In the Greek text Paul begins this section with this focus: "only worthy of the gospel of Christ. . . ." The meaning of the first word, "only" (translated *whatever happens* by TNIV), is expressed in Barth's paraphrase, "Just one thing!"[191] All of Paul's imperatives are subsumed under just one thing, *the gospel of Christ.* Paul does not impose a long list of rules; he presents the

190. See the Introduction, 19-25.
191. Barth, 45.

person of Christ. The good news of Christ, the story of Christ, is the rule for the community of believers. That is why, at the center of this ethical section (1:27–2:18), Paul sets forth the narrative of Christ (2:6-11). The imperatives are based on the indicatives of who Christ is and what he has already done. The *gospel of Christ* proclaims that Jesus is the exalted Lord of all and that this Lord of all emptied himself, humbled himself, and was obedient unto death on a cross. The *gospel of Christ* provides the motive and the pattern for all Christian behavior.

The TNIV phrase — *as citizens of heaven live* — highlights the concept of citizenship in Paul's imperative *(politeuesthe).* The imperative *(politeuesthe)* literally means "to be citizens" or to "discharge your obligations as citizens."[192] The verb is built on the noun *polis* ("city") and connotes the political duties of citizens of a city.[193] Paul's use of this political word only here in all of his letters was probably inspired by the pride of Roman citizenship in the Roman colony of Philippi. Residents of this colony enjoyed the privilege and responsibility of living under the protection of Roman law.[194] Paul appeals to this sense of civic pride in his directive to live as good citizens.

A major question in the interpretation of Paul's command is whether Paul is referring to heavenly citizenship, Roman citizenship, or both. Although the word *heaven* is not included in Paul's imperative, the TNIV's insertion of this word is derived from Paul's explicit assertion in 3:20 that "our citizenship is in heaven."[195] Bruce Winter, however, argues that Paul's focus in Philippians 1:27 is "the civic responsibility of Christians in the public place."[196] Winter asserts that "Paul's use of a cognate in Phil. 3:20 does not influence the translation of the verb in 1:27."[197] Hawthorne combines the insights of both of these positions by interpreting Paul's direction to be good citizens in the context of the dual citizenship of the Philippians. To *live as citizens in a manner worthy of the gospel of Christ* means to live as "a good citizen of an earthly state" and "as a good citizen

192. BDAG, 846.

193. The political connotation of this word is omitted by major English versions: KJV, RSV, NRSV, NIV, NASV.

194. Acts recounts the significance of Paul's own appeal to his Roman citizenship in Philippi (Acts 16:37-39).

195. For a defense of the position that Paul is referring to heavenly citizenship in 1:27, see Timothy C. Geoffrion, *The Rhetorical Purpose and the Political and Military Character of Philippians: A Call to Stand Firm* (Lewiston, N.Y.: Mellen Biblical Press, 1993), 48.

196. Winter, *Seek the Welfare of the City,* 85. For interpretations of the term πολιτεύεσθε *(live as citizens),* see also R. R. Brewer, "The Meaning of *politeuesthe* in Philippians 1:27," *JBL* 73 (1954), 76-83; E. C. Miller, "Πολιτεύεσθε in Philippians 1.27: Some Philological and Thematic Observations," *JSNT* 15 (1982), 86-96. Brewer interprets the term in its Greco-Roman context as a reference to living as citizens of Philippi. Miller interprets πολιτεύεσθε in the light of Hellenistic Jewish writings as a reference to living as the true Israel: "See to it that you are the true Israel, people who live not according to Torah, but who live a life worthy of the new law which is the Gospel about the Christ who is Jesus" (94).

197. Winter, *Seek the Welfare of the City,* 103 n. 45.

of this new state," the heavenly commonwealth.[198] Hawthorne's interpretation rightly appreciates the full range of Paul's concern in this section. Paul wants members of the church to be united (1:27; 2:2) so that they will "shine like stars" in the midst of their "crooked and depraved generation" (2:15). Their good conduct as citizens in their heavenly colony, the church, will be a brilliant witness in their life as citizens in Philippi, the Roman colony. Paul's report that his own life *served to advance the gospel* in Caesar's household (1:12-13) prepared the way for his challenge to *citizens of heaven to live in a manner worthy of the gospel* in Caesar's colony. Paul's imperative calls for Christians to be good citizens, worthy of the gospel of Christ, as members of a colony within a colony.[199] Paul's concept of dual citizenship can be conveyed by an expanded paraphrase: As good citizens of Philippi and as good citizens of heaven, live in a manner worthy of the gospel of Christ!

After the imperative to *live as citizens in a manner worthy of the gospel of Christ,* Paul slips in a parenthetical phrase: *whether I come and see you or only hear about you in my absence, I will know.* This phrase reminds the Philippians of his own expectation to visit Philippi soon (1:26; see also 2:24) and anticipates the announcement of his plan to send Timothy to Philippi to give him the latest news about the church in Philippi (2:19). Paul is informing the Philippians that he will know about them either by his own personal inspection of them or at least by an oral report about them. Paul is not threatening them with this phrase. He anticipates that he will *be cheered* (2:19) by news about them. Nevertheless, by reminding the Philippians that his personal relationship with them gives him knowledge of their conduct, Paul is making them accountable to him. One way or another, he will be checking on them to see how they are doing. He knew that imperatives without personal accountability do not transform the way we live.

After the parenthetical phrase, Paul defines three specific aspects of their life as citizens: (1) *that you stand firm in the one Spirit,* (2) *striving together with one accord for the faith of the gospel* (3) *without being frightened in any way by those who oppose you.* These three phrases unpack the obligations of good citizenship. The direction to *stand firm* translates a Greek verb that means "to be firmly committed in conviction."[200] To *stand firm* was not easy in the hostile environment that Paul describes. He speaks in the same sentence of opposition, suffering, and struggle.[201] The Christians in Philippi needed to persevere in their commitment to Christ when adversaries attacked them for their faith in Christ. Such hostility was intended to destroy

198. Hawthorne, 56.

199. Bockmuehl, 98: "Philippi may be a colony enjoying the personal imperial patronage of Lord Caesar, but the church at Philippi is a personal colony of Christ the Lord above all."

200. BDAG, 944; although the verb is in the indicative mood in 1:27 in the context of indirect speech, its association with the imperative, *live as citizens,* gives it imperatival force.

201. 1:27-30 is one sentence in the Greek text.

their faith and divide them from each other. At this point Paul does not focus on the identity of the opposition, but on an essential element of Christian faith: the unshakeable determination to *stand firm*. Christians must not flee, compromise, give in, back down, or be divided when they face hostile opposition. The command to *stand firm* was "used to indicate the duty of the soldier in battle, or to describe the taking of a position vis-à-vis that of an adversary."[202] Like soldiers on a battlefield, they must not yield an inch of ground no matter how hard their adversaries press against them. The importance of standing firm is stressed by Paul's repetition of his demand to stand firm at the end of this letter (4:1).[203]

The ability to *stand firm* is found *in the one Spirit*. By capitalizing *Spirit*, the TNIV indicates that Paul is referring to the Holy Spirit. Translations of this phrase as *one spirit* (without the capitalization of *spirit*) imply that Paul is referring to the human spirit or the community spirit. Some commentators support this interpretation of *one spirit* as an anthropological term on the basis that there is a synonymous parallelism between *one spirit* in this phrase and "one soul" in the next phrase.[204] If there is a synonymous parallelism between these two terms, *one spirit* and "one soul," then the meaning of the first term, *one spirit*, is explained by the second term, "one soul." But the premise that there is a parallelism between these two terms and that this parallelism is synonymous is an unwarranted assumption.[205] There are good reasons to take the term *spirit* as a reference to the Holy Spirit.[206] First, the closest parallel to the phrase *stand firm in the one Spirit* is found in 4:1: *stand firm in the Lord*. This parallel in 4:1 shows that Paul looks to the Lord for the ability to *stand firm*. Second, Paul's references in the immediate context to the *provision of the Spirit of Jesus Christ* (1:19) and *common sharing in the Spirit* (2:1) are evidence that Paul's use of the term *Spirit* in this context points to his confidence in God's *Spirit*, not the human *spirit*, for deliverance (1:19) and unity (2:1-4). Third, the use of exactly the same phrase, *in one Spirit*, in two other Pauline letters (1 Cor 12:13; Eph 2:18) clearly refers to the "believers' common experience of the one Spirit as the basis for unity."[207] So when Paul directs Christians in Philippi to *stand firm in one Spirit*, he is at the same time reassuring them that *the one Spirit* of God is their source of power to remain united and unshakeable in the face of opposition. Unity *in the one Spirit* is the gift of God, not the achievement of the

202. See Geoffrion, *The Rhetorical Purpose and the Political and Military Character of Philippians*, 55, for examples from Greek literature.

203. See also the same command to *stand firm* in 2 Thess 2:15; 1 Cor 16:13; Gal 5:1; Eph 6:13-17.

204. Hawthorne, 56; O'Brien, 150; Silva, 94. (TNIV translates "one soul" as *one accord*.)

205. See Fee, 164 n. 37: "It is purely gratuitous to assume that the parallel is synonymous in the sense of the second repeating or explaining the first."

206. See Fee, 164-66; also Barth, 47; Martin, 85; Bockmuehl, 99.

207. Fee, 165-66.

church.[208] The *one Spirit* of God unites and empowers Christians to stand their ground in the struggles of life.

Paul continues to paint his picture of Christians united together in battle by adding the dramatic expression, *striving together,* a military image of soldiers fighting side by side.[209] When Christians *stand firm in the one Spirit,* the result will be seen in the way they are *striving together with one accord for the faith of the gospel.* The TNIV phrase, *with one accord,* is a translation of "one *psychē,* one soul." The *psychē,* soul, is the "center of the inner human life in its many and varied aspects" and was often used as a reference to a "person."[210] A well-trained army presents a united front and fights as a single unit when the soldiers are fighting side by side as one person. Aristotle used the phrase "one soul" to portray unanimity in friendship: "Friends have one soul between them; friends' goods are common property; friendship is equality."[211] Paul's image of striving together with one soul conveys the ideal of such unity among Christians that they are no longer striving as separate individuals but striving together as one person.

When Christians are fighting against each other, rather than side by side, unity is lost. At the end of his letter, Paul urges two Christians, Euodia and Syntyche, who were fighting against each other, to be reconciled (4:2). Then he asks a mediator to help these two women to be reunited *since they have contended at my side in the cause of the gospel* (4:3). The clause, *they have contended at my side,* is a translation of the same word used in 1:27, translated there as *striving together.* With his image of *striving together with one accord* (1:27) and his reminder that the two women in conflict had previously *contended at my side* (4:3), Paul seeks to unify a divided church. The unity of "one soul" can be maintained only by unity in the *one Spirit.* Only when Christians *stand firm in the one Spirit* will they experience the unity of *striving together with one accord.* The Spirit of God initiates and empowers unity. Unity *in the one Spirit* is a gift to be appropriated by prayerful faith; unity of "one soul" is a task to be accomplished by persistent work.

Paul describes the work that unites the church in his phrase *for the faith of the gospel.* Christians are united when they fight side by side with one soul *for* the faith of the gospel.[212] Unfortunately, some members of the church in Philippi were fighting *against* each other rather than fighting for *the faith of the gospel.* Even though two women had been contending at Paul's side in the cause of the gospel, they were now opposed to each other

208. Barth, 47: "Unity in the 'Spirit' is no task *(Aufgabe)* but a gift *(Gabe)* that men need only call to mind again in order to be united."

209. BDAG, 964.

210. BDAG, 1099.

211. Aristotle, *Eth. nic.* 9.8.2.

212. This use of the word *for* takes the dative case of *faith* as a "dative of advantage." The dative of advantage or disadvantage specifies a relationship "in which action is directed toward someone either to his or her benefit or detriment" (Porter, *Idioms of the Greek New Testament,* 98).

and needed to be reconciled (4:2-3). The aim of fighting side by side is not *against* anyone, but *for the faith of the gospel.* This phrase, *for the faith of the gospel,* occurs only here in the NT. It may mean faith in the gospel, the faith (creed) that is the gospel, or the faith generated by the gospel.[213] Since the differences between these options are not really substantial, it may not be necessary to make a decision between them. Perhaps all these meanings are contained in Paul's phrase. The best way to understand Paul's point is to note that his use of the word *gospel* in this context stresses both the communication of the gospel and the conduct that is worthy of the gospel. His autobiographical report focuses on "the advance of the gospel" through his imprisonment (1:12-13) and on those who *proclaim the gospel,* whether by false motives or true (1:14-18). His ethical exhortation begins with the challenge to *live in a manner worthy of the gospel* (1:27). When Christians focus on proclaiming the gospel and living by the truth of the gospel, they will be soul mates, *striving together with one soul.*

28 After explaining what it means to *stand firm* in the positive sense of *striving together,* Paul strengthens their resolve by negatively stating what it means to *stand firm: without being frightened in any way by those who oppose you.* The Greek word translated *being frightened* does not occur elsewhere in the NT. It was used in Greek literature to describe horses that are startled and frightened on the battlefield. Plutarch, a contemporary of Paul, employs this word in his story of a Roman soldier's death in battle due to his frightened horse.[214] His horse, who was "agitated," threw him to the ground, and he was killed. Paul's instruction to *stand firm without being frightened* calls for Christians not to be agitated and terrified on the battlefield as horses often are. Christians are not to be intimidated *in any way.* No matter how powerful the opposition is, nothing should shake the resolve of those who *stand firm in the one Spirit.* Lined up side by side as one person, they should not be scared by any threats or any torture. They should not run from any battle, back down from any attack, compromise anything, or concede *in any way.*

Paul does not clearly identify *those who oppose* the Christians in Philippi. Some have supposed that they are the same people Paul describes in chapter 3 when he tells his readers to *watch out for those dogs* (3:2).[215] The "dogs" appear to be Jewish-Christian intruders who were seeking to persuade the Gentile Christians that it was necessary to become Jewish in order to belong to the righteous people of God. In chapter 1, however, *those who oppose* appear to be Roman non-Christians, since Paul refers to *those who oppose* in the same sentence that equates his struggle with the struggle

213. The discussion revolves around the genitive case of the word *gospel.* Is it an objective genitive (the gospel is the object of faith), a genitive of apposition or definition (the gospel is the faith), or a subjective genitive (the gospel generates faith)?

214. See Geoffrion, *The Rhetorical Purpose and the Political and Military Character of Philippians,* 67.

215. Hawthorne, 58; Silva, 92.

of his readers: *you are going through the same struggle you saw I had, and now hear that I still have* (1:30). The struggle Paul describes in chapter 1 is indicated by his references to his *chains*, the *palace guard*, and his possible *death.* The Christians in Philippi were facing the same Roman opposition as Paul was for their commitment to Christ. Paul's courageous witness to Caesar's bodyguard presents an inspiring example. He was not intimidated by the most powerful soldiers in the Roman Empire. Neither should the Christians in Philippi be intimidated by the elite corps of Roman soldiers and other top-ranking Roman officials who resided there.[216] The seemingly insignificant members of the church, the heavenly colony, should not be startled or frightened by opposition from the most powerful persons in the Roman colony.[217] The clash of empire and church will not shake or agitate those who *stand firm in the one Spirit, striving together with one accord for the faith of the gospel.*

Paul assures his readers that all of *this* — their commitment to stand firm, striving together without being frightened — *is a sign.*[218] A *sign* "serves as an indicator of something."[219] What exactly this *sign* indicates needs some clarification. Our TNIV translation says that this *sign* is an indicator to the opponents of the destruction of the opponents, but of the salvation of the Christians: *This is a sign to them that they will be destroyed, but that you will be saved.*[220] This translation constructs a perfectly balanced parallelism and contrast between the two phrases:

> *They will be destroyed.*
> *You will be saved.*

This contrast is seen in 1 Corinthians 1:18, where Paul says, "The message of the cross is foolishness to those who are perishing, but to us who are being saved it is the power of God." But Paul's own words in Philippians do not present such a clear contrast. A more precise translation of Paul's own words reads as follows: "This is to them a sign of destruction, but of your salvation" (my trans.). This sentence is elliptical: words have to be supplied to make sense of Paul's sentence. On the basis of the parallelism and con-

216. See the description of Philippi in the Introduction, 1-6.

217. See Fee, 167: "It seems very likely that the (Roman) citizens of Philippi, who would have honored the emperor at every public gathering, were putting special pressure on the Philippian believers; their allegiance had now been given to another *kyrios*, Jesus, who had himself been executed at the hands of the empire."

218. The antecedent of the pronoun *this* is not clear. The pronoun could refer back to a specific element of the preceding phrases: the faith, or steadfastness, or unity, or fearlessness, or opposition. Most interpreters, however, take the pronoun as a reference to the entire description of the steadfastness, unity, and fearlessness of the believers in the face of opposition.

219. BDAG, 332. This word, ἔνδειξις, also means "demonstration, proof."

220. RSV, NRSV, NIV, NASV, and NEB also translate this verse in various ways, all with the implication that the opponents will be destroyed.

trast in this sentence, translators see the possessive pronoun "of your" in the second phrase and supply the corresponding possessive pronoun "of their" in the first phrase. As a result of adding these words to Paul's words, most translations have constructed the contrast between the destruction of the opponents and the salvation of the Christians: "This is to them a sign [of their] destruction, but of your salvation."

A major problem in this reading of Paul's words is the difficulty of understanding how the opponents would see the faith of the Christians in the face of opposition as a sign of their own destruction. Why would the opponents think that they would be destroyed when they saw the unity and steadfastness of Christians? Some have attempted to answer this difficult question with psychological explanations.[221] But such explanations are wildly speculative at best. Others admit the difficulty of understanding how the opponents would understand this sign, but still assert that it is a sign of the opponents' destruction "whether the persecutors recognize it or not."[222] But such an assertion devalues the meaning of Paul's words: *this is a sign.* Surely, Paul is stating that the sign is an indicator of something that would be recognized.

This difficult problem of understanding how the opponents would recognize the Christians' loyalty to the gospel as a sign of their own destruction is removed if Paul is saying that the sign is recognized by the opponents as a sign of the destruction of Christians. Stephen Fowl, following the lead of Gerald Hawthorne, reads Paul's words in this way: "The Philippians' steadfastness in the face of opposition is a sign to the opponents of the Philippians' destruction."[223] Hawthorne offers his own paraphrase of verse 28: "In no way let your adversaries strike terror in you. For although they see your loyalty to the truth as inevitably leading to your persecution and death, you see it as leading through persecution to the salvation of your souls."[224] The pagan residents of Philippi saw the Philippian Christians' loyalty to the gospel and tried to frighten the Christians with threats something like, "Your loyalty to the gospel is a sure sign that you will be destroyed!" From the opponents' perspective, the Christians' refusal to give up their faith that Christ is Lord was all the evidence needed to prove them worthy of execution in a Roman colony dedicated to the worship of Caesar as Lord. Imperial authorities would not only threaten;

221. Beare, 68: "The apostle suggests that God is working secretly upon the minds and consciences of the persecutors, with premonitions of their own doom and persuasions of the good that awaits the persecuted."

222. O'Brien, 155.

223. Stephen E. Fowl, "Philippians 1:28b, One More Time," in *New Testament Greek and Exegesis: Essays in Honor of Gerald F. Hawthorne* (ed. Amy Donaldson and Timothy Sailors; Grand Rapids: Eerdmans, 2003), 175.

224. Hawthorne, 60. Fowl, "Philippians 1:28b, One More Time," suggests that the possessive pronoun, "of your," is a modifier of both "destruction" and "salvation" (175 n. 31).

they would also punish deviance from the imperial cult. *To stand firm, striving together with one accord for the faith of the gospel* in the Roman world was "a concrete manifestation to the opponents of the Christians' impending destruction, a destruction that would have entailed not only physical death but also the judgment of the gods."[225]

The steadfast faith of Christians, united in their witness to Christ, presented a *sign* that is interpreted in opposite ways by those inside and those outside the church. While Christian unity for the gospel is a *sign* to those outside the church of the Christians' destruction, it is a *sign* to those inside the church of salvation. Paul encourages believers in a hostile environment by assuring them that their unity in the process of suffering for faith in Christ is a *sign* that *you will be saved — and that by God.* They need not be frightened in any way by the opinion of their opponents that the consequence of their faith will be destruction. For they know that their steadfast faith in Christ is really the evidence of their present and eternal salvation. TNIV translates the noun "salvation" as a future tense verb, *you will be saved.* But in this context, Paul is pointing to the evidence of "salvation" in the present as well as future. When he expresses his expectation of "salvation" (TNIV, *deliverance*) in verse 19, he defines salvation in verse 20 as having *sufficient courage so that Christ will be exalted in my body, whether by life or by death.* Courage to live or die for the exaltation of Christ is a manifestation of salvation. Paul is urging Christians to exhibit the same courage in their steadfast, fearless stand for Christ in verses 27-28 and assures them that such a stand for Christ is also a clear sign that they are saved and will be saved, whether they live or die. Destruction may in fact be the experience of Christians, but destruction by Roman execution is not the end of the story. Christians know that salvation is theirs in Christ because they know the story of Christ — he was *obedient to death — even death on a cross! Therefore, God exalted him to the highest place* (2:8-9)

The certainty of salvation rests not on human striving but on God. All of their salvation evidenced by their standing and striving is *by God* and "from God." God is the source of all aspects of their salvation — of their ability to stand firm in the one Spirit, their striving together as one soul to declare and live by the gospel, and their courageous persistence when threatened with destruction by their opponents. Their courage was rooted in their faith that destruction by their opponents could not overturn the certainty of their salvation *by God.*

29 Paul goes on to explain that salvation by God does not exclude the experience of suffering. In fact, salvation by God includes suffering on behalf of Christ. *For,* Paul asserts, *it has been granted to you on behalf of Christ not only to believe on him, but also to suffer for him.* The verb translated *it has been granted* (TNIV) means "to give freely, give graciously."[226] The cognate

225. Fowl, "Philippians 1:28b, One More Time," 176.
226. BDAG, 1078.

noun of this verb is "grace." Suffering on behalf of Christ, just as much as believing in Christ, is a gift of God's grace. The key to understanding Paul's inclusion of suffering within salvation is his threefold repetition of phrases focusing on the relationship of the believer with Christ: *on behalf of Christ, on him, for him.* Salvation is Christ. *To live is Christ!* Believers in Christ are given the grace of walking with Christ in the way of Christ, who *humbled himself by becoming obedient to death — even death on a cross!* (2:8). In his suffering, Christ was nailed to a cross. To unbelievers the cross is simply a sign of destruction, but to believers the cross is the sign of salvation. Suffering *on behalf of Christ* will be seen by enemies of the cross as a *sign* of destruction, but believers will recognize suffering on behalf of Christ as a *sign* of salvation, of union with Christ.

The suffering in view here is not everyday headaches and heartaches. Suffering *on behalf of Christ* is caused by public identification with Christ in a world hostile to Christ. This verse on suffering is a continuation of the sentence that begins in verse 27 with the exhortation to *lives as citizens . . . in a manner worthy of the gospel of Christ.* As the citizens of heaven lived out their citizenship in Philippi in a way that proclaimed and reflected the truth of the gospel, they experienced suffering on behalf of Christ. The preposition, translated *on behalf of* and *for* (TNIV), is a "marker of the moving cause or reason" of the suffering.[227] Public identification with Christ was the "cause or the reason" for the kind of suffering that was given as a grace to the believers in Philippi. Believing in Christ caused suffering for Christ. God's grace gives both the ability to believe in Christ and the ability to suffer for Christ. In believing and suffering, Christ is the source and center of life.

30 After interpreting the meaning of their suffering in the light of their relationship to Christ, Paul now adds a note about their relationship to him in their suffering: *since you are going through the same struggle you saw I had, and now hear that I still have.* Suffering can more easily be accepted as a gracious gift from God when we see how it is a gift of God's grace in the life of someone we love. Paul reminds his friends of his experience of suffering so that they will have his example to follow in their own affliction. Their partnership with Paul brought them into the *same struggle* Paul had. Paul defines the nature of their suffering for Christ by his use of the term *agōn (struggle).* This term originally indicated a place or arena of an athletic contest, then the contest itself, and later any kind of struggle or conflict.[228] The word was used in Paul's era by the author of 4 Maccabees in a comparison of the suffering *(agōn)* of Jewish martyrs under the Syrian tyrant, Antiochus, to the contest *(agōn)* of athletes:

> Truly divine was the contest *(agōn)* in which they were engaged. On that day virtue was the umpire and the test to which they were put was

227. BDAG, 1031.
228. E. Stauffer, "ἀγών," *TDNT* 1:135.

> a test of endurance. The prize for victory was incorruption in the long-lasting life. The first to enter the contest was Eleazar, but the mother of the seven sons competed also, and the brothers as well took part. The tyrant was the adversary, and the world and the life of men were the spectators. Piety won the victory and crowned her own contestants.[229]

This analogy was effective since the *agōn* (contest) of athletes and the *agōn* (torture) of martyrs often occurred in the same arena before the same spectators.[230] Paul also draws from images of an athletic contest to portray his suffering: *Forgetting what is behind and straining toward what is ahead, I press on toward the goal to win the prize* (3:13-14). Paul ran his race *to know Christ — yes, to know the power of his resurrection and participation in his sufferings* (3:10). The purpose of this vivid picture of an athletic Paul running hard to win the prize is to motivate those who see it to run in the same race: *Join together in following my example* (3:17). Paul paints the picture of running with him in the same contest *(agōn)* when he tells his readers, *you are going through the same struggle (agōn) you saw I had, and now hear that I still have* (1:30). The readers of his letter may not have been literally *in chains* as Paul was, but Paul's entire account of suffering *in chains for Christ* (1:12-26) was designed to encourage them to know that their suffering put them in the same arena, running the same race, and engaged in the *same struggle* as Paul was.

The details of Paul's suffering were well known to the church in Philippi. As Paul tells them, *you saw . . . and now hear.* What the believers *saw* of Paul's struggle we may surmise from Paul's account in his letter to the church in Thessalonica written shortly after his first visit to Philippi: "We had previously suffered and been treated outrageously in Philippi" (1 Thess 2:2). Acts 16:16-40 provides us with more specifics in its account of Paul's suffering in Philippi. That account relates how Paul and Silas were seized, dragged into the marketplace, accused before the magistrates of advocating customs contrary to Roman laws, stripped, beaten with rods, thrown into the inner cell of prison, and had their feet fastened in the stocks. What the believers in Philippi heard of Paul's struggle during the time he wrote his letter to them we can only infer from his repeated references to his chains (1:7, 13, 14, 17) and his mention of the palace guard (1:13) and Caesar's household (4:22). All of this information indicates that Paul's suffering was caused by Roman opposition to his proclamation of Christ. Paul's gospel that Jesus Christ is now the exalted Lord who will come as the Savior from heaven to bring everything under his control directly confronted the Roman imperial gospel that Caesar is Lord and Savior. "Paul was preaching an anti-imperial gospel."[231] His battle cry to the

229. 4 Maccabees in *Old Testament Pseudepigrapha* (ed. James Charlesworth; New York: Doubleday, 1985), 2:562-63.

230. Stauffer, "ἀγών," *TDNT* 1:136.

231. Horsley, *Paul and Empire,* 140. Read more on the imperial cult in the Introduction, 2-3.

church in Philippi to *stand firm . . . for the faith of the gospel* is a call for loyalty and perseverance in the *same struggle.* Both Paul and the Philippians were engaged, by virtue of their commitment to the gospel of Jesus Christ, in the *same* life-and-death *struggle* with the religious and political powers of the Roman Empire. Paul was aware that this struggle made suffering inevitable and might in fact bring about his own death and that of his partners under the Roman powers. But his letter assures them that suffering for Christ was the way to advance the gospel (1:12), the way for Christ to be exalted (1:20), the way to experience God's grace (1:29), and the way of Christ himself, who *humbled himself by becoming obedient to death — even death on a cross!* (2:8).

Philippians 2

B. Think of the Interests of Others (2:1-4)

1 *Therefore*
A *if you have any encouragement from being united with Christ,*
B *if any comfort from his love,*
C *if any common sharing in the Spirit,*
D *if any tenderness and compassion,*
2 A *then make my joy complete by being like-minded,*
B *having the same love,*
B *being one in spirit*
A *and of one mind.*
3 A *Do nothing out of selfish ambition or vain conceit.*
B *Rather, in humility value others above yourselves,*
4 A *not looking to your own interests*
B *but each of you to the interests of others.*[1]

In these four verses Paul compellingly expresses in one long, complex sentence (in the Greek text) the same basic concern as the previous sentence (1:27-30). The urgent imperative of both sentences is to be united: *stand firm in one Spirit, striving together with one accord for the faith of the gospel* (1:27); *being like-minded, having the same love, being one in spirit and of one mind* (2:2). The previous sentence emphasizes the need to stand firmly united for the gospel in the face of those who oppose the church. This sentence focuses on the need to be humbly united with those who divide the church. Paul urges believers to be one so that they will be able to endure suffering caused by those outside the church and to heal divisions caused by those inside the church.

1. For this arrangement of the clauses, see David A. Black, "Paul and Christian Unity: A Formal Analysis of Philippians 2:1-4," *JETS* 28.3 (1985), 299-308. See also Gnilka, 102.

1 Paul links this sentence to the previous one with the word *therefore.* This word introduces "the result of or an inference from what precedes."[2] The result of the experience of unity with one another in the *same struggle* caused by *those who oppose* the church (1:27-30) should be an endeavor to seek unity with those who have different interests within the church (2:1-4). Paul spells out the motivation for seeking unity in the church in the four clauses that begin with the word *if.* In this context, the word *if* points to realities or certainties, not possibilities or probabilities.[3] Barth expresses the sense of this word in his translation "as surely as."[4] In these four clauses Paul is reminding believers of four certainties they can be sure are true. These confident indicatives of reality are the basis for the urgent imperatives to build unity.

Interpreters debate whether the emphasis in these four clauses is on "supernatural, objective realities"[5] or the "deepest experiences common to every Christian."[6] We gain a comprehensive view of the realities that Paul sets before his readers by combining these interpretations. The clauses call believers to reaffirm both the divine objective work of salvation and the human subjective experience of salvation in Christ. All four clauses reassure believers that God is binding them together with cords of love.

The first *if*-clause points to *any encouragement in Christ.* The TNIV clarifies the meaning of these words in the Greek text by filling in the gaps with additional words: *if* [*you have*] *any encouragement* [*from being united*] *with Christ.* Christ is the source of *encouragement;* in the community *encouragement* from Christ flows from one member to another. The word *encouragement* has three meanings: (1) "act of emboldening another in belief or course of action"; (2) "strong request"; and (3) "lifting of another's spirits."[7] All three meanings — exhortation, request, and comfort — have found worthy supporters on the basis of good evidence. We can see how the theme of exhortation in this context appears to support exhortation as the meaning of this word. Paul begins this section by exhorting believers to *live as citizens worthy of the gospel of Christ* and to *stand firm in one Spirit, striving with one accord for the faith of the gospel* (1:27). These imperatives are clarified and amplified throughout the entire passage: *make my joy complete by being like-minded* (2:2); *work out your salvation* (2:12); *do everything without grumbling or arguing* (2:14); and *be glad and rejoice with me* (2:18). If the word *en-*

2. BDAG, 736; Collange, 72.

3. See J. L. Boyer, "First Class Conditions: What Do They Mean?" *GTJ* 2 (1981), 75-114. Boyer lists the first-class conditional clauses in Phil 2:1 as examples of first-class conditions that assume the reality of the conditional clause.

4. Barth, 51.

5. O'Brien, 167, takes all four clauses as descriptions of God's work of salvation.

6. Hawthorne, 64. According to Hawthorne, the first two clauses focus on "the human side of things — Paul's encouragement of and love for the Philippians, the second on the divine — the unity among the Philippians created by the Holy Spirit and God surrounding them with the warmth of his affection" (67).

7. BDAG, 766.

couragement is understood as a reference to these exhortations, then the phrase *in Christ* points to the authority and power behind this exhortation: it is given to believers with the authority of Christ.[8] Closely related to the sense of exhortation is the connotation of request. The cognate verb to the noun *encouragement* means "I urge you." Paul uses this verb twice in his strong request for two women in the church in Philippi to be reconciled and reunited to each other: *I plead with Euodia and I plead with Syntyche to be of the same mind in the Lord* (4:2).[9] Since Paul's desire for his friends to be united motivates him to write this letter, it is easy to see how the word *encouragement* may be taken as a reference to his "admonition in Christ" to be like-minded.[10]

Although the interpretations of the word *encouragement* as exhortation and request make good sense in this context, there are also good reasons to understand the word as a reference to the *comfort* that believers have from being united together *in Christ*.[11] The phrases immediately before this assurance of *encouragement in Christ* inform believers that they have been granted *on behalf of Christ not only to believe on him, but also to suffer for him* (1:29). The comfort for those who suffer is the knowledge that suffering is a gift granted to them and that suffering is on behalf of Christ. Furthermore, there is the comfort that believers experience from being united in the *same struggle* — united with Paul in his struggle and united with one another (1:30). The theme of suffering runs through the whole letter. Paul refers repeatedly to his chains (1:7, 13, 14, 17) and reflects on the prospects of his death (1:20, 21, 23). The source of his comfort in chains and in the face of death is his relationship to Christ. He urges believers not to be frightened by those who oppose them (1:28). The source of comfort for Christians in the face of opposition is their unity in the one Spirit (1:27). Paul writes about suffering in a way that comforts and consoles the spirits of his readers by reminding them continually of the comfort they have from being united together in Christ. Ultimately, consolation in suffering comes from knowing that Christ himself suffered and was consequently vindicated by God (2:8-9). Those who suffer for their faith in Christ are strengthened by knowing that in Christ they will also be vindicated by God for their suffering.

Paul makes this same connection of suffering and comfort in 2 Corinthians: "For just as we share abundantly in the sufferings of Christ, so also our comfort abounds through Christ. . . . We know that just as you share in our sufferings, so also you share in our comfort" (2 Cor 1:5-7). This passage

8. Beare, 70; Müller, 85; Hawthorne, 65.

9. This verb often serves as an introduction to ethical imperatives in Paul's letters: 1 Thess 2:11-12; 5:14; 1 Cor 1:10; 4:16; 16:15; Rom 12:1; 15:30; 16:17; Eph 4:1.

10. O. Schmitz, "παρακαλέω," *TDNT* 5:795; Schenk, 179.

11. Bockmuehl, 106: the word "contains the ideas of both consolation and strengthening. . . . Union with Christ even in the midst of suffering opens up a treasury of consolation and strength."

is foundational for understanding the meaning of comfort in Paul's letters. Ten times Paul uses the nouns *encouragement* and *comfort* and their cognate verbs *encourage* and *to comfort* in this passage to set forth his theology of comfort. God is the "God of all comfort, who comforts us in all our troubles, so that we can comfort those in any trouble with the comfort we ourselves receive from God" (2 Cor 1:3-4). In Philippians we see Paul comforting those in trouble with the comfort that he had received from God. He tells of his experience of comfort from God as he sat in chains and faced execution (1:12-26). He assures his readers that as surely as they shared in the *same struggle* with him (1:30), they also share in the same *encouragement in Christ* with him (2:1). This line of interpretation leads to understanding the *in Christ* phrase to denote the corporate experience of union with Christ. The *comfort* that comes from corporate solidarity with one another in Christ assuages the pain caused by suffering. Peace replaces fear and joy overcomes grief when believers experience the reality of the presence of Christ in their community. The reality of this comfort *in Christ* is a strong motivation to aim for unity in the community.

Although the context gives support for all three meanings of *encouragement,* the use of the word in this sentence to motivate his readers favors the meaning of comfort. If Paul is reminding them of his exhortation or request to be united in order to motivate them to be united, then this sentence seems to be strangely repetitive and circular. But if he is focusing their attention on the comfort they experience together in Christ in order to motivate them to be united, then this sentence moves compellingly from a basis for pursuing unity to an appeal for unity.

The second *if*-clause draws attention to *any comfort from love.* TNIV seeks to draw out the meaning of this phrase by adding the pronoun *his* to the words found in the Greek text: *any comfort from [his] love.* The pronoun *his* refers back to *Christ* in the previous phrase and implies that Paul is reminding his readers of Christ's love for them.[12] The scope of love in this letter, however, includes Christ's love for the church, Paul's love for the church, and the love of believers for one another.[13] The previous reference to love commends those who preach out of love for Paul (1:16). Paul's prayer that love may abound more and more is a prayer for believers to grow in their ability to love each other (1:9). The experience of love in the community gives comfort, especially in times of suffering. While the accent is on the love of believers for one another, Paul reminds his readers that Christ is the source of this love. His own love for believers is rooted in the *affection of Christ Jesus* (1:8). And his prayer for believers to grow in their love for one another leads him to pray that they will be *filled with the fruit of*

12. Supported by Müller, 85; O'Brien, 172.

13. Beare, 71: "the mutual love which binds together the Apostle and the Christian believers of Philippi." Hawthorne, 65: "In this letter where Paul's affection for the Philippians seems so obvious and so much in the foreground, . . . it is but natural to suppose that it is Paul's love that provided consolation for the Philippians and is in view here now."

righteousness that comes through Jesus Christ (1:9-11). So Paul's reminder of *any comfort from love* (2:1) should be taken as an inclusive reference to the experience of love within the community empowered by Christ's love.

The basic meaning of the word translated *comfort* in this phrase is "to speak to someone in a friendly way."[14] As with the word *encouragement* in the previous phrase, this word *comfort* can also have the sense of admonishment. The way Paul pairs this word *comfort* with the word *encouragement* several times in his letters indicates that he uses these words as basically synonymous terms.[15] In Paul's use of synonymous parallelism in the first two *if*-clauses, the first clause appreciates the comfort experienced in the community from being united with Christ. The second clause values the comfort brought by love: Paul has expressed his love for the church in Philippi (1:8); he has prayed for their love for each other to increase (1:9); he has commended the love of believers for him (1:16); and he has indicated that all love comes through Jesus Christ (1:11). The entire breadth and depth of this love already so clearly described by him is the source of comfort in the community. Paul reminds believers of the *comfort from love* (2:1) so that they will continue *having the same love* for one another (2:2).

The third *if*-clause refers to *any common sharing in the Spirit.* The word translated *common sharing* is *koinōnia.* Paul's first reference to *koinōnia* is to joyful thanksgiving for *partnership in the gospel* (1:5). *Partnership* unites Paul and the church in Philippi in the joint venture of proclaiming the gospel. In this partnership, the church in Philippi gave financially to support Paul's mission (4:15-18). Now Paul deepens the understanding of his partnership with the church by calling it a *koinōnia of the Spirit. Koinōnia* is not simply a business relationship depending on the willingness and ability of the business partners to fulfill the terms of a business contract. The *koinōnia* of believers is more than *partnership;* it is "communion in the Spirit," *common sharing in the Spirit.*[16] Paul was aware that disunity in the church threatened his partnership. His joint venture with believers in the church in the mission of proclaiming the gospel would collapse if those believers were divided against each other. To strengthen the unity of the church, Paul draws on another meaning of *koinōnia,* that of common ownership.

In Paul's world, the term *koinōnia* referred not only to voluntary association for the purpose of a joint venture, a business partnership, but also to common possession as a result of inheritance.[17] Common possession did

14. G. Stählin, "παραμυθέομαι," *TDNT* 5:817; BDAG, 769.

15. Besides this instance in Phil 2:1, see also 1 Cor 14:3; 1 Thess 2:12; 5:14. According to Stählin, it is "difficult to find a convincing criterion by which to draw any sharp line of demarcation" between these two words (Stählin, "παραμυθέομαι," *TDNT* 5:821).

16. For a development of the concepts of business partnership and communion included in the meaning of *koinōnia,* see G. Walter Hansen, "Transformation of Relationships," in *New Testament Greek and Exegesis: Essays in Honor of Gerald F. Hawthorne* (ed. A. M. Donaldson and T. B. Sailors; Grand Rapids: Eerdmans, 2003), 189-92.

17. See Hansen, "Transformation of Relationships," 190.

not entitle each heir to only a piece of the property; each heir was part owner of the whole property. Believers in Christ are heirs to the Holy Spirit; they have common possession of the Holy Spirit. A helpful way of understanding this concept of common possession of the Spirit is to turn to the teaching of the OT that the Levites were not given an inheritance in the land because the Lord was their inheritance (Deut 10:9). God has given his Spirit to the church as their inheritance.

The phrase *common sharing in the Spirit* emphasizes the experience of the entire community rather than the individual experience of possessing the Spirit. What all believers have in common is their experience of sharing together in the gift of the Spirit. They all know that they *serve God by his Spirit* (3:3). They are called to *stand firm in the one Spirit* (1:27).

The fourth *if*-clause leads the readers to consider *any tenderness and compassion.* The Greek word translated *tenderness* refers to "the inward parts of a body, including especially the viscera, entrails."[18] A reference to the intestines in ancient Greek served as a metaphorical way of speaking about strong emotions. Paul used this term in this letter when he expressed how he longed for his friends with the *affection of Christ Jesus* (1:7). Paul's affection for his friends was really the expression of Christ's life flowing in and through him. He calls on them to remember how their lives have been touched by the tenderness of Christ so that they will tenderly care for *the interests of others* (2:4). To intensify their recollection of his *tenderness* Paul adds the synonym *compassion.* This word denotes the "display of concern over another's misfortune."[19] In other contexts, Paul employed this word to refer to God's compassion (Rom 12:1; 2 Cor 1:3).[20] Ultimately, God is the source of all compassion. In the context of this letter, however, Paul's use of this word focuses on the agents of God's compassion, "the sympathy of the Philippians."[21] The church in Philippi displayed their concern for Paul (4:10) by sending Epaphroditus to bring gifts to him while he was in prison (4:18). Paul motivates his friends to be united by reminding them of the *tenderness and compassion* "that he and they have toward one another."[22] These "descriptions of the access, the open, inner road between Paul and the Philippians" provide a strong incentive to build unity in the community.[23] The memory of past intimacy should heal present disunity. Paul pleads with them, "If we were such close friends concerned to help each other in the past, let us tear down the walls that divide us and be reunited in love."

18. BDAG, 938.

19. BDAG, 700. These same two words are also paired in a list of other qualities to describe the clothes of God's chosen people: "clothe yourselves with tenderness and compassion . . ." (Col 3:12).

20. Hawthorne (67) and O'Brien (175) take these uses of this word in other Pauline letters as evidence that Paul is referring to God's compassion in Phil 2:1.

21. R. Bultmann, "οἰκτίρω," *TDNT* 5:161.

22. Fee, 182.

23. Barth, 51.

2 The joy of close friendship inspires Paul's requests: *then make my joy complete by being like-minded, having the same love, being one in spirit and of one mind.* The initial request, *make my joy complete,* is not "simply prefatory to the main idea."[24] Paul designed the entire letter to build a stronger, deeper friendship with the Philippian believers.[25] Paul begins this letter by thanking God *with joy* for his partnership — *koinōnia* — with the Philippians (1:5); he ends the letter by telling them how he *rejoiced greatly* because of the way the church continued their partnership with him throughout his ministry even when he was in prison (4:10-18). The joy that comes from his relationship with his friends (2:17, 18) makes them his *joy and crown* (4:1). But because friendships are fragile and even close friends are all too easily divided by pride, selfishness, and preoccupation with personal interests, Paul appeals to the Philippians to make his joy complete *by being like-minded.* In this appeal he is voicing the heartfelt desire of a true, committed friend. He is not an aloof apostle, untouched by the painful divisions in the church. Disunity among his friends diminishes his joy. The unity of his friends with each other will complete his joy.[26]

Paul pens three phrases to explain what his friends need to do to complete his joy. The first one, translated *by being like-minded,* contains the verb *think,* one of Paul's favorite words in this letter.[27] This word appears first in Paul's opening thanksgiving for his friends when he tells them why it is right *to feel* the way he does about them (1:7). He uses this word twice to describe the kind of unity he desires to see in the church: *be like-minded . . . of one mind* (2:2). He introduces the Christ hymn with this word: *have the same attitude of mind* (2:5). In his challenge to follow his example, he speaks of those who *take such a view* of things and those who *think differently* (3:15). With tears he uses this word to describe those whose *mind is set* on earthly things (3:19). He employs this word in his plea to Euodia and Syntyche to be reconciled by calling on them *to be of the same mind* (4:2). Twice he uses this word when he commends his friends for their renewed *concern* and his realization that they *were concerned* (4:10). These ten occurrences of this word illustrate the range of meanings expressed by this verb: *feel, be minded, have the attitude of mind, take a view, think, set the mind on,* and *be concerned.* This spectrum of meanings indicates that this verb speaks of the dominant attitude and settled disposition of the entire person. So when Paul calls his friends to *think the same thing (being like-minded),* he is not ask-

24. Hawthorne, 67.

25. See the Introduction, 6-12, for a description of a letter of friendship.

26. Bockmuehl, 108: "What Paul asks has to do with the Philippians' relationships amongst each other; but he himself takes a keen interest in them as their pastor and friend. Their progress in the faith, expressed in unity and harmony (cf. earlier 1.25, 27), will fill up his own measure of joy — and, given their bonds of friendship, that in itself should be an incentive to pursue it."

27. The verb *think,* φρονέω, occurs ten times: 1:7; 2:2 (twice); 2:5; 3:15 (twice); 3:19; 4:2; 4:10 (twice).

ing them to have the same thoughts or feelings about everything. They are not called to be ditto marks of each other. Paul is not squelching human creativity, nor is he prohibiting personal diversity. He is calling his friends to "seek the same goal with a like mind."[28] He identifies the common goal of the community in the next phrases (2:2-4), and illustrates the common goal by the supreme example of Christ (2:5-8).

The next phrase, *having the same love,* defines what *being like-minded* means. In this phrase Paul moves from his prayer that *your love may abound more and more* (1:9) to an imperative, to *have the same love.*[29] His prayer expresses his dependence on God to work in the community so that love will increase. His imperative calls the community to the work of love. The work of the community is the love that Christ displayed *by taking the very nature of a servant* (2:7). Only a common commitment of all to love as Christ loves will restore unity to the divided community. Paul's description of the division between some who preach Christ *out of love* for Paul and others who preach *out of selfish ambition* (1:16-17) sheds light on his commands to have *the same love* and to do nothing *out of selfish ambition* (2:2-3).[30] *Having the same love* for one another requires giving up *selfish ambition* to compete with each other and out-perform each other.[31]

Paul extends his line of requests for unity with one more phrase, *being one in spirit and of one mind. One in spirit* is a translation of one Greek word, formed from the preposition *with* and the noun *souls.* The word means "souls together," people in harmony with one another, "harmonious."[32] This word echoes Paul's description of the citizens *striving together with one accord* (1:28). *One accord* is a translation of two Greek words literally meaning "one soul." The unity of believers empowers them to work together as one person. In the Hellenistic cultural context this description of harmonious relationships with the words "one soul" was a depiction of a deep, strong friendship. Aristotle used the phrase "one soul" to portray unanim-

28. G. Bertram, "φρονέω," *TDNT* 9:233.

29. Although the verb *having* (ἔχοντες) in this phrase is in the form of a participle, Paul is using the participle with a sense that is clearly imperatival. See C. F. D. Moule, *An Idiom-Book of New Testament Greek* (2nd ed.; Cambridge: Cambridge University Press, 1963), 179-80.

30. Schenk, 182.

31. Davorin Peterlin, *Paul's Letter to the Philippians in the Light of Disunity in the Church* (NovTSup 79; Leiden: Brill, 1995), 62, views the verbal links between Paul's depiction of the division between preachers (1:16-17) and his demand for love between the Philippians (2:2-4) as evidence that "the Philippians were sharply polarized, some for Paul, some against him." But Paul's confidence in the Philippians' obedience (2:12) and his gratitude for their support (4:10-18) do not support this theory that there was a polarization in Philippi for and against Paul and that this polarization caused Paul's appeal for unity in 2:1-4. Perhaps his appeal for unity in 2:1-4 was caused by the polarization between preachers in the context of Paul's imprisonment and not by what Paul heard about the church in Philippi. See Fowl, 81 n. 10. In any case, Peterlin's mirror-reading of 2:1-4 is questionable support for his theory of widespread division for and against Paul.

32. BDAG, 961.

ity in friendship: "Friends have *one soul* between them; friends' goods are common property; friendship is equality."[33] Paul picks up this cultural expression of friendship in his request for his friends to be "souls together" *(one in spirit).*

Of one mind is a translation of a Greek phrase that literally calls for believers in Christ to be "those who are thinking one thing." Paul uses the same word heard at the beginning of this series of phrases calling for unity. Repetition — *being like-minded . . . of one mind* — hammers home his challenge to be united by focusing on one common goal and concentrating together on one thing. Divisions can be overcome only by taking on a common yoke and pulling together in the same direction.[34] When believers are preoccupied with their personal agenda, they will pull in different directions and split the church into separate interest groups. By focusing on their own egocentric priorities, they will be disunited. Only by setting their minds on one thing will they be united by one common subject. Although the content of the one thing is not explicitly stated at this point, the entire letter to the Philippians asserts that Christ is the one common Subject that unites and binds believers together.[35] When Christians declare that *to live is Christ* (1:21), *acknowledge that Jesus Christ is Lord* (2:11) and desire *to know Christ* above all other things (3:8-10), then they will be *of one mind* because they will all be worshipping and serving together the One whom *God exalted to the highest place* (2:9). In other words, *being like-minded* and *of one mind* means more than simply being agreeable; it means agreeing that Jesus Christ is Lord and submitting to his Lordship (2:10-11). Paul explains what he means by *being like-minded* and *of one mind* when he calls his readers to *have the same attitude of mind Christ Jesus had* (2:5) and then discloses "the mind of Christ Jesus" in the narrative of the incarnation, humiliation, and exaltation of Christ (2:6-11).

3 Paul lists two negative attitudes to eliminate and one positive attitude to cultivate so that believers will be *of one mind. Do nothing out of selfish ambition or vain conceit. Rather, in humility value others above yourselves.* The Greek text simply states the double negative without a verb: "neither selfish ambition nor vain conceit." The addition of a verb of action *(do nothing)* correctly indicates that the phrase has the force of a moral imperative.[36] Since Paul is focusing on the *attitude of mind* (2:2, 5) in the immediate context, the imperatival sense of his double negative is a prohibition against two attitudes, two egocentric ways of thinking.[37] To be *of one mind* believers must

33. Aristotle, *Eth. nic.* 9.8.2.

34. Barth, 54-55.

35. O'Brien (179) suggests that the one thing is the gospel: "τὸ ἓν φρονοῦντες focuses on the need for the members of the congregation to be 'gospel oriented' as they relate to and care for one another."

36. Most translations add some verb of action. See NIV, TNIV, RSV, NRSV, GNB, NAB, and NASB.

37. Schenk, 182.

stop setting their minds on their own ambitions and their own glory. As long as Christians have the attitude that what matters most is self-fulfillment and self-advancement, they will never experience the unity *of one mind.* Paul confronts the cause of disunity by exposing these divisive attitudes.

Paul has already exposed the *selfish ambition* that motivated some preachers (1:17). Though they preached Christ, their ministry was self-seeking: they sought to puff up their own reputation and put down Paul while he was in prison (1:18). Now Paul points to those who are dividing the church in Philippi and admonishes them to purge themselves of this toxic attitude of *selfish ambition.* This attitude is brought to light and censured by Paul in other letters in his lists of the causes of conflict in the church (2 Cor 12:20; Gal 5:20). He notes that those "who reject the truth and follow evil" are "self-seeking" (Rom 2:8). This is the attitude of "those who, demeaning themselves and their cause, are busy and active in their own interests, seeking their own gain or advantage." They "cannot lift their gaze to higher things."[38]

The attitude of *selfish ambition* drives a person to *vain conceit.* The Greek word translated *vain conceit* combines two words: "empty glory." This word exposes those who polish their façade but are devoid of the inner reality of spiritual vitality to match their "exaggerated self-evaluation."[39] Their glory is only a false illusion. Paul challenges his friends to do nothing to obtain empty glory — the glory of position, prestige, power, and possessions. Paul uses the cognate adjective of this word in his admonition to the Galatian Christians: "Let us not become *conceited,* provoking and envying each other" (Gal 5:26). The *conceited* person constantly provokes and puts down others to gain the highest place. The empty glory gained by selfish ambition stands in absolute contrast to the glory given to God when Christ, who *made himself nothing* and *humbled himself* (2:7-8), is exalted by God to the highest place to receive universal worship (2:9-11). Only when every knee bows and every tongue acknowledges *that Jesus Christ is Lord, to the glory of God the Father* (2:10-11) will there be perfect unity. Four references to the *glory of God* (1:11; 2:11; 4:19, 20) demonstrate that Paul's ultimate goal was *soli Deo gloria,* the glory of God alone. Selfish ambition and vain conceit seek to take the glory that belongs only to God.

After censuring *selfish ambition* and *vain conceit,* Paul commends the attitude that builds unity: *Rather, in humility value others above yourselves.* No doubt this commendation of humility baffled Paul's first-century readers in Philippi. On the one hand, *hubris,* excessive pride, was condemned in Greek literature. According to Greek authors from Homer to Demosthenes, *hubris* — arrogance, insolence, and an exaggerated sense of superiority — destroyed great heroes and prosperous cities.[40] In the Aeschylean tragedy,

38. F. Büchsel, "ἐριθεία," *TDNT* 2:660.
39. BDAG, 538.
40. G. Bertram, "ὕβρις," *TDNT* 8:295-99.

The Persians, the ghost of King Darius warns against pride *(hubris):* "For presumptuous pride, when it has burgeoned, bears as its fruit a crop of calamity, whence it reaps a plenteous harvest of tears. . . . Zeus, of a truth, is a chastiser of overweening pride and corrects with a heavy hand."[41] On the other hand, however, Hellenistic authors viewed *humility* with contempt because it connoted lowliness, weakness, lack of freedom, servility, and subjection.[42] Plutarch insists that fate cannot make a great man "fearful and *poor-spirited*" (*Alex. fort. virt.* 4.2.336e), nor can severe afflictions make him "bad, fearful, *abject,* ignoble, or envious" (*Tranq. an.* 17.2.475e). Epictetus praises the man who "is incapable of flatteries and a mean and *petty disposition*" (*Diss.* 3.24.56).[43] These authors expressed an ideal of Greek culture that great men overcome the shame of lowliness and weakness by noble acts and thoughts.[44]

Whereas the Greeks despised humility because they sought to elevate humanity to nobility far above lowliness and weakness caused by afflictions, Paul desired humility because he believed that God exalted Jesus to be the Lord above all humanity. Reared within Judaism, Paul knew from many biblical texts that God humbles the proud and exalts the humble. For example, the prophet Isaiah warned that "The haughty eyes of people shall be brought low, and the pride of everyone shall be humbled; and the LORD alone will be exalted in that day" (Isa 2:11). And Proverbs taught that "humility goes before honor" (Prov 15:33).[45]

Paul saw the ultimate proof of the biblical teaching on humility in the narrative of Christ, *who humbled himself by becoming obedient to death — even death on a cross! Therefore, God exalted him to the highest place* (2:8-9). The humility of Christ is not the same as the humility scorned by the Greeks. Humility as exhibited by Christ is not passive inability or pathetic servility. Christ chose his destiny: *he made himself nothing* to become one with humanity, and *he humbled himself* to obey the will of God. In humility he expressed immense compassion for humanity by enduring suffering and death on a cross.

Since Christ *humbled himself,* followers of Christ seek to practice *humility* in their attitudes and actions to others. Paul explains to his readers that the way to practice humility is to *value others above yourselves.* The verb *value* focuses the mind "to engage in an intellectual process, to think, consider and regard."[46] Instead of being preoccupied with introspective, self-absorbed, egocentric thoughts, the mind turns outward to regard the value

41. Aeschylus, *Pers.* 821, 827 (Smyth, LCL).

42. W. Grundmann, "ταπεινός," *TDNT* 8:1-11.

43. Quotations from Grundmann, "ταπεινός," *TDNT* 8:5.

44. H.-H. Esser, "Humility," *NIDNTT* 2:260.

45. See the extended list of texts related to humility provided by Esser, "Humility," *NIDNTT* 2:260-61, including texts from Jewish apocalyptic literature, Qumran Scrolls, and rabbinic texts.

46. BDAG, 434.

of others. This direction of thinking is not obsessed with negative thoughts about oneself; it is freed from thinking about oneself to consider others. Paul uses this verb *value* in his depiction of Christ, who *did not consider equality with God something to be used to his own advantage* (2:6).[47] Because Christ was not captivated by egocentric thinking about his own equality with God, he emptied himself, taking the nature of a servant. Christ thought not of himself but of those he came to serve.

The object of this way of thinking is *others.* This word, usually translated as "one another," is Paul's favorite designation of members of the community of believers in Christ.[48] In his letters, his ethical exhortations list numerous responsibilities that members of the Christian community have toward one another: love one another; build up one another; bear with one another; forgive one another; bear one another's burdens; and be kind and compassionate to one another. So Paul's challenge to *value others* is really a call to think about the needs of the community. The health and welfare of the community become the focus of attention when members are considering one another in humility.

To *value others above yourselves* is to place the needs of others first on your personal agenda. The word *above* means to surpass or excel.[49] Paul uses the same word to speak of the *surpassing worth of knowing Christ Jesus* (3:8). Knowing Jesus Christ far surpasses the importance of everything else. The same word describes the peace of God, which *transcends all understanding* (4:7). The peace of God surpasses the comprehension of all human understanding and the power of all human understanding to guard the heart and the mind. When Paul uses this word in his encouragement to *value others above yourselves,* he is not counseling his readers to beat themselves up or put themselves down. Instead, he is urging them to build up and lift up others. The focus is not negative, but positive. Let the needs and interests of others surpass yours: put them in first place; give them the place of honor; respect them; listen to them; speak about them; serve them; strengthen them; encourage them. Putting others instead of ourselves in the center of our concern will cause a radical Copernican revolution in the community.

4 Paul clarifies how to *value others above ourselves* by explaining that this reorientation will be accomplished by *not looking to your own interests but each of you to the interests of the others. Looking* means "paying careful attention."[50] The TNIV translation seems to negate paying any attention at all to our own personal interests. But the simple word "and" in Paul's text indicates a contrast by conveying "not only, but also": we are not only to pay attention to our own interests, but also to the interests of others.[51] Paul does

47. See the use of the same verb in 2:25; 3:7, 8, 9.
48. See BDAG, 46.
49. BDAG, 1033.
50. BDAG, 931.
51. Although καί is not found in a few MSS (D*,C F G K), its inclusion is supported by

not advocate total self-neglect, but a reprioritizing of life so that *each of you* gives the largest share of attention to *others*.[52]

The Greek text does not contain the word *interests*. That word has been added twice to make some sense of the text: not looking each one to the . . . of your own, but also each one to the . . . of the others.[53] Martin suggests that the object of *looking* is not the interests of others, but the "good points and qualities in one's fellow-Christians."[54] The clue to this interpretation, according to Martin, is that the verb *look* is used by Paul to mean "regard as your aim." The same verb is employed by Paul when he urges his friends to follow his example and *to keep your eyes on those who live as we do* (3:17). And Paul uses the cognate noun with the sense of *goal* when he expresses his commitment to *press on toward the goal* (3:14). According to Martin's interpretation, 2:4 calls us to regard the good example of others as our aim. When we fix our sight on others, we will "not be so preoccupied with our own concerns and the cultivation of our own spiritual life that we miss the noble traits to be seen in others." Since the Christ-like qualities in others reflect the glory of Christ himself, our high regard for the good example of others who follow Christ leads us to follow the supreme example of Christ himself. Paul's advice to regard others (2:4) prepares the way for the portrayal of the supreme example of Christ (2:5-11).[55] Humility gained by

---

early and diverse MSS (𝔓[46] ℵ A B C D[2] Ψ 𝔐). Bockmuehl (113) accepts the inclusion of καί, but suggests that the meaning is "but actually" or "but rather" — not "but also."

52. Cf. Troels Engberg-Pedersen, "Radical Altruism in Philippians 2:4," in *Early Christianity and Classical Culture: Comparative Studies in Honor of Abraham Malherbe* (ed. John Fitzgerald, Thomas Olbricht, and L. Michael White; Leiden: Brill, 2003), 197-204. Engberg-Pedersen argues that Paul's use of the double conjunction, ἀλλὰ καί, advocates a radical altruism: his readers should turn their attention *away from* their own interests and look *instead* to the interests of others.

53. Commentators fill in the blanks in many different ways: "point of view" (Barth, 57-59); "rights" (Beare, 73; Bockmuehl, 113); "needs" (Fee, 190); "the things that interest and deeply concern" (Hawthorne, 69).

54. Martin, 94-95. "In others," Calvin says (246), "he will regard with honor whatever there is of excellence."

55. Ralph Martin, *A Hymn of Christ: Philippians 2:5-11 in Recent Interpretation and in the Setting of Early Christian Worship* (Downers Grove: InterVarsity Press, 1997), 94. O'Brien's criticisms (184-85) do not outweigh the merits of Martin's line of interpretation. (1) O'Brien draws too hard a line between the accusative case of the person who is the object of one's vision and admiration (as in Phil 3:7) and the accusative case of the general expression "the interests of others" (as in Phil 2:4). Investigation of the examples he cites in Greek literature does not support the fine distinction that he makes between these two uses of the accusative case with this verb. (2) O'Brien's objection that admiration of the virtues of other Christians negates the emphasis on humility (2:3) runs up against Paul's own commendation of the virtues of Timothy and Epaphroditus (2:19-30) and Paul's exhortation to follow his own example and the example of others (3:17; 4:9). Humility in oneself may even be developed by focusing on the virtues of others. (3) O'Brien's assertion that Martin's interpretation does not "harmonize with the example of Christ set forth in the following hymn" misses the connections that Paul makes in this letter between the example of Christ and the characteristics of Christ expressed in the lives of those who follow Christ (see 2:19-30; 3:4-15). (4) Finally,

looking up to the good example of others must always look past others to worship on bended knee before the Lord, who humbled himself to die on the cross and whom God exalted to the highest place.

C. Focus on Christ (2:5-11)

5 *In your relationships with one another,*
have the same attitude of mind Christ Jesus had:
6 *Who, being in very nature God,*
did not regard equality with God something to be used to his own advantage;
7 *rather, he made himself nothing*
by taking the very nature of a servant,
being made in human likeness.
8 *And being found in appearance as a human being,*
he humbled himself
by becoming obedient to death —
even death on a cross!
9 *Therefore God exalted him to the highest place*
and gave him the name that is above every name,
10 *that at the name of Jesus every knee should bow,*
in heaven and on earth and under the earth,
11 *and every tongue acknowledge that Jesus Christ is Lord,*
to the glory of God the Father.

1. *A Community Mindful of Christ (2:5)*

5 In this verse Paul constructs a bridge between his exhortation to be mindful of the interests of others (2:1-4) and the hymn of Christ (2:6-11).[56] As readers move across his bridge, their attention turns from *the attitude of mind* which they express in their *relationships with one another* to the *attitude of mind Christ Jesus had,* expressed in his humiliation on the cross. In his exhortation, Paul emphasizes the importance of the *attitude of mind* of

---

O'Brien dismisses Martin's interpretation because Martin does not accept or explain the inclusion of καί *(also)* in the second half of the verse. But Martin's interpretation can be sustained even with the inclusion of καί. The presence of the καί simply indicates that Paul does not call for a total negation of one's own value or worth. The way that Paul sets up himself repeatedly in this letter as an example to follow shows that he does not totally negate seeing his own good qualities, as the absence of the καί might imply.

56. The connection with 2:1-4 is strengthened by the addition of the conjunction γάρ *(for, since)* in some MSS (𝔓^{46} ℵ^{2} D F G 𝔐). The reading that lacks the conjunction has good MSS support (ℵ* A B C Ψ); if the conjunction were in the original, there is no good reason for omitting it.

believers by calling them to be *like-minded* and of *one mind* (2:2) in their community. In the hymn, he calls the community to focus on Christ by leading them to worship Christ, who took the form of a servant and was consequently exalted by God.

Paul's connection between the attitude of believers and the Christ hymn is difficult to define precisely because his sentence is elliptical: it lacks a verb in the second clause. A literal translation presents the difficulty caused by the absence of a verb.

5a) Think this in yourselves
5b) which also in Christ Jesus.

A myriad of possible ways to supply a verb can be summarized by considering two alternative translations.

1. *Let this mind be in you that was in Christ Jesus.*[57] This way of reading the sentence implies an ethical interpretation of the Christ hymn. Christ's attitude portrayed in the hymn is viewed as an ethical paradigm of the attitude that Christians should express in their community. According to this interpretation, Paul is urging believers to reshape their attitude in the life of their community by looking at the attitude seen in Christ's life. *In humility,* believers must *value others* (2:3) because Christ, the ultimate example of humility, *humbled himself* (2:8).

Criticisms against this interpretation proceed along grammatical and theological lines.[58] A grammatical analysis shows that verse 5 is a sentence with two parallel clauses. If we add the verb *was* in the second clause and take the phrase *in Christ Jesus* as a reference to the individual example of Christ, we lose sight of the parallelism of these two clauses. Since the verb *think* is in the first clause, it would be natural to supply the same verb in the second, parallel clause.[59] And since the phrase *in you* expresses Paul's concern for the way that believers are thinking in their community (*among* you) rather than *within* themselves individually, the parallel phrase *in Christ* would also be understood as an equivalent expression referring to union with Christ, the incorporation of believers into the body of Christ, rather than denoting the individual example of Christ.[60]

57. NRSV; similarly, KJV, NIV, and NASB.

58. For extensive criticisms of the ethical example interpretation, see especially Martin, *A Hymn of Christ,* 68-88.

59. Silva (108): "There is nothing in the first clause to suggest that a verb other than *phroneō* should be supplied in the second clause." O'Brien (257), however, insists that supplying the same verb in the second clause "leads to a tautology."

60. Hawthorne (80-81) tries to preserve the grammatical parallelism by interpreting the *in you/in Christ* phrases as expressions of agency: "This way of thinking must be adopted by you, which was also the way of thinking adopted by Christ Jesus." But his translation is based on using the passive form of the verb "to think" found in the Majority Text, a reading that Hawthorne himself admits is "the inferior reading" (80), "perhaps an effort to more easily explain" the "in Christ" as a parallel to "in you" (76).

Theological reflection on the Christ hymn leads critics of the ethical interpretation to resist reducing the hymn to the level of a moral example. They insist that only naïve ethical idealism would suggest that the unique events of Christ's incarnation, death on a cross, and exaltation by God could be imitated in a Christian's life.[61] These objections form the basis for an alternative translation.

2. *Think this way among yourselves which also you think in Christ Jesus.*[62] This translation emphasizes the parallelism by using the same verb, *think,* in both clauses and by understanding the phrases *in you* and *in Christ Jesus* as parallel references to the corporate union of Christians with Christ. Paul is calling Christians to "think the same in your community with each other as one is obligated to think in the community in Christ."[63] Karl Barth argues that the phrase *in Christ Jesus* "designates in point of fact the reality, the place, the area in which the people addressed exist. They exist in the fellowship of Christ Jesus; they are members of his body."[64] The Christ hymn proclaims the awesome Reality of the one in whom Christians exist as members of his body. Those who propose this way of reading verse 5 insist that the purpose of the hymn is doctrinal (the proclamation of the unique Christ event), not ethical (the presentation of a moral example to imitate).[65] When the hymn is viewed as a drama of salvation in Christ, "it becomes more and more impossible to think of the believer as treading in His footsteps."[66] By placing the proclamation of Christ in the hymn after his moral exhortation, Paul is pointing to the power for moral transformation. Christian behavior is motivated and empowered by salvation in Christ, not by the example of Christ. The NEB captures this perspective in the translation, "Let your bearing towards one another arise out of your life in Christ." Experiencing the risen Lord's presence in the community will change the way believers think of one another.[67]

This line of interpretation gains support from Paul's appeal to Euodia and Syntyche to be reconciled (4:2). He urges them *to be of the same mind in the Lord.* The similarity of 2:5 and 4:2 is striking. The same verb *to think* is followed by the same reference to union with Christ. Paul is urging these two women to change their attitudes toward one another to reflect the real-

61. E. Käsemann, "Kritische Analyse von Phil. 2,5-11," *ZThK* 47 (1950), 313-60; ET by Alice Carse, "A Critical Analysis of Philippians 2:5-11," in *God and Christ: Existence and Province* (ed. Robert W. Funk; Journal for Theology and the Church 5; New York: Harper & Row, 1968), 45-88. The theological context for Käsemann's rejection of the ethical interpretation of the hymn is explained by Robert Morgan, "Incarnation, Myth, and Theology: Ernst Kasemann's Interpretation of Philippians 2:5-11," in *Where Christology Began: Essays on Philippians 2* (ed. Ralph Martin and Brian Dodd; Louisville: Westminster John Knox, 1998), 43-73.

62. Martin, *A Hymn of Christ,* 71.

63. Müller, 92.

64. Barth, 59.

65. Gnilka, 108.

66. Martin, *A Hymn of Christ,* 83.

67. Schenk, 185.

ity of their union with the Lord. The reality of their union *in the Lord* should transform the way they *think* of one another.

No doubt the debate over the translation of verse 5 will continue.[68] But the second translation has the best support. The parallelism of the two clauses leads the reader to supply some form of the main verb in the second clause and to understand both *in* phrases as references to the new community of believers in union with Christ Jesus: "Think this way in your community which you also think in your union with Christ." Such a translation fits well within the structure of Pauline ethics where the ethical imperative is grounded in the doctrinal indicative. The indicative of the union of our minds in Christ compels us to obey the imperative to think in harmony with one another in our Christian community.

Our acceptance of the second translation, however, does not force us to drop the ethical interpretation in favor of the doctrinal interpretation. Setting up these two interpretations as antithetical interpretations presents a false dichotomy. True, the hymn proclaims the unique drama of salvation in Christ: Christians do not merely look to Christ as a great moral example whom they follow, but as the exalted Lord whom they worship and obey. Just as Paul himself aspires *to know the power of his resurrection* (3:10), so he exhorts all believers to participate in the life of the risen Lord by the way they think toward one another in their common life *in Christ Jesus* (2:5).

And yet, the hymn also portrays Christ as the supreme moral example: He is the great Original and Origin of a new humanity. The explicit verbal links between Paul's moral instruction and the Christ hymn point to the way in which Paul wants Christians to become like Christ: *in humility* (2:3) they are to become like him who *humbled himself by becoming obedient to death — even death on a cross!* (2:8). Paul aspires to *participation in his sufferings, becoming like him in his death* (3:10). Although Paul does not use the hymn to set forth a series of steps to follow in the imitation of Christ, he does use it to draw up a correspondence between the exalted Lord and humble Christian service. He calls Christians to shape their community to reflect the self-humbling service of the Lord whom they worship.[69] Despite the vast differences between the narrative of Christ and the narrative of believers in Christ, believers are, nevertheless, drawn into the drama of Christ and eagerly anticipate becoming like Christ, both in his humiliation (2:3, 8; 3:10) and in his vindication (3:21). Thus verse 5 is a call "to apply to their communal life the precedent that is theirs by virtue of the fact that they are in Christ."[70] In the

68. BDAG, 1066, offers translations for both sides of the debate: "Let the same kind of thinking dominate you as dominated Christ Jesus," or "Have the same thoughts among yourselves as you have in your communion with Christ Jesus."

69. G. W. Hansen, "Resurrection and the Christian Life in Paul's Letters," in *Life in the Face of Death: The Resurrection Message in the New Testament* (ed. R. N. Longenecker; Grand Rapids: Eerdmans, 1998), 210.

70. S. E. Fowl, *The Story of Christ in the Ethics of Paul: An Analysis of the Function of the Hymnic Material in the Pauline Corpus* (JSNTSup 36; Sheffield: JSOT Press, 1990), 92.

exaltation of Christ, God vindicated the self-humbling of Christ. Christ-like self-humbling is the supreme virtue of the new humanity in Christ. "The renunciation of rights and dignity, the humble self-surrender which led Jesus to the cross, these God had declared to be the only greatness recognized in heaven."[71] In verse 5, Paul is urging believers to express their new humanity in Christ in their *relationships with one another* by having *the same attitude of mind Christ Jesus had.*

Background Questions

Before we proceed with a verse-by-verse exposition of verses 6-11, we need to consider two preliminary questions in the interpretation of this passage.

1. Is Philippians 2:6-11 a hymn?
2. Is Paul the author of this hymn?

Is This Text a Hymn?

The literary form of this passage is significantly different from the literary form of its surrounding context. In 1:27–2:5; 2:12-18, Paul is engaged in ethical exhortation: second person imperatives direct the community's life. The style and vocabulary of his pastoral advice are familiar ground; parallels abound in his letters. But we enter new territory in 2:6-11. Instead of reading customary Pauline prose, we are suddenly hearing poetry. Precise definitions of poems and hymns are debated.[72] Yet, in a general sense, poetry is marked by certain common traits: "a certain rhythmical lilt ascertainable when the passage is read aloud, a correspondence between words and phrases which are placed in the sentences in an obviously carefully selected position, not always *ad sensum;* the use of *parallelismus membrorum* (i.e. an arrangement into couplets); and traces of a rudimentary metre and the employment of rhetorical devices such as *homoeoteleuton,* alliteration, antithesis and *chiasmus.*"[73] Philippians 2:6-11 contains all of these traits of poetry.[74] As a result, "There is at least one thing that calls forth almost universal agreement. It is that vv. 6-11 constitute a beautiful example of a very early hymn of the Christian church."[75]

71. G. B. Caird, *New Testament Theology* (ed. L. D. Hurst; Oxford: Oxford University Press, 1994), 189.

72. See Martin, *A Hymn of Christ,* 1-23; Morna Hooker, "Philippians 2:6-11," in *Jesus und Paulus: Festschrift für W. G. Kümmel* (ed. E. E. Ellis and Erich Grässer; Göttingen: Vandenhoeck & Ruprecht, 1975), 157; O'Brien, 188; Fee, 193-94. Philippians 2:6-11 does not measure up exactly to modern definitions of poems and hymns or to ancient Greek and Semitic examples of poetry. The terms "song" and "hymn" are used in a broad sense when applied to NT poetic material. Hymns and creeds are often included in the same category.

73. Martin, *A Hymn of Christ,* 12-13.

74. See the commentary below, 133-69.

75. Hawthorne, 76.

Although there is widespread agreement that Philippians 2:6-11 is a poem or a hymn, debate regarding the specific details of its literary form continues unabated.[76] Ernst Lohmeyer's analysis provides a good starting point in this discussion.[77] In his description of the literary form of the passage, he sets forth the Greek text in six stanzas, with three lines in each stanza. The translation that follows stays as close as possible to the Greek text so that the English reader can see the poetic structure and features presented by Lohmeyer.[78] The exposition of the Christ hymn below follows this translation and arrangement.

(1) The one existing in the form of God
did not consider it an advantage to exploit
to be equal to God,
(2) but he emptied himself,
taking the form of a slave,
becoming in the likeness of human beings;
(3) and in appearance being found as a human being,
he humbled himself,
becoming obedient unto death — even death on a cross.
(4) Therefore also God highly exalted him
and gave to him the name
that is above every name,
(5) that in the name of Jesus
every knee will bow,
in heaven and on earth and under the earth,
(6) and every tongue will acknowledge that
Jesus Christ is Lord,
to the glory of God the Father.

Like threads in a beautiful tapestry, the lines in this poem are carefully woven together to form a complete picture. In the six stanzas of three lines each, the first three stanzas depict the attitudes and actions of Jesus on his journey from his original glory of equality with God all the way to his death on the cross; the last three stanzas proclaim the actions of God resulting in the universal worship of Jesus to the glory of God. Thus, the hymn

76. For an extensive review, see especially Martin, *A Hymn of Christ*, vii-95.

77. Ernst Lohmeyer, *Kyrios Jesus: Eine Untersuchung zu Phil. 2,5-11* (Sitzungsberichte der Heidelberger Akademie der Wissenschaften, Philosophisch-historische Klasse, Jahrgang 1927/28, 4. Abhandlung; Heidelberg: Carl Winter, Universitätsverlag, 2. Auflage 1961). Martin (*A Hymn of Christ*, 30) says that most studies of the passage since 1928 have been amendments and modifications of Lohmeyer's work.

78. My translation and arrangement reflect the works of Ernst Lohmeyer (90) and Colin Brown ("Ernst Lohmeyer's *Kyrios Jesus*," in *Where Christology Began: Essays on Philippians 2* [ed. Ralph P. Martin and Brian J. Dodd; Louisville: Westminster John Knox Press, 1998], 8-9) with some alterations that are explained in more detail in the commentary below.

portrays a divine parabola of descent from eternal glory to the cross and ascent back again to eternal glory. As a narrative poem, beginning and ending in eternity, it is complete in itself.

The stanzas develop a logical sequence: "Each three-line stanza expresses a consequence that becomes the ground of action in the next."[79] The first stanza reveals the attitude of Christ in his original state of equality with God: he did not consider exploiting the advantage of his divine form. The second stanza tells us that the result of his attitude was his action to empty himself by taking the form of a slave and becoming like a human being. The third stanza tells of his consequent self-humbling and obedience unto death on a cross. Each stanza is creatively formed. The main verb *(he considered)* in the first stanza is framed by a participle *(existing)* and an infinitive *(to be)*. In the second stanza the main verb *(emptied)* is modified by two participles *(taking, becoming)* that follow one another without a conjunction like two mighty drumbeats. The main verb *(humbled)* in the third stanza is also framed by two participles *(being found, becoming)* in the first and third lines.[80] The extension of the third line amplifies the horrific nature of Christ's death: *death on a cross.* The first three stanzas descend downward to the nadir of Christ's journey.

A double conjunction, *therefore also,* separates the first three stanzas from the last three and signals God's great reversal. The attitudes and actions of Christ led him to death on a cross. Now God acts. God is the subject of two verbs in the fourth stanza: God *highly exalted* him and *gave* to him. The consequences of God's actions are portrayed in the next two stanzas by two verbs: *every knee will bow* (fifth stanza); *every tongue will acknowledge* (sixth stanza). Note the beautifully balanced parallelism between the first and second half of the hymn. Both the first and the fourth stanzas point to divine actions. In each half of the hymn, the two stanzas that follow the portrayal of divine action give the consequences of that action. The main verb *(he emptied himself)* in the second stanza and the main verb *(he humbled himself)* in the third stanza portray the results of the decision of *the one in the form of God* that he would not exploit the advantage of his equality with God. The verb *(every knee will bow)* in the fifth stanza and the verb *(every tongue will acknowledge)* in the sixth stanza describe the results of the decisions of God to exalt Christ and give him the *name.* The word *name* is repeated three times and like the repeated drumbeats at the end of a symphony lead to the grand climax heard in the acknowledgment of all creation that Jesus Christ has the divine name: *Jesus Christ is Lord!*

As Colin Brown aptly notes, "These observations force the conclusion that the passage is no ordinary piece of letter writing or even rhetorical prose, but a carefully crafted poem."[81] The balanced symmetry of the

79. Brown, "Ernst Lohmeyer's *Kyrios Jesus,*" 9.
80. Brown, "Ernst Lohmeyer's *Kyrios Jesus,*" 9.
81. Brown, "Ernst Lohmeyer's *Kyrios Jesus,*" 9.

whole, the development of the themes, and the choice and placement of each word all provide ample evidence that Paul has inserted a hymn into the middle of his directions for the life of the community.

So far we have been looking at this hymn in the form of six stanzas with three lines in each stanza. This arrangement works well to highlight the poetic structure of this passage. Other arrangements have been proposed.[82] Of the many options, two are especially noteworthy. Jeremias arranges the hymn in three stanzas with four lines in each stanza.[83] According to Jeremias, the three stanzas portray the preexistence, the earthly life, and the heavenly glory of Christ. The advantage of his arrangement is the way it draws attention to parallelisms in the hymn.

I

The one existing in the form of God
did not consider an advantage
  to exploit to be equal to God
but he emptied himself,
taking the form of a slave,

II

becoming in the likeness of men,
and in appearance being found as
  a man,
he humbled himself,
becoming obedient unto death.

III

Therefore also God highly exalted him
and gave to him the name that is above every name,
that in the name of Jesus every knee will bow,
and every tongue will acknowledge that Jesus Christ is Lord.

The first stanza begins with *form of God* and ends with *form of a slave;* the second stanza begins with *becoming in the likeness of men* and ends with *becoming obedient unto death.* Each line of the first stanza is in some way parallel to each corresponding line in the second stanza.[84] The third stanza contains two couplets: the parallelism of the first two lines speaks of God's exaltation of Christ; the parallelism of the last two lines reflects the universal worship of Christ.

The disadvantage of Jeremias's arrangement is his deletion of three lines to make his stanzas perfectly symmetrical.[85] In the absence of any other evidence, his own artistic arrangement serves as the only basis for his deletion. His analysis also requires accepting his interpretation of the third

82. See Martin, *A Hymn of Christ*, 30-38, and O'Brien, 188-93, for extensive reviews of the options and criticisms of each option.

83. Joachim Jeremias, "Zur Gedankenführung in den paulinischen Briefen," in *Studia Paulina in Honorem J. de Zwaan* (ed. J. N. Sevenster and W. C. van Unnik; Haarlem: Hohn, 1953), 152-54.

84. Silva, 113.

85. Jeremias deletes three lines: *even death on the cross, in heaven and on earth and under the earth,* and *to the glory of God the Father.* He claims that these lines could not have been part of the original hymn.

line of the first stanza *(he emptied himself)* as a reference not to the incarnation of Christ but to the death of Christ.[86]

After discarding Jeremias's arrangement of the hymn in three stanzas referring to the three stages of Christ's narrative, Martin presents the hymn as a series of couplets in six pairs, arranged in this way so that they could be chanted antiphonally.[87]

A (a) Who, though He bore the stamp of the divine Image,
(b) Did not use equality with God as a gain to be exploited;
B (a) But surrendered His rank,
(b) And took the role of a servant;
C (a) Accepting a human-like guise,
(b) And appearing on earth as the Man;
D (a) He humbled Himself,
(b) In an obedience which went so far as to die.
E (a) For this, God raised Him to the highest honour,
(b) And conferred upon Him the highest rank of all;
F (a) That, at Jesus' name every knee should bow,
(b) And every tongue should confess that 'Jesus Christ is Lord.'

The plethora of suggested arrangements of this hymn drives a few interpreters to doubt that this passage is a hymn or song, even though they are forced to admit that it represents "exalted prose."[88] Hawthorne, however, expresses the conviction of most interpreters that the diverse analyses "demonstrate beyond doubt the fact that these verses comprise an early hymn."[89] Because the line between "exalted prose" and a "hymn" is so fine and the poetic nature of this passage is so widely appreciated, we are justified to call this passage a hymn even if we cannot provide a precise definition of a hymn or know its exact, original structure. With no claim that we have found the original structure, we will, nevertheless, follow Lohmeyer's six-stanza arrangement as a guideline in our commentary on this text. His

86. For a defense of the interpretation that the phrase "he emptied himself" refers to the death of Christ, not to the incarnation of Christ, see Robert H. Gundry, "Style and Substance in 'The Myth of God Incarnate' according to Philippians 2:6-11," in *Crossing the Boundaries: Essays in Biblical Interpretation in Honour of Michael D. Goulder* (ed. Stanley E. Porter, Paul Joyce, and David E. Orton; Leiden: Brill, 1994), 290-93. See discussion of the meaning of the phrase *(he emptied himself)* in the commentary below, 146-51.

87. *A Hymn of Christ,* 36-38. Martin accepts Jeremias's deletion of three phrases on the grounds that these phrases break the symmetry of the couplets and appear to be Pauline additions to an early church hymn.

88. Robert Gundry ("Style and Substance," 288): "The concentricity, chiasms, and other related parallels in Phil. 2:6-11 rather favor the view that this passage represents Paul's own exalted prose." Fee (192-93): "Since the seminal work of Lohmeyer, the vast majority of interpreters have assumed the present passage to be an early hymn (whether by Paul or otherwise) in honor of Christ. Whether a hymn or not, and I have considerable doubts here, one can scarcely miss the poetic and exalted nature of much of this."

89. Hawthorne, 77.

arrangement is especially useful for two reasons. First, his arrangement recognizes that the verbs provide the narrative structure for the hymn. In the first half of the hymn, three independent verbs, one in each stanza, express the acts of Christ leading to his humiliation in death. In each of these three stanzas the independent verb is framed by a participle and an infinitive (stanza one) or by two participles (stanzas two and three). In the second half of the hymn, two independent verbs in the fourth stanza express the exaltation of Christ by acts of God leading to the worship of Christ reflected by the two verbs in stanzas five and six. Second, Lohmeyer's arrangement follows the logical sequence of the hymn. As Colin Brown observes, "If every three lines form a unit of thought, which in turn constitutes the premise for the next three lines, the passage has a logical structure that requires the three-line arrangement Lohmeyer discovered in it."[90] Thus, Lohmeyer's arrangement serves as a valuable guide to the narrative structure and the logical sequence of the hymn.[91]

Who Is the Author of This Hymn?

The same evidence that this text is a hymn compels many interpreters to assert that Paul was quoting a hymn that he did not author, a hymn that was used in the worship of the early church. Five major lines of evidence need to be reviewed to assess the validity of this assertion.

First, the contrast between the hymn and its immediate context appears to indicate that the hymn is a quotation from a different genre of literature. The hymn is inserted in the middle of Paul's pastoral direction for community life. It "interrupts the flow of Pauline prose writing."[92] In contrast to the focus on the readers of the letter in the second person imperatives of Paul's ethical exhortation, the third person indicatives in the hymn focus on the actions of Christ, God, and all created beings. In contrast to a list of directions for the church to follow, the hymn is a lyrical contemplation of Christ. Did Paul compose this beautiful hymn of praise in a spontaneous burst of inspiration, or did he quote a hymn that he had learned from the early church? Neither option can be conclusively proven. No one can prove that Paul was incapable of writing beautiful poetry such as this. But the way that this hymn is set in this letter like a perfectly cut, absolutely clear diamond in a gold ring suggests that Paul acquired this precious jewel from the Christ-centered worship of the church rather than from the creative work of his own mind. Without missing a beat, Paul moved from giving pastoral advice to quoting poetic adoration of the Lord Jesus Christ to the glory of God the Father.

90. Brown, "Ernst Lohmeyer's *Kyrios Jesus*," 23.

91. My exposition of the Christ hymn follows my translation, structured according to Lohmeyer's arrangement.

92. Martin, *A Hymn of Christ*, lvii.

Second, the completeness of the hymn is evidence that Paul was quoting a hymn. Once he started this hymn, he couldn't be stopped. He had to sing all six stanzas of the hymn because they were so intricately woven together. To restrict himself only to words or phrases that were directly germane to his context and leave out the rest of the hymn would have been impossible for him to do because it would have caused him to tear apart a beautiful tapestry depicting the entire drama of Christ's humiliation and exaltation. Even though the entire hymn is connected in a number of ways to its context, it is so complete in itself and so much more majestic than its context that it is very easy to see that this hymn could have existed independently on its own before it was inserted by Paul into this letter.

Third, the style of the hymn is so different from the rest of Paul's own composition that it appears to be written by someone else. The rhythmic cadence, the parallel patterns and lines, the framing of independent verbs with participles, and the bipartite structure of the entire hymn with the downward movement of humiliation perfectly counterbalanced by the upward movement of exaltation are all poetic elements that set this text apart from the usual style of Paul found in his letters.

Of course, it is impossible to prove that Paul could not have written this hymn since we have no way to know for sure the extent of Paul's talents as an author. Some gifted authors write completely different kinds of literature: one of my favorite authors, C. S. Lewis, for example. His literary criticism, philosophical treatises, personal letters, children's stories, science fiction, and poems all flowed from his own fertile mind. Perhaps, Paul's devotion to Christ, so pronounced especially in this letter, inspired him to compose this beautiful poem of praise to Christ. Even Ralph Martin, one of the strongest advocates of pre-Pauline authorship of this hymn, admits that "Paul is capable of an exalted and poetic style when the occasion serves."[93] And yet, Martin, along with many other Pauline scholars, concludes that the unique style of this hymn marks it as "a separate composition, inserted into the epistolary prose of Paul's writing."[94]

Fourth, the fact that key words of the hymn were never used by Paul anywhere else in his letters may indicate that Paul was not the author of this hymn. The words *harpagmon (advantage to exploit)* and *katachthoniōn (under the earth)* do not appear elsewhere in Paul's letters, in the NT, or even in the Greek Old Testament (LXX). The word *hyperypsōsen (highly exalted)* does not appear elsewhere in Paul's letters or in the NT. The word *morphē (form),* used twice in this hymn *(form of God; form of a slave),* is not found elsewhere in Paul's letters. The only other time it appears in the NT is in the longer ending of Mark (Mark 16:12).

Besides these four words in the hymn that are not found elsewhere in

93. Martin (*A Hymn of Christ,* 57 n. 3) points to such passages as 1 Corinthians 13 and Rom 8:31-39 as Pauline parallels to Phil 2:6-11.

94. Martin, *A Hymn of Christ,* 43.

Paul's letters, five other terms are used elsewhere in Paul's letters, but are used in a unique way in the hymn. In the hymn the expression *he emptied himself* is used in a positive sense to commend the self-giving, self-surrendering love of Christ (2:7).[95] But in the other four uses of the same verb in Paul's letters (Rom 4:14; 1 Cor 1:17; 9:15; 2 Cor 9:3) the word is used with a strongly pejorative sense to condemn something that Paul abhors. The word *appearance* (2:8) refers to the human appearance of Christ; in its only other occurrence in Paul's letters (1 Cor 7:31), the same word refers to the appearance of the world. In the hymn the word *obedient* describes Christ's obedience to God as the true servant of the Lord.[96] Paul uses the same word in 2 Corinthians 2:9, but it refers to a test of obedience to his apostolic instructions. The only other time this word is used in the NT, it denotes lack of obedience to Moses (Acts 7:39). The terms *in heaven and on earth* (2:10) are used in conjunction in other places in Paul's letters (Phil 3:19-20; 1 Cor 15:40; 2 Cor 5:1-2), but only to represent two contrasting modes of human existence and never in conjunction with the expression *under the earth.* Paul's letters refer to "the name of our Lord Jesus Christ" (1 Cor 1:2, 10; 6:11; Eph 5:20), "the name of our Lord Jesus" (1 Cor 5:4; 2 Thess 1:12; Col 3:17), "the name of the Lord" (Rom 10:13; 2 Thess 3:6; 2 Tim 2:19), but a reference simply to *the name of Jesus* is found only in this hymn (2:10).

All of this unusual vocabulary in the hymn of Christ causes some to believe that Paul was not the author of this hymn. Of course, there is no way to prove or disprove authorship on the basis of vocabulary. The collection of Paul's letters does not provide an adequate basis for knowing the extent of Paul's vocabulary. Perhaps, Paul's contemplation of Christ and his composition of a hymn of Christ led him to use an unusual vocabulary. Nevertheless, when careful readers of Paul's letters confront the extraordinary words in this hymn, it is quite understandable that they would conclude on the basis of the exceptional vocabulary that Paul was not the author of this hymn.[97]

Fifth, the theological content of the hymn drives some interpreters to pose a non-Pauline authorship for the hymn. The theological concepts in the hymn that are not formulated in the same way anywhere else in Paul's letters include the identification of Christ as a slave (2:7), God's acts of exalting Jesus Christ and giving him the name above every name (2:9), and the threefold division of heaven, earth, and under the earth (2:10).[98] Paul of-

95. See the discussion of this word in the commentary on v. 7.

96. See the discussion of this word in the commentary on v. 8.

97. Martin, *A Hymn of Christ,* 48.

98. See Martin, *A Hymn of Christ,* 49. Martin also adds to this list the concept of the equality of Christ with God (2:6) in contrast to the Pauline concept of the subordination of Christ to God (1 Cor 15:28). But the concept of the equality of Christ with God is clearly stated elsewhere in Paul's letters. Although some passages in Paul's letters portray Christ as subordinate to God (1 Cor 11:3; 1 Cor 15:28), Paul affirms in other passages the full equality

ten describes himself and fellow believers as slaves of Christ, but nowhere else does he call Christ a slave. Paul says often in his letters that God *raised* Jesus from the dead, but not that God *exalted* him. Paul's letters teach that God graciously gave gifts and granted his favor to Abraham, to Paul, and to the church. But this is the only place where Christ is the object of the verb *to give* and the recipient of a gift from God. Paul says that he was caught up to the third heaven (2 Cor 12:2) and that Christ descended to the lower parts of the earth (Eph 4:9), but nowhere else is there a reference to people *in heaven and on earth and under the earth.*

Besides the presence of these unusual theological formulations in the hymn, the favorite Pauline themes of redemption, resurrection, and the church are conspicuously absent in the hymn. The gospel according to Paul is that "Christ died for our sins" (1 Cor 15:3); "he died for all" (2 Cor 5:15); "he died for us" (1 Thess 5:10). The absence of any reference to the redemptive value of Christ's death "for us" is quite surprising. Another central theme of the gospel according to Paul is the resurrection of Christ: Jesus is declared "by his resurrection from the dead" to be Jesus Christ our Lord (Rom 1:4; 1 Cor 15:4). To many interpreters of Paul, the hymn does not sound like typical Pauline theology when it moves from death to exaltation with no mention of the resurrection from the dead.[99] Finally, the confession that Jesus is Lord is central in Pauline theology, but this confession is the confession of the believing, Spirit-led church: "If you confess with your mouth, 'Jesus is Lord,' and believe in your heart that God raised him from the dead, you will be saved" (Rom 10:9, NIV); "no one can say, 'Jesus is Lord,' except by the Holy Spirit" (1 Cor 12:3). The climax of the hymn is the universal confession of all creation that Jesus is Lord.

Of course, no one hymn can be a compendium of all the major themes in Paul's letters. Nor can new themes in the hymn mark it as non-Pauline, since the full extent of Paul's theology is not necessarily limited to the content of his letters. Nevertheless, the theological differences between the hymn and Paul's letters provide the basis for some interpreters of Paul to conclude that Paul was not the author of this hymn.

The arguments for and against Pauline authorship are finely balanced. However, despite a "swing back to Pauline authorship on the part of some,"[100] this commentary agrees with the general consensus that this text

---

of Christ with God. See my commentary on 1:2 and 3:7-11. See also Murray J. Harris, *Jesus as God: The New Testament Use of* Theos *in Reference to Jesus* (Grand Rapids: Baker, 1992), 144-72, for convincing evidence that the term Θεός is applied to ὁ Χριστός in Rom 9:5 and that this appellation fits well within Pauline Christology.

99. Martin, *A Hymn of Christ*, 50.

100. Fee, 193; N. T. Wright (*The Climax of the Covenant: Christ and the Law in Pauline Theology* [Minneapolis: Fortress, 1993], 98). "If someone were to take upon themselves to argue, on the basis of my conclusions, that the hymn was originally written by Paul himself precisely in order to give Christological and above all theological underpinning to the rest of Philippians, especially chs. 2 and 3, I for one should find it hard to produce convincing

is best identified as "Paul's adaptation of a Christological hymn that likely originated much earlier than the epistle in which it is preserved."[101] Identification of Paul's explicit quotations of scripture in his letters can be checked by comparing his quotations with their sources. For example, the first step in an evaluation of the claim that Paul quotes Job 13:16 in Philippians 1:19 is a careful comparison of these two texts.[102] But identification of Paul's quotations of early Christian texts in his letters is much more difficult since in most cases we cannot check his sources. In these cases, identification of Paul's quotations depends on a careful comparison of the style, vocabulary, and content of the text in question with the larger context of Paul's own letters. A significant contrast between the text in question and Paul's writing is a valid reason to claim that the text is a quotation. Our analysis of the Philippians 2:6-11 text demonstrates that there is a significant contrast between this text and the style, vocabulary, and content of Paul's letters. This contrast provides a reasonable basis for the claim that Paul was not the original author of this text.

If Paul was not the author of the hymn, then who was? Numerous attempts to answer that question have produced a wide spectrum of speculations. Only four prominent options are considered here. First, Ernst Käsemann developed the theory that the hymn is derived from a pre-Christian Gnostic redeemer myth.[103] The basic narrative structure of the descent and ascent of the redeemer figure in the Gnostic redeemer myth served as the structure for the hymn as it was composed by the early Christian community. But Käsemann's suggestion that a pre-Christian Gnostic redeemer myth is the background of the hymn has encountered some difficult obstacles. First, since all evidence for Gnostic redeemer myths comes from the second century of the Christian era, there is little basis for talking about a pre-Christian redeemer myth. Second, the conflict of a Gnostic redeemer against cosmic powers, an essential element of the Gnostic redeemer myth, is not found in the hymn. Third, the incarnation of Christ and God's exaltation of Christ are essential elements of the hymn, but are not found in Gnostic myths.[104] For these reasons, Käsemann's theory has not garnered much support.

Second, at the other end of the spectrum of theories of authorship, Jerome Murphy-O'Connor places the origin of the hymn within the Pauline circle: "We do not know in which community the hymn originated, but in all probability it was one which had been founded by Paul." Murphy-O'Connor concludes that "the hymn grew out of Pauline teach-

---

counterarguments." See also Robert Gundry ("Style and Substance," 288): "This passage represents Paul's own exalted prose."

101. Larry W. Hurtado, *Lord Jesus Christ: Devotion to Jesus in Earliest Christianity* (Grand Rapids: Eerdmans, 2003), 112.

102. See the commentary on this verse above.

103. E. Käsemann, "A Critical Analysis of Philippians 2:5-11," *JTC* 5 (1998), 62, 66, 72.

104. See O'Brien, 193-94.

ing."[105] But if the hymn so faithfully represents Pauline teaching, why not simply accept that Paul is its author?

Third, the style, language, and theological concepts of the hymn compelled Fitzmyer to suggest that an Aramaic-speaking, Jewish Christian was the author of this hymn.[106] According to this theory, the style and language of the hymn are best explained by translating the Greek text back into Aramaic. Lohmeyer also claims that the Christology of the hymn is "bound by an indissoluble spiritual tie to the mother soil of Jewish piety."[107] Some aspects of this theory have gained support. For example, the evidence that the Christology of early Jewish Christianity viewed Jesus as the servant of the Lord (see Acts 3:13, 26; 4:27) and the righteous one who suffered (Acts 3:14; 7:52) may shed some light on the development of these motifs in the hymn.[108] One of the main objections to Fitzmyer's theory is the difficulty of translating the hymn back into Aramaic. The poetic qualities and nuanced idioms of the hymn are directly related to its use of the Greek language. This is not proof of its original composition in Greek, but it certainly points in that direction.[109]

Fourth, Ralph Martin asserts that "in Stephen we have a candidate for the authorship of the hymn. He was a Hellenistic Jewish Christian, of wide sympathies and with depth of penetration into the mystery of Christ."[110] Stephen's participation in the early church in Jerusalem, combined with his commitment to the universal mission of the church, would have enabled him to express both the early Jewish-Christian elements and the universal perspective of the hymn. His speech begins with a reminder that "the God of glory appeared to our father Abraham while he was in Mesopotamia" (Acts 7:2) and ends with the quotation from Isaiah: "'Heaven is my throne, and the earth is my footstool. What kind of house will you build for me? says the Lord'" (Acts 7:49). Before his martyrdom, Stephen witnesses to the glory of God and Jesus, the Son of Man, standing at the right hand of God (Acts 7:54-56). These links between Stephen and the hymn may be clues that Stephen or someone from Stephen's circle was the author of the hymn.[111]

All theories about the authorship of this hymn are highly speculative. Fortunately, its interpretation does not depend on any theory regarding authorship. Since Paul sets forth this hymn in his letter, he puts his stamp of

105. Jerome Murphy-O'Connor, *Paul: A Critical Life* (Oxford: Oxford University Press, 1996), 226; similarly, Beare, 78: "If the Apostle uses it, it is not unlikely that it was first composed by a gifted writer of his own circle, who had learned from him to think of Christ as the 'Man from Heaven' (1 Cor. xv.47), who 'being rich, impoverished himself for your sakes' (2 Cor. viii.9)."

106. Joseph A. Fitzmyer, "The Aramaic Background of Philippians 2:6-11," *CBQ* 50 (1988), 470-83.

107. Lohmeyer, *Kyrios Jesus*, 88.

108. See early Richard Longenecker, *The Christology of Early Jewish Christianity* (SBT 17; London: SCM Press, 1970), 106.

109. Wright, *The Climax of the Covenant*, 98.

110. Martin, *A Hymn of Christ*, 304.

111. Martin, *A Hymn of Christ*, 304-5, 312-13.

approval on every word and incorporates all its points into his theology and his ethics. Whether or not he was the original author of the hymn, he in effect becomes its author by using it for his purposes. By quoting this hymn, he confirms all that it says. In fact, he conforms to all that it says. The narrative poem of Christ provides the theological and ethical direction for the meaning of life in Christ. As Pheme Perkins explains, "The hymn sets out the central Christian metaphor whose effects are to be detected in the experiences of Paul, Epaphroditus and the Philippians." For this reason, Perkins calls the hymn "the governing metaphor for Christian belief." Not only does the hymn govern Christian belief, but also Christian conduct. "Within the Philippian community itself, Paul applies the governing metaphor to relationships."[112] Life in Christ will transform the behavior as well the beliefs of Christians so that the narrative structure of the hymn of Christ will be reflected not only in the story of the apostle Paul but also in the story of the *koinōnia* of the Spirit.

With full recognition of the speculative nature of all theories about authorship, this commentary accepts, as a working hypothesis, Martin's suggestion that one of the early Hellenistic Jewish-Christian missionaries, perhaps Stephen himself, was the author of the hymn. According to this hypothesis, the hymn is one of the first missionary hymns of the early church. As the church was expanding beyond its Jewish borders, this hymn gave the church the vision of the universal worship of Jesus Christ as Lord of all. And it reminded the church that the way of her Lord to glory was the way of humble, obedient service, suffering, and death. Stephen, perhaps the original author of this hymn and a martyr for his faith in Christ, followed in the way of his Lord. And Paul quoted this hymn with the *desire to know Christ — yes, to know the power of his resurrection and the* koinōnia *of his sufferings, becoming like him in his death* (3:10). Furthermore, Paul assured followers of Christ that it was granted to them not only to believe in Christ *but also to suffer for him* (1:29). As the church worships Christ with this hymn on bended knee acknowledging that Jesus Christ is Lord, she has an attitude of submissive obedience before her Lord. When the church has that attitude of mind in her relationship with her Lord, then she will be marked by humility in the relationships between fellow believers (2:5).

2. *The Christ Hymn: Humility (2:6-8)*

6 The first stanza of the hymn speaks of Christ's preincarnate attitude of mind: he did not consider his divine form, his equality with God, an advantage to exploit.

112. Pheme Perkins, "Philippians: Theology for the Heavenly *Politeuma*," in *Pauline Theology I: Thessalonians, Philippians, Galatians, Philemon* (ed. Jouette M. Bassler; Minneapolis: Fortress, 1991), 97, 103-4.

(1) *The one existing in the form of God*
did not consider it an advantage to exploit
to be equal to God,[113]

This interpretation of the first stanza as a description of Christ's existence before his incarnation does not depend on the meaning of the participle *existing*. This word does not in itself denote preexistence.[114] It simply points to a state or circumstance of being.[115] The subject of the hymn is the one who exists in the state or circumstance of being in the form of God. The reason for the perspective that the participle *existing* speaks of Christ's preexistence, or, more precisely, his preincarnate state, is found not in the meaning of the word *existing*, but in the relationship of this verb in the first stanza to the verbs in the second stanza. Both stanzas are parts of one continuous sentence that tells the narrative of Christ all the way to his death on the cross. The present participle *existing* in the first stanza precedes three verbs in the second stanza: an aorist finite verb, *he emptied*, modified by two aorist participles, *taking* and *becoming*.

(1) *The one existing in the form of God*
did not consider it an advantage to exploit
to be equal to God,
(2) *but he emptied himself,*
taking the form of a slave,
becoming in the likeness of human beings;

In this narrative sentence *existing in the form of God* comes before the actions described by the verb forms *he emptied* himself, *taking* the form of a slave, and *becoming* in the likeness of human beings. This temporal relation of the present participle to the aorist finite verb and the two aorist participles points to the preexistence of *the one existing in the form of God* before he emptied himself, took the form of a slave, and became in the likeness of humans.[116]

The prepositional phrase *in the form of God* describes the sphere or location of Christ's preincarnate existence. While we should not read too much into the preposition *in*, we should at least recognize that the text does

113. My translation of the Christ hymn follows the word order of the Greek text as closely as possible.

114. Against Lightfoot (110), who asserts that "the word denotes 'prior existence' but not necessarily 'eternal existence.'"

115. BDAG, 1029.

116. Gerald F. Hawthorne, "In the Form of God and Equal with God (Philippians 2:6)," in *Where Christology Began: Essays on Philippians 2* (ed. Ralph P. Martin and Brian J. Dodd; Louisville: Westminster John Knox, 1998), 97. The arguments of those who dispute a reference in the first stanza to the preexistence of Christ will be considered in more detail below.

not say that Christ was the form of God, but that Christ was *existing in* the form of God. This combination of the word *existing* with the preposition *in* is also found in Luke 7:25: "those who are clothed [*existing*] *in* expensive clothes and luxury are in palaces." In the terms of this idiomatic expression, the first stanza of the hymn asserts that Christ was clothed *in the form of God.*[117]

The standard Greek lexicon defines *form* as "outward appearance and shape."[118] In Greek literature the word *form* speaks of the "external appearance" visible to human observation. The visible form of persons, animals, and plants can be described in terms of color, shape, and size.[119] Similarly, the word *form* in the Greek OT (LXX) refers to something that can be seen.[120] For example, "A form stood before my eyes" (Job 6:16). "The carpenter measures with a line and makes an outline with a marker; he roughs it out with chisels and marks it with compasses. He shapes it in the form of a man" (Isa 44:13). This lexical meaning of *form* seems to work well for both uses of the word *form* in the context of this hymn.[121] In the parallel phrases, *the form of God* and *the form of a slave,* the word *form* refers to outward appearance. The one existing in the outward appearance of God took the outward appearance of a slave. The form of slaves could be observed every day in the marketplace of Philippi. Their outward appearance indicated that they were slaves. But can the form of the immaterial, invisible God be described? In contrast to the gods in Greek religion who have sensual forms, in the Jewish religion "it is a fundamentally alien and impossible thought that God should have a form open to human perception, or that He should reveal himself in sensual form."[122] Anthropomorphisms abound in the OT. God has a face, eyes, ears, mouth, arms, fingers, and back. But all of these references to the form of God are clearly figurative expressions. The prohibition against making any image of God demonstrates the conviction that the transcendence of God must not be diminished by human attempts to objectify the divine form. Hence, interpreters are challenged to understand this apparent oxymoron: What is *the form of God?*

From an extended study of the use of the word *form* in classical philosophy, J. B. Lightfoot concludes that it "must apply to the attributes of the Godhead. In other words, it is used in a sense substantially the same which it bears in Greek philosophy."[123] In Aristotle's metaphysics, all of

117. Behm, "μορφή," *TDNT* 4:751 n. 52; Hawthorne, 81.

118. BDAG, 659.

119. Behm, "μορφή," *TDNT* 4:742-43.

120. Judg 8:18; Job 4:16; Isa 44:13.

121. As noted earlier, these are the only two occurrences of the word *form* in Paul's letters. The only other occurrence in the NT is in the longer ending of Mark regarding the resurrection appearances of Christ: "Afterward Christ appeared in a different form to two of them while they were walking in the country" (16:12).

122. Behm, "μορφή," *TDNT* 4:749.

123. Lightfoot, 132.

reality can be described in terms of form and matter. The *form* of something is perceived through observation and expresses the true *nature* and *essence* of a thing. Aristotle's technical definition of this term is the basis of Lightfoot's assertion that *form* "implies not the external accidents but the essential attributes."[124] According to Lightfoot, the phrase *in the form of God* means participation in the being and sharing in the essence of God.[125] Lightfoot's use of the Aristotelian connection of *form* with *being, nature,* and *essence* appears to have influenced many commentaries.[126] As helpful as this definition of the word *form* has been to many, doubts have been raised about the legitimacy of restricting the meaning of the word *form* to the technical meaning found in the metaphysics of Aristotle.[127] Yet, even though Lightfoot's use of Aristotle has been questioned, his conclusion that the word *form* refers to the "the true divine nature"[128] is substantially confirmed by a different approach.

A number of interpreters have defined the meaning of *the form of God* by referring to numerous references in the OT that indicate that the glory of God is the outward appearance of the presence and majesty of God.[129]

> "There was the glory of the LORD appearing in the cloud" (Exod 16:10).
> "The glory of the LORD settled on Mount Sinai" (Exod 24:16).
> "Moses said, 'Now show me your glory'" (Exod 33:18).
> "Then the cloud covered the tent of meeting, and the glory of the LORD filled the tabernacle" (Exod 40:34).
> "Moses said, 'This is what the LORD has commanded you to do, so that the glory of the LORD may appear to you'" (Lev 9:6).
> "And the glory of the LORD appeared to all the people" (Lev 9:23).
> "The priests could not perform their service because of the cloud, for the glory of the LORD filled his temple" (1 Kings 8:11).
> "The heavens declare the glory of God" (Ps 24:1).

124. Lightfoot, 110.

125. See Martin, *A Hymn of Christ,* 102, for an evaluation of Lightfoot's definition of *form.*

126. Hawthorne (84): "being in possession of all the characteristics and qualities of God"; Fee (204): "It denotes 'form' or 'shape' not in terms of the external features by which something is recognized, but of those characteristics and qualities that are essential to it. Hence it means that which truly characterizes a given reality."

127. For significant references in Greek literature where *form* means a physical appearance, see Silva, 123. Käsemann ("Critical Analysis," 59-61) rejects the use of classical parallels. He prefers to use parallels from Hellenistic mystery religions and defines the phrase *the form of God* in terms of the Gnostic "heavenly man" myth. The difficulties of interpreting the hymn against the background of second-century Gnostic literature have been reviewed above.

128. Lightfoot, 133.

129. See Martin (*A Hymn of Christ,* 103) for a review of interpreters who have taken this approach.

"'Holy, holy, holy is the LORD Almighty; the whole earth is full of his glory'" (Isa 6:3)

"'Arise, shine, for your light has come, and the glory of the LORD rises upon you'" (Isa 60:1-2).

"Like the appearance of a rainbow in the clouds on a rainy day, so was the radiance around him. This was the appearance of the likeness of the glory of the LORD" (Ezek 1:28).

"I saw the glory of the God of Israel coming from the east, . . . and the land was radiant with his glory" (Ezek 43:2).

"I looked and saw the glory of the LORD filling the temple of the Lord" (Ezek 44:4).

The glory of God dramatically overpowers people by filling the tabernacle, the temple, the land, the whole earth, and the heavens with radiant, transcendent light.

Paul develops his argument in Romans 1 from this perspective that the glory of God is the outward appearance of God's power and majesty. Paul critiques those who have suppressed the truth: "They . . . exchanged the glory of the immortal God for images" (Rom 1:23). He bases his accusation on the premise that "since the creation of the world God's invisible qualities — his eternal power and divine nature — have been clearly seen, being understood from what has been made, so that people are without excuse" (Rom 1:20). This revelation of God in creation is the glory of God that has been exchanged for idols. Paul personally experienced the glory of God when he encountered Christ: "For God, who said, 'Let light shine out of darkness,' made his light shine in our hearts to give us the light of the knowledge of God's glory displayed in the face of Christ" (2 Cor 4:6).

This evidence that both the OT and NT speak of the glory of God as the manifestation of God supports the definition of *the form of God* as the glory of God.[130] The form of God in which the preincarnate Christ was clothed was the glory of God.[131] In both the OT and NT, the glory of God is the manifestation of God's power, the revelation of God's nature in creation and redemption, and the radiance of God's being.[132] In the account of Moses' request to see the glory of God ("Show me your glory"), the Lord's response is: "I will cause all my goodness to pass in front of you, and I will

130. Fee (205) rejects the definition of *the form of God* as "the glory of God." He points to the parallelism of the phrases, *the form of God* and *the form of a slave,* and notes that it is impossible to apply glory to the role of the slave. But this criticism misses the antithetical nature of the parallelism. The hymn draws a contrast between the form of God and the form of a slave. The word *form* means outward appearance in both cases. But *the form of God* is glory; *the form of a slave* is humiliation.

131. Behm, "μορφή," *TDNT* 4:751. For similar definitions of *the form of God* as "the glory of God," see Martin, *A Hymn of Christ,* 104-5 and his quotes from H. A. W. Meyer and J. Weiss.

132. See G. Kittel, "δόξα," *TDNT* 2:238-48.

proclaim my name, the LORD, in your presence" (Exod 33:18-19). Here the manifestation of the glory of the Lord is closely united with a proclamation of the Lord's goodness and the Lord's name. The glory of God expresses the being of God. The same close association of the glory of God and the being of God is found in the description of Christ in Hebrews: "He is the radiance of the glory of God and the exact representation of his being" (Heb 1:3). This union of the glory of God with the being of God informs our understanding of the first line of the hymn of Christ: *existing in the form of God.* If we conclude that *the form of God* means the glory of God and that the glory of God is intimately related with the being of God, then we will also conclude that the phrase *existing in the form of God* points to Christ's *being in very nature God* (TNIV). Our conclusion sounds similar to the one that Lightfoot derived from his use of Aristotelian metaphysics. But our conclusion is derived from our use of the biblical connection between the perception of outward appearance connoted by the word *form* and the perception of the manifestation of God's presence described as the glory of God. By saying that Christ was in the form of God before being made in human likeness, the hymn places Christ's preincarnate existence in the glory of God. And by doing so, the hymn asserts the intimate union of Christ with the being of God. While the hymn does not present an Aristotelian metaphysical definition, it does proclaim the existence of Christ in essential equality with God.[133]

The third line of the first stanza confirms the view that the first line asserts the equality of Christ with God. The parallelism of the first and third lines, *existing in the form of God* and *to be equal with God,* leads the reader to define each line in terms of the other line. The meaning of the line *existing in the form of God* is clarified by the line *to be equal with God.*[134] As an interpretive key for the first line, the third line affirms the one existing in the form of God to be equal with God. The form of God is not something different from God or less than God, just as the glory of God is not something different from God or less than God. So the one existing in the form of God is not different from God or less than God. And yet, despite equality with God, the one existing in the form of God and God are two distinguishable persons. In the last stanza of the hymn, Jesus is worshipped as Lord, to the glory of God the Father. Although the Lord Jesus and God are two distinguishable persons, Jesus is not a separate, second god. The union of Jesus with God is so intimate that the worship of Jesus is an inclusion within and an extension of the worship of the one God.[135] In the first stanza of the hymn, union with God is attributed to the personal existence of the preincarnate Christ.

The line of interpretation developed so far understands the meaning

133. Silva, 116.

134. Käsemann ("Critical Analysis," 62): "Whoever overlooks this fact and separates these two terms in order to consider them in isolation, can hardly be credited with a methodologically sound procedure."

135. Hurtado, *Lord Jesus Christ,* 151-52.

of the phrase *one existing in the form of God* in terms of the phrase "one existing in the glory of God." Another line of interpretation defines the meaning of the phrase the *one existing in the form of God* in terms of the image of God in Adam. Those who equate the phrase *the form of God* with the phrase "the image of God" see an extended comparison of Christ and Adam in the hymn. According to Dunn, the hymn "is dominated by the Adam/Christ parallel and contrast." As a result, "the terms used in the hymn do not have an independent value; *their sense is determined by their role within the Adam Christology.*"[136]

Weighty arguments have been forged against this use of the Adam/Christ parallel as a framework for interpreting the hymn. One primary reason given for drawing parallels between Christ and Adam in the hymn is the claim that the two words, *form (morphē)* and "image" *(eikōn)*, were used as "interchangeable terms."[137] Extensive research, however, adequately demonstrates that it is "inappropriate to assume a strict equivalence" of these words.[138] Even though there is some overlap in the lexical range of meanings of these two words, the question still remains as to whether the phrase *in the form of God* is used interchangeably with the phrase "the image of God." Hurtado says, "The answer is clearly negative."[139] In the Genesis story of creation, the phrase "the image of God" expresses the unique position of human beings as created representatives of God within God's creation. The NT applies this phrase "the image of God" to human beings (1 Cor 11:7; Col 3:10) and to Christ (2 Cor 4:4; Col 1:15). But nowhere is the phrase *form of God* used interchangeably with the phrase "image of God." According to Hurtado, the claim that the phrase *form of God* is used in the hymn as an allusion to the Genesis story of Adam created in the image of God needs to be supported by "at least a word or two from the alluded to text so that readers can catch the allusion."[140] But, in fact, besides the word *God* not one word from the Greek text of the Genesis story of the creation and temptation of Adam can be found in the hymn.[141]

136. James D. G. Dunn, *Christology in the Making: An Inquiry into the Origins of the Doctrine of the Incarnation* (London: SCM Press, 1960), 119. Dunn's emphasis.

137. Martin, *A Hymn of Christ*, 108; Dunn, *The Theology of Paul the Apostle* (Grand Rapids: Eerdmans, 1998), 284: "The terms were used as near synonyms." Even O'Brien, who rejects the Adam-Christ parallel, says that "most exegetes recognize that the semantic fields of the two terms overlap considerably" (263). The overlap can be seen in the lexicon: BDAG (659) on *form* (μορφή): "form, outward appearance, shape." BDAG (281-82) on "image" (εἰκών): "an object shaped to resemble the form or appearance of something, likeness, portrait; that which represents something else in terms of basic form or features, form, appearance."

138. David Steenburg, "The Case against the Synonymity of MORPHĒ and EIKŌN," *JSNT* 34 (1988), 85.

139. Hurtado, *Lord Jesus Christ*, 122.

140. Hurtado, *Lord Jesus Christ*, 122.

141. Fee (209) rejects any attempt to find Adam/Christ parallels in the hymn "since there is not a single linguistic parallel to the Genesis narrative."

These arguments against an Adam/Christ parallel in the hymn caution us to resist building the entire interpretation of the hymn on the foundation of this parallel. And yet, the "network of associations between Philippians 2 and Genesis 1–3" is strongly supported by evidence in Paul's letters where we find Adam/Christ parallels (Rom 5:12-19; 1 Cor 15:45-48), the word "image" in connection with Christ (Rom 8:29; Col 1:15), and the close connection of "image" and "glory" in the description of Christ (2 Cor 3:18; 4:4-6).[142] The equation of *the form of God* and "the image of God" can be accepted when it is expanded to include the middle term, *the glory of God.* Evidence for the equation of the rare reference to *the form of God* with the common reference to *the glory of God* has already been presented above. Paul equates "the light of the gospel that displays the glory of Christ, who is the image of God" with "the light of the knowledge of God's glory displayed in the face of Christ" (2 Cor 4:4, 6). Thus we have the expanded connection of *the form of God*–"the glory of God"–"the image of God."[143] All three terms (*form,* "glory," and "image") are united by Paul in one verse: "we all, who with unveiled faces contemplate the Lord's *glory,* are being trans*form*ed into his *image* with ever-increasing *glory*" (2 Cor 3:18). The way Paul connects these three terms in his letters leads to the conclusion that he would have heard the reference in the hymn to *the form of God* as an allusion to "the glory of God" and as an echo of "the image of God." We cannot enter into the long discussion of the difference between quotations, allusions, and echoes at this point. But we can learn "the discipline of tuning our ears to the internal resonances of the biblical text."[144] Once we have gained the sensitivity to hear the echo in the hymn of the biblical account that Adam was created in the image and likeness of God (Gen 1:26-27), then we will begin to hear more echoes of the Genesis story in the hymn and see more parallels between Christ and Adam in the hymn.[145]

Christ	**Adam**
Existing in the form of God	created in the image of God
Did not grasp equality with God	tempted to be like God
Took the form of a slave	enslaved to sin
Obedient to death	death after disobedience

The parallels drawn between Christ and Adam lead some to assert that the hymn does not make any reference to a preincarnate, personal pre-existence of Christ. Here is Dunn's logic: Since the narratives of Adam and Christ are parallel and since "Adam was certainly not thought of as pre-existent," therefore, "no implication that Christ was pre-existent may be in-

142. Silva, 116.

143. Martin, *A Hymn of Christ,* 106-19.

144. Richard B. Hays, *Echoes of Scripture in the Letters of Paul* (New Haven: Yale University Press, 1989), 21.

145. See Dunn's list of parallels in *The Theology of Paul the Apostle,* 284.

tended."[146] Similarly, Brown concludes that the phrase *in the form of God* refers to "one whose earthly life was a manifestation of God."[147] In this interpretation of the hymn, the hymn presents Christ's narrative against the backdrop of Adam's narrative. As human beings bearing the image of God, Adam and Christ made very different choices: Adam succumbed to the temptation to be like God (Gen 3:5), but Christ did not consider equality with God something to be grasped (Phil 2:6). Instead of grasping for equality with God, Christ "freely embraced the outcome which Adam's grasping and disobedience brought upon humankind. He freely embraced the lot of humankind as a slave to sin and death, which was the consequence of Adam's grasping."[148] Dunn stresses that the hymn draws these parallels between Christ and Adam in order to focus on the choices that they both made and the consequences of their choices. According to him, questions about the historicity of Adam or the preexistence of Christ are not addressed by the hymn.[149]

When the parallels between Christ and Adam are pressed to this point of denying any reference in the hymn to the preexistence of Christ, the narrative of the hymn is neglected and lost. The narrative in the hymn collapses when the story is retold to depict the choice of Christ as the choice of a human being who *emptied himself, taking the form of a servant, becoming in the likeness of human beings.* The hymn emphasizes the decision to become a human being by adding the phrase, *and being found in appearance as a human being.* If the first line — *the one existing in the form of God* — portrays the choice of one who is already a human being without any reference to his pre-human existence, then the subsequent lines in the narrative — *becoming in the likeness of human beings and being found in appearance as a human being* (2:7, 8) are strangely redundant.[150] What is the point of saying that a human being chose to become a human being and was found in appearance as a human being? But these repeated references to being made and found in human likeness are hugely significant if they depict the consequences of the choice of *the one existing in the form of God* before he became a human being.

Our recognition of the relation between the phrases *the form of God* and the "image of God" and between the parallels of Adam and Christ in the hymn does not necessarily lead to a denial of any reference to the preexistence of Christ in the hymn. Wright strongly agrees with Dunn that the terms of the hymn must have their sense determined by the contrast be-

146. Dunn, *Christology in the Making,* 119.

147. Brown, "Ernst Lohmeyer's *Kyrios Jesus,*" 27.

148. Dunn, *The Theology of Paul the Apostle,* 287-88.

149. Dunn, *Christology in the Making,* 120.

150. I. H. Marshall, "Incarnational Christology in the New Testament," in *Christ the Lord: Studies in Christology Presented to Donald Guthrie* (ed. H. H. Rowdon; Leicester: Inter-Varsity Press, 1982), 6; Martin, *A Hymn of Christ,* xxi: "The hymn's thought cannot start from Adam of Genesis but must go behind that Adam to Him who was the archetype of Adam. Only on this basis can the symmetry be established, and any real meaning given to the choice of Christ (in verse 6) which brought Him into the stream of humanity."

tween Christ and Adam, but then effectively argues that this contrast requires the preexistence of Christ. "The contrast between Adam and Christ works perfectly in my view: Adam, in arrogance, thought to become like God; Christ, in humility, became human."[151] G. B. Caird maintains that the incarnation is the main point of the Adam/Christ contrast in the hymn: "The whole balance of Philippians 2:5-11 depends on the reversal of Adam's conduct by the incarnation: Adam, being created in human form, grasped at equality with God; Christ, 'though he was in the form of God,' stooped to accept equality with the human race."[152] Theological reflection on the parallels between the Christ hymn and Genesis 1–3 led Ridderbos to observe that the hymn "describes Christ's pre-human, divine mode of existence and his disposition shown in it with features that make him known to us already in his pre-existence as the second Adam."[153] Thus, even before his incarnation, as *the one existing in the form of God* he was already the divine original for the creation of humanity in the image of God. Humanity is a copy of the divine original. By his incarnation, death, and exaltation, Christ opens the way for humanity to share in the glory of the original. Paul eagerly anticipated the time when the Lord Jesus Christ will "transform our lowly bodies so that they will be like his glorious body" (Phil 3:21).

The one existing in the form of God made a choice:

> *He did not consider it* harpagmos *(an advantage to exploit)*
> *To be equal with God.*

Defining the nature of this choice is difficult because the meaning of the Greek word *harpagmos* is unclear. This word is found nowhere else in the NT or Greek OT (LXX), and only rarely in Greek literature. The translation *an advantage to exploit* is one of many possible definitions of the word *harpagmos.* Of the many alternatives, four definitions deserve special attention.[154]

(1) *Grasping for something already possessed.* The KJV expresses this definition: "[Christ] thought it not *robbery* to be equal with God."[155] This active meaning of the word conveys the sense of an act of aggression: "a violent

151. Wright, *The Climax of the Covenant,* 91-92.

152. Caird, *New Testament Theology,* 97. Caird's point, that it was the human form that Christ took, not the Satanic form, refutes the position taken by some that the contrast in the Philippians passage is not between Christ and Adam but between Christ and Satan. For a representative of that position, see J. M. Furness, "Behind the Philippians Hymn," *ExpT* 79 (1967-68), 178.

153. Herman Ridderbos, *Paul: An Outline of His Theology* (Grand Rapids: Eerdmans, 1975), 76-78. Ridderbos convincingly argues against any interpretation of Christ's preexistence that involves the idea of a "heavenly man" as developed in different ways by Cullmann or Käsemann. "The speculative idea of Christ as the pre-existent heavenly man brings us into conflict with the text itself" (77).

154. Wright (*Climax of the Covenant,* 62-90) charts ten meanings and refers to many more.

155. Lightfoot (133-34) lists this meaning first in his extended note and quotes as support early Latin authors Tertullian, Ambrosian Hilary, Ambrose, and Augustine.

seizure of property."[156] When the term is defined in this way, it implies that Christ did not consider his equality with God to be his by an act of robbery since it was already his by inherent right.[157] In other words, Christ knew that his equality with God did not come to him by grasping but by being in the form of God. An objection raised against this definition is based on the context, which emphasizes the example of Christ's humility. In the context, the hymn of Christ draws attention "not to the right which He *claimed,* but the dignity which He *renounced.*"[158] This first definition seems to run contrary to the purpose of the hymn by giving a meaning to the opening stanza that emphasizes Christ's claim to his divine right to equality with God: be humble like Christ, who, existing in the form of God, knew that he was equal to God.

The active meaning of *harpagmos* as an act of *grasping for something already possessed* is framed in a somewhat different way by some who propose that the hymn presents the true nature of God as "characterized not by selfish grabbing, but by open-handed giving."[159] Thus, Christ's recognition that his equality with God is not robbery is not to be interpreted as claiming his divine right of equality with God, but as knowing that equality with God consists not in getting for oneself, but in giving of oneself. For those who understand the hymn in this way, the participial clause in the opening line should not be translated as a concessive participle (*although* he was in the form of God), but as a causative participle: "precisely *because* he was in the form of God he reckoned equality with God not as a matter of getting but of giving."[160] Giving, not grasping, expresses the very nature of God. God's essence is self-giving surrender.

According to some, the active meaning runs into "beaucoup trouble" because there is no object to the word.[161] If the word refers to an act of grasping, there should be a reference to the object of grasping. The reader is left wondering: grasping what? Wright deflects this criticism of the active meaning by insisting that "an abstract noun like 'snatching', 'grasping', or 'getting' does not need an object; it refers, intransitively, to a particular way of life."[162] Foerster, however, rejects the definition of *harpagmos* as an activity of grasping on the basis that "the lack of an object makes this impossible."[163]

(2) *Something to be grasped that is already possessed.* This passive mean-

156. BDAG, 133.

157. Wright, *Climax of the Covenant,* 63.

158. Lightfoot, 134.

159. Hawthorne, 85. See also C. F. D. Moule, "Further Reflections on Philippians 2,5-11," in *Apostolic History and the Gospel* (ed. W. W. Gasque and R. P. Martin; Grand Rapids: Eerdmans, 1970), 264-76.

160. C. F. D. Moule, "The Manhood of Jesus in the NT," in *Christ, Faith, and History* (ed. S. W. Sykes and J. P. Clayton; Cambridge: Cambridge University Press, 1972), 97.

161. Collange, 89. Also Martin, 135-36.

162. Wright, *Climax of the Covenant,* 89.

163. W. Foerster, "ἁρπαγμός," *TDNT* 1:474.

ing of the word is used by the RSV and NIV translations: "a thing to be grasped," "something to be grasped." Lightfoot fills in the implications of this meaning with his colorful paraphrase: "He, though existing before the worlds in the form of God, did not treat His equality with God *as a prize, a treasure to be greedily clutched and ostentatiously displayed;* on the contrary, He resigned the glories of heaven."[164] This understanding of *harpagmos* implies that the *prize, treasure,* consisted of the rights and privileges of divinity, not divinity itself. Lightfoot was concerned to demonstrate that his definition supports the view that Christ possessed equality with God in his preincarnate state and that Christ did not give up his equality with God in his incarnation, but only "the glories of heaven."[165] The basic elements of Lightfoot's analysis have been widely affirmed with some variations and modifications. Barth succinctly states a similar understanding of the term: "Christ, being equal with God, has no need to assert himself in that or cling to it, but can renounce the outward appearance and credit that correspond to such being, without surrendering the being itself."[166]

(3) *Something to be grasped that is not possessed.* A different interpretation is given by some who view the choice made by Christ from the perspective of the Adam-Christ contrast. In contrast to Adam who attempted to be like God (Gen 3:5), Christ did not regard equality with God as something to be grasped. From this perspective, Christ's choice was a refusal to grasp something that he did not possess. Rather than connecting this choice described in the hymn to a particular event in Christ's earthly life, such as the temptation in the wilderness or the confession of his Messiahship at Caesarea Philippi, Dunn suggests that at every stage of his life and ministry Christ choose not to grasp for equality with God as Adam did but to accept the fallen lot of Adam's race.[167]

Martin proposes a mediating position between the position that Christ had equality with God but did not cling to it and the position that Christ did not have equality with God and did not grasp for it.[168] By making a distinction between (a) the phrase *being in the form of God* and (b) the phrase *to be equal to God,* Martin maintains that Christ possessed (a) divinity but did not possess (b) equality with God in his preincarnate state. Equality with God, according to Martin, means to exercise cosmic Lordship. This Lordship was implicit in Christ's preexistent state as *the one existing in the form of God,* but "the meaning of the verse is that He did not reach out from his favored place and grasp at that authority. He chose, on the contrary, to

164. Lightfoot, 134.

165. Lightfoot, 134-37.

166. Barth, 62-63.

167. Dunn, *Christology in the Making,* 120-21. See the references by Martin, *A Hymn of Christ,* 142-43, to other proponents of this view.

168. Latin terms are often used in this debate. *Res rapta* means a thing possessed which one holds on to; *res rapienda* means a thing which one does not possess, which one wants to grasp.

be installed as World-Ruler and Cosmocrat at the completion of a mission of self-humbling and lowly obedience."[169]

Martin's position, however, conflicts with the structure of the hymn in at least two ways.[170] First, Martin's distinction between the phrases *existing in the form of God* and *to be equal to God* contradicts the grammatical structure of the phrase *to be equal to God*. In the Greek phrase the significance of the article with the infinitive *to be* is that it points back to the previous phrase, *existing in the form of God*.[171] "This means that 'the being equal with God' is precisely another way of saying in the form of God.'"[172] Second, Martin's position (that cosmic Lordship belongs potentially to Christ but is not actually his until after the cross and exaltation) conflicts with the theological structure of the hymn.[173] The theological point of the hymn is not that Christ is elevated to the position of cosmic Lordship (equality with God) which he did not have before his humiliation, but that Christ reveals the essence of equality with God and cosmic Lordship by his humiliation. The exaltation of Jesus is "the affirmation, by God the Father, that the incarnation and death of Jesus really was the revelation of the divine love in action."[174]

(4) *Something to be selfishly exploited that is already possessed.* In an extensive study of this phrase, Hoover insists that "in every instance which I have examined this idiomatic expression refers to something already present and at one's disposal. The question . . . is not whether one possesses something, but whether or not one chooses to exploit something."[175] This interpretation takes the hymn's reference to equality with God as a description of Christ's divine nature and position in his preincarnate state. The hymn asserts Christ's decision not to regard his equality with God as *harpagmos:* something to be exploited for his own selfish advantage. When *harpagmos* is understood as *something to be selfishly exploited*, Christ's decision does not imply that he gave up his equality with God but that he expressed his equality with God. "The pre-existent son regarded equality with God not as excusing him from the task of (redemptive) suffering and death, but actually as uniquely qualifying him for that vocation."[176] The obedience of the Son in his death on the cross revealed the true nature of God.

The first stanza of the hymn lifts the veil between time and eternity to reveal the choice of one existing in the form of God and equal with

169. Martin, *A Hymn of Christ*, 152-53.

170. Wright (72-73) subjects Martin's view to six criticisms.

171. In Greek grammar this is called "the anaphoric significance of the article, i.e. its reference to something previously mentioned" (see BDF §399).

172. Hawthorne, "In the Form of God and Equal with God," 104.

173. See Wright, *The Climax of the Covenant*, 84-87.

174. Wright, *The Climax of the Covenant*, 86.

175. R. W. Hoover, "The HARPAGMOS Enigma: A Philological Solution," *HTR* 64 (1971) 95-119. This quote is from 118.

176. Wright, *The Climax of the Covenant*, 83-84.

God. This person did not view his divine being and rank as something to use for his own selfish advantage. Such a view was inconsistent with his character. This first stanza states that this negative choice — this decision to say No to selfish exploitation of an advantageous position — was the choice of this divine person. The negative choice — the divine No — reveals the divine character of this person. In contrast to the natural human tendency to say Yes to every opportunity to exploit personal advantages of position and power for selfish purposes, this person said No to the exploitation of his divine position and his unlimited power for his own selfish pursuits. The great rulers, heroes, and gods of the citizens of Philippi were famous for exploiting their positions of power. When did the emperors Caligula and Nero, the great conqueror Alexander the Great, or the gods Apollo and Zeus ever not regard their positions as advantages to exploit? But the one existing in the form of God said No to selfish exploitation of his position in the form of God and said Yes to the form of a servant.

7 *but he emptied himself,*
taking the form of a slave,
becoming in the likeness of human beings;

A shocking metaphor depicts the next choice in the narrative of Christ's journey to the cross. He *emptied himself!* It should be no surprise that this verb has fueled centuries of debate. What does it mean that the one existing in the form of God and equal with God *emptied himself?* A historical review of responses to this question yields a wide spectrum of interpretations.[177] Three interpretations merit careful evaluation. (1) *The kenotic theory:* Christ emptied himself by divesting himself of divinity: divine attributes, divine glory, or divine power. (2) *The incarnation view:* Christ emptied himself by becoming a human being in the form of a slave. (3) *The Servant of the Lord portrait:* the metaphor of emptying is an echo of the scriptural picture of the Servant of the Lord, who "poured out his life to death" (Isa 53:12). These are not mutually exclusive interpretations; our own conclusion combines elements from all three.

(1) *The kenotic theory.*[178] This theory attempts to answer the question, Of what did Christ empty himself? The originators of the kenotic theory find the answer in the previous lines of the hymn: Christ emptied himself of the form of God, of his equality with God. The surrender of the form of God simply means that Christ emptied himself of his divine nature.[179] Usually, a reference to the kenotic theory points to this view that Christ exchanged the form of God for the form of a servant. A kenotic Christology based on this

177. See especially Martin, *A Hymn of Christ,* 169-96. Martin lists seven major categories of interpretation, with various alternatives within each category.

178. The name of this theory is derived from the Greek word *to empty* (κενόω).

179. Martin (*A Hymn of Christ,* 166 n. 1) quotes H. A. W. Meyer and C. Gore as proponents of this view.

view denies to some extent or other the fullness of Christ's divine nature as a result of his incarnation. Objections to this form of the kenotic theory arise from several important observations of the text. First, the verb *emptied* does not require a second object in addition to the pronoun *himself.*[180] Thus, the question — Of what did he empty himself? — does not require an answer since the answer is already supplied in the pronoun *himself.* Second, the strong adversative *but* that introduces the verb *emptied* separates this verb from the phrase *the form of God* so that the phrase *the form of God* cannot be the object of the verb.[181] Third, the verb *emptied* is defined by the participles that follow it: *he emptied himself by taking and becoming.* Thus, Christ's self-emptying was accomplished "not by subtracting from but by adding to."[182] Fourth, the verb *emptied* is used metaphorically; to press for a literal meaning of "emptying" ignores the poetic context and nuance of the word. For all these reasons the original version of the kenotic theory has been discredited.

Modified versions of a kenotic theory still surface, but they are presented in ways that do not suggest any diminishment of Christ's divine nature. These definitions of *kenosis* (emptying) still attempt to answer the question, Of what did he empty himself? Lightfoot, for example, says that "He divested Himself not of His divine nature, for this was impossible, but of the glories, the prerogatives, of Deity."[183] Similarly, Martin asserts that "it would be wrong to insist that the text teaches the surrender of divine attributes and the exchanging of Christ's deity for his human nature." But he goes on to say that "he who existed eternally in a heavenly station surrendered that high place and gave up the position of being the 'Image of God' and humbled himself to accept the role of the servant." According to Martin, "His kenosis then is His willingness to step out of the Father, and this He must do in order to take human form. It entails a suspension of His role as the divine Image by His taking on an image which is Man's."[184]

These modifications of the kenotic theory recognize that the contrast between the first and second stanzas of this hymn implies the extent of surrender involved when Christ emptied himself. The reaction against the kenotic theory goes too far when it insists that the hymn "gives no clue whatsoever as to what it was that Christ emptied himself of."[185] While there is no basis for saying that Christ emptied himself of his divine nature, as the founders of the kenotic theory said, the contrast between the form of God and the form of a slave gives an important clue as to what Christ emptied himself of. The insights of the modified versions of the kenotic theory can be validated and retained by looking at the meaning of Christ's self-emptying as defined by the incarnation view.

180. Martin, *A Hymn of Christ*, 167.
181. O'Brien, 218.
182. Hawthorne, 86.
183. Lightfoot, 112.
184. Martin, *A Hymn of Christ*, 194-96.
185. Hawthorne, 85.

(2) *The incarnation view.* Christ's voluntary act of self-surrender is defined by the two phrases: *taking the form of a slave* and *becoming in the likeness of human beings.* Since these two phrases essentially describe the incarnation — Christ became a human being in the form of a slave — Christ's act of emptying himself is equated with the incarnation. The particular form of his incarnation as a human being is emphasized by the first phrase, *taking the form of a slave.* The meaning of the word *form* here is the outward appearance that reveals the inward nature; the same meaning of the word is expressed in the phrase *the form of God.* But there is an absolute contrast between the outward appearance of God and the outward appearance of a slave. *The form of God* is the glory of God: the glorious splendor of the highest position, the power displayed in the creation of the universe, and the sovereignty expressed in his universal rule over all his creation. *The form of a slave* is the exact opposite of glory: a slave does not have a high position, unlimited power, unrivaled sovereignty. A slave has the lowest position; he is powerless; he has no rights. He has no glory: no honor; only shame.[186] This contrast points to the extent of Christ's self-emptying. Since slavery in the world of Paul and his readers was "the extreme in respect of the deprivation of rights,"[187] the hymn tells us that Christ deprived himself of his divine rights when *he emptied himself, taking the form of a slave.* Although Christ did not exchange the form of God for the form of a slave, he "gave up the appearance of his divinity" when he took the form of a slave.[188] While still existing in the form of God, he experienced all the powerlessness and poverty of a slave. In a sense, O'Brien is right when he says that Christ "displayed the nature or form of God in the nature or form of a slave, thereby showing clearly not only what his character was like, but also what it meant to be God."[189] But in another sense, Christ cloaked or hid the form of God in the form of a slave. By taking the form of a servant, his existence in the form of God was concealed. In the words of Calvin, "Christ, indeed, could not renounce his divinity, but He kept it concealed for a time, that under the weakness of the flesh it might not be seen."[190]As Barth says, "He put himself in a position where only he himself knows himself in the way the Father knows him. . . . The step that brings him into that unrecognizable condition, into the *incognito,* is grounded entirely in himself alone. That is how he takes on the 'form of a servant,' the appear-

186. For a description of the social setting of the colony of Philippi for understanding the loss of honor and sense of shame incurred by taking the form of a slave and suffering death on a cross, see J. H. Hellerman, "The Humiliation of Christ in the Social World of Roman Philippi, Part 1," *BSac* 160 (2003), 321-36; J. H. Hellerman, "The Humiliation of Christ in the Social World of Roman Philippi, Part 2," *BSac* (2003), 421-33.

187. Moule, "Further Reflexions on Philippians 2:5-11, in *Apostolic History and the Gospel,* 268. Moule makes a convincing case for this interpretation of the term *slave* in the context of the practice of slavery in the Hellenistic world.

188. BDAG, 539.

189. O'Brien, 224.

190. Calvin, 248.

ance and the credit (or rather lack of credit) of a being that is not God, that is not the Lord."[191]

Thus, the *kenosis* of Christ, the self-emptying of Christ, is the incarnation in the form of a slave of the one existing in the form of God. The TNIV conveys the meaning of the *kenosis* of Christ: *he made himself nothing by taking the very nature of a servant, being made in human likeness.* Calvin hits the same note in his commentary: "The Image of God shone forth in Christ in such a manner that He was nevertheless abased in outward appearance and brought to nothing in the estimation of men; for He bore the form of a servant, and assumed our nature."[192] That the verb *emptied* means made nothing or rendered powerless can be observed in Paul's use of same verb in other letters: "lest the cross of Christ be *emptied of its power*" (1 Cor 1:17); "faith *has no value*" (Rom 4:14, NIV).[193] The verb *emptied* "does not refer to the loss of divine attributes but — in good Pauline fashion — to making something powerless, emptying it of apparent significance."[194] When Christ emptied himself by taking the form of a slave, he made himself powerless with no apparent significance in the world.

(3) *The Servant of the Lord portrait.* The text *he emptied himself, taking the form of servant* bears resemblance to Isaiah's portrayal of the Servant of the Lord who "poured out his life unto death" (Isa 53:12). Jeremias claims that the expression *he emptied himself* is an exact translation of the Hebrew text of "he poured out his life."[195] A comparison of the Servant Song in Isaiah and the hymn of Christ discloses other connections: the servant is highly exalted (Isa 52:13; Phil 2:9); the form of the servant (Isa 52:14; Phil 2:7); the humiliation of the servant (Isa 53:3-4; Phil 2:8); "therefore" God exalted the servant (Isa 53:12; Phil 2:9).[196] The verbatim quotation of Isaiah 45:23 ("every knee will bow, every tongue will swear") at the end of the hymn (Phil 2:10-11) adds to the evidence that the line *he emptied himself, taking the form of a servant* is an allusion to the line in the Servant Song that the Servant of the Lord "poured out his life unto death."[197]

On the basis of this evidence, Jeremias interprets the phrase *he emptied himself* as a reference to the death of Christ, not to the incarnation of Christ.[198] The structure of the hymn, however, makes this interpretation difficult to sup-

191. Barth, 63.

192. Calvin, 249.

193. See also two texts where boasting is rendered powerless: "*deprive* me of my boast" (1 Cor 9:15); "that our boasting about you should not *prove hollow*" (2 Cor 9:3).

194. Wright, *The Climax of the Covenant,* 84.

195. J. Jeremias, "παῖς θεοῦ," *TDNT* 5:711.

196. Jeremias, "παῖς θεοῦ," *TDNT* 5:712 n. 446.

197. Silva, 125; also Fee, 212. But see O'Brien's review of the arguments (268-71) and conclusion (271) that "the evidence presented by Jeremias and others has not been sufficient to establish with certainty the identity of Is. 53:12 and Phil. 2:7."

198. Jeremias, "παῖς θεοῦ," *TDNT* 5:711 n. 445. He is strongly supported by R. H. Gundry, "Style and Substance in 'The Myth of God Incarnate' according to Phil 2:6-11," 274, 290-93.

port. The hymn appears to follow a chronological order of events: the preincarnate choice not to exploit the advantage of equality with God, incarnation, humiliation, and death on the cross. If the self-emptying is a reference to the cross, then the hymn presents events out of chronological order: the cross, incarnation, the cross. While chronological order cannot be presupposed, the evidence that the self-emptying is an allusion to Isaiah 53:12 is not a good reason for breaking the apparent order in the hymn by taking the self-emptying as a reference to the cross. This allusion does not require pressing for a complete correspondence between the hymn of Christ and the Servant Song. The hymn is saying essentially the same thing as "he poured out his life unto death," even though in the hymn the self-emptying is the incarnation that led to death, rather than death itself. An allusion usually paraphrases rather than quotes. But as a paraphrase, this allusion still effectively evokes the memory of an ancient portrait to enrich the meaning of the expression *he emptied himself.* The portrait of the Servant of the Lord in the Servant Song of Isaiah and the portrait of Christ in the hymn of Christ, though they are different in many respects, portray the same story of the same person.[199]

An objection raised against the identification of the Servant in Isaiah with the slave in Philippians 2:7 is based on the contrast between the honor associated with the title "Servant of the Lord" in Isaiah and the humiliation associated with the form of the slave in the hymn of Christ.[200] But this objection overlooks the graphic portrayal of humiliation endured by the Servant of the Lord in Isaiah 53.[201] The Philippian readers were probably first reminded of the humiliation of slaves in their own contemporary Roman context when they heard the hymn about the humiliation and death of a slave. But their understanding of the suffering of Christ depicted by the hymn would have been deepened by hearing the song of the suffering of the "man of sorrows" in Isaiah 53.

> He had no beauty or majesty to attract us to him, nothing in his appearance that we should desire him. He was despised and rejected by men, a man of sorrows, and familiar with suffering. Like one from whom men hide their faces he was despised, and we esteemed him not. Surely he took up our infirmities and carried our sorrows, yet we considered him stricken by God, smitten by him and afflicted. (Isa 53:2-4, NIV)

Clear echoes of this ancient song of the Servant of the Lord can be heard again in this early Christian hymn of the one who, existing in the form of God, *made himself nothing by taking the very nature of a servant.*[202]

199. Longenecker, *The Christology of Early Jewish Christianity,* 106, points to "a verbal and a conceptual affinity between Phil 2:6-11 and Isaiah 53."

200. O'Brien, 270.

201. Gundry, "Style and Substance in 'The Myth of God Incarnate' according to Phil 2:6-11," 293.

202. Fee, 212.

The meaning of the phrase *he made himself nothing* (TNIV) contains some elements of all three alternative interpretations considered above. Christ did not empty himself of his divinity, his divine form and equality with God, but he did surrender his divine rights and cloaked his divine glory by becoming human in the form of a slave. His existence in the form of God was both manifested and concealed in the form of a slave. His act of self-emptying was the incarnation; the result of the incarnation was humiliation, suffering, and death. While his slave-like form would have been understood by the Philippians against the background of contemporary slavery in the Roman world, it was most eloquently described in the Song of the Servant in Isaiah 53. Like the Suffering Servant in that song, Christ "poured out his soul unto death."

The two parallel participial phrases, *taking the very nature of a servant* and *becoming in the likeness of human beings,* both describe how Christ's act of self-emptying was accomplished by the simultaneous action of *taking* and *becoming. Taking the form of a slave* specifies the *form* of his incarnation. His incarnation was not in the form of a lord or in the form of an emperor to be served by others, but in the form of a slave, "a person without advantage, with no rights or privileges of his own for the express purpose of placing himself completely at the service of all."[203] The term *slave* does not designate a certain class of people to which Christ belonged, but the specific mission of his incarnation.[204] Christ became a human being not in order to be served, but to serve.[205] Whether or not this hymn reflects the tradition of the incident in the life of Jesus, in which Jesus takes the role of slave and washes his disciples' feet (John 13),[206] that incident illustrates the meaning of this line in the hymn. "Jesus knew that the Father had put all things under his power, and that he had come from God and was returning to God; so he got up from the meal, took off his outer clothing, and wrapped a towel around his waist. After that, he poured water into a basin and began to wash his disciples' feet, drying them with the towel that was wrapped around him" (John 13:3-5). Jesus deliberately stripped himself of the rights and privileges of his divine majesty as Lord and took the form of a slave to serve the needs of others.

The participle *becoming* is used in this context to "indicate entry into a new condition" or "state of being."[207] In contrast to the present tense participle, *existing,* in the first stanza that speaks of continuous existence in the form of God, the aorist participle, *becoming,* speaks of "an entrance into an

203. Hawthorne, 87.

204. Collange, 93.

205. Mark 10:45: "the Son of Man did not come to be served, but to serve, and to give his life a ransom for many."

206. Hawthorne (87) suggests that the incident of John 13 shaped the hymn, but in the revised edition Martin (Martin and Hawthorne, 103) points to significant differences between the hymn and John's theology that make Hawthorne's suggestion untenable.

207. BDAG, 198.

existence like that of human beings."[208] The use of the word *becoming* in this context is similar to its use in other contexts (John 8:58; Rom 1:3; Gal 4:4) to denote "being born."[209] While the hymn does not offer a narrative of the birth and infancy of Christ, it does contemplate the entrance of Christ into human history.

Christ's entrance into history was *in the likeness of human beings.* The word *likeness* means "having common experience" and "being similar in appearance."[210] In some contexts, the word stresses (a) the actual identity of two objects or events: "if we have been united with him in the *likeness* of his death" (Rom 6:5). In this passage, the word *likeness* means that in baptism we have experienced "the *same* death that he died."[211] In other contexts, the word points to (b) an external resemblance between two completely different objects: "The *appearances* of the locusts were like horses prepared for battle" (Rev 9:7, my trans.). Since this word can indicate actual identity or merely external resemblance, the question naturally arises regarding the extent of similarity between Christ and human beings. Did *becoming in the likeness of human beings* result in (a) such complete identification with fallen humanity that there was no difference between Christ and fallen humanity?[212] Or did *becoming in the likeness of human beings* result only in (b) an outward façade of similarity that merely cloaked the inner, essential dissimilarity of Christ, the divine being, to fallen humanity? Both of these extremes are negated by the context. The extreme of (a), total identification with no difference, would mean that Christ retained nothing of his divine form and equality with God and was subject to the power of sin and did sin. But the hymn's portrayal of the one existing in the form of God entering human history and its announcement of the divine vindication of Christ's perfect obedience rule out (a). Christ did retain his divine form and equality with God in the likeness of human beings, and Christ was sinless in his perfect obedience.[213] In these essential ways Christ was dissimilar to fallen humanity. The opposite extreme of (b) is also ruled out by the hymn. This extreme would mean that Christ's appearance in the likeness of human beings was only a charade: he did not actually become a human being; he was a divine being in a human mask.[214] But the whole point of the second and third stanzas of the hymn (2:7-8) is the extent of Christ's identification with fallen humanity in his self-emptying, his slave form, his human like-

208. O'Brien, 224.

209. Martin, *A Hymn of Christ,* 202.

210. BDAG, 707.

211. BDAG, 707; Martin, 201.

212. The question of the *likeness* of Christ to fallen humanity is raised by a parallel passage: God sent his own Son "*in the likeness* of sinful humanity" (Rom 8:3).

213. J. Schneider, "ὁμοίωμα," *TDNT* 5:197.

214. In early church history, this extreme was called Docetism, a teaching that Christ only appeared to be a human being, but never actually assumed a human nature.

ness, his human appearance, his humiliation, his obedience, and his death on a cross. The hymn tells the story of one existing in the form of God who entered into human experience as a human being; it is not a farce or comedy of one who was faking identification with humanity.[215]

The phrase *in the likeness of human beings* guards the mystery of Christ's incarnation from the two extremes of (a) and (b).[216] The ambiguity of the phrase *in the likeness* preserves both the similarity of Christ to human beings in his full humanity and the dissimilarity of Christ to fallen humanity in his equality with God and his sinless obedience.[217] Even when Christ acquired his human nature and entered human experience, he continued to exist in the form of God and remained equal with God.[218] I have translated the Greek word for men *(anthrōpoi)* in our text as *human beings* since the Greek word in this context is gender inclusive: Christ identified with all of humanity, not just the male gender. The point of the text is not that Christ was made in the likeness of the male gender, but that he was made *in human likeness* (TNIV). In the past, when the English word "men" was understood by all to be gender inclusive in some contexts, the use of the English word "men" as a translation of the Greek word *anthrōpoi* was accurate. But in the present time, when the English word "men" is considered by many to be gender exclusive in all contexts, the term *human* or *human beings* needs to be used in this context to convey the meaning of the text: Christ identified with all human beings, both men and women.

8 *and in appearance being found as a human being,*
he humbled himself,
becoming obedient unto death — even death on a cross.

The next phrase in the text, *and in appearance being found as a human being,* stresses by repetition the genuineness of Christ's humanity. In his "outward *appearance,* form, and shape,"[219] Christ was *found* in every respect to be fully human. The word *found* here indicates that the reality of Christ's humanity was discovered "intellectually through reflection, observation, examination or investigation."[220] The word "expresses the truth that this fact could be

215. Bonnard, 44.

216. Martin (*A Hymn of Christ,* 206) observes, "The coming of the Lord of glory to earth is wrapped in mystery; and His advent upon the scene of time is no everyday occurrence. There is an unexplained element, not only in His appearance but in His life upon earth."

217. Fee, 213.

218. Schneider ("ὁμοίωμα," *TDNT* 5:197): "As man Christ is in the depths of His essence a being of another kind."

219. BDAG, 981; Schneider, "σχῆμα," *TDNT* 7:954: "σχῆμα always denotes the outward form or structure perceptible to the senses and never the inward principle of order accessible only to thought." The only other use of this word in the NT is in 1 Cor 7:31: "The *form* of this world is passing away." In this context, the word points to the present manifestation of this world, the present observable structure and order of this world.

220. BDAG, 412.

seen by anybody."[221] Solid empirical evidence led all who observed Christ to conclude that he was an authentic, not a counterfeit, human being. Here again the Greek word *anthrōpos* is best translated as *human being,* since the point of the text is not Christ's male gender, but his humanity.

These last two phrases of verse 7 emphasize the reality of Christ's humanity in different ways: the first one speaks of his historical entrance into humanity; the second one points to the empirical evidence of his humanity. These parallel phrases present a historical sequence and a progression of thought.[222] The historical event of *being made* is followed by the personal experience of *being found.* Although these two phrases are linked together in synthetic parallelism, the conjunction *and* at the beginning of the second phrase serves as the introduction of a new sentence and indicates that this phrase modifies the following verb, he *humbled himself.*[223] As the one existing in the form of God, he emptied himself by *being made in human likeness. And* as one who was *found in appearance as a human being,* he humbled himself.

The hymn narrates a second downward step of the divine person. Just as the one in the form of God *made himself nothing,* the same person, *found* by examination to be a human being, *humbled himself.* As a human being, "he takes in that capacity the same step into the depths once again."[224] The decision not to exploit the advantageous position of equality with God but to empty himself is confirmed by the subsequent decision not to exploit his advantageous position as a divine person made in human likeness but to humble himself. The one who could have rightfully claimed the highest position in human history and justly received supreme honors deliberately sought the lowest position and submitted himself to extreme humiliation.

This reference to Christ's humiliation may be another echo of the Servant Song in Isaiah 53.[225] The Greek text of Isaiah 53:8 says that the Servant of the Lord was taken away "in humiliation,"[226] and the entire song graphically describes the extent of his humiliation. Beyond this obvious parallel

221. Schneider, "σχῆμα," *TDNT* 7:956.

222. Müller (105) draws attention to the synthetic parallelism: ἀνθρώπων — ἄνθρωπος and γενόμενος — εὑρεθείς.

223. According to Fee (214 n. 3), O'Brien (226), Gnilka (121), and Müller (105), the conjunction *and* (καί) connects the two main verbs, *emptied* and *humbled,* not the participles, *becoming* and *being found.*

224. Barth, 64.

225. See W. D. Davies, *Paul and Rabbinic Judaism: Some Rabbinic Elements in Paul's Theology* (London: S.P.C.K., 1948), 274. Davies tabulates the parallels:

Isa 52:13:	He shall be exalted	Phil 2:9:	God has highly exalted him
Isa 53:7:	He was oppressed, yet he opened not his mouth	Phil 2:8:	He humbled himself
Isa 53:8:	ἤχθη εἰς θάνατου	Phil 2:8:	ὑπήκοος μέχρι θανάτου
Isa 53:12:	He poured out his soul unto death	Phil 2:6:	ἑαυτὸν ἐκένωσεν

On the basis of these parallels, Davis says, "We shall assume that Paul identified Jesus, the Messiah, with the Suffering Servant of Deutero-Isaiah."

226. Isa 53:8: ἐν τῇ ταπεινώσει Phil 2:8: ἐταπείνωσεν ἑαυτόν

of the humiliation of the servant in both passages, careful investigation highlights significant differences between the two songs.[227] In Isaiah, the title "my servant" (Isa 52:13) connotes a position of honor, but the reference to *a slave* in the Christ hymn (Phil 2:7) depicts a position with no rights or privileges. Isaiah's Servant Song presents the Servant suffering passively without protest as a slaughtered lamb (Isa 53:7). The Christ hymn, however, emphasizes that the servant actively *humbled himself, becoming obedient unto death* (Phil 2:8). The clause, "he poured out his soul unto death" (Isa 53:12), does not provide a genuine parallel to the Christ hymn since the clause *he emptied himself* (2:7) and the phrase *unto death* (5:8) refer to two separate events: the event of the incarnation and the event of the cross. Although these differences between these two songs make it difficult to hear a perfect echo of the Servant Song in the Christ hymn, the clear parallel of the humiliation of the servant in both songs identifies Jesus with the Suffering Servant of Isaiah 53.

The servant's humbling of himself in the Christ hymn perfectly embodies the teaching of Jewish wisdom literature that "humility comes before honor" (Prov 15:33; 22:4), the gospel traditions of Jesus' teaching that "whoever humbles himself will be exalted" (Matt 23:12; Luke 14:11; 18:14), and the teaching of the early church to "humble yourselves before the Lord, and he will lift you up" (Jas 4:10; similarly, 1 Pet 5:6).[228]

In the immediate context of the Christ hymn, the line "Christ *humbled himself*" is an explicit connection between the hymn and Paul's exhortation: *in humility value others above yourselves* (2:3). Paul encourages the practical expression of humility by pointing to the perfect exemplar of humility of Christ as portrayed in the hymn.[229] As an exemplar, the hymn does not give a "model to be copied" in every detail.[230] The narration of the unique events of the incarnation, crucifixion, exaltation, and universal worship of Christ does not provide a step-by-step pattern to be imitated.[231] And yet, Paul does draw a parallel between the ethical behavior of the church and the life of Christ by first requiring the church to practice humility and then

227. Hooker, *NIB* 11:503.

228. Müller, 105-6.

229. See Fowl, *The Story of Christ in the Ethics of Paul,* 92; Hansen, "Transformation of Relationships," 202-3.

230. Martin (215) strongly objects to an ethical interpretation of the hymn: "The hymn has little to say about the ethical intention of Jesus as though the author were holding up His virtues as a model to be copied." Martin sets his own rule for the interpretation of the hymn: "It is of the utmost importance to isolate the meaning of the terms in the hymn from the use which is made of them by Paul in the verses that proceed and follow. The text of the hymn must be taken on its own, irrespective of the application which is made in the neighboring verses." Martin may be right that the hymn, isolated from its context, does not provide an ethical example. But when we interpret the hymn in the context and observe the verbal link between the exhortation to practice humility and the self-humbling of Christ, it is hard to miss Paul's ethical application of the hymn.

231. Hansen, "Transformation of Relationships," 203.

pointing to the precedent for their behavior in the self-humbling obedience of Christ.

The phrase *by becoming obedient unto death* explains how Christ *humbled himself.* Humiliation was not something that happened to Christ against his will. The one existing in the form of God and equal with God could not be humbled or humiliated by any person or power unless he willingly submitted to that humiliation.[232] His submission to humiliation could be explained only as being the result of his own active obedience. He chose to be submissive as a slave rather than to be sovereign as the Lord. By his obedience the one existing in the form of God confirmed his decision to take the form of a slave. The form of God is glory; the form of a slave is humiliation. By his obedience Christ both manifested and concealed the glory of God in the humiliation of a slave. The *extent* of Christ's obedience is emphasized by the phrase *unto death.* This is not a measurement of the time of obedience, but of the degree of obedience.[233] The point is not so much how long, but how much Christ became obedient. "Jesus' obedience took him to the nth degree, to death itself."[234]

The hymn does not specify the object of Christ's obedience. The hymn "is interested rather in the fact that he obeys, in the attitude of submission and dependence he adopts."[235] That Christ became obedient to God may be inferred from the subject of the next sentence *(God exalted him)* and from the final line of the hymn *(to the glory of God the Father).*[236] This inference is supported by other texts that emphasize the obedience of the Son to the will of God the Father.[237] Since Christ's obedience to the will of God is so well grounded in biblical teaching, it is reasonable to assume that God was the object of Christ's obedience celebrated in this hymn of Christ. The context of the hymn may also imply that others besides God were the objects of his service and beneficiaries of his obedience. Since Paul's introduction to the hymn called believers in Christ to "look not only to your own interests, but also to the interests of others" (2:4), we may infer that Paul uses the hymn to demonstrate that Christ's obedience unto death was in "the interests of others."[238] This inference is supported by other texts that point to Christ's death as the ultimate act of service to others.[239] As a slave, Christ served God by serving others and giving his life as "a ransom for many" (Mark 10:45). Although the hymn itself does not explicitly say so, Paul sets the hymn in a context to show that Christ's death was "his ultimate act of obe-

232. Barth, 64.
233. BDAG, 644.
234. Fee 216 n. 9.
235. Barth, 65.
236. Bruce, 79: "It was to the Father's will that he rendered obedience as far as death."
237. Especially Mark 14:35-36; John 4:34; 6:38; Heb 5:8; 10:7.
238. Hawthorne, 89.
239. Especially Mark 10:45; John 15:13; Eph 5:25; 1 John 3:16.

dience to God in his self-giving service to people."[240] In his application of the hymn (2:12), Paul encourages his readers to express the life of Christ in their community by their obedience to God in their service to each other.

The first half of the hymn ends with the dramatic phrase — *even death on a cross! Death, Death!* Like the crescendo of a drum roll, the reverberation of the word *death* brings the first half of the hymn to a deafening silence before the *cross.* The last word to be heard is the word *cross. Death on a cross* was not a heroic death, a noble death, but a shameful death, a disgraceful death. The cross displayed the lowest depths of human depravity and cruelty.[241] It exhibited the most brutal form of sadistic torture and execution ever invented by malicious human minds.[242] Roman law reserved the cross for the worst criminals and the most violent insurrectionists, and only those who were slaves or foreigners. A Roman citizen would never be executed by crucifixion. Cicero called death on a cross "a most cruel and disgusting punishment."[243] The cross is "the worst extreme of the tortures inflicted upon slaves." "To bind a Roman citizen is a crime; to flog him is an abomination; to slay him is almost an act of murder; to crucify him is — what? There is no fitting word that can possibly describe so horrible a deed."[244] For Christians in a Roman colony, the phrase *death on a cross* "would emphasize the abject degradation of Christ's lowly obedience, and drive home the lesson that His identification with men reached the lowest rung of the ladder."[245] No greater contrast can be imagined than the contrast between the first and last lines of the first half of the hymn: *existing in the form of God . . . death on a cross.* The one existing in the form of God suffered the most extreme humiliation in human experience by his death on a cross.

The cross served as the instrument by which Christ *emptied himself* and *humbled himself.* Christ willingly accepted the cross to fulfill his purpose for *taking the form of a servant* and *being made in human likeness.* Every decision and action of *the one existing in the form of God* led deliberately to the final climax of *death on a cross.* The hymn celebrates Christ's choice to be *obedient to death — even death on a cross.* The extreme humiliation by death on the cross was the ultimate fulfillment of the divine intention of the one who was equal to God.[246]

240. Hawthorne, 89.

241. Bonnard, 45.

242. See Martin Hengel, *Crucifixion* (Philadelphia: Fortress, 1977), 21-32, for a detailed description of "crucifixion as a barbaric form of execution of the utmost cruelty." In his summary, Hengel says, "Crucifixion satisfied the primitive lust for revenge and the sadistic cruelty of individual rulers and of the masses. It was usually associated with other forms of torture, including at least flogging. At relatively small expense and to great public effect the criminal could be tortured to death for days in an unspeakable way" (87).

243. Cicero, *Against Verres* 2.5.64 §165 (LCL: Cicero, *The Verrine Orations* 2.651).

244. Cicero, *Against Verres* 2.5.66 §§169-70 (LCL: Cicero, *The Verrine Orations* 2.655-57).

245. Martin, 221.

246. O'Brien, 231.

The way that the line *even death on a cross* provides a fitting climax for the entire first half of the hymn (and, as we will see, the basis for the second half of the hymn) indicates that it was an integral part of the original hymn before Paul used the hymn for his own purposes.[247] The argument of many interpreters that these words must be viewed as a Pauline addition because they break the metrical symmetry of the hymn and reflect Pauline purposes and theology are refuted by observing that "the words in fact constitute the climax to which the last three verses have been pointing."[248] The line *death on a cross* does not reflect Paul's usual way of referring to the cross. Invariably, Paul's references to the death of Christ on the cross point to the redemptive benefit of the cross "for us." The cross of Christ, according to Paul, was the way that Christ "gave himself for me" (Gal 2:20), the way that Christ "redeemed us from the curse of the law by becoming a curse for us" (Gal 3:13), and the way that "the world has been crucified to me, and I to the world" (Gal 6:14). None of these redemptive benefits of the cross "for us" are explicitly mentioned in the hymn. Although these benefits for us may be inferred from the surrounding context, the portrayal of the cross in the hymn itself is centered exclusively on Christ. The reason for the cross given by the hymn itself is not the redemptive benefit for us, but the decisive action of Christ to empty himself and humble himself.

To celebrate the cross of Christ as the achievement of the decisive action of the one existing in the form of God is the great paradox of the first half of the hymn. It is logical to celebrate the creation of the stars and galaxies, the oceans and the mountains, the birds and flowers, and the human senses to enjoy all of this as the achievement of the creative action of the one existing in the form of God. Other hymns do celebrate the creative power of God in this way. The psalmist sings that "the heavens declare the glory of God" (Ps 19:1); the song of the Word declares that "through him all things were made; without him nothing was made that has been made" (John 1:3); another song of Christ proclaims that "by him all things were created: things in heaven and on earth, visible and invisible, whether thrones or powers or rulers or authorities; all things were created by him and for him" (Col 1:16). These hymns make perfect sense; what they celebrate is consistent with the glory of God. But the first three stanzas of the hymn of Christ in Philippians 2 go in another direction; they contradict any reasonable expectations for the celebration of the glory of God. The first

247. Bruce, 79: "The phrase *even death on a cross* forms the climax of the first part of the hymn. It is not a later addition calculated to Christianize the composition; it is integral to the sense, and rhythmically it forms a coda to the first part as the phrase *to the glory of God the Father* does to the second part."

248. G. B. Caird, *Paul's Letters from Prison: Ephesians, Philippians, Colossians, Philemon in the Revised Standard Version* (Oxford: Oxford University Press, 1976), 122. See also Hengel, *Crucifixion*, 62-63; Fee, 217; O'Brien, 230. Beare (85) misses the integral connection of this line to the entire hymn when he comments that it "stands outside the formal structure of the hymn and is substantially irrelevant to its theme."

three stanzas do not lift up our eyes to the heavens to see the wonders of creation; they do not even lift up our hearts by showing us wonderful miracles of healing and deliverance; they take us down, down, down to the deepest, darkest hellhole in human history to see the horrific torture, unspeakable abuse, and bloody execution of a *slave* on a *cross*.[249] This hymn celebrates the death of a *slave* on a *cross* because, although he is forever the one existing in the form of God, he is on that cross by his own deliberate choice to *empty himself* and *humble himself.*

3. *The Christ Hymn: Exaltation (2:9-11)*

9 *Therefore also God highly exalted him*
and gave to him the name
that is above every name,

The first sentence of the hymn ends with Christ's death on a Roman cross — the lowest place. The second sentence begins with a complete reversal: *Therefore also God highly exalted him.* Christ's actions led to his total humiliation by death on the cross. Now God's actions lead to the universal worship of Christ by every tongue confessing that he is Lord. Although the hymn changes direction from downward to upward, Christ remains the central theme of the entire hymn, both as the subject of his own actions that led to his humiliation as an obedient slave on a cross and as the object of God's actions that lead to his exaltation as the Lord worshipped by all.[250]

A double conjunction, *therefore also,* bridges the transition from the first sentence to the second sentence, from humiliation to exaltation. *Therefore,* as an inferential conjunction,[251] indicates that Christ's action of self-humbling is the reason for God's actions of exalting him and giving him the name above every name. The use of the conjunction *also* in this way "marks an element of reciprocity"[252] evident in the change of pronouns: Christ humbled *himself;* God exalted *him.* The combination of the conjunctions introduces God's exaltation of Christ as the result of the Christ's obedience unto death.[253] Since this double conjunction introduces God's actions as the *result* of Christ's obedience, does it also mean that God's actions were the *reward* for Christ's obedience?

249. See Joseph H. Hellerman, *Reconstructing Honor in Roman Philippi:* Carmen Christi *as* Cursus Pudorum (SNTSMS 132; Cambridge: Cambridge University Press, 2005): "It is hardly an accident that crucifixion, the most dishonorable form of public humiliation which the socially conscious Roman elite could employ in their efforts to punish and discourage rebellion among the lower classes, finds itself so closely associated with slavery, the lowest class in the stratified world of Roman antiquity."

250. Martin, *A Hymn of Christ,* 230.

251. BDAG, 250.

252. Martin, *A Hymn of Christ,* 233.

253. BDF §442 (12).

Strong voices give a resounding No to the view of Christ's exaltation as a reward for his obedience. Calvin insists that "we ought to avoid such profane speculations as obscure the grace of Christ." To guard against such speculations, Calvin asserts that the inferential expression *(therefore also)* "denotes here a consequence rather than a reason." What motivated Calvin's definition of the conjunction was his concern to stop anyone from thinking that "a man could merit divine honours and acquire the very throne of God."[254] Barth also excludes any idea of reward, but he does so by denying that the conjunction denotes any sense of sequence or consequence: "It does not say that he who was humbled and humiliated was afterward exalted, was indeed . . . rewarded for his self-denial and obedience. But what it says is that precisely he who was abased and humbled, even to the obedience of death on a cross, is also the Exalted Lord."[255] According to Barth, the conjunction does not bridge a transition in the narrative of Christ from the event of humiliation to the event of exaltation; instead, it simply connects two views of Christ: "he who became a man and was crucified . . . is he who is exalted." Hawthorne develops another way to avoid the idea of reward or merit by suggesting that the conjunctions indicate that God's exaltation of Christ was the "natural or logical outcome of his humility. In other words, these conjunctions affirm what Jesus taught, namely that in the divine order of things self-humbling leads inevitably to exaltation. This is an inflexible law of God's kingdom that operates without variance, equally applicable for Christians at Philippi as for Christ himself."[256]

These ways of denying the idea of reward in God's exaltation of Christ contribute noteworthy insights. They accurately insist that God's exaltation was not *quid pro quo:* God's exaltation was not a recompense granted on the basis of strict justice in return for Christ's self-humiliation. Since the statement that God *exalted* Christ is amplified by the parallel statement that God *gave* him the name above every name, the verb *gave (charizomai),* indicating an act of grace, defines the verb *exalted* as an act of grace. God's exaltation of Christ was by the "libre grâce de Dieu," the free grace of God.[257] Thus, Calvin rightly rejects the argument that the hymn shows how anyone can merit divine honor on the basis of obedience. Barth's approach properly establishes the identity of the exalted Christ with the crucified Christ. Hawthorne helpfully reminds us that Christ illustrates his own rule that "whoever humbles himself will be exalted."

Although these insights correct flawed ideas of reward, they do not provide the basis for excluding a proper concept of reward. Calvin's redefinition of the conjunctions to mean consequence rather than reason is "extremely doubtful."[258] Even the sense of consequence does not eliminate the

254. Calvin, 250.
255. Barth, 66.
256. Hawthorne, 90.
257. Collange, 95.
258. Martin, 232.

concept of reward. Barth's denial that the conjunctions indicate a sequence rejects what the narrative affirms: the exaltation comes *after* the humiliation and is in some way a response to the humiliation. Hawthorne seems to view the humiliation and exaltation of Christ as an impersonal, automatic series of events that illustrate an "inflexible law." But the hymn speaks of the exaltation of Christ in terms of God's personal acts, not in terms of the logical outcome of an abstract principle. The hymn says that after Christ humbled himself by becoming obedient unto death, God personally intervened when he exalted Christ and gave him the name above every name. Does it not appear that the hymn presents God's exaltation of Christ as a personal reward for Christ's obedience?

Yes. But our Yes must be qualified in several important ways. First, the hymn does not view the reward as the motive for Christ's obedience. Thus, Christ's obedience does not exemplify obeying in order to deserve a reward. Second, the hymn does not present the reward as redemption from sin. The hymn does not lead to the supposition that obedience can earn the reward of salvation from sin, nor does the hymn offer any hope that redemption can be received as compensation for obedience.[259] The reward given to Christ was vindication by God: God vindicated Christ's *death on a cross* by exalting him *to the highest place.* Third, the hymn views the reward as a gracious gift. God gave the name above every name not as compensation for Christ's work, but as proof of divine approval of his work. Fourth, the hymn views the reward as divine confirmation of Christ's true identity, not as an acquisition of a new position. The true identity of the one existing in the form of God and equal to God was hidden by the humiliation of death on a cross, but was revealed by God's act of exalting him and giving him the name of Lord. As long as these four qualifications of the concept of reward are kept in mind, God's exaltation of Christ may be properly understood as God's way of graciously rewarding Christ by vindicating him after his death on a cross and by revealing his divine nature after his humiliation.[260]

The verb *exalted* is an unusual compound word found only here in the NT. By adding the prefix *above* to the verb *exalt,* the word designates the highest possible exaltation. TNIV conveys the meaning of the word, to "raise someone to the loftiest height,"[261] by adding the words *to the highest place.* The word *exalted* has a superlative, not a comparative sense: the thought is not that God exalted Christ to a higher position than he possessed before his incarnation, but that God exalted him to the highest posi-

259. Silva (128) observes, "The Christ-hymn, though it certainly describes Christ's sacrificial work, does not have as its primary object setting forth the vicarious character of his obedience. In other words, we need not fear that an emphasis on the gracious character of God's act in exalting Jesus subverts the principle of Christ's meritorious obedience on behalf of His people."

260. See Martin, *A Hymn of Christ,* 231-35.

261. BDAG, 1034.

tion after his humiliation.[262] This superlative sense of the word *hyper-exalted* is confirmed by the rest of the sentence: Christ is given a name *above* (the preposition *hyper* is the prefix in the verb *hyper-exalted*) every name; every knee in heaven and on earth and under the earth will bow to him. The word *hyper-exalted* stresses the incomparable transcendence and absolute majesty of Christ. The same word *hyper-exalted* is found in the Greek text of Psalm 97:9: "For you, O LORD, are the Most High over all the earth; you are exalted [*hyper-exalted*] far above all gods." As O'Brien comments on this text, "The point is not that Yahweh is one stage higher than other deities, but that he is in a class by himself. He is truly the incomparable one."[263]

The verb *he exalted* is linked to and defined by the next verb, *he gave:* God supremely exalted Jesus when he graciously gave Jesus the name that is above every name.[264] Jesus received that name as the result of God's gracious decision to "give freely as a favor."[265] Some have proposed that the name given is the name *Jesus.* Moule suggests that "God, in the incarnation, bestowed upon the one who is on equality with him an earthly name which, because it accompanied that most God-like self-giving, has come to be, in fact, the highest of names, because service and self-giving are themselves the highest of divine attributes. Because of the incarnation, the human name 'Jesus' is acclaimed as the highest name; and the Man Jesus thus comes to be acclaimed as Lord, to the glory of God the Father."[266] The view that the name *Jesus* is the name given by God appeals to the support of the next line: *in the name of Jesus.* Advocates of this view point out that the name *Jesus* is truly a name, not a title, such as the title *Lord.*

Solid evidence, however, leads most interpreters to advocate the view that the name that God gave Jesus is the name *Lord.* The narrative sequence of the hymn points to the name that was given at the exaltation: at the incarnation the name Jesus was given; when God exalted Jesus he then gave him the name *Lord.* The *name* of a person can have the sense of a title that "is rightfully borne and encodes what a person really is."[267] The sense of title applies especially to the divine names that express "qualities and powers."[268] The hymn dramatically postpones the announcement of the divine name given to Jesus until the last line, which declares that every tongue will confess that Jesus Christ is *Lord.* The echo this line gives of Isaiah 45:23-24 confirms that the divine name *Lord* is the name that is above every name:

262. Beare, 85; Hawthorne, 91; O'Brien, 236; Fee, 221.

263. O'Brien, 236.

264. Significant MSS witnesses (𝔓[46] ℵ A B C 33 1175) have the article τό, *the name* (τὸ ὄνομα); several MSS and the Majority Text (D F G 𝔐) lack the definite article τό, *name* (ὄνομα). The early and diverse MSS strongly support the inclusion of the article.

265. BDAG, 1078.

266. Moule, "Further Reflexions on Philippians 2:5-11," 270. Vincent (62): "The name conferred is Jesus Christ, combining the human name, which points to the conquest won in the flesh, and the Messianic name, 'the Anointed of God.'"

267. BDAG, 713.

268. BDAG, 712.

"Before me every knee will bow;
by me every tongue will swear.
They will say of me, 'In the LORD alone are righteousness
and strength.'"

Isaiah 41–45 stresses the uniqueness of the divine name LORD *(Yahweh)*:[269] "I am the LORD your God" (41:13); "I am the LORD; that is my name" (42:8); "I, even I, am the LORD, and apart from me there is no savior" (43:11); "This is what the LORD says — Israel's King and Redeemer, the LORD Almighty: I am the first and the last; apart from me there is no God" (44:6); "I am the LORD, and there is no other" (45:18). By quoting Isaiah 45:23 in Philippians 2:10-11, the hymn appropriates the unique divine name LORD for Jesus. The parabolic shape of the hymn can be followed by tracing the names or titles of Jesus: the one existing in the form of God goes down to the lowest place by taking the form of *slave* and back up to the highest place when God gives *Jesus* the name that is above every name so that every tongue will confess that he is *Lord.*

Consideration of the context for Paul's letter to the Philippians provides another reason for the view that the name *Lord* is the name that God gave Jesus. In a Roman colony, Philippians would hear the acclamation that Jesus is Lord as a shocking allusion to the declaration of the Roman imperial cult that Caesar is Lord.[270] In the ideology of the imperial cult, Jupiter and the gods gave divine authority and divine names to Augustus Caesar. In the theology of the hymn of Christ, God gave the divine name to Jesus so that he will be the LORD acclaimed and worshipped by all. By quoting this hymn, Paul presents the exaltation of Jesus as Lord in language that reflects and subverts the Roman imperial cult.[271]

10 *that in the name of Jesus*
every knee will bow
in heaven and on earth and under the earth,

The two verbs expressing the actions of God, *exalted* and *gave*, are followed by a purpose clause containing two verbs, *bow* and *acknowledge.* These verbs vividly demonstrate that the purpose for God's exaltation of Jesus is the universal worship of Jesus as Lord. The purpose clause begins with the prepositional phrase, *in the name of Jesus.* Some take this phrase as a reference to the occasion of worship: at the name of Jesus, "when the name of Jesus is mentioned every knee should bow."[272] Others consider this phrase as an explanation of the means of worship: *in the name of Jesus*

269. *Yahweh*, the sacred Hebrew name for God, is invariably translated in the Greek Bible as κύριος, rendered in NIV with capital and small capital letters as LORD.

270. Richard A. Horsley, ed., *Paul and Empire: Religion and Power in Roman Imperial Society* (Harrisburg: Trinity Press International, 1987), 140-41.

271. N. T. Wright, *Paul in Fresh Perspective* (Minneapolis: Fortress, 2005), 72-74, 93.

272. BDAG, 713.

"speaks of Jesus as the Mediator through whom created beings offer their worship to God."[273] But the context rules out these two interpretations of the phrase by defining the meaning of the phrase as a description of the worship of Jesus as Lord. The phrase *in the name of Jesus* refers backward to the previous phrase, God *gave him the name that is above every name,* and looks forward to the acclamation of every tongue that *Jesus Christ is Lord.* By referring to *the name of Jesus,* the hymn is focusing on the name *Lord* that belongs to *Jesus* as a result of God's exaltation of Jesus and God's gracious gift of the name *Lord* to Jesus. The bestowal of the divine name *Lord* on the crucified and now exalted person *Jesus* brings about the universal worship of *Jesus* as *Lord.* The phrase *in the name of Jesus* ties together the theme of humiliation in the first half of the hymn and the theme of exaltation in the second half of the hymn. By *being made in human likeness* the one existing in the form of God became a real human being named Jesus. Jesus is the name of the one who took *the form of a slave.* Jesus is the name of the one who *humbled himself by becoming obedient unto death on a cross.* God exalted the crucified Jesus and gave him the divine name *Lord* so that all creation would worship Jesus as Lord.

The use of the phrase *in the name of Jesus* to introduce the allusion to Isaiah 45:23 invests this phrase with added depth of meaning. In the prophetic words of Isaiah 45, God calls, "Turn to me and be saved, all you ends of the earth; for I am God, and there is no other" (45:22). And God predicts: "Before me every knee will bow" (45:23). In place of the words "before me," the hymn inserts the phrase *in the name of Jesus.* The prediction that every knee should bow at the name of Jesus fulfills the prediction that every knee will bow before God. By applying this text to Jesus, the hymn boldly asserts that Jesus bears the name of God and is to be worshipped as Lord, to the glory of God the Father. The hymn's description of the worship of Jesus as Lord in the language of an OT text that portrays the worship of God clearly expresses "the conviction that he is directly and uniquely associated with God."[274]

Bowing the knee "expresses supplication, abasement, worship, subjection" before one in authority.[275] Slaves bowed before their lords to show their subjection and willingness to obey.[276] The people of God bow before God: "Come, let us bow down in worship, let us kneel before the LORD our Maker; for he is our God and we are the people of his pasture, the flock under his care" (Ps 95:6-7). The hymn celebrates the bowing of every knee before the exalted Lord Jesus. By bowing before the Lord Jesus to worship him, the church anticipates the bowing of all creation: every knee *in heaven and on earth and under the earth.* In ancient cosmology these three spheres of

273. Beare, 87.
274. Hurtado, *Lord Jesus Christ,* 112.
275. H. Schlier, "γόνυ," *TDNT* 1:738.
276. Ibid., 739.

the universe were under the control of invisible spirit-powers. An amalgam of Egyptian, Greek, and Jewish sources sets forth a list of names and formulas for use in the deliverance of those possessed by demons: "Say thou whatsoever thou art, in heaven, or of the air, or on earth, or under the earth. . . . Say thou whatsoever thou art, for I adjure thee by God the light-bringer, invincible, who knoweth what is in the heart of all life, who of dust hath formed the race of men."[277] The hymn of Christ puts all three realms of the universe under the authority of the Lord Jesus Christ. All angels and demons, all human beings, and, indeed, all creation will bow at the name of Jesus.[278] The whole universe will openly express total submission before the Lord Jesus Christ.

11 *and every tongue will acknowledge that*
Jesus Christ is Lord,
to the glory of God the Father.

The expectation that *every tongue will acknowledge that Jesus Christ is Lord* does not mean that all creation will gladly offer praise and thanksgiving that Jesus Christ is Lord.[279] The verb *acknowledge* simply means "to declare openly in acknowledgment."[280] The acknowledgment of every tongue to God in Isaiah 45 includes "all who have raged against him," who "will come to him and be put to shame" (45:24). The acknowledgment of every tongue that Jesus Christ is Lord does not mean universal participation in the confession of faith made by the church, but "the open and irrevocable admission that this is the rightful Lord of the universe because God has installed Him on the seat of uncontested authority."[281] So the picture given by the hymn of every tongue acknowledging that Jesus Christ is Lord is not a picture of the universal church worshipping Jesus but of every creature in all of creation acknowledging that Jesus Christ is Lord. And yet, the hymn leads Christians to worship Jesus by expressing their faith that the crucified and exalted Jesus would receive universal acknowledgment from all creatures that Jesus Christ is the Lord. When the church worships Jesus as Lord, they give a preview of the universal acknowledgment of his Lordship by all creation celebrated in the hymn.

The universal acclamation that *Jesus Christ is Lord* is the climax of the

277. Paris Magical Papyrus, lines 35-43, in *The New Testament Background: Selected Documents* (rev. ed.; ed. C. K. Barrett; San Francisco: Harper, 1989), 35.

278. See Martin, *A Hymn of Christ*, 257-64, for a review of the debate regarding the intended reference of the three plural adjectives; "of heaven and of earth and of under the earth" (ἐπουρανίων καί ἐπιγείων καί καταχθονίων). The limited restriction to demonic powers only or to human beings only is unwarranted. According to Martin, "The phrase is a rhetorical pleonasm, expressed with the amplitude of poetic licence, for the whole universe. It is as though the writer were saying that the range of Christ's victory and sovereignty is all-embracing and complete" (258).

279. The meaning given by Lightfoot, 115.

280. BDAG, 351. See also O. Michel, "ὁμολογέω," *TDNT* 5:214.

281. Martin, *A Hymn of Christ*, 264.

hymn. By placing *Lord* first in this acclamation, the Greek text puts the emphasis on that name. That name was dramatically withheld until every tongue in the whole creation reveals that name. The hymn announced that God exalted the crucified one and gave him a name that is above every name, but it did not immediately reveal that name. Then the hymn portrayed the supreme sovereignty of the name given to Jesus in the scene of every knee bowed before Jesus because he bears that name. But still it did not reveal that name. The hymn elaborately described the absolute authority of the one who bears that name over all three realms of creation: *in heaven and on earth and under the earth.* But still that name remains unspoken. Finally, the almost unbearable suspense is broken when the hymn summons all creation to acknowledge in one voice that name that is above every name: *Lord Jesus Christ!*[282]

The lines that so dramatically lead up to the revelation of the name *Lord* invest that name with three dimensions of meaning: sovereignty, identity, and destiny. First, God's exaltation of the crucified servant to the highest position of absolute authority over all creation invests the name *Lord* with the meaning of *divine sovereignty.*[283] The way that the hymn expands the allusion to Isaiah 45:23 ("before me every knee shall bow, by me every tongue swear") by adding the phrase encompassing all three realms of creation *(every knee will bow, in heaven, and on earth, and under the earth)* emphasizes that the sovereignty of Jesus is a divine sovereignty that surpasses all human and angelic sovereignty. As Bauckham observes, "For Jewish monotheism sovereignty over all things was definitive of who God is. It could not be seen as delegated to a being other than God. Angels might carry out God's will, as servants subject to his command in limited areas of his rule, but God's universal sovereignty itself was intrinsic to the unique divine identity as sole Creator and Ruler of all."[284] When every knee bows in heaven and on earth and under the earth at the name of Jesus, all creation is thereby acknowledging that divine sovereignty belongs to Jesus, who has been given the name that is above every name, the name Lord. The second commandment in the Decalogue explicitly prohibits bowing down before anything in the heavens above or on the earth below or in the waters under the earth because the Lord God is a jealous God (Exod 20:4-5; Deut 5:8-9). Only the Lord God exercises universal sovereignty over all of creation; only to the Sovereign Creator will every knee bow (Isa 45:23). By giving Jesus the name *Lord,* God gave Jesus divine sovereignty over all creation so that every knee in all of creation would bow to him.

282. Most MSS ($\mathfrak{P}^{46}$ א A B C D Ψ 𝔐) support the reading Lord Jesus Christ (κύριος Ἰησοῦς Χριστός); a few MSS (F G) omit Χριστός, perhaps to harmonize with v. 10: *at the name of Jesus.*

283. Richard J. Bauckham, "The Worship of Jesus in Philippians 2:9-11," in *Where Christology Began: Essays on Philippians 2* (ed. Ralph P. Martin and Brian J. Dodd; Louisville: Westminster John Knox, 1998), 130.

284. Bauckham, "The Worship of Jesus in Philippians 2:9-11," 130.

Second, by giving Jesus the name *Lord,* God declared the *divine identity* of Jesus. Some scholars, observing the parallels between the Christ hymn and Hellenistic myths of the descent and ascent of gods in the Greek religion, have asserted that the enthronement of Jesus as Lord is similar to the coronation of a deity in the context of Hellenistic polytheism.[285] But the use of language from Isaiah 45:23 demonstrates that Jewish monotheism is the background for this hymn. Hence, an understanding of the Jewish context of the name *Lord* is needed to appreciate the significance of that name. In the Jewish religion, the name *Lord (kyrios)* is actually a substitute name for the Hebrew divine name YHWH (Yahweh). Whenever Jews saw the divine name YHWH in their Hebrew text, they would not pronounce it for fear of blaspheming or taking in vain the unique divine name of God. Instead they would say a substitute name, the Hebrew name *ʾādôn,* meaning "Lord," for the unpronounceable divine name YHWH. As a result, when the Jews translated their Hebrew scriptures into Greek in the third century B.C. (that translation is called the Septuagint or LXX), they used the Greek name *kyrios* ("Lord") at least 6,156 times for the unique divine name YHWH.[286] Since YHWH was the unique proper name for God, that was *the name that was above every name* (Phil 2:9). The Jewish prophets proclaimed God's exclusive claim to his own unique name: "I am the LORD, and there is no other; apart from me there is no God" (Isa 45:5-6, 18, 21). Jesus was given the name that belonged to God alone. By bearing the name Lord, Jesus was not identified as one of many lords in the pantheon of Hellenistic gods and lords nor as merely a political rival of Lord Caesar. The name Lord identified Jesus with the one and only God of Jewish monotheism, the Creator and Sovereign of all.[287]

Third, the name Lord points not only to the present sovereignty and identity of Jesus but also to his future destiny. The acknowledgment of every tongue that Jesus Christ is Lord is a future event.[288] *Already* God has given the name Lord to Jesus, but *not yet* does Jesus receive universal acknowledgment as Lord. This *already–not yet* tension inherent in the name Lord is the structure of the eschatological vision of the exaltation of Jesus in the hymn of Christ. The vision of Isaiah 45 anticipated the ultimate vindication of the Lord when every knee bows to him and every tongue swears to him: "'In the LORD alone are deliverance and strength'" (Isa 45:23-24). By

285. See W. Bousset, *Kyrios Christos* (trans. John Steely; Nashville: Abingdon, 1970), and the response by Martin, *A Hymn of Christ,* 281.

286. G. Quell, "κύριος," *TDNT* 3:1058-59.

287. Bauckham, "The Worship of Jesus in Philippians 2:9-11," 132.

288. Even though the Greek verb ἐξομολογήσηται *(acknowledge)* is aorist subjunctive, it may still point to the future as a "futuristic aorist" (see BDF §333). The variant reading ἐξομολογήσεται, a future indicative, is supported by many MSS including A C D F G K L P and may have been inserted to harmonize the text with the indicative form (ὀμεῖται) in some manuscripts in Isa 45:23. The aorist subjunctive is supported by early and good witnesses, including 𝔓[46] א B, but it may be explained as a harmonization with the subjunctive verb (κάμψῃ) in v. 10.

proclaiming God's gift of the name *Lord* to *Jesus,* the hymn gives assurance to the church that this ultimate vindication belongs to the *Lord Jesus Christ.* In the midst of present suffering and persecution for her faith in Jesus Christ, the church sings this hymn about the vindication of her faith when every tongue will acknowledge that *Jesus Christ is Lord.* In fact, "the church is the earthly center from which the full Lordship of Christ becomes visible."[289] When the church worships Jesus by bowing before him and proclaiming that he is Lord, she embodies the vision of the future submission of all creation to the Lord Jesus. The proclamation that Jesus is Lord announces his destiny: because he has been given the name Lord, he will rule over all creation. Jesus, crucified on a Roman cross, not Caesar seated on a Roman throne, is destined to receive universal acknowledgment that he alone is the sovereign Lord. "In the hymn the Church is caught up from earth to heaven, from the scene of conflict and duress into the presence of the all-conquering Lord, from the harsh realities of what is to the glorious prospect of what will be, because it is so already in God's sight."[290]

The final line of the hymn declares that God's exaltation of Jesus rebounds *to the glory of God the Father.* This last line summarizes the message of the entire hymn.[291] The one existing in the form of God did not strive to be exalted and worshipped as Lord for his own glory apart from God, but just the opposite: he emptied himself, humbled himself, and was obedient unto death on a cross. As a result, God exalted him and gave him the name Lord. All that Jesus did in his self-emptying, self-humbling, and obedient death on the cross led to the glory of God the Father because the self-giving of Jesus expressed the very nature of God: "The one true God consists, through and through, of self-giving love."[292] All that God did in exalting Jesus and giving him the name Lord to be worshipped by all creation led to the glory of God the Father because the Lordship of Jesus Christ expresses the very nature of God: God is Lord because God the Lord creates all and rules over all.

The hymn offers no explanation of the mystery of the unity of God the Father and the Lord Jesus Christ. The Jewish monotheistic belief that "the LORD our God, the LORD is one" (Deut 6:4) is maintained, but in a revised form: now the one God is the Lord Jesus Christ and God the Father. The renaming of both God as God the Father and the Lord as the Lord Jesus Christ turns the ancient Jewish monotheism into a new christological monotheism.[293] The hymn asserts the full equality of Jesus with God (2:6)

289. Oscar Cullmann, *Christ and Time: The Primitive Christian Conception of Time and History* (rev. ed.; trans. Floyd V. Filson; Philadelphia: Westminster, 1964), 154.

290. Martin, *A Hymn of Christ*, 269.

291. Martin (*A Hymn of Christ*, 272-75) gives reasons why this last line is a Pauline addition to the hymn, but then he admits that "it simply reiterates the Leitmotiv of the whole hymn" (276).

292. N. T. Wright, *What St. Paul Really Said* (Oxford: Lion Hudson, 1997), 69.

293. Wright, *The Climax of the Covenant*, 94, 130.

and proclaims that Jesus bears the unique proper name of God, the name Lord (2:9-11). Yet, there is no division or competition between the Lord Jesus and God the Father, for the Lord Jesus obeys the will of God the Father, and the universal worship of Jesus as Lord fulfills the will of God the Father.[294] The Father receives glory through the obedience and the worship of his Son.[295] The hymn's portrayal of the worship of God as the worship of Jesus as Lord *to the glory of God the Father* demonstrates "an evident concern to understand the reverence given to Jesus as an extension of the worship of God."[296]

The hymn has come full circle from the first line about the one existing in the form of God expressing the glory of God to the last line about the exalted Jesus bringing glory to God the Father. The whole hymn is totally God-centered, and God-glorifying. In the downward journey to the death of Jesus on the cross and in the upward journey to the universal acclamation of Jesus as Lord, the very nature of God is revealed. "The meaning of the word 'God' includes not only Jesus, but specifically, the crucified Jesus."[297] The worship of God includes the worship of Jesus, who died as a slave on the Roman cross and now sits on the highest throne as Lord of all creation.

D. Work Out Your Salvation (2:12-18)

12 *Therefore, my dear friends, as you have always obeyed*
— not only in my presence, but now much more in my absence —
continue to work out your salvation with fear and trembling,
13 *for it is God who works in you to will and to act in order to fulfill his good purpose.*
14 *Do everything without grumbling or arguing,*
15 *so that you may become blameless and pure, "children of God*
without fault in a warped and crooked generation."
Then you will shine among them like stars in the sky
16 *as you hold firmly to the word of life.*
And then I will be able to boast on the day of Christ
that I did not run or labor in vain.
17 *But even if I am being poured out like a drink offering*
on the sacrifice and service coming from your faith,
I am glad and rejoice with all of you.
18 *So you too should be glad and rejoice with me.*[298]

294. Hurtado, *Lord Jesus Christ*, 641.

295. Silva, 133.

296. Hurtado, *Lord Jesus Christ*, 151.

297. Wright, *What St. Paul Really Said*, 69.

298. After following my translation of the Christ hymn, I return again to the TNIV for my exposition of the text.

When Paul finishes the Christ hymn, he returns to giving practical guidelines for life in the community. His ethical appeal in this section continues to develop what he introduced earlier as the way to *live in a manner worthy of the gospel of Christ* (1:27). By presenting the person and work of Christ in the great Christ hymn, Paul strengthens his appeals for unity in the church (1:27; 2:2) and establishes a solid foundation for his encouragement to *work out your salvation . . . without grumbling or arguing* (2:12, 14). True worship of Christ inspires our work; singing the praise of Christ motivates us to build the community in Christ. Christ above all is the unifying center of our life together. "The more genuine and the deeper our community becomes, the more will everything else between us recede, the more clearly and purely will Jesus Christ and his work become the one and only thing that is vital between us. We have one another only through Christ, but through Christ we do have one another, wholly, for all eternity."[299]

12 Paul moves quickly and easily from theological contemplation to practical implication. The word *therefore* points to the intended results of all that the Christ hymn proclaims.[300] Christ's death on the cross and his universal Lordship are not abstract theological concepts far removed from the nitty-gritty problems of everyday life. Reflection on the cross of Christ, the exaltation of Christ, and the universal worship of Christ leads to reconciliation in the community of those who confess that Jesus Christ is Lord.

The first application of the hymn that Paul pinpoints is obedience: *my dear friends, as you have always obeyed.* This application picks up the language of the hymn: Christ *humbled himself by becoming obedient to death — even death on a cross!* (2:8). Christ's obedience established the ultimate moral standard of obedience for followers of Christ. Paul does not set up this standard in an accusing way but in an affirming way. He embraces his readers by calling them *my dear friends,* literally, "my beloved." This strong expression of love for his friends continues the theme of friendship in this letter.[301] In his thanksgiving Paul calls on God as the witness of his love for his friends: *God can testify how I long for all of you with the affection of Christ Jesus* (1:8). And in his closing appeal he expands his expression of affection for his friends: *my brothers and sisters, you whom I love and long for, my joy and crown* (4:1). The warmth and depth of Paul's words of love for his friends

299. Dietrich Bonhoeffer, *Life Together* (trans. John W. Doberstein; New York: Harper & Row, 1954), 26.

300. BDAG, 1107. The specific reference of ὥστε is not clear. Is the obedience of the Philippians the intended result of the entire hymn (Lohmeyer, 99; Schenk, 213), the phrase in the hymn about Christ becoming obedient unto death (Bonnard, 49), or the last line of the hymn about the acknowledgment of all created beings that Jesus Christ is Lord (Meyer, 108), or does ὥστε connect the ethical exhortations in 2:12-18 with the initial imperative in 1:27 and all that follows from that imperative (O'Brien, 274)? Of all these possible options it seems best to take the imperative of 2:12 as the intended result of all that the entire hymn proclaims: the self-giving, self-humbling obedience of Christ, the exaltation of Christ, and the universal worship of Christ.

301. See the Introduction, 6-12, on the language of friendship in Philippians.

give his encouragement to continue in obedience with genuine persuasive power.

Paul also affirms his friends by telling them that they *have always obeyed — not only in my presence, but now much more in my absence.* His praise for their practice of obedience is based on his memory of their initial, enthusiastic acceptance of the gospel (4:15) and their faithful partnership with him in the proclamation of the gospel (1:5). For Paul, obedience is measured by conformity to the gospel of Christ. His overarching imperative is to *live in a manner worthy of the gospel of Christ* (1:27). By complimenting his readers for their obedience after leading them through the hymn to Christ, Paul implies that they are already obeying the gospel encapsulated in the hymn by following the example of Christ's obedience (2:8) and by acknowledging Jesus Christ as the Lord of their lives (2:9-10). Although Christ is not explicitly stated as the object of their obedience, the very close connection between the hymn and the affirmation of their obedience points to Jesus Christ the Lord, whom all must worship and obey to the glory of God the Father.[302] Of course, obedience to Christ entails obedience to Paul since Paul proclaims the gospel of Christ, but Paul emphasizes that he is merely a servant of Christ (1:1) while Christ is the Lord of all (2:9-10). Paul desires to be totally eclipsed by Christ: *to live is Christ* (1:21). When Paul commends believers for their obedience, he is affirming their commitment to live the kind of life that corresponds to the gospel of Christ by obeying Christ. Obedience is defined not in legal terms but in relational terms as knowing Christ, being like him, and serving him.

Paul moves from commending to commanding. *As you have always obeyed . . . continue to work out your salvation.* His commendation for past success is intended to motivate his friends to work even harder in the present and future. The addition of the word *continue* by TNIV brings out the sense of the elliptical sentence and the imperative *work out. As you have always obeyed . . . continue to work out.* As you have run well, you must continue to run even better all the way to the finish line. As you are already marked by your courageous commitment to Christ, you must continue to live out the meaning of that commitment in every area of your lives.

"It is this 'long obedience in the same direction' which the mood of the world does so much to discourage."[303] When the path of obedience to Christ becomes steep and dangerous, pleasure seekers look for an easier way. Religious tourists hunting for sensational entertainment, instantaneous enlightenment, and emotional excitement will jump on the newest

302. NRSV makes Paul the object of obedience by inserting the pronoun "me": "as you have always obeyed me." See also Beare (89): "obedience to the Apostle's counsels and directions, accepted as carrying all the authority of the God who gave him the grace of the apostolate." But most interpreters agree that the implied object is God or Christ. See Lightfoot, 115; Martin, 139.

303. Eugene Peterson, *A Long Obedience in the Same Direction* (2nd ed.; Downers Grove: InterVarsity Press, 2000), 17.

rides and take quick shortcuts, but they will not be found with pilgrims on the long, hard road following in the footsteps of Christ, who was *obedient to death — even death on a cross.* Paul's call to unflagging, Christ-like obedience will not be popular in a world that so highly values going fast and having fun and so quickly rejects enduring pain and submitting to authority. But the essential characteristic of the wise who build their community on Christ is their consistent obedience to him.

The way to continue obeying Christ is to *work out.* The imperative means "to cause a state or condition, bring about, produce, or create."[304] A few examples will illustrate Paul's use of this word. "The law *brings* wrath" (Rom 4:15); "suffering *produces* perseverance" (Rom 5:3); "sin, seizing the opportunity afforded by the commandment, *produced* in me every kind of coveting" (Rom 7:8); "our light and momentary troubles *are achieving* for us an eternal glory" (2 Cor 4:17). Paul uses this word to call his friends to bring about, produce, achieve, or create something. The object Paul says they are supposed to produce is *your salvation!* This is a surprise for anyone acquainted with Paul's letters. Earlier in this letter, Paul assures the readers that their salvation is God's work: *you will be saved — and that by God* (1:28). Paul is consistent in his emphasis that salvation is not achieved by human work, but by God's grace; salvation is not produced by works but by faith in God. "To anyone who does not work but trusts God who justifies the ungodly, their faith is credited as righteousness" (Rom 4:5). Paul views justification and salvation as results of faith: "it is with your heart that you believe and are justified, and it is with your mouth that you profess your faith and are saved" (Rom 10:10). Salvation from eschatological judgment is a gift received from God through Christ: "For God did not appoint us to suffer wrath, but to receive salvation through our Lord Jesus Christ" (1 Thess 5:9). That is Paul's central thesis. How then can he command his friends: *work out your salvation?*

In order to understand what Paul is saying here, we need to remind ourselves that his interest in this context is social harmony in the community of believers. The entire context for Paul's imperative to *work out your salvation* has to do with unity in the church. His previous imperatives call for unity: *stand firm in the one Spirit, striving together with one accord* (1:27); *make my joy complete by being like-minded, having the same love, being one in spirit and of one mind* (2:2). His subsequent imperative also focuses on social harmony: *do everything without grumbling or arguing* (2:14). In the light of Paul's focus in this context on unity in the church, the command to *work out your salvation* "is to be understood in a corporate sense. The entire church, which had grown spiritually ill (2:3-4), is charged now with taking whatever steps are necessary to restore itself to health, integrity, and wholeness."[305]

The plural form of the verb *work out* and the pronoun *your* can be seen

304. BDAG, 531.
305. Martin and Hawthorne, 139.

as corroboration that Paul's command should not be interpreted in a merely individualistic sense as a requirement for each individual to work for personal, eternal salvation but in a corporate sense as a call for the whole community to rebuild social harmony. Paul's consistent emphasis on unity in the church in this context compels us to see that Paul's call to *work out your salvation* has an ecclesiological reference: it is a call to restore harmony in the church by serving one another.[306] This contrast between an individualistic sense and a corporate sense to the command to *work out your salvation* does not posit an antithesis between individual responsibility and corporate responsibility. Restoring unity in the church by serving one another is the responsibility of each individual Christian. Paul's command in verse 14 to *do everything without grumbling or arguing* confronts each member with the challenge to desist from attitudes and words that tear apart the social fabric of the community.

In the light of this evidence that Paul's concern is social relationships in the community, some interpreters take the word *salvation* in this context to mean the good health of the community rather than personal justification by God and eternal salvation from judgment. A few examples support this redefinition. The term *salvation* is used in Greek literature for good health, corporate well-being, and social harmony. In an annual feast to Zeus in Magnesia, the priest prays "for the *salvation* of the city, country, citizens, wives, children and other residents, for peace for wealth, for the growth of the grain and other fruits and cattle."[307] Plato thought that it was the duty of the ruler to *save* the state, "not just to preserve it from outer destruction but also to maintain it as a constitutionally ordered state."[308] And in the NT the term is used to mean good health (Mark 3:4; Acts 4:9; 14:9; 27:34). Paul may have intended this meaning of social well-being and corporate health in this context when he called for the Philippians to work out their salvation.[309]

Although good evidence indicates that Paul's concern in this section of his letter is social harmony in the community, the redefinition of the word *salvation* simply in terms of the health of the community does not adequately reckon with Paul's customary use of this word. This word is primarily "for Paul a future, eschatological term."[310] Paul's focus on future sal-

306. Martin and Hawthorne, 139-40.

307. W. Foerster, "σῴζω," *TDNT* 7:967.

308. Foerster, "σῴζω," *TDNT* 7:968.

309. Martin and Hawthorne, 140.

310. Foerster, "σωτηρία," *TDNT* 7:992. "In the light of Paul's consistent use of σωτηρία to denote personal, eternal salvation it is unlikely that the term here points to the present corporate health or well-being of the Philippians" (O'Brien, 278). "Out of the nearly twenty occurrences of this noun in the Pauline corpus, not one instance requires the translation 'well-being'; the vast majority require — and all of them admit — the theological sense" (Silva, 136). "The concept of salvation belongs unquestionably to the apostle's eschatological perspective, and its basic reference is futuristic" (J. Paul Sampley, "Reasoning from the Horizons of Paul's Thought World: A Comparison of Galatians and Philippians," in *Theol-*

vation can be seen in this letter in his reassurance given to persecuted believers — *you will be saved* (1:28) — and in his expectation of *a Savior* from heaven who *will transform our lowly bodies so that they will be like his glorious body* (3:20-21). In our immediate context, Paul's exhortation to *work out your salvation* is placed in an eschatological framework between his description of the day when every knee will bow before Jesus and every tongue confess that Jesus Christ is Lord (2:9-10) and his anticipation of the future *day of Christ* (2:16). The future, triumphant *day of Christ* is the consummation of the salvation inaugurated by the death and exaltation of Christ celebrated in the hymn to Christ (2:6-11). The gospel according to Paul is the good news of salvation through the death, resurrection, and ultimate, universal victory of Christ. The saving power of God is operative through the gospel: "it is the power of God that brings *salvation* to everyone who believes" (Rom 1:16). For those who believe the gospel and receive God's grace, the eschatological day of salvation is today: "now is the time of God's favor, now is the day of salvation" (2 Cor 6:2). Since Paul regularly employs the word *salvation* "in the supernatural-eschatological sense,"[311] we should attempt to see if that meaning works in this context before adopting a meaning outside the range of Paul's normal usage. In fact, we can appreciate how well the full theological-eschatological sense of *salvation* works in this context when we understand that from Paul's perspective ethical behavior is motivated and empowered by the eschatological reality of salvation.[312] On the basis of his readers' present experience of salvation and their anticipation of future salvation, Paul urges them to express in their community life a dramatic demonstration of the salvation given and promised to them. "What Paul is referring to, therefore, is the *present* outworking of their *eschatological salvation* within the *believing community* in Philippi."[313] Paul's concept of eschatological salvation can be seen in his declaration that *our citizenship is in heaven* (3:20). The church is an eschatological community, a colony of heaven. But in order for the heavenly reality to be a present, earthly experience, believers need to *work out* the *salvation* promised to them. Paul desires to see an ecclesiological fulfillment of the eschatological promise of salvation.

This understanding of working out salvation as a present expression of God's promise of salvation does not contradict but rather implements

---

ogy and Ethics in Paul and His Interpreters: Essays in Honor of Victor Paul Furnish [ed. Eugene H. Lovering Jr. and Jerry L. Sumney; Nashville: Abingdon, 1996], 122).

311. K. H. Schelke, "σωτηρία," *EDNT* 3:327.

312. This link between eschatological salvation and ethics can be heard when Paul tells the Thessalonian believers, "since we belong to the day, let us be sober, putting on faith and love as a breastplate, and the hope of *salvation* as a helmet" (1 Thess 5:8). We see the same connection between eschatological salvation and ethics in Rom 13:11-12: "The hour has already come for you to wake up from your slumber, because our *salvation* is nearer now than when we first believed. The night is nearly over; the day is almost here. So let us put aside the deeds of darkness and put on the armor of light."

313. Fee, 235.

Paul's earlier instruction to look after the interests of others (2:4). Building the community to be an earthly demonstration of heavenly citizenship takes both individual and corporate effort, since every believer must work together and serve one another to be united as the people saved by God.

Paul modifies his imperative to *work out your salvation* with two phrases. First, he says that working out salvation should be done *not only in my presence, but now much more in my absence.*[314] Like parents moving their children from dependence to independence, Paul urges his converts to continue in their obedience during his absence even more resolutely than they did in his presence. They should not be dependent on having him present to inspire them in their work. Evidently, quarreling and complaining occurred in the church in Paul's absence. So he wrote this letter to the church and appealed to *God's holy people in Christ* to stop fighting and to work together in unity while he was away from them. Paul's first command to the church to *stand firm* in unity during his absence (1:27) is restated in this exhortation to express the reality of salvation in community life even more wholeheartedly during his absence than in his presence.

Paul's reference to his absence is not a euphemism for "his impending departure from this life."[315] In fact, Paul expresses confidence that he will visit the Philippians soon (2:24). The repetition of presence-absence language in this letter expresses Paul's friendship love: he fondly remembers being present with them, he thinks of them with love and thanksgiving during his absence, and he longs to be present with them again.[316] This letter is a way for Paul to be present with his friends and inspire them to be united during his absence.

Paul also modifies his imperative to *work out your salvation* by adding a prepositional phrase: *with fear and trembling.* In the OT this kind of language indicates awe in the presence of God (Exod 15:16; Isa 19:16) or fear of the Jewish people because of God's presence with them (Deut 2:25; 11:25). Paul uses the same phrase to depict his own attitude when he first preached the gospel in Corinth "in weakness and with great fear and trembling" (1 Cor 2:3) and to describe the attitude of the Corinthian believers when they were obedient to Paul's instructions through Titus, "receiving him with fear and trembling" (2 Cor 7:15). The same phrase is used in Ephesians to direct slaves to obey their masters with fear and trembling (Eph 6:5). The use of this phrase in these texts demonstrates that an attitude of *fear and trembling* is an attitude of humility and submission in God's presence or in the presence of other people. According to some interpreters, this

314. Strong textual evidence (𝔓[46] ℵ A C D F G 𝔐) supports the reading, "not as in my presence only" (μὴ ὡς ἐν τῇ παρουσίᾳ μου μόνον); only a few MSS (B 33 1241) support the omission of ὡς: μὴ ἐν τῇ παρουσίᾳ μου μόνον *(not only in my presence).* The variant reading, probably caused by an accidental omission, has little impact on translations. TNIV *(not only in my presence)* does not translate the word ὡς.

315. Beare, 89.

316. See the Introduction, 6-12, on friendship.

phrase in Paul's letter to the Philippian believers calls for them to have an attitude of humility and respect toward one another.[317] Such instruction regarding the attitude of Christians toward one another appears to fit with his previous direction — *in humility value others above yourselves* (2:3) — and his subsequent command to stop *grumbling or arguing* (2:14). But the phrase is more likely a strong reminder of the only appropriate attitude to have in the presence of God.[318] The previous sentence pictures the worship of all creation on bended knee in the presence of Jesus Christ the Lord (2:9-11) because God has highly exalted him, and the subsequent sentence points to the presence of the all-powerful *God who works in you* (2:13). When we worship and serve the God who highly exalted Jesus and the God who works in us, our attitude in God's presence should be one of humble submission before God. The fear of the Lord is the best way to dispel the attitude of *selfish ambition or vain conceit* (2:3) that so quickly ruins social harmony in the church. In order to build the community, believers need to work together with the attitude of humility that they are doing everything in the presence of God. Then their work will express their worship of the Lord Jesus Christ, to the glory of God the Father.

Paul's way of combining the fear and love of the Lord reflects both his Jewish roots and his experience of Christ. The fear of the Lord in the worship experience of Israel did not mean the terror and dread of God alone but unites the sense of awe and reverence with love and trust.[319] Israel was called to fear and love God at the same time: "And now, O Israel, what does the Lord your God ask of you but to fear the Lord your God, to walk in all his ways, to love him, to serve the Lord your God with all your heart and with all your soul" (Deut 10:12). Both fear and love motivated Paul: "We know what it is to fear the Lord. . . . Christ's love compels us" (2 Cor 5:11, 14). Meditating on the picture in the Christ hymn of all created beings bowing before Jesus and acknowledging him to be Lord should certainly generate fear in our hearts of the awesome majesty and power of the Lord of all the universe — not fear that drives us away from the Lord, but fear that draws us close to him to worship, adore, and love him. Although believers are repeatedly commanded to "fear not" (see, e.g., Luke 1:13, 30; 2:10; 5:10; 8:50), assured that God has not given "a spirit of fear" (2 Tim 1:7), and informed that "perfect love casts out fear" (1 John 4:18), fear and love are still paradoxically united in Christian experience.[320] *Fear and trembling* united with trust and love in the presence of our Lord Jesus Christ and God the Father inspire us to work out our salvation.

317. Barth, 71; Hawthorne, 100; Martin and Hawthorne, 141.

318. Gnilka, 149; Judith M. Gundry Volf, *Paul and Perseverance: Staying In and Falling Away* (Louisville: Westminster/John Knox, 1990), 269.

319. Bruce K. Waltke, "The Fear of the Lord: The Foundation for a Relationship with God," in *Alive to God: Studies in Spirituality Presented to James Houston* (ed. J. I. Packer and Loren Wilkinson; Downers Grove: InterVarsity Press, 1992), 24.

320. W. Mundle, "Fear," *NIDNTT* 1:624.

13 Immediately after his imperative to *work out your salvation with fear and trembling,* Paul encourages his readers by asserting, *for it is God who works in you to will and to act in order to fulfill his good purpose.* Paul is well aware that the work of building the community of believers is frustrating when selfish ambitions and self-interest (1:15-17; 2:3-4) shred the fabric of the community. Workers burn out and give up in such discouraging situations. But Paul gives the builders of the Christian community in Philippi a very good reason to have supreme confidence that their work is not in vain: *for* God originally initiated, presently sustains, and ultimately will complete all their work by his indwelling power.[321] *God works in you.* The verb *works in* means "to put one's capabilities into operation, work, be at work, be active, operate, and be effective."[322] All the capabilities of God are in operation, active, and effective in the work of believers.

God's working in believers precedes and empowers their work, but it does not obviate the need for their work. Paul is not telling Christians to "let go and let God" or "get out of God's way so God can do it." Such slogans for the Christian life express a passivism not consonant with Paul's call to the persistent obedience of working out salvation in the life of the church. Nor is Paul advocating a God of the gaps: "Go as far as you can, then leave the rest for God" or "God helps those who help themselves." These attitudes endorse an activism that admits the need for only a little boost or a small subsidy from God. Paul, however, teaches the absolute necessity of the empowering presence of God not only to do any work but also to have a desire to do the work.

By his indwelling presence *in you,* in individual believers and in the community as a whole,[323] God directs, strengthens, and sustains even the will-to-work. The word *will* has a wide range of meanings: "to have a desire for something, wish to have, to want something; to have something in mind for oneself, or purpose, resolve; to take pleasure in."[324] Contemporary Christians speak of a purpose-driven church and a purpose-driven life;[325] Paul speaks here of a God-driven purpose. Even our purpose, our willing and desiring to live and work for God, comes from God. God is the great originator of human willing as well as human working. That is why Paul says that we work *with fear and trembling, for* it is God who works in us to will and to work. The true understanding that the same God who exalted the Lord Jesus (2:9) is the God who now works in us even to will to work

321. The conjunction *for* (γάρ) is a "marker of cause or reason" (BDAG, 189) for working out salvation with fear and trembling.

322. BDAG, 335.

323. This phrase *in you* has a corporate reference in this context, but it requires individual appropriation as well: "The resolve of each of them to see to it that God's purposes are accomplished in their community" (Fee, 238).

324. BDAG, 447-48.

325. See Rick Warren, *The Purpose Driven Church* (Grand Rapids: Zondervan, 1995); *The Purpose Driven Life* (Grand Rapids: Zondervan, 2002).

(2:13) fills us with fear and trembling in his presence. We humbly bow before God to let his creative, gracious will regenerate and energize our will to serve him. When our own human ambitions work in us to will and to work, our human wills fight against each other and tear apart the church. In any human organization, human wills run in conflicting directions. When our wills are not bound to God's will, we are bound to divide. Only when our wills are bound to God's will are we free to unite.

Verses 12 and 13 are linked together as effect and cause: our work is the effect; God's work is the cause of our work. We work because God works. Paul takes great care to clarify this connection between God's work and our work by using the same verb in verse 13 for God's work and our work: *It is God who works in you . . . to work.* God is named here as the One who works: He is the Infinite Worker. When our finite work is empowered by God's work, then our work is an expression of God's work.[326] The priority of God's work does not vitiate our responsibility to work. We are not puppets on God's strings; we are fully responsible human beings obligated to *continue to work out our salvation.* God's total sovereignty is the air we breathe and the ground we walk on to fulfill our human responsibility to work. God's indicative — God works — makes it possible to fulfill the imperative given to us — work! Without God's prior work directing and empowering our work, all our work is meaningless and in vain. All human effort is in vain unless it is energized by God. "Unless the LORD builds the house, the builders labor in vain" (Ps 127:1). Recognizing God the Creator as the source of all our creativity leads us to pray with the psalmist as we work:

> May the favor of the Lord our God rest upon us;
> establish the work of our hands for us —
> yes, establish the work of our hands. (Ps 90:17)

Because of God's gracious work in us, we work *to fulfill his good purpose.* Since Paul's emphasis in this context is social harmony, some interpreters take the noun translated as *good purpose* in the sense of the goodwill of human beings toward one another.[327] Although this interpretation may seem to be confirmed by the absence of the pronoun *his* in the Greek text, the presence of the article with the abstract noun has a reflexive sense and refers back to God, the subject of the sentence.[328] And as Hawthorne acknowledges, the noun "usually refers to the 'benevolent purpose' or the 'good will' of God.[329] To refer again to human will immediately after the reference to human will would be tautological.[330] The emphasis in the im-

326. This truth is encapsulated in Eph 2:10: "We are God's handiwork, created in Christ Jesus to do good works, which God prepared in advance for us to do."

327. Hawthorne, 101.

328. Silva, 142.

329. Hawthorne, 100.

330. G. Schrenk, "εὐδοκία," *TDNT* 2:747 n. 33.

mediate context on the sovereignty of God's work leads most interpreters to see this noun as a reference to God's good will.[331] The goal of God's work is the fulfillment of the good purpose of God. God fulfills his own good purpose by working in us to will and to work out our own salvation. When God's creative work is demonstrated by Christians living and working together in harmony and unity, his purpose is fulfilled.

14 Paul now gives instructions for working out salvation in the community in one long, complicated sentence that stretches through three verses (2:14-16). Each part of the sentence needs to be interpreted in the light of the whole sentence. Paul begins with an imperative modified by a prohibition: *Do everything without grumbling or arguing.* The all-inclusive imperative, *do everything,* demonstrates that we should work out our salvation in every dimension of life. Paul used the same comprehensive imperative to tell the Corinthian believers that every activity of life should be done for the glory of God: "So whether you eat or drink or whatever you do, *do everything* for the glory of God" (1 Cor 10:31; see also Col 3:17). Any attempt to divide the activities of life into spiritual and sacred categories is negated by this view that *everything* in life should be transformed by salvation.

The comprehensive command is modified by a phrase that prohibits *grumbling or arguing. Grumbling* refers to whispering complaints, talking in secret against someone, and making negative comments about others behind their backs.[332] *Arguing* in this context means quarreling and debating in ways that are divisive and raise doubts.[333] These words clearly echo descriptions of Israel wandering in the wilderness: "All the Israelites grumbled against Moses and Aaron. . . . The LORD said to Moses and Aaron: 'How long will this wicked community grumble against me? I have heard the complaints of these grumbling Israelites'" (Num 14:2, 26; also Exod 16:7-12; Num 17:5-25). Since Paul believed that the story of Israel was instructive for the church (1 Cor 10:11: "These things happened to them as examples and were written down as warnings for us"), he used the story of the Israelites in the wilderness to warn the Christians in Corinth: "Do not grumble, as some of them did — and were killed by the destroying angel" (1 Cor 10:10). Paul's use of the same language in his letter to the Philippian Christians indicates that he is taking his instructions for the church from the narrative of Israel.

Although his basic prohibition against *grumbling or arguing* points to specific problems in the church, his allusion to the grumbling of Israel in the wilderness does not describe the object of grumbling in the church. Are the Christians in Philippi grumbling against God, against their leaders, against Paul, or against all of the above? Since Paul does not say how close the parallels are between the church and Israel or give us the content of the grum-

331. Bockmuehl, 154; Martin and Hawthorne, 143; O'Brien, 288.
332. BDAG, 204; K. H. Rengstorf, "γογγυσμός," *TDNT* 1:735-36.
333. BDAG, 232-33; G. Schrenk, "διαλογισμός," *TDNT* 2:97.

bling and arguing, we can only speculate. Some clues in the context seem to point to similarities between the church and Israel and lead us to conjecture what the Philippian Christians were complaining about. Like Israel in the wilderness, the Christians in Philippi were suffering. In fact, Paul says that suffering for Christ was granted to the Philippian believers (1:29). Some Christians were probably complaining about their suffering, just as the Israelites complained about their suffering in the wilderness. Although there are no clear signs that the church was actively rebelling against God as Israel did, Paul's call to obey God (2:12) and his affirmation of God's gracious working in the church to accomplish God's purpose (2:13) can be seen as an antidote for the Philippians' attitude of complaining against God in a time of suffering.[334] We may also speculate that just as some Israelites complained not only against God but also against their leaders appointed by God, so also some Christians in Philippi were probably complaining about the leaders in their church. Although Paul's letter does not contain quotes of their complaints, his call for unity (1:27; 2:2), his denunciation of selfish ambition (1:17; 2:3), his instruction to welcome and honor their leader Epaphroditus and people like him (2:29), his appeal to Euodia and Syntyche to be reconciled (4:2), his unusual mention of overseers and deacons in his salutation (1:1), and his instruction to follow those who live as Paul and his companions do (3:17) are all clues that some complaints have been leveled against the leaders of the church in Philippi. We may also conjecture that just as some Israelites blamed Moses for their suffering in the wilderness, so some Philippian believers may have complained that Paul was to blame for their own suffering for their faith in Christ. Some clues in the context that support this conjecture can be seen in Paul's defense of his own suffering on the grounds that it *served to advance the gospel* (1:12-14), his description of some who sought to stir up trouble for him while he was in chains (1:15-17), his appeal to make his joy complete by being like-minded (2:2), his command to stop grumbling (2:14) so that his ministry will not be in vain (2:16), and his claim that he was being poured out as a drink offering on the sacrifice and service of the Philippians' faith (2:16).[335]

While we cannot be entirely sure what the Philippian Christians were complaining about, we can be sure that Paul viewed complaining and quarreling as serious flaws that could destroy the unity of the Christian community in Philippi. On account of these flaws in the church, Paul urgently appealed for unity (2:1-5), centered the focus of the church on Christ — the ultimate basis of unity (2:6-11), called the church to practice Christ-like obedience with fear and trembling (2:12), and encouraged confidence in God's work in the community (2:13). The fulfillment of the challenge to

334. Martin and Hawthorne, 144.

335. Peterlin, *Paul's Letter to the Philippians,* 71-75. This theory of opposition to Paul, however, runs contrary to Paul's strong commendations of the church in Philippi, especially in 1:5 and 4:10-18.

work out your salvation can be observed in those who *do everything without grumbling or arguing*. In this context an essential evidence of *salvation* is deliverance from the common, debilitating habits of *grumbling or arguing*.[336]

15 The reason for purging *grumbling or arguing* from community life is *that you may become blameless and pure, "children of God without fault in a warped and crooked generation."* This purpose clause calls the Christian community to fulfill its mission in the world by cleaning up the conversation in the community. When Christian conversation is laced with complaints and personal attacks, Christians have lost their distinctive quality as the children of God in a world characterized by that same kind of negative tone. Three adjectives set a high standard for the character of the children of God: *blameless (amemptoi), pure (akeraioi),* and *without fault (amōma)*. The first letter in each word, *alpha* (α), the first letter in the Greek alphabet, is a prefix that negates the root word: no blame, no flaw, and no fault. To understand Paul's application of these words here we must keep in mind that he is addressing the entire Christian family and talking about the quality of their life together. These words describe the way the children of God relate to one another; an individualistic application of these words misses the point. To go into isolation and abstain from all kinds of immoral behavior is not the way to reach the high standard set by these words. In this context, these adjectives focus on the way Christians talk with and about one another. To be a *blameless* Christian community means that no one can find the faults of gripping and bickering in the words or tone of conversation in the community.[337] To be a *pure* Christian community means that Christians do not mix their good words with negative complaints or specious arguments.[338] Their speech is like good, undiluted wine. When *children of God* are *without fault*, their conversations will not be marked by the blemishes of bitter criticisms or angry quarrels.[339]

These three adjectives describe the *children of God*, one of Paul's favorite designations for Christians. By faith in Christ, Christians experience the witness of the Spirit that they are God's adopted children, and by the Spirit of Christ they address God as "*Abba*, Father" (Gal 3:26; 4:5-6; Rom 8:14-17). Paul's designation of Christians as *children of God* at this point puts special emphasis on the quality of their relationships. *Children of God* demonstrate who they are when they *become blameless, pure, and without fault* in the way they relate and talk with each other *without grumbling or arguing*. Paul is not

336. Barth, 75.

337. The Greek root word (μέμφομαι) in the word *blameless* (ἄμεμπτοι) means "to find fault" (BDAG, 629).

338. The Greek word for *pure* (ἀκέραιοι) is based on a Greek word (κεράννυμι) that means "to mix components, mostly of water with wine (to dilute the high alcoholic strength)" (BDAG, 540).

339. The Greek word for *without fault* (ἄμωμα) was used in the Greek OT (LXX) in the requirement that sacrificial animals should be "without blemish" (Num 6:14; BDAG, 56); hence Christ is described as the sacrificial lamb "without blemish" (1 Pet 1:19).

describing the way to *become* the children of God; he is urging the children of God to express the reality of who they are in the life and conversation of their Christian community. His command is under the overarching grace of God, who alone can empower his adopted children to *become* who they are. The only way for children of God to *become* who they are is by the power of the Father, the *God who works in you to will and to act in order to fulfill his good purpose.*

The next phrase presents a contrast to the Christian community: the children of God live *"in a warped and crooked generation."* A sharp line distinguishes the Christian community from its surrounding culture. Inside the community, relationships are to become *blameless, pure, and without fault;* outside the community, relationships are *warped and crooked.* Paul envisions a church that looks and sounds strikingly different from the world. Here again Paul is taking a line from the story of Israel but with a surprising twist. The words *"children"* and *"a warped and crooked generation"* are found in Deuteronomy 32:5 (LXX), but with a different meaning: "His degenerate children have dealt falsely with him, a perverse and crooked generation."[340] This text from Deuteronomy calls the children of God blemished *(mōmēta)* and equates them with a warped and crooked generation; Paul calls for the children of God to be unblemished *(amōma)* and distinguishes them from a warped and crooked generation. Some interpreters view Paul's use of this OT text as an assertion that the church has taken the place of Israel as the children of God.[341] Support for this view may seem to come from Paul's claim for the church, that *it is we who are the circumcision* (3:3). But Paul's ironic echo of Deuteronomy 32:5 does not provide a foundation for the position that the church has replaced Israel.[342] Although Paul is certainly contrasting the church and Israel, he is not explicitly saying that the church is replacing Israel as the children of God. The church learns from the negative example of Israel's disobedience in the wilderness, but the Gentile church does not take the place of Israel. Instead, according to Paul, the Gentile church is grafted into Israel until "all Israel will be saved" (Rom 11:26). Israel received the gift of "adoption" as sons (Rom 9:4), and "God's gifts and his call are irrevocable" (Rom 11:29). As the grumbling children of God in the wilderness, Israel became a warped and crooked generation. Paul instructs the members of the church to avoid grumbling so that they will become blameless children of God in a warped and crooked generation. Paul's reference to "the world" in the next phrase — a parallel to his depiction of a *"warped and crooked generation"* in this phrase — shows that Paul's main point here is not to declare the replacement of Israel but to draw a strong contrast between the children of God and the world, between the

340. The LXX reads: ἡμάρτοσαν οὐκ αὐτῷ τέκνα μωμητά γενεὰ σκολιὰ καί διεστραμμένη.

341. Hawthorne, 102: "The church now has the privilege of replacing Israel as God's children"; also Silva, 144-45.

342. Bockmuehl, 156-57.

Christian community and its non-Christian environment. The surrounding culture is *warped,* "morally bent or twisted, unscrupulous, dishonest,"[343] and *crooked,* having departed from the standard of moral values.[344] The purity of the church should be remarkably different from the perversion of the world.

The difference between the church and the world is immeasurably heightened by the next phrase: "among whom you shine like stars in the world" (my trans.).[345] The word *stars* refers to the heavenly bodies, the sun, moon, and all the stars in the sky.[346] Christians are like heavenly stars in a dark world. Here again we can hear an echo of the Greek OT (LXX): "Those who understand will shine like the stars of heaven, and those who have the strength of my words as the stars of heaven forever and ever" (Dan 12:3).[347] In the context of the apocalyptic vision of Daniel, those who "shine like stars" are those who have been raised from the dust to everlasting life (Dan 12:2). Paul envisions the fulfillment of this eschatological vision in the present mission of the church in the world. By changing "stars of heaven" (Dan 12:3) to *stars in the world,* Paul sets forth the worldwide scope of the Christian mission.[348] The heavenly light of the small community of believers in Philippi shines far beyond their own city to illuminate the way home for a warped and crooked generation lost in the darkness of this world.[349] In Paul's day, sailors did not have GPS to guide them through the night; they looked to the stars to plot their course to a safe harbor. The middle or passive voice of the verb *shine* may mean "to become visible, appear" or have the active sense, "to shine, flash."[350] Both interpretations really have the same meaning: when a star appears in the night sky, it shines in the darkness.[351] Although the form of the verb *shine* could be taken as an imperative,[352] "you must shine," its location in a dependent clause favors taking

343. BDAG, 930.

344. BDAG, 237.

345. TNIV *(Then you will shine among them like stars in the sky)* turns this subordinate, prepositional phrase into a new, independent sentence, makes the present tense a future tense, and translates *world* (κόσμῳ) as *sky.*

346. BDAG, 1073. In the LXX φωστῆρες refers to the heavenly bodies that God placed in the heavens on the fourth day (Gen 1:14, 16; see also Wis 13:2; Sir 43:7).

347. This is a literal translation of the LXX text. "Those who understand will shine like the stars of heaven (καὶ οἱ συνιέντες φανοῦσιν ὡς φωστῆρες τοῦ οὐρανοῦ), and those who have the strength of my words as the stars (καί οἱ κατισχύοντες τοὺς λόγους μου ὡσεὶ τὰ ἄστρα) of the heaven forever and ever" (Dan 12:3).

348. Bockmuehl (158) suggests that Paul's use of the word *world* "could be due to an alternative translation of the Hebrew word *ʿôlām* in Dan 12:3.

349. Note the parallelism of the two prepositional phrases: *in a warped and crooked generation* and *in the world.*

350. BDAG, 1046-47. See Matt 2:7; 24:27.

351. Silva, 146.

352. Beare, 92: "The imperative appears to be required here, rather than the indicative"; Hawthorne, 103: "It is unlikely that Paul is merely reminding the Philippians of what they are already doing. There would be no purpose in that."

the verb as an indicative: "you are shining."[353] The indicative gives the Philippians a vision of who they are, stars shining in the world, so that they will be motivated to fulfill the imperative, *Do everything without grumbling or arguing.* In an important parallel to Paul's words, the indicative in the teaching of Jesus, "You are the light of the world," is the basis for the imperative: "let your light shine before others, that they may see your good deeds and glorify your Father in heaven" (Matt 5:14-16).

16 By adding the clause, *as you hold firmly to the word of life,* Paul explains more fully how to become blameless children of God who shine like stars in the world.[354] The verb *hold firmly* may characterize a defensive or an evangelistic stance. The evangelistic implications of the image of *stars in the world* and the expression *word of life* lead some to visualize believers in Christ shining like stars by holding firmly the word of life as the source of light and life for a dark world.[355] This line of interpretation gives us a positive alternative to the prohibition against *grumbling or arguing.* Instead of being preoccupied with complaining, the church should be occupied with proclaiming the word of life. Complaining turns off the light of the church in the world; proclaiming the word of life shines the light of the life of Christ into the darkness of the world.

Although the context supports a call to proclaim the word of life, the primary meaning of the verb *hold firmly* connotes defending the word of life. This verb means (1) "to maintain a grasp on someone or something," (2) "to be mindful or especially observant," or (3) "to remain at a place."[356] In order not to be overwhelmed or snuffed out by the opposition of the world, the church needs "to maintain a grasp" on the word of life. Paul's concern is that the persecuted church will *stand firm in the one Spirit . . . without being frightened . . . by those who oppose* (1:27-28). The *children of God* develop a purity of belief and behavior unalloyed by the culture of *a warped and crooked generation* only by holding on resolutely to the *word of life.* A strong defense of the *word of life* keeps its light shining bright in the dark world for all to see. So this defensive posture of holding firmly the word of life leads to evangelistic results.

Although Paul does not use the full expression, *the word of life,* elsewhere, he often refers to the *word* as a synonym for the gospel he preaches.[357]

353. O'Brien, 296; Silva, 147.

354. The participial clause, the word of life holding (λόγον ζωῆς ἐπέχοντες), is viewed as an instrumental modifier (1) of the purpose clause, *so that you may become* (O'Brien, 297; Bockmuehl, 158) or (2) of the relative clause, *among whom you shine* (Fee, 247). Since these phrases are so closely connected — the relative clause is parallel and adds definition to the purpose clause — I take the participial clause as an instrumental modifier of both phrases. Another view is offered by Hawthorne (105), who says that the participle is imperatival and the beginning of a new sentence.

355. See Fee, 247; Fee (247 n. 33) also suggests that Paul's phrase expresses the meaning of the Hebrew text of Dan 12:3 ("those who lead many to righteousness").

356. BDAG, 362.

357. See 1:14; 1 Thess 1:5, 6, 8; 2:13; 1 Cor 1:18; 2:4; 2 Cor 2:17; 4:2; 5:19; 6:7.

The *word* is about the *life* of Christ and generates *life* in all who hear and believe in Christ. The immediate reference of this expression in this context is the Christ hymn.[358] Paul calls for the attitude of believers to be transformed by focusing on Christ (2:5-11). He urges the church to demonstrate their firm grasp of the message about Christ by the way they live out the life of Christ in their relationships with one another. This is another way of saying that believers in Christ are to *live in a manner worthy of the gospel of Christ* by *striving together with one accord for the faith of the gospel* (1:27). Since the *word of life* is the source of life for the church, the existence of the church depends upon a firm grasp of the word of life. If the word of life is lost, the church will be like a black hole rather than a shining star in the world.

After painting his portrayal of blameless children of God shining like stars in the world by holding firmly to the word of life, Paul gives believers in Christ a personal reason for living up to this portrayal: *And then I will be able to boast on the day of Christ that I did not run or labor in vain.*[359] Paul expected the members of the church to be motivated by the prospect that the quality of their life would be the basis of Paul's *boast* about them on *the day of Christ.* The word *boast* means "the act of taking pride in something or that which constitutes a source of pride."[360] This reference to boasting sounds strange in a section where Paul denounces *vain conceit,* advocates *humility* (2:3), recounts the story of Christ who *humbled himself* (2:8), and foresees the day when all will worship Christ, *to the glory of God the Father* (2:11). But however strange this reference may sound, it fits in well with Paul's theme of boasting in his letters.[361] Paul excludes all boasting about keeping the law (Rom 3:27; cf. Eph 2:8-9) or about human leaders (1 Cor 3:21) and explicitly says that no one may boast before God (1 Cor 1:29).[362] The only boasting that Paul allows is boasting in the Lord (1 Cor 1:31; Phil 3:3), boasting in the cross of Christ (Gal 6:14), and boasting in tribulations (Rom 5:3) and infirmities (2 Cor 12:9). In addition, Paul often boasts about his converts (2 Cor 7:4; 8:24; 9:2; 1 Thess 2:19; 2 Thess 1:4), and expects his converts to boast about him (2 Cor 1:14; 5:12). Paul's theme of boasting turns the whole concept of human boasting upside down. Human boasting takes pride in human power and human accomplishments. But Paul's boasting gives all the glory to God for God's demonstration of grace and power through human weakness and tribulation. When Paul speaks of boasting on the day of Christ about his ap-

358. Barth, 77.

359. In the Greek text (εἰς καύχημα ἐμοί εἰς ἡμέραν Χριστοῦ), these words (presented as an independent sentence in TNIV) form a purpose clause at the end of the sentence beginning in v. 14 with the imperative: *Do everything without grumbling or arguing.* This clause at the end of the sentence expresses the purpose of the entire sentence, not merely the purpose of the last phrase *(as you hold firmly to the word of life).* See Vincent, 70; O'Brien, 298.

360. BDAG, 537.

361. 35 of the 37 NT occurrences of the verb *I boast,* 10 of the 11 NT occurrences of the noun *boast,* and 11 of the 12 NT occurrences of the noun *boasting* are in Paul's letters.

362. See Simon J. Gathercole, *Where Is Boasting? Early Jewish Soteriology and Paul's Response in Romans 1–5* (Grand Rapids: Eerdmans, 2002).

ostolic work in the community of believers (2:16), his boasting is based upon his belief that *it is God who works in you to will and to act in order to fulfill his good pleasure* (2:13). His boasting is not self-glorying or self-praise, but "boasting in the grace of God."[363] If the Philippians were following the flow of Paul's letter, the prospect of Paul's boasting about them on the day of Christ would not cause them to swell with pride about their own work or Paul's work but to bow in humility with thankfulness for God's work through Paul's ministry in their community.

Paul was filled with eager expectation of *the day of Christ.*[364] The anticipation of *the day of Christ* motivated Paul to work hard because he expected the quality of his work to be evaluated by Christ on that day. Since Paul anticipated appearing "before the judgment seat of Christ" (2 Cor 5:10; cf. 1 Cor 4:1-5; Rom 14:10-12) to give an account of his ministry, he urged believers to give ample evidence that he *did not run or labor in vain.* The pictures of a runner and a laborer are Paul's favorite self-portraits. He saw striking similarities between his ministry and these pictures of running in a Roman stadium and laboring with the working class in the Roman Empire.[365] His word for *labor* connotes becoming weary from exerting oneself physically, mentally, or spiritually, working hard, toiling, striving, and struggling.[366] Paul was used to strenuous exertion and exhaustion in his work as an apostle. This work was filled with the stress and the sweat, the discipline and the pain portrayed in these pictures. He ran his race to "get the prize," not "like someone running aimlessly" (1 Cor 9:24-26). He wanted to be sure that he "was not running and had not been running in vain" (Gal 2:2). When he compared himself to the other apostles, he was convinced that by the grace of God he had "worked harder than all of them" (1 Cor 15:10). But he knew that the testing of his hard work on the day of Christ would reveal whether or not his work was *in vain.* He suspected that the quality of the work of some was like straw rather than gold and that "their work will be shown for what it is" and "burned up" on the day of Christ (1 Cor 3:11-15). Paul, however, was confident that all of the suffering endured in the long race and difficult work of his career as an apostle would not be in vain because he was confident that God, who was constantly working in the community of believers (2:13), would complete the good work that he had initiated (1:6). But even though he is confident in God's work, he still urges the believers in Christ to give evidence of God's work in their community so that he can boast on the day of Christ that he *did not run or labor in vain* in Philippi. The review of his ministry on the *day of Christ* presents an incentive to the church to *become blameless and pure, children of God.*

363. R. Bultmann, "καυχάομαι," *TDNT* 3:651.
364. See also 1:6, 10.
365. Vincent, 70; Martin and Hawthorne, 147.
366. BDAG, 558.

17 The suffering experienced by Paul in his ministry and characterized in the pictures of running and working is now portrayed as offering a sacrifice in a temple: *But even if I am being poured out like a drink offering on the sacrifice and service coming from your faith, I am glad and rejoice with all of you.* The introductory words to this picture *(But even if)* point to a progression of thought from the two previous pictures.[367] The previous pictures display the suffering of extreme exertion: the runner expends every ounce of energy to reach the finish line; the worker toils and struggles to complete the work. Now this picture goes even further to display the suffering of the ultimate sacrifice: the apostle pours out his life in his ministry. Just in case readers think that Paul resents the suffering of extreme exertion that he has endured in his ministry, he now corrects that misconception: *But even if* I suffer the ultimate sacrifice of martyrdom *(I am being poured out like a drink offering),* I do not resent this suffering at all but rather *I am glad and rejoice with you all.*[368] Paul responds to suffering, no matter how extreme and ultimate, with rejoicing.

In this picture a priest offers a burnt offering of a sacrificial animal on the altar and also pours out a drink offering of wine. The picture reflects both Jewish and Greek sacrificial rituals. The expression *I am being poured out like a drink offering* "means to pour out a portion of a drink on the ground or on a cultic site as an offering to the gods"; it was used widely in Greek literature to depict the common practice of pouring out wine at feasts and religious ceremonies as libations to Zeus and other Olympian deities.[369] The same verb was used in the Greek OT (LXX) to depict the Jewish rituals of pouring out a drink offering to God.[370] For example, instructions are given in Numbers 28:7: "In the sanctuary you shall pour out a drink offering of strong drink to the LORD." Probably, Paul was drawing the picture from his own Jewish background, but his Gentile readers would have easily understood the imagery in their own religious context.[371]

367. O'Brien (303) argues that this conjunction (ἀλλά) "marks a progression beyond the preceding words." His claim that "it has an ascensive force" is disputed by Fee (250 n. 49) on the grounds that the ascensive usage is restricted to ἀλλά with καί. See BDF §448.6. Barth (79-81) takes the conjunction *(But)* as the introduction of a whole new section "that does not contain any direct teaching" but discusses "points of a purely personal, human kind" regarding his relationship with the Philippian congregation. However, the close connection of this picture of sacrifice with the two previous pictures of suffering as a runner and a worker indicates that this sentence is a completion of the same train of thought.

368. The expression *even if* (εἰ καί) introduces a concessive clause that presents the real possibility of martyrdom (see BDF §§374, 457).

369. O. Michel, "σπένδομαι," *TDNT* 7:528.

370. Michel, "σπένδομαι," *TDNT* 7:531; see examples in Num 15:5; 28:7.

371. Since Paul's use of sacrificial language in other places (see Phil 4:18; 1 Cor 9:13; 10:18; Rom 12:1; 15:16) is so closely connected to the Jewish sacrificial system, he is probably using Jewish imagery here (see Fee, 251 n. 51). But according to Vincent (72), "The fact that Paul is writing from Rome to a Gentile church seems to indicate that the metaphor is cast in the mould of heathen rather than Jewish sacrificial usage." But the religious context of Paul's readers does not necessarily indicate the source of his own language.

Although the picture of *being poured out like a drink offering* presents a dramatic metaphor of Paul's suffering, its ambiguity causes us to ponder its meaning. Was Paul depicting his own martyrdom or was he portraying his years of suffering in his work as an apostle? Proponents of the interpretation of this metaphor as a reference to Paul's sufferings in his ministry as an apostle rather than to his martyrdom observe the following points: (1) the present rather than future tense of the verb *(I am being poured out)*; (2) the evidence that this verb never denotes killing or pouring out of blood; (3) Paul's confidence that he will visit Philippi soon (2:24); (4) the combination of this metaphor with the two previous metaphors in a way that makes all three pictures a dramatic presentation of Paul's suffering in his ministry; and (5) the unlikely juxtaposition of martyrdom and rejoicing.[372]

All of these observations do not overthrow the view that Paul is referring to the real possibility of his martyrdom. The present tense is used in a concessive clause not to state what is currently happening to the apostle or to forecast a certain future, but to portray a real possibility: *even if* I am martyred. The present tense of the same verb in 2 Timothy 4:6 clearly points to martyrdom: "For I am already being poured out like a drink offering, and the time for my departure is near." The second phrase in 2 Timothy 4:6 interprets the metaphor as a reference to imminent martyrdom. In Philippians 2:17, however, the metaphor does not point to the certainty of imminent martyrdom, but only to the supposition of a possibility of martyrdom: even if I suppose that the worst possible scenario happens and I am martyred. Since Paul is not forecasting the imminent certainty of his death, he does not contradict himself when he informs his readers of his imminent visit in 2:24. The observation that the term Paul uses does not refer to the shedding or pouring out of blood in sacrificial contexts does not negate the view that Paul is using sacrificial language metaphorically, not literally, to depict the possibility of martyrdom: his life being poured out as sacrifice to God.[373] This metaphor bears striking resemblance to the metaphor used in the portrayal of Christ: Christ emptied himself (2:7). Just as Christ's self-emptying led to death on a cross, so Paul views the possibility of following in the way of Christ by *being poured out* unto death. Paul rejoices not in the act of martyrdom itself, but in the possibility of being one with Christ in *being pouring out* as Christ *emptied himself* to be obedient unto death on a cross. And Paul's joy also results from being one with the Philippians in their sacrifice since he considers *being poured out like a drink offering* as a sacrifice that is intimately united with their *sacrifice and service.*[374]

372. See Collange, 100-101; Fee, 252-55; Martin and Hawthorne, 148-49.

373. Besides the metaphorical use of this verb in 2 Tim 4:6 as a reference to martyrdom, this verb is unquestionably used metaphorically to refer to martyrdom by Ignatius in *Rom.* 2:2: "Grant me nothing more than that I be poured out to God, while an altar is still ready."

374. For advocacy of this view, see Barth, 82; Beare, 93-94; Gregory L. Bloomquist, *The Function of Suffering in Philippians* (JSNTSup 78; Sheffield: JSOT Press, 1993), 171; Silva, 150; O'Brien, 305-6; Bockmuehl, 161.

This language about *sacrifice and service* describes Paul's own ministry in Romans 15:16: "the grace God gave me to be a minister of Christ Jesus to the Gentiles. He gave me the priestly duty of proclaiming the gospel of God so that the Gentiles might become an offering acceptable to God, sanctified by the Holy Spirit." On the basis of this text in Romans, Calvin says that the phrase *sacrifice and service* is a picture of the Philippians being offered up as a *sacrifice* by Paul in an act of priestly *service.*[375] Most interpreters, however, hold to the view that both nouns refer to the sacrifice and service of the Philippians because (1) one article unites two nouns joined by *and* in an expression of a single idea or event in Paul's prepositional phrase, *on the sacrifice and service,* (2) Paul refers later to the sacrifice and service of the Philippians (2:30; 4:18), and (3) the sacrificial imagery in this context presents Paul's drink offering as an addition to the sacrifice and service of the Philippians.[376]

The preposition *on* in this imagery of sacrifices made by Paul and the Philippians may have alluded to the practice in both Jewish and Greek ceremonies of pouring the drink offering directly on the sacrifice that was on the altar. But in this context this preposition may have less of its primary spatial meaning and more of the sense of "in addition to."[377] In the Jewish sacrificial ritual, the drink offering was poured out as an additional sacrifice to the burnt offerings.[378] The drink offering completes the main offering of a burnt sacrifice on the altar and makes it pleasing to God. The possibility of *being poured out like a drink offering* makes Paul rejoice because his sacrifice would be in addition to and a completion of the sacrifice he is urging believers to make as an expression of their faith. Paul is not calling for a sacrifice on the part of others that he is unwilling to make himself.

TNIV adds the words *coming from* to the simple expression *your faith* to clarify the implication that faith inspires and empowers *sacrifice and service.*[379] The word *sacrifice,* a term used to designate Jewish (see Mark 12:33; Heb 5:1) and pagan sacrifices (1 Cor 10:18) and the sacrificial death of Christ (Eph 5:2; Heb 9:26; 10:12), was used metaphorically by Paul to depict the sacrifice of oneself to do the will of God (Rom 12:1-2).[380] The term *service* was the label for the work of priests in the temple (Luke 1:23; Heb 9:21) and the high-priestly work of Christ (Heb 8:6).[381] The specific kind of *sacrifice (thysia) and service (leitourgia)* given by the Philippians is disclosed by Paul's

375. Calvin, 260.

376. Lightfoot, 119; Vincent, 71; Hawthorne, 105, Silva, 150; Fee, 254.

377. BDAG, 365, gives "in addition to" as meaning for ἐπί found in 1 Cor 14:16; 2 Cor 7:13, and Phil 2:27: *sorrow upon sorrow.*

378. See Num 15:5, 7, 10; 28:7: "In the sanctuary you shall pour out a drink offering."

379. This interpretation takes τῆς πίστεως as a subjective genitive or genitive of source (see Beare, 95; Hawthorne, 105; Silva, 151; Fee, 255). Vincent (71) argues for an objective genitive ("a sacrifice which consists of your faith"), and O'Brien (310) suggests that the genitive is epexegetical, referring to the readers' life of faith.

380. BDAG, 462-63.

381. BDAG, 591.

use of the same terms in his commendation of Epaphroditus (2:25-30) and in his receipt of the gifts sent by the Philippians (4:17-18). He commends Epaphroditus, *who was sent to take care of my needs* (2:25), for risking his life to make up what was lacking in the Philippians' *service to me* (2:30). In his receipt, Paul says, *I am amply supplied, now that I have received from Epaphroditus the gifts you sent. They are a fragrant offering, an acceptable sacrifice, pleasing to God* (4:17-18). The Philippians gave sacrificial gifts to Paul (4:14-16) in their service to him. Although their financial contributions are specifically in view, Paul elevates the significance of their sacrificial financial support by using terms that "suggest an aura of high status" for those who render any type of service.[382] The Philippians were engaged in priestly *service* as they fulfilled their responsibilities in their *partnership in the gospel* (1:5) by sending Epaphroditus with monetary gifts that were genuine *sacrifices* motivated by their *faith* in Christ.

Paul had such a high view of the service of these friends that even the prospect that he might *be poured out as a drink offering* as an appropriate addition to their sacrifice caused him to be *glad and rejoice* with them. He rejoices because he is contemplating the possibility of completing the sacrifice they have already made. Not the absence of suffering, but the presence of sacrifice inspired by faith in Christ generated Paul's joy. And since his friends are also rejoicing in the opportunity to express their faith in sacrificial service, Paul knows that when he is rejoicing he is rejoicing together with all of them. Rather than begrudging their sacrifice, Paul's friends are delighted to serve him. Such joyful service is contagious. Paul shares in their joy.[383]

18 Paul is not content to share in their joy; he desires them to share in his joy as well: *So you too should be glad and rejoice with me.* He does not want his friends to be depressed by his imprisonment and suffering. If they are able to be joyful in their sacrificial service to Paul, then they should be able to rejoice in Paul's desire to be poured out as a drink offering as a completion of their sacrifice. Paul's emphasis on joy in the midst of suffering does not advocate a masochistic attitude: "I am happy because I am miserable." The larger setting of his imperatives to rejoice with him in suffering establishes partnership in the gospel (1:5), partnership in the Spirit (2:1), and partnership in the sufferings of Christ (3:10) as the ultimate basis of joy. The prefix *with* in the verbs *I rejoice with* and *you rejoice with* points to this theme of partnership. Partnership in Christ by the Spirit

382. BDAG, 591.

383. Lightfoot (119) suggests that the verb *I rejoice with* (συγχαίρω) means "I congratulate" simply because of the fact that since "joy is enjoined on the Philippians in the second clause, it must not be assumed on their part in the first." BDAG (953) lists the meaning "to express pleasure over another's good fortune, congratulate" as a secondary sense of this verb, but Lightfoot's suggestion is not convincing since Paul uses the verbs *rejoice* (χαίρω) and *rejoice with* (συγχαίρω) so often in this letter with the primary meaning of experiencing joy (O'Brien, 311 n. 55).

with one another makes shared suffering with Christ and with one another a joyful experience.[384]

Paul began this section of specific ethical instructions with a negative prohibition against complaining: *Do everything without grumbling or arguing* (2:14). He now ends on a positive note by encouraging his friends to rejoice with him in all aspects of their partnership together in Christ. Even in the midst of suffering, sacrifice, and service, joy is a distinguishing mark of partners in Christ.

V. RECOMMENDATIONS OF CHRIST-LIKE SERVANTS (2:19-30)

After giving direct exhortation, Paul now presents the dynamic examples of two men, Timothy and Epaphroditus, who embody the Christ-like attitudes he has been encouraging his readers to have in their relationships with one another. This abrupt shift from imperatives to illustrations causes some interpreters to suggest that Paul is closing his letter by announcing his travel plans in this section in the conventional way that ancient letter writers often did at the end of a letter.[385] According to this view, "When Paul wrote these words he had not the slightest intention of adding further long paragraphs of warning and exhortation. He is bringing his letter to an end."[386] But concluding his letter does not appear to be Paul's purpose in this section. In fact, Paul's travelogues do not primarily function as a conclusion to his letters.[387] A comparison of this section with similar sections in other Pauline letters shows that this travelogue contains two common features of Paul's travelogues: his intention to recommend and dispatch an emissary to the readers, in this case two emissaries, Timothy and Epaphroditus, and his plan for a personal visit.[388] The underlying purpose of these travelogues is to display "the presence of apostolic authority and power — of which the travelogue in the narrow sense is

384. Hawthorne, 106; Bockmuehl, 162-63.

385. For detailed analysis of the function of a travelogue in papyrus letters and in the Pauline letters, see Robert W. Funk, "The Apostolic *Parousia:* Form and Significance," in *Christian History and Interpretation: Studies Presented to John Knox* (ed. W. R. Farmer, C. F. D. Moule, and R. R. Niebuhr; Cambridge: Cambridge University Press, 1967), 249-68; John L. White, *The Form and Function of the Body of the Greek Letter* (SBLDS 2; Missoula, Mont.: Scholars Press, 1972), 143-45; W. G. Doty, *Letters in Primitive Christianity* (Philadelphia: Fortress, 1973), 36-37; T. Y. Mullins, "A Visit Talk in New Testament Letters," *CBQ* 35 (1973), 350-58.

386. Beare, 95.

387. His travelogues sometimes appear in the middle of the body of his letter: 1 Cor 4:14-21; Gal 4:12-20; 1 Thess 2:17–3:11.

388. See Rom 15:14-33; 1 Cor 4:14-21; 2 Cor 12:14–13:10; Gal 4:12-20; 1 Thess 2:17–3:11; Phlm 22.

only one element."[389] Since the letter functioned as a substitute for Paul's physical presence, Paul added weight to the apostolic authority of the letter by promising that he would visit the congregation soon in person to make sure that the imperatives in his letter were implemented. Meanwhile his emissaries spoke with his authority when they conveyed and explained the contents of his letter.

This analysis of the purpose of Paul's travelogues illuminates our understanding of the function of this section in Paul's letter to the Philippians. Unable to be present in person, Paul backs up the authority and power of his letter with a promise of a personal visit: *I am confident in the Lord that I myself will come soon* (2:24), and with recommendations of his personal emissaries, Timothy (2:19-23) and Epaphroditus (2:25-30). In his recommendations, Paul shows how these two men exhibit the same character traits that he has been encouraging the Philippians to develop. By his *genuine concern* for the welfare of the Philippians in a time when *everyone looks out for their own interests* (2:20-21), Timothy illustrates the altruistic attitude Paul desired the Philippians to have, *not looking to your own interests but each of you to the interests of others* (2:4). When Epaphroditus *almost died* because he *risked his life* in the service of Christ (2:30), he mirrored Christ, who took *the very nature of a servant* and was *obedient unto death* (2:7-8). Paul's portrayal of the same traits in Timothy and Epaphroditus that he saw in Christ and wanted to see in the Philippians gives the readers reliable guides to follow. To *have the same attitude of mind Christ Jesus had* (2:5) seems intangible until that attitude is exhibited in contemporary servants of Christ. As we read Paul's travel plans for these two servants of Christ, we do not merely gain historical knowledge about ancient itineraries; we are guided in our service of Christ by the recommendations of two extraordinary servants of Christ.

A. Timothy (2:19-24)

> [19]*I hope in the Lord Jesus to send Timothy to you soon, that I also may be cheered when I receive news about you.* [20]*I have no one else like him, who will show genuine concern for your welfare.* [21]*For everyone looks out for their own interests, not those of Jesus Christ.* [22]*But you know that Timothy has proved himself, because as a son with his father he has served with me in the work of the gospel.* [23]*I hope, therefore, to send him as soon as I see how things go with me.* [24]*And I am confident in the Lord that I myself will come soon.*

19 Paul's use of the verb *I hope* (vv. 19 and 23) to express his desire to send Timothy does not imply that Paul lacked confidence that he would ac-

389. Funk, "The Apostolic *Parousia*," 249. Funk shows how Paul made his apostolic presence, apostolic *parousia*, felt in his congregations in three related ways: the letter, his emissary, and his own personal presence.

tually send Timothy. Although the English word may connote a high degree of uncertainty, the Greek word implies confidence of a future event.[390] Paul often used the same verb to assure his friends of his intentions to be with them.[391] Paul's statement that his hope is *in the Lord Jesus* indicates that he makes his travel plans under the direction of the Lord Jesus, submits his plans to the Lord Jesus for approval, and depends upon the Lord Jesus for the realization of his plans. As *servants of Christ Jesus* (1:1), Paul and Timothy did not make plans without seeking the direction and approval of the Lord.

Paul communicates his sense of the future by saying that he plans to send Timothy *soon*.[392] Although Timothy's departure was delayed until Paul could see how things would go for him in his personal situation, presumably in his imprisonment and upcoming trial (2:23), the delay would not be for long. Paul is also confident that his own visit to Philippi will be *soon* (2:24). Paul envisions only a brief interval before his circumstances will dramatically improve: *soon* he will be able to send Timothy to Philippi since he will no longer need his assistance; *soon* he will be free to visit his friends in Philippi. Paul does not appear to gain his positive view of his future from a sanguine temperament, a resolute commitment to an optimistic perspective on life no matter what, or a careful analysis of the latest news. He claims that he is positive about the future because he places his *hope in the Lord Jesus* (v. 19) and he is *confident in the Lord* (v. 24). Whether he means that he simply trusts in the goodness of the Lord or that he has received a special revelation from the Lord regarding his future, we cannot be sure. But we do know that when Paul looked at the horizon he focused on the Lord Jesus. As a result he was filled with hope and confidence.

Paul explains his reason for sending Timothy to Philippi by saying that he desires to be *cheered* when he receives news regarding the condition of the church in Philippi. Used only here in the NT, the word *cheered* means "to be heartened, be glad, have courage."[393] Although Paul assumes that the church will be encouraged by Timothy's report regarding his own situation,[394] he places his emphasis on the potential impact that Timothy's re-

390. BDAG, 319.

391. Paul used the same verb to express his plans to visit the churches in Corinth (1 Cor 16:7) and Rome (Rom 15:24) and his friend Philemon (Phlm 22). Paul's theological use of the word is well stated by Bultmann: "Hope is not concerned with the realization of a human dream of the future but with the confidence which, directed away from the world to God, waits patiently for God's gift, and when it is received does not rest in possession but in the assurance that God will maintain what he has given" (R. Bultmann, "ἐλπίζω," *TDNT* 2:532).

392. The adverb *soon* (ταχέως) is used here to "focus on brevity of interval rather than on speed of activity" (BDAG, 992).

393. BDAG, 417. The use of the imperative (εὐψύχει) is found in salutations of letters of condolence and in Hellenistic grave inscriptions in Paul's day.

394. The expression *I also* (κἀγώ) implies Paul's confidence that the Philippians will be cheered by what Timothy tells them about the progress of the gospel through Paul's witness in prison.

port regarding the church will have on his personal sense of well-being. This emphasis on his deep concern for the welfare of the church puts pressure on the church to cheer him up by following his directive to be *one in spirit and of one mind* (2:2). The church now knows that they will encourage Paul by their unity or discourage him by their disunity. Not as a dispassionate spectator but as a tenderly caring parent, Paul opens his heart to the church. His words "combine a subtle, unobtrusive admonition and an expression of affectionate solidarity between apostle and congregation."[395]

20 The first reason Paul gives for sending Timothy rather than someone else is that there is *no one else like him, who will show genuine concern for your welfare.* In this recommendation of Timothy, Paul uses the adjective *equal-soul (isopsychos)* to highlight Timothy's most important quality: I have no one else of *equal soul,* no one else of the same mind, no one else with a kindred spirit.[396] This depiction of Timothy's special qualification to serve as Paul's agent points not to the absolute uniqueness of Timothy (there is no one equal to Timothy) but to the closeness of Timothy and Paul (there is no one else who is as equal to me as Timothy is).[397] Paul's reason for choosing Timothy is that Timothy shares his mind and his heart.[398] That Timothy's kindred spirit with Paul makes him the best choice to represent Paul comes into view again in Paul's description of their intimate relationship *as a son with his father* (v. 22).

Since Timothy was as a son to Paul, Paul assured the Philippians that Timothy would have the same concern as Paul did for their welfare: he *will show genuine concern for your welfare.* Paul's use of the word *genuine* draws attention again to his close relationship to Timothy. The adjectival form of this word *genuine* refers to "one who is considered a valid member of a family, legitimate, true."[399] This adjective is used in 1 Timothy 1:2 to describe Timothy as Paul's "true son in the faith." As Paul's true son, Timothy will have a familial concern for the Philippians; he will genuinely care for them just as much as Paul does.

Being genuinely concerned can turn into being anxiously worried. Paul admonishes his readers not to go to that extreme: *Do not be anxious about anything* (4:6: *mēden merimnate*). But Paul uses the same verb in his recommendation of Timothy, who *will be genuinely concerned (merimnēsei)* for

395. Barth, 85.

396. BDAG, 48; perhaps there is a play on words with the preceding εὐψυχῶ (MM 307). Paul will be made "good of soul" *(eu-psychos)* only by a report from the one who is "equal of soul" *(iso-psychos).*

397. The absence of an expressed object for ἰσόψυχον ("equal of soul") leaves room to argue that the adjective means no one else is equal to Timothy (see Lightfoot, 120; Gnilka, 158; Müller, 126). But Paul's focus in this context on the closeness of his relationship with Timothy *(as a son with his father)* supports the interpretation that Timothy is qualified because he is "equal of soul" to Paul (see Hawthorne, 110; O'Brien, 318; Fee, 266).

398. Beare, 96.

399. BDAG, 202. Fee (266 n. 29) doubts that the adverb used here in 2:20 can be shown to carry the same sense as the adjective.

the welfare of the Philippians. Paul draws a line between obsessive anxiety and genuine concern.[400] Caring for the needs of friends should not lead to anxiety; freedom from anxiety should not lead to a lack of concern for friends. In fact, members of the body of Christ should have concern for each other (1 Cor 12:25: *to auto hyper allēlōn merimnōsin*).[401]

21 Paul moves from his specific reason for choosing Timothy on the basis of Timothy's kindred spirit demonstrated by his genuine concern to a general criticism of *everyone: For everyone looks out for their own interests, not those of Jesus Christ.* What motivated Paul to make such a universal denunciation of *everyone?* When he says *everyone,* does he mean the entire population, all Christians, all eligible candidates among Paul's circle of co-workers, or only all co-workers who were not responsive to Paul's call to serve Christ? Does his judgment that *everyone looks out for their own interests,* mean that everyone is totally selfish or simply that they were unwilling to give up their self-interests to be Paul's agents to Philippi? These and many subsidiary questions perplex interpreters.[402]

A generous interpretation takes *everyone* as a reference to certain co-workers who should have been available but were unwilling to be sent by Paul to Philippi because they were preoccupied with their own interests.[403] This restriction of everyone takes into account Paul's positive words about co-workers in Rome who preached Christ out of goodwill and love (1:15-16) and his final greetings from the Lord's people who were with him (4:22). Paul could not have meant to insult these highly valued co-workers and good friends by his general condemnation of everyone. By *everyone* he must have meant those he had already described as preachers of Christ out of envy, rivalry, and selfish ambition (1:15-17). They are the ones who look out *for their own interests, not those of Jesus Christ.* This limitation of Paul's reference to everyone works well in the context of the letter and sets up the contrast Paul draws between Timothy's genuine concern for the welfare of the church and the selfish ambitions of others. By making this comparison, Paul reinforces his imperatives: *Do nothing out of selfish ambition* and *value others above yourselves, not looking to your own interests* (2:3-4). The exemplary willingness of Timothy to serve Jesus Christ by serving others provides an exceptional standard by which Paul rebukes *everyone* who *looks out for their own interests, not those of Jesus Christ.* In the light of his exhortations to the believers in Philippi, he has some of them in mind when he makes his judgment of everyone.

400. The present tense imperative in 4:6 calls the readers to stop their obsessive habit of worrying about everything, while the future tense in 2:20 indicates that Timothy will care for the practical needs of the Philippians when he arrives (O'Brien, 319).

401. See Bultmann, "μεριμνάω," *TDNT* 4:592.

402. After reviewing many alternative interpretations, Vincent (74) concludes: "Without more information a satisfactory explanation seems impossible." Hawthorne (111) agrees.

403. Beare, 97; Bockmuehl, 166; O'Brien, 321; Gnilka, 159.

22 The second reason Paul gives for sending Timothy to the church in Philippi is the church's knowledge of Timothy: *you know that Timothy has proved himself.* The word Paul uses here to speak of Timothy's proven character refers to "the experience of going through a test with special reference to the result."[404] From Paul's perspective, proven character is produced by perseverance in the experience of suffering (see Rom 5:3-4), and the evidence of proven character is faithful service that validates a confession of the gospel of Christ (see 2 Cor 9:13).[405] Timothy had proved himself to the Philippians by enduring trials and remaining faithful in his service with Paul as a minister of the gospel. Although Paul does not tell *how* the Philippians acquired their knowledge of Timothy's proven character,[406] he states that *what* the church knew was that *as a son with his father he has served with me in the work of the gospel.*[407] In this brief phrase Paul features the character traits of loyalty and humility. Timothy's loyalty to Paul was not the loyalty of a cold professional, but the intimate loyalty of *a son* to *his father.* As one who had been nurtured in the faith and directed in his work by Paul for many years, Timothy enjoyed a rare intimacy with his mentor that could be appropriately characterized as a father-son relationship (see also 1 Tim 1:18; 2 Tim 2:1).[408] Just as many Greco-Roman moralists and Jewish teachers in his Mediterranean culture required, Timothy fulfilled his filial duty by honoring and obeying Paul as a son should honor and obey his father.[409] Since the

404. BDAG, 256.

405. All seven NT uses of δοκιμή occur in Paul's letters (Rom 5:4 [twice]; 2 Cor 2:9; 8:2; 9:13; 13:3; Phil 2:22). See W. Grundmann, "δοκιμή," *TDNT* 2:258-59.

406. The account in Acts does not help much since it implies only that Timothy was with Paul during his first visit to Philippi (Acts 16:1-3; 17:14-15) but does not give any record of Timothy's experience during that visit.

407. With the verb of knowing (γινώσκετε), the conjunction ὅτι (translated *because* by TNIV; "how" by NRSV) points to the basis or content of knowledge: you know *that;* you know *how.* See BDF §397 (1).

408. See Paul's other references to his relationship as father (1 Thess 2:11; 1 Cor 4:15), mother (1 Thess 2:7; 4:19), and parent (2 Cor 6:15; 12:14) to those whom he brought to faith in Christ.

409. See C. S. Keener, "Family and Household," *DNTB* 354-56; C. J. H. Wright, "Family," *ABD* 2:766-69. Sir 3:1-8 is a typical passage in Jewish wisdom literature:

> [1]Listen to me your father, O children;
> act accordingly, that you may be kept in safety.
> [2]For the Lord honors a father above his children,
> and he confirms a mother's right over her children.
> [3]Those who honor their father atone for sins,
> [4]and those who respect their mother are like those who lay up treasure.
> [5]Those who honor their father will have joy in their own children,
> and when they pray they will be heard.
> [6]Those who respect their father will have long life,
> and those who honor their mother obey the Lord;
> [7]they will serve their parents as their masters.
> [8]Honor your father by word and deed,
> that his blessing may come upon you.

Philippians were cognizant of Timothy's filial loyalty, they could be sure that Timothy's words and actions would faithfully represent Paul's heart and mind. Timothy's filial loyalty was also the basis of Paul's recommendation of Timothy to the Corinthian church: "I have sent to you Timothy, my son whom I love, who is faithful in the Lord. He will remind you of my way of life in Christ Jesus, which agrees with what I teach everywhere in every church" (1 Cor 4:17). Timothy was Paul's favored agent because he was faithful to Paul's teaching.

Since Paul's teaching was gospel-centered, what mattered most to him was Timothy's loyalty to the gospel. In fact, in a surprising, yet totally Pauline shift of direction, Paul does not say that Timothy served me, but that he *served with me in the work of the gospel.* The gospel was the final authority for Paul as well as for Timothy. They were both *servants of Christ Jesus* (1:1) *in the work of the gospel.*[410] Of supreme importance to Paul was *partnership in the gospel, confirming the gospel,* the need *to advance the gospel,* the responsibility *to proclaim the gospel, the defense of the gospel,* and the call to *live in a manner worthy of the gospel of Christ* (1:5, 7, 12, 14, 16, 27). *The work of the gospel* is the work of preaching the gospel, "the work of evangelism."[411] But according to Paul's call to the Christian community to live in a manner worthy of the gospel (1:27), the work of the gospel provides not only the foundation for the community but also the continuing direction for community life. "We are obedient to the Gospel and meet its demands when we are active in the ministry of love. This active love is the obedience of the confession of the Gospel."[412] Timothy served loyally with Paul in the work of proclaiming the gospel to bring people to faith in Christ and in the work of guiding the church to live out the implications of the gospel in the community of believers.

Timothy's loyalty in his roles as a son to Paul and as a slave with Paul in the work of the gospel was evidence of the character trait of humility. Sons and slaves are subservient to the demands of fathers and masters. Timothy humbled himself to be an obedient son and slave. In his humility he was like Christ, who *made himself nothing by taking the form of a slave* and *humbled himself by becoming obedient to death* (2:7-8). In Paul's recommendation of Timothy, he uses the same language as the hymn to Christ so that his readers will know that Timothy has *the same attitude of mind Christ Jesus had* (2:5). Timothy serves as a Christ-like example for the church to show what a Christ-like character looks like in everyday life.

23 After writing his recommendation of Timothy, Paul reiterates his plan to send Timothy to Philippi and adds a note to explain why he is not sending Timothy immediately: *I hope, therefore, to send him as soon as I see*

410. The verb *served* (ἐδούλευσεν) denotes the work of *slaves* (δοῦλοι): "to act or conduct oneself as one in total service to another, perform the duties of a slave" (BDAG, 259).

411. O'Brien, 325.

412. G. Friedrich, "εὐαγγέλιον," *TDNT* 2:734.

how things go with me. Unfortunately, the reason Paul gives for the delay is frustratingly vague. What *things* does Paul have mind in his phrase *how things go with me?*[413] Most commentators speculate that Paul is referring to the outcome of his trial.[414] He did not want to send Timothy until he saw whether he would be sentenced to execution or set free. Timothy would be sent with news of the verdict as soon as it was given. Perhaps Paul simply meant that he needed Timothy to stay with him in the time of uncertainty when he could not see how things would turn out because there was *no one* else (v. 20) who was *as a son* (v. 22) to Paul. Or it could be that the *things* Paul had in mind were the conflicts with those who *preach Christ out of envy and rivalry* and supposed that they could *stir up trouble* for Paul (1:15-17).[415] We can imagine that Timothy was a comfort to Paul and a mediator between Paul and his opponents in these conflicts. Reasonable hypotheses can be formulated to fill in the gaps left by Paul's ambiguous note, but in the end we must admit our ignorance. Paul did not clarify what *things* he was waiting to *see* before he would send Timothy.[416] The only clear point in his note about the timing of Timothy's visit is that after he saw how things would go for him, he would send Timothy to Philippi "at once."[417]

24 Even though Paul gives reasons why Timothy is uniquely qualified to serve as his agent, he recognizes that no one can really take his place. So he hastens to emphasize the importance of his own personal presence.[418] *I am confident in the Lord that I myself will come soon.* This stress on his personal presence — *I myself* — communicates Paul's deep personal commitment to his friends. He is not simply sending a letter or even his closest friend as substitutes for himself in order to avoid personal involvement. No matter what suffering he is enduring in the present and no matter how much it will cost to travel to Philippi again, he himself will be with them again. Not only does this emphasis on personal presence indicate Paul's commitment to his friends, but it also points to the seriousness of the crisis in the church. Evidently, Paul believes that true unity in the church can be fully restored only by his own personal presence. But Paul hopes that his letter and the visits of his agents will promote the process of restoration of

413. Actually the Greek phrase τὰ περί ἐμε does not even contain the word *things.*

414. See Fee, 269; Bockmuehl, 167; Barth, 84; Beare, 97.

415. Collange, 104; O'Brien, 327: "Timothy may have been needed to assist the apostle in some delicate pastoral situation."

416. Some (Barth, 86, with apparent support from O'Brien, 326) suggest that Paul is focusing on the outcome of his trial since the verb *see* (ἀφίδω) means "to see something from a distance." But BDAG (158) gives the meaning "to develop a more precise knowledge about something."

417. The adverb *soon* (ἐξαυτῆς) means "at once, immediately, soon thereafter" (BDAG, 346).

418. Emphasis on personal presence is indicated in two ways: first, by the use of the conjunctions μέν (v. 23) . . . δέ (v. 24), which not only tie vv. 23 and 24 together but also place special emphasis on v. 24 (see BDF §447); second, by the use of the intensive pronoun αὐτός (see BDF §288).

unity in the church. And by promising that he will make a personal visit, Paul enhances the authority of his letter and his agents.

In spite of the uncertainty he expresses in this letter regarding his future, Paul is totally convinced *(I am confident)* that he will soon be with his friends. In a parallel passage, after his famous soliloquy about the alternatives of living and dying, Paul uses the same verb — *I am confident* — to express his certainty that he will remain alive and be with the Philippians again (1:25). We can see the high level of certainty expressed by this verb when we note that Paul uses the same verb *I am confident* to express his settled conviction that God will complete the work that he began in the Philippian community (1:6).

Paul's addition of the phrase *in the Lord* to his statement of confidence may mean that his confidence is conditioned by the will of the Lord or that it is informed by the word of the Lord. In other words, he may be saying, "I am confident if that is what the Lord wills to happen."[419] Or he may be saying, "I am confident because the Lord has given me his word that this will happen."[420] Given Paul's strong sense of certainty about his future plans, his expression *in the Lord* appears to mean that Paul is sure that the Lord has already given his stamp of approval on these plans or was in fact the original source of inspiration for these plans.

Paul's plan to visit Philippi after his release from prison is a small but important piece of the puzzle of dating Paul's life. If Paul wrote this letter from prison in Rome after writing his letter to Rome, a trip back east to Philippi would seem to be in conflict with his strong statement in Romans 15:17-24 that his work in the regions east of Rome was finished. Of course, Paul was notorious for changing his travel plans (2 Corinthians 1). If, however, Paul wrote this letter from prison in Caesarea or in Ephesus, another trip to Philippi can fit easily with either his voyage from Caesarea to Rome or his last trip from Ephesus to Corinth.[421]

B. Epaphroditus (2:25-30)

> [25]*But I think it is necessary to send back to you Epaphroditus, my brother, co-worker and fellow soldier, who is also your messenger, whom you sent to take care of my needs.* [26]*For he longs for all of you and is distressed because you heard he was ill.* [27]*Indeed he was ill, and almost died. But God had mercy on him, and not on him only but also on me, to spare me sorrow upon sorrow.* [28]*Therefore I am all the more eager to send him, so that when you see him again you may be glad and I may have less anxiety.* [29]*Welcome him in the*

419. Calvin, 263. O'Brien, 327: "Paul's plans are subject to the wishes of his Lord and master."

420. Barth, 86.

421. See the Introduction, 19-25.

Lord with great joy, and honor people like him, [30]because he almost died for the work of Christ. He risked his life to make up for the help you yourselves could not give me.

After his praise of Timothy's Christ-like character, Paul gives a solid recommendation of Epaphroditus, who appears to be the bearer of this letter on his return to Philippi. Woven into his commendation are the reasons why he thought it *necessary* to send this messenger from the Philippian church back home. The first reason is Epaphroditus's need: *for he longs for all of you* (v. 26); the second reason is the Philippians' need: *so that when you see him again you may be glad* (v. 28). In the process of recommending Epaphroditus and giving the reasons for sending him home, Paul describes the sorrowful experience of the very serious illness that Epaphroditus suffered in *the work of Christ* when *he risked his life* to serve Paul. Twice Paul says that Epaphroditus *almost died* (vv. 27, 30). The willingness of Epaphroditus to risk his life to the point of almost dying in the service of others made him another shining example of one who had *the same attitude of mind Christ Jesus had* (2:5). Although Epaphroditus bore the name of a Greek goddess, he had the character of Christ, who took *the form of a servant* and was *obedient to death* (2:7-8). Paul's preeminent desire to know Christ leads him to see the story of Christ reenacted in the service and suffering of Epaphroditus.

Perhaps two other motives for Paul's strong endorsement of Epaphroditus can be read between the lines. If the Philippians were disappointed that their messenger, Epaphroditus, had prematurely abandoned the mission they had given him to serve Paul, then Paul's words serve to assure them that *indeed he was ill* (v. 27) and that he had risked his life to make up for the service that the Philippians themselves could not give him (v. 30). Instead of criticizing Epaphroditus, the church should *welcome him in the Lord with great joy* and honor him (v. 29). Perhaps, Paul's emphatic support of Epaphroditus was written to build a "golden bridge for his retreat."[422] If so, then we see how a magnanimous leader works to turn an embarrassing situation into a cause for honor and rejoicing.

Another possible aim of this paragraph may be to express Paul's attempt to prevent potential criticism against himself for sending back Epaphroditus instead of sending his special agent, Timothy.[423] To forestall this misunderstanding Paul explains why *it is necessary* for him to send Epaphroditus. Perhaps Paul's presentation of the reasonableness of his decision is given in self-defense against an attack on his honor and integrity. If so, then we see how a wise leader foresees possible misunderstandings that would hurt his effectiveness and works to give an adequate explanation of his decision.

422. Barth, 87.

423. Silva, 159: "Was Epaphroditus a consolation prize, sent simply because Timothy, whom the Philippians expected, had to stay with Paul?"

While reading between and behind the lines leads some to speculate that these polemical motives guided Paul, on the surface he is simply expressing his deep affection and great appreciation for Epaphroditus. "Thus rather than read ulterior motives into words of affection we should take them at face value."[424] In Epaphroditus we really do see an exceptional servant of Christ who risked his life in the work of Christ and thus exhibited the character of Christ.

25 By placing the expression *it is necessary* first in the sentence, Paul draws a striking contrast to what he said about his *hope* to send Timothy *soon* (vv. 19, 23) and his *confidence* that he would visit *soon* (v. 24). In the case of Timothy and Paul, Paul's hopes that their visits would be *soon* were qualified by the uncertainty of how things would turn out for him. Although Paul's hopes for the future were rooted in the Lord Jesus and filled with confidence, their fulfillment was delayed. The length of time indicated by *soon* was left open. But Paul *thought it necessary* to send Epaphroditus home immediately, without delay. The word *necessary* indicates that urgent, pressing needs forced or required him to send Epaphroditus home without delay.[425] In his commendation of Epaphroditus, Paul spells out the content of his thought process regarding the urgent needs that made his decision necessary.[426]

Before explaining the necessity of sending Epaphroditus, Paul honors him by giving him five titles: *my brother, co-worker and fellow soldier, who is also your messenger, whom you sent to take care of my needs.* Paul depicts his relationship with Epaphroditus in the first three designations. Calling him *my brother* means more than recognizing him as a Christian or even as a member of the same family, the family of believers in Christ.[427] All too often people who recognize each other as Christians and members of the family of God do not have any commitment to each other or affection for each other. Paul's use of the possessive personal pronoun *(my)* to modify the first three titles for Epaphroditus emphasizes their affectionate relationship. Paul speaks of the *sorrow upon sorrow* he would have experienced if Epaphroditus had not recovered from his illness (v. 27).

Paul calls Epaphroditus *my co-worker* after he calls him *my brother.* This priority and connection must be kept in mind to appreciate the deeply

424. Fee, 273.

425. See illustrations of the usage of ἀναγκαῖος in Greek literature given in C. Spicq, "ἀναγκαῖος," *TLNT,* 1:97: Homer, *Il.* 8.57: "Necessity forces them"; Philo, *Decalogue* 99: "Man, inasmuch as he depends upon a thousand things that the necessities of life require, has the obligation of taking care of acquiring the necessities as long as he lives." See also A. Strobel, "Ἀναγκαῖος," *EDNT* 1:78; BDAG, 60.

426. The verb "I think" (ἡγησάμην), "to engage in an intellectual process" (BDAG, 434), is a present tense translation of an epistolary aorist: the use of the past tense to reflect the "standpoint of an orally delivered message" (BDF §334).

427. Vincent, 75, simply equates "a brother" with being a Christian. See also von Soden, "ἀδελφός," *TDNT* 1:145: "ἀδελφός in the NT denotes 'fellow-Christians.'"

personal relationship Paul had with his *co-worker.*[428] By calling Epaphroditus his *co-worker,* Paul includes him in his inner circle of associates; he has a place on the team who lived, traveled, and served with Paul for the advance of the gospel. Later in his commendation of Epaphroditus, Paul says that this *co-worker almost died for the work of Christ* (v. 30). The *work of Christ* in this context is the help offered to Paul as the agent of the church in Philippi. Paul says that Epaphroditus was *sent to take care of my needs* (2:25). Paul's co-workers were his assistants who served him under his authority. The term *co-worker* does not connote unconditional equality with Paul.[429] Ultimately, however, the co-worker recognizes the authority of God. Paul puts himself and all who work with him in the same category: "We are God's co-workers" (1 Cor 3:9).

The third title Paul applies to his *brother* and *co-worker* is *my fellow soldier.* In Paul's experience and theology, the work of Christ leads inevitably into warfare and suffering on behalf of Christ (1:29). Certainly suffering was the consequence of Epaphroditus's service in the work of Christ. He *almost died for the work of Christ* (2:30). As a fellow soldier with Paul, Epaphroditus endured opposition and persecution with Paul. He probably stayed with Paul in prison as he took care of Paul's needs. As he worked and served with Paul, they were bound together with ties stronger than Roman chains.

The next two descriptive terms point to the responsibilities given to Epaphroditus by the church in Philippi: "your messenger and servant to my need" (my trans.). The way that TNIV takes the second term as an explanation of the first *(your messenger, whom you sent to take care of my needs)* brings out the meaning of *messenger (apostolos).* Epaphroditus was an "apostle" sent by the church on a specific mission to take care of Paul's needs. Paul is not using the word *apostle* with the special sense applied only to the "foundation-laying preachers of the gospel, missionaries and church founders possessing the full authority of Christ."[430] The Twelve and Paul were apostles in this special sense, but there were also "messengers of the churches" (see 2 Cor 8:23) in the general sense of "messengers without extraordinary status."[431]

The second term completes the meaning of the first: this "apostle" was a "servant." The term "servant" refers in a general sense to "one engaged in administrative or cultic service," such as an official serving in the government (Rom 13:6) or a priest fulfilling religious duties (Christ the true High

428. Bengt Holmberg, *Paul and Power: The Structure of Authority in the Primitive Church as Reflected in the Pauline Epistles* (Philadelphia: Fortress, 1978), 60.

429. G. Bertram, "συνεργός," *TDNT* 7:874.

430. D. Müller, "Apostle," *NIDNTT* 1:132. Paul claims to an apostle in this special sense of unique authority given by Christ himself: Gal 1:1, 12-17; 1 Cor 1:1; 9:1-2; 2 Cor 1:1; 2:12. Paul does not say that Epaphroditus is an apostle equal to himself, as Hawthorne (117) claims.

431. BDAG, 122; O'Brien, 332: "envoys commissioned by the congregations for specific purposes."

Priest; Heb 8:2), and in a special sense to "one engaged in personal service, aide, assistant."[432] Epaphroditus was sent as an apostle by the Philippian church to be a personal assistant to Paul. His specific assignment was *to take care* of Paul's *needs*. Paul's words at the end of this letter clearly state that his *needs* were fulfilled by *gifts: I have received full payment and have more than enough. I am amply supplied, now that I have received from Epaphroditus the gifts you sent me* (4:18). But Epaphroditus fulfilled his mission as Paul's personal assistant in more ways than as the bearer of gifts from Philippi. Paul's appreciative commendation points to other aspects of personal service. As Paul's *brother, co-worker and fellow soldier,* Epaphroditus was able to make up for the service that the Philippians themselves were unable to give (2:30). Surely, this service included but was not limited to financial support. The Philippians sent Epaphroditus to care for Paul in every way possible.[433]

26 To explain why he is sending Epaphroditus home immediately, Paul describes Epaphroditus's emotional attachment to his home church: *For he longs for all of you and is distressed because you heard he was ill.* This disclosure of such strong emotions evokes negative reactions by some interpreters. Was Epaphroditus so emotionally immature that he was overwhelmed by "homesickness"?[434] Did Epaphroditus have a "nervous disorder"?[435] Isn't such an emotional reaction strange "for the behavior of a grown man"?[436] Such negative interpretations are not warranted by Paul's language here. The words *longs for* and *distressed* certainly connote deeply felt passion and strong emotion, but they do not characterize abnormal behavior. When Paul says of himself that *God can testify how I long for all of you* (1:8), he uses the same word to describe his own deep affection for his Philippian friends as he uses to depict how Epaphroditus *longs for* the same people. Paul was not disclosing immaturity or diagnosing a pathological abnormality in either case; he was passionately expressing the "strong desire" that he and Epaphroditus had for reunion with friends.[437] He views longing for friends as a normal dimension of friendship love. When Paul says that his friend Epaphroditus *is distressed,* he is using a word not used elsewhere in the NT except in the description of Jesus in the Garden of Gethsemane when he "began to be deeply distressed and troubled."[438] Although the Gospel writers use this word to emphasize the extreme emotional anguish of Jesus in the Garden, they certainly do not portray Jesus as emotionally immature or psychologically abnormal.[439] Neither does Paul's

432. BDAG, 591-92.
433. See Gnilka, 161.
434. Hawthorne, 117.
435. Martin, 130.
436. Barth, 88.
437. BDAG, 377.
438. Mark 14:33//Matt 26:37.
439. Bockmuehl, 171, argues (*pace* O'Brien, 334) that the word describes anguish not as a result of shock "but to perceived inability to change a state of affairs."

use of the word insinuate in any way a negative assessment of the emotional condition of Epaphroditus. Paul's description of the affection and angst of Epaphroditus follows and confirms his positive commendation of Epaphroditus. That commendation is not a cover-up for Epaphroditus's "emotional instability"[440] or "his frailness."[441] In the light of Paul's positive recommendation of Epaphroditus, we can infer that he had a positive view of his strong emotions of longing for friends during his prolonged separation and distress when he underwent the traumatic experience of serious illness complicated by the inability to clarify reports his friends have heard of his illness.[442] These emotions are stated as a legitimate reason for sending this *messenger* back home immediately. Paul in no way disapproves of the emotions of his *brother, co-worker and fellow soldier.* He understands these strong emotions and validates them.

Paul explains that the emotional distress of Epaphroditus was caused by knowing that the Philippians heard that he was ill, but Paul does not explain why this knowledge caused Epaphroditus distress. Was he distressed because his illness had distressed his friends and he was unable to communicate with them to clarify his situation (no cell phones or e-mail!)? Or was he in turmoil because he knew that his friends would be disappointed in him if they thought that his illness hindered the successful completion of his mission to care for Paul? The ambiguity of this text gives rise to many conjectures, but offers no evidence to confirm any of them.[443]

440. Martin and Hawthorne, 165, suggests: "Perhaps it was an emotional instability that made him unsuitable for the work for which he was commissioned, a despondency that brought him to death's door, hinted at in the reference to his homesickness and distraught anxiety for all those at Philippi, although this thought of depression leading to suicidal tendencies or a psychosomatic condition that brought him near death may seem strained."

441. Barth, 88.

442. Distress may be seen as an amplification of the meaning of longing. Or the two emotions may be viewed as separate responses to different circumstances: first the longing simply as a result of his separation; then the distress as a result of his illness and reports of his illness received at home. See O'Brien, 334.

443. Another set of speculations stimulated by this verse focuses on the question of the number of trips made between Paul's prison and Philippi. If Epaphroditus became sick while in prison with Paul and he learned that the Philippians had heard of his sickness through a message from Philippi, we can speculate that there were five trips between Paul's prison and Philippi: (1) a messenger goes from Paul's prison to inform the church in Philippi of Paul's imprisonment; (2) Epaphroditus is sent to take care of Paul in prison and becomes sick while in prison with Paul; (3) a messenger goes to Philippi and informs the Philippians of this sickness; (4) a messenger returns to the prison and relays the reaction of the Philippians to the sickness; (5) Epaphroditus is sent back home to Philippi. On the basis of this speculation regarding the number of trips back and forth between Paul's prison and Philippi, some conjecture that the prison was probably in Ephesus, only a few days away, rather than in Rome, a few weeks away. See Beare, 98. Alternatively, the number and length of trips are reduced significantly if we imagine that (1) Epaphroditus became sick on his way to Paul's prison (perhaps not far from home); (2) one of his traveling companions re-

27 Paul now clarifies the report the church had heard of Epaphroditus's illness: *Indeed he was ill, and almost died.* Apparently, Paul felt that the report that *he was ill* minimized the seriousness of the illness. *For indeed,* Paul exclaims, *he was ill!* He was so ill that he was near to death; he was so ill that he looked like death![444] While Paul's emphasis on the near-death experience of Epaphroditus offers no assistance to speculative medical diagnoses, it does help to explain the emotional trauma experienced by Epaphroditus and Paul. Anyone who has had the experience of being with a close friend who is dying can easily imagine the agony that these two friends experienced.

Paul repeats his report of the near-death experience in v. 30: *he almost died for the work of Christ* (v. 30). The repetition of the word *death* in the story of Epaphroditus emphasizes the parallel to the narrative of Christ, who was *obedient to death — even death on a cross!* (2:8). This striking echo of the Christ hymn in Paul's account of the illness of Epaphroditus sets this servant of Christ before the Philippians as one who clearly reflects Christ, the one who endured death as the servant of God.[445] The church sees in the experience of Epaphroditus that intense suffering is an opportunity to reflect *the same attitude of mind Christ Jesus had* (2:5).

Paul continues his report with a declaration of God's mercy: *But God had mercy on him!* Near death! *But God!* This juxtaposition of death and God gives God all the glory for the recovery from illness. The focus is God-centered. The intense prayers of Paul and of the church could have been recounted: What desperate intercession was made for hours, days, and sleepless nights? The details of recovery could have been dramatically portrayed: Did he open his eyes, stand up, raise his arms to heaven, and praise God? All human actions are obscured from view. Only God's merciful action is seen. *God had mercy on him.* Paul emphasizes the sovereign mercy of God: "It does not, therefore, depend on human desire or effort, but on God's mercy" (Rom 9:16). Certainly this record of God's merciful intervention when Epaphroditus was near death encourages believing prayer for those who are terminally ill, but this account also encourages depending only on God's mercy: trusting in God's mercy when recovery does not occur; giving credit only to God's mercy when recovery does occur.

Paul also openly expresses his own deep experience of God's mercy in the recovery of Epaphroditus: *God had mercy on him, and not on him only but also on me, to spare me sorrow upon sorrow.* Paul's honesty about his sorrow presents a counterpoint to his constant emphasis on joy in this letter.

---

turned home with the news; and (3) Epaphroditus knew how his home church would respond to this news without anyone informing him. See Fee, 277-78. For a discussion of these speculations, see the Introduction, 19-25.

444. BDAG, 770, defines the adjective παραπλήσιον as "coming alongside or near, coming near, resembling, similar." The adjective serves here as an "improper preposition" (BDF §184).

445. Bloomquist, *The Function of Suffering in Philippians*, 177.

Paul freely admits that *sorrow,* even *sorrow upon sorrow,* is the experience of one who is *in Christ* and whose motto is *to live is Christ.* Paul's joy "has nothing to do with stoic apathy."[446] Rejoicing in the Lord does not mean denying the reality of sorrow caused by tragic circumstances of life.

Paul does not spell out the specific circumstances that caused his sorrow when he says that he was spared sorrow upon sorrow. The sorrow he was spared seems to refer to the death of Epaphroditus. But what caused the other sorrow? The illness of Epaphroditus,[447] his imprisonment,[448] and the rivalry of other preachers (1:15-17)[449] are all good, reasonable guesses. While Paul does not clearly identify the cause of the sorrow he had before facing the oncoming new wave of sorrow in the near-death illness of his friend, he does open himself for all to see how deeply he would have grieved over the death of his friend. The same Paul who exclaimed that *to die is gain* (1:21), promised *the peace of God, which transcends all understanding* (4:7), and had *learned the secret of being content in any and every situation* (4:12), nevertheless tells his readers how the emotion of sorrow almost overwhelmed him — "wave upon wave of grief."[450] Some happy Christians may want to admonish Paul for his sorrow, "You should not be sorrowful because death is but an open door into the presence of Christ. You need to claim the peace of God to guard your heart and mind in Christ Jesus. You need to learn to be content even in the time of death." But Paul's admission of sorrow is not a confession of sin. The emotion of sorrow is a God-given, Christ-like emotion, especially in the face of death, "the last enemy to be destroyed" (1 Cor 15:26).

28 Paul emphasizes his eagerness to send Epaphroditus home: *Therefore I am all the more eager to send him.* The conjunction *therefore (oun)* expresses the consequence of the recovery from terminal illness: because God had mercy on Epaphroditus, Paul wants to send him back "with special urgency."[451] The sense of increased urgency — *all the more eager* — may imply a change in plans: if Epaphroditus had not been ill, Paul would not have been so eager to send him home; but since he had been deathly ill and was now miraculously well, Paul was *more eager* to send him home. In other words, the original expectation of the church and Paul may have been for Epaphroditus to stay with Paul indefinitely or at least until the outcome of his trial, but as a result of the trauma of his illness and relief at his recovery, Paul decided to send him home sooner than expected.[452]

Two expected outcomes of Paul's decision benefit the church and

446. Barth, 88.

447. Beare, 98.

448. Vincent, 76.

449. Bockmuehl, 175.

450. Hawthorne, 118.

451. BDAG, 939, defines the comparative adverb σπουδαιοτέρως (TNIV: *all the more eager*) "quick in doing something, with haste, with special urgency."

452. Bockmuehl, 175.

Paul: *so that when you see him again you may be glad and I may have less anxiety.* Paul's desire that the Philippians *may be glad* (literally, "rejoice") is consistent with his persistent appeal to them to *rejoice in the Lord* (2:18; 3:1; 4:4). Only when they see Epaphroditus and fully appreciate how *God had mercy on him,* will they fully recover from the upsetting news of his illness and rejoice in the Lord over his miraculous healing. When Paul expresses his desire for the church to rejoice *again,*[453] he is not simply concerned for the happiness of believers. His focus in this passage as always is God-centered; rejoicing in Paul's theology is praise for God's mercy and delight in God's presence. By sending Epaphroditus home, Paul knows that he will lead the church into joyful worship for the merciful intervention of God.

Paul will also benefit from Epaphroditus's return home by having *less anxiety.* Although TNIV is supported by the lexical definition of the Greek word as "free from anxiety,"[454] this translation does not adequately indicate the way that this word connects to Paul's previous expression, *sorrow upon sorrow.* God spared Paul *sorrow upon sorrow;* now the return of Epaphroditus to the joyful welcome of his church will cause Paul to have even *less sorrow.*[455] Paul's use of the comparative expression *less sorrow* indicates that he does not expect to be freed from all sorrow, but that he will have comparatively less sorrow. Although the joyful reunion of Epaphroditus with his home church will assuage his sorrow, he will still have sorrow. Paul does not disclose the cause of his continuing experience of sorrow. Paul's imprisonment, his adversaries, and his rivals are all candidates for the causes of his sorrowful condition. Whatever the reason for his sorrow may be, Paul still lives within the realm of sorrow. His prescription for joy does not include the removal of all sorrow but such a focus on presence of the Lord within the experience of sorrow that rejoicing in the Lord becomes the predominant theme of life.

29 Now that Paul has spelled out the reasons and benefits of his decision to send Epaphroditus home early, he urges the church to plan a joyful reunion to honor him: *Welcome him in the Lord with great joy, and honor people like him.* Speculations that Paul directed the Philippian believers to give Epaphroditus a joyful welcome with honor because they were inclined to do the opposite — be critical of him and dishonor him — are all unconfirmed theories.[456] Paul may have given this direction because he sensed

453. The adverb *again* (πάλιν) could modify the verb *see* (Hawthorne, 119; Silva, 162; or the verb *rejoice* (Vincent, 77; Fee, 280; O'Brien, 339). The latter view is supported by the observation that this adverb is usually placed before the verb it modifies and the repetition of the imperative *to rejoice.* Paul calls the church to rejoice again and again.

454. BDAG, 48.

455. The word ἀ-λυπό-τερος contains the ἀ-privative that negates the root word λυπή *(sorrow)* and has the comparative form ending -τερος.

456. Hawthorne, 119: "Paul anticipated problems at Philippi over Epaphroditus' unexpected return. Hence, he wards off this criticism with apostolic authority." Such mirror-reading of the text is imaginative, but cannot be confirmed by the text itself.

that the church's disappointment that Epaphroditus had to cut short his mission to care for Paul would dampen their enthusiasm to welcome him home. On the other hand, he may have been encouraging the church to expand and intensify the warm welcome they were already inclined to give. He urges them to give Epaphroditus a really great banquet and a permanent place of honor rather than a simple potluck supper and a quick nod for his service. The command to *welcome him in the Lord* highlights *in the Lord* as the primary, central relationship of believers. Their welcome needs to embrace Epaphroditus as one who belongs to the community of believers in the Lord; he needs to be included with *all God's people in Christ Jesus at Philippi* (1:1). "Give him, as saints ought to do, the reception due to a saint, with all joy."[457] We can easily imagine that this encouragement to celebrate Epaphroditus's homecoming *with great joy* calls for a prolonged standing ovation, wholehearted embracing, and many other expressions of overwhelming gratitude to God that Epaphroditus is well again and that he has successfully completed his mission.

Paul uses the welcome that Epaphroditus should receive as a model for the way to *honor people like him.* All such people should be highly honored and respected, "highly regarded because of status or personal quality."[458] Since Paul draws such close parallels between Epaphroditus and Christ, the honor given to such people as Epaphroditus is really honor given to Christ since such people reflect Christ.

30 Paul's closes his commendation of Epaphroditus by drawing attention again to his Christ-like character and faithful service for Christ: *he almost died for the work of Christ.* Ultimately, the work that Epaphroditus did was commissioned and directed by Christ. True, the church sent him to care for Paul and Paul sent him back to the church. But behind the church and Paul, Christ was accomplishing his will and doing his work through Epaphroditus. When the work of a servant of Christ is seen in this light as the *work of Christ,* then that work takes on a new dimension of value and meaning. By stating that Epaphroditus "came near to death" (TNIV: *he almost died*) for the work of Christ, Paul deliberately draws a clear verbal parallel with the Christ hymn: Epaphroditus *came near to death*//Christ *was obedient unto death.* The humble, self-sacrificing attitude of Christ, the Servant, is seen in this servant of Christ.

Paul expands his description of the self-sacrificing attitude of Epaphroditus: *He risked his life to make up for the help you yourselves could not give me.* An entertaining interpretation suggests that Paul coined the word *risked* with the sense of gambling as a wordplay on the name of Epaphroditus. According to this interpretation, the name of Epaphroditus means favorite of Aphrodite, the goddess of fortune, and his name was pronounced by gamblers when they threw the dice as a good luck charm: "hoping by

457. Chrysostom, "Homily on Philippians 10.2.29," *ACCS* 8:265.
458. BDAG, 340.

this 'invocation' to be blessed with a gambler's luck in the throw of the dice because the divine hand was behind it." Paul coined this gambling term to say that, in keeping with his name, Epaphroditus gambled with his life in the work of Christ and won because God's blessing was upon him.[459] As fascinating as this interpretation is, however, it rests on thin evidence. The verb means to "expose to danger, risk."[460] The lexicons do not offer any references to gambling. The suggestion that gamblers used the name Epaphroditus as an invocation for divine blessing is not supported by solid evidence.[461] So Paul was probably not alluding to a gambler's risk when he speaks of the willingness of Epaphroditus to risk his life for the work of Christ. Perhaps instead of hearing his words as an echo of a gambler, we should hear his commendation as an echo of the word of Christ: "Those who want to save their life will lose it, but those who lose their life for me and for the gospel will save it" (Mark 8:35). Epaphroditus did not make his own safety and security his number one priority; he courageously risked everything, including his own life, to fulfill the mission given to him. He put himself in harm's way and exposed himself to great dangers to accomplish his work. His example stands as a constant challenge to all followers of Christ who seek personal security above personal sacrifice in the service of Christ.

His reason for risking his life was *to make up for the help you yourselves could not give me.* The TNIV offers a smooth rendering of a difficult phrase; a more literal translation of the Greek word order runs as follows: "to supply your lack of service to me" (my trans.).[462] At first glance this phrase may look like a rebuke for lack of service. But in fact Paul's words communicate deep gratitude for the church and for their messenger, Epaphroditus. The goal of Epaphroditus's mission, defined here by the verb *to make up, to supply,* envisions him as the one who will "supply what is lacking" or "fill a gap."[463] Epaphroditus supplied what was lacking in the *service* of the Philippians to Paul. This term for *service* connotes sacred work and gives "an aura of high status for those who render any type of service."[464] Paul has already used the same term to refer to the service of the Philippians: *I am being poured out like a drink offering on the sacrifice and service coming from your faith* (2:17). By using this elevated language for the support of the Philippians, Paul shows his respect and appreciation for their sacrificial gifts delivered through Epaphroditus. He uses the imagery of temple sacrifices for these gifts at the end of his letter: *They are a fragrant offering, an ac-*

459. Hawthorne, 120, following the work of Harrington C. Lees, "Entre nous," *ExpT* 37 (1925-26), 46. Also Vincent, 77: "a gambler's word. He gambled his life. The word might have been suggested to Paul by seeing the soldiers throwing dice."

460. BDAG, 759; LSJ, 1305.

461. Silva, 163.

462. ἀναπληρώσῃ τὸ ὑμῶν ὑστέρημα τῆς πρός με λειτουργίας.

463. BDAG, 70.

464. BDAG, 591.

ceptable sacrifice, pleasing to God (4:18). Thus, Paul is using complimentary language when he says that Epaphroditus supplied what was lacking in the priestly service of the Philippians. When Paul refers to *your lack (hymōn hysterēma) of service to me,* he is not criticizing them, but simply recognizing the fact of their personal absence.[465] Their lack was simply the inability of the whole church to be with Paul in prison. But the presence of their messenger, Epaphroditus, made up for their absence: the one filled the gap for the many. The sacred *service* of the Philippian church in their partnership with Paul is the *work of Christ.* Epaphroditus risked his life to fulfill that work and complete that service by bringing gifts from the church and by being in prison with Paul in the place of the church.

Through all the troubles and disappointments of his life, Paul is able to see and delight in the radiance of Christ reflected in the character and service of his friends. When he draws their portraits, he shows how ordinary people give themselves sacrificially to serve the needs of others as Christ did. In this way his friends become an extension of his imperative to *have the same attitude of mind Christ Jesus had* (2:5).

465. BDAG, 1044.

Philippians 3

VI. DISCLOSURES OF PERSONAL EXPERIENCE (3:1-21)

Paul turns inward in this chapter and reveals intimate aspects of his personal journey. His autobiographical sketch of his conversion to Christ discloses a dramatic contrast between his previous persecution of the church as a Pharisee and his present quest to know Christ. The Christ-centered focus of the entire letter is passionately expressed as Paul tells of his strong desire to gain Christ, be found in Christ, pursue Christ, and ultimately be totally transformed by Christ. This deeply personal tone fills the passage with highly charged emotions: passionate longing to know Christ and painful tears for those who are enemies of the cross of Christ.

Paul weaves theological reflections into his personal disclosure. He contrasts his accomplishment of *righteousness based on the law* with the *righteousness that comes from God on the basis of faith;* he describes how he presses on *toward the goal to win the prize for which God has called* him *heavenward in Christ Jesus;* he expresses his eager anticipation of the *Lord Jesus Christ, who by the power that enables him to bring everything under his control, will transform our lowly bodies so that they will be like his glorious body.* In other words, Paul explains the whole process of salvation — justification, sanctification, and glorification — in terms of his own personal experience. All of his experience is centered *in Christ.* Christ is the center of Paul's theology.

These personal and theological features make this chapter a gold mine for all who are interested in Paul and his theology. Other features fill this chapter with landmines of controversies: Who are the opponents — *those dogs* and *enemies of the cross of Christ?* Is this chapter an interpolated fragment? How could Paul view himself as *faultless?* Does the phrase *faith in Christ* mean the faithfulness of Christ or the faith of believers in Christ? These and many other perplexing questions challenge us as we read through the chapter.

A. Boasting in Privileges (3:1-6)

> [1]*Further, my brothers and sisters, rejoice in the Lord! It is no trouble for me to write the same things to you again, and it is a safeguard for you.*
> [2]*Watch out for those dogs, those evildoers, those mutilators of the flesh.* [3]*For it is we who are the circumcision, we who serve God by his Spirit, who boast in Christ Jesus, and who put no confidence in the flesh —* [4]*though I myself have reasons for such confidence. If others think they have reasons to put confidence in the flesh, I have more:* [5]*circumcised on the eighth day, of the people of Israel, of the tribe of Benjamin, a Hebrew of Hebrews; in regard to the law, a Pharisee;* [6]*as for zeal, persecuting the church; as for righteousness based on the law, faultless.*

The first verses of chapter 3 raise a perplexing problem. At first Paul seems to be writing a conclusion, but then he doesn't conclude. When he says, *Further* (literally, "finally," as in NRSV), the reader expects him to begin his final paragraph, but this is not the final paragraph. After what looks like a conclusion, he starts to address a different subject in a different tone of voice. He turns abruptly from commending his close friends (2:19-30) to condemning dangerous *dogs.* If 3:2-21 were cut out, there would be a smooth transition from 3:1 to 4:1. The move from "finally, rejoice" (3:1) to the tender words and personal appeals of 4:1-3 keeps the letter on the same track and in the same tone. The jump from a conclusion — "finally, rejoice!" — to a curse — *watch out for those dogs!* — presents a shocking break in the line of discourse.

One response to this sudden change of directions is an imaginative hypothesis regarding fragments of letters that have been combined into the one letter now called Philippians. According to Beare, the "seriousness of the break and the complete lack of connection between this chapter and the remainder of the letter" require the view that 3:1-21 is "an interpolated fragment." Beare insists, "It can hardly be doubted that we have here a fragment of another letter, undoubtedly a letter of Paul's, but written on a different occasion and for a different purpose." He admits that "there is no means of discovering where and when the letter containing this fragment was written." But he claims that "we may reasonably feel that if the fragment is found in a letter to the Philippians, it will be because the collector of the Pauline letters found it in the church chest at Philippi."[1]

Another response to the abrupt shift in 3:1-4 is acceptance of it as the result of the author's prerogative, perhaps even his predilection, to change directions. After all, Paul was not bound by any ancient or modern prescriptions for writing letters or well-reasoned essays. If he goes off on a tangent, inserts a parenthetical aside, or responds to a sudden inspiration to address an urgent need, then an alert reader is obligated to note his change

1. Beare, 101.

of direction and move along with him. Despite the "seriousness of the break," many lines of continuity can be traced between 3:2-21 and the sections that precede and follow it. The need for the proposed radical surgery of cutting out this section as "an interpolated fragment" becomes less urgent when we see how well it fits within the unity of the entire letter.[2]

1 Recent scholarship demonstrates that verse 1 is a common expression used in letters of Paul's day as a transition from one subject to the next.[3] Labeled as the "epistolary hesitation formula," this common expression contains three characteristic elements found in verse 2: the verb *to write* and the word translated *trouble,* better translated as "a cause of hesitation," with the negative *no.* The adjective translated *trouble* (TNIV; NIV) or "troublesome" (NRSV) means "a state involving shrinking from something, holding back, hesitation, reluctance"[4] and occurs in numerous papyrus letters in adjective or verb form with a negative to express either a request for the recipient not to hesitate or a notification that the writer does not hesitate.[5] By using this conventional form, Paul is saying, "To write the same things to you is not a cause of hesitation for me" or "I do not hesitate to write these things to you again."[6] Paul uses the "hesitation formula" as "an expression of friendship."[7] Because he is a friend, Paul does not hesitate *to write the same things again.*

The nearest reference point for *the same things* in the immediate context is the command: *rejoice in the Lord!*[8] Since this command echoes similar imperatives to rejoice (2:17-18, 29; and later in 4:4), Paul uses the plural in his "hesitation" expression — *I do not hesitate to write the same things* — to emphasize that he is well aware of the repetition of his command to rejoice and yet he does not hesitate to repeat this command. In his cultural context, his repeated appeals to rejoice emphatically demonstrate his friendship love: a friend is one who shares in another's joys and sorrows.[9] Paul ex-

2. Bockmuehl, 176: "The biblical critic's wielding of the scalpel is generally more dangerous to the patient than the application of Ockham's razor to the critic's hypotheses." See the Introduction, 15-19, for an evaluation of various hypotheses regarding the unity of the letter.

3. Jeffrey T. Reed, "Philippians and the Epistolary Hesitation Formulas: The Literary Integrity of Philippians, Again," *JBL* 115 (1996), 63-90.

4. BDAG, 702.

5. Reed, "Philippians and the Epistolary Hesitation Formulas," 66-72, gives examples from thirty-three papyrus letters.

6. Reed, "Philippians and the Epistolary Hesitation Formulas," 75.

7. Reed, "Philippians and the Epistolary Hesitation Formulas," 76.

8. Other suggestions for the reference of *same things* include things written in a former letter or letters (Vincent, 91), things told to them during his ministry in Philippi (Silva, 171, 172; O'Brien, 352), and things written to warn his readers against troublemakers such as the *dogs* in v. 2 (Lightfoot, 126). For Hawthorne (124) and Bockmuehl (180), the *same things* are the repeated appeals to rejoice.

9. Frederic M. Schroeder, "Friendship in Aristotle and Some Peripatetic Philosophers," in *Greco-Roman Perspectives on Friendship* (ed. John T. Fitzgerald; Atlanta: Scholars Press, 1977), 38.

pands the meaning and experience of joy by adding *in the Lord.* The Lord is the source, object, and sphere of joy. This theologically motivated joy *in the Lord* realistically faces and transcends all the sorrows and sufferings caused by living for Christ in a Roman prison and a Roman colony. Yet, this theological orientation of joy does not minimize the social dimension of this joy. Joy in the Lord is a corporate experience, a community celebration. Paul has just informed the Philippians that he is sending Epaphroditus back home so that when they see him they may rejoice (2:28), and he has implored them to *welcome him in the Lord with great joy* (2:29). Now he repeats this command: *Further, my brothers and sisters, rejoice in the Lord* (3:1). Joy in the Lord holds the community together.

In the light of this repeated command to rejoice, the suggestion that *rejoice* in this context really means "farewell" is unfounded.[10] Although, this verb is used at the beginning of Greek letters as a greeting and may mean farewell in conversations or on tombstones,[11] Paul's repeated use of this verb as an imperative to rejoice leads the reader to expect that the verb has the same meaning here unless there is good reason to adopt another meaning. Some see the opening word of 3:1, *further* (NRSV, "finally"), as a good reason to take this verb to mean "farewell" rather than *rejoice* because the word "finally" (TNIV, *further*) is seen as a marker of the conclusion of the letter.[12] But this word "finally" is not necessarily an indication that the letter writer has reached his final paragraph and is ready to say "farewell." The term means "that which remains over," that which is left.[13] In some cases it refers to the last item in a sequence, "finally," but in other contexts it marks a transition to a new section and signifies an additional inference from the previous section. Since this term is used at the beginning, middle, and end of Hellenistic letters, its meaning is defined, depending on its place in the letter, as a sign of an inferential addition to previous points (see 1 Thess 4:1; 2 Thess 3:1) or as a sign of the conclusion of the letter (2 Cor 13:11).[14] In the present context, this term works well as a marker for an additional command that flows inferentially out of the two previous commands: *Welcome him in the Lord with great joy, and honor people like him* (2:29); *Further, . . . rejoice in the Lord!* (3:1). By beginning the sentence with the adverb *further,* Paul signals that he is moving from the specific directives in his commendation of Epaphroditus to a general exhortation. When the

10. Beare, 100: "Finally, my brethren, I bid you farewell in the Lord."

11. BDAG, 1075; the use of this verb at the end of a letter to mean "farewell" is not substantiated. See L. Alexander, "Hellenistic Letter-Forms and the Structure of Philippians," *JSNT* 37 (1989), 97: "The place for this verb is not at the end of the letter but at the beginning."

12. Beare, 100; Jerome Murphy-O'Conner, *Paul: A Critical Life* (Oxford: Clarendon, 1996), 219.

13. BDAG, 602; the term can also mean "from now on, in the future." BDF §160 defines it as "for the rest, moreover, now, already."

14. Reed, "Philippians and the Epistolary Hesitation Formulas," 83.

Philippian church welcomes Epaphroditus home with great joy and honors him, they will be motivated *further* to respond wholeheartedly to Paul's additional appeal to *rejoice in the Lord.*

Paul ends this verse by assuring them: *it is a safeguard for you.* This clause and the clause, *it is no trouble for me* ("it is not a cause of hesitation for me"), serve as parallel predicate nominatives for the clause, *to write the same things.*

A diagram of this sentence with a literal translation shows the close link between these two phrases.

> *"To write the same things to you*
> *for me is not a cause of hesitation*
> *and for you a safeguard."*

The two phrases are connected by a correlative conjunction that could be translated, on "the one hand . . . and on the other hand";[15] both phrases begin with a personal pronoun, *for me . . . for you;*[16] both phrases end with an adjective combined with a negative particle. Often the adjective translated *safeguard* is defined in relation to the warnings that follow in verse 2: *watch out for those dogs, those evildoers, those mutilators of the flesh.* If that is Paul's reference point, then he is concerned *to write the same things* as a *safeguard* against such threats.[17] But if, as presented above, Paul's reference point for *the same things* is his series of commands *to rejoice,* then this adjective may have a different shade of meaning. The semantic field of this adjective includes three meanings: (1) describing stability, firmness; (2) describing an expression that ensures certainty; (3) describing someone's safety, security.[18] Although arguments can be made for the use of the third meaning,[19] the first meaning fits best with Paul's reason for repeating his imperative to rejoice. *To write the same things to you again,* to repeat his imperatives to rejoice, is not a cause of hesitation for Paul and is a basis of stability for them.[20] The stability or firmness of believers in the midst of suffering is one of Paul's primary goals: repeatedly he calls for them to *stand firm* (1:27; 4:1). Now he asserts that his appeals to rejoice in the Lord are designed to give them stability. When believers *rejoice in the Lord,* they are strengthened to *stand firm* even in the midst of *sacrifice* (2:17-18) and *sorrow* (2:27-29). Paul could easily have demonstrated that building stability on rejoicing in the Lord is a scriptural theme: "The joy of the LORD is your strength" (Neh 8:10); "Sing for joy to God our strength" (Ps 81:1); "O LORD, the king re-

15. BDAG, 629; BDF §447.

16. The dative case of these pronouns is a dative of advantage, which "serves to designate the person whose interest is affected" (BDF §188).

17. Silva, 171.

18. BDAG, 147.

19. See especially Bockmuehl, 181.

20. Reed, "Philippians and the Epistolary Hesitation Formulas," 78; Schenk, 248.

joices in your strength" (Ps 21:1); "I will rejoice in the Lord, I will be joyful in God my Savior. The Sovereign Lord is my strength" (Hab 3:18-19). Although Paul does not offer these texts, he does give the example of his own consistent practice as convincing proof of this scriptural principle that rejoicing in the Lord is the foundation for stability.

2 In a sudden shift of attention, Paul blurts out three terse warnings: *Watch out for those dogs, those evildoers, those mutilators of the flesh.*[21] These warnings raise some difficult questions: Who are these dogs, and where are they? Why does Paul warn against them? Why does Paul use these derogatory names for them, and what do these names mean? What does Paul mean when he says to *watch out for* these people?

As abrupt as these warnings appear to be in the flow of Paul's discourse, their place in the structure of his letter can best be understood by seeing how they serve in a familiar pattern as a series of negative condemnations of bad examples linked with a series of positive commendations of good examples.[22] Paul first guides his readers by using three present tense imperatives that call for association with and imitation of good examples: *welcome him, honor people like him, rejoice in the Lord* (2:29–3:1). Now, after a conventional expression (the epistolary hesitation formula) marking a turning point in the letter, three more present tense imperatives call for dissociation from and repudiation of bad examples: *Watch out for dogs, watch out for evildoers, watch out for mutilators.*[23] Paul builds the structure of this letter with this contrast of positive and negative: good preachers of Christ motivated by love/bad preachers motivated by selfish ambition (1:15-18); citizens of heaven/those who oppose (1:27-28); humility/selfish ambition (2:3-4); children of God/warped and crooked generation (2:14-15); honor them/watch out for them (2:29–3:2); keep your eyes on those who live as we do/many live as enemies of the cross of Christ (3:17-19); their mind is set on earthly things/our citizenship is in heaven (3:19-20). The recurrence of this positive/negative pattern allays suspicion that an unrelated fragment from another letter has been inserted here or that Paul has turned in a completely different direction. His negative warnings of evil workers who harm the church purposefully present a contrast to the previous positive endorsements of co-workers who have sacrificed their lives for the good of the church.

The command to *watch out* may be interpreted as a warning to beware of something hazardous or as an instruction to observe and pay close attention to something.[24] On the basis of the grammatical structure of this imperatival construction, some have argued that Paul is not warning against actual adversaries but calling for careful study of an alternative way of life:

21. TNIV omits the verbs given in the Greek text in the last two warnings.

22. Reed, "Philippians and the Epistolary Hesitation Formulas," 86.

23. TNIV omits the verbs in the second two phrases.

24. BDAG, 179.

"Paul is not so much warning the Philippians to be on guard against their opponents, as he is asking them to pay careful attention to them, to study them, so as to understand them and to avoid adopting their destructive beliefs and practices."[25] But the meaning of the verb "look," *watch out for*, is based not only upon grammatical considerations but also upon its immediate context. If the direct object of the verb is something hazardous (Watch out for the fire!), then the verb takes on the aspect of a warning.[26] Since Paul repeats the imperative *watch out* three times and each time attaches dangerous direct objects — *dogs, evildoers, mutilators* — to the verb, the direct objects color the verb with the meaning of a warning to be aware of or *watch out for* something hazardous. Paul is not calmly advising his readers to do some academic analysis of possible alternatives; he is urgently warning them to *watch out for* harmful adversaries.

The derogatory names given to these adversaries mask and, at the same time, reveal their true identity. Although Paul puts dog masks on them, the terms clearly point to their Jewish identity. Paul's contrast between mutilation and the true circumcision and his boasting of his own Jewish privileges indicate that these people evidently exalted the importance of circumcision and boasted of their Jewish credentials. Although they were posing as Christian teachers, they placed their emphasis on belonging to the Jewish people.[27] They heaped scorn upon those outside the Jewish family by calling them by traditional Jewish names for outsiders: *dogs* and *evildoers*. Now Paul turns the tables on them and calls them by the same derisive names that they have used for those whom they have excluded. In this satirical twist, Paul gives them a bitter taste of their own poisonous prejudice.

Although the Jewish-Christian identity of the *dogs* can be detected, their location is difficult to find. Is Paul referring to specific individuals in

25. Hawthorne, 125, following the study of G. D. Kilpatrick, "ΒΛΕΠΕΤΕ, Philippians 3:2," in *In Memoriam Paul Kahle* (ed. M. Black and G. Fohrer; BZAW 103; Berlin: A. Töpelmann, 1928), 146-48. According to Kilpatrick, the verb βλέπω means "beware of" only when (1) it is followed by an objective clause with an aorist subjunctive or future indicative introduced by the negative particle μή (see Matt 8:4; 18:10; Mark 1:44; Heb 3:12) or (2) it is followed by a prepositional phrase introduced by the preposition ἀπό. Since Phil 3:2 does not have this grammatical structure, Kilpatrick argues that it cannot mean "beware of."

26. Silva, 172; Reed, "Philippians and the Epistolary Hesitation Formulas," 85.

27. Against Hawthorne, 125: "These opponents were not Judaizers, i.e. Jewish Christians, but Jews." The evidence in Paul's other letters against Judaizing opponents confirms that the Judaizers were Jewish Christians: their aim was not to deny Christ, but to persuade Paul's Gentile converts to complete their conversion to Christ by joining the Jewish people through the rite of circumcision and observance of the law. To counteract their teaching of the necessity and superiority of a Jewish identity Paul engaged in extensive arguments against them, especially in his letter to the Galatian churches. Presenting a different perspective on the opponents, H. W. Bateman, "Were the Opponents at Philippi Necessarily Jewish?" *BSac* 155 (1998), 39-61, argues that the opponents were local Gentile Judaizers, not ethnic Jews, and not Christians. See also J. L. Sumney, "*'Servants of Satan,' 'False Brothers,' and Other Opponents of Paul* (JSNTSup 188; Sheffield: Sheffield Academic, 1999), 160-87.

Philippi who "threatened the Philippian community,"[28] to itinerant agitators misleading other Pauline churches who had not yet traveled to Philippi,[29] to ambitious preachers of Christ currently attempting to "stir up trouble" in Paul's place of imprisonment (1:15-17),[30] or to all "the Judaizing opponents who have dogged his ministry for so many years"?[31] Some clues that point to the location of these opponents may be found by comparing this letter to other Pauline letters that refer to similar opponents. In comparison to his other letters against these opponents, his letter to the Philippians does not give a detailed description of them and their teaching, an extended argumentation against them, or an assertion of Paul's apostolic authority in defense of the gospel. Instead of the polemical tone of those letters, a warm, affectionate tone dominates this letter. These contrasts indicate that Paul's attack is not directed against specific individuals within the Philippian church, but is a warning against potential visiting teachers similar to the ones who were so disruptive in other Pauline churches. Yet, his warning is too vehement to be merely a historical reference to harmful teachers in the past who pose no real threat in the present. Furthermore, since the warning is given to guard the Philippian Christians against people who could actually harm *them,* it is not a reference to people who are seeking to harm *Paul* in his place of imprisonment, but who pose no threat in Philippi. The tentative conclusion that can be drawn from these lines of investigation is that Paul is warning against false teachers who, though not yet in the church in Philippi, are nevertheless a clear and present danger. Perhaps Paul is writing this letter soon after confronting the Galatian believers for being misled by false teachers who have infiltrated their churches. The heat of that conflict can be felt in his warnings to the Philippian believers.[32] He is deeply concerned to warn them about the *dogs* that had recently harmed his churches in Galatia and may be prowling near Philippi.

Dogs were not lovable, huggable pets and companions in Paul's Jewish culture. They were regarded "as the most despicable, insolent and miserable of creatures."[33] Dogs were despised because they would eat anything, including dead animals, human corpses, and their own vomit.[34] Enemies of Israel were insulted by being compared to and called *dogs.*[35] By

28. Silva, 173.

29. Frank S. Thielman, "Ephesus and the Literary Setting of Philippians," in *New Testament Greek and Exegesis: Essays in Honor of Gerald F. Hawthorne* (ed. Amy M. Donaldson and Timothy B. Sailors; Grand Rapids: Eerdmans, 2003), 219.

30. Lightfoot, 69.

31. Bockmuehl, 180; Fee, 294-95.

32. See the Introduction, 23-25, and the arguments there for dating Philippians during Paul's time in Ephesus when he wrote his letter to the Galatian churches.

33. O. Michel, "κυών," *TDNT* 3:1101.

34. Exod 22:31; Jer 15:5; Prov 26:11: "As a dog returns to its vomit, so a fool repeats his folly."

35. Pss 22:16, 20; 59:6, 14: "They return at evening, snarling like dogs, and prowl about the city."

emphasizing the boundary line between the Jewish people and Gentiles and demanding that Gentile Christians must identify with the Jewish people, Judaizers were excluding Gentile believers from the people of God and either actually or by implication calling them *dogs.* Even though the Gentile believers were followers of Jesus, they were regarded as unclean as dogs since they did not conform to the purity laws of the Jews. Until these Gentile converts came within the circle of Judaism, they were considered by the Judaizers to be outside the circle of the holy people of God; therefore, they were regarded as unclean *dogs.*

Paul draws another circle with Christ at the center. The Gentile believers are *holy people in Christ* (1:1) and are becoming *blameless and pure, "children of God without fault in a warped and crooked generation"* (2:14). True purity is in Christ: those who belong to Christ are the holy people of God. Since the Judaizers recognize only the purity that comes from belonging to the Jewish people, they despise the purity that comes from belonging to Christ. By despising true purity in Christ, they put themselves in the place of dogs. Following this line of thought, Paul calls the Judaizers by their own favorite title for impure Gentiles: *Watch out for those dogs!*

Paul also calls the Judaizers *evildoers.* Paul's reversal of the Judaizers' self-understanding gives this title an ironic tone. Since Jews did the works of the law, they portrayed themselves "servants of righteousness" (see 2 Cor 11:15) in contrast to the enemies of the people of God, who do not obey the law and are therefore evildoers (see Ps 14:4-6). Paul paints over their beautiful self-portrait to depict them as evildoers in two ways. First, they are evildoers because their emphasis on the works of the law turns into a self-reliance that obscures the need for salvation in Christ.[36] Second, they are evildoers because their work to convert Gentile Christians to Judaism by requiring circumcision and works of the law harms Christians by misleading them to supplement faith in Christ with works of the law.[37] Since these missionaries are drawing Gentile converts away from faith in Christ, they are evildoers. They may boast of their good works, but the results of their mission are so devastating that a warning must be posted: *Watch out for those evildoers.*

The harm that dogs and evildoers cause now comes into clear focus: they are *mutilators of the flesh.* The TNIV translation adds the words *of the flesh.* Literally, Paul says, "Beware of the mutilation."[38] The term "mutilation" is a sarcastic twist on the significance of circumcision: circumcision, the sign of the Jewish covenant, has no more value than mutilation if it replaces faith in Christ as the basis of belonging to the people of God. The Law and the Prophets taught that circumcision as an outward sign has no value unless it is a sign of a spiritual attitude of submissive obedience to the will and word of God (Deut 10:16; 30:6; Jer 4:4; Ezek 44:7). Paul reflects

36. Hawthorne, 125.

37. Beare, 105.

38. BDAG, 528, defines κατατομή as "mutilation, cutting in pieces."

the same assessment of circumcision: "A person is not a Jew who is one only outwardly, nor is circumcision merely outward and physical. No, a person is a Jew who is one inwardly; and circumcision is a circumcision of the heart by the Spirit" (Rom 2:28-29). By placing such a great emphasis on the Jewish rite of circumcision as the only way to belong to the people of God, the Judaizers had turned circumcision into something as worthless as the pagan rite of mutilation of the flesh. When Gentile Christians, under pressure from the Judaizers, accepted circumcision as the way to be included in God's blessing upon the Jewish people, they were acting exactly like pagans in the surrounding culture who tried to gain favor with the gods by physical mutilation.[39] Paul warned the Philippian Christians against *those mutilators of the flesh.* His warning applies to all ministers who draw people away from faith in Christ by insisting on the primary importance of religious rituals. Without faith in Christ and the inner work of the Spirit, even the most sacred rite is merely a physical act and a meaningless performance with no spiritual value at all.

3 In direct contrast to those who turned circumcision into mutilation by requiring Gentile Christians to be circumcised, Paul now asserts, *For it is we who are the circumcision.* The reason that Gentile believers in Christ should reject the requirement to be circumcised is that they already are *the circumcision.*[40] Their new identity in Christ gives them the right to be called by the names for the people of God, even the name *the circumcision.* This name points to the physical sign of belonging to the covenant people of God.[41] This sign was so highly valued by the Jews that they called themselves *the circumcision.*[42] By saying *we are the circumcision,* Paul marks all believers in Christ, both circumcised Jews and uncircumcised Gentiles, with the sign of the covenant people of God: all now belong to the covenant people; all are now included within the special covenantal relationship that God made with his people.

Paul's bold claim that all believers in Christ are included in *the circumcision,* in the people of God, does not imply that the Jewish people are excluded from the people of God.[43] Paul is not relegating all of Israel to *those*

39. For a description of pagan rites of self-mutilation in Paul's day, see David W. J. Gill, "Behind the Classical Façade: Local Religions in the Roman Empire," in *One God, One Lord: Christianity in a World of Religious Pluralism* (ed. A. Clarke and B. Winter; Exeter: Paternoster, 1992), 72-87. In a barbaric ritual, the priests of Cybele castrated themselves and placed their testicles in a box in the temple of Cybele (80-81).

40. The conjunction *For* indicates that Paul is now giving the reason to *watch out for those dogs, those evildoers, those mutilators of the flesh.*

41. See Gen 17:11: "You are to undergo circumcision, and it will be the sign of the covenant between me and you."

42. See Rom 3:30; 4:9, 12; 15:8; Gal 2:7-9, 12, where the Jewish people are identified as *the circumcised* and the Gentiles are called *the uncircumcised.*

43. Barth, 93-94, goes too far when he says, "Verse 3 declares that the people of God that bore that mark simply do not exist any more. We are the one real people of God. Ours are in truth the prerogatives whose name and semblance alone are still with Israel."

dogs. Those dogs are those who refuse to recognize that Gentile believers in Christ have full covenant membership in the people of God. The question of the relationship between Israel, the ancient people of God, and the church receives extensive treatment by Paul in Romans 11. Here Paul simply asserts "that faith in Christ places Gentile believers on the same footing before God as Jewish believers, co-opting them into the Abrahamic covenant which circumcision symbolizes."[44]

In Paul's sketch of those whom he calls *the circumcision,* he emphasizes three of their characteristic activities: (1) they *serve God by his Spirit;* (2) they *boast in Christ Jesus;* (3) they *put no confidence in the flesh.* This (TNIV) translation of the verb *serve* adds the word *God* because the verb connotes "the carrying out of religious duties, especially of a cultic nature."[45] Paul's deliberate contrast with the characterization of the *evildoers* as those who engage in "the mutilation" of the flesh emphasizes that *the Spirit* of God guides and empowers the work of believers in Christ.[46] Perhaps, Paul's reference to the Spirit responds to the evil workers' claim to have the presence and power of the Spirit in their ministry.[47] It is more likely, however, in the light of the emphasis in Paul's letters on the role of the Spirit of God in Christian life and ministry, that we will gain a better understanding of this reference to the Spirit by rooting it in Paul's own theology rather than by seeing it as a reaction to the position of his opponents. For example, in Galatians Paul teaches that the presence of the Spirit is the distinguishing mark of belonging to the family of God's people (Gal 3:1-5; 4:6), and the power of the Spirit, not the law, is the only adequate guide and power for life and service (Gal 5:16-25).[48] In keeping with his consistent emphasis elsewhere, Paul puts the empowering presence of the Spirit of God at the head of his list of distinguishing characteristics of the believer in Christ.

The second characteristic activity of *the circumcision* is *boasting in Christ Jesus.* Throughout the entire letter Paul models and encourages this activity of boasting in Christ Jesus. He states that the desired outcome of his own ministry is that *boasting in Christ Jesus will abound* (1:26). He es-

44. Bockmuehl, 191.

45. BDAG, 587.

46. The dative case of πνεύματι could be taken as locative, "serving in the Spirit," but is probably better understood as an instrumental use of the dative, "serving by the Spirit." To reduce the use of πνεύματι here to signify "the contrast between a true spiritual worship and mere external ordinances" (Beare, 105) misses the significance of qualification of "Spirit" by the genitive "of God" (πνεύματι θεοῦ). The *Spirit of God,* not the human spirit or human spirituality, is the source of inspiration and direction for those who serve God.

47. See Andrew T. Lincoln, *Paradise Now and Not Yet: Studies in the Role of the Heavenly Dimension in Paul's Thought with Special Reference to His Eschatology* (Grand Rapids: Baker, 1991), 90. Fee (299 n. 60) insists that this kind of "mirror reading" is not good evidence for an understanding of the theology of the opponents.

48. See G. Walter Hansen, *Galatians* (IVPNTCS; Downers Grove: InterVarsity Press, 1994), 120-24, 168-82.

chews doing anything *out of selfish ambition or vain conceit* (2:3). Especially in the great Christ hymn, he leads the reader to exult in the one being in the form of God, the one taking the form of the servant, and the one exalted by God and worshipped as Lord by all creation (2:5-11). He considers all of the highest privileges and greatest accomplishments of his life to be as garbage compared to knowing Christ (3:4-8). Paul's preoccupation with boasting in Christ Jesus exemplifies the words of Jeremiah 9:24: "Let those who boast boast in the Lord" (1 Cor 1:31).

The third characteristic of the people of God is that they *put no confidence in the flesh.* The term *flesh* has a wide range of meanings: from "the material that covers the bones" to "an unregenerate and sinful state."[49] In this context, Paul's characterization of the Judaizers (v. 2) and his description of his own Jewish heritage (vv. 4-6) lead to an understanding of *flesh* in terms of Jewish descent and the Jewish ritual of circumcision. *Confidence in the flesh* gives ultimate significance to national identity and physical ceremony. The person who puts confidence in the flesh says, "Belonging to my tribe and observing my ritual make me secure in my relationship with God." In contrast to those who put such confidence in the *flesh,* the true people of God, *the circumcision, put no confidence* in national status and religious ceremony. Boasting in Christ Jesus excludes putting confidence in the flesh.[50] Although national identities and sacred ceremonies are not viewed as bad in themselves, they are rejected as the foundation for one's relationship with God or with fellow believers.

4 Paul now shifts from first person plural to first person singular: *we put no confidence in the flesh, though I myself have reasons for such confidence.* This shift of emphasis opens the way for one of the most stunning first-century self-portraits.[51] In the next two verses (vv. 5-6) Paul defines *confidence in the flesh* in terms of his pure Jewish pedigree, his upper-class social status, his blameless moral life as a Pharisee, and his personal piety based on the law. By presenting this self-portrait, Paul demonstrates that he meets every qualification for greatness and excellence in Jewish society. Nobody can surpass him. He challenges and overwhelms the competition: *If others think they have reasons to put confidence in the flesh, I have more.* Precisely because others think they have *reasons to put confidence in the flesh,* Paul seems to contradict his assertion that we *put no confidence in the flesh* by setting forth his own impeccable résumé to defeat the Judaizers on their own turf. If they are playing a one-upmanship game by comparing reasons to put confidence in the flesh, then Paul will beat them by showing them the superiority of his credentials and achievements. Paul's ultimate aim is not to win this game of competition for status in the flesh but to ridicule

49. BDAG, 914-16.

50. E. Schweizer, "σάρξ," *TDNT* 7:130: "The direct opposite of σάρξ here is Χριστὸς Ἰησοῦς."

51. Bonnard, 61.

those who value status in the flesh.[52] After listing his superior advantages in the flesh (vv. 5-6), he declares that they are worth nothing to him now: *whatever were gains to me I now consider loss for the sake of Christ* (v. 7). He paints this portrait of himself as the perfect Jew to demonstrate to the believers in Christ in Philippi that (1) neither they nor the Jewish teachers could ever reach the level of his perfection and that (2) all these Jewish perfections have no value whatsoever compared to the value of knowing Christ. The purpose of this demonstration is to convince the Philippian believers to reject any propaganda for perfection by belonging to the Jewish people and by observing Jewish customs.

5-6 The seven features of Paul's self-portrait of his Jewish perfections give an impressive display of his privileges by birth and his personal accomplishments. The first perfection in the list is the fact that he was *circumcised on the eighth day.* By placing his circumcision on the eighth day as the first item in this list, Paul emphasizes that he had a "first class" circumcision in a Jewish family that fulfilled the requirement of the law (Gen 17:12; Lev 12:3) to circumcise their newborn son on the eighth day. His circumcision on the eighth day was superior to the circumcision of a Gentile proselyte at the time of conversion to Judaism.[53] Even if the Gentile believers in Christ decided to reach for perfection within Judaism by getting circumcised, they would not be able to attain the perfection of a circumcision on the eighth day. They would have a second-rate circumcision compared to Paul's eighth-day circumcision.

As a second reason for confidence in the flesh, Paul presents his pure pedigree: he is *of the people of Israel.* This phrase means that he was of the "race of Israel." The translation of *genos* as *people* does not adequately express the significance of this Greek word *genos.* The term denotes "ancestral stock, common ancestry, nationality."[54] Paul is claiming genealogical purity; his blood is untainted by any Gentile blood. The name *Israel* is the main self-designation of the Jewish people and conveys a religious message: we, the descendants of the patriarch Israel, are God's chosen people.[55] In another context, Paul challenged this assumption that genealogical membership in Israel guaranteed membership in Israel as the people of God. "Not all who are descended from Israel are Israel" (Rom 9:6). In his analogy of the olive tree that represents Israel (Rom 11:13-24), Paul describes how genealogical members of Israel have been broken off from the tree because of their unbelief in Christ while Gentiles have been grafted into the tree because of their belief in Christ. In this context, however, Paul

52. Gregory L. Bloomquist, *The Function of Suffering in Philippians* (JSNTSup 78; Sheffield: JSOT Press, 1993), 178.

53. The dative case of circumcision is a dative of reference (BDF §197): with reference to circumcision an eighth-day one. This grammatical construction implies that circumcision on the eighth day is superior to circumcision later in life, such as proselyte circumcision.

54. BDAG, 194.

55. BDAG, 481; K. G. Kuhn, "Ἰσραήλ," *TDNT* 3:360.

is asserting his genealogical membership in Israel. Gentile proselytes could belong to the *people (laos)* of Israel by faith in Christ, but they could never belong to the "race" *(genos)* of Israel. Any attempt to persuade Gentile Christians that they would attain perfection by joining the Jewish people was misleading. If perfection is measured on the basis of the *flesh,* Gentile proselytes would always be second-rate members compared to those who were "of the race of Israel."

Paul adds another proof of his superiority in the flesh by tracing his descent from *the tribe of Benjamin.* Tracing family lineage from tribal origins in this way to demonstrate noble ancestry occurs in the first sections of Josephus's autobiography: "The family from which I am derived is not an ignoble one, but has descended all along from the priests; and as nobility among several people is of different origin, so with us to be of the sacerdotal dignity, is an indication of the splendor of a family."[56] Just as Josephus was proud of his membership in the tribe of Levi, the tribe of priests, so Paul appears to be proud that he belongs to the tribe of Benjamin. He also points to his ancestry and tribal legacy in Romans 11:1: "I am an Israelite myself, a descendant of Abraham, from the tribe of Benjamin." The favored place of the tribe of Benjamin in the history of Israel begins with Benjamin himself: he was loved in a special way by Jacob as the son of his favorite wife, Rachel, and the only son to be born in the promised land (Gen 35:16-18). The tribe of Benjamin produced the first king of Israel (1 Sam 9:1-2), maintained loyalty to the tribe of Judah when the other ten tribes deserted the Davidic monarchy (1 Kings 12:21), and inherited within its territory the city of Jersusalem (Judg 1:21). Paul's Hebrew name, Saul (Acts 13:9), may reflect the pride of his parents in one of the most famous members of their tribe. Paul expresses this pride in his tribe as a reason he has for more confidence in the flesh than others.

Paul also claims superiority in the flesh on the basis of his cultural orientation: he is *a Hebrew of Hebrews.* This claim is not simply an indication that Hebrew (Aramaic) is his mother tongue. His fluency in Hebrew revealed his educational background and his cultural position. Ever since the Hellenization of the Mediterranean world in the third and second century B.C., the Jewish people were divided by language and culture. The Jews who were highly assimilated into the Hellenistic culture lost their use of the Hebrew language and their commitment to the Hebrew culture; they also accepted and participated in the political structures, social patterns, educational curriculum, ideological values, religious rites, and physical features of Hellenism.[57] In contrast to these Hellenized Jews, Jews who were antagonistic to Hellenistic culture fiercely protected their linguistic and cultural heritage against the corrupting influences of Hellenism: they

56. Josephus, *Life* 1–2.

57. See John M. G. Barclay, *Jews in the Mediterranean Diaspora from Alexander to Trajan (323 BCE–117 CE)* (Edinburgh: T&T Clark, 1996), 82-124.

were proud to be Hebrews. Jewish hostility against Hellenized Jews is clearly expressed in 1 Maccabees, the history of the Jewish revolt against the forces of Hellenism in 169 B.C.:

> In those days certain renegades came out from Israel and misled many saying, "Let us go and make a covenant with the Gentiles around us, for since we separated from them many disasters have come upon us." This proposal pleased them, and some of the people eagerly went to the king, who authorized them to observe the ordinances of the Gentiles. So they built a gymnasium in Jerusalem, according to Gentile custom, and removed the marks of circumcision, and abandoned the holy covenant. They joined with the Gentiles and sold themselves to do evil.[58]

By his claim to be *a Hebrew of Hebrews,* Paul clearly places himself on the side of those in Israel who "chose to die rather than to be defiled by food or to profane the holy covenant."[59] Of course, as a well-educated Hebrew in the Hellenistic world, Paul was fluent in Greek: he wrote his letters in Greek with methods of persuasion advocated by the Hellenistic rhetorical handbooks of his day.[60] But his fluency in Greek does not indicate that he had abandoned his Hebrew culture. Even the strict rabbinic schools in Jerusalem were effectively fluent in Greek and significantly influenced by their use of Greek literature and Greek rhetorical methods.[61] A simple contrast between Palestinian and Hellenistic Judaism fails to account for the extent of Hellenistic influence throughout the entire Hellenized world, including Palestine. The fact that Paul was a Jew of the Dispersion does not immediately put him in the category of Hellenized Jews. Even though his commitment to Christ caused a break with orthodox Judaism, his similarity to the Jews who were adamantly antagonistic to Hellenistic culture can be seen in the way he connects idolatry and immorality (see Rom 1:18-32) and divides humanity between the sons of God and the rest (Rom 8:12-21).[62] Paul was *a Hebrew of Hebrews:* he had not lost his use of Hebrew, his mother tongue, nor deviated from his cultural heritage.

The first four features of Paul's self-portrait reveal the superiority of the privileges that he had inherited and retained from his orthodox Jewish parents. The next three features display Paul's own personal achievements: his membership in an elite group of spiritual leaders within Judaism, his participation in the nationalistic effort to defend Judaism, and his perfection in his obedience to the law.

When Paul positions himself within Judaism by saying that he is, *in regard to the law, a Pharisee,* he is aligning himself with influential moral

58. 1 Macc 1:11-15.

59. 1 Macc 1:63.

60. See G. W. Hansen, "Rhetorical Criticism," in *DPL* 822-26.

61. See Martin Hengel, *Judaism and Hellenism* (London: SCM Press, 1974).

62. Barclay, *Jews in the Mediterranean Diaspora,* 392.

leaders who "are esteemed most skillful in the exact explication of their laws."[63] They sought to reform Jewish society by promoting their strict applications of the law to everyday life. Their interpretations of the law emphasized purity rules and Sabbath observance.[64] Their name, Pharisees, comes from an Aramaic term denoting "the separated ones, separatists."[65] Although their strict observance of the oral law separated them from the rest of Jewish society, it did not lead them into the monasticism of the Essenes. Instead they led others in their Jewish society away from the attractions of Hellenistic culture into a life governed by the rigorous requirements of the oral law. Paul belonged to this group of morally superior leaders: as a Pharisee his life was totally law-centered, law-controlled, and law-promoting. No matter how far the Philippian Christians might try to go in their attempt to observe the law in their quest for holiness, they could never achieve the superiority attained by Paul in his Pharisaic devotion to the law.

Paul puts his position as a Pharisee at the radical end of the spectrum of devotion to the law when he says, *as for zeal, persecuting the church.* Especially since the Maccabean revolt against Hellenistic forces, the challenge to protect the purity of Israel called for righteous leaders who would show zeal for the law. Mattathias, the patriarch of the Maccabean rebels, "burned with zeal for the law, just as Phinehas did" (1 Macc 2:26) and summoned the Jews of his day to do the same: "Let everyone who is zealous for the law and supports the covenant come out with me" (1 Macc 2:27). On his deathbed, Mattathias commanded his own sons to "show zeal for the law, and give your lives for the covenant of our ancestors" (1 Macc 2:50). Paul uses the word *zeal* here with this sense of intense dedication to keeping the law.[66] Although Paul does not explicitly say that his *zeal* is for the law, in the context, the word *zeal* is sandwiched between two phrases emphasizing the importance of the law in such a way that the law is the object of his zeal. In a parallel phrase, Paul clearly says that "in his previous life in Judaism" he was "extremely zealous for the traditions of my fathers" (Gal 1:13-14). *Zeal* was the code word in Paul's time for "a fervent commitment to defending the purity of Israel's religious practice and of her communal institutions, even at the cost of life itself."[67] The militant expression of zeal by the

63. Josephus, *J.W.* 2.8.14; see also *Ant.* 18.1.2.

64. Anthony J. Saldarini, "Pharisees," *ABD* 5:289-303.

65. BDAG, 1049.

66. See BDAG, 427; the term can also have a negative connotation of jealousy and envy and is used by Paul with this sense in his lists of vices (1 Cor 3:3; 2 Cor 12:20; Gal 5:20; Rom 13:13).

67. Bockmuehl, 199. See also Terence L. Donaldson, *Paul and the Gentiles: Remapping the Apostle's Convictional World* (Minneapolis: Fortress, 1997), 286: "The basic pattern of zeal was derived from the popular Old Testament prototypes — Phineas (Num 25), Elijah (1 Kgs 18-19), and Simeon and Levi (Gen 34). Zeal was more than just a fervent commitment to the Torah; it denoted a willingness to use violence against any — Jews, Gentiles, or the wicked in general — who were contravening, opposing, or subverting the Torah."

Zealots in their attempt to overthrow Roman domination in the 60s by physical violence shows how zeal for the law could be used as a basis for armed rebellion. This use of the term *zeal* with the meaning of physical violence reflects a narrow sense of the much wider usage that connotes a fierce nationalistic defense of the life and legacy of Israel.

Paul expressed his zeal for his national heritage by *persecuting the church.* According to his letter to the Galatians, he "intensely persecuted the church and tried to destroy it" (Gal 1:13). The account of Paul's persecution of the church in Acts attests that Paul's aggressive attack on the church included threats of murder and imprisonment (Acts 8:3; 9:1; 22:4-6; 26:10-11). According to Acts, Paul was identified (7:58) with those who attacked the Jewish Christians for speaking against the temple and against the law (6:11-14). Apparently, these accusations incited the zeal of Paul to punish these renegade Jews for their unfaithfulness to the law. Because these Jewish Christians had replaced the centrality and sovereignty of the holy law of God with the worship of a crucified Messiah, Paul was inflamed with zealous rage to stop their subversive influence within Israel by giving them the just punishment that Stephen their leader had recently received at the hands of the Sanhedrin (Acts 7:54–8:1). Paul's persecution of the church demonstrated his zeal to defend the identity of the people of God as the people who are faithfully keeping the law against the alternative preached by the church that the people of God are identified by following the crucified and risen Christ.[68]

The object of Paul's persecution was *the church.* This word was used in the Greek and Roman world for a regularly summoned legal assembly (Acts 19:39) and for a casual gathering of people (Acts 19:32, 40).[69] In the OT (LXX) the word occurs about a hundred times as a reference to an assembly, most times an assembly of Israelites. Significantly, this word is used for the assembly of Israelites at Sinai gathered to worship and to hear the law (Deut 4:10; 9:10; 18:16; cf. Acts 7:38).[70] Paul uses the term *church* for a specific assembly of Christians meeting in one place (Rom 16:5), for the totality of Christians living in a geographical area but not necessarily in one meeting place (Phil 4:15; 1 Cor 4:17), and for the global community of Christians (1 Cor 6:4; 12:28).[71] Paul's description of his zealous persecution of the

68. Donaldson, *Paul and the Gentiles,* 292: "His persecuting zeal was fueled by a perception that the Christ proclaimed in the gospel represented a rival boundary marker for the people of God." Cf. Fabian E. Udoh, "Paul's Views on the Law: Questions about Origin (Gal 1:6–2:21; Phil 3:2-11)," *NovT* 42 (2000), 218: "We know nothing . . . about what Paul perceived in those he persecuted. Donaldson's thesis that he perceived the Christ-Torah antithesis derives exclusively from Paul's Christian statements about the Law." If, however, we grant Paul at least some credit for an honest portrayal in Philippians 3 of his pre-Christian position, then we do know that his motive for persecuting the church was his zeal for the law.

69. BDAG, 303.

70. K. L. Schmidt, "ἐκκλησία," *TDNT* 3:527-29.

71. BDAG, 304.

church may refer to his harassment of Christians living in Jerusalem, Judea, and the surrounding areas.[72] But his depiction of Christians in this context as the true circumcision (3:3) supports the interpretation of church here as a reference to "the new Israel, the true heir and successor of God's chosen people and so the universal society."[73] As Paul boasts about his unsurpassed zeal that far excelled the Judaizers who were working to purify his churches, he presents the bitter irony that his extraordinary zeal for the purity of the people of God (ancient Israel) caused him to persecute the true people of God (the new Israel). From the perspective of boasting about his Jewish achievements in the flesh, Paul could list his persecution of the church as uncontested evidence for his extreme zeal for the law. But from the perspective of his new life in Christ, his persecution of the church was viewed as the greatest of his sins and the reason why he was the least of the apostles and did not even deserve to be called an apostle. Only by the grace of God was he forgiven the heinous sin of attacking the church of God (1 Cor 15:9-10).

Paul concludes his list of *reasons to put confidence in the flesh* with a stunning claim: *as for righteousness based on the law, faultless. Righteousness* in this phrase means the "quality or characteristic of upright behavior, uprightness."[74] As a Pharisee Paul determined and evaluated the quality of his upright behavior by the OT law as it was interpreted and amplified in the oral law. He reports that "the exertion with which he observed scrupulously the law's prescriptions, interpreted in their most rigid sense, led him to attain a perfection which was without lapse or defect."[75] Within the framework of the entire law, however, *faultless* does not mean sinless, since "a blameless observance of the law involved using the means of atonement for sin."[76] And yet, the claim to be *faultless* clearly communicates Paul's

72. O'Brien, 378.

73. Martin and Hawthorne, 187.

74. BDAG, 24.

75. Jacques Dupont, "The Conversion of Paul, and Its Influence on His Understanding of Salvation by Faith," in *Apostolic History and the Gospel: Biblical and Historical Essays Presented to F. F. Bruce on His 60th Birthday* (ed. W. W. Gasque and R. P. Martin; Grand Rapids: Eerdmans, 1970), 182-83.

76. See Frank Thielman, *Paul and the Law* (Downers Grove: InterVarsity Press, 1994), 154-55; see E. P. Sanders, *Paul and Palestinian Judaism*, 298-305, for his exposition of the Dead Sea Scrolls' teaching on the need and provision of atonement for all who observe the law. For example, 1Q 3:8-9: "By the spirit of uprightness and of humility his sin is atoned. And by the compliance of his soul with all the laws of God his flesh is cleansed by being sprinkled with the cleansing waters and being made holy with the waters of repentance. May he, then, steady his steps in order to walk with perfection." See also Richard N. Longenecker, *Paul: Apostle of Liberty* (Grand Rapids: Baker, 1976), 97: "We know of a nomistic, even antilegalistic, piety which existed amidst the strictness of Qumran. And the Dead Sea Scrolls often speak expressly of being 'blameless' or 'free from fault' in the keeping of the commandments of the Lord, yet without that blamelessness being viewed as a legalism or mere externalism. For the men of Qumran it was only through a spiritual apprehension of God's truth, the working of his Holy Spirit, and an attitude of uprightness, humility, and

"palpable satisfaction" with his upright behavior based on the law.[77] Paul is saying more than, I have "no qualms of conscience, no feelings of shortcomings."[78] He is pointing to an objective feature of his portrait, as observable and verifiable as his circumcision and his persecution of the church.[79] He was confident that the public record of his moral performance according to the law was impeccable.

The difficulty of harmonizing Paul's claim to being *faultless* according to righteousness based on law with his teaching in other letters that "all who rely on observing the law are under a curse" (Gal 3:5; see Gal 3:19-25; 5:3; Rom 5:20) can best be addressed by observing Paul's specific polemical purpose in this context.[80] Paul is not presenting a general theological principle about human ability to be faultless by observing the law. His argument is designed to disarm the promoters of the law by boasting that he has more reasons than they do for *confidence in the flesh.* Paul presents his superiority *in the flesh* as an *ad hominem* argument to defeat his opponents on their own grounds. If they want to promote the advantages of belonging to the nation of Israel and the perfection that comes from observing the law, then he will demonstrate that his position and performance as one *of the people of Israel* is far superior to theirs. But he will quickly say that he considers all of these *gains* to be a *loss* for the sake of Christ (3:7). And he will contrast his own righteousness that comes from the law with the righteousness that comes from God on the basis of faith (3:9). His reason for listing his *reasons for confidence in the flesh* is to persuade the Philippian Christians to *boast in Christ Jesus and put no confidence in the flesh* (3:3). By asserting that

---

submission that one could acceptably keep God's commandments and thus be accounted before Him as blameless." The interpretative translation NIV *(as for legalistic righteousness, faultless)* is misleading and has been corrected in the TNIV *(as for righteousness based on the law, faultless).*

77. Donaldson, *Paul and the Gentiles,* 138-39. Similar satisfaction is expressed by a certain ruler when Jesus reminds him of the commandments: "All these I have kept since I was a boy" (Luke 18:21).

78. K. Stendahl, *Paul among Jews and Gentiles* (Philadelphia: Fortress, 1976), 13.

79. O'Brien, 380; Dupont ("The Conversion of Paul, and Its Influence on His Understanding of Salvation by Faith," 183): "As he saw himself, Paul was, at the eve of his conversion, a man well satisfied, contented with his membership of the elect race and of an elite group of his people, and confident of attaining by his religious observance an ideal of righteousness which would make him beyond reproach in the eyes of God, men and his own conscience."

80. Stephen Westerholm, *Israel's Law and the Church's Faith: Paul and His Recent Interpreters* (Grand Rapids: Eerdmans, 1988), 161: "His description of his life under the law as 'blameless' (Phil 3:6) perhaps reflects his pre-conversion assessment, though the polemical context in which the claim is made — a comparison with Paul's detractors, self-proclaimed devotees of the law — should be kept in mind as well. There is no warrant for detaching Phil 3:6 from its context, then elevating the isolated claim to Paul's 'real' assessment of human capacities, setting aside Romans 1–3, 5, 7, etc. in the process." See also A. J. Thompson, "Blameless before God? Philippians 3:6 in Context," *Them* (2002), 5-12. Thompson argues against K. Stendahl and E. P. Sanders that Paul's self-estimation of his blamelessness before his conversion was exposed by his postconversion perspective to be less than adequate.

his own birth into the Jewish nation and his own faultless behavior based on the law have the value of garbage compared to the surpassing value of knowing Christ (3:8), Paul seeks to convince the Philippians that belonging to the Jewish nation and perfection according to the law are not worth pursuing since even as Gentile believers they are already in Christ.

Although Paul's reasons for confidence in the flesh are specifically related to his Jewish origins and achievements, they reflect the universal elements of human pride. In every age and place, an arrogant pledging of allegiance to their nation and a complacent polishing of their trophies of perfect performance eclipse the centrality and sovereignty of Christ in the lives of Christians.[81] No matter how precious the social privileges and how perfect the moral accomplishments may be, all that ultimately, eternally matters for a follower of Christ is Christ.

B. Losing All to Know Christ (3:7-11)

> [7]*But whatever were gains to me I now consider loss for the sake of Christ.* [8]*What is more, I consider everything a loss because of the surpassing worth of knowing Christ Jesus my Lord, for whose sake I have lost all things. I consider them garbage, that I may gain Christ* [9]*and be found in him, not having a righteousness of my own that comes from the law, but that which is through faith in Christ — the righteousness that comes from God on the basis of faith.* [10]*I want to know Christ — yes, to know the power of his resurrection and participation in his sufferings, becoming like him in his death,* [11]*and so, somehow, attaining to the resurrection from the dead.*

Immediately after presenting the portrait of himself as a Pharisee to show that he looked better than others *in the flesh* (3:4-6), Paul juxtaposes a strikingly different self-portrait (3:7-11) to demonstrate that he now considers even his most valuable assets in the flesh to be liabilities in the light of his knowledge of Christ Jesus his Lord.[82] He even considers his extraordinary achievement of a faultless record of righteousness based on the law (3:6) to be worthless in contrast to the righteousness that comes from God

81. See Fee, 310: "Confusion of being a Christian with being a member of a given nation has a long history in the church; it is one of the pernicious bequests of the conversion of Constantine, which plagues not only officially 'Christian' states, but perhaps even more insidiously a country like the United States, where the American flag often holds pride of place in Christian sanctuaries and where patriotic holidays are sometimes the more significant days in the American church calendar."

82. Although the adversative conjunction *but* (ἀλλά) emphasizes the radical contrast between the two portraits, it may be an insertion later in the textual tradition. The conjunction is not found in early and diverse witnesses (𝔓[46] ℵ* A G 0282. 33. 81). Yet, ἀλλά is included by other significant witnesses and by the vast majority of MSS (ℵ[2] B D F Ψ and the 𝔐). The external evidence is not conclusive. "The verse seems to cry out for a transitional particle, but this very fact may have led scribes to add the conjunction" (Silva, 182).

(3:9). As he describes his own personal experience of new life in Christ, Paul provides a theological outline of the entire scope of salvation in Christ: justification, receiving righteousness from God by faith in Christ (v. 9); sanctification, knowing the power of Christ's resurrection and participation in his sufferings (v. 10); and glorification, attaining to the resurrection from the dead (v. 11).

In this portrait, Paul's whole life revolves around Christ: nine times by name or pronoun in these five verses, Christ fills all of Paul's vision. Although Paul does not explicitly label the total transformation in his life as his conversion, his negative assessment of his position and achievements in his previous way of life because of his present passion to know Christ demonstrates that a profound reorientation occurred.[83] True, Paul always remained a Jew who believed in the God of Abraham, Isaac, and Jacob and affirmed the divine authority of the Hebrew scriptures, but he was radically transformed by his supreme ambition to know the crucified, risen Christ and to become like him (3:10).[84]

Paul draws striking parallels between his transformation (3:5-11, 21) and Christ's incarnation–crucifixion–exaltation (2:5-11) to reveal how his personal experience conforms to the narrative of Christ. (1) When Paul *considers* the privileges of his previous, superior position to be a loss (3:7, 8), he is like Christ, who did not *consider* equality with God something to be used to his own advantage (2:6). (2) Paul gives up everything valuable so that he will be *found* in Christ (3:8-9), just as Christ made himself nothing so that he would be *found* in appearance as a human being (2:8). (3) Paul's desire to be *conformed* to Christ in his death (3:10) reflects Christ's decision to take the *form* of a servant and become obedient unto death (2:7-8). (4) Paul's longing to know Christ Jesus his *Lord* (3:8) anticipates the day when all will acknowledge that Jesus Christ is *Lord* (2:11). (5) Paul's reenactment of the narrative of Christ also includes his expectation that he will know the power of his resurrection, attain to the resurrection from the dead (3:10), and ultimately be transformed by Christ so that his lowly body will be like his Christ's glorious body (3:21). Paul carefully crafts the story of his transformation to convince his readers that his choice to renounce his confidence in the flesh is the choice they too must make in order to know Christ and be conformed to Christ in his humiliation and exaltation. Readers who follow Paul's example will not put their confidence in the privileges of belonging to the Jewish community (or any other community), but will choose the way of humility and service as Christ did.[85] Although Paul's story discloses his per-

83. Against Stendahl, *Paul among Jews and Gentiles*, 7-23, who argues that "the usual conversion model of Paul the Jew who gives up his former faith to become a Christian is not the model of Paul but of ours" (9).

84. See G. Walter Hansen, "Paul's Conversion and His Ethic of Freedom in Galatians," in *The Road from Damascus: The Impact of Paul's Conversion on His Life, Thought, and Ministry* (ed. Richard N. Longenecker; Grand Rapids: Eerdmans, 1997), 213-37.

85. Pheme Perkins, "Philippians: Theology for the Heavenly *Politeuma*," in *Pauline*

sonal passion, his story also offers a practical paradigm for the way to become like Christ. Those who follow Paul by emptying themselves of all their pride in their ethnic origin, national heritage, social class, and religious work will be like Christ, who *emptied himself, taking the form of a servant.*[86]

This parallelism between Christ and Paul also points to the infinite difference between the apostle and his Lord. Even though Paul desires to be conformed to Christ in his death, he recognizes the absolute superiority and sovereignty of Christ. Paul confesses that Christ Jesus is *my Lord,* considers *everything a loss* compared to the surpassing value of knowing Christ, and trusts in Christ alone for the righteousness that comes from God. In this witness to his faith in Christ, Paul gives to Christ the worship and obedience that belong only to God. "This confession is so strong that though Paul does not literally use the words 'Christ is God,' his depiction of the utter incomparability of Christ can lead to no other conclusion."[87] Paul's outpouring of his devotion to Christ in 3:7-11 personalizes the worship of Christ in the Christ hymn of 2:6-11 as the one who did not use his equality with God to his own advantage, who made himself nothing by taking the form of a servant and becoming human, who was obedient to death on a cross, whom God exalted to the highest place to receive universal worship as the Lord of all, to the glory of God the Father. The uniqueness of Christ's narrative of incarnation–crucifixion–resurrection became the motivation, not the obstacle, for Paul's desire to be united with Christ in his suffering and his victory.

7 Paul introduces his new self-portrait with a simple, strong thesis statement: *But whatever were gains to me I now consider loss for the sake of Christ.* Looking back, this statement makes an emphatic contrast with Paul's picture of himself as one who has good *reasons to put confidence in the flesh* (v. 4); looking forward, this statement sets forth the terms that are expanded and developed in the enlarged picture of Paul's new life in Christ (vv. 8-11). The relative clause, *whatever were gains to me,* refers back to Paul's list of reasons for his superiority in the flesh and suggests that Paul could have added other impressive items to this list.[88] These privileges and

---

Theology: Volume 1 (ed. J. M. Bassler; Minneapolis: Fortress, 1991), 98-99: "Paul himself exemplifies the practical choice of 'lowliness' in his rejection of the former marks of his status as a member of Israel in order to 'know the Lord' (3:4-11). He insists that Christians cannot accept those who seek to reinstate the physical marks of belonging to the earthly *politeuma* of the Jewish community."

86. David A. deSilva, "No Confidence in the Flesh: The Meaning and Function of Philippians 3:2-21," *TrinJ* 15 n.s. (1994), 28: "The pattern of Paul's rejection of claims before God parallels Christ's refusal to cling to equality with God: both reach or will reach their eventual exaltation by emptying themselves and by pursuing the goal of obedience to God without seeking to secure any claims on God's reward."

87. V. Koperski, *The Knowledge of Christ Jesus My Lord: The High Christology of Philippians 3:7-11* (Kampen: Kok Pharos, 1996), 323.

88. The indefinite relative pronoun *whatever* (ἅτινα) implies that there is wider scope of the things that *were gains* to Paul than the seven items listed in vv. 4-6. See Fee, 315 n. 9.

achievements really *were gains* to Paul from the perspective of reasons to put confidence in the flesh. Using business accounting terms, Paul clearly states that he had gained profits as a result of his heritage and his strict observance of the law.[89] The plural, *gains*, gives the picture of Paul evaluating and tabulating each of his assets on a net worth balance sheet. His exceptional net worth put him far ahead of his contemporaries. As he asserts in verse 4, he had *more* than all of them. For years, Paul had considered himself incredibly wealthy in terms of social and religious equity.

But now the main clause sets forth the shocking reversal in Paul's evaluation of his assets: these *I consider a loss for the sake of Christ*. Paul's radically new evaluation was the result of "an intellectual process."[90] His encounter with Christ did not shut off his mind, but it set him free to think with a whole new depth and clarity about his life from a totally different perspective.[91] His conversion was not an escape from reason but an illumination of reason. Once Christ became the goal of his life, he could finally see and understand the true value of his life in the light of Christ.

For the sake of Christ means that Christ is the reason why Paul considers his former *gains* as a *loss*.[92] The perfect parallelism of this sentence sets forth Paul's life in the form of a balance sheet.

Whatever	*were*	*to me*	*gains,*
these	*I consider*	*because of Christ*	*loss.*

The shift from plural *gains* to singular *loss* indicates that Paul is not giving different values to each of his assets, discounting them at different rates: some are marked down 50 percent; others down 90 percent. Because of Christ, Paul has added up all of his assets and considered them to be one huge liability. After his conversion to Christ, Paul recalculates the value of all of the advantages of his family and his accomplishments, his social class and his moral achievements, and then he enters the new bottom line: they all add up to one overwhelming disadvantage, one huge loss.[93]

8 Paul now expands his thesis statement regarding his evaluation of his former gains to be a loss because of Christ. The strange combination of

89. A gain, κέρδος, refers to "that which is gained or earned, a gain, profit" (BDAG, 541).

90. To *consider* (ἥγημαι) means "to engage in an intellectual process, think, consider, and regard" (BDAG, 434). The perfect tense of ἥγημαι emphasizes the present result of a past process of consideration. See BDF §§340-42.

91. Collange, 129; Bonnard, 63.

92. The TNIV (NIV, RSV) translates the Greek phrase διὰ τὸν Χριστόν as *for the sake of Christ*. The preposition διά with the accusative case is a "marker of something constituting cause, the reason why something happens, results, or exists" (BDAG, 225). Paul's use of the same preposition (διά) with the accusative case in reference to Christ in v. 8 expands the meaning of this phrase and emphasizes that Christ is "the cause, the reason" for Paul's total reevaluation of his life.

93. *Loss* (ζημίαν) means "damage, disadvantage, loss, forfeit" (BDAG, 428).

conjunctions at the beginning of verse 8 emphasizes the expansion: *What is more* (TNIV; similarly, NRSV: "More than that"), conveys the sense of Paul's use of five conjunctions to intensify and go further in asserting his loss because of Christ.[94] The change from the perfect tense, *I have considered,* to the present tense of the verb, *I consider,* stresses Paul's present attitude toward his gains and losses: he did not have any second thoughts about his previous decision; in fact, he reaffirmed and renewed his choice every day.[95] His present *I consider* continues and extends his past *I have considered* into his present and future experience.[96] Paul's renewed commitment to his past decision to live for Christ models for his readers how to *stand firm in the one Spirit, striving together with one accord for the faith of the gospel* (1:27). "Paul here attempts to inspire them by recounting how an overpowering experience in the past continues to motivate him in the present and give him hope for the future while he endures present trials."[97]

Paul also expands the scope of his reevaluation because of Christ by changing the object of his consideration from *whatever* things and *these things* in verse 7 to *everything* and *all things* in verse 8. The pronouns *whatever* and *these* in verse 7 clearly refer to Paul's list in verses 5-6. These things, the privileges of his birth and the perfection of his righteousness based on the law, are considered *a loss* because of Christ. But now Paul goes further: he considers *everything a loss* because of Christ. This expansion enables Paul to move beyond the specifics of his own story and extend the list of things that are considered a loss to cover all things "that might compete with Christ for his allegiance."[98] In the context, *everything* refers to all things that encourage *confidence in the flesh.*[99] Paul is reinforcing his assertion that to *boast in Christ Jesus* requires putting *no confidence in the flesh* (v. 3). All rivals of Christ are totally devalued.

Paul explains with greater depth the reason for this drastic devaluation of everything. The simple phrase in verse 7, *for the sake of Christ,* is amplified in verse 8 to *because of the surpassing worth of knowing Christ Jesus my Lord.*

94. ἀλλὰ μενοῦν γε καί is a combination of particles not found elsewhere in Greek literature. Probably the strangeness of this combination caused some copyists (𝔓[46 vid] א*) to omit the final particle καί (so Fee, 317 n. 15). The combination of ἀλλὰ καί is used "to introduce an additional point in an emphatic way" and can be translated, "not only this, but also" (BDF §448); the combination of μενοῦν γε is used "to either heighten or correct" (BDF §450).

95. Silva, 179 n. 19, observes that although the perfect tense also refers to the present time, the contrast between the perfect tense in v. 7 and the present tense of this verb twice in v. 8 indicates that Paul makes a distinction between the present significance of a past decision and a present choice to renew his past decision.

96. Schenk, 264.

97. Koperski, *The Knowledge of Christ Jesus My Lord,* 157.

98. Martin and Hawthorne, 190.

99. Silva, 179, argues that "we need not absolutize the meaning of *panta* to appreciate its full force. The thrust of the word is clearly established by the context: everything on which Paul might place his fleshly confidence." Similarly, according to O'Brien, 387, πάντα includes "anything in which he was tempted to trust and which therefore stood over against the personal knowledge of Christ."

When Paul speaks of *surpassing worth,* he is stating that the quality or value of knowing Christ excels and surpasses all alternatives. This surpassing greatness, "a decisive, superior, victorious factor,"[100] far outweighs the value of anything else. When you put the value of knowing Christ on one side of the balance scale and everything else on the other side, *everything* else has no value whatsoever compared to *the surpassing worth of knowing Christ.*[101]

Knowing Christ Jesus my Lord changed Paul's view of *everything.* This knowledge is above all the "personal acquaintance" of Christ Jesus.[102] Paul did not gain this knowledge of Christ Jesus through his own theological reflection but by receiving the revelation of Christ Jesus (2 Cor 4:6; Gal 1:12) and by acknowledging him as *my Lord.*[103] Knowledge of Christ Jesus as *my Lord* includes the submission of every thought and every act (2 Cor 10:5-6) to Christ Jesus the Lord. As Paul's prayer for his readers that their *love may abound more and more in knowledge and depth of insight, so that you may be able to discern what is best* (1:9) shows, true knowledge combines insight with love. In Paul's passionate desire *to know Christ* (3:10), his yearning for an intimate experience of Christ in his life — *the power of his resurrection and participation in his sufferings* — involves love for Christ and insight into the enduring significance of the work of Christ. This use of the word *knowledge* to refer to a personal relationship, moral action, and intellectual reflection continues and deepens the OT references (Jer 9:23, 24; 31:34; Hos 4:1; 6:6) to the knowledge of God.[104] In his polemic against the Judaizers, Paul emphasizes that the surpassing greatness of the knowledge of God is experienced in the acknowledgment that Christ Jesus is Lord.

Paul reminds his friends that knowing Christ cost him everything: *for whose sake I have lost all things.* When Paul says, *I have lost all things,* he is using the verb form of the noun *loss* that he has already used twice and is referring to "the loss of something with the implication of undergoing hardship or suffering."[105] The aorist tense of the verb *I have lost* focuses on his conversion, when his encounter with Christ and subsequent obedience to

100. BDAG, 1033.

101. The genitive case of the knowledge (τῆς γνώσεως) is an epexegetic genitive or a genitive of apposition, defining the content of the surpassing worth as the knowledge.

102. BDAG, 203.

103. E. Schütz, "Knowledge," *NIDNTT* 2:403.

104. See O'Brien, 388; Martin and Hawthorne, 138. Against Beare, 114: "We must agree with M. Dibelius that *gnōsis* 'is used in the technical sense given it in Hellenistic mysticism.'" Beare qualifies this by saying that "the words *gnōsis* and *ginōskō* ('knowledge' and 'know') retain religious and moral overtones of the greatest importance, carried over from the Hebraic usage." R. Bultmann ("γινώσκω," *TDNT* 1:710) says that "Paul undoubtedly borrows from the Gnostics in describing the γνῶσις Χριστοῦ Ἰησοῦ as a distinctive mark of the Christian." But Bultmann qualifies this after his exposition of the text by asserting that "this is all very different from Gnosticism." After Koperski, *The Knowledge of Christ Jesus My Lord,* 22-65, provides a review of the proponents of the Hellenistic and Gnostic background and the proponents of the Jewish background, he concludes that Paul's use of the term *knowledge* "does seem to come primarily, even perhaps exclusively, from his Jewish heritage" (65).

105. BDAG, 428.

him caused Paul to renounce all of the privileges and advantages of his high social standing and religious achievements.[106] Whether Paul was forcefully stripped of all his privileges or willingly gave them up as a result of his conversion, the main point of his statement is clear: because of his commitment to Christ, Paul forfeited everything and suffered hardship. Paul is not speaking theoretically about the possibility of losing everything. He knew firsthand that following Christ caused him to be excluded from the security and privilege of belonging to the Jewish community. He presents his own experience of suffering for his faith in Christ to thwart any attempt on the part of the Judaizers to offer the Philippian Christians the advantages of belonging to the Jewish community.[107] As a result of acknowledging that Jesus Christ is Lord, the Philippian Christians are in conflict with their Roman and Jewish neighbors who deny the Lordship of Jesus. They should expect that their allegiance to Christ Jesus as Lord will cause them to suffer hardship.

Paul takes his revaluation of his advantages in the flesh another radical step further by declaring, *I consider them garbage.* The word *garbage* denotes "excrement, manure, garbage, kitchen scraps." In some Greek texts this term refers "specifically to human excrement."[108] Paul not only considers all things as *loss,* but in this shocking statement he intensifies his renunciation of all things by referring to them as *garbage.* "The choice of the vulgar term stresses the force and totality of this renunciation."[109] Paul gives the reason for this vulgar reference to all his privileges when he says, *I consider them garbage, that I may gain Christ.* Because his goal is to *gain Christ,* anything that stands in the way of that goal must be rejected as utterly worthless and repulsive as garbage. Paul highly valued and greatly appreciated the privileges of belonging to the Jewish community (see Rom 3:1-2; 9:1-5). But he considered these good things as a *loss* and as *garbage* because they led to putting *confidence in the flesh* and stood in the way of the *surpassing worth of knowing Christ Jesus my Lord.* What Paul renounced was not the wickedness of the flesh but all the goodness of his flesh. "That goodness is over and done with and abides under judgment; [it] must not have any form of lurking place alongside of Christ."[110] The choice is clear: Are all

106. The passive voice may have the full force of the passive and indicate that Paul was "disowned by his family and disinherited, or had property confiscated, and been deprived of all his rights in the national community of Judaism" (Beare, 115). Or the passive may have shifted its meaning and refer to Paul's "voluntary renunciation of everything" (O'Brien, 389). See BDF §159 (2).

107. Mikael Telbe, "The Sociological Factors behind Philippians 3:1-11 and the Conflict at Philippi," *JSNT* 55 (1994), 119: "The implication for the Philippian believers is, therefore, that it is not in keeping with knowing Christ to seek identity with the Jewish community as a means of mitigating the conflict and escaping the suffering; instead they are to identify with Christ and to face the unavoidable suffering as true disciples of Christ."

108. BDAG, 932.

109. F. Lang, "σκύβαλον," *TDNT* 7:446.

110. Barth, 98.

privileges of the flesh my *gains* (v. 7), or will I seek *to gain Christ?* I can *gain Christ* only by considering all the *gains* of my flesh to be as worthless as *garbage.* Now Paul's new balance sheet of his net worth is complete. Paul has transferred all his former gains, all of his assets, over to the liability column. He made this transfer *in order to gain Christ,* the one incomparable asset of surpassing worth.

9 To explain why he *considers* his advantages as a loss and as garbage, Paul expresses his purpose with two verbs: *that I may gain Christ and be found in him.* The chiastic arrangement of the verbs in this purpose clause aids in the interpretation of each line:

that	*Christ*	*I may gain*
and	*be found*	*in him*

The second verb amplifies the meaning of the first verb: to *gain Christ* means to *be found in him.* Paul has already used the verb *be found* in his portrait of Christ in the Christ hymn: as a result of Christ's decision that he would *not consider equality with God something to be used to his own advantage, he made himself nothing . . .* and was *found in appearance as a human being* (2:6-8). By using the same verb, Paul draws attention to the parallel between the goal of Christ's self-emptying and the goal of his own loss: just as Christ was found to be in human form, Paul desires to be found in Christ. Although linguistically the passive voice of this verb may refer to human observation of Paul or to God's assessment of Paul,[111] the participial phrase that follows and modifies this verb points to God's assessment, *the righteousness that comes from God.* As a result of having the righteousness that comes from God, Paul expects to be found by God in Christ. Since the future *day of Christ* (1:6, 10; 2:16), the day of *the resurrection from the dead* (3:11), fills Paul's horizon, that day may be his point of reference: he hopes to be found in Christ on the day of Christ.[112] Paul's focus in the immediate context, however, is on the present experience of having righteousness from God and knowing Christ.[113] The present and future often coalesce in Paul's vision. Paul lives every day in the light of the last day. The future expectation to be found in Christ rests on the present experience of being found in Christ.

111. See H. Preisker, "εὑρίσκω," *TDNT* 2:769.

112. See Judith M. Gundry-Volf, *Paul and Perseverance: Staying In and Falling Away* (WUNT 2.37; Louisville: Westminster John Knox, 1991), 258: "Only the righteousness which comes from God can give Paul the assurance that he will 'be found in him' on the last day (3:9)." O'Brien, 392: "The apostle's great ambition is to 'be found in him' on that occasion when every knee shall bow to Jesus Christ as Lord." Also Gnilka, 194; Collange, 115. Although Collange says that the verb is future tense, it is aorist tense and as such may refer to past, present, or future. (See BDF §§331-33 with examples of ingressive, complexive, gnomic, and futuristic aorists. See also S. E. Porter, *Idioms of the Greek New Testament* [Sheffield: JSOT Press, 1992], 35-39.)

113. Beare, 116.

Now Paul explains the basis of being found in Christ by adding a compact participial clause that contrasts two kinds of righteousness: my own righteousness from the law and the righteousness from God through faith in Christ.[114] He begins by renouncing his possession of the first kind of righteousness with an emphatic *not: not having.* In the context of the long sentence (vv. 8-11), the way that Paul repudiates this kind of righteousness is to view it as *a loss* and as *garbage.* Like the Hebrew prophet, Paul considers "all our righteous acts as filthy rags" (Isa 64:6). He defines the kind of righteousness that he rejects with two modifiers. First, the possessive pronoun, *my own,* stands before the noun *righteousness* in an emphatic position and qualifies this righteousness as Paul's own *personal* possession. Second, *from the law* defines this kind of righteousness as being the result of his own obedience to the law. This connection of righteousness with the law repeats his boast in verse 6: *as for righteousness based on the law, faultless.* Since Paul fulfilled the law's prescription for righteous behavior, he possessed righteousness from the law. He claims it to be *my own righteousness* because he had achieved it by keeping the law. He owned it because he had earned it.

This interpretation of Paul's claim to personal righteousness on the basis of his own achievement is vigorously disputed. E. P. Sanders rejects the interpretation that *my righteousness* means "my individual righteousness, based on the merit achieved by the performance of good deeds" and redefines *my righteousness* as "the peculiar result of being an observant Jew, which is *in and of itself a good thing.*"[115] From Sanders' perspective, Paul's righteousness is the result of being included within God's covenant with the Jewish people and maintaining his place of membership in God's covenant people by observing the law. Dunn asserts that "my own" cannot mean "achieved by me." Instead Paul was expressing the "conviction that righteousness was Israel's, to be practiced by covenant-loyal Jews and defended as Israel's by its practitioners."[116] The phrase *my righteousness* is "*membership* language," according to Wright. "When Paul says he does not have a righteousness 'of my own', based on Torah, the context of the previous verses must mean that he is speaking of righteousness, a covenant status, which was his as a Jew by birth, marked with the covenant badge of circumcision, and claiming to be a part of the inner circle of that people by being a zealous Pharisee. That which he is refusing in the first half of verse 9 is not a moralistic or self-help righteousness, but the status of orthodox

114. Whether the participial clause is a causal modifier, indicating the reason for being found in Christ, or a modal modifier, indicating the manner of being found in Christ, it provides an explanation of the basis of being in Christ in either case. See BDF §§417, 418 for the uses of an adverbial participle.

115. E. P. Sanders, *Paul, the Law, and the Jewish People* (Philadelphia: Fortress, 1985), 44-45 (his italics).

116. James D. G. Dunn, *The Theology of Paul the Apostle* (Grand Rapids: Eerdmans, 1998), 370.

Jewish covenant membership."[117] In other words, Paul's own righteousness is a national righteousness possessed by Paul as a member *of the people of Israel* (v. 5).

This recent reinterpretation clarifies Paul's repudiation of his own righteousness as a rejection of the exclusivist position that only circumcised, law-observant members of the people of Israel could possess righteousness. The point of Paul's argument in this context is that Gentile believers in Christ do possess righteousness even though they do not belong to the ethnic group of people called Jews. This Jew/Gentile distinction is the social context of Paul's language. But Paul's argument goes beyond the immediate social problem in its renunciation of all self-achieved righteousness. To limit Paul's reference to his own righteousness to his membership in the Jewish nation ignores Paul's emphasis on his own personal achievement. Kim appropriately challenges the reinterpretation by asking, "If Paul was not conscious of his personally achieved righteousness but only of the 'national righteousness' of Israel in Phil 3:2-20, should he not have referred to it as 'our own righteousness,' including his Jewish opponents in his claim, insofar as they, by virtue of their being zealous Jews, evidently also participated in the 'national righteousness'?"[118] Paul's claim to have more reasons to have confidence in the flesh (v. 4) than all his opponents is based on his boast that his achievement of a faultless righteousness based on law (v. 6) gave him a personal righteousness that far surpassed the national righteousness of his opponents. "Paul's 'own' righteousness is the result of his personal zeal in fulfilling the law's demands."[119] Thus, Paul's reason for superior confidence in the flesh is not merely based on his national status but also on his personal achievement.[120] His rejection of his own personal righteousness derived from his observance of the law reveals his profound revulsion at his own personal righteousness. His zealous pursuit of his own righteousness caused him to persecute the church. He did not view his own righteousness as "in and of itself a good thing." He considered it to be *garbage*.

But, Paul says, there is another kind of righteousness, not a righteousness that he achieved, but a righteousness that he received: *that which is through faith in Christ — the righteousness that comes from God on the basis of faith*. Usually we would expect that a word has the same meaning in both cases when the same word is used side by side in the same sentence.[121] But

117. N. T. Wright, *What St. Paul Really Said* (Oxford: Lion Hudson, 1997), 124.

118. Seyoon Kim, *Paul and the New Perspective: Second Thoughts on the Origin of Paul's Gospel* (Grand Rapids: Eerdmans, 2002), 77.

119. S. Westerholm, *Perspectives Old and New on Paul: The "Lutheran" Paul and His Critics* (Grand Rapids: Eerdmans, 2004), 312.

120. See Simon Gathercole, *Where Is Boasting? Early Jewish Soteriology and Paul's Response in Romans 1–5* (Grand Rapids: Eerdmans, 2002), 181-82.

121. J. A. Ziesler, *The Meaning of Righteousness in Paul* (Cambridge: Cambridge University Press, 1972), 149-51, argues against a difference in meaning; in both cases righteous-

by setting up this strong contrast between his own *righteousness that comes from the law* and the *righteousness that comes from God on the basis of faith,* Paul presents two different meanings for the word *righteousness.* Paul's own righteousness from the law denotes his own upright behavior determined by the law.[122] The righteousness that comes from God does not come from Paul's good moral conduct or from a superior level of conduct empowered by God, but from God's judicial verdict of a righteous standing before God. The righteousness from the law refers to Paul's obedience to the law; the righteousness from God refers to a right relationship granted by God, not on the basis of obedience to the law, but on the basis of faith in Christ.[123]

Paul's unique way of qualifying righteousness as *the righteousness that comes from God* puts this expression in the category of Paul's references in Romans to righteousness credited, received, or obtained as a gift.[124] This gift of righteousness from God needs to be distinguished from God's own righteousness.[125] The righteousness of God, revealed, made known, and demonstrated (Rom 1:17; 3:5, 21, 22, 25, 26), refers to God's own character of justice and faithfulness and God's act of salvation. But this line between God's own righteousness (God's character and God's act) and God's gift of righteousness cannot be drawn in a way that separates the Giver from the gift.[126] Since those who receive the gift of God's righteousness have a new righteous status and have come into a right relationship with God, they now have direct experience of God's character and God's act of salvation. *Having . . . the righteousness that comes from God* opens the way to *gain Christ and be found in him* and *to know him.* The gift of righteousness from God includes union with Christ. Paul ties together the concepts and experience of judicial acquittal (God's judicial decision to grant a righteous status) and personal membership in Christ and the body of Christ. The way to be included in Christ is by having the righteousness from God. If inclusion in

---

ness refers to ethical behavior, but from different sources: first from Paul's efforts; second from God's power. But Ziesler has to bring in the relational aspect of the second use of righteousness to make sense of the passage.

122. BDAG, 248.

123. Westerholm, *Perspectives Old and New on Paul,* 275. Westerholm (263-84) helpfully distinguishes between ordinary righteousness (when one does what is right, one has ordinary righteousness) and extraordinary righteousness (when unrighteous sinners are treated as righteous by God because of what Christ has done, they have received extraordinary righteousness by faith in Christ).

124. See Rom 4:3-6, 22-24; 5:17; 9:30; 10:4.

125. Wright, *What St. Paul Really Said,* 104. See Wright's helpful chart of meanings for righteousness (101), where he distinguishes between A. God's own righteousness (A1. Righteousness as a moral quality; A2. Righteousness as God's salvation-creating power) and B. A righteousness given to humans (B1. Righteousness as a righteous standing from God; B2. Righteousness as a quality that comes before God). Wright defines *righteousness . . . from God* in terms of B1, not A1 or A2.

126. See E. Käsemann, *Perspectives on Paul* (Philadelphia: Fortress, 1971), 82: The apostle did not "permit righteousness to be considered as a gift which could be detached from the giver and transferred to our possession."

Christ were dependent on righteousness from the law, only those who were faultless in observing the law could be members of Christ. But since inclusion in Christ is based on the gift of righteousness from God, inclusion in Christ is open to all through faith in Christ.

The phrase *through faith in Christ* explains how this extraordinary righteousness is received. The ambiguity of the Greek phrase *(pisteōs Christou)* translated *faith in Christ* is the subject of an extensive debate between two options: the genitive case of *Christ (Christou)* could be either an objective genitive or a subjective genitive. If Christ is the object of the verbal noun *faith,* then the expression speaks of human faith in Christ; if Christ is the subject of the verbal noun *faith,* then the expression speaks of Christ's faith or faithfulness. Although many recent interpreters present weighty arguments in favor of the view that this phrase means "the faithfulness of Christ," the traditional understanding of the phrase as a reference to faith in Christ still rests on solid evidence.[127] If we limit ourselves to the evidence in Philippians, we observe that Paul's use of the noun *faith* three times (1:25, 27; 2:17) and the verb *believe* once (1:29) to refer to the faith of the Philippians in Christ in the context of their experience of suffering prepares the reader to take his use of the noun *faith* in this verse (3:9) as a reference to faith in Christ that empowers Paul *to know the power of his resurrection and participation in his sufferings* (3:10). Paul backs up his challenge to the Philippians — *it has been granted to you on behalf*

127. A good way to enter into the extensive discussion on this subject is to read the debate between James Dunn (advocate of *faith in Christ*) and Richard Hays (advocate of *faithfulness of Christ*), reprinted in appendices 1 and 2 of Richard B. Hays, *The Faith of Jesus Christ* (2nd ed.; Grand Rapids: Eerdmans, 2002), 249-97. Arguments for "faithfulness of Christ" include: (1) faith (πίστις) followed by the genitive of a person other than Christ almost always refers to the faith or faithfulness of that person, e.g., faithfulness of God (Rom 3:3); faith of Abraham (Rom 4:12, 16); (2) the usual meaning of faith (πίστις) in Hellenistic literature is faithfulness; (3) the obedience of Christ, an important theme in Paul's theology (Phil 2:8; Rom 5:18-19), is aptly expressed in the references to the faithfulness of Christ; (4) an awkward redundancy is avoided in texts (Gal 2:16; 3:22; Rom 3:22; Phil 3:9) when the interpretation of the ambiguous phrase is taken as a reference to the faithfulness of Christ alongside a clear reference to belief in Christ. Arguments for *faith in Christ* include: (1) since Christ is the only object of faith in Paul's letters, it is not surprising that when faith is followed by the genitive of a person other than Christ the genitive is subjective and refers to the faithfulness of that person; (2) since Paul uses the references to human faith in Gen 15:6 and Hab 2:4 as a basis for his phrase "faith of Christ" (see Gal 3:6-12), this phrase refers to human faith in Christ; (3) although Paul refers to the obedience of Christ (Rom 5:19; Phil 2:8), he never explicitly calls Christ's obedience the faith or faithfulness of Christ; (4) the so-called redundancy of Paul's language does not require the interpretation "faithfulness of Christ," but clarifies the meaning of this ambiguous phrase as *faith in Christ.* Although this debate has spawned a great number of public conferences, books, and articles, in the end participants on both sides agree that Christ's work is the basis for the gift of righteousness from God and that faith in Christ is the way to receive the saving work of God in Christ. For excellent support of the traditional sense of *faith in Jesus Christ,* see Westerholm, *Perspectives Old and New on Paul,* 305-6; Moisés Silva, "Faith versus Works in Galatians," in *Justification and Variegated Nomism, Volume 2: The Paradoxes of Paul* (ed. D. A. Carson, Peter T. O'Brien, and Mark A. Seifrid; Grand Rapids: Baker Academic, 2004), 227-36.

of Christ not only to believe on him, but also to suffer for him (1:29) — with his own experience of *faith in Christ* and *participation in his sufferings* (3:9-10). Note that Paul specifically designates the act of believing as granted by God. Paul does not view faith as a human work or virtue. If he did, then righteousness through faith in Christ would be just another kind of self-achieved righteousness. Faith is a human response empowered by God's grace.[128] Second, the two uses of the noun *faith* in this verse serve to clarify the role and emphasize the importance of faith in Christ. The first use points to faith as the agency or means by which righteousness from God is received: *through faith in Christ.* The second use indicates the basis or foundation upon which this experience of being found in Christ having the righteousness from God rests: *on the basis of* faith. The article in this second use *(the faith)* is anaphoric, referring back to the first use. By referring twice to *faith in Christ* in his definition of the *righteousness from God,* Paul highlights the crucial difference between righteousness achieved by keeping the law and righteousness received by dependence on Christ. Paul is not advocating faith by itself as the means or basis of this extraordinary righteousness. Faith in Christ looks away from self-achievement and looks to Christ.

10 Paul's goals are all Christ-centered: *to gain Christ, be found in him,* and *know him.*[129] By restating his goals in these different ways, Paul keeps the focus completely on Christ and emphasizes that his relationship with Christ totally eclipses everything else in his life. Paul repeatedly expresses his desire to know Christ: *because of the surpassing worth of knowing Christ Jesus my Lord* (3:8), the aim of every step in the journey is *to know Christ* (3:10) until that final step when Christ will be fully known in *the resurrection from the dead* (3:11).[130] Here we see the main contrast that Paul is drawing be-

128. Beare, 119: "Faith for Paul is the necessary correlative of grace; see the striking phrase of Rom 3:16: 'for this reason it is of faith, that it may be based upon grace'. It is not a claim upon God, but a confession of total dependence upon God, and a continual recognition of helplessness to do anything of ourselves to better our condition before God; and a continual willingness to receive as a gift from God that which we can by no means procure or help to procure for ourselves."

129. Although the genitive of the articular infinitive expresses purpose, its connection to other elements in the sentence is ambiguous. The goal expressed in the articular infinitive *to know him* (τοῦ γνῶναι αὐτόν) may be parallel to the goals expressed by the ἵνα clause (*to gain Christ and be found in him;* see Barth, 103; Koperski, *The Knowledge of Christ Jesus My Lord,* 177; Silva, 189; O'Brien, 401), or it may be an epexegetical use to explain the meaning of the ἵνα clause (see BDF §400.8), or it may express the ultimate goal after the statement of the penultimate purpose in the ἵνα clause (see Fee, 327).

130. The aorist tense of the infinitive *to know* may be ingressive, denoting the beginning; complexive, denoting linear actions or repeated actions as a whole; or futuristic, denoting a future condition (see BDF §332). According to Beare, 123, the emphasis "is not on a gradual growth in knowledge, but on its final attainment, which must await the resurrection of the dead (v. 11)." Vincent, 103-4, says that Paul "is here speaking rather of his coming into a knowledge of the riches of Christ in the process of his experience." Fee, 326, asserts that knowing Christ is "both 'already' and 'not yet.'" Lohmeyer, 139-42, interprets knowing Christ as the experience of martyrdom.

tween his former life in Judaism and his present life in Christ: his overarching goal is no longer a faultless observance of the law; now his daily and ultimate purpose is to know Christ. Since the desire *to know him* is the goal of one who is *found in him,* this knowledge is relational and experiential. The purpose of life *in Christ* is personal, intimate knowledge of Christ.

Paul explicates the meaning of knowing Christ in terms of two objects of knowledge: *to know the power of his resurrection and participation in his sufferings.*[131] By using one definite article, Paul unites *the power* and *participation* to form a single entity.[132] Knowing *the power of his resurrection* and *participation in his sufferings* are two inseparable aspects of his experience of knowing Christ. It is impossible to know the power of his resurrection without participation in his sufferings. The unity of these two aspects of the knowledge of Christ leads to viewing them as contemporaneous: since knowing participation in his sufferings is the present experience of Paul, then knowing the power of his resurrection takes place in the present context of sufferings. Knowing the power of Christ's resurrection provides the incentive and strength to participate in the sufferings of Christ.[133] Certain elements in the context, however, also point to the future experience of knowing the power of Christ's resurrection. The structure of verses 10-11 presents a parallelism between two references to resurrection:[134]

A *the power of his resurrection*
  B *participation in his sufferings*
  B *becoming like him in his death*
A *attaining to the resurrection from the dead*

This parallelism indicates that the knowledge of the power of Christ's resurrection will be given in the future time concurrent with the resurrection from the dead. At that future time the *power of his resurrection* will be fully manifested when *the Lord Jesus Christ, by the power that enables him to bring everything under his control, will transform our lowly bodies so that they will be like his glorious body* (3:20-21).[135] Paul's emphasis on the future victory of Christ in this passage fills the present suffering with meaning and purpose.

131. After expressing his goal in the phrase *to know Christ,* Paul uses the conjunction *and* (καί) not to add two more objects of knowledge, but to clarify what it means *to know Christ.* This is an epexegetical use of *and* (καί) to explicate the meaning of the previous phrase. See BDF §442 (9); Gnilka, 195.

132. The definite articles before *participation* and *suffering* in some later manuscripts are not found in early witnesses (𝔓[46] א* A B).

133. O'Brien, 404.

134. Bloomquist, *The Function of Suffering in Philippians,* 180.

135. Koperski, *The Knowledge of Christ Jesus My Lord,* 187: "The power of Christ's resurrection is the power which will ultimately transform the body of our lowliness so that we are given the form of the glorious body of Christ (cf. 3:20-21), and it seems at first that this is what Paul intended to say in 3:10, probably with the intention of contrasting the final destiny of the opponents in 3:2 with that of Christians, as he has done in 1:28."

He presents a dynamic polarity between the present experience of Christ and the future consummation in Christ. The present knowledge of the resurrection of Christ guarantees the future promise of the complete knowledge of Christ by participation in his glorious resurrection life. Both the future and present aspects of the knowledge of Christ's resurrection power are essential components of Paul's portrayal of the Christian life. Without the future prospect of knowing Christ's resurrection power in his transformation of our lowly bodies to be like his resurrection body, our present suffering would be ultimately pointless and futile. Without the present knowledge of Christ's resurrection power in the midst of our suffering, we would have no assurance of the future victory.

The precise content of the knowledge of the *power of his resurrection* comes into sharper focus when we recall that the Christ hymn asserts that after Christ's death on the cross, *God exalted him to the highest place* (2:9). The *power of his resurrection* is ultimately God's power. Paul's announcement of Christ's resurrection was a testimony of what God did: "we have testified about God that he raised Christ from the dead" (1 Cor 15:15; Eph 1:19-20); "by his power God raised the Lord from the dead (1 Cor 6:14). These references demonstrate that the use of the passive voice in the gospel witness that "he was raised on the third day" (1 Cor 15:4) points to God, who raised him from the dead. Furthermore, the word *power (dynamis)* in Paul's vocabulary, related to his teaching on salvation, usually refers to the effective power of God.[136] "The gospel is "the power of God" (Rom 1:16); creation bears witness to God's "eternal power" (Rom 1:20); the message of the cross is "the power of God" (1 Cor 1:18). The power of God is demonstrated in the life of the believer by the power of the Holy Spirit (Rom 15:13; 1 Cor 2:4-5).[137] Paul knows by experience that the power of God that was demonstrated in the resurrection is now demonstrated by the power of the Spirit in his life and ministry.[138] In contrast to all his attempts to experience the power of God through strict observance of the law, Paul now knows the power of God by knowing Christ and the power of his resurrection.

Paul's own experience of knowing Christ began with knowing the power of his resurrection in his initial encounter with Christ. That transforming encounter led Paul to suffer for *defending and confirming the gospel* (1:7). But in his experience of suffering, Paul grew in the knowledge of

136. BDAG, 262-63; O. Betz, "Might," *NIDNTT* 2:604-6. See Rom 1:16, 20; 1 Cor 1:18; 2:5; 2 Cor 4:7; 6:7; 13:4; Gal 3:5; Eph 1:9, 21; 3:7, 16, 20; Col 1:11, 29; 1 Thess 1:5; 2 Tim 1:8.

137. 1 Cor 2:4-5: "My message and my preaching were not with wise and persuasive words, but with a demonstration of the Spirit's power, so that your faith might not rest on human wisdom, but on God's power."

138. Rom 8:11: "if the Spirit of him who raised Jesus from the dead is living in you, he who raised Jesus from the dead will also give life to your mortal bodies because of his Spirit who lives in you." Beare, 122: "The power of the resurrection is the life-giving power of God, the power which he manifests in raising Christ from the dead, and which he now manifests in the new life which the Christian receives from the risen Christ and shares with him."

Christ by *participation in his sufferings.* This *participation (koinōnia)* was not merely an attitude of self-identification with Christ. He was not simply engaged in psychologically reframing his story. Rather, Paul speaks as one who intentionally participated in the narrative of Christ so that his story was a genuine reenactment and a purposeful extension of the narrative of Christ. Participation is not a passive sharing similar to sharing in a common humanity or ethnic background, "but rather involves a relationship which one decides to enter."[139] By deciding to consider his status as a loss for the sake of Christ (3:7-8), Paul entered into relationship with Christ, who did not consider his status as something to be used to his own advantage but emptied himself (2:7-8). As a result of his choosing to participate in the narrative of Christ, Paul's sufferings were in reality the sufferings of Christ.

Paul's development of the concept of *participation (koinōnia)* places the human *partnership* for the sake of the common venture of advancing the gospel (1:5) within the divine-human communion with the Spirit (2:1) and communion with the Spirit within the divine-human participation in the sufferings of Christ (3:10). The *partnership in the gospel* resulting from *common sharing in the Spirit* leads to *participation* in the sufferings of Christ. Just as human partnership in the gospel requires an active participation of the partners, so sharing in the Spirit and participation in the sufferings of Christ involve deliberate decisions as well.

The term *participation (koinōnia)* points to the solidarity of all believers who have chosen to participate in the sufferings of Christ.[140] Paul is not presenting his participation as an individualistic enterprise reserved only for martyrs. This participation in the sufferings of Christ cannot happen in isolation from others. According to Paul, all believers are called to share in the sufferings of Christ (1:29-30; 1:7). By their experience in community of *participation in his sufferings,* believers grow in their knowledge of Christ. The longing to know *participation in his sufferings* is a longing for a *community* experience. By suffering together for the sake of Christ, believers are drawn together in Christ.

The genitive case of the word *sufferings* after the term *participation (koinōnia)* is best taken as an objective genitive since the genitive after this term designates the objects shared in common by the partnership, the *koinōnia.*[141] In his use of the plural word *sufferings,* Paul indicates a wide range of afflictions endured by believers as a result of their identification with Christ.[142] Paul's references to his chains (1:7, 13, 14, 17), his past and

139. Koperski, *The Knowledge of Christ Jesus My Lord,* 248.

140. G. Walter Hansen, "Transformation of Relationships," in *New Testament Greek and Exegesis,* 191-92.

141. H. Seesemann, *Der Begriff KOINŌNIA im Neuen Testament* (Giessen: Töpelmann, 1933), 83-85.

142. Against the interpretation of Hawthorne/Martin, 198, that equates these sufferings with the death of Christ and participation in his sufferings as another way of saying that believers are crucified with Christ and baptized into his death.

present struggles (1:30), and the suffering experienced by the Philippian believers (1:28-29) all provide specific descriptions of the sufferings of Christ. Although Paul does refer in other places (see Rom 6:3-10) to our inward union with Christ in his death, his primary emphasis in this context is on the outward sufferings of Christians.[143] Paul, however, does not draw a sharp line between inward union with Christ in his death and outward sufferings for Christ. As he tells his readers, the gift of believing Christ is linked with the gift of suffering for him (1:29). In Paul's experience, knowing Christ by believing in him led to knowing Christ by suffering for the sake of Christ. Paul is not a masochist who had suffering as his goal. Suffering was not a goal in itself, but it was the inevitable consequence of believing in Christ. For the sake of Christ Paul *lost all things* (3:8).

By his participation in the sufferings of Christ, Paul is *becoming like him in his death.* The participle, *being conformed,* expresses the result of *sufferings.*[144] Although this participle occurs only here in the NT, its root word, *form,* takes us back to the Christ hymn: being in the *form* of God, Christ took the *form* of a servant (2:5, 7). As a servant, Christ was *obedient unto death* (2:8). Here again we can see how Paul is intentionally identifying his experience with the narrative of Christ. Living *in Christ* means living in the story of Christ, being conformed to the pattern of Christ's narrative.

Being conformed to his death can be interpreted in several ways: (1) Paul may be referring to his martyrdom. Just as the sufferings of Jesus led to his death on the cross, so also Paul's sufferings led to his execution.[145] Paul's reference to resurrection from the dead in the next verse may indicate that he is thinking about his physical death and resurrection. Yet, Paul seems to be viewing his whole life, not just the end of his life, as a process of being conformed to Christ's death by his participation in Christ's suffering. In other words, this last phrase in verse 10 explains what is happening to Paul during his whole experience of participation in Christ's sufferings.

(2) *Being conformed to his death* may also be interpreted as a reference to the inward experience of dying to sin by being united with Christ in his death: "For we know that our old self was crucified with him so that the body ruled by sin might be done away with, that we should no longer be slaves to sin" (Rom 6:6).[146] Certainly Paul is concerned in this letter with being free from sin, *pure and blameless* (1:10; 2:14). But the difficulty with interpreting this phrase in the light of the parallel with Romans 6:1-6 is that it limits the reference of *being conformed to his death* to the beginning of life in Christ since this passage refers to being united with Christ's death through

143. See Koperski, *The Knowledge of Christ Jesus My Lord,* 256-65.

144. Beare, 124: "The hazards and batterings to which he is subjected in his work for Christ are the concrete external means by which he is being conformed to Christ's death."

145. Lohmeyer, 139-42.

146. Silva, 190: "The parallels with Rom. 6:1-11 ('we who died to sin,' 'baptized into his death,' 'buried with Him,' etc.) make it clear that Paul is not thinking primarily of his physical death." See also Hawthorne and Martin, 198-99.

baptism: "all of us who were baptized into Christ Jesus were baptized into his death" (Rom 6:3). Paul is not referring to the beginning of his life in Christ, but to his entire experience of participation in Christ's sufferings as a process of being conformed to his death.[147]

(3) *Being conformed to his death* may be interpreted as a reference to Paul's obedience in his faithful proclamation of the gospel of Christ. The link between *partnership (koinōnia)* in the gospel and *participation (koinōnia)* in his sufferings connects sufferings to the proclamation of the gospel, and those sufferings for the sake of the gospel are the means by which Paul is conformed to the death of Christ. Paul's reference to Christ's death is primarily a reference to Christ's obedience: *he humbled himself by becoming obedient unto death* (2:8). The main point of application that Paul takes from the Christ hymn is obedience: immediately after the hymn he calls his readers to obedience (2:12). Their obedience will cause them to *shine like stars in the sky* as they *hold firmly to the word of life* (2:15-16). Paul calls them to express their obedience by living *in a manner worthy of the gospel of Christ* (1:27). Their obedience will inevitably cause them to face opposition and to suffer (1:28-29). And their suffering will continually shape them to be like Christ, who was obedient unto death.

These three interpretations do not need to be set against each other as separate alternatives. Paul's experience of being conformed to Christ's death may well include his sense of facing his own execution, his awareness that he was baptized into the death of Christ to be freed from sin, and his appreciation that his sufferings for the gospel are shaping his obedience so that he will reflect Christ, who was obedient unto death.

11 Death does not have the last word. Paul expresses his hope that he will participate in Christ's victory over death: *and so, somehow, attaining to the resurrection from the dead.* Paul can endure the process of being conformed to Christ's death through participation in his sufferings in the present because he knows the power of Christ's resurrection in the present and he anticipates his own resurrection from the dead in the future. Paul distinguishes between his present experience of the power of Christ's resurrection and the future resurrection by adding the prepositional prefix *from* to the noun *resurrection* and by adding the prepositional phrase *from the dead.*[148] The repetition of the preposition *from* emphasizes that this resurrection is a resurrection *from* among those who are physically dead.[149] Paul's

147. Fee, 334 n. 67: "Paul's concern is first of all with his and the Philippians' ongoing sufferings as God's way of bringing them into conformity to Christ in his death, and thus with the whole of life as reflecting a cruciform existence."

148. The majority of MSS have τῶν νεκρῶν, but τὴν ἐκ νεκρῶν is solidly supported by all early and diverse witnesses (𝔓[46] ℵ A B D P Ψ).

149. Gnilka, 197. Lincoln, *Paradise Now and Not Yet*, 92: "ἡ ἐξανάστασιν τὴν ἐκ νεκρῶν (verse 11), as compared with the more straightforward ἡ ἀναστάσεως of verse 10, is an expression used only here by Paul, and emphasizes in the strongest way that he has the final bodily resurrection in view."

focus here is not on the present experience of union with the resurrected Christ that makes him exclaim: *For to me, to live is Christ* (1:21).[150] Instead Paul is emphasizing the futurity of the final and complete victory over death. His emphasis on the futurity of resurrection from the dead is yet another way of combating the false teaching of perfectionists who are claiming their attainment of complete perfection in the present.[151]

Along with his emphasis on the futurity of resurrection, Paul seems to express some sense of uncertainty regarding his attainment of the future resurrection from the dead in his phrase *and so, somehow, attaining to.*[152] This note of uncertainty may be an expression of Paul's self-distrust similar to that in 1 Corinthians 9:27: "I strike a blow to my body and make it my slave so that after I have preached to others, I myself will not be disqualified for the prize."[153] Paul was concerned to avoid a prideful presumptuousness.[154] He did not want his readers to think that he had earned or deserved the future resurrection from the dead as a result of knowing the present power of Christ's resurrection and participation in his sufferings. Any thought that Paul was triumphantly claiming that he could attain to the resurrection from the dead flatly contradicts his emphasis in this passage that he did not value his own righteousness based on his achievement of keeping the law, but *the righteousness that comes from God on the basis of faith* in Christ. Although Paul has no doubt about the reality of the future resurrection from the dead, as can be seen in his confident expectation that Christ *will transform our lowly bodies so that they will be like his glorious body* (3:21), he does express an attitude of humility when he contemplates his own personal participation in this awesome future event.[155] How could I, Paul, ever hope to

150. See the focus on the present experience of resurrection with Christ in Rom 6:4-11; Col 3:1-3; Eph 2:6.

151. Gundry-Volf, *Paul and Perseverance,* 254.

152. BDAG, 279, gives the meaning "if perhaps, if somehow" to the conditional particles εἴ πως. The verb *to attain* (καταντήσω) means "to reach a condition or goal, to arrive at" (BDAG, 523). This expression conveys "a degree of contingency often underrated by commentators" (Bockmuehl, 217).

153. Silva, 192-93. Other interpreters of Paul's expression of uncertainty (εἴ πως) offer alternative meanings: (1) while the goal of the resurrection is certain, the way or route by which the apostle will reach it is unclear. . . . he might reach the resurrection through martyrdom (or by some other kind of death), or he might be alive at the coming of Christ" (O'Brien, 413); (2) "By introducing his hope to 'attain to the resurrection from the dead' with εἴ πως, Paul removes the realization of this hope from the realm of human possibility and confesses it to be only a 'divine possibility.' Christian perfection as attainment of the resurrection depends on an act of God" (Gundry-Volf, *Paul and Perseverance,* 258).

154. "If you think that you are standing firm, be careful that you don't fall" (1 Cor 10:10).

155. For other explanations of Paul's uncertainty, see R. E. Otto, "'If Possible I May Attain the Resurrection from the Dead' (Philippians 3:11)," *CBQ* 57 (1995), 324-40, argues that Paul's uncertainty relates to the challenge of remaining faithful in martyrdom and attaining to the special resurrection accorded to martyrs. But Otto fails to demonstrate that Paul explicitly restricts his reference to a special resurrection accorded to martyrs. A. Perri-

be involved in the ultimate triumph of God over death? *Somehow I might attain to it* is all that he can say.

No other power — neither the power of the Roman Empire nor the power of the Jewish religion — can compete with the power that can raise the dead. Paul wants his readers to know Christ, whom God has already exalted above all earthly powers, so that they will turn away from earthly attractions and cling to Christ alone.

C. Pressing On toward the Goal (3:12-14)

> [12]*Not that I have already obtained all this, or have already arrived at my goal, but I press on to take hold of that for which Christ Jesus took hold of me.* [13]*Brothers and sisters, I do not consider myself yet to have taken hold of it. But one thing I do: Forgetting what is behind and straining toward what is ahead,* [14]*I press on toward the goal to win the prize for which God has called me heavenward in Christ Jesus.*

Paul knows that his passionate intention *to know Christ* does not in itself make him perfect. His decision to *consider everything a loss because of the surpassing worth of knowing Christ* was only the beginning of a daily discipline to *press on toward the goal.* The authenticity of faith in Christ cannot be measured only by the intensity of one's initial decision to receive Christ. Receiving Christ is a lifetime adventure.

Paul's description of his daily discipline of *straining toward what is ahead* serves as a double-edged sword. On the one hand, Paul is correcting an attitude of moral perfectionism by stressing that he himself has *not already obtained all this or already arrived at* [his] *goal* (3:12). Unlike his previous attitude when he considered himself to be *faultless* as to *righteousness based on the law* (3:6), he now ardently denies any claim to perfection. His denial of perfectionism contradicts not only those Jewish Christians in his day who were claiming and promising perfection by way of membership in the Jewish people, but also perfectionists in every age who are advertising their procedures as the way to procure instant perfection.[156] On the other hand, Paul is also correcting an attitude of moral libertinism by emphasiz-

---

man, "The Pattern of Christ's Sufferings: Colossians 1:24 and Philippians 3:10-11," *TynBul* 42 (1991), 62-79, proposes that Paul uncertainty comes from his view that the *parousia* might occur before he dies and prohibit him from completing his participation in the sufferings of Christ and attaining to the resurrection from the dead.

156. Most commentators see Paul's denial of perfection as a warning against Jewish-Christian Judaizers who advocate circumcision and the law as the way to attain perfection (see O'Brien, 418; Silva, 197; Martin and Hawthorne, 205; Bockmuehl, 221). Beare (130) suggests that Paul is correcting perfectionists within the Christian community "who imagine that they have been admitted to the highest level of the Christian life and have no more progress to make."

ing that he is passionately pressing on toward the goal to win the prize for which God has called him. Paul offers his example to counter many who live as *enemies of the cross . . . : their god is their stomach, their glory is in their shame, and their mind is on earthly things* (3:17-19).[157] The pressures of the surrounding pagan culture dampen and even extinguish the enthusiasm and determination of Christians to press on to maturity in their obedience to the call of God. Many succumbed to these pressures, gave up their commitment to Christ, and fell back into the popular immorality of their culture. In this section Paul seeks to inspire them to get back in the race and live up to their commitment to Christ. Paul's dramatic imagery of his race cuts both ways: perfectionists who claim to have already arrived at the goal and libertines who have dropped out of the race are both called to get back on track and *press on.*[158]

12 Paul begins with a double *not already* to emphasize that he is still running the race and has *not already* reached the finish line: *not that I have already obtained all this, or have already arrived at my goal.*[159] Since the transitive verb *obtained* requires an object, translations usually supply one. But the Greek text does not include an object. A plausible meaning of this verb in this context is "to enter into a close relationship, receive, make one's own, apprehend/comprehend." This meaning supports the suggestion that Christ is the object of the verb: Paul has not already fully apprehended Christ.[160] Two times at the end of this sentence Paul uses an intensified form of the same verb to confirm that his desire is *to take hold of that for which Christ Jesus took hold of me.*[161] Ever since Paul was grasped and apprehended by Christ, he has desired to grasp and comprehend Christ. But "to know the incomprehensible greatness of Christ demands a lifetime of arduous inquiry."[162] Paul's desire to *gain Christ and be found in him* (3:8-9) and *to know Christ* (3:10) engages him in an intimate relationship with Christ that is a dynamic process of intellectual apprehension and moral transformation.[163]

157. The discussion of these verses below includes a description of these people.

158. Silva, 197: "In sorting out the various viewpoints we must note that perfectionism and antinomianism are not mutually exclusive principles." Silva points out that 1 John and Galatians were also written to combat both perfectionism and antinomianism. In the Galatian churches, the intrusion of Judaistic teachers who promoted law-keeping actually incited the sinful tendencies to break the law and indulge in immoral behavior (Gal 5:13-26).

159. Lincoln, *Paradise Now and Not Yet,* 93, says that Paul's "double 'not already'" counters "any propaganda which announces that the fullness of resurrection existence and heavenly glory can be experienced now."

160. BDAG, 584, gives this meaning for the verb λαμβάνω in Phil 3:12 and supplies Christ as the object of the verb: "the mystical apprehension of Christ."

161. The addition of the prepositional prefix κατα to the verb λαμβάνω gives the word καταλαμβάνω the meaning of "to grasp" both in the sense of "to seize, arrest" (John 8:3) and "to understand, comprehend" (Acts 25:25; Eph 3:18). See BDAG, 519-20.

162. Martin and Hawthorne, 206.

163. O'Brien, 421; Martin and Hawthorne, 206: "Paul means to say that he does not lay claim to having fully grasped the meaning of Christ at this point in his experience. Christ —

His first denial that he has already fully grasped Christ leads to his second denial that he has "already become perfect."[164] Although this is the only time that the verb "become perfect" is found in Paul's letters, the cognate adjective "perfect" occurs seven times with a range of meanings. The adjective means "meeting the highest standard" of goodness and virtue (Rom 12:2), "being mature, full grown" (1 Cor 14:20; Eph 4:13), "being fully developed in a moral sense" (Col 4:12), and "being a cult initiate" (probably Phil 3:15; Col 1:28).[165] The use of the adjective in 1 Corinthians 13:10 points to the future when "the perfect comes and what is in part disappears." In that context, Paul contrasts the present imperfection and the future perfection: "Now we see only a reflection as in a mirror; then we shall see face to face. Now I know in part; then I shall know fully, even as I am fully known" (1 Cor 13:12). This contrast comes very close to the point of Paul's denial that he has "already become perfect" in Philippians 3:12: precisely because he has not yet already fully grasped Christ, he has not already become perfect. Only when he sees Christ face to face will he be totally transformed by Christ's power to be like him (3:20-21). Paul anticipates that he will become perfect in the "future-eschatological" sense, but only on the day of Christ and by the power of Christ.[166] Until then, he honestly admits his imperfection.

His imperfection, however, does not discourage him from pursuing growth in his relationship with Christ: *but I press on to take hold of that for which Christ Jesus took hold of me.* The adversative conjunction *but* reveals Paul's unrelenting determination to press on despite the limitations caused by his present imperfection. Rather than causing him to give up and quit, Paul's sense of incompleteness compels him to *press on.* This term *press on* means "to move rapidly and decisively toward an objective."[167] Paul used the same word to prove that he was zealous to the point of *persecuting the church* (3:6). Previously, his zeal for the law drove him to run after and pursue the church. Now he is running after and pursuing Christ, to know

---

the full significance of this person — is the missing object of the verb ἔλαβον." Other suggestions for a direct object for the verb ἔλαβον include: (1) the resurrection from the dead, based on the immediately previous phrase in 3:11 (J. Harold Greenlee, "Saint Paul — Perfect but Not Perfected 3:12," *Notes on Translation* 4 [1990], 53-55); (2) all that is included in vv. 8-11 (Vincent, 107); (3) the prize for which God has called me heavenward as stated in 3:14 (Beare, 129); (4) the righteousness that comes from God referred to in 3:9 (A. F. J. Klijn, "Paul's Opponents in Philippians III," *NovT* 7 [1964]: 278-84, especially 281-82). This last suggestion draws some support from the variant textual reading (ἢ ἤδη δεδικαίωμαι — "or already have been justified") inserted after ἔλαβον in 𝔓[46] and D. But the MSS evidence strongly favors the omission of this phrase (Silva, 204; O'Brien, 418).

164. TNIV offers *already arrived at my goal* as a translation of the verb τετελείωμαι. This perfect passive use of the verb τελειόω points to the present results of a process that has already been completed. Paul strongly asserts that the process to "become perfect" (see BDAG, 996, for this meaning of τελειόω in Phil 3:12) has *not already* been completed.

165. BDAG, 995-96.

166. Silva, 201.

167. BDAG, 254.

Christ. When Paul uses the verb *to take hold of* to state the object of his pursuit, he does not provide an object for this verb. Yet the context indicates that Paul is pursuing the apprehension of Christ. The ultimate reason for Paul's pursuit of the apprehension of Christ is Christ's apprehension of Paul: "because I was apprehended by Christ."[168] Christ's apprehension of Paul means that Paul has been captured by Christ, taken hold of by Christ, and Christ will not let go of him. *Because* he has been apprehended by Christ, Paul has all the reason, the endurance, the assurance, and the joy he needs to pursue Christ even if he has not already comprehended Christ.[169] He is running hard after Christ with his heart wide open to receive Christ because Christ has already received him and arrested him by his love. Divine grace is the source and goal of the human pursuit.

13 Paul emphatically repeats his denial of perfection: *Brothers and sisters, I do not consider myself yet to have taken hold of it.* The direct address, *brothers and sisters,* reminds his readers of his personal, familial relationship with them and emphasizes the importance of his assertion that he is not yet perfect. He reaches out, places both hands on their shoulders, looks in their eyes, and says, "I really mean what I just said, I'm not perfect yet." The verb *consider* indicates that his admission of imperfection is not the result of an emotional upset or chronic melancholy. It means "to give careful thought to a matter" and "to hold a view about something" after thorough evaluation.[170] After a careful assessment of himself, Paul draws a perfectly rational conclusion: *I have not yet taken hold of it.*[171] The use of the two personal pronouns at the beginning of the sentence, *I myself,* places strong emphasis on the personal nature of Paul's self-evaluation and implies a contrast to the opinion that others have of themselves.[172] Apparently, others consider themselves to be perfect; in their self-assessment, they are totally satisfied with themselves and confident that they have already arrived at the apex of human achievement. "In strong contrast with self-righteousness and religious conceit," Paul has a sane estimate of his own spiritual, moral progress.[173] A

168. TNIV translates the idiom ἐφ' ᾧ *that for which;* this idiom can also express a causal connection: "because" (see BDF §235 [2]). The causal meaning for this idiom seems to fit better in this context (*contra* Bockmuehl, 221), since Paul's point is that Christ's arrest and apprehension of him caused his lifelong pursuit of Christ.

169. Barth, 108.

170. BDAG, 597-98.

171. The textual evidence is very finely balanced between the reading "I do *not* (οὐ) consider that I have made it on my own" (NRSV) and the reading "I do *not* consider myself *yet* (οὔπω) to have apprehended." The major uncials ℵ A D support οὔπω *(not yet);* 𝔓[46] B and the Majority Text (𝔐) support οὐ *(not).* The meaning is the same either way. The context supports the insertion of *not yet* since the previous sentence emphasizes *not already.* But this point may be the reason why scribes changed οὐ to οὔπω on the basis of the context (Silva, 204).

172. Lightfoot, 152: "St. Paul is not contrasting his own estimate of himself with other people's estimate of him, but his estimate of himself with others' estimate of themselves."

173. Vincent, 109.

close examination of his life reveals that he has not *taken hold of it.* For the third time, Paul uses the verb *take hold of.* Paul seems to employ both basic meanings of this verb: "to win, attain" and "to understand, comprehend."[174] Here again the TNIV adds an object, *it,* to complete the meaning of a transitive verb, but Paul did not supply an object. In accordance with his use of the same verb in the previous sentence and in keeping with the entire context, Paul has the knowledge of Christ and his personal relationship with Christ in mind. He has not yet attained to complete conformity to the standard of Christ's obedience unto death on the cross, nor has he completely understood the full significance of Christ.[175] He recognizes that his partial knowledge of Christ is a very long way from knowing Christ as much he desires to know Christ.

In the light of his realization that he has not yet attained the knowledge of Christ that he desires, he has only one goal: *But one thing I do.* TNIV adds the verb *I do* to make a complete sentence, but Paul's elliptical interjection makes sense as it stands in this context: *But one thing!*[176] The highest priority in his life captivates his full attention and demands total concentration. The tyranny of urgent needs, the clamor of popular voices, the top news of the day all take a pale second place to the one overarching goal of Paul's life. All his thoughts, emotions, and decisions are focused on this fixed point: *One thing!*

Paul paints a picture of his pursuit of *one thing* with two bold brushstrokes, two parallel participial clauses: *Forgetting what is behind and straining toward what is ahead.*[177] These two clauses give a dramatic portrayal of a runner who refuses to look back over his shoulder, but keeps straining every fiber of his being forward toward the goal. Paul does not tell us what the things behind him are, nor does he teach us how to forget these kinds of things. Perhaps he is thinking all the way back to his days as a zealous persecutor of the church (3:5-6).[178] We know that Paul forgot all the accomplishments and failures of the time before his encounter with Christ in the sense that he considered all those things as worthless as garbage compared to knowing Christ (3:7-8). But Paul's reference in this context to *what is behind* points to those things in his life as a believer in Christ. His point is that even though he believes in Christ he has not yet fully apprehended Christ. *What is behind* is everything that he has already achieved and attained in his walk with Christ.[179] For a long time, for at least twenty years, he has known Christ and served him. He could easily point back to a long list of achieve-

174. BDAG, 519-20.

175. Martin and Hawthorne, 208.

176. BDF §481; BDAG, 292: "Just one thing!"

177. The parallelism is accentuated in the Greek text by the use of the conjunctions μὲν . . . δέ, which could be translated, "on the one hand . . . and on the other hand." Schenk, 263.

178. Martin and Hawthorne, 209.

179. Barth, 109; O'Brien, 429.

ments in his ministry as an apostle, to special revelations given to him by the Lord, and to major theological arguments developed in his messages and in his letters. He has already accomplished so much, taught so much, and walked in the Spirit so faithfully that he of all people could say that he had reached the goal, arrived at the apex, and fully apprehended all that he was called to attain. But instead, Paul forgets what he has achieved so far. Of course, he didn't forget these things in the sense that he was unable even to call them to mind. In fact, his letters are full of references to his past experiences as a believer in Christ.[180] But he did not let his mind dwell on these things; he did not keep turning over in his mind the good old days of active service before he was imprisoned; he did not constantly remind himself of all his achievements nor continually recount those special high points of his intimate relationship with Christ.[181] He forgets, continually and intentionally forgets, what is behind in order to press on. He is not distracted by all the trophies of the past. He is able to move exuberantly into the future because he decisively throws away the burdens of the past. Forgetting is not a passive loss of memory; no, it is an active, continuous discipline of the mind and heart.[182] Although he did not actually forget the past, he emphatically chose to disregard it. He forcefully rejected it. He openly declared a nonobservance of his past achievements.[183]

Paul's practice of *forgetting* the past gave him the freedom for *straining* toward the future. This is the only time this word *straining* appears in the NT. This verb means to "exert oneself to the uttermost."[184] It graphically portrays Paul running a race: his body "is bent forward, his hand is outstretched towards the goal, and his eye is fastened upon it."[185] Every thought and every emotion reaches out in eager anticipation of arriving at the goal. While Paul clearly refutes perfectionism in his self-portrait, at the same time he also resists the trend to turn from perfectionism to hedonism. The temptation to drop out of the race and simply "enjoy life" seduced many to *set their mind on earthly things* (3:19). In contrast, Paul's image of himself as a runner inspires passionate perseverance in the life of faith in Christ.[186] Faith is not simply a decision in the past or a static state of existence; faith is running a race, *straining toward what is ahead.*[187] Paul desires to

180. For example, he refers to special revelations (2 Cor 12:1-4), a long list of things he has suffered in the course of his work (2 Cor 11:23-33), his accomplishments as an apostle (Rom 15:19-24), and his hard work as an apostle (1 Cor 15:10).

181. Vincent, 109: "He does not use the memory of what God has wrought in him and through him to encourage self-satisfaction and relaxation."

182. Müller, 171.

183. Schenk, 263.

184. BDAG, 361.

185. Vincent, 110.

186. Fee, 347: "Perfectionism is hardly an issue; but perseverance with regard to Christ and the gospel is."

187. Bockmuehl, 222: "Faith for Paul has an essentially incomplete and future dimension."

encourage *progress and joy in the faith* (1:25). *Progress in the faith* requires stretching beyond past and present accomplishments and reaching out to seize every opportunity to grow in faith.

14 The two clauses, *forgetting* and *straining toward,* modify the main verb, *I press on,* by explaining how Paul is able to *press on.*[188] Paul's manner of running is characterized by forgetting and straining toward. Now he expands his picture of his race to include imagery of the finish line, the goal of the race. In this race Paul is not yet at the finish line; he has not completed the race; so he must *press on.* For the second time, Paul uses this verb to connote moving "decisively toward an objective."[189] The repetition reminds the reader of Paul's daily pursuit of his goal: he keeps on running; he never gives up, slacks off, or sits back in smug self-satisfaction. Instead of saying, "I ran the race and I reached the goal," or, "I ran the race, am burned out, and I give up," he says, "I am running the race toward the goal." Even though he has not yet reached the goal, the not yet "does not by any means appear to be a check or a sedative."[190] The not yet is an incentive to *press on toward the goal.*

The word *goal* simply means the "mark" or "target."[191] The runner keeps looking at the goal, concentrates on the goal, and disregards everything else but the goal. Although the actual content of the goal is not specifically defined by Paul, the image of the goal carries forward the thrust of Paul's point: running the race of faith in Christ demands concentration on the finish line. Whether the finish line is being with Christ at death, as Paul contemplates in 1:23 *(to depart and be with Christ),* or the return of Christ from heaven, as Paul envisions in 3:20 *(we eagerly await a Savior from there),* Paul is determined to run the race well all the way to the finish line. Again, the imagery implies that Paul has not yet completed the race; there are still more laps to run before he reaches the finish line. At the same time, however, the imagery of concentrating on the finish line emphasizes that faith in Christ demands the constant discipline of keeping our eyes on the completion of the race. Running half the race and then sitting on the sidelines to watch others run is not an option.

The reason for running this race of faith in Christ is *to win the prize for which God has called me heavenward in Christ Jesus.*[192] In the Hellenistic games, the *prize* was "an award for exceptional performance."[193] This im-

188. Martin and Hawthorne, 209 defines the two participles in v. 13 as "circumstantial participles of manner."

189. BDAG, 254.

190. Barth, 107.

191. BDAG, 931: the same word (σκοπόν) also denotes a target in archery. The cognate verb (σκοπέω) means "to pay careful attention to; to keep one's eyes on."

192. The TNIV paraphrase, *to win the prize,* accurately translates the prepositional phrase "unto the prize" (εἰς τὸ βραβεῖον) in a way that helpfully expresses the sense of purpose expressed by the preposition εἰς. BDAG, 290, lists a meaning of εἰς as "to denote purpose" and gives numerous examples, including Luke 5:4; Rom 9:17; 14:9; 2 Cor 2:9.

193. BDAG, 183.

age of running to win a prize appears in Paul's challenge to the Corinthian believers: "Do you not know that in the race all runners run, but only one gets the prize? Run in such a way as to get the prize" (1 Cor 9:24). Paul precludes any illusion that his own performance merits *the prize* by asserting that *God has called me heavenward in Christ Jesus.* All of Paul's strenuous effort responds to and is empowered by the gracious initiative of God's call.[194] A precise explanation of the connection between *the prize* and *the call of God* confronts the difficulty of defining the genitive case of *the call* as it relates to *the prize* ("the prize of the upward call of God"). If this is a genitive of apposition, then the prize is the upward call of God.[195] The difficulty with this definition of call is that it places the reception of the call in the future. But Paul uses the word *call* as a technical term to refer to the act of God that "brings the one called into fellowship with Christ (1 Cor 1:9) and at the same time into fellowship with other members of his body."[196] The call of God stands at the beginning, not the end, of the race that Paul runs.

Another way of relating *the prize* and *the call* draws from the imagery of the Hellenistic games, where the judge would call the winner up to receive a prize.[197] But this definition of *call* overstates its cultural connotations and understates its theological content in Paul's letters.[198] Although Paul employs the imagery of running in the Olympic games, his language conveys his theological perspective: God's call initiates the relationship of believers in Christ, beginning with conversion and continuing to the future communion with Christ after death. The attainment of the prize of being with Christ at the end of the race is the fulfillment of God's call at the beginning of the race.[199]

If God's call is the invitation to press on toward the prize of communion with Christ, then the genitive case of *call* is a subjective genitive: God's call gives believers the promise of the prize.[200] This interpretation fits well with Paul's use of the term *call* as the "effectual, efficient divine calling which now takes place through the gospel and by which God has called the

194. E. Stauffer, "βραβεῖον," *TDNT* 1:638: "This certainly does not mean that man decides his own destiny by his own willing and running (R. 9:16). The prior decision is made by God alone, who issues the call. . . . By this divine act, however, man is summoned to supreme activity."

195. NEB: "I press towards the goal to win the prize which is God's call to the life above, in Christ Jesus." Lincoln, *Paradise Now and Not Yet,* 94: "Such an upward call to heavenly existence is not attained in this life, he is saying, but is the goal for which we aim, the prize which lies ahead at the end of the race."

196. L. Coenen, "Call," *NIDNTT* 1:275. See K. L. Schmidt, "καλέω," *TDNT* 3:492.

197. Collange, 118.

198. Fee (349 n. 49) notes that this definition "seems more fanciful than real, since there is no evidence that such an announcement was ever termed a κλῆσις, and this word is an especially Pauline one, full of theological grist that this suggestion would neutralize."

199. J. Eckert, "καλέω," *EDNT* 2:243.

200. Vincent, 111; Bockmuehl, 223.

church to faith itself as well as to the whole of the new life of faith."[201] God's call draws men and women into relationship with his Son through the preaching of the gospel and gives them the experience and the prospect of living and growing *in Christ Jesus*. God's call unites believers with Christ and the members of the body of Christ; "the upward call of God in Christ Jesus" points to the relationship Paul already enjoys, and *the prize*, the continuation of the relationship that he anticipates.[202] The word *heavenward* indicates both the direction of the call and the origin of the call. God's call is a calling from above and a calling to a heavenly reward.[203] In his encounter with the risen Christ, Paul experienced God's call from above. As a result he pressed on all his life with the eager anticipation of the future prize of being with Christ and knowing Christ in the heavenly realm, free from all earthly limitations.

The future goal of winning the prize captured Paul's complete attention, set him free from the tyranny of the past, and filled his present life with the incentive to press on to take hold of all that Christ had called him to be and do. *Forgetting what is behind*, Paul is *straining toward what is ahead* in order to know Christ.

D. Mentoring Others (3:15-17)

> 15*All of us, then, who are mature should take such a view of things. And if on some point you think differently, that too God will make clear to you.*
> 16*Only let us live up to what we have already attained.* 17*Join together in following my example, brothers and sisters, and just as you have us as a model, keep your eyes on those who live as we do.*

In Paul's self-portrait, his eyes are always focused on Christ: he reevaluates his life before Christ in the light of the surpassing worth of knowing Christ (3:4-9); he concentrates in the present on being like Christ (3:10); and he looks into the future with eager anticipation of winning the prize, the reward of being with Christ (3:11-14). His Christ-centered vision determines the way that he views his past, his present, and his future. Now Paul directs the Philippian church to *take such a view of things*. When they adopt his Christ-centered perspective on life, they *will join together in following* his example and align themselves with all who live as he does.

15 Paul gives direction for *all of us who are mature*. The apparent contradiction between the use of the verb *teleioō* to deny perfection in verse 12

201. Herman Ridderbos, *Paul: An Outline of His Theology* (Grand Rapids: Eerdmans, 1975), 235.

202. Fowl, 163, quotes patristic commentators who emphasize the "ever-deepening communion with the triune God in a way that shows how we can never be sated in our desire for communion with God. The more one attains, the more one desires."

203. Vincent, 111; Barth, 109.

("I have not already become perfect") and the use of cognate noun *teleioi* to claim perfection in verse 15 ("all of us who are perfect") forces the reader to consider the meaning and relationship of these assertions regarding perfection. A reasonable approach toward resolving this contradiction is to see how these texts mirror the historical context. Behind the entire passage stands the specter of opponents who advocated perfectionism by assimilation with the Jewish people through circumcision and keeping the law (3:1-4).[204] Paul eschews perfectionism by relating his own personal revolution from his *faultless* law-centered life to his present Christ-centered life (3:4-11) and by stressing that he has not already attained perfection in his race toward the goal of knowing Christ (3:12-14). Now he turns the entire concept of perfectionism on its head by asserting that "what characterizes perfection is not to consider oneself perfect."[205] Christian perfection "consists, stated paradoxically, in Christian imperfection, in running towards the goal."[206]

In this context, Paul defines the meaning of the word *teleioi* as *mature*.[207] His definition of maturity is contained in the encouragement that we *should take such a view of things* as he has just expressed in the previous paragraph. Maturity is taking Paul's view of things, having Paul's attitude, and adopting Paul's way of thinking. The clause "let us have this attitude" brings us back to the earlier exhortation in 2:5: *In your relationships with one another, have the same attitude of mind Christ Jesus had.* The practical way to have the attitude of Christ Jesus is to have Paul's attitude. When Paul decided to *consider everything a loss because of the surpassing knowledge of knowing Christ* (3:7-8), his attitude reflected that of the one who *made himself nothing, . . . humbled himself and was obedient unto death — even death on the cross!* (2:7-8). The mature attitude exhibited by Paul combines genuine humility, knowing that we have not already arrived at the goal, and wholehearted commitment, straining toward the goal. By including himself with his readers in his exhortation, "let us have this attitude," Paul is calling for unity of mind in the community as he did in 2:2: *be like-minded . . . of one mind.* The attitude of those who *press on toward the goal to win the prize* (3:14) is not an individualistic, competitive attitude of runners who run alone to beat everyone else. This attitude draws people together as they focus in their community on knowing Christ and following Christ. Paul does not of-

204. See Lightfoot, 153; Lincoln, *Paradise Now and Not Yet*, 94; and Martin and Hawthorne, 211-12, for diverse explanations of the perfectionism opposed by Paul in this passage. Various brands of perfectionism include the perfectionism of Jewish Christian Gnostics by initiation into mystic rites, non-Christian Jews on the basis of their birth in the covenant people and their obedience of the law, Christian Jews by circumcision and lawkeeping, and Christian martyrs by death for their faith. Fee, however, rejects any attempt to reconstruct the perfectionism of Paul's alleged opponents. See Fee, 344 n. 24.

205. Bockmuehl, 226.

206. Barth, 111.

207. TNIV; BDAG, 995.

fer his self-portrait to put himself above or beyond others but to unite others with him in the common pursuit *to know Christ.* He is drawing together the friends of the cross before he refers to the *enemies of the cross* (3:18).[208]

After his encouragement to the mature to join with him by thinking the same way he does, Paul addresses those who *on some point think differently.* By using the word *think* twice in this sentence, Paul emphasizes the importance of having the same attitude on the major points of principle and recognizes the reality of a difference of attitude on some minor points.[209] The difference of attitude is not radical, but only a difference *on some point.*[210] Paul is not referring here to essential differences such as he addresses in his description of the *enemies of the cross of Christ* in verses 18-19. But he recognizes that there will be differences on some points even when members of the community sincerely desire to have the same attitude in the pursuit of Christ as Paul has. Paul does not demand total uniformity or coerce absolute agreement on every point.[211] Without any sign of anxiety or resentment, he allows his readers freedom to discover how to develop a mature attitude with the assurance *that God will make clear* to them how to handle their differences. Paul's confidence in God — God will reveal this to you — echoes his repeated expressions of confidence in God's work in the community: *he who began a good work in you will carry it on to completion* (1:6); *it is God who works in you to will and to act in order to fulfill his good purpose* (2:13).[212]

How God will reveal his direction to resolve minor points of difference Paul does not explain. He seems content to leave the means of God's guidance undefined and open. His move from a law-centered life to life in Christ gives him freedom from detailed prescriptions for every conceivable

208. Fowl, 164.

209. Both the grammar and the whole context of the letter indicate that some already have a different attitude. The conditional conjunction εἴ followed by the present indicative φρονεῖτε introduces a condition of reality; the phrase can be translated, "*since* you think somewhat differently" (Martin and Hawthorne, 210). And since the context of the letter includes the appeal (4:2) to two women to *be of the same mind* (τὸ αὐτὸ φρονεῖν), there is clearly a difference of attitude within the community.

210. Vincent, 113: "The reference is loose, and concerns minor points in the characteristics of the τέλειοι generally considered. It was entirely possible that many of his readers, although having a genuine faith in Christ, and fully accepting the doctrine of justification by faith, might not have apprehended his profound views of mystical union, or have had the same clear ideas as himself concerning certain practical applications of doctrine; even that they might not have felt the impulse to higher spiritual attainment in its full stringency, and might have been inclined to regard his conduct and sentiments in certain particulars as exaggerated. Such facts are familiar to every Christian pastor."

211. Fowl, 164-65, refers to the similarities between epistolary conventions of friendship letters addressing differences in a friendship and Paul's expression here regarding the difference of opinion. See also Jeffrey T. Reed, *Discourse Analysis of Philippians: Method and Rhetoric in the Debate over Literary Integrity* (LNTS; Sheffield: Sheffield Academic, 1997), 268.

212. Lightfoot, 153, captures Paul's confidence in God: "If you are sound at the core, God will remove the superficial blemishes."

situation. Paul is no longer bound by the tradition that produced the Mishnah with its applications of the law to all known circumstances. Although the unity of the church is one of Paul's highest priorities, he knows that true unity will be achieved only by God's revelation, not by his rhetorical power.[213]

16 After a short sideways glance at those who differ from him, Paul returns to emphasize the main point of his exhortation.[214] He encourages the entire church, including himself, to maintain their progress in the faith: *Only let us live up to what we have already attained.* Paul's encouragement expresses his positive appreciation for the community in his reference to *what we have attained.* The verb *attained* signifies that they have already arrived at a point in their journey and reached a level of understanding and conduct in their faith that sets a high standard for their future belief and behavior.[215] Even though he recognizes the difference of perspective on some points, yet he applauds their unity in their commitment to *know Christ* (3:10) and to *press toward the goal to win the prize* (3:14). Paul's appeal to *live up to* means "to be in line with" the standard set by their progress so far.[216] He uses the same term when he urges the Galatian churches to "keep in step with the Spirit" (Gal 5:25) — and when he describes those who "keep in step with this rule" (Gal 6:16).[217]

Paul now points to the real progress that has been attained and that sets the course of direction for the whole community. Now they must all continue "on in this direction! — no extravagances to right or to left!"[218] Paul's affirmation of the attainment that they have already achieved assures his readers that he is not criticizing them for lack of progress or coercing them to move in a new direction. These believers are not being forced to conform to some standard outside themselves; they are being called to live up to their own experience of God's gracious work in their community *to will and to act in order to fulfill his good purpose* (2:13).

By his use of the first person plural, Paul reminds his readers of the *partnership* that they have experienced in their progress in the faith. An in-

213. Fowl, 165.

214. Paul changes from first person plural — *all of us . . . should take such view of things* — to second person plural — *if you think differently* — and back to first person plural — *let us live up to what we have already attained.* This change gives his direct address to those who differ from him the sound of a parenthetical aside. The adverbial conjunction, only (πλήν), used for "breaking off a discussion and emphasizing what is important" (BDAG, 826), brings readers back to the main point.

215. BDAG, 1053. The same verb is used by Paul in his reference to his "arrival" at Corinth in his journeys (2 Cor 10:14) and in his reference to the people of Israel who had not *attained* their goal in their pursuit of the law as the way to righteousness (Rom 9:31).

216. BDAG, 946.

217. Perhaps memory of Gal 6:16 caused the insertion in the Majority textual tradition: "Let us keep in step with the same rule, thinking the same thing" (Beare, 131). This later addition, however, is not found in the early and diverse witnesses (𝔓[16,46] א A B).

218. Barth, 112.

dividualistic understanding of *what we have already attained* does not do justice to Paul's theme of the attainment of the community as a whole in their experience and expression of partnership in the gospel. They have already attained progress in their *partnership in the gospel* (1:5), their *common sharing in the Spirit* (2:1), and their *participation in [Christ's] sufferings* (3:10). Paul's primary concern is that this corporate attainment of partnership could be destroyed by *selfish ambition* (1:17; 2:3). What has already been attained must be maintained by humility (2:3), the kind of humility seen in Christ, who humbled himself by becoming obedient to death (2:8), and the humility seen in Paul, who lost all things to gain Christ, becoming like him in his death (3:8-10).

17 Paul has already stressed that his example only partially reflects the perfect, transcendent paradigm of Christ's humility: *not that I have already obtained all this, or have already arrived at my goal.* Although his example is admittedly imperfect, it is, nevertheless, tangible and accessible to the church he founded. So he takes the role of a mentor: *Join together in following my example, brothers and sisters.* By addressing his readers as *brothers and sisters* when he calls for them to follow his example, Paul reminds them of their equality as siblings in the same family, pressing on together in the same direction toward the common goal of knowing Christ.[219] Literally, Paul calls them to *become* "fellow imitators of me." The compound word "fellow imitators" is not attested elsewhere in Greek literature and may be Paul's own creation.[220] This phrase could mean that they are to become "fellow imitators" with Paul of Christ.[221] The entire letter conveys Paul's sense of mutuality and equality with his friends in Philippi.[222] When he calls them to follow his example, he is urging them to join with him in his own journey to know Christ. When they are fellow imitators of Paul, they will be united in their common pursuit of *one thing* (3:13): *to know Christ — yes, to know the power of his resurrection and participation in his sufferings, becoming like him in his death* (3:10). Paul coined the term "fellow imitators" as yet another way to urge the community to be united in their life in Christ. To view Paul's call to be fellow imitators of his example as a "defense of his own apostleship"[223] or as

219. Hawthorne, 159.

220. Bockmuehl, 228.

221. Fee (364 n. 10) offers Paul's use of other "*syn*-compounds" to emphasize mutuality in this letter as support for this interpretation. συγκοινωνούς μου ["my fellow partners"] τῆς χάριτος πάντας ὑμᾶς ὄντας — *you all share in God's grace with me* (1:7); συγχαίρω πᾶσιν ὑμῖν· συγχαίρετέ μοι — *I rejoice with all of you . . . rejoice with me* (2:17-18); συνεργὸν καί συστρατιώτην μου — *my co-worker and fellow-soldier* (2:25); συνεργῶν μου — *my co-workers* (4:3).

222. In all of Paul's uses of the noun μίμηται the genitive pronoun refers to the object of imitation (1 Thess 1:6; 2:14; 1 Cor 4:16; 11:1; Eph 5:1). Hence the genitive pronoun μου, "of me," in the clause, Συμμιμηταί μου γίνεσθε — "become fellow imitators of me," identifies the object of imitation. BDAG, 958, translates the phrase as "join with others in following my example."

223. A. Reinhartz, "On the Meaning of the Pauline Exhortation: *'mimētai mou ginesthe'* — Become Imitators of Me," *SR* 16 (1987), 393-404.

a way to construct and enforce "the hierarchy, Christ–Paul–Christians"[224] turns Paul's entire self-portrait in this chapter upside down. Paul's emphasis in this chapter is his loss of privilege and position for the sake of Christ. Imitating Paul does not lead to defending one's position and asserting power, but to having *the same attitude of mind Christ Jesus had: . . . he made himself nothing; he humbled himself* (2:5-8). Paul offers himself as an example of one who followed the way of Christ, the way of the cross. Imitating Paul is the way to imitate Christ.[225]

Paul also encourages the community to "pay careful attention" to other examples of followers of Christ: *keep your eyes on those who live as we do.*[226] Timothy and Epaphroditus represent the kind of people Paul has in mind (2:19-30). They reflect the self-giving nature of Christ by the way they served Paul and the community of believers in Philippi. The way they "walk" demands careful observation and faithful imitation. Although TNIV uses the term *live,* Paul uses his favorite ethical term for Christian behavior: those who "walk."[227] In the OT, the term "walk" is used frequently to depict a personal relationship with God and obedience to the commands of God.[228] The heroes of faith walked with God: "Enoch walked with God" (Gen 5:24); "Noah was a righteous man, blameless among the people of his time, and he walked with God" (Gen 6:9); God commanded Abraham, "walk before me . . . and be blameless" (Gen 17:1). The people of Israel receive promised blessings if they "keep the commands of the LORD and walk in his ways" (Deut 28:9). The prophet Isaiah commends the one "who walks righteously and speaks what is right" (Isa 33:15). The psalmist prays, "Teach me your way, O LORD, and I will walk in your truth" (Psalm 86:11). From the Hebrew word *halakh* ("walk") comes the term *Halakah* for a vast amount of rabbinic legal literature dealing with the application of biblical commandments to different contexts of life.[229] Drawing from his Jewish heritage, Paul draws his readers' attention to all those who set an example

224. Elizabeth A. Castelli, *Imitating Paul: A Discourse of Power* (Louisville: Westminster/John Knox, 1991), 96.

225. See D. M. Stanley, "'Become Imitators of Me': The Pauline Conception of Apostolic Tradition," *Bib* 40 (1959), 859-77; J. H. P. Reumann, "Justification and the *Imitatio* Motif in Philippians 3.2-21," in *Promoting Unity: Themes in Lutheran-Catholic Dialogue* (ed. G. Anderson and J. R. Crumley Jr.; Minneapolis: Augsburg, 1989), 17-28.

226. BDAG, 931. The verb is σκοπέω.

227. BDAG, 803. In at least twenty of its thirty NT occurrences, περιπατέω is used by Paul to depict Christian conduct. See Rom 6:4; 8:4; 13:13; 14:15; 1 Cor 3:3; 7:17; 2 Cor 4:2; 5:7; 10:2-3; 12:18; Gal 5:16; Phil 3:17-18 (twice); Col 1:10; 2:6; 3:7; 4:5; 1 Thess 2:12; 4:1 (twice), 12; 2 Thess 3:6, 11.

228. G. Bertram, "πατέω," *TDNT* 5:942-43.

229. E. P. Sanders, *Paul and Palestinian Judaism: A Comparison of Patterns of Religion* (Philadelphia: Fortress, 1977), 76: "The Mishnah is the *halakic* work par excellence. . . . The purpose of *halakah* is to determine whether or not a biblical passage does in fact constitute a commandment, if there can be any doubt; to establish the application of a biblical commandment; to define its precise scope and meaning; and to determine precisely what must be done in order to fulfill it."

by their walk with God. His purpose is not to set forth a detailed application of law, but to encourage the development of personal relationships with mentors who model the way to walk with Jesus Christ.[230] In this chapter, he considers his former life when he was faultless according to righteousness based on law (3:6) as garbage compared to knowing Christ (3:8-10). The church needs to pay close attention to mentors who press on toward the goal of knowing Christ.

The Philippian Christians are called to look for those who walk *just as you have us as a model.* Paul's use of first person plural *us* may be a reference to himself: he is the model for those whose walk is an example for his readers.[231] But in the light of his enthusiastic recommendation of Timothy and Ephaphroditus (2:19-30) and his strong commendation of his true companion and his other co-workers (4:3), his first person plural probably "refers to Paul and his team of associates."[232] Paul values the exemplary walk of others who follow the *model* set by him and his team of co-workers. This *model* serves as an "archetype" for the moral life of Christians.[233]

E. Mourning over the Enemies of the Cross (3:18-19)

> [18]*For, as I have often told you before and now tell you again even with tears, many live as enemies of the cross of Christ.* [19]*Their destiny is destruction, their god is their stomach, and their glory is in their shame. Their mind is set on earthly things.*

In opposition to those who "walk" in the way Paul does, *many [walk] as enemies of the cross of Christ.* By repeating the verb "walk" (TNIV, *live*), Paul places a fork in the road. We must make a radical choice between two different ways to live: the Christ-centered life or the self-centered life. Paul's description of the way of self-indulgence warns us against the constant danger of following dominant cultural fashions opposed to the way of the cross.

18 The conjunction *for* connects this warning to the previous command, *keep your eyes on those who live as we do,* and gives the reason for that command. Close adherence to positive examples is necessary because negative examples clamor for attention and lead to destruction. Since the *enemies of the cross* present such an alluring and harmful alternative to the way of the cross, Paul warns against them. Paul does not speak directly to the

230. Paul draws a contrast between walking according to the law and walking in the Spirit: "walk in the Spirit. . . . if you are led by the Spirit, you are not under the law" (Gal 5:16-18).

231. Fee, 365; Martin and Hawthorne, 218; Reumann, "Justification and the *Imitatio* Motif in Philippians 3.2-21," 23.

232. Lincoln, *Paradise Now and Not Yet,* 95; Bockmuehl, 229.

233. BDAG, 1020.

many people who *live as enemies of the cross;* they are not included with *God's holy people in Christ Jesus at Philippi* (1:1) to whom Paul addresses this letter. But even though these *enemies* are outside the Christian community, their influence on the community is so strong that Paul frequently repeats his warning: *I often told you before and now tell you again.*[234]

Since Paul does not name these people, they escape definitive identification. Some commentators see signs of Jewish Christians in Paul's description of them. According to this perspective, these are the same people Paul warns his readers about at the beginning of the chapter: *Watch out for those dogs, those evildoers, those mutilators of the flesh* (3:2).[235] That warning points to the corrosive influence of Judaizers, Jewish Christians who require circumcision and compliance with the law.[236] The stinging epithets, *dogs, evildoers, and mutilators,* contradict the Judaizers' own image of themselves. In the same way, if Paul is thinking of Judaizers again in his warning against the enemies of the cross, his description of them turns the Jewish self-concept upside down: since they are preoccupied with food laws, *their god is their stomach;* since they exalt the importance of circumcision, *their glory is in their shame;* since they focus on their ethnic Jewish privileges, *their mind is set on earthly things.*[237] The difficulties faced by this interpretation, however, are the absence of any clear connection between Jewish food laws and idolatry in Paul's letters, the absence of any evidence that Paul viewed circumcision or male genitals as shameful, and the absence of Paul's dismissal of Jewish privileges as earthly things. In fact, Paul expresses his approval of observing Jewish food laws in certain circumstances (1 Cor 9:20; Rom 14:1-17), views the Jewish practice of the circumcision of *Jews* (not *Gentiles*) as a sign of faithfulness to the law (1 Cor 7:18-19; Phil 3:5-6), and lists Jewish privileges as the irrevocable gifts of God (Rom 9:4-5; 11:29).[238]

A more plausible identification of *the enemies of the cross* emphasizes Paul's focus on the way these people *live,* or "walk." The problem with these people is not a theological denial of the cross of Christ, but an ethical divergence from the way of the cross of Christ. The narrative of the cross presents a way to walk in humility as a servant, *by becoming obedient unto*

234. Note the similarity to Paul's reminder of previous warnings in Gal 5:21: "I warn you, as I did before, that those who live this way will not inherit the kingdom of God."

235. O'Brien, 454-57; Martin and Hawthorne, 221; Barth, 113-14; Witherington, 97-98; D. K. Williams, *Enemies of the Cross: The Terminology of the Cross and Conflict in Philippians* (JSNTSup 223; London: Sheffield Academic, 2002), 224: "The unity of Paul's argument can be seen in the way that vv. 18-19 resumes the polemic of v. 2, with outright 'name-calling'. This is a part of Paul's *rhetorical strategy.* Paul uses derogatory language to malign his opponent's religious perspective in v. 2. But in vv. 18-19 Paul uses pejorative language not to characterize the 'theology' but the *praxis* of the opposing group. Therefore, there are not two or three different groups but only one."

236. See the commentary above on 3:2.

237. Lincoln, *Paradise Now and Not Yet,* 95-97; Müller, 176-81; Williams, *Enemies of the Cross,* 225-27.

238. Bockmuehl, 231.

death — even death on a cross! (2:7-8). The narrative of Christ (2:6-11) is framed by exhortations to *do nothing out of selfish ambition or vain conceit* (2:3) and to *work out your salvation* (2:12). Paul's story of his personal renunciation of his elite position in order to participate in the sufferings of Christ (3:4-10) provides an example of the way to walk in the way of the cross. In this context, *enemies of the cross* are those who "seek to avoid suffering that might come their way as the result of their convictions about Christ."[239] Their selfish ambitions are opposed to the way of the cross.[240]

When Paul speaks of these people who are walking contrary to the way of the cross of Christ in their pursuit of their own self-interests, he speaks *with tears.* Literally, Paul writes, "but now I speak even weeping." Paul reserves such an outpouring of emotion for those who have professed belief in Christ.[241] Although he refers to these people in the third person as outsiders, they are still close to his heart. Paul's pastoral concern for those whose *mind is set on earthly things* causes him intense emotional pain. Though his words are harsh, his heart is broken. He mourns over the enemies of the cross.

19 In a play on words, Paul contrasts *all of us who are mature (teleioi)* with the *enemies of the cross,* whose *destiny (telos) is destruction.*[242] These people think that they have already arrived at the *goal (telos)* and are already "perfect" *(teleioi).* They think that being perfect elevates them above the experience of suffering. But Paul paints a different portrait of those "who are perfect" *(teleioi):* they freely admit that they *have not already arrived at the goal* (3:12); they willingly participate in the sufferings of Christ (1:29; 3:10). Those who think that they have already arrived at the goal and avoid participation in the sufferings of Christ are actually traveling toward the goal of destruction. Paul sees their destruction as the inevitable consequence of choosing a self-indulgent lifestyle and opposing the way of the cross of Christ. In their deliberate refusal to suffer with Christ, they have separated themselves from salvation in Christ.

239. Fowl, 171; Paul A. Holloway, *Consolation in Philippians: Philosophical Sources and Rhetorical Strategy* (SNTSMS 112; Cambridge: Cambridge University Press, 2001), 144: "One becomes an 'enemy of the cross' when one rejects the proposition that those who seek to know Christ must suffer as he did and that his 'cross' is to be enthusiastically embraced as leading to the *summum bonum* of knowing Christ."

240. Fee, 371: "They have abandoned Christ by adopting a lifestyle that is totally opposed to the redemptive work of the cross." See also Lightfoot, 155; Beare, 133-36; Bockmuehl, 230-32.

241. Vincent, 116-17: "This deep emotion would more probably be excited by recreant Christians than by heathen whose sensuality and worldliness were familiar to the Apostle. He would be most sorrowfully affected by the reproach and injury to the church wrought by professing Christians, and by their own unhappy and perilous condition." Paul uses the same verb to encourage sharing in the grief of fellow believers — "cry with those who cry" (Rom 12:15); he uses the noun *tears* in his reference to a letter written to believers in Corinth: "I wrote you out of great distress and anguish of heart and with many tears, not to grieve you but to let you know the depth of my love for you" (2 Cor 2:4).

242. Silva, 212; O'Brien, 455.

The self-indulgence of these people expresses itself in their appetites, their pride, and their mind: *their god is their stomach, and their glory is in their shame. Their mind is set on earthly things.* Though the word *stomach* refers literally to the "organ of nourishment," here it refers metaphorically to the "seat of the inward life, of feelings and desires."[243] In Romans 16:18, Paul describes people who "are not serving our Lord Christ, but their own appetites" (literally, "their stomachs"). In the context of addressing the problem of sexual immorality in 1 Corinthians, Paul quotes those who legitimize giving in to sexual desires by saying, "Food for the stomach, and the stomach for food" (1 Cor 6:13). Paul's response to such rationalization is that "the body is not meant for sexual immorality but for the Lord" (1 Cor 6:13). These passages indicate that Paul uses the term *stomach* to represent "unbridled sensuality, whether gluttony or sexual licentiousness."[244] For those who have no higher authority for the way they live than the dictates of their bodily appetites, *their god is their stomach.* They worship their appetites.

Even though serving bodily appetites leads to shameful behavior, these people take pride in their shame; they broadcast and brag about their shameful indulgence of their physical appetites: *their glory is in their shame.* The word *shame* may allude to sexual immorality as it does in Paul's comment that "men committed shameful acts with other men" (Rom 1:27) and in the reference to "shameful nakedness" in Revelation 3:18.[245] Paul's reference to people who "find their glory in that which causes them shame"[246] sounds strangely similar to media coverage of celebrities made famous by their shameful acts.

The reason why these people are enslaved by their sensual appetites and boast about their shameful acts is that *their mind is set on earthly things.* In this final characterization of the enemies of the cross, Paul uses a favorite verb. The verb to *set [one's] mind on* something expresses Paul's goal for the community: *being like-minded, of one mind* (2:2). The same verb introduces the narrative of Christ: *have the same attitude of mind Christ Jesus had* (2:5). This verb concludes Paul's story of his loss of all things to know Christ: *All who are mature should take such a view of things* (3:15). Paul uses this verb in his appeal to the two women who are fighting each other: *be of the same mind in the Lord* (4:2). In all of these uses of the verb, Paul encourages a Christ-centered, unifying attitude. But in his description of the enemies of the cross, Paul employs this verb to depict a self-centered, divisive attitude.

243. BDAG, 550.

244. J. Behm, "κοιλία," *TDNT* 3:788. But Behm's suggestion that Paul may be "alluding to the observance of laws of food" (see also Hawthorne, 166) finds no support in Paul's letters and neglects the evidence that Paul allows Jewish Christians to keep food laws as long as they do not censure those who do not (Rom 14:1-17) and Paul himself keeps the food laws when he eats with Jews (1 Cor 9:20).

245. R. Bultmann, "αἰσχύνη," *TDNT* 1:190.

246. BDAG, 30.

People with this orientation of life are obsessed with getting *earthly things* for their own personal gratification.[247] In contrast to pursuing the heavenward call of God in Christ Jesus (3:14), they are concentrating on their earthly possessions and pleasures. These people had probably been members of the Christian community in Philippi, but now they "have turned full circle; having abandoned the way of the cross, they have their mind once again set on earthly things."[248]

This negative example (3:18-19) establishes an antithesis to Paul's appeal to *join together in following my example* (3:17).[249] Paul's readers have to make the choice: either they will follow the *enemies of the cross* by setting their minds on earthly things or they will follow Christ by having *the same attitude of mind Christ Jesus had* (2:5). Paul does not offer any middle ground or middle way. Similar to Christ's challenge, "You cannot serve both God and money" (Luke 16:13), Paul's challenge will not allow his readers the possibility of serving two masters. Either *their god is their stomach* or they will *consider everything a loss because of the surpassing worth of knowing Christ* (3:7). Either they will pursue *earthly things* or they will pursue the "heavenward call of God in Christ Jesus."

F. Expecting Christ's Ultimate Victory (3:20-21)

> [20]*But our citizenship is in heaven. And we eagerly await a Savior from there, the Lord Jesus Christ,* [21]*who, by the power that enables him to bring everything under his control, will transform our lowly bodies so that they will be like his glorious body.*

Paul turns from those who set their minds on *earthly things* (3:19) to focus our attention on *our citizenship in heaven* (3:20). In these lyrical lines, Paul unites a proclamation of our present citizenship in the heavenly commonwealth with an announcement of the ultimate victory of our Savior, the Lord Jesus Christ.

20 The emphatic first place of the pronoun *our* stresses the contrast between those who are earthly minded and those who are heavenly minded. Although most translations insert the adversative conjunction *but* in order to highlight this contrast, Paul's use of the causal conjunction "for"

247. BDAG, 369, defines *earthly things* (τὰ ἐπίγεια) as those things that "are characteristic of the earth as opposed to heavenly"; in the context of Phil 3:19, the word carries the "implication of personal gratification."

248. Bockmuehl, 232.

249. Timothy C. Geoffrion, *The Rhetorical Purpose and the Political and Military Character of Philippians: A Call to Stand Firm* (Lewiston, N.Y.: Mellen Biblical Press, 1993), 154-55: "The picture is one of two opposing armies: those who remain steadfast in their devotion to Christ stand opposite those who have not stood firm and are now 'enemies of the cross' (3:18; cf. 1:28). Their ways of thinking (φρονέω) and their destinies are diametrically opposed."

connects this sentence with the imperatives of verse 17.[250] By replacing the causal conjunction "for" with an adversative conjunction *(but)*, translators accurately point to the contrast between the enemies of the cross (3:18-19) and the citizens of heaven (3:20-21), but they miss the explanatory function of this sentence as a compelling reason to follow the imperatives in 3:17.[251] The passage presents two imperatives followed by two motivating reasons to follow Paul's commands:

Imperatives: *Join together in following my example*
Keep your eyes on those who [walk] as we do
Reasons: *For many [walk] as enemies of the cross*
For our citizenship is in heaven

Paul seeks to motivate his readers to imitate him and those who walk like him by painting two pictures: his dark picture of those who set their minds on earthly things portrays their future destruction; his radiant picture of us who belong to a heavenly state depicts the future triumphant return of our Savior and the transformation of our bodies by his power. Paul's eschatological vision establishes the basis for his ethical imperatives. The future shines a bright light on the present to guide our moral choices.[252] From Paul's eschatological perspective, we are already citizens of the heavenly order of reality. Our *citizenship in heaven* is not based upon wishful thinking or an imagination of future possibilities, but on *the righteousness that comes from God*.[253] The *righteousness that comes from God* means that by God's judicial decision we belong to the heavenly community.

The term *citizenship (politeuma)* connotes an active, "constitutive force regulating its citizens."[254] By extension the term refers to the state and the citizens under the sovereign power of the government. According to Aristotle, "The government *(politeuma)* is everywhere sovereign in the state."[255] Paul's use of the word emphasizes the membership of Christians in the

250. Cf. O'Brien, 459: γάρ "provides the reason for Paul's derogatory judgment of his opponents."

251. Bockmuehl (233) concurs that "the link is at once contrastive and explanatory."

252. Richard Hays, *The Moral Vision of the New Testament: Community, Cross, New Creation: A Contemporary Introduction to New Testament Ethics* (San Francisco: HarperCollins, 1996), 27: "The dialectical character of Paul's eschatological vision (already/not yet) provides the ethical framework for moral discernment: he is sharply critical not only of the old age that is passing away but also of those who claim unqualified participation already in the new age. To live faithfully in the time between the times is to walk a tight rope of moral discernment, claiming neither too much nor too little for God's transforming power within the community of faith."

253. Barth, 115: "We stand under God's righteousness, and so now: under the righteousness established in heaven. It is his judicial order that obliges us and protects us. Further — it is not conditioned by our wishes and capabilities, but is unconditionally grounded in itself. Further — it is not imagination but reality."

254. Lincoln, *Paradise Now and Not Yet*, 99.

255. Aristotle, *Politica* 3.6.1278b. See H. Strathmann, "πόλις," *TDNT* 6:519-22.

heavenly kingdom governed by Christ.[256] Our governing power, our executive authority is in heaven. The implication of asserting our citizenship in the heavenly state is that we are a "colony of heavenly citizens" here on earth.[257] This concept of belonging to a community of foreigners who pledge allegiance to the government in their home country became a metaphor for living in exile. Josephus referred to the community of Diaspora Jews in Alexandria as a commonwealth *(politeuma)*.[258] The Jews in this community gathered to hear the elders who came from Jerusalem for the interpretation of the law. Although the Jews resided in Alexandria, they belonged to a community *(politeuma)* that recognized the final authority of the interpreters of the law who came from Jerusalem. Philo developed a somewhat different philosophical application of the term *politeuma*. In his Platonic reinterpretation of Judaism, Philo used the term *politeuma* as a reference to the heavenly realm of virtues and ideas. Those who live by these ideals belong to this heavenly state *(politeuma)*.[259] These Jewish metaphorical applications of the term *politeuma* may have influenced Paul's assertion that Christians belong to a heavenly community.[260] Perhaps, Paul's Jewish Christian opponents (see 3:2) claimed the term as their own to assert their authority.[261] But a contest with Jewish claims or Jewish-Christian opponents does not appear to be the primary concern of Paul's language here. His terminology carries special significance for the church in the Roman colony called Philippi. Because Augustus conferred on Philippi all the rights and privileges of being governed under the Roman form of constitutional government, Philippi was on an equal footing to cities in Italy. The official language of Philippi was Latin, the language of Rome. The fact that the majority of inscriptions found in Roman Philippi are in Latin confirms the Roman orientation of the citizens of Philippi.[262] In contrast to the allegiance of Roman Philippians to their governing power, their *politeuma*, in Rome, Paul sets forth the parallel and opposing claim of Christians that their governing power, their *politeuma*, is in heaven.[263]

The close connection between Roman colonial language and Paul's terminology comes into even sharper focus in the next phrase: *we eagerly await a Savior from there, the Lord Jesus Christ.* In the Roman Empire, Caesar Augustus was acclaimed to be the "savior of the world" because he restored order and peace not only in Italy but also throughout the provinces

256. Strathmann, "πόλις," *TDNT* 6:535.

257. BDAG, 845.

258. Josephus, *Ant.* 12.2.13.108. See Strathmann, "πόλις," *TDNT* 6:527.

259. Strathmann, "πόλις," *TDNT* 6:528.

260. Lincoln, *Paradise Now and Not Yet*, 97: "Paul's counter-claim is that he and those who are faithful to the apostolic tradition are those whose commonwealth is in heaven."

261. Paul C. Böttger, "Die eschatologische Existenz der Christen: Erwägungen zu Philipper 3,20," *ZNW* (1969), 244-63.

262. Gill, "Macedonia," in *The Book of Acts in Its Greco-Roman Setting*, 411-13.

263. Lincoln, *Paradise Now and Not Yet*, 100.

and regions under his sovereign rule.[264] Paul's use of the term *Savior* in his letter to Christians in Roman Philippi "sharply opposes Jesus Christ as Lord to the imperial savior."[265] By applying the imperial title *Savior* to Jesus Christ, "Paul explicitly (and we must assume deliberately) speaks of Jesus in language which echoes, and hence deeply subverts, language in common use among Roman imperial subjects to describe Caesar."[266] Paul redirects the focus of his readers from the savior in Rome, Caesar Augustus, to the Savior in heaven, Jesus Christ the Lord. In contrast to the enemies of the cross who set their minds on earthly powers (3:18-19), the Christians in Philippi are called to focus their trust and hope in the Lord and Savior above all earthly powers. The enemies of the cross followed the natural inclination of residents in Philippi to look to the emperor in Rome to exert his sovereign power to solve their problems, satisfy their appetites, rescue them from trouble, and protect them from danger. But the Christian who followed the example of Paul (3:17) looked to Jesus Christ to be their Lord and Savior.[267] Such a change of allegiance would inevitably cause them to participate in the sufferings of Christ (3:10).[268] Their sufferings will cause them to *eagerly await* their *Savior* from heaven who has *the power that enables him to bring everything under his control* (3:20-21). Their hope for the future is not fixed on Caesar, the savior and lord of the Roman Empire, but on Jesus Christ, the heavenly Lord and Savior.[269]

Although Paul uses Caesar's titles "savior" and "lord" for Jesus in this context in order to subvert the use of these titles in the Roman Empire as an expression of absolute, undivided allegiance to Caesar, Paul's Jewish heritage provides the meaning for these titles. Especially significant is the use of these titles in the text of Isaiah 45:15, 21-23, already observed as the OT backdrop of the Christ hymn (Phil 2:9-11):

> "Truly you are a God who hides himself,
> O God of Israel, the Savior. . . .

264. W. Foerster, "σωτήρ," *TDNT* 7:1012; MM, 621; BDAG, 985.

265. Richard A. Horsley, *Paul and Empire: Religion and Power in Roman Imperial Society* (ed. Richard A. Horsley; Harrisburg, Pa.: Trinity Press International, 1997), 141.

266. N. T. Wright, *What Saint Paul Really Said* (Grand Rapids: Eerdmans, 1997), 88.

267. N. T. Wright, *Paul in Fresh Perspective* (Minneapolis: Fortress, 2005), 72: "My proposal is that Philippians 3, though important in its own right as a statement of how Paul understood his own pilgrimage, constitutes an example which Paul is holding out to them, an example of how they, too, must hear the call of God in Jesus to sit light to their civic status and be prepared to hail Jesus, not Caesar, as Lord."

268. Since Paul's "radical political critique" (Wright, *Paul in Fresh Perspective*, 73) comes in the context of his teaching on suffering for the sake of Christ (2:29-30), it cannot be read as a call for political revolution. The radical political critique of earthly claims to absolute authority the church makes by giving their ultimate allegiance to the Lord Christ leads to participation in the sufferings of Christ (3:10). See the criticism of Wright's political perspective by Martin and Hawthorne, lxx-lxxi.

269. Peter Oakes, *Philippians: From People to Letter* (SNTSMS 110; Cambridge: Cambridge University Press, 2001), 139-45.

> Who told this long ago?
> Was it not I, the LORD?
> There is no other God besides me, a righteous God and a Savior;
> There is no one besides me.
> Turn to me and be saved, all you ends of the earth!
> For I am God, and there is no other.
> By myself I have sworn, from my mouth has gone forth in
> righteousness
> A word that shall not return:
> To me every knee shall bow, every tongue shall swear."

This text expresses Paul's lifelong Jewish conviction that God alone is Savior and Lord and informs his application of those titles to Jesus.[270] Jesus, not Caesar, is the rightful bearer of the divine titles, Savior and Lord. Jesus, not Caesar, should be trusted as Savior and worshipped as Lord.

When Paul uses the verb *eagerly await* in his letters, he is expressing the ultimate eschatological hope of Christians.[271] Christians still "eagerly await through the Spirit the righteousness for which we hope" (Gal 5:5). Christians "wait eagerly for our adoption, the redemption of our bodies" (Rom 8:23); all "creation waits in eager expectation for the children of God to be revealed" (Rom 8:19), anticipating that "creation itself will be liberated from its bondage to decay and brought into the freedom and glory of the children of God" (Rom 8:20-21). Christians "eagerly wait for our Lord Jesus Christ to be revealed" (1 Cor 1:7). By using the first person plural *we eagerly await a Savior* (Phil 3:21), Paul characterizes the whole Christian community as a community of hope: all the members of this community are looking forward to the appearance of their Savior. Paul has already described his own orientation: *forgetting what is behind and straining toward what is ahead* (3:13-14). Now he unites all believers with him in his attitude of eager anticipation. Even though their present experience includes suffering, they are all still dominated by hope. Their hope contrasts with the hope of those who set their minds on earthly things. The only hope for a mind preoccupied with an earthly agenda is the intervention of an earthly savior. If Caesar would come from Rome, the mother city, and visit Philippi, a treasured Roman colony, he would bring order and peace. Although the eschatological hope of the Christian community echoes the imperial eschatology with its use of Caesar's titles, Savior and Lord, the Savior and Lord anticipated by the Christian community is coming from heaven, not from Rome.[272]

270. For the use and meaning of σωτήρ in the OT, see G. Fohrer, "σωτήρ," *TDNT* 7:1012-13.

271. BDAG, 100; W. Grundmann, "ἀπεδέχομαι," *TDNT* 2:56.

272. See N. T. Wright, "Paul's Gospel and Caesar's Empire," in *Paul and Politics: Ekklesia, Israel, Imperium, Interpretation: Essays in Honor of Krister Stendahl* (ed. Richard A. Horsley; Harrisburg, Pa.: Trinity Press International, 2000), 174.

21 The political overtones of Paul's eschatology continue in the next phrases of his assertion of hope: *who, by the power that enables him to bring everything under his control, will transform our lowly bodies so that they will be like his glorious body.* Christians anticipate sharing in the glory of their Savior and in his universal subjugation of all things under his control. No matter how glorious Caesar is or how great the power of his rule over all things in his empire, Caesar is no match for the Savior and Lord from heaven. Writing from a Roman prison to a Roman colony, Paul spells out a greater vision of the future than any Caesar could ever accomplish.

Our Savior from heaven *will transform our lowly bodies so that they will be like his glorious body.* The verb *transform* envisions a dramatic, supernatural event when Christ will "change the form" of our body from *lowly* to *glorious.*[273] In the *lowly* present form we have a "body of humiliation"; in the *glorious* future form our body will *be like his glorious body.*[274] By defining the *lowly* form of our present body in terms of "humiliation,"[275] Paul points to the "unpretentious state or condition" of our present bodily experience.[276] Although Paul does refer to the body as the "body of sin" (Rom 6:6) and the "body of death" (Rom 7:24), he does not express Gnostic or dualist contempt for the body, as if the body itself were inherently corrupt and evil.[277] The body is the outward, physical expression of the whole person — the outward expression of sinful desires or the outward expression of the Holy Spirit's directions.[278] The term "humiliation" echoes the use of the verb "humbled" in the Christ hymn. After *taking [the form] of a servant, being made in human likeness, and being found in appearance is a human being,* Christ *humbled himself by becoming obedient to death — even death on a cross!* (2:7-8). Christ himself experienced "humiliation" in his incarnation.[279] Life in our

273. BDAG, 641.

274. J. Schneider, "μετασχηματίζω," *TDNT* 7:957: "As already in the case of Christ (2:8), δόξα will follow ταπείνωσις. The body of glory will replace the body of humiliation which Christians now bear."

275. The genitive of quality in the phrase τὸ σῶμα τῆς ταπεινώσεως (the body of humiliation) defines the nature of the present body. See BDF §165.

276. BDAG, 990.

277. The KJV translation, "vile body," misrepresents the meaning of the word by implying essential moral corruption.

278. Robert H. Gundry, *SŌMA in Biblical Theology: With an Emphasis on Pauline Anthropology* (Grand Rapids: Zondervan, 1987; reprint of Cambridge: Cambridge University Press, 1976), 50: "The *sōma* denotes the physical body, roughly synonymous with 'flesh' in the neutral sense. It forms that part of man in and through which he lives and acts in the world. It becomes the base of operations for sin in the unbeliever, for the Holy Spirit in the believer. Barring prior occurrence of the Parousia, the *sōma* will die. That is the lingering effect of sin even in the believer. But it will also be resurrected. That is its ultimate end, a major proof of its worth and necessity to the wholeness of human being, and the reason for its sanctification now."

279. P. Doble, "'Vile Bodies' or Transformed Persons? Philippians 3:21 in Context," *JSNT* 86 (2002), 3-27. Doble argues that the "body of humiliation" is the body disciplined to humility of the kind advocated by Paul in 2:2-5 and exemplified by Christ in 2:6-8.

present body is filled with the "humiliation" of weakness, suffering, and death. Writing from prison, Paul is acutely aware that his chains and his imminent execution are elements of his personal humiliation. He does not deny the present reality of his humiliation; he acknowledges the form of his present bodily existence. Paul paints a brutally realistic portrait of *our lowly bodies* without any removal of blemishes or addition of halos.

In contrast to the present body of humiliation, the body of the future *will be like his glorious body.* The line of continuity in our present and future forms of existence is existence in a *body.* Paul's hope is not to be rescued from his body, but to have his body transformed; he does not contemplate a future out of the body or bodiless human existence.[280] The future of Christians will be as somatic as was the bodily resurrection of Christ. Here, as in other letters, Paul eagerly anticipates the "redemption of our bodies" on the basis of the bodily resurrection of Christ from the dead (Rom 8:11-23; see also 1 Corinthians 15).[281] The "resurrection of Christ is a new affirmation of God's first decision that Adam should live." . . . Adam "has not been allowed to uncreate what God created. . . . In the resurrection of Christ creation is restored."[282] Paul's hope is not for redemption from creation but for the redemption of creation, including the redemption of our bodies. Our bodies will be changed, but not discarded.[283] This assurance of a continuity of bodily existence does not address a host of questions: Will there be a continuity of DNA, a continuity of memory, a continuity of personality? Attempts to answer these and many related questions go beyond Paul's simple assertion of a continuity of somatic existence. Where Paul does address the question of continuity he sets forth a simple analogy of the continuity between a seed and the full grown plant (1 Cor 15:36-38). But this analogy does not provide much more information about the nature of the continuity between the present and the future body. What is the extent of that continuity? Is there a material continuity or only a continuity of personal iden-

280. Lincoln, *Paradise Now and Not Yet,* 103: "Final salvation will definitely embrace bodily existence and μετασχηματίζω involves not a creation of something entirely new but the transformation of something already there, in this case 'our body of humiliation.'"

281. Gundry, *SŌMA in Biblical Theology,* 182: "The resurrection of Christ was and the resurrection of Christians will be physical in nature. Anything less than that undercuts Paul's ultimate intention that redeemed man possess physical means of concrete activity for the eternal service and worship of God in a restored creation. Otherwise, God's purpose in the creation — material as it is — would be thwarted. To dematerialize resurrection, by any means, is to emasculate the sovereignty of God in both creative purpose and redemptive grace."

282. Oliver O'Donovan, *Resurrection and Moral Order* (Leicester: Inter-Varsity Press, 1986), 14-15; Gundry, *SŌMA in Biblical Theology,* 182: "God will restore the broken nature of believers at their resurrection not only because of his grace, but also because the nature of man qua man as a unity of body and spirit represents God's creative purpose."

283. George E. Ladd, *A Theology of the New Testament* (rev. ed.; ed. Donald A. Hagner; Grand Rapids: Eerdmans, 1974), 609: "Rather than being discarded, the body, which often humiliates us, is to be transformed and glorified (Phil. 3:21)."

tity? The best we can say is that the seed analogy suggests a continuity of "identity with a difference."[284]

Paul's emphasis on the continuity of bodily existence raises doubts that Paul ever contemplated a time of bodiless existence. Paul asserts that personal human existence is somatic existence. And yet, Paul also emphatically asserts in this letter that *to die is gain* (1:21), and he expresses his *desire to depart and be with Christ, which is better by far* (1:23). Paul's definition of death as personal communion *with Christ* does not support the view that there is a cessation of personal existence, euphemistically called sleep, until the return of Christ and the resurrection of the body.[285] We cannot press Paul's assertion that human existence means somatic existence so far that it denies Paul's own expectation of personal communion with Christ at the time of death. The traditional way to resolve the tension between Paul's emphasis on bodily existence and his expectation of communion with Christ at the time of death is the hypothesis of an intermediate state of bodiless human existence, a continuation of life as a soul without a body. But this hypothesis radically conflicts with Paul's expectation of a continuity of somatic human existence. Other hypotheses include instantaneous resurrection of the body at the time of death or an intermediate body at the time of death before the resurrection of the body.[286] Paul does not hypothesize to resolve the apparent conflict between his expectation of personal communion with Christ at the time of death and his insistence on the continuity of somatic human existence. But this unsolved mystery does not diminish his eagerness to be with Christ when he dies and his eagerness for his body to be transformed.

The radical discontinuity in our bodily existence will be the difference between humiliation and glory: our body of humiliation will be conformed to his glorious body. The adjective "conformed" indicates that our future body will have "the same form" as Christ's glorious body.[287] Christ is always the perfect prototype, the divine paradigm for Paul. He desires "to be conformed to his death" in the present (3:10); he anticipates being "conformed to his glorious body" in the future (3:21). All that Paul says here about the body of the risen Christ is that his resurrected body expresses "his glory": it is the "body of his glory." As Paul describes some of the characteristics of the resurrection body of Christians in Corinthians 15, he re-

284. Murray J. Harris, "Resurrection and Immortality in the Pauline Corpus," in *Life in the Face of Death: The Resurrection Message of the New Testament* (ed. Richard N. Longenecker; Grand Rapids: Eerdmans, 1998), 155.

285. See the commentary above on 1:21-23.

286. See Gundry, *SŌMA in Biblical Theology;* Murray J. Harris, *Raised Immortal: The Relation between Resurrection and Immortality in New Testament Teaching* (London: Marshall Morgan & Scott, 1983); C. F. D. Moule, "St. Paul and Dualism: The Pauline Concept of Resurrection," *NTS* 13 (1966), 106-23.

287. BDAG, 958; a seventh-century addition to the Beza text (D), followed by the Majority Text, inserts the phrase εἰς τὸ γένεσθαι αὐτό ("so that it might become") before the adjective σύμμορφον. The addition attempts to smooth out the syntax, but it is clearly a secondary text.

veals some of the qualities of the prototype resurrection body, the body of the risen Christ. The resurrection body is a "spiritual body" (1 Cor 15:44-46). The "spiritual body" is a body perfectly "animated and guided by the spirit."[288] In contrast to the corruptibility, dishonor, and weakness of the natural body, the spiritual body will be incorruptible, glorious, and powerful (1 Cor 15:42-43). Any deterioration or decay experienced in our natural bodies will be impossible since the spiritual body will be constantly renewed by the Spirit. Our natural bodies with all their indignities and imperfections will be replaced by unblemished, beautiful bodies. We will have perfect health and unlimited energy through the constant rejuvenation of the Spirit. In all of these characteristics of their resurrection bodies, Christians will display the likeness of the risen Christ, the last Adam, the heavenly man (1 Cor 15:45-49).[289]

The essential difference between the risen Christ and all who become like him in their resurrection bodies is his unrivaled power. Paul draws attention to the uniqueness of Christ's sovereign power: Christ has the ability to *transform our lowly bodies to be like his glorious body by the power that enables him to bring everything under his control.* Here again Paul's language echoes the claims of Caesar. The Roman emperors claim absolute power over the bodies of their subjects. Paul sits in chains by Caesar's decree. But only Christ has the power to bring everything under his control. The power of earthly tyrants to humiliate the followers of Christ will be overcome by Christ when he subjects all things to himself and transforms our bodies of humiliation to be like his glorious body.[290] Christ, not Caesar, will exercise universal dominion by his power; Christ, not Caesar, will exercise his power to transform our bodies so that our humiliation will be transformed into glory. In his exercise of power to control all things, Christ will display the sovereign power of God. Paul eagerly awaits the one who is exalted by God to the highest place so that all things will be subjected to him (Phil 2:9-11). By the subjection of all things under his control Jesus Christ will deserve the universal acclamation that he alone is the Lord, far above all earthly powers.

Paul unites individual and cosmic transformation in his vision of the future event when the Lord from heaven *will transform our lowly bodies to be like his glorious body by the power that enables him to bring everything under his control.*[291] Paul's reasoning is from the cosmic to the individual: since the

288. Harris, "Resurrection and Immortality in the Pauline Corpus," 153: "The adjective *pneumatikon* ('spiritual') does not mean 'composed of spirit,' as though 'spirit' were some ethereal, heavenly substance." See also Gundry, *SŌMA in Biblical Theology*, 165: "A *pneumatikon sōma* is not a bodily form with spirit as its substance; it is a physical body renovated by the Spirit of Christ and therefore suited to heavenly immortality."

289. See an elaboration of the qualities of the resurrection body by Harris, *Raised Immortal*, 119-33.

290. Fowl, 175.

291. The order of these clauses represents the order in the Greek text: ὃς μετασχηματίσει τὸ σῶμα τῆς ταπεινώσεως ἡμῶν σύμμορφον τῷ σώματι τῆς δόξης αὐτοῦ, κατὰ τὴν ἐνέργειαν τοῦ δύνασθαι αὐτὸν καί ὑποτάξαι αὐτῷ τὰ πάντα. The preposition *by* (κατά) sets forth

Lord has the power to bring the entire universe under his control, he certainly has the power to accomplish our personal transformation. The work of the cosmic subjugation of all things includes within it the accomplishment of our personal transformation.[292] While this future event may include some process, the future event cannot be replaced by historical process. Paul weeps over those who set their minds on earthly things, eagerly watching the news of the historical process of Caesar attempting to bring all things under the control of the Roman Empire. Christians have a different gospel: they eagerly wait for the good news of their Savior, the Lord Jesus Christ, coming from heaven to transform their bodies by his power to bring all things under his control. Although a process of universal dominion often occurs in the history of the world — Caesars often seek to be saviors of the world by subjugating all things under their control — Paul does not allow the pseudo-saviors of the world to eclipse the true Savior who will come from heaven to exercise his sovereign power over all things and transform the humiliation of his people into glory. Even when we are locked in Caesar's dark prisons and bound in Caesar's chains, *we eagerly await a Savior.*

A combination of 2:6-11 and 3:20-21 tells the complete story of the way of salvation that leads through suffering to glory. The story begins with Christ in eternity, *being in very nature God* (2:6), continues with the incarnation, *being made in human likeness* (2:7), and moves to the cross, *obedient to death — even death on a cross!* (2:8). The story then tells of the dramatic reversal when God turns the humiliation of the cross into exaltation *to the highest place* with *the name that is above every name,* so that *every tongue will acknowledge that Jesus Christ is Lord, to the glory of God the Father* (2:9-11). In 3:20-21 the story announces the coming of the *Lord Jesus Christ* from heaven *to bring everything under his control* and *transform our lowly bodies so that they will be like his glorious body.* The story of salvation tells us of a great "interchange" between Christ and us: Christ came to share in our suffering so that we would share in his glory. He became like us in order to transform us to become like him.[293] This story does not end in heaven, but on earth. The Savior, the Lord Jesus Christ, comes from heaven to restore all of creation.

Since 3:20-21 announces the grand climax of the story of salvation, this text seems to function as the final verse of the Christ hymn (2:6-11). Re-

---

the power of cosmic subjugation as the *norm,* "in accordance with," and the *cause,* "because of, as a result of," for the work of personal transformation. See BDAG, 512-13; O'Brien, 465 n. 139.

292. Barth, 116-17: "With the same power that the *kyrios* (the Lord) uses in order to make *ta panta* (all things) subject to himself and through him to the Father, he will transform us, make us new. Us? Yes, us who, praising him here and now as *kyrios,* wait for the revelation of his *kyriotēs* (lordship). We wait for our inclusion in this his one indivisible, divine, sovereign act that comprehends at once both the living and the dead." See also Harris, *Raised Immortal,* 167.

293. See M. D. Hooker, "Interchange in Christ," *JTS* 22 (1971), 349-61.

markable parallels between the words and concepts of the two passages appear to confirm that 3:20-21 belongs with the Christ hymn.

2:6-11	3:20-21
in form	*conform*
being	*is*
humbled	*humiliation*
every knee shall bow	*to bring everything under his control*
Jesus Christ is Lord	*Lord Jesus Christ*
glory of God	*his glory*

A number of unusual words in 3:20-21 not often or ever used elsewhere in Paul's letters also seem to confirm that Paul is quoting a fragment of an early Christian hymn.[294] In addition, the conjunction "for" and the relative pronoun *who* appear to signal a "liturgical confession."[295] None of this evidence definitively proves the hypothesis that 3:20-21 is a pre-Pauline Christian hymn.[296] The close connection of this passage with the Christ hymn (2:6-11) may simply indicate that Paul's heart reverberates with the words and themes of that hymn as he composes these lines to express his eager anticipation of the coming of our *Savior, the Lord Jesus Christ.* Just as he and Silas were praying and singing hymns to God at midnight in the jail in Philippi (Acts 16:25), so also, as he is writing this letter from a Roman prison to the Christians in Philippi, Christian hymns of praise can be heard ringing through the lines of his letter and lifting his readers to envision a bright future when all the humiliation of suffering will be transformed to glorious participation in Christ's complete victory over all things.

294. As evidence that 3:20-21 is a pre-Pauline hymn, J. C. Becker, "Erwägungen zu Phil. 3:20-21," *TZ* 27 (1971), 16-29, points to the following unusual vocabulary: *citizenship* (πολίτευμα), *in the heavens* (ἐν οὐρανοῖς), *to be* (ὑπάρχει), *savior* (σωτῆρα), the Lord Jesus Christ (κύριον Ἰησοῦν Χριστόν) as a complete title, *transformed* (μετασχηματίσει) for the resurrection of the body, "body of humiliation" (τὸ σῶμα τῆς ταπεινώσεως). On the basis of the unusual vocabulary and the parallels with the Christ hymn, Becker concludes that 3:20-21 is part of the pre-Pauline Christ hymn.

295. Hawthorne, 169: "A careful examination of the language and style of writing found in this section and a study of its unusual words and rhythmic patterns, and so on, suggest that it is another Christological hymn, perhaps composed early in the church's existence, found and used by Paul because it precisely expressed his own ideas. . . . Thus, when translating, one is fully justified in setting this section forth in poetic form to call attention to its hymnlike characteristics."

296. See Gundry, *SŌMA in Biblical Theology*, 177-81, for a detailed refutation of the hypothesis that Paul is quoting from an early Christian hymn. He argues that the parallel words ignore the significant difference of order and contexts, the conjunctions are often used by Paul in nonliturgical settings, and the unusual vocabulary is not so unusual after all when cognate words are considered. After reviewing all the evidence for and against the hymn hypothesis, O'Brien, 471, concludes: "The arguments from the form, language, and ideas of Phil. 3:20-21 in favor of the view that the passage is pre-Pauline and either a hymn or hymnic piece are inadequate. We judge that the passage is the apostle's own composition even if phrases such as 'the Lord Jesus Christ' were taken over from earlier tradition."

Philippians 4

VII. FINAL APPEALS (4:1-9)

A. Be of One Mind in the Lord (4:1-3)

[1]*Therefore, my brothers and sisters, you whom I love and long for, my joy and crown, stand firm in the Lord in this way, my dear friends!*

[2]*I plead with Euodia and I plead with Syntyche to be of the same mind in the Lord.* [3]*Yes, and I ask you, my true companion, help these women since they have contended at my side in the cause of the gospel, along with Clement and the rest of my co-workers, whose names are in the book of life.*

With a lavish outpouring of love Paul challenges the community to *stand firm in the Lord* and pleads with two women *to be of the same mind in the Lord.* His affectionate address does not diminish the intensity of his plea for unity, nor does his plea for unity detract from the depth of his love for this community.[1] Paul passionately loves a divided community. He warmly embraces the community and urges the two opposing leaders of warring factions to be reconciled.

1 Paul's inferential conjunction, *therefore,* points back to the reasons to obey his imperatives.[2] His experience of the righteousness that comes from God through faith in Christ (3:7-17), the tragic destiny of the enemies of the cross (3:18-19), the present reality of our heavenly citizenship, and

1. On the basis of the expressions of strong affection in 4:1, Fowl, 177, following Bockmuehl, 237, dismisses the possibility of serious problems within the church. And grounding himself on 4:2-3, Davorin Peterlin, *Paul's Letter to the Philippians in the Light of Disunity in the Church* (NovTSup 79; Leiden: Brill, 1995), 105, following Silva, 221, sees a major division within the church leadership as the primary focus of the entire letter.

2. BDAG, 1107, translates Ὥστε followed by imperatives as "for this reason." Paul's use of the same conjunction in 2:12 points back to the Christ hymn as the reason to obey his imperative, *work out your own salvation.*

the expectation of Christ's return to restore all things (3:20-21) are compelling motives to *stand firm* and to *be of the same mind* (4:1-3).[3] Paul's commands are not arbitrary assertions of his personal authority. He always bases his imperatives on the solid ground of the indicatives of what Christ has done and will do. Grace always precedes, surrounds, empowers, and concludes the life of obedience. The letter begins with the greeting — *Grace and peace to you from God our Father and the Lord Jesus Christ* — and ends with the blessing — *The grace of our Lord Jesus Christ be with your spirit.* Paul's strong exhortations can be understood and implemented only in the context of the *grace of our Lord Jesus Christ.*

Before Paul challenges his friends to *stand firm,* he reminds them of his deep affection for them. The way he addresses his friends leaves no room to doubt his genuine love for them. He piles up five terms of endearment to describe his close relationship with them: *my brothers and sisters, beloved, longed for, my joy and crown,* and *beloved.* Paul often addresses all the members of the Christian community as *brothers and sisters.*[4] In the larger framework of Paul's theology, the familial relationship of brothers and sisters in the Christian community springs from the gift of adoption as children in God's family through the redemptive work of God's Son (Gal 4:4-7). Paul reminds the Philippian believers that they are *children of God* (2:12). Brothers and sisters in God's family enjoy equality and mutuality: they stand on the same level as siblings and share in a reciprocal relationship.[5] No longer does Paul have a spiritual hierarchy: Jews above Gentiles; faultless Hebrews above clueless Hellenists (3:5-6). His frequent use of the vocative address, *brothers and sisters,* points to a true friendship among equals.

Although siblings are not always on the best of terms with each other, Paul emphasizes that his Christian *brothers and sisters* are "beloved" by repeating the word "beloved" twice in the same sentence. A major theme in Paul's letters is how God demonstrates divine love for all believers in Christ.[6] But here Paul is expressing his own all-inclusive, unconditional love for his brothers and sisters. Paul repeatedly tells his friends, "I love you. I really love you." Not only does he love his family at a distance, but because of the distance they are *longed for.* This is the only time that this term occurs in the NT. "Its rarity perhaps adds intensity to the emotion of

3. Since 4:1 is an application of the preceding argument, some commentators emphasize its backward reference as a conclusion to 3:1–4:1 (Silva, 216-17; Witherington, 102-3; Hooker, 532). Most of them put it at the beginning of a new section of exhortations (O'Brien, 473; Fee, 385; Bockmuehl, 237). All recognize the transitional function of 4:1.

4. Paul addresses his readers directly as *brothers* seven times in this letter: 1:12; 3:1, 13, 17; 4:1, 8, 21. Since the term includes all the members of the community and since he addresses two women in 4:2, it is appropriate to translate the term as inclusive of men and women: *brothers and sisters.*

5. Ernest Best, *Paul and His Converts* (Edinburgh: T&T Clark, 1988), 132-35.

6. Paul uses *beloved* and *chosen* from OT passages to express God's unconditional sovereign love and election of believers in Christ (Rom 1:7; 9:25). See E. Stauffer, "ἀγαπάω," *TDNT* 1:49.

'homesick tenderness,' especially to the pain of separation that Paul feels and expresses here."[7]

Even as he is bound in chains and suffers the pain of separation from his friends, he nevertheless says that they are his *joy and crown.* Throughout this letter Paul expands the theme of joy. Joy fills Paul's life because he lives *in the Lord* and enjoys community with his *brothers and sisters.* Since his joy is relational and not situational, it cannot be shaken or diminished by the circumstances of his life. Paul tells his friends that because of them he joyfully celebrates a great victory: they are his *crown.* The combination of joy and crown, *my joy and crown,* indicates that "Paul envisions a grand celebration, perhaps like that at the end of the Olympic games, where the victors are given their wreaths and there is much rejoicing."[8] Since Paul refers to his friends in Thessalonica as "the crown in which we will glory in the presence of the Lord Jesus when he comes" (1 Thess 2:19), he may have the time of the Lord's return in mind when he refers to his Philippian friends as his *joy and crown.*[9] He told them earlier to *hold firmly to the word of life* so that he would *be able to boast on the day of Christ* (2:16). And his announcement of the Lord's imminent appearance from heaven to transform our lowly bodies (3:20-21) sets the immediate context for this reference to his friends as his *joy and crown.*[10] Yet Paul seems to have the present, not the eschatological future, in mind when he refers to his friends as *my joy and crown.*[11] Certainly, Paul affirms throughout the letter that they are his source of joy (1:18-19; 2:17). And he takes pride in their partnership (1:6; 2:1; 4:15) and citizenship (1:27; 3:30) with him. They are already his *joy and crown.*

Paul's outpouring of love, longing, joy, and pride goes beyond the terms that are "standard in discourse between friends."[12] In this warm embrace of his vibrant friendship with them, Paul challenges his friends: *stand firm in the Lord in this way, dear friends!* In this call to *stand firm* Paul repeats

7. Hawthorne, 178. See BDAG, 377. Paul uses cognate verb forms in 1:8 and 2:26.

8. Witherington, 102; see BDAG, 944.

9. Lightfoot, 157; Barth, 117; Fee, 388.

10. Calvin, 285: "He calls them his joy and crown, because, delighted that those who had been won through his efforts were persevering in the faith, he hoped for that triumph of which we have spoken, when the Lord will crown those things which have been done under his guidance."

11. Vincent, 130; O'Brien, 476; Bockmuehl, 257: "Paul's phrase is likely to have both present and future application: even now, the Philippians are his pride and joy, and he feels sure that they will be his 'boast on the day of Christ' (2:16)."

12. John T. Fitzgerald, "Philippians in the Light of Some Ancient Discussions of Friendship," in *Friendship, Flattery, and Frankness of Speech: Studies on Friendship in the New Testament World* (NovTSup 82; ed. John T. Fitzgerald; Leiden: Brill, 1996), 148, claims that "the terms of affection and longing that occur here are standard in discourses involving friends." But he cannot substantiate this claim by showing parallels to such a list of superlative terms. Fee, 388 n. 18, is certainly right to remonstrate that "it would be unfortunate indeed if, in recognizing that Paul is here using language common to friendship in the Greco-Roman world, one were to see this as a merely formal phenomenon and not the outpouring of his heart for his friends."

his initial exhortation to *stand firm in one Spirit* (1:27). In both contexts his challenge to *stand firm* comes with references to our citizenship, our opposition, and our unity.

> Citizenship:
> *as citizens of heaven live in a manner worthy of the gospel* (1:27)
> *our citizenship is in heaven* (3:20)
>
> Opposition:
> *those who oppose you* (1:28)
> *enemies of the cross* (3:18)
>
> Unity:
> *in the one Spirit, striving together with one accord* (1:27)
> *be of the same mind in the Lord* (4:2)

These parallels provide guidelines for the definition of the imperative to *stand firm.* First, we stand firm as citizens of heaven: as a community of exiles on earth we are to remain steadfast in our loyalty and obedience to our government in heaven. In anticipation of the day of universal acclamation, we declare with our words and our lives our allegiance to Jesus Christ our Lord. Second, we stand firm in our commitment to the cross of Christ in the face of those who oppose us as the enemies of the cross. Our commitment to Christ causes hostility and suffering. But we are not intimidated; our resolve to stand firm is intensified by our participation in the suffering of Christ. Third, we stand firm by being united in one mind and one Spirit. We cannot stand firm divided and alone; we stand firm when we are linked arm in arm, heart with heart in our community of brothers and sisters. This understanding of what it means to stand firm is capsulated in the prepositional phrase *in the Lord.* To *stand firm in the Lord* means that we remain strong and resolute in union with our Lord by exhibiting his Lordship over our lives, by following our Lord's way to the cross, and by walking in unity with each other in our corporate union with our Lord.[13]

Paul clarifies the meaning of his challenge to *stand firm* with an adverb, *in this way.* If this adverb points backward, then Paul is calling the community to stand firm by following his example and the example of others who live as he does (3:17).[14] If the adverb points forward, then Paul is instructing the community how to stand firm in the imperatives that follow in 4:2-9: *be of the same mind* (4:2); *Rejoice!* (4:4); *let your gentleness be evident* (4:5); *do not be anxious . . . present your requests* (4:6); *think about such things* (4:8); and *put it into practice* (4:9).[15] Perhaps the best way to interpret the ad-

13. Collange, 125; Schenk, 329.

14. So Fee, 388; O'Brien, 476.

15. Martin and Hawthorne, 240: "In a series of imperatives he puts meaning into the word οὕτως, 'thus.'"

verb is to take it as a link between the example that Paul has given in his own pursuit of Christ and the exhortations he is about to give for the way to live in union with Christ.[16]

2 After his challenge to the entire community to *stand firm,* Paul turns to address two women who are in conflict: *I plead with Euodia and I plead with Syntyche to be of the same mind in the Lord.* By repeating the verb *plead,* Paul speaks directly to each woman separately and does not take sides. No doubt the conflict between these two leaders caused a division between members of the community as people were forced to declare their allegiance to one or the other. But Paul avoids favoritism by respectfully pleading with each one individually. The verb *plead* conveys an appeal, request, and encouragement and implies treating someone in "an inviting and congenial manner."[17] Paul encourages these women who are "beloved" with a tender, friendly tone to be reconciled with one another.[18]

Euodia and *Syntyche* were common Greek names, appearing on first-century grave inscriptions.[19] Although attempts to identify these women with other biblical characters or social groups have failed,[20] Paul's reference to their names indicates that they were well-known members of the church who were causing a serious division by their personal animosity. If their personal squabble was an unusual occurrence within a basically unified church, then pointing to them by name seems to be unjustified and inexplicable.[21] Why would Paul speak to these two women so urgently if their conflict did not have any impact on the church? But if their conflict seriously threatened the unity of the church, then his reference to them by name in a letter to be read to the whole church appropriately and understandably identifies a major cause of the problem of disunity addressed in numerous ways throughout the entire letter.[22] Paul's call for these two

16. Silva, 217: "Whatever the precise syntactical force of *houtōs,* however, one should not assume that a backward and a forward reference are mutually exclusive. On the contrary, the bridging or transitional function of 4:1 is very clear."

17. BDAG, 765.

18. Schenk, 271, insists that the term *plead* (παρακαλῶ) does not have the sense of admonition ("Mahnung"), but rather the character of friendly enlivening stimulation ("freundschaftlichen Ermunterung"), as indicated by addressing these women as ἀγαπητοί.

19. BDAG, 409, 976.

20. Although the name "Lydia" may have referred to a woman's place of origin rather than served as a proper name, there is no good reason to identify either Euodia or Syntyche with Lydia. The hypothesis of a missionary couple fails on the basis that Paul addresses each of these woman individually, not as a couple, and the feminine form of their names followed by a feminine pronoun demonstrates that these were two women, not a man and a woman. The Tübingen hypothesis (that these two names are allegorical references to the Jewish-Christian and Gentile-Christian factions of the church) merely illustrates how some hypotheses travel far beyond any supporting evidence.

21. O'Brien, 479: "Since only two members are singled out by name, this personal discord may have been exceptional in the congregation."

22. D. E. Garland, "The Composition and Unity of Philippians," *NovT* 27 (1985), 173: "It is my contention that Paul carefully and covertly wove his argument to lead up to the

women to *be of the same mind* in the Lord repeats his major challenge to the entire community to be *like-minded, having the same love, being one in spirit and of one mind* (2:2). Paul's use of the same language when he requests the two women to *be of the same mind* as he used when he urged the entire church to *be like-minded* connects the problem of disunity in the church with the conflict between these two women. His general call for harmony in the church prepared the way for naming these two women. "The church was polarized around Euodia and Syntyche, who were the focus of disunity."[23] The only way for the church to be united is for these two women to *be of the same mind in the Lord.*

To be of the same mind means to think the same thing, have the same attitude, have the same opinion, and be intent on the same goal.[24] Paul has already defined this term (1:7; 2:2 [twice], 5; 3:15, 19) as a basic orientation and attitude toward life. When one's attitude of mind is *in the Lord,* union with the Lord informs and inspires the attitude. Paul wants these two women to have the right attitude toward each other by focusing on their life in union with the Lord. When their common bond in the Lord becomes central, their attitude toward each other will be the same as Christ Jesus expressed on the way to the cross: they will not claim their rights for their own advantage; they will take the form of a servant; they will humble themselves (2:5-8). Beyond these general characteristics of a Christ-like attitude, Paul does not disclose the specific changes that will be necessary for Euodia and Synthyche to make in order for them *to be of the same mind.*

If the conflict was caused by theological differences, then harmony will depend upon finding a way to resolve or transcend these differences on the basis of a common union in the Lord. Some speculate that these two women represent different theological perspectives: a perfectionist, legalist Jewish perspective and a permissive, antinomian Hellenist perspective.[25] Such speculation fails to provide adequate evidence that Paul addressed false theological positions held by members of the church in Philippi. Others speculate that the conflict was caused by diverse attitudes toward Paul: one woman and her followers withdrew support; the other woman supported Paul.[26] This hypothesis conflicts with Paul's repeated expressions of

---

impassioned summons in 4:2. He wrote primarily to defuse the dispute between these two women that was having disastrous repercussions for the unity of the church."

23. Peterlin, *Paul's Letter to the Philippians in the Light of Disunity in the Church,* 221; but Peterlin, 228, says that the conflict between Euodia and Syntyche was "not the cause or the root of disunity in the church." According to him, 228 n. 9, "To say this would be going beyond the available evidence and limit the reconstruction of the events to one simple scenario." Peterlin claims that his "reconstruction is more complex as it tries to take into account the complexity of information."

24. BDAG, 1065-66.

25. Müller, 137 n. 3, points to F. C. Baur and the Tübingen hypothesis as the source of this theological explanation of the conflict.

26. Peterlin, *Paul's Letter to the Philippians in the Light of Disunity in the Church,* 223: "At Philippi it all in the end came down to one of the two named women deacons, a prominent

thanksgiving for *all* the members of the church and their partnership with him (1:3-8; 4:10-18). Perhaps the way to understand the conflict between these two women is to find the reason for it in Paul's references to selfish ambition and rivalry (1:15-17; 2:3), on the one hand, and his references to humility (2:3, 8; 3:21), on the other. Whatever the specific issues may have been, the conflict was basically caused by pride, selfish ambition, and a spirit of rivalry. These two church leaders were engaged in a power struggle to expand their spheres of influence and control over the church. The only way out of such a conflict of self-interest is to have the mind of Christ: the humble attitude of a servant willing to suffer the ignominy of the cross in order to care for the interests of others in obedience to God.

3 Apparently, Paul did not think that these two women would resolve their conflict on their own. Perhaps they did not have the will or the ability to meet face to face and work through their issues. So Paul calls for another person to be a go-between, a moderator to guide them to reconciliation: *Yes, and I ask you, my true companion, help these women.* Paul's request for third-party intervention shows how deep the division between these two women was and how wide the negative impact of their division was in the church. Far from being a minor, unimportant dispute in an otherwise harmonious community, this conflict receives special attention because it was spreading like a virulent, aggressive form of cancer in the body. Paul's use of the emphatic particle *yes* with the verb of request, *I ask,* stresses his sense of urgency as he enlists the help of his *true companion.*[27]

Conjectures about the identity of Paul's *true companion* abound. Timothy and Epaphroditus are two obvious candidates on the basis of Paul's recommendation of them in this letter. Since the adjective *true* describes the *companion* (4:3) and the cognate adverb *genuine* describes the way that Timothy *will show concern* for the welfare of the Philippians (2:20), Timothy deserves to be called Paul's true companion. He is *as a son with his father* in his relationship with Paul (2:22). Epaphroditus could also claim to be Paul's true companion in the light of his titles and qualities: *co-worker and fellow soldier, messenger* (2:25); *he almost died for the work of Christ* (2:30). The account of Paul's visit to Philippi in Acts 16:11-40 suggests that Paul's true companion might be his traveling companion, Silas, or his first convert and hostess, Lydia. Since the first "we" section in Acts (16:11) begins with Paul's visit to Philippi, Luke becomes a possibility. The term *companion* might refer to a specific person with this proper name, *Syzyge.* Or the name could serve as a metaphorical reference to the entire Philippian church,

---

member of church leadership, withdrawing her support and using her influence to convince her house-congregation to do likewise. It appears to me that a small and tightly-knit house-congregation had little choice in such a matter anyway. Other church leaders (and their house-congregations) were possibly convinced too and joined her in her action. Thus the withdrawal of support for Paul united the 'anti-Pauline lobby' in a very practical and tangible way."

27. BDAG, 665.

Paul's partner in the gospel (1:5; 4:15-18). Even the possibility that this name refers to Paul's wife receives consideration since the term *companion* means yokefellow and sometimes refers to a wife. All of these hypotheses have their advocates, but "it is no longer possible to determine with certainty just whom the apostle has in mind."[28] No doubt the church knew the true identity of this person and was impressed that Paul asked this person to *help these women.*

The primary meaning of this verb *help* carries a strong sense of physical action: "seize, grasp, apprehend, catch, and take hold of together."[29] The verb refers to the arrest of Jesus (Mark 14:48; Matt 26:55; Luke 22:54; John 18:12), and the arrest of Peter (Acts 12:3). The same verb refers to the "catch" of many fish (Luke 5:9) and to the *help* given by the disciples to pull in the nets and fill the boats with fish (Luke 5:7). The only time Paul uses this verb in his letters is in this urgent request for his true companion to take strong personal action to bring these two women together. The two women have moved so far apart that the only hope for reconciliation is for Paul's companion to take hold of them and draw them back together again.

Paul gives his companion strong motivation for taking such courageous action. The reason for reconciling these women is that *they have contended at my side in the cause of the gospel.* To say that they *contended* by Paul's side means that they "struggled along with" Paul; they "fought" at his side.[30] Paul uses the same verb in his challenge to all members of the church to *stand firm in one Spirit, striving together with one accord for the faith of the gospel* (1:27). These women were famous for striving together at Paul's side in his gospel mission. They were not passive spectators; they were actively involved participants who struggled and suffered along with Paul to advance the gospel in the face of harsh opposition. Paul emphatically states that these two women were full members of his mission team, *along with Clement and the rest of my co-workers.*[31] Although a background check on Clement is unavailable, his Latin name may indicate his Roman origin. Apparently, he had such a good reputation in the church that Paul wanted to single him out by name as an example of one who contended at his side along with the two women. Along with these three fellow combatants, an army of *co-workers* receive the honor of being mentioned in Paul's letter. Although constraints of time and space do not allow Paul to list their names, they are all significant members of Paul's team. The women need to be rec-

28. BDAG, 954.

29. BDAG, 955. The verb occurs sixteen times in the NT, only once in Paul's letters.

30. BDAG, 964.

31. Two MSS (𝔓[16 vid] א*) support a variant reading, *my co-workers and the rest* (τῶν συνεργῶν μου καὶ τῶν λοιπῶν). This variant reading seems to exclude the women and Clement from the list of co-workers. And in this variant reading, the reference to *the rest* seems to include the whole community and not just Paul's co-workers. The reading in the text, *and the rest of my co-workers* (καὶ τῶν λοιπῶν συνεργῶν μου), is well supported by early and diverse MSS (𝔓[46] א[2] A B D F G Ψ 𝔐).

onciled because they belong to a great team of close associates of Paul. When Paul thinks of those who have served faithfully with him, Euodia and Syntyche come immediately to his mind. For this reason, Paul's true companion should make every effort to help these two women to be of the same mind.

Although Paul does not take time to mention the names of all his co-workers, their *names are in the book of life.* A number of references in Jewish literature to names written in God's book demonstrate that Paul is drawing on a well-established tradition.[32] In the Lukan tradition of the words of Jesus, his disciples are to "rejoice that your names are written in heaven" (Luke 10:20). The letter to the Hebrews also refers to the "church of the firstborn, whose names are written in heaven" (12:23). The promise of having their names written in the book of life sustains the persecuted recipients of the book of Revelation (3:5; 13:8; 17:8; 20:15). The reference to the book of life sounds an eschatological note consonant with the reminder of *citizenship in heaven* (3:20). The citizens of the Roman colony of Philippi who have their names recorded in a civic register of citizens know that they have a duty to live in harmony and peace with one another. The citizens of the colony of heaven in the Roman colony of Philippi who have their names written in the book of life in heaven are called by their Lord above all powers to live in peace with one another.[33] The anticipation of the Lord's appearance from heaven is the primary motivation for unity among those whose names are written in the book of life.

B. Rejoice in the Lord (4:4-9)

> *4Rejoice in the Lord always. I will say it again: Rejoice! 5Let your gentleness be evident to all. The Lord is near. 6Do not be anxious about anything, but in every situation, by prayer and petition, with thanksgiving, present your requests to God. 7And the peace of God, which transcends all understanding, will guard your hearts and your minds in Christ Jesus.*
>
> *8Finally, brothers and sisters, whatever is true, whatever is noble, whatever is right, whatever is pure, whatever is lovely, whatever is admirable — if anything is excellent or praiseworthy — think about such things.*
> *9Whatever you have learned or received or heard from me, or seen in me — put it into practice. And the God of peace will be with you.*

In this final burst of commands, Paul fires off one imperative after another in rapid succession. At first sight these directives may appear to be a rote repetition of the standard requirements for living the Christian life.[34]

32. Exod 32:32; Ps 69:28; Ezek 13:9; Dan 12:1; 1QM 12:3.
33. Fee, 397.
34. Compare 1 Thess 5:16-22.

Verse 8 might even look like a page out of a Hellenistic book on ethics. But closer observation will show that these commands are integrally related to the major themes of the entire letter and the specific conditions of the church in Philippi. These guidelines lead the church to be "an alternative political body, ruled by a different Lord, to that body constituted by citizens of Philippi under the dominion of Caesar."[35] Paul's practical advice guides the spiritual formation of the citizens of heaven.

4 The command to *rejoice in the Lord always* extends the theme of joy and rejoicing developed throughout the letter. Every other reference to joy in this letter encourages an appropriate response to the circumstances described in the immediate context. In 1:18 Paul rejoices that Christ is preached even though some preachers are motivated by selfish motives. In 2:2 Paul urges the Philippians to make his joy complete by being like-minded and of one mind. Paul calls the Philippians to rejoice with him in 2:17-18 because they are joined together in sacrifice and service. Paul tells the Philippians to welcome Epaphroditus with great joy because he almost died for the work of Christ (2:29). Rejoicing in the Lord is encouraged in 3:1 as a safeguard against the *dogs,* the Judaizers, who require conformity to their standards. In 4:10 the generous gift of the church to Paul causes him to rejoice greatly in the Lord. Since each reference to joy in this letter is tied to a specific reason or context for joy, the command to *rejoice always in the Lord* in 4:4 calls for a thoughtful response to the circumstances and reasons for joy. Although the addition of the adverb *always* indicates that rejoicing does not depend on specific circumstances and no grammatical conjunction ties this command to the context, we can still see some connection. Paul's previous correlation of unity and joy in 2:3 provides a basis for linking his command to rejoice with his appeal to Euodia and Syntyche to be of one mind (4:2). The reconciliation of two estranged friends leads to joyful celebration. And joyful praise to the Lord leads friends to set aside grievances in order to worship the Lord in unity. In contrast to a bitter, belligerent spirit that drives people apart, a sweet, exuberant spirit brings people together.

The command to rejoice in this context also comes as the first of a series of imperatives and in that way serves to set the tone for all that follows. Written from prison to Christians who are suffering for their commitment to Christ, this command calls for the development of a cheerful attitude in every circumstance to be the dominant theme in the Christian life. The fulfillment of all other goals in the Christian walk flows out of the practice of rejoicing *in the Lord.*

The simple phrase *in the Lord* provides the essential key to joy in every circumstance. No matter what anxiety circumstances cause, there is still "a defiant 'Nevertheless!'" *in the Lord* we rejoice.[36] Our relationship with the Lord is so central and determinative in our lives that all other factors

35. Fowl, 181.
36. Barth, 120.

cannot shake our sense of enthusiasm in the Lord. Paul is drawing on the rich heritage of his own Bible here. The Psalms command us, "Rejoice, the LORD is king" (Ps 97:1). The call of the Psalms to "make a joyful noise to the LORD" (Ps 100:1) ushers the people of God into corporate worship. People caught up in joyful worship of the Lord are united in heart and lifted above the circumstances of life in a vision of the awesome majesty of the Lord. The high point of this letter envisions all people bowing and proclaiming that *Jesus Christ is Lord* (2:11). Such a vision empowers even persecuted prisoners and residents in the Roman Empire to *rejoice in the Lord.*

Lest there be any detractors or recalcitrant members of the church who resist the encouragement to rejoice in the Lord, Paul repeats the command, *I will say it again: Rejoice!* He doubles the command in case there are those who object that rejoicing in a time of suffering is inappropriate. A time of suffering is a time when rejoicing in the Lord is the only way to survive. In no way is Paul simply advocating a positive mental attitude or urging his readers to "cheer up" and "have a nice day."[37] His double emphasis on joy comes from his own experience of knowing the resurrection power of Christ and participation in his sufferings (3:10) in his Roman prison.

5 Those who are truly rejoicing in the Lord at all times will be characterized by *gentleness to all.* "This is how other people are to experience the Christian's joy in the Lord."[38] Gentleness means "not insisting on every right of letter of law or custom, yielding, gentle, kind, courteous, and tolerant."[39] Aristotle describes the gentle person as "the one who by choice and habit does what is equitable, and who does not stand on his rights unduly, but is content to receive a smaller share although he has the law on his side."[40] Such leniency needs to be evident in the lives of Christians "as opposed to the non-recipients of grace, who can still be stiff and bristly."[41] The Pastorals include gentleness as an essential qualification for leadership in the church (1 Tim 3:2) and call for members of the church to be gentle to everyone (Tit 3:3). James teaches that the wisdom that comes from heaven is considerate (Jas 3:17).

Gentleness should not be reserved only for close friends and family or only for fellow Christians; it should *be evident to all.* Paul calls for Christians to have a reputation of being courteous. Especially in a society hostile to the Christian faith, Christians are called to respond to opposition with *gentleness* to all. Paul's use of this term in his letter to the Philippians is strikingly similar to the use of the same term in the Wisdom of Solomon 2:19. In that text those who oppose the righteous say, "Let us test him with

37. Bockmuehl, 244.

38. Bockmuehl, 244; Barth (121) quotes Luther: "Before God be glad at all times, but before men be lenient."

39. BDAG, 371; H. Preisker, "ἐπιεικής," *TDNT* 2:589: Gentleness is the "mitigation of strict legal claims out of regard for special circumstances in individual cases."

40. Aristotle, *Eth. nic.* 5.10.8.

41. Barth, 121.

insult and torture, so that we may find out how gentle he is, and make trial of his forbearance." Paul recognizes that suffering for faith in Christ tests the quality of gentleness. Harsh attacks quickly spark defensive responses. So Paul encourages the small, beleaguered group of Christians in Philippi to let their *gentleness be evident to all* even when they are stripped of their honor and treated unjustly.

The assurance that *the Lord is near* provides needed encouragement to maintain the attitude of gentleness to all in a time of suffering. The phrase reminds the readers again of the imminent coming of the Savior from heaven to transform humiliation into glory (3:20-21).[42] The shame of persecution will soon be exchanged for the honor of participating in Christ's victory. The NT church is often encouraged in times of suffering by the assurance that *the Lord is near:* "when you see these things happening, you know that he is near, right at the door" (Mark 13:29); "You too, be patient and stand firm, because the Lord's coming is near" (Jas 5:8); "the time is near" (Rev 1:3; 22:10). The church eagerly prays, "Come, Lord! — *Marana tha!"* (1 Cor 16:22). Even when Christians suffer under the rule of Caesar as Lord, they can express courteous leniency toward all because they believe that Christ the Lord is coming soon *to bring everything under his control* (3:21).

6 Assurance that the *Lord is near* also encourages Christians to stop being anxious.[43] The present tense prohibition, *Do not be anxious,* indicates that the readers must stop what they are habitually doing.[44] The same verb is used with a positive connotation in Paul's prediction that Timothy *will show genuine concern* for the welfare of the church in Philippi (2:20). But evidently the Philippians had crossed the line from having genuine concern to being overly concerned and distressed by their concerns.[45] From the contents of the letter, we learn that concerns for the welfare of Paul and

42. Most commentaries interpret the term *near* as a temporal reference. See Vincent, 133: "The phrase expresses the general expectation of the speedy coming of Christ." Fee, 408: "It seems likely that this is primarily intended as the last in the series of eschatological words to this suffering congregation, again reminding them of their sure future, despite present difficulties." O'Brien, 489: "The Philippians are to adopt an unabrasive spirit under provocation because their Lord is coming to vindicate their cause." The adverb *near* (ἐγγύς) refers in some contexts to spatial proximity (Mark 1:38; 6:36; John 19:42; Eph 2:13; see BDAG, 271). Collange, 126, develops the spatial sense of *near* by tying this phrase together with 2:6-8: the Lord drew near to humanity in his incarnation and humiliation (2:6-8). O'Brien, 489, comments that "both interpretations are theologically correct, and it may be unnecessary to choose between them. The apostle may have intended to include both ideas of time and space with his use of ἐγγύς: the Lord who may return at any time came near in his incarnation (2:6-8), and is continually near to his people ('at hand', AV) to guide and bless them."

43. Despite the lack of conjunctions, these short staccato statements are connected by an inner logic. See Silva, 225; Fee, 408; O'Brien, 490; Müller, 197.

44. See BDF §336 (3) for a discussion and illustrations of the present tense prohibition.

45. See BDAG, 632, for the negative and positive meanings of μεριμνάω: "1. to be apprehensive, have anxiety, be anxious, be unduly concerned (Phil 4:6); 2. to attend to, care for, be concerned about (Phil 2:20)."

Epaphroditus (1:12; 2:26) and threats of persecution for faith in Christ (1:29-30) caused the believers in Philippi to be anxious. Paul understands that anxious thoughts naturally multiply in times of trouble.[46] But he calls for his friends to make a concerted effort to stop their obsession with worrying. His comprehensive prohibition allows them no exception: *nothing,* absolutely *nothing,* is a proper object of the continuous stress of worry.

A comprehensive positive — *but in everything* — establishes a total contrast with the comprehensive negative — *nothing.*[47] Only by praying with thanksgiving *in every situation* is it possible to stop being anxious about *anything.* The continuous positive focus of praying with thanksgiving to God *in everything* breaks and replaces the habit of worry. "To begin by praising God for the fact that in this situation, as it is, he is so mightily God — such a beginning is the end of anxiety."[48] The string of three synonyms for prayer — *prayer, petition, requests* — with the additional emphasis on *thanksgiving* encourages all types of prayer. The first term, *prayer,* often signifies intercessory prayer for others.[49] True intercessory prayer for others overcomes anxious thoughts about them. The second term, *petition,* denotes "an urgent request to meet a need, exclusively addressed to God."[50] In this letter Paul uses this term when he refers to his prayers for the Philippians (1:4) and their prayers for him (1:19). Since he and the Philippians were *going through the same struggle* (1:30), their prayers for each other included urgent requests for God to meet the needs caused by suffering for faith in Christ. Paul knew that the petitions of his friends in Philippi for him and God's provision of the Spirit of Jesus Christ would bring about his deliverance (1:19). His experience of the effectiveness of petitions to God gave him confidence that God would meet all the needs of the Philippians (4:19). Based upon this confidence in the effectiveness of petitions, Paul encourages the Philippians to turn their worries into petitions to God. The third term for prayer, *requests,* refers to naming specific items. This term occurs in only two other places in the NT. Pilate granted the *request* that Jesus be crucified (Luke 23:24). The readers of 1 John are encouraged to pray because God hears whatever we ask according to his will. "And if we know that he hears us — whatever we ask — we know that we have the *requests* we asked of him" (1 John 5:15). Both of these uses of the term *request* indicate specific items that are requested. By his use of this

46. R. Bultmann, "μεριμνάω," *TDNT* 4:591: "The exhortations not to worry presuppose that every man naturally cares for himself and his life, that he is concerned about himself, that he is always intent on something and concerned about something. This is by no means ruled out as illegitimate. Indeed, it is accepted that man is concerned about himself and that he strives after things. But the why and wherefore of his concern and striving are given a new orientation, and so, too, is his understanding of himself and his life."

47. Müller, 198.

48. Barth, 122.

49. BDAG, 878; H. Schönweiss, "Prayer," *NIDNTT* 2:867-69. See Rom 1:10; 15:30; 1 Thess 1:2; Phlm 4, 22; Col 4:2, 12; Eph 1:16.

50. BDAG, 213.

term, Paul encourages being specific in prayer to God — not mouthing vague generalities and amorphous meditation, but giving voice to the specific desires of our hearts.

Literally, Paul says, "let your requests be made known to God."[51] By telling us to let our requests be made known to God, Paul is not presupposing that God does not know our needs before we give voice to them.[52] He is calling for full self-disclosure in God's presence. By expressing our specific requests to God, we "acknowledge our total dependence upon God."[53] The preposition *to* in the phrase *to God* pictures this kind of prayer as a "movement or orientation toward" God.[54] Prayer orients our lives toward God; we grow in an open relationship with God by presenting our specific needs and desires to him.

With thanksgiving gives the right attitude and perspective in prayer.[55] Paul's own prayers exemplify the practice of praying with thanksgiving: *I thank my God every time I remember you. In all my prayers for all of you, I always pray with joy because of your partnership in the gospel from the first day until now* (1:3-5). Though Paul had good reasons to be anxious for the welfare of the Philippians given their experience of suffering and their lack of unity, his prayers for them exude an attitude of joyful gratitude to God for them. His confident petitions for God's future blessings rest on his grateful remembrance of God's faithfulness: *being confident of this, that he who began a good work in you will carry it on to completion until the day of Christ Jesus* (1:6). "Thanksgiving means giving God the glory in everything, making room for him, casting our care on him, letting it be his care."[56] Conversely, a lack of thanksgiving to God leads to idolatry: exchanging the glory of God for images of created things. As a result, thinking and praying become futile (Rom 1:21-25). Absence of thanksgiving to God in prayer turns off the power in prayer. Without thanksgiving, prayer becomes merely a way of complaining to God about all the bad things that are or might be happening. The only way to fulfill Paul's challenge to *do everything without grumbling or arguing* (2:14) is to pray *in every situation, with thanksgiving* (4:6).

7 After his instructions on prayer, Paul makes a promise that those who pray in this way will experience *the peace of God.*[57] The conjunction *and* is used in this context "to introduce a result that comes from what precedes."[58] The transcendent experience of God's peace is the assured result

51. τὰ αἰτήματα ὑμῶν *(your requests)* is the subject of the imperative verb γνωριζέσθω ("be made known"). TNIV turns *your requests* into the object of the imperative verb: *present your requests.*

52. Matt 6:32 offers the assurance that "your heavenly Father knows that you need them" as the antidote to worry.

53. O'Brien, 493.

54. BDAG, 874.

55. Müller, 198.

56. Barth, 122.

57. Müller, 198: not a wish, but a promise.

58. BDAG, 495.

of praying as verse 6 describes prayer. The condition for experiencing God's peace is not that God grants all of our requests but that we have made known all our requests to God with thanksgiving. God's peace is not the result of the power of our prayers or the effectiveness of our prayers. Prayer is not auto-suggestion, a form of self-hypnosis that produces God's peace. Prayer is our openness about our needs before God, our emptiness in his presence, our absolute dependence upon him with an attitude of constant thanksgiving and complete trust.[59] When we pray with that attitude, the focus is not at all upon what we are doing or will do, but on what God will do. God will do something supernatural beyond our best abilities and thoughts: the peace of God will guard us. "Peace is always the gift of God rather than humanly devised or achieved."[60]

The peace of God denotes "the peace that God himself has."[61] In this sense, *the peace of God* refers to "the calm serenity that characterizes God's very nature and that grateful, trusting Christians are welcome to share."[62] "Peace then is God's very character; verse 9 refers appropriately to *the God of peace.*"[63] Although the peace of God refers primarily to the peace God has and is in himself, the peace of God also refers to the peace that God gives: "the inward peace of the soul which comes from God, and is grounded in God's presence and promise."[64]

The *peace of God* is the opposite of anxiety.[65] "God himself is not beset with anxieties, for he knows the end from the beginning and directs all things in accordance with his will."[66] When we trust God in prayer, God gives to us his peace to guard our hearts and minds against anxious thoughts.[67] But the *peace of God* in a larger and deeper sense is more than the absence of anxiety. Peace in the Hebraic sense of *shalom* means "well-being," especially well-being in terms of health and harmony in personal relationships.[68] *Shalom* seldom if ever denotes the spiritual attitude of inward peace. It is "not something concealed and inward; it manifests itself in the form of external well-being." *Shalom* "is an emphatically social con-

59. D. Martyn Lloyd-Jones, *The Life of Peace: An Exposition of Philippians 3 and 4* (Grand Rapids: Baker, 1992), 174-75.

60. Bockmuehl, 247.

61. Barth, 123.

62. Martin and Hawthorne, 246; this interpretation takes the genitive, *of God* (τοῦ θεοῦ), as a descriptive genitive.

63. Bockmuehl, 248; O'Brien, 496: "It is best, in our judgment, to regard the phrase as designating, in the first instance, that peace which God himself possesses or has."

64. Vincent, 135.

65. The phrase *the peace of God* occurs only here in the NT; a similar phrase, *the peace of Christ,* occurs in Col 3:15.

66. Beare, 147.

67. Fowl, 184: "The peace of God, which comes through prayer, counters anxiety because it 'guards believers' thoughts and hearts in Christ.'" Lloyd-Jones, *The Life of Peace,* 174: "He will keep you absolutely safe from those things that are keeping you awake and preventing your sleep."

68. Hooker, 541.

cept."[69] In Paul's letters, it refers to the relationship of peace with God (Rom 5:1) and the relationship of peace with one another (Rom 14:17; 1 Cor 7:15; Eph 4:3; 2 Tim 2:22).[70] In the context of Paul's letter to the Philippians, his promise of the peace of God continues the theme of *being like-minded, have the same love, being one in spirit and of one mind* (2:2; 4:2). By means of corporate prayer with thanksgiving (4:6), God will give peace in the troubled relationships (4:7).[71] Ultimately, the command to *be of the same mind* will be fulfilled by the gift of God's peace when the church turns to God in prayer.[72]

The peace of God *transcends all understanding.* This description of God's peace is defined in two ways. First, to transcend all understanding is taken by some to mean that human reasoning cannot comprehend God's peace. Calvin advocates this meaning on the grounds that "nothing is more foreign to the human mind, than to hope in the depth of despair, in the depth of poverty to see riches, and in the depth of weakness not to give way."[73] Similarly Silva comments, "God's peace transcends our intellectual powers precisely because believers experience it when it is unexpected, in circumstances that appear to make it impossible: Paul suffering in prison, the Philippians threatened by quarrels within and enemies without."[74] To be anxious because of suffering and quarrels is reasonable; to have the peace of God in the face of opposition transcends human reason.

Second, the phrase *transcends all understanding* is taken by others to mean that the peace of God is far superior to human reason. All the exceptional human abilities of perceptive insights and reflective intelligence cannot resolve conflicts and reduce anxiety as effectively as God's peace does. The healing power of God's peace far surpasses the powers of the human mind. "The peace of God surpasses every human thought or device as a means of insuring tranquility of heart."[75] "God's peace is able to produce exceedingly better results than human planning."[76] By the use of their human understanding the Philippians were exacerbating their divisions and intensifying their anxiety. Now Paul calls them to pray together with thanksgiving and to subject their minds to the gift of God's peace.[77]

Although both interpretations can be supported from the Greek words and the context, the interpretation that points to the superiority of

69. G. von Rad, "εἰρήνη," *TDNT* 2:406.

70. W. Foerster, "εἰρήνη," *TDNT* 2:415-16.

71. Lightfoot, 161, comments that the promise of the peace of God is "again an indirect allusion to their dissensions."

72. Fee, 410: "In contrast to other letters, he does not express 'peace' as an imperative but as an indicative, closely related to their trusting God in prayer." See the imperatives to live in peace in Rom 14:19; 2 Cor 13:11; 1 Thess 5:13.

73. Calvin, 290.

74. Silva, 226.

75. Vincent, 136.

76. Martin and Hawthorne, 247.

77. Collange, 127.

God's peace over human planning and ingenuity seems to fit best with the promise that God's peace *will guard your hearts and minds in Christ Jesus.* Paul's image of guarding comes from the presence of the Roman garrison housed in Philippi to keep the peace of Rome, the *pax Romana,* for the benefit of the Roman Empire.[78] The verb *guard* conveys the general meaning of "to provide security, guard, protect, and keep."[79] This verb is used by Paul with a specific reference to the military function of guarding the city gates of Damascus (2 Cor 11:32) and probably has the same military overtones in Philippians 4:7, "in order to ring bells with his readership at Philippi where a military garrison was stationed to guard the *pax Romana.*"[80] Although the peace imposed on the city of Philippi expressed the superior intelligence and planning of the Roman Empire, the effectiveness of God's peace-keeping force far surpassed even the best military minds of the Roman army. The garrison guarding the Roman peace could only exert external pressure, but God's peace guards the interior lives, the *hearts and minds,* of believers in Christ.

The *heart* is "the center and source of the whole inner life, with its thinking, feeling and volition."[81] The *mind* (or, a better translation, *thought*) is "that which one has in mind as a product of intellectual processes."[82] Paul uses the term *thoughts* five times in 2 Corinthians with a negative sense as a reference to corrupt thoughts opposed to Christ and Christian knowledge (2:11; 3:14; 4:4; 10:5; 11:3). In Philippians 4:7, however, the term appears to have a neutral sense of thoughts that proceed from the hearts of Christians.[83] In his letter to the church in Philippi, Paul recognizes the sad fact that the hearts and the thoughts even of Christians are susceptible to envy, rivalry, selfish ambition, vain conceit, and selfish interests (1:15; 2:3-4). But he assures the church that through prayer, God will keep the peace in the community by guarding the innermost "emotions, affections, thoughts, and moral choices" of the members of the community.[84] By referring to the *hearts and minds*[85] of believers, Paul is giving a holistic summary

78. Fowl, 184; O'Brien, 498; Fee, 411 n. 58: "This is a military metaphor, where a garrison, such as the one always stationed in Philippi, 'guards the Roman *pax.*'"

79. BDAG, 1066-67.

80. Bockmuehl, 248.

81. BDAG, 508; J. K. Chamblin, "Psychology," *DPL* 769; J. Behm, "καρδία," *TDNT* 3:612.

82. BDAG, 675.

83. Behm, "νόημα," *TDNT* 4:960-61.

84. Martin and Hawthorne, 247.

85. A few MSS (263 590 809) omit "and your thoughts" (καὶ τὰ νοήματα ὑμῶν); several MSS (F G it) replace the word *minds* (νοήματα) with "bodies" (σώματα); one papyrus (𝔓) adds the words "and the bodies" after the word *minds* (καὶ τὰ νοήματα καὶ τὰ σώματα); the reading in the text, *your hearts and your minds* (τὰς καρδίας ὑμῶν καὶ τὰ νοήματα ὑμῶν), is strongly supported by early and diverse MSS (𝔓^{46} ℵ A B D Ψ 𝔐). Both the combinations of heart and body (Rom 1:24) and heart and thoughts (2 Cor 3:14-15) occur in Paul's letters. Scribal error can be imagined in either direction. Perhaps early scribal harmonization with 1 Thess 5:23

of the interior life of the church and all its members. A narrowly personal reduction of the reference to *hearts and minds* to an individualistic sense — peace in *my own* heart and mind — misses the need for relational peace addressed throughout the letter, especially in 2:1-4 and 4:2-3.[86] God gives peace and keeps peace in the community in Christ Jesus. This community of believers residing in Philippi lives *in Christ Jesus.* This significant phrase, *in Christ Jesus,* appears eight times in this letter (1:1, 26; 2:5; 3:3, 14; 4:7, 19, 21) as the unifying thread of the entire discourse.

8 *Finally,* Paul wraps up his directives for the Christian life with one long sentence containing two appeals: *think about such things* — the virtues of a good life (4:8) — and *put it into practice* — what they learned from Paul (4:9).[87] As a result of God's peace guarding the hearts and minds of believers, their minds focus on all that is *excellent or praiseworthy.* Paul defines all that is excellent with a list of six adjectives and two nouns arranged in an impressive rhetorical fashion. As a result of repeating the relative pronoun *whatever (hosa)* before each of the six adjectives and omitting any conjunctions between these six clauses, Paul's list of these six virtues appears to be expansive and comprehensive.[88] Then two parallel conditional clauses summarize this list in terms of two nouns. This list of eight virtues presented in the six adjectives and two nouns leads up to the imperative and its direct object: *think about these things.*

Whatever is true
Whatever noble
Whatever right
Whatever pure
Whatever lovely
Whatever admirable
If any excellence
If any praiseworthy

Think about such things.

Paul's list of eight virtues bears a striking resemblance to lists of virtues in Greek literature. "It is almost as if he had taken a current list from a textbook of ethical instructions, and made it his own."[89] The term *excellence (aretē),* a term not found elsewhere in Paul's letters, means "excellence of

("spirit, soul, and body") caused a change from "thoughts" to "bodies" (so Fee, 402 n. 11). The external MS evidence strongly supports the reading *hearts and "thoughts."* See Bockmuehl, 248-49.

86. Bockmuehl, 248.

87. The expression *finally* serves in this context not to conclude the letter but to finish a list of imperatives (O'Brien, 499).

88. According to BDF §460 (3), the lack of conjunctions (polysyndeton) "produces the impression of extensiveness and abundance."

89. Beare, 148.

character, exceptional civic virtue." "The term is a favorite subject in Stoic thought relating to morality."[90] By the use of this term, usually translated *virtue* in Greek literature, Paul seems to signal that he is developing a list of virtues roughly parallel to virtue lists in Greek literature.[91] In *The Republic,* Plato presents four cardinal virtues: prudence, justice, fortitude, and temperance. In *Nicomachean Ethics,* Aristotle develops an elaborate list of moral and intellectual virtues. He defines twelve moral virtues as means between the vices of excess and defect.[92] The Stoics derived extensive lists of virtues from Plato's four cardinal virtues. These lists played an important role in the popular moral teaching of the Stoics.[93] Dio Chrysostom lists the virtues "in the hope of being able to win souls from evil, delusion, and wicked desires and to lead them to love virtue and to long for a better life."[94] Just as Paul encourages his readers to think about the virtues, Plutarch also affirms the benefit of thinking about virtues: "It is true that the thought and recollection of good men almost instantly comes to mind and gives support to those who are making progress towards virtue, and in every onset of the emotions and in all difficulties keeps them upright and saves them from falling."[95] Paul's use of the term *excellence* or *virtue (aretē)* in his virtue list probably indicates that he is drawing upon his readers' familiarity with the popular discussion of virtues in their culture.

In addition to this unusual use of the term *excellence/virtue (aretē)* in Paul's list of virtues, two of the eight terms — *lovely* and *admirable* — do not occur elsewhere in the NT, one term — *noble* — occurs only in the Pastorals (1 Tim 3:8, 11; Tit 2:2), and, as we will see in our exposition of the list, some of the terms, *true, right,* and *pure,* are used in ways that differ from Paul's normal usage but conform to their use in Hellenistic ethics. All of these observations support the conclusion that Paul "has taken over terms that were current coin in popular moral philosophy, especially in Stoicism."[96] Paul's challenge to *think about* these Hellenistic virtues indicates his desire for the church to appreciate all that is good in the surrounding culture. Although the church experiences opposition from the culture (1:28), this opposition should not lead to a totally negative judgment and repudiation of culture. "The world knows very well what is good. Christians are to know it too, no less well than the world but better — that is assuredly the apostle's view."[97] But Paul does not simply advocate a pursuit of popular mo-

90. BDAG, 130.

91. BDAG, 130; C. G. Kruse, "Virtues and Vices," *DPL* 962-63; John T. Fitzgerald, "Virtue/Vice Lists," *ABD* 6:857-59.

92. *Eth. nic.* 2.6-9.

93. A. J. Malherbe, *Moral Exhortation: A Greco-Roman Sourcebook* (LEC 4; Philadelphia: Fortress, 1986), 138-41.

94. Dio Chrysostom, *Oration* 4.83-96, quoted in Malherbe, *Moral Exhortation,* 140.

95. Plutarch, "Progress in Virtue" 85 B, in *Mor.* 1.453 (Babbitt, LCL).

96. O'Brien, 502; see also Martin and Hawthorne, 250; Bockmuehl, 250.

97. Barth, 124; Bockmuehl, 250: "In his positive estimation of this rhythmically arranged list of Hellenistic virtues, therefore, Paul in effect asserts the moral sanity of Chris-

rality; he qualifies and elevates the virtues in his continuation of the same sentence in the next verse (4:9) by redefining these virtues in terms of his teaching and example. Ultimately, life in Christ brings to fulfillment the highest moral aspirations in the surrounding culture.

The challenge to *think about whatever is true* requires the search for truth in the most comprehensive sense. Although Paul normally associates truth with the truth about God (Rom 1:18, 25) and the truth of the gospel of Christ (Gal 2:5, 14; 5:7; 2 Cor 4:2; 11:10), in the context of this list of virtues he affirms *whatever is true* to be the proper subject of Christian thought.[98] Thinking about *whatever is true* requires discernment to see the difference between what is true and what is false. Paul distinguishes between true and false motives (1:18). Paul expects that the one who loves not only thinks about the truth but also "rejoices with the truth" (1 Cor 13:6). Paul's command to *think about whatever is true* endorses the claim that "all truth is God's truth."[99] In obedience to this command, Christians work out an integration of *whatever is true* with "the truth of the gospel" in all areas of life.

Paul's encouragement to *think about whatever is noble* leads to a life of respectful admiration of people who are noble, serious, dignified, honorable, and above reproach.[100] In the Pastorals, deacons (1 Tim 3:8), women (3:11), and older men (Tit 2:2) are to be *noble,* worthy of respect. Calling for a focus on all that is noble also implies a deliberate turning away from all that is ignoble, dishonorable, and vulgar.[101] In Greek literature the virtue *noble* is also attributed to divine beings in the sense that they are "worthy of reverence, august, sublime, and holy."[102] In this context the virtue connotes whatever is awe-inspiring, lofty, and majestic: "things that lift the mind from the cheap and tawdry to that which is noble and good and of moral worth."[103]

Attention to *whatever is right* means fulfilling all that is "obligatory in view of certain requirements of justice."[104] In Paul's theological discourse, this term carries the meaning of being righteous before God. In this sense, "'There is no *just* person, not even one'" (Rom 3:10). The only way to be *right,* righteous before God, is through the redemptive work of Christ: "through one person's obedience, all will be constituted just" (Rom 5:19). Only by faith in Christ can one be just: "'The just shall live by faith'" (Rom 1:17; Gal 3:11). But Paul can also use this term in a broadly secular sense. He claims that *it is right* for him to feel the way he does about the

tian faith — professing 'the moral atmosphere of the Incarnation to be common sense', as G. K. Chesterton put it (*Orthodoxy,* ch. 9)."

98. Bockmuehl, 252; O'Brien, 504.

99. Arthur F. Holmes, *All Truth Is God's Truth* (Grand Rapids: Eerdmans, 1977). According to Holmes, "The early church claimed that all truth is God's truth wherever it be found" (p. 8). He also quotes Clement of Alexandria and Justin Martyr for support (p. 14).

100. BDAG, 919.

101. O'Brien, 504.

102. BDAG, 919.

103. Martin and Hawthorne, 251.

104. BDAG, 247.

Philippians (1:7). He uses the term with this basic Hellenistic meaning in this list of virtues.[105] The person who has the virtue of being *right* or *just* in Greco-Roman society is "one who upholds the customs and norms of behavior, including especially public services that make for a well-ordered, civilized society."[106] The NT offers several examples of this secular sense of the term. The master of the vineyard offers to give "whatever is just" at the end of the day (Matt 20:4). Masters are directed to give their slaves "whatever is just" (Col 4:1). According to Philo, this is the cardinal virtue.[107] "The just person *(ho dikaios)* is the stay of the human race; he brings his personal property to the community and gives unstintingly for the good of those who find a use for it. He then seeks from God, who alone possesses all wealth, that which he does not have."[108]

To *think about whatever is pure* requires focusing on those things that are morally blameless. Originally the word signified "the awe-inspiring holiness of the gods and their realm."[109] As a cultic term it designated persons and things purified in the temple for religious rites. This original external religious meaning of the word was extended to include inward moral significance.[110] Paul desires to present the church to Christ "as a pure virgin" (2 Cor 11:2). Paul's call to moral purity reverberates throughout the early church. 1 Timothy 5:22 repeats the challenge: "Keep yourself pure." Titus 2:5 urges the younger women "to be self-controlled and pure." James 3:17 describes the wisdom that comes from above as "first of all pure." 1 Peter 3:2 encourages wives to win over their husbands to the faith by the "purity and reverence" of their lives. 1 John 3:3 calls for those who have the hope of Christ's appearance to "purify themselves, just as he is pure." Polycarp's *To the Philippians* challenges the young men to be "blameless in all things, caring for purity, and curbing themselves from evil" (5:3) and the virgins to "walk with a blameless and pure conscience" (5:5).[111] For Paul, purity in all of life begins in the thought life: *think about whatever is pure.*

Thought must also be given to aesthetic appreciation: *think about whatever is lovely.*[112] The term translated *lovely,* appearing only here in the NT, means "causing pleasure or delight, pleasing, agreeable, and lovely."[113] In the story of Queen Esther's encounter with the king, this word points to

105. Bockmuehl, 254.
106. BDAG, 246.
107. *TLNT* 1:321.
108. Philo, *Migr. Abr.* 219.
109. H. Balz, "ἁγνός," *EDNT* 1:22.
110. Hauck, "ἁγνός," *TDNT* 1:122; BDAG, 13.
111. See also *1 Clem.* 1:3; 21:8; 29:1; 48:1.
112. Bockmuehl, 253: "Of all the words in Paul's list, this one gives the clearest indication that the range of qualities that should shape a Gentile Christian mind includes a dimension not just of moral but of aesthetic truth as well. It extends to all that is beautiful in creation and in human lives." Fee, 418: "In common parlance, this word could refer to a Beethoven symphony, as well as to the work of Mother Teresa."
113. BDAG, 886.

the beauty of Esther's face (LXX Esth 5:1b). Consideration of this virtue leads to an enjoyment of genuine beauty that gives pleasure.

The term translated *admirable* occurs only here in the NT and does not appear in the LXX. The word denotes whatever is "praiseworthy, commendable."[114] The nominal form of this adjective refers to a "good report" (2 Cor 6:8). Related to the term *euphonic*, the term *(euphēma)* means "fair-spoken, fair-sounding."[115] Whatever words, works, or persons are well spoken of by people deserve our careful consideration.

After pointing to these six virtues in this list of adjectives, Paul now reinforces the significance of these virtues in his two conditional phrases: *if anything is excellent, if anything is praiseworthy.* These two phrases qualify the six qualities already listed in terms of moral excellence.[116] The form of the conditional phrases assumes the certainty of the condition and could be translated: *since* there are things that are excellent and praiseworthy. We have already observed that the term *excellence, virtue (aretē)* connects this list of excellent qualities with the whole concept and practice of Hellenistic virtue ethics. The term *praiseworthy* usually refers to human beings who are worthy of "praise, approval, and recognition."[117] Paul desires to direct the attention of the Philippians to those people who embody all the virtues in their character and conduct. Since the entire letter points above all to Christ and the next verse recalls his own teaching and example, Paul expects his readers to see how the noblest aspirations and highest standards of Hellenistic culture are uniquely fulfilled in Christ and in those who are in Christ. But his challenge to *think about such things* also calls for a discerning evaluation of all that is virtuous and praiseworthy in their own culture.

The command to *think* requires his readers "to give careful thought to a matter, consider, ponder, and let one's mind dwell on something."[118] Paul is calling for followers of Christ to be attentive, reflective, meditative thinkers. Developing a Christian mind and character requires a lifetime of discerning and disciplined thought about all the things that are excellent and praiseworthy.

9 All the virtues listed in verse 8 now receive redefinition in terms of Paul's teaching and practice: *Whatever you have learned or received or heard from me, or seen in me — put it into practice.* Paul does not pose a contrast or disjunction between the qualities listed in verse 8 and the content of his teaching and conduct (v. 9). He is not correcting a wrong view of the virtues

114. BDAG, 414.

115. LSJ, 737.

116. Fee, 416 n. 13: "The two words 'moral excellence' and 'praiseworthy' do not 'summarize' the preceeding virtues, they qualify them."

117. BDAG, 357. After the word *praiseworthy* (ἔπαινος), several MSS (D F G) have the word (ἐπιστήμης). Apparently, this word was added by copyists to provide a definition of praiseworthy: "praiseworthy of understanding." The reading in the text is strongly supported by early and diverse MSS.

118. BDAG, 598.

in light of his teaching and practice of the gospel, nor is he presenting two unrelated subjects: think about the virtues (v. 8) and practice my teaching and example (v. 9). The definite relative pronoun *whatever* at the beginning of verse 9 refers back to its antecedent at the end of verse 8: *such things.*[119] Usually, sentences beginning with the definite relative pronoun "introduce a further and specific elaboration of the preceding subject at hand."[120] Paul's use of the definite relative pronoun *whatever* indicates that his teaching and way of life exemplify those things that are considered to be *excellent* and *praiseworthy.* Paul points to the virtues as the focus of his teaching and the form of his life. We can paraphrase Paul's line of thought in this way: "*Think about such things* as acts of selfless love in the service of others because they are *excellent* and *praiseworthy.* And my message and life are devoted to what is most *excellent* and *praiseworthy:* the self-emptying, self-humbling love of Christ on the cross. *Put into practice* the selfless love of Christ that you have *learned* from me and *seen* in me so that your lives will be *excellent* and *praiseworthy.*"

To remind his readers of the transformative experience of receiving his teaching and observing his example Paul strings together four verbs: *you learned and you received and you heard and you saw.* The verbs *learned and received* refer primarily to his teaching of the gospel, and the verbs *heard and seen* refer to the paradigmatic value of his life.[121] But since Paul presents his life story in parallel to the gospel narrative of Christ, this distinction between these verbs should not be pressed. To *learn* means "to gain knowledge or skill by instruction" and "to come to a realization, with implication of taking place less through instruction than through experience or practice."[122] Although this verb "consistently has an intellectual focus," learning "includes also the conduct of one's life."[123] A few verses later Paul witnesses to his own process of learning through experience: *I have learned to be content whatever the circumstances* (4:11). The Philippians *learned* of the gospel through Paul's instruction and through their personal experience with Paul as they saw him embody the gospel in his life.

The verb *receive* is often used by Paul as a technical term for receiving tradition.[124] Paul *received* the gospel narrative of Christ's death, burial, and

119. O'Brien, 508.

120. Bockmuehl, 254. See 1 Cor 2:13; Gal 2:10; 1 Pet 3:21; Acts 11:30; 26:10.

121. Vincent, 140; O'Brien, 508-9; Calvin, 291, interprets the first three verbs as all referring to Paul's teaching, and the fourth verb as a reminder of his life.

122. BDAG, 615.

123. G. Nebe, "μανθάνω," *EDNT* 2:384; examples of the intellectual focus: "teaching that you have learned" (Rom 16:17), "that you may learn the meaning of the saying, 'Do not go beyond what is written'" (1 Cor 4:6), "you can all prophesy in turn so that everyone may learn and be encouraged" (1 Cor 14:31).

124. BDAG, 768; G. Delling, "παραλαμβάνω," *TDNT* 4:13: "'to receive the fixed form, in the chain of Christian tradition,' of the account of the institution of the Lord's supper and of the passion, death and resurrection of Jesus or 'to inherit the formulated laws of Christian morality,' the Christian Halaka."

resurrection (1 Cor 15:3); he *received* the words of institution of the Lord's Supper (1 Cor 11:23); the Thessalonian believers *received* the word of God that they heard from Paul (1 Thess 2:13); they also *received* ethical tradition to guide their relationships (2 Thess 3:6). Since the verb received is also used for receiving Christ — "you received Christ Jesus as Lord" (Col 2:6), it connotes more than an intellectual reception of traditional teaching. The verb *receive* also refers to "the reception of an inner understanding of the nature and spirit of the moral life of the Christian which grows out of the contagious power of example."[125] The Philippian believers *received* Paul's teaching of the early church traditions of the gospel of Christ, including the hymn of Christ (2:6-11), and they also *received* the power of Christ's life through their personal experience with Paul, who exemplified his motto: *For to me, to live is Christ.*

Personal observation of Paul's example receives special emphasis in the verbs of sensory experience: *heard and seen in me.* Paul combines these two verbs earlier in the letter to remind the Philippians in their own struggle that he also suffered for the gospel of Christ: *you are going through the same struggle you saw I had, and now hear that I still have* (1:30). His reminder of what the Philippians have *heard and seen* in him refers to the way that his life displays the life of Christ: *the power of his resurrection and participation in his sufferings* (3:10).[126] In his participation in the sufferings of Christ, Paul thought about *whatever was true, noble, right, pure, lovely, and admirable:* he rejoiced that his chains *served to advance the gospel* (1:12).[127] Paul's response to suffering in his own life provides a tangible pattern for the Philippians to follow. Although the prepositional phrase *in me* follows and modifies the last verb, *seen,* the phrase directs the Philippians to remember that all that they had *learned and received and heard and seen* was embodied *in* Paul.[128] Paul not only preached the gospel, but he also showed the way to live the gospel.

Paul's command, *put it into practice,* challenges his readers to move beyond contemplation to action. The imperative calls for them to "bring about or accomplish something through activity."[129] The time has come to get out of the chair of theoretical reflection about Christ and the Christian life and *press on toward the goal* (3:14). Paul knew that these recent converts needed more than an instruction manual; they needed a mentor to know

125. Delling, "παραλαμβάνω," *TDNT* 4:13.

126. Fee, 420: "Paul is once again calling them to the kind of cruciform existence he has been commending and urging on them throughout. Only as they are 'conformed to Christ's death,' as Paul himself seeks continually to be, even as they eagerly await the final consummation at his coming, will they truly live what is 'virtuous' and praiseworthy' from Paul's distinctively 'in Christ' perspective."

127. Paul A. Holloway, *Consolation in Philippians: Philosophical Sources and Rhetorical Strategy* (SNTSMS 112; Cambridge: Cambridge University Press, 2001), 155.

128. O'Brien, 511.

129. BDAG, 860.

how to *have the same attitude of mind Christ Jesus had* (2:5). The call to be like Christ is not enough; Paul sets forth his own life as a model for following Christ. His imperative to practice his Christ-centered life repeats his previous challenge: *Join together in following my example, brothers and sisters, and just as you have us as a model, keep your eyes on those who live as we do* (3:17). This challenge appears often in Paul's letters to his churches.[130] Paul's call for imitation of his example was entirely appropriate in the context of his day and conformed to the understanding of the teacher-student relationship in both the Jewish and Greco-Roman cultures.[131] The Jewish author of the *Testament of Benjamin* extols the value of imitating good men: "Pattern your life after the good and pious man Joseph. . . . See then, my children, what is the goal of the good man. Be imitators of him in his goodness because of his compassion, in order that you may wear the crown of glory."[132] Dio Chrysostom encourages the imitation of a teacher: "Whoever really follows anyone surely knows what that person was like, and by imitating his acts and words he tries as best he can to make himself like him. But that is precisely, it seems, what the pupil does — by imitating his teacher and paying heed to him he tries to acquire his art."[133] As a good teacher in his day would customarily do, Paul sets before his students his art: his portrayal of the suffering of Christ and his participation in Christ's sufferings present what is most excellent and praiseworthy. He calls for believers to imitate him and acquire his art.

Although Paul takes the role of the teacher when he challenges his readers to *think* and to *practice,* he writes to them as a friend and gives them this challenge to strengthen his friendship with them. According to the moral teachers of Paul's era, the best form of friendship was based on virtue.[134] According to Aristotle, "The perfect form of friendship is that between the good, and those who resemble each other in virtue."[135] Since "virtue is a permanent quality,"[136] friendships based on virtue are permanent. Cicero also points to virtue as the priority of true friendship: "Let this be ordained as the first law of friendship: Ask of friends only what is honorable; do for friends only what is honorable."[137] Two types of inferior

130. 1 Cor 4:16; 7:7-16; 11:1; Gal 4:12; Phil 3:17; 1 Thess 1:6; 2:14; 2 Thess 3:7-9. See S. E. Fowl, "Imitation of Paul/of Christ," *DPL* 428-31; D. M. Stanley, "Imitation in Paul's Letters: Its Significance for His Relationship to Jesus and to His Own Christian Foundations," in *From Jesus to Paul: Studies in Honour of Francis Wright Beare* (ed. Peter Richardson and John C. Hurd; Waterloo, Ont.: Wilfrid Laurier University Press, 1984), 113-26.

131. See numerous quotations from Hellenistic and Jewish sources in Best, *Paul and His Converts,* 61-62.

132. *Testament of Benjamin* 3:1; 4:1, in J. H. Charlesworth, *The Old Testament Pseudepigrapha* (New York: Doubleday, 1983-85), 1:825-26.

133. Dio Chrysostom, *Discourse* 55.4, 5.

134. Fitzgerald, "Philippians in the Light of Ancient Friendship," 141-60.

135. Aristotle, *Eth. nic.* 8.3.6.

136. Aristotle, *Eth. nic.* 8.3.6.

137. Cicero, *Amic.* 13.44.

friendship described by Aristotle are friendship based on utility and friendship based on pleasure.[138] Friends who look only for some benefit to be gained from their friendship have a friendship of utility. Friends who enjoy each other only because they enjoy the pleasure of witty people have a friendship of pleasure. In these types of friendship, friends do not love each other for being what they are in themselves but for some benefit or pleasure to be gained through the friendship. Since utility and pleasure change with time, "Friendships of this kind are easily broken off, in the event of the parties themselves changing, for if no longer pleasant or useful to each other, they cease to love each other."[139]

By calling the Philippian believers to think about the virtues and to practice his embodiment of the virtues in his Christ-centered teaching and life, Paul places his friendship with them on the firm basis of virtue, above all, virtue in Christ.[140] In the next paragraph, Paul discusses his partnership with them and their generous support of him (4:10-18). But he does not want them to misconstrue their friendship with him in terms of a utilitarian friendship. He is eager to keep them from denigrating their friendship to merely *the matter of giving and receiving* (4:15). So before he turns to that financial *matter,* he emphasizes that their friendship is grounded in virtue.

When believers *think about these things* and *put them into practice,* they will enjoy the presence of the God of peace: *And the God of peace will be with you.* The simple conjunction, *and,* with the future indicative, *will be,* presents a promise.[141] Those who focus their minds on all that is true and set their wills to do all that Paul has taught by word and example will experience the promise of the presence of the God of peace. Paul uses this name for God, *God of peace,* in prayers for his churches: "May God himself, the God of peace, sanctify you" (1 Thess 5:23; Rom 15:33). And this name, *God of peace,* introduces promises: "The God of peace will soon crush Satan under your feet" (Rom 16:20); "And the God of peace will be with you" (2 Cor 13:11). *Peace* in the biblical sense is "nearly synonymous with messianic salvation."[142] Through the Messiah, God will bring the condition of peace: reconciliation with God and harmony in all relationships.[143] Peace is not so much a subjective tranquility as an objective reality created by the reign of God through the Messiah.[144] The promise of God's presence assures the

138. Aristotle, *Eth. nic.* 8.3.1-4.

139. Aristotle, *Eth. nic.* 8.3.3.

140. Fitzgerald, "Philippians in the Light of Ancient Friendship," 157.

141. The conjunction *and* (καί) is used here as in v. 7, *and the peace of God,* "to introduce a result that comes from what precedes" (BDAG, 495); BDF §442 (2): the consecutive use of καί means "and so, so."

142. BDAG, 288.

143. Isaiah 50:7: "How beautiful upon the mountains are the feet of the messenger who announces peace, who brings good news, who announces salvation, who says to Zion, 'Your God reigns.'"

144. Herman Ridderbos, *Paul: An Outline of His Theology* (Grand Rapids: Eerdmans, 1975), 184: "For in Paul (as in the whole of Scripture) 'peace' refers not only or in the first

church that God, the source and sustainer of peace, will lead them to experience the reality of reconciliation with God and with one another. The God of peace will bring good order and harmony in their community worship of God and in their life together: "For God is not a God of disorder but of peace — as in all the congregations of the people of God" (1 Cor 14:33). For a church disturbed by the problem of disunity between prominent leaders (Phil 4:2), Paul's promise of the presence of the God of peace comes as a welcome reassurance that God will restore and renew broken relationships.

The promise of the presence of the *God of peace* (4:9) explains the promise of the *peace of God* (4:7): when the *God of peace will be with you,* then *the peace of God . . . will guard your hearts and minds in Christ Jesus.*[145] Only God's presence brings his peace. When the *God of peace* is present, the *peace of God* rules in the hearts and minds of his people. In the larger context of Paul's teaching, God's peace comes with the presence of God's Spirit: the fruit of the Spirit is peace (Gal 5:22).

VIII. THANKS FOR GIFTS FROM PARTNERS (4:10-20)

10I rejoiced greatly in the Lord that at last you renewed your concern for
me. Indeed, you were concerned, but you had no opportunity to show it. 11I
am not saying this because I am in need, for I have learned to be content
whatever the circumstances. 12I know what it is to be in need, and I know
what it is to have plenty. I have learned the secret of being content in any and
every situation, whether well fed or hungry, whether living in plenty or in
want. 13I can do all this through him who gives me strength.

14Yet it is good of you to share in my troubles. 15Moreover, as you Phi-
lippians know, in the early days of your acquaintance with the gospel, when I
set out from Macedonia, not one church shared with me in the matter of giv-
ing and receiving, except you only; 16for even when I was in Thessalonica,
you sent me aid more than once when I was in need. 17Not that I desire your
gifts; what I desire is that more be credited to your account. 18I have received
full payment and have more than enough. I am amply supplied, now that I
have received from Epaphroditus the gifts you sent. They are a fragrant offer-
ing, an acceptable sacrifice, pleasing to God. 19And my God will meet all
your needs according to the riches of his glory in Christ Jesus.

20To our God and Father be glory for ever and ever. Amen.

---

place to disposition, but is the denotation of the all-embracing gift of salvation, the condition of *shalom,* which God will again bring to unrestricted dominion."

145. Martin and Hawthorne, 254, claims that the promise in v. 9 "is an advance in thought over the promise provided in v. 7. There it was said that God's peace would be with them; now it is said that God himself who gives peace, or who is himself peace, will be with them." But according to O'Brien, 512, "Since the gift of his peace cannot be separated from his presence as the giver, these two assurances are closely related in meaning."

At the end of his letter, Paul acknowledges the initial support of the church in his ministry (*in the early days . . . not one church shared with me in the matter of giving and receiving, except you only*) and the recent gifts that the church sent to him through Epaphroditus (*I have received full payment*).[146] But the lack of any explicit expression of gratitude gives some interpreters the idea that Paul's words convey a "thankless thanks."[147] And his careful qualifications of his acknowledgment of these gifts with strong statements of independence (*I am not saying this because I am in need. . . . not that I desire your gifts*) make him look like a reluctant recipient of these gifts. The way Paul acknowledges the gifts from his friends in Philippi raises perplexing questions and leads to diverse interpretations. Is Paul's language here the result of the fact that "the church to which Paul was writing was divided over their allegiance to him, and he knew it"?[148] Is his reserved acknowledgment of gifts written in this way because these gifts were a "violation of one of Paul's strict principles, entailing giving of a personal gift to him which was not only unsolicited, but which the Macedonian churches knew from personal experience he opposed"?[149] Is Paul using the technical terminology of a business partnership contract?[150] Does Paul's response to the gifts from the Philippians reflect the social and rhetorical conventions in the Greco-Roman world where "verbal gratitude in written form was not a social expectation, except when writing to someone who was socially superior" and "material gratitude, that is, gratitude in the form of return, was a social obligation."[151]

These lines of interpretation will be explored in the following discussion of this intriguing passage. More significantly, however, our study of this passage will yield rich insights into Paul's personal spiritual experience, his friendship with the Philippian believers, and his theological perspective on giving and receiving between Christians. Paul radically transforms the social convention of partnership in the light of the gospel of Christ.[152]

146. See the Introduction, 15-19, for discussion of the position that this section, 4:10-20, is a separate letter.

147. Lohmeyer, 178.

148. Peterlin, *Paul's Letter to the Philippians in the Light of Disunity in the Church*, 216.

149. Martin and Hawthorne, 259.

150. J. Paul Sampley, *Pauline Partnership in Christ: Christian Community and Commitment in Light of Roman Law* (Philadelphia: Fortress, 1980), 52-53: "The passage is somewhat unusual because of the frequency of commercial technical terms. From many of Paul's letters we know that he used technical terms of law and commerce, but the frequency of them in Philippians 4:10-20 is unparalleled."

151. G. W. Peterman, *Paul's Gift from Philippi: Conventions of Gift Exchange and Christian Giving* (SNTSMS 92; Cambridge: Cambridge University Press, 1997), 83-86.

152. See G. Walter Hansen, "Transformation of Relationships," in *New Testament Greek and Exegesis: Essays in Honor of Gerald F. Hawthorne* (ed. Amy M. Donaldson and Timothy B. Sailors; Grand Rapids: Eerdmans, 2003), 181: "Paul not only used but also radically transformed the contemporary concepts of partnership, citizenship, and friendship in order to rebuild the fractured fellowship of the church."

10 Paul reports his great joy when he received the gifts from the Philippians: *I rejoiced greatly in the Lord that at last you renewed your concern for me.* The theme of rejoicing runs through the entire letter and comes to its most exuberant expression here. The beginning of the letter strikes the note of rejoicing: *I always pray with joy because of your partnership in the gospel* (1:4). And rejoicing repeatedly bursts forth from the apostle's heart.[153] But now Paul quantifies the intensity of his joy: the adverb *greatly,* used only here in the NT, strengthens the verb *rejoiced* to the point that Paul's joy surpasses the joy of his friends.[154] He asked his friends to rejoice; he *rejoiced greatly.*[155] The past tense of the verb, *rejoiced,* may indicate that the action is a past action from the perspective of the recipients when they are hearing the letter but a present action from the perspective of Paul when he is writing the letter.[156] In the context of this paragraph, however, the past tense appears to be a reference back to the time when he received the gifts from the church through Epaphroditus (4:18).[157] Paul's awareness of the Lord's faithfulness in the provision of these gifts causes him to rejoice greatly *in the Lord.* Good gifts never divert Paul's central focus from rejoicing in the Lord, the ultimate Provider of all good gifts. His focus on the Lord's provision is the basis of his assurance to the Philippians: *God will meet all your needs according to the riches of his glory in Christ Jesus* (4:19). This central focus on God transforms the transaction of giving and receiving among Christians from a human, horizontal exchange to a divine-human, triangular interaction. God initiates giving, empowers givers, supplies gifts, and meets needs. Participating in the activity of God by giving and receiving leads to rejoicing greatly in the Lord.

The basis of Paul's great joy is that the Philippians renewed their concern for him: *at last you renewed your concern for me.* The verb *you renewed* paints a botanical image of a plant blooming again after a period of dormancy.[158] Like a fruit tree blossoming again, the Philippians caused their concern to grow and blossom again. Paul's phrase *at last* points to the culmination of a time of inactivity or dormancy when the Philippians' concern for him was apparently not growing and blossoming.[159] In metaphorical language, Paul speaks of his joy when wintertime is finally past and springtime brings a renewal of the Philippians' concern for him.

153. 1:5, 18; 2:1, 17-18; 3:1; 4:1, 4, 10.

154. BDAG, 623.

155. Silva, 232, offers the translation: "Have I asked you to rejoice in the Lord? You should know that I myself rejoice greatly in the Lord."

156. Vincent (141) and Martin and Hawthorne (260) label this verb as an epistolary aorist. See BDF §334.

157. O'Brien, 516; Fee, 428; Silva, 235.

158. BDAG, 63. This verb, ἀναθάλλω, occurs only here in the NT. If it is used intransitively, it would be translated, "you blossomed again"; if it is used transitively here, it means "you revived your care for me." The presence of the τό in the phrase τὸ ὑπὲρ ἐμοῦ φρονεῖν indicates that the infinitive φρονεῖν is in the accusative case as the direct object of the transitive use of the verb ἀναθάλλω. See BDF §399 (1); Vincent, 142; Peterman, 130.

159. BDAG, 434: the phrase ἤδη ποτέ is a "marker of culmination, *now at length.*"

A familiar word appears again in Paul's reference to *concern:* ten times in his letter to the Philippians Paul uses this word to speak of a way of thinking, a feeling, an attitude, a mind-set.[160] The relational aspect of this word is highlighted in Paul's expression of his affection for the Philippians: *It is right for me to feel this way about all of you* (1:7). Paul chooses the same word to designate a way of thinking in harmony with one another: *being like-minded . . . of one mind* (2:2). Paul selects this word again to explain that *being like-minded* comes from having *the same attitude of mind Christ Jesus had* (2:5). According to Paul, those who are mature think this way: *take such a view of things* (3:15). Paul urges the two women who are in conflict *to be of the same mind* (4:2). All of these uses of the word point to the crucial importance of having the *attitude of mind* that builds relationships. Now Paul tells his friends how delighted he is that they have caused their thoughts about him to grow and bloom again (4:10). They thought about him in the sense of being concerned about him.[161] Their gifts tangibly demonstrated the reality of their concern for him. Paul *rejoiced greatly in the Lord* for these gifts because through them the Philippians displayed in their *concern* for him the attitude of mind that he calls for them to have toward each other in his earlier exhortations in this letter (2:2; 4:2).[162]

Sampley views Paul's frequent use of this verb, "to think in harmony with one another," as evidence that Paul views his relationship with the Philippians as a voluntary business partnership, a consensual *societas.* A partnership ceases to exist when partners no longer have the same attitude of mind toward one another.[163] He provides documentation to show that a partnership requires partners to be of the same mind. For example, he quotes from the legal code of Gaius: "A partnership lasts as long as the parties remain of the same mind."[164] Peterman objects to Sampley's thesis: "Though *societas* demands being of the same mind, being of the same mind does not demand *societas.*"[165] But Peterman's objection to Sampley's thesis that Paul views his relationship with the Philippians in terms of a voluntary business partnership (a *societas*) does not adequately appreciate the close connection that Paul makes between partnership *(koinōnia)* and being of the same mind in this letter and especially in this passage. Paul closely and significantly links his double reference to the Philippians' concern for him (4:10) with his double reference to their partnership with him (4:15, 16). While we can debate the way Sampley defines Paul's language as technical terminology for a legally binding consensual *societas,* we must not miss the way that Paul ties together being of the same mind and concern

160. Φρονέω: 1:7; 2:2 (twice), 5; 3:15 (twice), 19; 4:2, 10 (twice).

161. BDAG, 1065.

162. See S. E. Fowl, "Know Your Context: Giving and Receiving Money in Philippians," *Int* 56 (2002), 45-58.

163. Sampley, *Pauline Partnership in Christ,* 15.

164. Sampley, *Pauline Partnership in Christ,* 15.

165. Peterman, *Paul's Gift from Philippi,* 131.

for one another with partnership. Paul views the Philippians' concern for him as a significant expression and essential element of their partnership with him.[166]

Paul's expression of joy over the Philippians' concern for him is not an explicit way of saying "thank you" to the Philippians.[167] Nevertheless, when Paul tells his friends that their concern for him causes him to rejoice greatly in the Lord, he is implicitly communicating to them how grateful he is for their gifts.[168] In fact, he clearly desires to remove a possible misunderstanding of his words as anything less than positive appreciation for their gifts. In case his readers might think that his commendation *(at last you renewed your concern for me)* contains a subtle rebuke for the period of dormancy between their initial gifts and their recent gifts, he corrects that possibility of misreading his words by adding an explanatory clause: *indeed, you were concerned, but you had no opportunity to show it.* This clause emphatically assures the Philippians of Paul's confidence that they were always concerned for him, even during the period of time when they could not send him any financial support. The imperfect tense of the verb, *you were concerned,* points to the continuity of their concern for Paul: at no time did they cease to have a real interest in his welfare. The conjunction at the beginning of this clause, usually translated *indeed,* conveys "the concessional or correctional force" of the clause.[169] In other words, precisely "because indeed" (the meaning of the complex conjunction) they always were concerned for him, Paul rejoiced when *at last* they had the opportunity to express their concern by sending gifts.

Why the Philippians *had no opportunity* to show their concern for a period of time remains a mystery. The verb means "to lack an opportune time for doing something."[170] In some way the circumstances in the life of the church in Philippi and/or in the life of Paul prevented the church from

166. See Hansen, "Transformation of Relationships," 187: "We cannot be certain that Paul used κοινωνία as a technical, legal term referring to the Roman *societas.* Yet Paul's description of the partnership for the advance of the gospel (κοινωνία εἰς τὸ εὐαγγέλιον, 1:5) certainly sounds like a Roman *societas:* it was a voluntary association of equal partners in a joint venture for a specific goal."

167. Schenk (43) argues on the basis of the etymological connection between "I rejoice" (χαίρω) and "I give thanks" (εὐχαριστέω) that Paul's expression of joy is a direct way of saying, "Thank you very much" for the gifts sent by Epaphroditus. But Peterman (*Paul's Gift from Philippi,* 128) points out that Schenk does not adequately demonstrate that rejoicing and giving thanks share the same semantic field.

168. Silva, 235: "Without leaning on the etymological connection between χαίρω and εὐχαριστέω (as Schenk does), we should recognize that this expression of joy certainly communicates thankfulness."

169. Silva, 234. According to BDF §235 (2), the prepositional construction, ἐφ' ᾧ, at the beginning of the clause "most frequently denotes the basis for a state of being, action, or result, especially with verbs of emotion." Following this prepositional construction, the conjunction καί takes on an intensive meaning, *indeed* (BDAG, 495-96).

170. BDAG, 34. The α-privative with the word καιρός connotes no opportune time. The word ἀκαιρεῖσθαι occurs only here in the NT.

expressing their concern. Perhaps the Philippian believers had no opportunity to express their concern because of "a very severe trial" and "their extreme poverty" (2 Cor 8:1-2).[171] Or perhaps Paul's imprisonment in Caesarea, journey to Rome, and imprisonment in Rome made him temporarily inaccessible to the Philippians.[172] We can only speculate what circumstances robbed the Philippians of an opportunity to show their love for Paul. Paul assures them that he fully understands that during the whole time of their lack of financial support they still continued to have a deep concern for him. Continuity of financial support is not a condition for continuity of friendship.

11 Paul continues to clarify his expression of gratitude by emphatically asserting that his rejoicing was not because his needs were met by timely financial support: *I am not saying this because I am in need.* Paul begins this sentence with a strong negative — "not that!" — to stop anyone from misunderstanding him.[173] He repeats his negation of misconceptions in verse 17: *not that I desire your gifts.* Paul is obviously determined to stop his friends from thinking that he values their renewed concern for him because his needs are supplied by their support. "Not that! Not that!" He is not talking about his need. The word *need,* occurring only here and in Mark 12:44, denotes "the condition of lacking that which is essential."[174] Paul does not deny that he was in the condition of lacking basic essentials, but he does deny that his impoverished condition gave rise to great joy when gifts arrived to rescue him from his poverty.[175] No, his great joy had nothing to do with the fact that the receipt of gifts met his dire needs.[176]

By his strong denial that he rejoiced because his needs were met, Paul refuses to take the role of one who is making a request for gifts from the church.[177] If he drew attention to his needs in a way that implied that he depended on the church for support, he would put himself in a socially inferior position as dependent on the church's patronage and he would be obligated to repay the gifts in some material way.[178] If his needs became his

171. Bockmuehl, 260.

172. Martin and Hawthorne, 262.

173. οὐχ ὅτι, "not that," is a Pauline way of forcefully correcting misconceptions of his previous statements: *not that I have already obtained all this* (Phil 3:12); *not that I desire your gifts* (Phil 4:17); "not that we lord it over your faith" (2 Cor 1:24); "not that we are competent in ourselves to claim anything for ourselves" (2 Cor 3:5); "not that we do not have the right" (2 Thess 3:9).

174. BDAG, 1044.

175. Gnilka, 174.

176. U. Wilckens, "ὕστερος," *TDNT* 8:599: "It is not the joy of a poor person whose need has been met."

177. Against Sampley, 55: "Any expression of 'need' was likely to have the force of 'request.'" Sampley thinks that Paul plays on this association of need and request to make his requests as the Philippians' partner in *societas.* But Paul explicitly denies that he speaking about his need (4:11).

178. See Peterman, *Paul's Gift from Philippi,* 52-89.

focus, he would lose his equality with his friends and he would incur the burden of social reciprocity with mutual financial obligations. Paul transforms the nature of his partnership with the Philippians by turning their attention to his experience of the presence and power of God in the midst of his experience of needs. The triangular nature of the partnership — God, Paul, and the Philippians — changes the expectations of social reciprocity.[179] The partnership is not simply a mutual human exchange of material support; now both sides of the partnership look to God, who *will meet all your needs* (4:19).

Paul's denial that he depends on the support of the Philippians to meet his needs is based on a major lesson he learned from his own experience: *for I learned to be content whatever the circumstances.* The aorist tense of the verb *learned* encompasses all the varied experiences of his life described in the next verse.[180] He did not learn this lesson in a day but throughout a lifetime of ups and downs. The laboratory of his life experience provided continuous opportunities for him to learn the attitude of contentment. His emphatic use of the personal pronoun *I* highlights his claim that he did his homework, mastered his lessons, and passed his tests. Although the attitude of contentment was not natural nor did it come easily, this quality of contentment eventually became an essential attribute of his character.

To be content was a central concept in ethical discussion from the time of Socrates, especially among Cynic and Stoic philosophers. In Stoic philosophy it denotes the one who "becomes an independent man sufficient to himself and in need of none else."[181] The goal for the Stoic was that "a man should be sufficient unto himself for all things, and able, by the power of his own will, to resist the force of circumstances."[182] The Stoic philosopher Seneca advocates the goal of being content: "The happy man is content with his present lot, no matter what it is, and is reconciled to his circumstances."[183] By the exercise of reason over emotions, the Stoic learns to be content.[184] For the Stoic, emotional detachment is essential in order to be content.[185]

In his use of the adjective *content* to describe the attitude he learned, Paul appears to have used a popular term from the vocabulary of the

179. Hansen, "Transformation of Relationships," 188.

180. See BDF §332 (1): The complexive (constative) aorist tense "is used for linear actions which having been completed are regarded as a whole." Porter, *Idioms of the Greek New Testament* (Sheffield: JSOT Press, 1992), 35: "The aorist tense-form occurs in contexts where the user of Greek wishes to depict an action as a complete and undifferentiated process."

181. G. Kittel, "αὐτάρκεια, αὐτάρκης," *TDNT* 1:466.

182. Vincent, 143.

183. Seneca, *De vita beata* 6:2 (LCL translation).

184. Abraham J. Malherbe, "Paul's Self-Sufficiency," in *Friendship, Flattery, and Frankness of Speech* (NovTSup 82; ed. John T. Fitzgerald; Leiden: E. J. Brill, 1996), 126; see also J. N. Sevenster, *Paul and Seneca* (NovTSup 4; Leiden: Brill, 1961), 113-14.

185. Peterman, *Paul's Gift from Philippi*, 136: "Emotional calm, or detachment ἀπαθής cannot be separated from αὐτάρκης."

Stoics.[186] In some important ways, however, Paul redefines this popular philosophical term. Paul refers to his experience of learning to be content in order to demonstrate that his friendship with his readers is not based on need.[187] Friendship based on need is inferior to true friendship between those who are self-sufficient or content, according to the ancient definitions of friendship.[188] Aristotle says that friendships based on utility or pleasures are inferior because in these types of friendship friends are interested only in some benefit or pleasure to be gained through friendship.[189] Since needs and pleasures change with time, "Friendships of this kind are easily broken off, in the event of the parties themselves changing, for if no longer pleasant or useful to each other, they cease to love each other."[190] Cicero asserts, "It is far from being true that friendship is cultivated because of need; rather, it is cultivated by those who are most abundantly blessed with wealth and power and especially virtue, which is man's best defense; by those least in need of another's help; and by those most generous and most given to acts of kindness."[191] According to Cicero, only the self-sufficient person can develop true friendships: "To the extent that a man relies upon himself and so is so fortified by virtue and wisdom that he is dependent on no one and considers all his possessions to be within himself, in that degree is he most conspicuous for seeking out and cherishing friendships."[192] Paul's statement that he *learned to be content* is his way of claiming that his friendship with the Philippian believers is true friendship, not a friendship based on utility; he was not looking to his friends with self-interest, depending on them to meet his needs, for he had *learned to be content.*

12 Paul describes the ups and downs of his life so that his readers will have a clear picture of the "school" where he learned to be content. His first two descriptions contrast opposite conditions in his experience: *I know what it is to be in need, and I know what it is to have plenty.* A more literal translation gives an even clearer sense of this contrast: "I know both how to be humbled and I know how to prosper." By his repetition of the verb *know,* Paul emphasizes the results of his learning process: *I have learned; I know; I know.*

The objects of his acquired knowledge are two infinitives: "to be humbled; to abound." "To be humbled" means to lose prestige or status, to be humiliated, and to be subjected to strict discipline.[193] This verb may be

186. Hawthorne and Martin, 264; Kittel, "αὐτάρκεια, αὐτάρκης," *TDNT* 1:467: Paul's use of this term in Phil 4:11-13 "appears to be fully identical with the philosophical αὐτάρκης ἐν παντί." See also Troels Engberg-Pedersen, "Stoicism in Philippians," in *Paul in His Hellenistic Context* (ed. Troels Engberg-Pedersen; Minneapolis: Fortress, 1995), 270, 278-79.

187. See Malherbe, "Paul's Self-Sufficiency," 137.

188. Hansen, "Transformation of Relationships," 201.

189. Aristotle, *Eth. nic.* 8.3.1-5 (Rackham, LCL).

190. Aristotle, *Eth. nic.* 8.3.3 (Rackham, LCL).

191. Cicero, *Amic.* 14.51 (Falconer, LCL).

192. Cicero, *Amic.* 9.30 (Falconer, LCL).

193. BDAG, 990.

focusing on Paul's own actions in regard to himself: he humbled himself and disciplined himself.[194] If Paul is describing his own deliberate choice to humble himself, then he is picturing himself as one who exemplifies the attitude of Christ Jesus, who *humbled himself* (2:8). Even if the verb is in the passive voice and depicts the loss and humiliation imposed by external forces, there is still an emphasis in this context on Paul's willingness to accept with contentment the adverse circumstances of abasement and deprivation. Since the verb "to be humbled" is contrasted with the verb "to have abundance" in the next line and is redefined by the substitution of the synonym *to be in need* in the last line, the verb acquires the sense "to live in poor circumstances."[195] In the context of his discussion of the Philippians' gift, Paul appears to have financial humiliation in view.[196] Paul learned to be content when he lived in poverty.

Paul also learned to be content when living in prosperity. The need to learn contentment in the midst of wealth may not be immediately apparent. Biblical wisdom, however, teaches that "the surfeit of the rich will not let them sleep" (Eccl 5:12), that "the love of money is the root of all kinds of evil," and that wealthy people tend to "set their hopes on the uncertainty of riches" rather than on God (1 Tim 6:10, 17). A first-century moralist, Plutarch, also warns that wealth breeds discontentment: "The owner of five couches goes looking for ten, and the owner of ten tables buys up as many again, and though he has lands and money in plenty is not satisfied but bent on more, losing sleep and never sated with any amount."[197] In the light of this natural propensity to covet more even in prosperity, Paul's contentment in a time and place of abundance is a rare virtue.[198]

Learning to have the attitude of contentment in poverty and in prosperity is so unusual that Paul employs a rare word, found only here in the NT, to depict this process of learning: *I have learned the secret.* The Greek word was a technical term in the Hellenistic mystery religions for being initiated into the mysteries by going through sacred rituals.[199] It was also used metaphorically for gaining insider knowledge. This term draws a line between those on the outside who do not know and those on the inside who

194. The middle voice is a possibility, but usually the reflexive idea is expressed by the active voice and a reflexive pronoun as in Phil 2:8.

195. W. Grundmann, "ταπεινός," *TDNT* 8:18.

196. Peterman, *Paul's Gift from Philippi,* 140.

197. Plutarch, *Mor.* 524B.

198. Calvin, 292: "He who knows how to use present abundance soberly and temperately with thanksgiving, prepared to part with everything whenever it may please the Lord, giving also a share to his brother according to his ability, and is also not puffed up, that man has learned to excel and to abound. This is an excellent and rare virtue, and much greater than the endurance of poverty."

199. BDAG, 660. In 3 Macc 2:30 τοῖς μεμυημένοις refers to "those who are initiated in the mysteries." Josephus uses the term in a metaphorical sense when he describes the execution of a woman because she "initiated people into the worship of strange gods" (*C. Ap.* 2.267).

know. By using this term, Paul claims that he has gained insight by being on the inside. The next verse explains that being on the inside means being in Christ, "in the one who empowers me" (4:13). Contrary to the cliché that experience is the best teacher, contentment is not learned merely by experience in all the circumstances of life but by being in Christ in *any and every situation. Whether well fed or hungry, whether living in plenty or in want,* Paul has *learned the secret of being content* because he has learned to keep his focus on his relationship with Christ, not on the fluctuating circumstances of his life.

Since the theme of suffering receives such emphasis in his letter to the Philippians, Paul's references to being *well fed* and *living in plenty* seem strangely out of place. How can Paul be content while *living in plenty* when he seeks to *have the attitude of mind* of the one who *humbled himself by becoming obedient to death* (2:5, 8) and when he wants *to know Christ, . . . to know participation in his sufferings, becoming like him in his death* (3:10)? Such aspirations of participation with Christ in his sufferings would seem to cause Paul to have an aversion to prosperity. The apparent contradiction between *living in plenty* and suffering with Christ makes contentment in plenty look hypocritical. One way around this contradiction is to redefine plenty as spiritual abundance, not material prosperity.[200] Another way to avoid the apparent contradiction is to suggest that plenty for Paul was not excessive material abundance by any modern measure. He is simply saying that as a result of the gifts from Philippi he has *more than enough;* he is *amply supplied* (4:18).[201] Even with the provisions from Philippi, his life in prison was not like living in a five-star luxury hotel. As noteworthy as these two ways of understanding Paul's contentment in prosperity are, however, they still do not adequately resolve the apparent contradiction between living in plenty and participating in Christ's sufferings. Spiritual abundance is certainly Paul's customary reference when he uses the verb "to abound."[202] But in this context he is speaking about material abundance: being *well fed.* And while Paul's experience of abundance cannot be compared to contemporary definitions of prosperity, being *well fed* does connote being filled, even gorged with food.[203] We can understand Paul's experience of contentment in prosperity when we observe that he *rejoiced greatly in the Lord* (4:10), not in material abundance, and that he sought benefits for others more than abundance for himself (4:17). His joy in the Lord was not heightened by prosperity or diminished by poverty. His concern for the welfare of others was not distracted by living in plenty or in want. His contentment in prosperity did not

200. Martin and Hawthorne, 265: "the overflowing abundance that Paul envisions as characteristic of the new age, inaugurated by Christ's coming (Phil 1:9, 26)."

201. F. Hauck, "περισσεύω," *TDNT* 6:61: "Through the riches that he has in Christ, the very modest improvement in his circumstances through the gift of the congregation is more than abundance, Phil 4:18."

202. 1 Thess 3:10, 12; 5:13; 2 Cor 7:4; Rom 5:20; Eph 3:20.

203. BDAG, 1087.

lead him to self-indulgence or self-aggrandizement: having material things did not become his reason for joy; acquiring material things did not make him greedy; protecting material things did not make him anxious.

Paul's references to his experiences of being *hungry* and living *in want* provide additional details to the picture of his suffering and struggle (1:30; 2:17; 3:10).[204] To be hungry means "to feel the pangs of lack of food."[205] To be in want means to "be lacking, go without."[206] Since physical pain is inherent in these experiences of hunger and need, contentment does not mean the absence of pain. Paul did not seek to be apathetic or unfeeling, as the Stoics did. He felt the discomfort of hunger and the deprivation of poverty. He did not learn *the secret of being content* by becoming indifferent to difficult conditions and detached from abrasive circumstances.[207] Contrary to the philosophy of the Stoics, Paul did not seek to live by reason in order to be anesthetized to physical and emotional pain. He freely relates his tears (3:18) and his great joy (4:10). He was passionately involved in pouring out his life as a sacrifice for others (2:17) as a servant of Christ Jesus (1:1). Paul's contentment in *any and every situation* flows out of his life in Christ.

13 Paul's thoughts begin and end with Christ. He begins this paragraph by recounting his great joy *in the Lord* (4:10). Now he ends with an exclamation of the wonder of Christ's empowerment in his life: *I can do all this through him who gives me strength.*[208] The TNIV wisely adds the pronoun *this* to limit the meaning of *all* in light of the context. Paul is not claiming omnipotence, the ability to do all things without exception. Any use of this verse to support a claim or goal of a triumphant, victorious Christian life without weaknesses or limitations conflicts with the immediate context and the wider teaching of Paul.[209] The contextual meaning of *all* refers to the previous claim *to be content whatever the circumstances* (4:11). In all the situations of his life — in poverty and in prosperity, when well fed and when hungry, Paul can be content. He has the power to endure all these extreme situations, all these ups and downs, without anxiety, with the peace of God guarding his heart and mind in Christ Jesus (4:6-7).[210]

204. Paul gives more extensive lists of his sufferings in 1 Cor 4:11-13; 2 Cor 4:8-9; 6:4-5; 11:23-29.

205. BDAG, 792.

206. BDAG, 1044.

207. Fowl, Philippians, 195: "Paul never seeks detachment from his circumstances."

208. Some MSS (א^2 D^2 and 𝔐) add Χριστω to make the reference to Christ explicit. Diverse and early MSS strongly support the shorter reading. Whether or not the addition is accepted, the entire letter and immediate context clearly indicate that Paul refers to the empowerment of Christ.

209. Martin and Hawthorne, 266: "Those translations that give the impression that Paul meant he could do anything and that nothing was beyond his powers (KJV, ASV, Moffatt, Goodspeed, RSV, Knox, NEB, NASB, NIV) are misleading to the point of being false." Vincent, 145, unjustifiably expands the meaning of *all* beyond the meaning determined by the context when he says, "Not all the things just mentioned, but everything."

210. Gnilka, 176.

Paul claims no power in himself. All his strength is "in the one who empowers" him. Although the preposition "in" can express agency *(through),* Paul's frequent use of the *in Christ* phrase to express union with Christ supports interpreting this preposition as an expression of the relationship of incorporative union: in living union with *the one who gives me strength.*[211] To *be found in Christ* (3:9) is worth far more to Paul than anything else. All his activities, all his emotions, and all his thoughts are within the sphere of Christ's presence: *For to me, to live is Christ* (1:21); *I am confident in the Lord* (2:24); *I want to know Christ — yes, to know the power of his resurrection and participation in his sufferings* (3:10); *I rejoiced greatly in the Lord* (4:10). This intimate communion with Christ is the source of Paul's strength.

By implicitly naming Christ as *him who gives me strength,* Paul denies anyone or anything else the rightful claim to be his source of strength. He rejoices in the gift from the church in Philippi, but he will not allow the church or their gift to take the place of Christ.[212] Although material gifts convey subtle claims to increase power, elevate position, enhance prestige, and guarantee peace, these claims cannot touch Paul. His all-consuming desire to know Christ sets him free from depending on other powers, either his own inner powers or the power of friends and their money. Christ, "the one who gives strength," provides more than sufficient power for Paul to advance the gospel even in chains (1:12) and to press on toward the goal of Christ-likeness even with his imperfections (3:12-14). When Paul looked at himself, he saw chains, weakness, and humiliation. But when he looked at Christ, he saw "the one who gives strength" to *become like him* (3:10) in and through suffering. Paul's contentment in all circumstances was not a passive acceptance — a whatever-will-be-will-be attitude — but an active pursuit of the goal to know Christ and to preach Christ.

14 The Philippians could have taken Paul's assertion that he was content without their support to mean that he did not value their support. Paul precludes such a negative perception of his contentment by expressing his appreciation of their relationship with him: *Yet it was good of you to share in my troubles.* The adversative conjunction *yet* at the beginning of the sentence stands as "a marker of something that is contrastingly added for consideration." By using this conjunction, Paul is "breaking off a discussion and emphasizing what is important."[213] Paul turns from his discussion of learning to be content (4:11-13) and returns to the important theme of partnership. The verb *share* belongs to the string of words in this letter pointing to the *partnership* of the Philippians and Paul in their activity of

211. Vincent, 145; O'Brien, 527; Fee, 434 n. 48; see the study of the phrase "in Christ, in the Lord" in J. D. G. Dunn, *The Theology of Paul the Apostle* (Grand Rapids: Eerdmans, 1998), 396-401, and his conclusion (401): "All of which makes it hard to avoid talk of something like a mystical sense of the divine presence of Christ within and without, establishing and sustaining the individual in relation to God."

212. Peterman, *Paul's Gift from Philippi,* 142.

213. BDAG, 826.

advancing the gospel (1:5, 7; 4:15), in the common life they *share in the Spirit* (2:1), and in their mutual *participation in the sufferings* of Christ (3:10; 4:14).[214] In this instance the prepositional prefix "with" is added to the verb *share* to intensify the emphasis on the mutuality and solidarity of the Philippians and Paul in their interests and activities as partners.[215] Paul's use of this compound verb, "share with," brings their focus back again to the important relationship they have in their life together as participants in the benefits of the gospel and partners in the advancement of the gospel.

Their partnership is demonstrated by the way they "share with" him in his *troubles*. By sending Epaphroditus to bring their support to Paul while he was in chains, the Philippians actively participated in his *troubles*. Indeed, Epaphroditus almost died in his service to Paul (2:30). Paul's *troubles* included both his external circumstances of oppression as a prisoner in Roman chains and his inward experience of distress.[216] Even though Paul insisted that he was content without the Philippians' support, nevertheless he still assures them that he greatly values their presence with him and support of him in his time of suffering. His focus is more on their close relationship with him than on the support they gave him.[217] Their service as partners with him in his suffering (4:14) demonstrated that they were partners with him in God's grace (1:7). The phrase, *share in my troubles* (4:14), echoes and explains the phrase, *share in God's grace with me* (1:7).[218] This close connection between God's grace and suffering comes into sharp focus in Paul's statement that suffering is given by God's grace: *it has been granted to you on behalf of Christ not only to believe on him, but also to suffer for him* (1:29).

Paul's commendation — *it was good of you* — expresses his approval of the Philippians' faithful and sacrificial partnership with him in his troubles. This idiomatic expression (literally, "you did well") conveys Paul's praise for conduct that meets "high standards of excellence."[219] Paul's approval sounds like appreciation.[220] But instead of an explicit "thank you," which would have sounded like a client thanking a patron, Paul's moral

214. See the commentary on the word *partnership*, κοινωνία, and its cognates in 1:5, 7; 2:1; 3:10; 4:14, 15.

215. On συγκοινωνέω, "to share with," see BDAG, 952: "to be associated with someone in some activity, in the sense of taking a sympathetic interest."

216. *Trouble* (θλῖψις) can refer to "trouble that inflicts distress, oppression, affliction" and to the "inward experience of distress, affliction, trouble" (BDAG, 457). Paul discloses his "inward experience of distress in this letter" with this same term in 1:17: *supposing they can stir up trouble for me while I am in chains.*

217. Lightfoot, 164: "It was not the actual pecuniary relief, so much as the sympathy and companionship in his sorrow, that the Apostle valued."

218. Peterman, *Paul's Gift from Philippi*, 146: "The συγκοινωνήσαντές μου τῇ θλίψει of 4:14 is very similar to the συγκοινωνούς μου τῆς χάριτος of 1:7."

219. BDAG, 505. See Acts 10:32; 2 Pet 1:19; 3 John 6.

220. Hawthrone, 202: "Paul comes as close to saying 'Thank you' as ever he does in this letter."

commendation "sounds more like a teacher congratulating a student."[221] By expressing his approval in this way, Paul carefully avoids the social debt incurred by an explicit statement of gratitude.[222] At the same time, however, he rewards the Philippians for the high moral value of their partnership with him in his suffering. It was excellent! It was beautiful! Such praise would assuage any hurt feelings caused by Paul's assertion that he was content without any support. His contentment without the Philippians' support did not diminish his commendation for their support.[223]

15-16 Paul's expands his commendation with an elaboration of the history of the Philippians' partnership with him. Since he is recounting the Philippians' own story, he acknowledges that they already know what he tells them: *as you Philippians know.*[224] This simple phrase not only indicates that the Philippians already know this account of their partnership but also that Paul has not forgotten the details of their support. By informing them of his memory of what they already know, Paul emphasizes how much he values their support: what you yourselves know, I do not and will never forget. What you did so well, I will always treasure in my memory.

Naming the *Philippians* also expresses "affectionate remembrance."[225] And the personal name communicates more than Paul's affection; it also shows his respect for his readers in Philippi. In his direct address to the *Philippians,* Paul uses a Greek transcription of the Latin name *Philippenses* designating the citizens of the Roman colony, Philippi, then called *Colonia Iulia Augusta Philippensium.*[226] Calling attention to the Roman pedigree of the Philippians by using their Roman name is Paul's way of showing that he respects their pride in their city.[227] To his praise for their partnership he adds a genuine compliment for their citizenship in Roman Philippi.[228]

A timeline accounts for the support provided by the Philippians. They became Paul's partners soon after they heard the gospel: *in the early days of your acquaintance with the gospel.* This translation in TNIV helpfully

221. Peterman, *Paul's Gift from Philippi,* 145.

222. Peterman, "'Thankless Thanks': Epistolary Social Conventions in Philippians 4:10-20," *TynBul* 42 (1991), 261-70.

223. Beare, 153: "Paul is trying, still rather curtly, to overcome any touch of ungraciousness in his assurance that he could have got along quite well without the gifts which they had been good enough to send."

224. The clause, *you Philippians know* (Οἴδατε δὲ καὶ ὑμεῖς, Φιλιππήσιοι), contains an emphatic use of the pronoun *you* (ὑμεῖς): "even you yourselves know!" The emphatic use of the conjunction καί serves to increase the emphasis on the knowledge of the Philippians. Cf. Vincent, 147: "καί marks the comparison of the Philippians with the apostle himself."

225. Vincent, 147.

226. For a comment on the significance of Paul's use of the name Φιλιππήσιοι, see David W. J. Gill, "Macedonia," in *The Book of Acts in Its Graeco-Roman Setting* (ed. David W. J. Gill and Conrad Gempf; vol. 2 of The Book of Acts in Its First-Century Setting, ed. Bruce W. Winter; Grand Rapids: Eerdmans, 1994), 411-13.

227. Martin and Hawthorne, 269. Gnilka, 177, suggests that this name was the Philippians' own self-designation; Bockmuehl, 263, speculates that Paul coined this name.

228. Beare, 154.

interprets the phrase, "in the beginning of the gospel," as a reference to the Philippians' beginning with the gospel, not Paul's beginning of evangelistic activity.[229] This interpretation of the phrase concurs with a similar temporal expression in the opening section of the letter where Paul thanks God for the Philippians' *partnership in the gospel from the first day until now* (1:5). Although the temporal reference to the beginning of the gospel points to the Philippians' beginning, the reference also reminds the Philippians of what they already know: they heard and received the gospel from Paul; they are indebted to Paul for the gospel itself. Their giving to support Paul's gospel ministry was a response to receiving the gospel from Paul.

A second temporal reference to the Philippians' partnership with Paul indicates that their support came after his departure from Macedonia: *when I set out from Macedonia.* A fascinating corroboration of this point comes from Paul's letter to the church in Corinth: "when I was with you and needed something, I was not a burden to anyone, for the brothers and sisters who came from Macedonia supplied what I needed" (2 Cor 11:9). When Paul reminds the Philippians of the support he received after his departure *from Macedonia,* he is referring to the support from the Philippians for his ministry in Corinth.[230]

In fact, the Philippians' support for Paul after he left them was exceptional: *not one church shared with me in the matter of giving and receiving, except you only.* Once again Paul employs *partnership* terminology to depict his unique relationship with the Philippians. Their church was the only one that "became a partner" (TNIV, *shared*) with Paul. Paul's use of the verb "became a partner" to explain the nature of the Philippians' *partnership* with him (1:5) points to the financial dimension of the partnership with the Philippians and also to the deeper experience of reciprocity in his friendship with them. When Paul writes that the church in Philippi "became a partner" with him *in the matter of giving and receiving,* he borrows Hellenistic commercial language for the "settlement of an account of debt and credit."[231] Numerous examples in Greek and Jewish-Hellenistic sources attest that the phrase *giving and receiving* has both a technical meaning referring to financial transactions and a nontechnical meaning referring to the giving and receiving of gifts, services, and mutual discourse between

229. Against G. Delling, "ἀρχή," *TDNT* 1:482: "Phil 4:15 refers to the first period of Paul's evangelistic activity."

230. See Fee, 441. According to Peterman (*Paul's Gift from Philippi,* 150), Paul could not receive support from the church in Philippi until he departed from Macedonia, "for it was his settled policy not to accept support from a church while present with them." Peterman supports this interpretation from his study of the Corinthian correspondence (see *Paul's Gift from Philippi,* 163-71). But the temporal reference in Phil 4:15 by itself does not support such a generalization regarding Paul's financial policy.

231. BDAG, 601. The words *in the matter of* translate the prepositional phrase εἰς λόγον. This phrase is a commercial, technical term for the "settlement of an account."

friends.[232] Some interpreters take Paul's language only in a literal, technical sense as a formal business report, an "accounting of receipts and expenditures."[233] Others see Paul appropriating conventional business language "as an idiomatic expression indicating friendship."[234] Since Paul says that he received gifts from the Philippians in the past (4:15-16) and that he is amply supplied after receiving their recent gifts brought by Epaphroditus (4:17-18), his account *of giving and receiving* certainly refers to material, financial transactions. But his language has far more than a literal, financial meaning. In the entire letter and especially in the immediate context, Paul expands and transforms the terms of his partnership with the Philippians so that the financial terms become metaphors for spiritual transactions.[235] Even in this sentence, the reminder that the partnership began *in the early days of your acquaintance with the gospel* points to the spiritual foundation and motivation for the partnership. The spiritual dimension becomes Paul's primary focus in verses 17-19. He will not allow himself to be restricted or reduced to a commercial relationship with his friends. Certainly, as he acknowledges, he is the joyful recipient of generous gifts from his friends. But they too have received the gospel and even the outpouring of his life (2:17) from him. And, he assures them, they will receive from God *according to the riches of his glory in Christ Jesus* (4:19). The particular reference point of Paul's account *of giving and receiving* is the exceptional generosity of the church in Philippi. But that particular point stands as a metaphor for the generosity of God expressed in the gospel of Christ.[236]

16 Paul adds another line to prove that he treasures the memory of the generosity of the Philippians: *for even when I was in Thessalonica, you sent*

232. Peterman (*Paul's Gift from Philippi*, 51-89) illustrates the use of the *giving and receiving* (δόσεως καὶ λήμψεως) terminology in extensive quotes from Seneca (especially *De beneficiis*, which is all about giving and receiving), Sirach, Epictetus, Plato, Aristotle, Xenophon, Plutarch, Cicero, and Philo. Peterman concludes that "δόσεως καὶ λήμψεως is not a technical phrase referring invariably to commercial transactions. The nature of friendship and social reciprocity in the first century allowed the use of financial language to refer to the mutual obligations of such relationships. These mutual obligations may have a financial character (as pointed out especially by Philo, *Cher.* 122–23) but they are essentially social obligations."

233. Beare, 154-55. Also, Sampley (*Pauline Partnership in Christ*, 55): "The last section of the Letter to the Philippians is a formal receipt tendered by Paul to the Philippian Christians for their gift-payment in response to his need-request." Hawthorne (204): "It is almost as though he viewed the entire matter as a strictly business affair."

234. Peter Marshall, *Enmity in Corinth: Social Conventions in Paul's Relations with the Corinthians* (WUNT 23; Tübingen: J. C. B. Mohr, 1987), 163: "Gifts and services, while of great importance in the initiating and maintaining of a reciprocal relationship, are one part of the total nexus of relations involved in giving and receiving."

235. Hawthorne (204) poses a false dichotomy between material and spiritual references: "It is unlikely that Chrysostom and those many commentators who follow him can be right in saying that this expression means that the Philippians gave (δόσις) material goods and in turn received (λῆμψις) spiritual goods from Paul, because this mixes two different things, material and spiritual, and thus alters the normal meaning of δόσις and λῆμψις."

236. See Hansen, "Transformation of Relationships," 188-89.

me aid more than once when I was in need.[237] This line backtracks from his account of their generosity after he departed from Macedonia: before leaving the province, they supported him in Thessalonica, a Macedonian city. Apparently, Paul presents this episode out of chronological sequence because the point of his report of the previous episode was that no other church contributed to his support *after* he departed from Macedonia. Since the church in Thessalonica did not partner with him in the *matter of giving and receiving* after his departure from Macedonia, that church is not mentioned. Now, however, he calls attention to the support of the Philippians while he was in the Macedonian city of Thessalonica in order to stress the immediacy and frequency of their support. *Even* immediately after he left Philippi, the Philippians *sent him aid* when he was in Thessalonica.[238] And they sent him aid *more than once*.[239]

Paul's account of the generous support of the Philippian church communicates his deep gratitude without explicitly expressing his thankfulness. In this way, he avoids incurring the inferior status and social obligation that comes with a direct expression of gratitude while at the same time he assures the Philippians that he greatly values all that they have done to care for him many times in the past when he was in need. They would be wrong to think that their recent gift was all that mattered to him. By transcribing this history of their partnership, he lets them know that every one of their gifts over the entire history of their relationship remains permanently etched in his memory.

17 After recounting this history of the gifts received from the church in Philippi, Paul again asserts that he does not seek their gifts out of self-interest: *not that I desire your gifts*. This denial echoes and reinforces his previous denial in verse 11: *I am not saying this because I am in need*. His protests against a false image of him as an anxious accountant — hovering over his spreadsheet, scheming how to raise more money without appearing to do so — may be aimed at actual criticisms.[240] Did some Philippians complain that Paul was inappropriately, cleverly and not so cleverly, soliciting for their financial support?[241] If so, he forcefully resists such an unfair carica-

237. Copyists made revisions of the phrase *when I was in need* (εἰς τὴν χρείαν μοι). The reading in the text (εἰς τὴν χρείαν μοι) is supported by good evidence (א B F G Ψ 𝔐). An early papyrus (𝔓46) dropped the preposition εἰς to make τὴν χρείαν the direct object of the verb ἐπέμψατε. A few MSS changed the dative pronoun μοι into a genitive pronoun, μου. These stylistic revisions do not change the clear meaning of the text.

238. The emphatic use of καί, *even, indeed*, stresses that the church in Philippi immediately assumed the role of Paul's special partner. 1 Thess 2:2 and Acts 17:1 attest that Paul's stay in Thessalonica occurred immediately after his time in Philippi.

239. According to BDAG, 97, the Greek phrase καὶ ἅπαξ καὶ δίς, literally, "once and twice," means "again and again, more than once."

240. Lightfoot, 166: "Again the Apostle's nervous anxiety to clear himself interposes."

241. Peterlin, *Paul's Letter to the Philippians in the Light of Disunity in the Church*, 214: "Paul's greater argumentativeness in 4:10-20, as well as the sharpened and particular criti-

ture: *Not that! Not that!* More likely, however, Paul is not responding to accusations that he is improperly raising funds for his personal needs. His warm, unreserved commendation of the church for their exceptional partnership with him militates against the theory that the church is divided over the issue of supporting him. What Paul is doing here is guarding against the cultural pressures that would turn this partnership into patronage, with himself in the subservient position of a client dependent on his patron. Paul maintains the partnership as a friendship between equals by rejecting a utilitarian motive for his relationship with his friends.[242] He does not seek their friendship for personal self-aggrandizement.

Paul insists that his motive is not his self-interest but their interest: *what I desire is that more be credited to your account.* Literally, Paul says, "I desire the fruit increasing to your account." The word "fruit" in a financial sense means "advantage, gain, profit."[243] By combining this term with the financial sense of *account,* Paul speaks in the language of an investments manager: he desires continuously increasing profits, daily compounding interest, and accumulating dividends for the Philippians' account. The metaphorical reference of these terms comes into view in Paul's prayer that the Philippians will be *filled with the fruit of righteousness that comes through Jesus Christ — to the glory and praise of God* (1:11). Paul's focus in that context on *the day of Christ* (1:10) leads his readers to expect that the final evaluation of the "fruit" in their *account* will occur on that day when Christ appears in glory (2:16; 3:20-21). Only then will the value of the benefits of their generous support of Paul be completely assessed. But the Philippians can expect that their investments in Paul's life and ministry will yield daily profits until the final day of reckoning the total amount of fruit credited to their account. The fruit flowing out of their relationship with God through Christ Jesus will be continuously increasing.[244]

Although the exact nature of the fruit is not explicitly defined, Paul's assurance that *God will meet all your needs* (4:19) opens up the spectrum of

---

cism of Paul by the Philippians in relation to this matter, suggests that the issue of the collection of money for Paul is at the heart of the tension between Paul and the Philippians, and consequently of the controversy over Paul within the church." Peterlin's hypothesis requires highly speculative mirror-reading of Paul's words. He has to admit that Paul "nowhere attacks the critics" (215). Yet, he imagines Paul in a boxing match with his adversaries, "accepting the punches and calmly correcting unfair imputations." For an overview of Paul's relationship with the church in Philippi, see the Introduction, 3-12, 25-26.

242. Peterman, *Paul's Gift from Philippi,* 159: "Paul has not become socially obligated, and thereby in a sense inferior, by accepting their gifts. Rather, because he has accepted their gifts, they have been elevated to the place of partners in the gospel. Though Paul is in receipt of their gift and can mention his own benefit from it (4:18a), in 4:17b he rather makes it appear that they are actually the ones benefited."

243. BDAG, 510. MM, 321, offers evidence for the commercial meaning of *profits* for the corresponding cognate word καρπεία in a third-century-B.C. papyrus document: "with respect to the *profits* which we should obtain from the temple" (*The Flinders Petrie Papyri* 3.53).

244. Bockmuehl, 265: "The profit is understood to accumulate until the last day."

possibilities. Certainly, Paul's primary desire for himself and his readers is to *have the same attitude of mind Christ Jesus had* (2:5), *to know Christ* (3:10), and to *press on toward the goal to win the prize for which God has called me heavenward in Christ Jesus* (3:14). When he anticipates the prospect of *fruitful labor* (1:22), he must be expecting that his work will produce Christ-likeness in his followers. In the context of his entire letter the term "fruit" points to "the blessing which is continually accruing to faithful ministry in the rich development of Christian character. Every act of Christian ministry develops and enriches him who performs it."[245] Every act of love increased their capacity to love more. The increase in fruit to the Philippians' account is the answer to Paul's prayer that *love may abound more and more* (1:9). Sacrificial gifts produce spiritual growth in the givers as well as support for the recipients.

But while the fruit accruing to their account refers to spiritual growth in the Philippians, it also refers to all of God's provisions to supply all their needs. God met Paul's needs while he was suffering in many ways, including the gifts sent by the Philippians. Paul assures the Philippians that the fruit of their gifts will be that God will meet all their needs in many ways as well. He does not promise relief from suffering, but he does promise God's presence and provision in the midst of their suffering. They can be confident that a return on their investment in Paul will be God's care for them. They need not be anxious about anything, for the peace of God will guard them (4:7) and the God of peace will be with them (4:9). Of course, Paul is not teaching a health-and-wealth gospel. He is not assuring his readers that they will experience great material prosperity as a result of their gifts. But he is expressing his genuine desire that they will experience the full spectrum of God's care just as he has.

18 Paul continues his use of commercial metaphors to document his receipt of the gift from Philippi: *I have received full payment*. The verb *I have received* serves as a commercial, technical term for "a receipt for a sum paid in full."[246] Here, finally, is Paul's receipt for the gifts.[247] Even though he did not seek the gifts, he carefully certifies that all the gifts were delivered and that he has accepted them.[248] Paul emphasizes that he is completely satisfied by

245. Vincent, 149. O'Brien, 539: "The apostle employed this commercial language to show that he has set his heart on an ongoing, permanent gain for the Philippians in the spiritual realm. The advantage (καρπός) that accrues to them as a result of their generous giving is God's blessing in their lives by which they continually grow in the graces of Christ until the parousia."

246. BDAG, 102.

247. Adolf Deissmann *Light from the Ancient East* (trans. Lionel R. M. Strachan; 4th ed.; Grand Rapids: Baker, 1978), 110-12, offers evidence from Greek papyri and ostraca to demonstrate that this verb is a "technical expression regularly employed in drawing up a receipt." Pictures of inscriptions show the use of the verb in a receipt for rent and a receipt for taxes. According to Deissmann's illustrations from ancient Greek inscriptions, ἀπέχω is regularly combined with πάντα in receipts: "I have received everything."

248. Peterman (*Paul's Gift from Philippi*, 143) argues that "a technical meaning for ἀπέχω should not be stressed." He gives the following reasons: (1) Paul's letter is not a com-

their gifts: *I have more than enough. I am amply supplied.* The first verb echoes Paul's use of the same term twice in his testimony that he learned to be content in the extremes of poverty and plenty: *I know what it is to have plenty . . . living in plenty* (4:12). Now that Paul has received the gifts from Philippi he is living in plenty; indeed, he has *more than enough:* he has abundance, he is rich, in fact, he is wealthy.[249] Since he does not describe his own needs or the value of the gifts, he offers no way to measure how much his income exceeds his expenses. But in case his readers are not convinced, he adds a second verb to expand and intensify the meaning of the first verb: *I am amply supplied.* Paul claims to be in a state of being filled to overflowing.[250] He is completely satisfied by the overwhelming abundance of the gifts sent by Epaphroditus. Perhaps Paul exaggerates the abundance of the gifts as a way of "pleading for no more gifts."[251] More likely, Paul is paving the way for his promise that God, *according to the riches of his glory in Christ Jesus,* will meet all of the needs of the Philippian friends who gave so sacrificially to care for his needs.[252] His witness to the abundance of God's provision assures them that they will have the same experience of God's provision.

Paul transforms the meaning of the gifts from Philippi by recasting them in terms of sacred, sacrificial imagery: *They are a fragrant offering, an acceptable sacrifice, pleasing to God.* From a social perspective, these gifts demonstrated the friendship of the Philippians by amply supplying all that Paul needed; from a theological perspective, these gifts demonstrated the faith of the Philippians by pleasing God as true sacrifices. The social act of friendship is a religious act of worship. Each of the terms carries the weight of a long history in religious contexts. The first expression, *a fragrant offering,* literally, "an odor of fragrance," depicts a sacrifice pleasing to God.[253] When Noah offered burnt offerings on the altar after the flood, "the LORD smelled the pleasing odor" (Gen 8:21). The Torah instructs Aaron and his sons to burn the whole ram on the altar; "it is a burnt offering to the LORD; it is a pleasing odor" (Exod 29:18). The ultimate value of the temple sacrifices is their "pleasing odor to the LORD" (Lev 1:9, 13, 17). In the NT, the sacrificial death of Christ is a pleasing odor to God (Eph 5:2). By describing the gifts from the church in Philippi as a *fragrant offering,* Paul elevates their value to the highest level as sacrifices that are pleasing to God.

The second phrase, *an acceptable sacrifice,* is a well-known expression in religious language. The word *sacrifice* served as the common term in the

---

mercial document; (2) the social context of the letter lends a social coloring to the term; (3) Paul's so-called receipt does not fulfill the function of a formal receipt since his receipt does not imply that pre-arranged conditions have been met; (4) Paul's stress is more on the completeness of gifts received than on the formalities of the reception.

249. BDAG, 805.

250. BDAG, 828.

251. Martin and Hawthorne, 272.

252. Beare, 155.

253. BDAG, 417.

OT for offerings of grain or animals to God. The psalmist recognizes that "the sacrifice acceptable to God is a broken spirit" (Ps 51:17). Paul describes the expressions of the Philippians' faith as *the sacrifice and service coming from your faith* (2:17). By describing their gifts as an *acceptable sacrifice,* he puts their gifts in the category of the sacred offerings accepted by God.

The third phrase, *pleasing to God,* also employs sacrificial language. Paul challenges the Roman Christians to offer their bodies as "living sacrifices, holy and pleasing to God" (Rom 12:1). The writer to the Hebrews urges followers of Jesus, "do not forget to do good and share with others, for with such sacrifices God is pleased" (Heb 13:16). In Phil 4:18, Paul sees the gifts of the Philippians as an *acceptable sacrifice, pleasing to God.* Their gifts can receive no higher value than this: they are a fragrant odor to God; they are acceptable sacrifices to God; they are pleasing to God.[254] These gifts can no longer be measured simply in terms of financial value or social value. God's pleasure in the gifts reframes them with spiritual, divine significance. The Philippians have not only provided *more than enough* for Paul, but they have also presented sacrifices *pleasing to God.* The meaning of the gifts is derived not so much from the way they benefit Paul, the one who received these gifts, but from the way that the Philippians, those who gave these gifts, fulfilled the will of God and pleased God by their gifts.[255]

Paul's own sense of abundance when he received the gifts comes from more than his own personal pleasure in the gifts. He knows that the gifts are pleasing to God.[256] Since he lives for the Philippians' *progress and joy in the faith* (1:25), nothing can give him more pleasure than the knowledge that the Philippians are expressing their faith by giving sacrificially in ways that are pleasing to God. Once again the threefold cord of the relationship of God, Paul, and the Philippian church is tightly woven. *Giving and receiving* flows back and forth among the three participants in this relationship in multiple ways and forms. Gifts to one another are sacrifices to God. When friends give to one another, they give pleasure to God.

19 The previous sentence ends with God; this one begins with God. *And my God will meet all your needs according to the riches of his glory in Christ Jesus.* The gifts from the Philippians were *pleasing to God; God* will return more than they gave. Friendship requires reciprocal giving and receiving. But since he is chained in a Roman prison, Paul cannot return gifts in kind to the Philippians. Within the corporate life of believers *in Christ Jesus,* however, they will receive a return for their gifts from *my God.* When God is the all-encompassing person in friendship, he dramatically changes the dynamics of reciprocal giving and receiving.

The intimate closeness of God with Paul receives special emphasis

254. Vincent, 151, connects *to God* (τῷ θεῷ) with all three expressions. Cf. O'Brien, 540.

255. Müller, 209.

256. Barth, 127: "He feels himself enriched through the gift because he knows it is an offering made to God and well pleasing to God."

through the possessive pronoun *my.* This pronoun also recalls Paul's own experience of God's personal care for all his needs. God provided *more than enough* so that he was *amply supplied.* Now his experience of God's care for his needs gives him confidence to assure the Philippians of God's care: *And my God,* the God who cares for me and meets my needs, *will meet all your needs.* The juxtaposition of the pronouns *my* and *your* — *my God . . . your needs* — indicates that Paul expects his God to act on his behalf to meet their needs.[257]

The definition of *needs* in the context as the material needs of Paul caused by the *troubles* of his persecution and imprisonment (4:14-18) implies that Paul's reference to the *needs* of the Philippians also focuses primarily on their material needs.[258] Paul clearly expresses his solidarity with the Philippians in their experience of suffering (1:29-30). Although suffering comes as an unavoidable consequence of serving Christ, Paul experienced God's care in his suffering and expects God to care for his friends in their suffering. The gospel of Jesus Christ does not promise the absence of suffering, but it does promise the presence of the *God of peace* (4:9) in suffering. My God will be with you, my God will take care of your material needs, Paul promises his friends in Philippi.

And yet, Paul's prayer for the Philippians and his pastoral instruction demonstrate that the needs of the Philippians include more than their material needs.[259] Paul prays that their *love may abound more and more in knowledge and depth of insight* (1:9). He urges them to be *like-minded* (2:2), to have *the same attitude of mind Christ Jesus had* (2:5), *to rejoice in the Lord* (3:1; 4:4), and *to let [their] gentleness be evident to all* (4:5). These prayers and challenges point to the spiritual needs of the Philippians. By stressing that God would meet *all* their needs, Paul is including the whole spectrum of needs, both material and spiritual.

The same verb that Paul uses in the passive voice to express his own experience of ample provision — *I am amply supplied* (4:18) — he now uses in the active voice to promise God's work of providing for the Philippians

257. Lightfoot, 167; O'Brien, 545.

258. Martin and Hawthorne, 273: "The needs that are under consideration here are similar to those kinds of needs that Paul himself had experienced due to hardships, suffering, deprivations, and afflictions (θλίψεις [v. 14]) that could be alleviated only by earthly goods and services and by human associates."

259. Bockmuehl, 266: "God's 'full provision' should be understood to cover material needs, but presumably also their need for the qualities which Paul has been encouraging in this letter: joy and steadfastness in Christ, humility and concord amongst each other." Martin and Hawthorne (273) poses a false dichotomy between the material and spiritual needs by asserting that Paul is concerned only with material needs in this context and "has not suddenly shifted to discuss spiritual needs." Silva (240) challenges this exclusive concern with material needs: "Should we view material and spiritual resources as mutually exclusive categories? While Paul does not ignore the realities of physical discomfort and suffering, his main concern is to help the Philippians find their true contentment in the peace and power of God (4:6-7, 11-13)."

— *my God will meet,* "will supply."[260] The future tense does not set a date when God *will meet all your needs.* God's provision will always be on time, but his time may not be our time. Paul's expectation of God's provision includes both the present time while his people are in the midst of trouble (4:14-18) and the future time of final consummation when our Savior *will transform our lowly bodies so that they will be like his glorious body* (3:21).

The verb *will meet* receives additional definition in the three prepositional phrases that follow. First, God's supply will be *according to his riches.* The measure of God's supply will be according to the measure of God's riches. Paul measured his own net worth in terms of the riches of God: "poor, yet making many rich; having nothing, and yet possessing everything" (2 Cor 6:10). He describes the mission of Christ in terms of transference of God's riches: "though he was rich, yet for your sake he became poor, so that you through his poverty might become rich" (2 Cor 8:9). Paul specifies the nature of the riches of God as "the riches of his kindness, tolerance and patience" (Rom 2:4) and "the riches of the wisdom and knowledge of God" (Rom 11:33). The other prison epistles, Colossians and Ephesians, feature the riches of God in Christ Jesus: "the glorious riches of this mystery, which is Christ" (Col 1:27); "that they may have the full riches of complete understanding, in order that they may know the mystery of God, namely Christ, in whom are hidden all the treasures of wisdom and knowledge" (Col 2:2); "the riches of God's grace that he lavished on us" (Eph 1:7-8); "the riches of his glorious inheritance" (Eph 1:18); "the boundless riches of Christ" (Eph 3:8); "I pray that out of his glorious riches he may strengthen you with power through his Spirit in your inner being" (Eph 3:16). All of these references to the boundless, glorious riches of God provide the basis for understanding Paul's confidence that God will fulfill his promise to meet all our needs, not with a stingy, meager pittance, but with a lavish, abundant provision befitting the limitless wealth of God. Of course, Paul's promise is not a get-rich-quick scheme. The prominent theme of suffering in this letter emphasizes that participation in the sufferings of Christ (3:10) will characterize the lives of all true believers in Christ (1:29-30). But true believers will also be confident that they will experience God's riches both in this life and in the life to come.

Second, the phrase *in glory* points to the transcendence of God's

260. The external manuscript evidence ($\mathfrak{P}^{46}$ ℵ A B D^2 𝔐) solidly supports the future indicative, *will meet* (πληρώσει). Other manscripts (D* F G Ψ 075, 6, 33, and few others) offer aorist optative, *may* [God] *meet* (πληρώσαι). Since the future indicative is better attested by early and diverse witnesses, it is probably the original reading. However, some interpreters support the less-well-attested aorist optative as the reading that "better reflects the apostle's own reverent attitude. He does not say categorically what God will do for his friends, but he prayerfully asks God to come to their aid" (Martin and Hawthorne, 258). This support for the aorist optative "wards off disappointment or disillusion when material, physical needs are not met." But the limitation of the meaning of *needs* to material needs is not warranted by the context. See the commentary above.

riches and the final experience of God's riches.[261] God's riches are not in the market, in real estate, or in gold. They are *in glory,* absolutely transcending and infinitely surpassing all earthly wealth. God's riches in glory can be fully received only *in glory,* on the *day of Christ* (1:6, 10; 2:16), when Christ *will transform our lowly bodies so that they will be like his glorious body* (3:21).

Third, the phrase *in Christ Jesus* gives the address of those who will receive God's provision. Those who are incorporated into Christ Jesus and live in union with him by faith are the ones who will experience God's provision according to his riches in glory.[262] Paul opens this letter with the address of the recipients: *to all God's holy people in Christ Jesus* (1:1). Now he closes the body of the letter with the same phrase to designate Christ Jesus as the location of all the recipients of God's riches. By giving this address, *in Christ Jesus,* Paul again transforms the nature of his friendship-partnership with the Philippians. They are not simply engaged in a correspondence and exchange of gifts between Philippi and a Roman prison. They relate to each other as residents in Christ Jesus. This transcendent residence brings them together within the domain in which alone they experience the giving and receiving of God's riches.[263] The enrichment of the Philippians will come as their lives are transformed by the cross and the resurrection of Christ.[264] By his example, Paul encourages his friends to desire the greatest of God's riches in Christ Jesus: *I want to know Christ — yes, to know the power of his resurrection and participation in his sufferings* (3:10).

20 Promising God's *riches in glory in Christ Jesus* leads to ascribing *glory* to God: *To our God and Father be glory forever and ever. Amen.* Paul's promise of God's riches names God as *my God* to express his intimacy with God and his expectancy that God will act on his behalf to meet the needs of the Philippians. Now Paul's praise to God as *our God* includes the Philippians in his worship of God for meeting the needs of all those who are in Christ Jesus. God's provision in and through Christ Jesus is the occasion

261. The enigmatic phrase *in glory* receives a myriad of diverse interpretations. Lightfoot, 454, explains that the words *in glory* have a temporal significance: They "show that the needs here contemplated are not merely temporary." God "shall supply by placing you in glory." Vincent, 151, takes the phrase *in glory* as an adverbial modifier of the verb, expressing the "mode or manner of fulfillment." God will meet your needs gloriously "in such wise that his glory will be manifested." TNIV takes the phrase *in glory* as an adjectival modifier of riches: *the riches of his glory.* Bockmuehl, 267, says that the phrase means that God's riches "derive from his heavenly presence and power." Fee, 453 n. 16, takes the phrase *in glory* to be locative, "referring to the ineffable and eternal 'glory' in which God dwells, as the context within which God lavishes his riches on his own in Christ Jesus."

262. This interpretation of the phrase *in Christ Jesus* in the locative sense does not contradict the instrumental sense of the phrase *through Christ Jesus* (see O'Brien, 549). Those who are in Christ Jesus receive God's provision through Christ Jesus.

263. Vincent (151) states that the phrase *in Christ Jesus* designates "the domain in which alone the πληρώσει can take place."

264. Collange, 133.

and the content of the praise to *our God and Father.*[265] *God the Father* receives the glory in Paul's worship. Just as the Christ hymn ends with the acknowledgment that Jesus Christ is Lord, *to the glory of God the Father* (2:11), so also the letter ends with those who experience God's glorious riches in Christ Jesus joining in the doxology: *To our God and Father be glory.*[266] By ascribing *the glory* to God, Paul praises the "divine honor, the divine splendor, the divine power, the visible divine radiance of God."[267] The glory of God is the revelation of God's attributes in the creation of the world, in the redemption accomplished through Christ, and in the final consummation of all things.[268] Paul is not adding to the glory of God but affirming the glory of God visibly displayed in the supply of God's riches in glory in Christ Jesus.

This doxology voices eternal praise to God: *forever and ever!* Literally, the phrase extends praise to God "into the ages of the ages." Paul's praise to the glory of God is not only for this age but for the age to come as well.[269] A familiar hymn expresses this perspective: "When we've been there ten thousand years, / bright shining as the sun, / we've no less days to sing God's praise / than when we'd first begun."

The doxology closes with *Amen,* a "strong affirmation of what is stated."[270] The responsive pronouncement of the Amen by the congregation of believers to a doxology or thanksgiving was an established custom in the early church.[271] The *Amen* gives the church the opportunity to endorse the doxology: *Amen.* Yes. So shall it be! In their *Amen* believers in Christ joyfully assert their faith that God fulfills all his promises in Christ, and in their *Amen* they affirm that they give all the glory to God forever and ever.[272]

265. Larry Hurtado, *Lord Jesus Christ: Devotion to Jesus in Earliest Christianity* (Grand Rapids: Eerdmans, 2003), 152.

266. See the close connection of God's redemption in Christ and praise to our God and Father in Gal 1:5, 2 Cor 1:20, and Rom 11:36.

267. G. Kittel, "δόξα," *TDNT* 2:247.

268. H. Hegermann, "δόξα," *EDNT* 1:346: "δόξα expresses for Paul the basic nature of God as it appears in his revelation, perceived by the illuminated reason in his creative power (Rom 1:20, 23), from the eye of faith in his judging and salvific power in historical manifestations. It becomes the object of faithful hope for the definitive shining forth at the end."

269. P. T. O'Brien, "Benediction, Blessing, Doxology, Thanksgiving," in *DPL* 69.

270. BDAG, 53.

271. H.-W. Kuhn, "ἀμήν," *EDNT* 1:70; 1 Cor 14:16: "Otherwise when you are praising God in the Spirit, how can others, who are now put in the same situation as an inquirer, say 'Amen' to your thanksgiving, since they do not know what you are saying?"

272. O'Brien, "Benediction, Blessing, Doxology, Thanksgiving," in *DPL* 69; 2 Cor 1:20: "For no matter how many promises God has made, they are 'Yes' in Christ. And so through him the 'Amen' is spoken by us to the glory of God."

IX. GREETINGS AND GRACE (4:21-23)

[21]Greet all God's people in Christ Jesus. The brothers and sisters who are with me send greetings. [22]All God's people here send you greetings, especially those who belong to Caesar's household.

[23]The grace of the Lord Jesus Christ be with your spirit. Amen.

Paul's final greetings and blessing communicate the warmth of his love for his friends and the depth of his commitment to Christ. He reaches out through his words to embrace each member of the church, to express the strong bond of friendship between his present circle of friends and the community in Philippi, and to assure believers that the grace of the Lord Jesus Christ is with them.

21 The imperative *greet* is Paul's customary way of sending his greetings to the churches addressed in his letters.[273] In three of his letters, the readers are instructed to *greet one another.*[274] But in this letter Paul calls upon the leaders of the church to greet the members of the church for him.[275] He wants each individual member of the church to receive greetings from him.[276] Paul would not be satisfied if the leaders looked at the whole church and said, "Paul greets all of you." He tells the leaders to communicate to each person: "Paul remembers you and sends his warm greetings to you." This way of sending his greetings to each person individually takes the place of greeting members of the church by name.[277] Perhaps, Paul does not follow his custom of naming individuals because he does not want to give an additional reason for envy and rivalry in an already divided church.

Although he avoids naming individuals, he gives each member of the church the highest possible position by addressing them as *God's people,* literally, "every saint in Christ Jesus."[278] Just as he began the letter by addressing all the members of the church as "saints" (1:1), so now he ends the letter by greeting every member as a "saint." The term "saint" echoes the OT description of Israel as God's holy people (Exod 19:4). Through God's

273. Rom 16:16; 1 Cor 16:20; 2 Cor 13:12; Col 4:15; 1 Thess 5:26.

274. Ἀσπάσασθε ἀλλήλους: Rom 16:16; 1 Cor 16:20; 2 Cor 13:12.

275. The second person plural form of the imperative *greet* indicates that Paul is asking more than one person to greet the members of the church. The address to *overseers and deacons* in the opening salutation (1:1) points to these leaders as the probable recipients of the letter and the ones responsible to pass on Paul's greetings to the other members in the church. See O'Brien, 552; Martin and Hawthorne, 280.

276. The TNIV translation of πάντα ἅγιον as *all God's people* obscures Paul's direction to greet "every saint." Since the word "saint" (ἅγιον) is singular, Paul is concerned that each saint, not simply the group as a whole, will receive greetings from him. NRSV provides a more accurate translation, "every saint."

277. See especially Romans 16, where Paul greets twenty-five individuals by name.

278. The TNIV translation of πάντα ἅγιον ἐν Χριστῷ Ἰησοῦ as *God's people in Christ Jesus* captures the sense of belonging to God by God's choice but misses the position given by God as "a holy one," "a saint."

choice and Christ's redemption, believers in Christ now enjoy the same covenantal relationship given by God to Israel. Paul's designation of believers as "saints" in this context does not refer to their behavior or the moral quality of their lives, but to their position as people set apart from this world by God's grace: they belong to God; they are God's possession.[279] By naming each member of the church as a "saint" when he sends his personal greetings, Paul reminds all the believers that they are already "saints," "holy ones," because of their relationship to God *in Christ Jesus.*

The phrase *in Christ Jesus* presents the basis for calling believers "saints."[280] Their union with Christ sets them apart and marks them as *God's people.*[281] Paul warns earlier in this letter against the danger of identifying God's holy people by the marks of the purity of their ancestral lineage or their faultless record of keeping the law (3:2-6). Although Paul could boast that he was *circumcised on the eighth day, of the people of Israel, of the tribe of Benjamin, a Hebrew of the Hebrews, in regard to the law a Pharisee,* and *as for righteousness based on the law, faultless,* he considered all of these qualifications a loss *because of the surpassing worth of knowing Christ* (3:5-7). Being a saint is not based on spiritual heritage or moral accomplishments, but on a transforming relationship with Christ.

Paul not only asks for his greetings to be given to every saint in Christ Jesus, but he also sends greetings from the *brothers and sisters* who are with him. Paul never lives in isolation. Even as a prisoner in chains, he lives in a community. Although he addresses all the members of the church in Philippi as *brothers and sisters* (1:12; 3:1, 13, 17; 4:1, 8), he makes a distinction between greetings from *brothers and sisters* (4:21) and greetings from *all God's people* (4:22; literally, "all the saints") in this context.[282] Evidently, *brothers and sisters* form a smaller group within the larger circle of "all the saints."[283] The *brothers and sisters* are people like Timothy and Epaphroditus (2:19-30) who live and work in close association with Paul.

22 Paul also sends greetings from *all the Lord's people,* literally, "all the saints," who are with him in the city of his imprisonment. Whether or

279. BDAG, 11; H. Balz, "ἅγιος," *EDNT* 1:19.

280. Lightfoot (167) takes *in Christ Jesus* (ἐν Χριστῷ Ἰησοῦ) with the verb *greet* (Ἀσπάσασθε): Greet in Christ Jesus. But the close proximity of the phrase *in Christ Jesus* to the noun "saint" and the use of the phrase *in Christ Jesus* to modify "saints" in 1:1 indicate that this phrase modifies the noun "saint" rather than the verb *greet.* See Vincent, 153.

281. According to Collange's interpretation (134), saints are marked by the seal of being in Christ.

282. Lightfoot, 167: "Apparently the Apostle's personal companions and fellow-travelers are meant, as distinguished from the Christians resident in Rome who are described in the following verse."

283. The more restricted use of *brothers* in this context may not be gender inclusive, since Paul may simply be referring to *brothers,* such as Timothy and Epaphroditus, or to a wider circle of co-workers, including some *sisters.* See the comments in the Introduction, 5-6, 35, and on 1:12 for a rationale for the gender-inclusive meaning of *brothers* when the term refers to all the members of the church.

not they knew that Paul was speaking on their behalf, they are included in Paul's warm exchange of greetings. Paul builds bridges between communities of faith. He works to build an association of churches related to one another as *God's people.* Since they are chosen and redeemed by God, their union in Christ transcends social, political divisions.

Paul sends special greetings from *those who belong to Caesar's household.* The household of Caesar consisted of slaves and freed slaves (freedmen) of the emperor. They functioned as managers of the properties and enterprises of the emperor throughout the empire.[284] Some members of Caesar's household were involved in the administration of the government; they served as civil servants under imperial direction.[285] If Paul sent his letter to the Philippians from Rome, then his letter to the Romans, sent to Rome a few years earlier, may contain some of the names of Caesar's household in the long list of names in Romans 16.[286] The names of Aristobulus (Rom 16:10) and Narcissus (Rom 16:11) deserve special attention since they were connected with the household of the Emperor Claudius.[287] Since Paul does not provide the names of the members of Caesar's household who sent greetings to Philippi, speculation cannot provide certainty. What is certain, however, is that Paul wants the Philippians to know that his imprisonment *actually served to advance the gospel* (1:12). Even the imperial guard heard the gospel (1:12). As a result, Paul can claim that members of Caesar's household are "saints" who send their greetings to the "saints" in Philippi. These simple greetings bear an implicit message to the Philippians: imperial power cannot stop the power of the gospel. Even while Paul in a Roman prison and the believers in Philippi are suffering under imperial authorities, the gospel is claiming the allegiance of imperial agents. The greetings from those who belong to Caesar's household point to the day when *every knee shall bow, . . . and every tongue confess that Jesus Christ is Lord* (2:10-11).[288]

23 Paul closes his letter with the blessing of grace: *The grace of the Lord Jesus Christ be with your spirit.*[289] This blessing of grace repeats the opening blessing: *Grace and peace to you from God our Father and the Lord Jesus*

284. John F. Hall, "Caesar's Household," *ABD* 1:798. According to Bockmuehl (270), members of the imperial household were present in Philippi. Inscriptions in Philippi mention the *familia Caesaris* and list three of Caesar's freedmen. See P. R. C. Weaver, *Familia Caesaris: A Social Study of the Emperor's Freedmen and Slaves* (Cambridge: Cambridge University Press, 1972), 300.

285. P. T. O'Brien, "Caesar's Household, Imperial Household," *DPL* 83.

286. Lightfoot, 171-178.

287. P. T. O'Brien, "Caesar's Household, Imperial Household," *DPL* 84.

288. Bockmuehl, 270: "Concealed behind this innocuous greeting is a powerful symbol of the day when even in Rome, the seat of imperial power, 'every knee shall bow' to Christ (2:11)."

289. All of the letters in the Pauline corpus close with some form of the blessing of grace. See Rom 16:20; 1 Cor 16:23; 2 Cor 13:14; Gal 6:18; Eph 6:24; Col 4:18; 1 Thess 5:28; 2 Thess 3:18; 1 Tim 6:21; 2 Tim 4:22; Tit 3:15; Phlm 25.

Christ (1:2). The sole focus on the Lord Jesus Christ in the final benediction implies that Christ has the authority to convey the grace of God to the church. Although Paul does not explicitly define the *grace of the Lord Jesus Christ* in this letter, two parallels with definitions of grace in 2 Corinthians draw out the meaning of this phrase. The Christ hymn, especially Philippians 2:6-8 *(he made himself nothing . . . he humbled himself)*, presents a striking parallel with his definition of grace in 2 Corinthians 8:9: "For you know the grace of our Lord Jesus Christ, that though he was rich, yet for your sake he became poor, so that you through his poverty might become rich" (2 Cor 8:9). And Paul's expression of his desire to *know Christ, to know the power of his resurrection* (Phil 3:10), runs parallel to the assurance of grace that Paul received from the Lord: "My grace is sufficient for you, for my power is made perfect in weakness" (2 Cor 12:9). These parallels to the definitions of *the grace of the Lord Jesus Christ* point to Christ's sacrificial death on the cross and the power of his resurrection.[290] Within the theological framework of his letter to the Philippians, Paul's blessing of *the grace of the Lord Jesus Christ* expresses his desire for believers to experience the self-giving love of Christ demonstrated on the cross in their relationships with one another in Christ and *the power of his resurrection* as they live in a manner worthy of the gospel of Christ in the midst of their suffering on behalf of Christ.

The blessing relates grace *with your spirit*.[291] The singular form of spirit is a distributive singular rather than a collective singular and could be translated as "with the spirit of each one of you."[292] The word *spirit* may have special reference to inner self-awareness, as in 1 Corinthians 2:11 ("for who knows a person's thought except the person's *spirit* within?"). Or it may simply refer to the whole person.[293]

Amen![294] Paul ends with his own affirmation, It is true! And he calls for the church to respond with their confirmation, Yes![295] Believers joyfully appropriate the blessing of the grace of the Lord Jesus Christ. Conflicts within the church and persecution from without cannot diminish the experience of God's grace in and through the Lord Jesus Christ.

To readers past and present, Paul ends his letter of joy with the blessing of grace: *The grace of the Lord Jesus Christ be with your spirit! Amen!*

290. Collange, 135.

291. Some MSS (ℵ^2 Ψ 𝔐) have *with* "all of you" (μετὰ πάντων ὑμῶν) instead of *with your spirit* (μετὰ τοῦ πνεύματος ὑμῶν). The reading in the NA^{27} text, however, has superior witnesses (including, 𝔓^{46} ℵ* A D) and concurs with Gal 6:18 and Phlm 25.

292. Martin and Hawthorne, 281-82. See BDF §140.

293. Schweizer, "πνεῦμα," *TDNT* 6:435.

294. Although the NA^{27} does not include *Amen*, the textual tradition (𝔓^{46} ℵ A D Ψ 𝔐) strongly supports it.

295. Collange, 135.

Index of Authors

Index of Subjects

Index of Scripture References

Colossians

1 Thessalonians

Index of Extrabiblical Literature